BAKER'S
Student
Encyclopedia
of
Music

R. Right (Ger., *rechte*); *r.h.,* right hand (*rechte Hand*). In French organ music, *clavier de récit* (swell manual).

rabāb (Arab.). Middle Eastern bowed FIDDLE, first recorded in the 10th century and based on a Persian plucked LUTE. It is held upright between the legs and rests on the ground on a short, metal spike. The rabāb has a pear-shaped body, sickle-shaped pegbox, and between three and five strings.

Related forms of it are played in southern Asia and Indonesia, the latter as a GAMELAN instrument called *rebab;* it was introduced there in the 16th century as a result of the Arab invasions. By the 11th century, the rabāb had reached Europe; it evolved into the REBEC.

Rachmaninoff, Sergei (Vassilievich), greatly renowned Russian-born American pianist, conductor, and composer; b. Semyonovo, April 1, 1873; d. Beverly Hills, March 28, 1943. Rachmaninoff came from a musical family. His grandfather was an amateur pianist, a pupil of JOHN FIELD, and his father also played the piano (*Rachmaninoff's Polka* was written on a theme improvised by his father). His mother likewise played piano, and it was from her that he received his initial training at their estate, Oneg, near Novgorod.

After financial setbacks, the family estate was sold and Rachmaninoff was taken to St. Petersburg, where he studied piano and harmony at the Conservatory from 1882–85. Acting on the advice of his cousin Alexander Siloti—yet another family pianist—he enrolled as a piano student of Nikolai Zverev at the Moscow Conservatory in 1885. He then entered Siloti's piano class and commenced the study of counterpoint and harmony in 1888.

At this time, Rachmaninoff met PIOTR ILYICH TCHAIKOVSKY, who appreciated his talent and gave him friendly advice. Rachmaninoff graduated from the Conservatory as a pianist in 1891 and as a composer in 1892. He won the gold medal in composition for his opera *Aleko,* based on a story by Aleksandr Pushkin. His Prelude in C-sharp Minor (from the *Morceaux de fantaisie,* op.3, no. 2)

Young musicians place flowers on Rachmaninoff's grave. (UPI/ Corbis-Bettmann)

quickly followed. Published in 1892, it became one of the most celebrated piano pieces in the world. His First Symphony, given in Moscow in 1897, proved a failure, however. Discouraged, Rachmaninoff destroyed the manuscript, but the orchestral parts were preserved.

In the meantime, Rachmaninoff launched a career as a piano virtuoso. He also took up a career as a conductor, joining the Moscow Private Russian Orchestra in 1897. He made his London debut in the triple capacity of pianist, conductor, and composer with the Philharmonic Society in 1899. Although he attempted to compose after the failure of his First Symphony, nothing significant came from his pen. Plagued by depression, he underwent hypnosis with Nikolai Dahl and then began work on his Second Piano Concerto. He gave the first complete performance of the score with Siloti conducting in Moscow in 1901. This concerto became perhaps the most celebrated work of its genre written in the 20th century. It is no exaggeration to say that it became a model for piano concertos by a majority of modern Russian composers and also of semipopular virtuoso pieces for piano and orchestra written in America.

In 1902 Rachmaninoff married his cousin Natalie Satina, with whom he spent some months in Switzerland, then returned to Moscow. After conducting at Moscow's

After Rachmaninoff's death, the score of his First Symphony was restored and performed in Moscow in 1945.

Bolshoi Theater from 1904 to 1906, he spent most of his time in Dresden, Germany, where he composed his Second Symphony, one of his most popular works. Having composed another major work, his Third Piano Concerto, he took it on his first tour of the U.S. in 1909. His fame was so great that he was offered the conductorship of the Boston Symphony Orchestra, but he declined. The offer was repeated in 1918, but again he turned it down.

Rachmaninoff lived in Russia from 1910 until after the Revolution of October 1917, at which time he left Russia with his family, never to return. From 1918 until 1939 he made annual tours of Europe as a pianist, as well as the U.S., where he spent much of his time. He also owned a villa in Lucerne from 1931 to 1939, where he composed one of his most enduring scores, *Rhapsody on a Theme of Paganini,* in 1934. In 1932 he was awarded the Gold Medal of the Royal Philharmonic Society of London.

After the outbreak of World War II in 1939, Rachmaninoff spent his remaining years in the U.S. He became a naturalized U.S. citizen a few weeks before his death in 1943, having made his last appearance as a pianist in Knoxville, Tennessee.

Among Russian composers, Rachmaninoff occupies a very important place. The sources of his inspiration lie in the ROMANTIC tradition of 19th-century Russian music. The link with Tchaikovsky's lyrical art is very strong: melancholy moods prevail, and minor keys predominate in his compositions, as in Tchaikovsky's. However, there is an unmistakable stamp of Rachmaninoff's individuality in the broad, rhapsodic sweep of the melodic line, and particularly in the fine resonant harmonies of his piano writing. His technical resourcefulness is unexcelled by any composer since Franz Liszt.

Despite the fact that Rachmaninoff was an émigré and stood in avowed opposition to the Soviet regime (until the German attack on Russia in 1941 impelled him to modify his stand), his popularity never wavered in Russia. After his death, Russian musicians paid spontaneous tribute to him. Rachmaninoff's music is much less popular in Germany, France, and Italy. On the other hand, in England and America it constitutes a potent factor on the concert stage.

Rachmaninoff worked on several operatic projects but only completed *Aleko, the Miserly Knight,* op.24, after Pushkin (1903–05), and *Francesca da Rimini,* op.25, based on Dante's *Inferno* (1900–05). For orchestra, he wrote three symphonies, four piano concertos, the *Paganini Rhapsody,* and several symphonic poems, including *Prince Rostislav* in 1891, *The Rock,* from 1893, and *The Isle of the Dead,* op.29, in 1909. He also composed the *Symphonic Dances,* op.45, in 1941. His best-known chamber work is the Cello Sonata in G minor, op.19, from 1901.

Rachmaninoff's Russian orthodox choral music is among his finest creations: *Liturgy of St. John Chrysostom,* op.31, from 1910, and *All-Night Vigil,* op.37, from 1915. He also composed *The Bells,* a choral symphony for soprano, baritone, chorus, and orchestra, op.35, based on the famous poem by Edgar Allan Poe, in 1913.

As a virtuoso pianist, Rachmaninoff followed the 19th-century tradition of composing music to show off his abilities. Unlike most of his predecessors, however, he wrote some excellent music in this vein, including the *Fantaisie-tableaux:* two suites for two pianos, opp. 5 and 17 (1893; 1900–01), 6 *Moments musicaux,* op.16 (1896), *Variations on a Theme of Chopin,* op.22 (1902–03), 10 Preludes, op.23 (1901–03), two sonatas, opp. 28 and 36 (1907; 1913, revised 1931), 13 Preludes, op.32 (1910), *Études-tableaux,* opp.33 and 39 (1911, 1916–17), and *Variations on a Theme of Corelli,* op.42 (1931). He also composed 82 songs (1890–1916).

racket (Ger. *Rackett, Rankett;* Fr. *cervelas, cervelat;* It. *rocchetta, cortalo*). Obsolete wind instrument of the 16th and 17th centuries. Its DOUBLE REED is partly covered by its MOUTHPIECE, called a *pirouette.* The body, made of ivory or wood, is shaped like a small tree stump, while the tube consists of a connected series of narrow channels bored up and down the body. FINGERHOLES are bored obliquely into the channels, thus requiring a player to use the tip and middle joints of a finger to cover a hole. The racket also has ventholes and a water escape.

As a closed pipe, it sounds an octave lower than its length, but it cannot be overblown, so that the RANGES on the three types of racket are only an octave and a PERFECT

MUSICAL INSTRUMENT

FIFTH. The lowest racket (great bass) has a range C_1–G_0; the highest (soprano), G_0–d_1. The racket has had an occasional role in the EARLY MUSIC REVIVAL of the 20th century.

PEOPLE IN MUSIC

Raff, (Joseph) **Joachim,** greatly renowned Swiss teacher and composer; b. Lachen, near Zurich, May 27, 1822; d. Frankfurt am Main, June 24, 1882. Raff was educated at the Jesuit Gymnasium in Schwyz. He was a schoolteacher in Rapperswill from 1840 to 1844 but pursued music during that time.

In 1843 Raff sent some of his piano pieces to FELIX MENDELSSOHN, who recommended them for publication. In 1845 he met FRANZ LISZT in Basel, who gave him further encouragement and assistance in finding employment. From 1850 to 1856 Raff was Liszt's assistant in Weimar, where he became an ardent supporter of the new German school of composition. He then went to Wiesbaden as a piano teacher and composer, where he married the actress Doris Genast. He subsequently was director of the Hoch Conservatory in Frankfurt from 1877 to 1882, where he also taught composition. Students flocked from many countries to study with him, including the American EDWARD MACDOWELL.

Raff was a composer of prodigious output, a master of all technical aspects of composition. He wrote 214 opus numbers that were published and many more that remained in manuscript. In spite of his fame, his music was little played after his death.

Raff is best known for his 11 symphonies, including No. 5, *Leonore,* his most famous work, which he wrote in 1872. He also composed several concert OVERTURES, two violin CONCERTOS, a piano concerto, two cello concertos, and four orchestral SUITES. His vocal music consists of six operas, various choral works with orchestra, and many unaccompanied choral works. He was also an active composer of chamber works, piano pieces, and arrangements.

raga (Sanskrit, colors; sing., *rāg*). A system of MODES used in the classical music of northern India, representing not only a succession of certain INTERVALS (not necessarily corresponding to the TEMPERED SCALE), but a meaningful relationship to spiritual values. In Indian theory, correspondences exist not only with human moods, such as joy or sorrow, loneliness and waiting, love and revulsion, but also with a definite time of the day or season of the year. The playing of the ragas by native musicians assumed, therefore, a mystical and magical quality of meditation and communication.

Indian musicians portrayed in an early manuscript. (Smithsonian Institution)

The modes of the ragas are usually PENTATONIC in their primary structure. Supplementary tones may be added, increasing the GAMUT to that of seven degrees. A rāg may exceed a range of a OCTAVE by a few pitches. Also, many ragas differ in pitch going up from going down, as does the Western melodic minor scale. The hierarchy of the primary and secondary tones of the ragas is strictly observed, and transitions from one rāg to another, corresponding to Western MODULATIONS, cannot be made within the same performance. The goal of improvisation is the expression of the intended meaning of a rāg. Each note must be thoroughly explored, with the appropriate ornamentation, and the movement from note to note must follow the appropriate rules of the rāg.

Melodic improvisation requires the support and challenge by the tablā player, who also has a system to work within, the TALA. The rhythmic structure of the tala is additive and cumulative: additive in the sense that divisions containing different numbers of beats in each are added to form a fixed rhythmic unit of considerable complexity, often making an arithmetic progression (e.g., 4 + 5; 2 + 3 + 4 + 5; 3 + 5 + 7), and cumulative (cyclical) in the sense that such rhythmic units are repeated to form larger units.

To an uninitiated listener, it appears magical that a group of native performers, playing without scores and without a visible signal by a principal player or conductor, could strike several drums or sound several instruments together after a long interval of time. This ability is explained by the fact that professional musicians can conceive such units, usually up to a 16-beat (*tīn-tāl*) cycle, but even potentially larger. To this capacity must be added the constant rhythmic variations that are skillfully but instinctively fitted into the main metrical divisions.

The standard form of the classical Indian improvisation is as follows: (1) the opening *ālāpa,* for the melodic and drone instruments; after a musical tuning check, the rāg is introduced in its basic form and improvised upon in a slow, arhythmic, meditative manner; (2) the *joḍ* (*jhālā*) or *tānam,* an improvisation with a regular pulse produced on the drone strings and repeated motives or sung with repetitive nonsense syllables; (3) the *gat* adds the tablā and tāl to the melodic instrument; the drone continues but is virtually inaudible. This final section alternates between a brief precomposed piece and free improvisation, with a friendly rivalry between melodic instrumentalist and drummer. The work concludes with a cadential formula repeated three times, assuring a smooth, satisfying close.

One of the most famous practitioners of Indian music in the West is RAVI SHANKAR. Shankar's career was given a considerable boost when GEORGE HARRISON of the BEATLES became interested in learning the SITAR, Shankar's instrument.

ragtime. A syncopated, primarily African-American music, popular from about 1896 to 1918. During this period, the term included vocal and instrumental music and dance styles associated with the music. As an instrumental genre it existed as both a popular ballroom style and as a highly significant contribution to early JAZZ. In today's usage, the ragtime genre refers almost exclusively to piano works.

The usual explanation for the term *ragtime* (first used in 1896 by the black performer Ernest Hogan) is a derivation from "ragged time," i.e., SYNCOPATION. Syncopation was a prevalent component of American popular music in the 19th century, especially with the dance music and song of the black slaves and ex-slaves, and its adaptation into blackface MINSTRELSY, notably in the music of STEPHEN FOSTER, DANIEL D. EMMETT, and others. After the Civil War, black performers reasserted their musical birthright by moving into the world of minstrelsy, creating and performing vaudevillelike revues featuring the CAKEWALK, buck and wing, and walk-around dances.

As African-American minstrelsy moved into the theater in the late 19th century, songs and later instrumental pieces in syncopated QUADRUPLE or DUPLE time became popular. The other major influence came from the MARCH, a truly popular genre in the U.S. after the Civil War in the hands of JOHN PHILIP SOUSA, Patrick S. Gilmore, and others. In the cakewalk, walk-around, and related black popular genres, the march piano's left-hand accompaniment in the bass—the lowest single note on the downbeat, a single note on the third beat, triads in higher registers on the offbeats—became standard. The melody, in eighth notes, became more syncopated, using, among others, these rhythms:

Ragtime was the first African-American genre to attain wide popularity in the U.S. without the strongly racist overtones that accompanied blackface minstrelsy. It first emerged in piano playing for American saloons, barrooms, bordellos, and burlesque houses. In the vernacular such pianists were referred to as "perfessors" (professors). Later, in the compositional hands of SCOTT JOPLIN, Tom Turpin, James Scott, Joseph Lamb, and many others, ragtime acquired a "classic" quality of elegance in moderate tempo (cf. Joplin's warning that "ragtime should never be played too fast") or a lively and even humorous quality more suitable for dancing.

The rapid motion and cross-accents of ragtime proved irresistible to classical composers. CHARLES IVES cultivated ragtime rhythms early in the century. Ragtime became very popular in Europe as well: CLAUDE DEBUSSY made use of ragtime rhythms in his *Golliwog's Cake Walk* (from *CHILDREN'S CORNER,* 1908) and IGOR STRAVINSKY (see next entry) and others wrote pieces closely modeled on ragtime.

Rag-Time. Ensemble piece by IGOR STRAVINSKY, 1918, in which he included the CIMBALOM.

Raindrop Prelude. Common and unsubstantiated nickname for FRÉDÉRIC CHOPIN's Prelude in D-flat major (op.28, no. 15, 1836–39).

Legend states that Chopin composed the prelude while waiting for George Sand and her children to return from a shopping trip on the island of Majorca, where they were living. A slow steady rain was falling, stimulating Chopin's OSTINATO on the dominant A♭ of the TONIC key. The A♭ changes enharmonically to G♯ in the piece's middle section.

Chopin specifically denied this story, which was circulating already during his lifetime, but picturesque sentimental tales are notoriously hard to kill.

Rainey, Ma (born Gertrude Pridgett), prominent African-American blues, jazz, and vaudeville singer; b. Columbus, Ga., April 26, 1886; d. Rome, Ga., Dec. 22, 1939. Rainey made her first appearance in public in Columbus when she was 12.

After touring with the Rabbit Foot Minstrels and Tolliver's Circus, she organized her own Georgia Jazz Band. Rainey was named "the Mother of the Blues" because she was one of the first female blues singers to tour widely in the South. She recorded first in 1923 and continued to tour through the end of the decade. BESSIE SMITH cited her as a key influence on her style.

The Depression had a major impact on both touring acts and the recording industry. Rainey struggled on but finally retired in 1935 to Columbus, Ohio. She died four years later in her native Georgia.

Rainy Day Women #12 & #35. BOB DYLAN's biggest pop hit. In this song, Dylan ironically attacks his critics, implying that the artist will be faulted no matter what he does.

Raitt, Bonnie, American popular music singer and guitarist; b. Los Angeles, Nov. 8, 1949. Her father was John (Emmet) Raitt (b. Santa Ana, Calif., Jan. 29, 1917), a versatile popular singer best known for his Broadway appearances in *Oklahoma!, Carousel, Pajama Game,* and *Annie Get Your Gun.*

Bonnie took up the guitar when she was 12. After attending Radcliffe College from 1967 to 1969, she departed the academic scene to pursue a career as a recording artist, mixing BLUES, ROCK, and BALLADS. She made a number of fine albums, including *Give It Up* (1972) and *Sweet Forgiveness*

PEOPLE IN MUSIC

A Broadway show, *Ma Rainey's Black Bottom,* was a success in the late '80s. It was based on Rainey's life and music.

PEOPLE IN MUSIC

(1977). However, she never attained the commercial heights expected of her. Her career was derailed for a time by alcoholism, but she fought her way back to sobriety and success.

In 1990 Raitt captured four Grammy Awards, including best album of the year for *Nick of Time* (1989). The album brought her renewed success and a number of top hits. She has continued to tour and record through the '90s.

Rake's Progress, The. Opera by IGOR STRAVINSKY, 1951, first performed in Venice. The LIBRETTO, in English, was written by W. H. Auden and Chester Kallman, its title taken from a series of satirical lithographs by the 18th-century British artist William Hogarth.

The story is a parable. The title character, Tom Rakewell (rake being a British slang word meaning a rogue or ne'er-do-well), is led into a series of adventures. He marries a bearded circus lady and invests a fortune in a device that grinds stones into flour and makes bread. Tom gambles for his soul with the devil, and though the devil loses, he causes Tom to lose his mind. The moral pronounced in the epilogue is very much in the manner of 18th-century fabulists: "For ideal hearts and hands and minds, the devil finds work to do."

The music imitates the BAROQUE style, with formal ARIAS, RECITATIVES, and choral INTERMEZZOS. But the rhythmic scheme is alive with angularities and asymmetries in the characteristic modern vein. The COUNTERPOINT allows for DISSONANCE, and the work moves freely between various KEYS. The orchestration is economical, with the HARPSICHORD (with a written-out part) serving as the primary voice.

Rákóczy March. A celebrated Hungarian piece with great patriotic associations.

Francis II Rákóczy (1676–1735) was the leader of the 1703 Hungarian rebellion against the Austrians, but the tune bearing his name did not appear until a century later. János Bihari, a Hungarian Gypsy violinist attached to a Hungarian regiment during the Napoleonic wars, is credited with its composition. It was first printed in 1820 in a collection of popular Army marches and quickly became a favorite.

FRANZ LISZT played it as a piano solo during his tour of Hungary in 1838 and later incorporated it in his *HUNGARIAN RHAPSODY* No. 15. HECTOR BERLIOZ arranged the *Rákóczy March* for orchestra in 1846 under the title *Marche Hongroise* and also included it as a separate number in his dramatic legend *La Damnation de Faust* (1846).

PEOPLE IN MUSIC

Raksin, David, American composer for films; b. Philadelphia, Aug. 4, 1912. Raksin studied piano in his childhood and also learned to play woodwind instruments from his father, a performer and conductor. When barely past puberty, he organized his own jazz band.

In 1931 Raksin entered the University of Pennsylvania, and in 1934–35 he also studied composition privately with Isadore Freed. In 1935 he went to Hollywood to assist Charlie Chaplin with the music for his film *Modern Times* (which he later orchestrated with Edward Powell). He also studied privately with ARNOLD SCHOENBERG, who was living in Los Angeles at the time.

Raksin composed more than 100 film scores, some of which attained great popularity. His greatest success was the theme song for *Laura,* which generated more than 300 different cover recordings. Apart from his activities as a composer and conductor, he also appeared as an actor and commentator in television programs.

Using material from his film music, Raksin composed several symphonic suites, among them *Forever Amber* and *The Bad and the Beautiful.* Other scores were *Force of Evil, Carrie, The Redeemer,* and *Separate Tables.* He also wrote incidental music, symphonic pieces, and vocal works, including *Oedipus memneitai* (Oedipus remembers) for bass-baritone narrator/soloist, six-part mixed chorus, and chamber ensemble in 1986. Raksin taught film and television composition at the University of California, Los Angeles, and was on the faculty of the University of Southern California School of Public Administration from 1968 to 1989.

In April 1992 Raksin received the Golden Soundtrack Award for Career Achievement from ASCAP, to whose Board of Directors he was subsequently elected. He also served as president of the Composers and Lyricists Guild of

America from 1962 to 1970 and of the Society for the Preservation of Film Music from 1992 to 1995.

Rameau, Jean-Philippe, great French composer, organist, and music theorist; b. Dijon (baptized), Sept. 25, 1683; d. Paris, Sept. 12, 1764. Rameau's father was organist at the Cathedral of St. Étienne in Dijon. He learned to play the harpsichord as a small child, and from age 10 to 14 he attended the Jesuit College des Godrans in Dijon. However, Rameau took up singing and composing instead of concentrating on his academic studies.

At 18, Rameau's father sent him to Milan, where he stayed for only a brief time before joining the orchestra of a traveling French opera troupe as a violinist. In 1702 he received a temporary appointment as organist at Avignon Cathedral. Later that year he became organist at Clermont Cathedral. By 1706 he was in Paris, where he published his first *Livre de pièces de clavecin* (Book of harpsichord pieces). He was active there as a church organist until 1708.

Rameau succeeded his father as organist at Notre Dame Cathedral in Avignon in 1709. He became organist to the Jacobins in Lyons in 1713 and then was organist at Clermont Cathedral from 1715 to 1723, where he wrote his famous *Traité de l'harmonie* (Treatise on harmony; 1722). Though little understood at the time, this work attracted considerable attention and also opposition, so that when he settled permanently in Paris in 1723 he was by no means unknown.

The fact that he failed in 1727 in a competition for the position of organist at St. Vincent-de-Paul did not injure his reputation: It was generally known that another organist, Louis Marchand (probably out of jealousy), had exerted his powerful influence in favor of Louis-Claude Daquin, who was in every respect inferior to Rameau.

In 1732 Rameau became organist at Ste. Croix-de-la-Bretonnerie and soon was recognized as the foremost organist in France. In 1726 his *Nouveau système de musique théorique* (New system of music theory) appeared, which was an introduction to the *Traité*. The leading ideas of his system of harmony are:

- chord-building by THIRDS

- classification of a chord and all its INVERSIONS as one and the same, thus reducing the multiplicity of CONSONANT and DISSONANT combinations to a fixed and limited number of ROOT CHORDS

- the invention of a fundamental bass (*basse fondamentale*), an imaginary series of root tones forming the real basis of the varied chord progressions employed in a composition

The stir that these novel theories occasioned, and his reputation as the foremost French organist, by no means satisfied Rameau's ambition. His ardent desire was to bring out a dramatic work at the Paris Opéra.

He had made a modest beginning with incidental music to Alexis Piron's comedy *L'Endriague* in 1723. After contributing further incidental music to two more of Piron's comedies in 1726, he became music master to the wife of a prominent courtier. The latter obtained from the famous French philosopher François-Marie Voltaire a LIBRETTO for *Samson,* which Rameau set to music. However, it was rejected on account of its biblical subject and is now lost. A second libretto, by Abbé Pellegrin, was accepted, and *Hippolyte et Aricie* was produced at the Opéra in 1733. Its reception was cool, despite its undeniable superiority over the operas of JEAN-BAPTISTE LULLY and his followers.

Rameau considered abandoning composing any further works for the theater, but the persuasions of his friends, who also influenced public opinion in his favor, were effective. In 1735 he brought out the successful opera-ballet *Les Indes galantes* and in 1737 his masterpiece, *Castor et Pollux,* a work that for years held its own alongside the operas of CHRISTOPH WILLIBALD GLUCK.

A career of uninterrupted prosperity commenced. Rameau was recognized as the leading theorist of the time, and his instruction was eagerly sought. For the next 30 years his operas dominated the French stage. He was named *Compositeur du cabinet du roi* (Composer of the King's chamber) in 1745, and was ennobled four months before his death.

From the beginning of his dramatic career, Rameau roused opposition and at the same time found ardent admirers. Practically the same charges were made against Rameau's works as would be made a century later against RICHARD WAGNER: unintelligible harmony, lack of melody, preponderance of discords, and noisy instrumentation.

It is regretable that Rameau was indifferent to the quality of his librettos. He relied so much upon his musical inspiration that he never could be made to realize the importance of a good text, hence the inequality of his operas. Nevertheless, his operas mark a decided advance over Lully's in musical characterization, expressive melody, richness of harmony, variety of MODULATION, and expert and original instrumentation.

Rameau wrote 30 sung dramas, premiered in Paris or Versailles, in various styles. He composed a relatively small amount of secular and sacred vocal music. His best known instrumental pieces are harpsichord works. He also wrote several other theatrical treatises.

Ramey, Samuel (Edward), outstanding American bass; b. Colby, Kans., March 28, 1942. Ramey attended Kansas State University, then studied voice with Arthur Newman at Wichita State University, earning his bachelor of music degree in 1968. After singing with the Grass Roots Opera Company in Raleigh, North Carolina, in 1968–69, he continued his studies with Armen Boyajian in N.Y.

Ramey made his professional operatic debut as Zuniga in CARMEN at the New York City Opera in 1973, and within a few seasons established himself as its principal bass. He also made guest appearances at several European opera festivals. In 1984 he made a brilliant debut at the Metropolitan Opera in N.Y. as Argante in GEORGE FRIDERIC HANDEL's RINALDO, and in 1987 he made his debut at the Salzburg Festival as Don Giovanni. He subsequently appeared with leading opera houses around the world and was engaged as a soloist with major orchestras.

Among Ramey's notable roles are Leporello, Don Giovanni, Figaro, Gounod's Mephistopheles, the four villains in LES CONTES D'HOFFMANN, Attila, and Boito's Mefistofele. He sang the role of Figaro for the sound-track recording of the award-winning film *Amadeus* in 1984.

PEOPLE IN MUSIC

PEOPLE IN MUSIC

Rampal, Jean-Pierre (Louis), celebrated French flutist, conductor, and teacher; b. Marseilles, Jan. 7, 1922. Rampal studied flute as a child with his father, who was first flutist in the Marseilles orchestra and a professor at the Conservatory. He then studied medicine until being drafted for military service by the German occupation authorities in 1943. When he learned that he was to be sent to Germany as a forced laborer, he went AWOL.

Rampal subsequently attended flute classes at the Paris Conservatory, winning the *premier prix* (first prize) in five months. He played solo flute in the orchestra of the Vichy Opéra from 1946 to 1950, while also beginning to tour, often in duo recitals with the pianist and harpsichordist Robert Veyron-Lacroix. He was solo flutist in the orchestra of the Paris Opéra from 1956 to 1962, and also became a popular artist on the Paris Radio.

Rampal subsequently toured throughout the world with phenomenal success as a virtuoso, appearing as soloist with all the major orchestras and in innumerable recitals. In later years he also appeared as a guest conductor. He taught at the Paris Conservatory and gave master classes worldwide.

Rampal's repertoire is vast, ranging from the BAROQUE masters to JAZZ, from the music of Japan to that of India, from arrangements to specially commissioned works. Of the last, such composers as FRANCIS POULENC and André Jolivet wrote pieces for him. Through his countless concerts and recordings, he did more than any other flutist of his time to bring his instrument into the mainstream of musical life.

Rampal was made a Chevalier of the Légion d'honneur in 1966 and an Officier des Arts et Lettres in 1971. With D. Wise, he published *Music, My Love: An Autobiography,* in 1989.

MUSICAL INSTRUMENT

rank. A row of ORGAN PIPES. A mixture STOP is said to have two, three, or more ranks, according to the number of pipes sounded by each key.

rant. An old country dance, or a REEL. It was used in instrumental suites by 17th-century English composers.

ranz des vaches (Fr.; Ger. *Kuhreigen*). One of the airs sung or played on the ALPINE HORN in the Swiss Alps as a call to cattle. The tune itself is marked by an asymmetrical rhythm. It appears to lean towards the Lydian MODE, with the characteristic augmented fourth as the key melodic INTERVAL. A version of the ranz des vaches appears in print in the 1546 *Bicinia gallica* of Georg Rhau.

răhns dā văh′sh

The ranz des vaches is also supposed to have magic and curative qualities. It is often combined with religious melodies.

rap. A style of urban African-American popular music that emerged in the mid-1970s. It is characterized by (often) improvised, sung-spoken rhymes performed to a rhythmic accompaniment. Rap is frequently performed A CAPPELLA, with sexual, socially relevant, or political lyrics. The music itself became known as HIP HOP.

Rap music with a more overt political message has been labeled gangsta (or gangster) rap. This music has been criticized by some in the white establishment for its advocacy of violent solutions to social problems.

Rape of Lucretia, The. Chamber opera by BENJAMIN BRITTEN, 1946, first performed at the Glyndebourne Festival.

Based on an ancient legend, the opera glorifies the "Christian" virtue of the heroine. Lucretia, awaiting her husband returning from war, is confronted by Tarquinius, the Roman commander. Imperiously he demands that she submit to him. When she refuses, he rapes her. Later, when her husband returns, she recounts her tragedy and shame to him before sinking a dagger into her breast.

The score is philosophically restrained, quite in opposition to the melodramatic Italian style of treating similar subjects.

Rappresentazione di anima e di corpo, La (Representation of the soul and body). RAPPRESENTAZIONE SACRA by Emilio de' Cavalieri (c.1550 – 1602). This MONODIC work represents the first theatrical application of the SECONDA PRATTICA to religious themes. The title reflects the content, a dramatic parable of the soul and body. The text includes characters with the abstract names Virtue and Valor taking part, much like a medieval mystery play. First performed 1600, Rome.

rappresentazione sacra (It., sacred performance). A religious spectacle developed in Florence beginning in the 15th century. Musically, it contained a succession of polyphonic CANZONAS. The first MONODIC example of the genre was *LA RAPPRESENTAZIONE DI ANIMA E DI CORPO,* 1600, by Emilio de Cavalieri. This work was a predecessor to the Italian *historia* and ORATORIO, as well as the Viennese *sepolochro.*

Rasoumowsky (Razumovsky) Quartets). The name given to LUDWIG VAN BEETHOVEN's three string quartets, op.59. Count Rasoumowsky was the Russian ambassador to Vienna who liked to play the violin. The result demonstrates how immortality could be bought by commissioning a great composer to dedicate a piece to an important official or a wealthy person.

In the first two quartets of this group, Beethoven used a Russian popular song that he picked up from a German collection. For this reason the *Rasoumowsky Quartets* are also known as the *Russian Quartets.*

RICHARD STRAUSS uses a ratchet in *TILL EULENSPIEGEL* (1895) and *DON QUIXOTE* (1898).

ratchet (Ger. *Ratsche*). An IDIOPHONE that consists of a wooden tablet. Scraped by a cogwheel, it produces a grating sound.

Ratsmusiker (Ger.). Town musicians, engaged by German municipalities to blow fanfares from the platform of the city hall.

PEOPLE IN MUSIC

Rattle, Simon (Denis), brilliant English conductor; b. Liverpool, Jan. 19, 1955. Rattle began playing piano and percussion as a child, appearing as a percussionist with the Royal Liverpool Philharmonic when he was 11 and with the National Youth Orchestra. He also took up conducting in his youth and was founder-conductor of the Liverpool Sinfonia from 1970 to 1972. He concurrently studied at the Royal Academy of Music in London from 1971 to 1974.

After winning first prize in the John Player International Conductors' Competition in 1974, Rattle was assistant conductor of the Bournemouth Symphony Orchestra and Sinfonietta until 1976. He made his first tour of the U.S., conducting the London Schools Symphony Orchestra that year.

Simon Rattle (left) *and Calvin Simmons at the Glyndebourne Opera House, 1976. (Hulton-Deutsch Collection/Corbis)*

In 1977 he conducted at the Glyndebourne Festival, then was assistant conductor of the Royal Liverpool Philharmonic and the BBC Scottish Symphony Orchestra in Glasgow, holding both positions until 1980.

Rattle made his first U.S. appearance as a guest conductor with the Los Angeles Philharmonic in 1979, becoming its principal guest conductor beginning in 1981. He also appeared as a guest conductor with other U.S. orchestras, as well as with European ensembles. In 1980 he became principal conductor of the City of Birmingham Symphony Orchestra, leading it on its first tour of the U.S. in 1988, the same year in which he made his U.S. debut as an opera conductor leading ALBAN BERG's *WOZZECK* in Los Angeles. In 1990 he made his debut at London's Covent Garden conducting Leoš Janáček's *The Cunning Little Vixen.*

In 1991 Rattle was named music director of the City of Birmingham Symphony Orchestra, which post he held until 1998. In 1987 he was made a Commander of the Order of the British Empire. His life is captured in Nicolas Kenyon's *Simon Rattle: The Making of a Conductor,* published in 1987.

Ravel, (Joseph) **Maurice,** great French composer; b. Ciboure, Basses-Pyrénées, March 7, 1875; d. Paris, Dec. 28, 1937. Ravel's father was a Swiss engineer and his mother of Basque origin. The family moved to Paris when he was an infant.

PEOPLE IN MUSIC

Ravel began to study piano at the age of 7 with Henri Ghis and harmony at 12 with Charles-René. After further piano studies with Emile Descombes, he entered the Paris Conservatory as a pupil of Eugène Anthiome in 1889. He won first medal in 1891 and passed to the advanced class of Charles de Bériot. He also studied harmony with Emile Pessard.

Ravel left the Conservatory in 1895. That same year, he completed work on his song *Un Grand sommeil noir,* the *Menuet antique* for piano, and the *Habanera* for two pianos

Maurice Ravel. (New York Public Library)

(later orchestrated for the *Rapsodie espagnole*). These pieces, written when Ravel was 20, already reveal great originality in the treatment of old MODES and of Spanish motifs. However, he continued to study, and in 1897 returned to the Conservatory to study composition with GABRIEL FAURÉ and counterpoint and orchestration with André Gédalge. His well-known PAVANE POUR UNE INFANTE DÉFUNTE for piano was written during that time, in 1899.

In 1899 Ravel conducted the premiere of his overture SHÉHÉRAZADE in Paris. Some elements of this work were incorporated into his song cycle of the same name of 1903. In 1901 he won the Second Prix de Rome with the CANTATA *Myrrha,* but ensuing attempts to win the Grand Prix de Rome were unsuccessful. Ravel left the Conservatory in 1903.

During the first decade of the new century, Ravel began composing in his mature style. He was irritated by the criticism that his work resembled that of CLAUDE DEBUSSY. Nonetheless, he composed many important and original works during this period, including his first opera, *L'HEURE ESPAGNOL* (1911), a number of songs, and *Rapsodie espagnole,* an orchestral work.

In 1909 Ravel began a fruitful association with Serge Diaghilev's Ballets Russes. For Diaghilev he wrote one of his masterpieces, *DAPHNIS ET CHLOÉ,* which took him three years to complete, from 1909 to 1912. Another ballet, *BOLÉRO,* commissioned by Ida Rubinstein and performed at her dance recital at the Paris Opéra in 1928, became Ravel's most spectacular success as an orchestral piece. Its relentless OSTINATO-driven CRESCENDO was irresistible to all but the composer.

Ravel was also an original orchestrator who developed textures both sensuous and transparent. In addition to orchestrating eight of his own piano works, some songs, and *TZIGANE* (1924), he arranged works by NIKOLAI RIMSKY-KORSAKOV, ERIK SATIE, ROBERT SCHUMANN, EMMANUEL CHABRIER, and MODEST MUSSORGSKY, most notably the latter's *PICTURES AT AN EXHIBITION* (originally for piano; 1922).

Said to be, for the most part, extremely shy, Ravel never married. He lived a life of semiretirement, devoting most of his time to composition. He accepted virtually no pupils, although he gave friendly advice to RALPH VAUGHAN WILLIAMS and GEORGE GERSHWIN. He was never on the faculty of any school, was not a brilliant performer, and appeared as a pianist only in his own works. Although he accepted engagements as a conductor, his conducting technique was poor.

When World War I broke out in 1914, Ravel was rejected for military service because of his frail physique, but he was anxious to serve. His application for air service was denied, but he was received in the ambulance corps at the front. His health gave way, and in the autumn of 1916 he was compelled to enter a hospital to recuperate. In 1922 he visited Amsterdam and Venice, conducting his music. In 1923 he appeared in London; in 1926 he went to Sweden, England, and Scotland; and in 1928 he made an American tour as a conductor and pianist. In the same year he received an honorary doctor of music degree at Oxford University.

Ravel came to hate his *Boléro,* despite its great success. He felt it was a rather limited piece of music.

In 1932 Ravel was apparently uninjured in an automobile accident. This event seemed to contribute to his final illness, however, and he developed difficulties in muscular coordination, attacks of aphasia, and headaches. At the time he thought he had "cerebral anemia," but the illness is now believed to have been Pick's disease, a form of dementia caused by atrophy of the frontal and temporal lobes of the brain. His last work, *Don Quichotte à Dulcinée* for baritone and orchestra, composed in 1932–33, was followed by several abortive projects. He declined steadily. He underwent brain surgery in December 1937, but it was unsuccessful, and he died nine days later.

Inspired evocation of the past was one aspect of Ravel's creative genius. In this style are his *Pavane pour une infante défunte*, *Le Tombeau de Couperin* (1914–17), and LA VALSE (1920). Luxuriance of exotic colors marks his ballet *Daphnis et Chloé*, his opera *L'Heure espagnole*, the song cycles *Shéhérazade* and *Chansons madécasses* (1925–26), and his virtuoso piano pieces *Miroirs* (1904–5) and *Gaspard de la nuit* (1908). Other works are deliberately austere, even ascetic, in their pointed classicism: the piano concertos, the piano Sonatine, and some of his songs with piano accompaniment.

Among Ravel's other notable works are *L'Enfant et les sortilèges* (fantaisie lyrique, 1920–25), two violin sonatas (1897; 1923–27), *Introduction et Allegro* for harp, flute, clarinet, and string quartet (1907), Piano Trio (1914), Sonata for violin and cello (1920–22), and *3 poèmes de Stéphane Mallarmé* for voice and ensemble (1914). He also composed works for voice and piano, including *5 Popular Greek Songs* (1904–6) and *Histoires naturelles* (1907), and *2 Hebrew Songs* (1914).

Razor Quartet (*Rasiermesserquartett*). String quartet by FRANZ JOSEPH HAYDN, late 1780s, in F minor (op.55, no. 2).

The nickname has an apocryphal story behind it: Haydn was so disturbed by the bluntness of his straight razor that he exclaimed, "I will give my best string quartet for a new razor!" A London publisher named John Bland supposedly overheard him and offered and later made the exchange.

re (It.; Fr. *Ré*). The second of the Aretinian (Guido d'Arezzo) syllables, and the name of the note *D* in France, Italy, etc.

Re pastore, Il. Opera by WOLFGANG AMADEUS MOZART, 1775, premiered in Salzburg. The setting follows the conventional pastoral drama, in which true love is tested by obstacles. Not a major work of Mozart's, but it has some fine set numbers.

Read, Daniel, important American tunebook compiler and composer; b. Attleboro, Mass., Nov. 16, 1757; d. New Haven, Conn., Dec. 4, 1836. Read worked on a farm as a youth. He studied mechanics and was employed as a surveyor at 18. At 17 he began to compose. He served in the Continental Army as a private, and at 21 he settled in New Stratford. Later he went to New Haven. In 1782–83 he maintained a singing school on the North River. He also was a comb maker.

At his death, Read left a collection of some 400 tunes by him and other composers. He published *The American Singing Book, or a New and Easy Guide to the Art of Psalmody, Devised for the Use of Singing Schools in America* (New Haven, 1785; fifth edition, 1795), the *American Musical Magazine* (containing 12 numbers of New England church music; compiled with Amos Doolittle; New Haven, 1786–87), Supplement to *The American Singing Book* (New Haven, 1787), *The Columbian Harmonist* (three volumes, 1793–1835), and *The New Haven Collection of Sacred Music* (New Haven, 1818).

realism. A musical aesthetic adopted by 19th-century composers determined to bring music closer to humanity. It differs from simple imitation of sounds in CHARACTER PIECES or PROGRAM MUSIC—such as *The Music Box, The Nightingale, The Brook,* and *The Cuckoo*—in its attempt to reflect in musical terms the reality of existence.

Realism finds its most logical application in vocal music, particularly in OPERA. The emergence of DRAMMA PER MUSICA was prompted by the desire to express the inflections of common speech in music. Among early opera composers

rā

PEOPLE IN MUSIC

GIULIO CACCINI stated his aims as creating a melody "by means of which it would be possible to speak in musical tones." His contemporary JACOPO PERI spoke of applying in opera "the accents which we unintentionally employ at moments of profound emotion." CHRISTOPH WILLIBALD GLUCK and HECTOR BERLIOZ declared similar beliefs decades later.

RICHARD WAGNER sought to intensify the power of ordinary speech, but his use of LEITMOTIVS precluded true realism. It was left to the Russian composers of the National School, particularly ALEXANDER DARGOMYZHSKY and MODEST MUSSORGSKY, to declare their determination to articulate in popular Russian accents the ARIAS and particularly the RECITATIVES in their operas. In this they opposed the Italian and the German ideals of music for music's sake.

Italian operatic realism found its application in the school of VERISMO. A specific type of realism motivated by political purpose arose in the Soviet Union under the somewhat specious name of SOCIALIST REALISM.

realization. 1. A written-out BASSO CONTINUO part, designed for those inexperienced in performing with FIGURED BASS. 2. An edited ARRANGEMENT of an old work; an adaptation for a specific purpose. This term came into use in the 20th century, favored particularly by English composers and arrangers. An arrangement required complete fidelity to at least the melody, rhythm, and harmony of the original, whereas a realization has a greater degree of freedom in transcribing the original work. 3. The creation of a whole, playable composition from an unfinished score or sketches. 4. The modern practice, responsive to CHANCE compositional procedures, of carrying out instructions, either explicitly or implicitly indicated in a given score, to perform a composition.

MUSICAL INSTRUMENT

rebec. A precursor of the VIOLIN, which originated in Islamic nations in Asia. It found its way to Spain and into France, where it remained popular until displaced by the violin. It had only three strings and was pear-shaped and long-necked. Also known by the Arabic name RABĀB.

recapitulation. A return of the EXPOSITION of a movement in SONATA FORM.

recessional. A hymn sung in church during the departure of choir and clergy after a service.

recital. A concert at which either (1) all pieces are executed by one soloist (or solo performer with accompanist), or (2) all pieces are by one composer. The term is not applied to a concert by a trio, quartet, etc.

recitative (Fr. *récitatif;* Ger. *Recitativ;* It. *recitativo*). A musical narrative, as contrasted with ARIAS and other formal parts in an OPERA or ORATORIO, which carries the action from one aria to another.

In early opera, *recitativo secco* (dry) was the common practice, with singers reciting a musical phrase following the accents and inflections of the spoken language accompanied by and alternating with a bare minimum of CHORDS played on the HARPSICHORD. In CLASSIC opera, WOLFGANG AMADEUS MOZART and others experimented with *recitativo accompagnato* (accompanied), where the vocal line was supported by an economical use of the full orchestra. In the 19th century, the demarcation between the accompanied recitative and the aria began to blur, until in RICHARD WAGNER's music dramas they coalesced into the ENDLESS MELODY.

Recitativo instrumentato is a recitativelike effect in instrumental music. It is achieved either by an instrument playing solo in an ensemble piece or, in piano playing, a crisp delivery of the melody, free in tempo and rhythm.

reciting note. In PLAINCHANT, the TONUS on which most of each verse (PSALM or CANTICLE) is continuously recited; usually the *dominant* above the tonus.

record album. 1. Originally, the bound holder for 78-rpm discs, whether for a single work or a collection. 2. A long-playing 33⅓-rpm disc.

record player. *See* PHONOGRAPH.

recorder (Fr. *flûte à bec;* Ger. *Blockflöte;* It. *flauto diritto*). An end-blown vertical FLUTE with a whistle mouthpiece popular

The word "recital" was invented by the manager of FRANZ LISZT's concert appearances in London. He hoped to convey a suggestion of a narrative and so to please romantically inclined music lovers.

res′ĭ-ta-tēv′

MUSICAL
INSTRUMENT

The recorder used in JOHANN SEBASTIAN BACH's *Fourth BRANDENBURG CONCERTO* is called a *flauto d'Eco.*

during the BAROQUE period; later superseded by the transverse flute.

Recorders ranging from bass to treble were used as solo instruments in chamber ensembles, under such names as sopranino, descant, treble, and bass.

Alto recorder player. (James P. O'Brien/School of Music, University of Arizona) ▶

After being dormant for over a century, the recorder enjoyed a spectacular revival in the 20th century that was fostered by performers and instrument makers. At first, the movement was primarily pedagogical in nature (e.g., the works by PAUL HINDEMITH and colleagues) but later involved the reincarnation of EARLY MUSIC in "authentic" form. This rebirth also engendered the composition of many new works for the instrument.

records. *See* RECORD ALBUM.

reco-reco (Braz.). *See* GÜIRO.

Red Mass. A solemn Roman Catholic votive MASS, in which the celebrants wear red vestments, celebrated at the openings of congresses, courts, and councils, as well as for some martyred saints.

Red Pony, The. Soundtrack by AARON COPLAND, 1948, for the film based on John Steinbeck's story about a young boy

gans for four electric organs and maracas in 1970, he made his first impact on the classical world.

In the summer of 1970 Reich traveled to Accra, Ghana, where he practiced under the tutelage of indigenous drummers. This experience bore fruit with the composition *Drumming* in 1971, which became quite popular. In 1973 he studied Balinese GAMELAN with a native teacher at the University of Washington in Seattle. In 1974 he received grants from the NEA and from the N.Y. State Council on the Arts, the first of many awards and honors. Becoming conscious of his ethnic heredity, he went to Jerusalem in 1976 to study the traditional forms of Hebrew cantillation.

Slowly but surely Reich rose to fame. His group was invited to perform at the Holland Festival and at radio stations in Frankfurt and Stuttgart. His increasing success led to a sold-out house when he presented a concert of his works at N.Y.'s CARNEGIE HALL in 1980. In 1986 he took his ensemble on a world tour.

Reich's music was MINIMALIST in philosophy. He deliberately reduced his harmonic and contrapuntal vocabulary and defiantly explored the fascinating potential of repetitive patterns. He used these techniques in his most successful works: *Music for Mallet Instruments, Voices, and Organ* (1973), *Music for 18 Musicians* (1976), *Music for a Large Ensemble* (1978), *Tehillim* (1981), *The Desert Music* (1984), and *Sextet* for percussion, piano, and synthesizers (1985).

Reich's techniques have been variously described as minimalist (derived from a minimum of chordal combinations), phase music (shifting from one chord to another, a note at a time), modular (built on symmetric modules), and pulse music (derived from a series of measured rhythmic units). Another term is PROCESS MUSIC, suggesting tonal progressions in flux. This system of composition is similar to SERIALISM in its use of repeated melodic progressions and periodic silences.

Despite his apparent disregard for musical convention, or indeed for public taste, Reich likes to trace his musical ancestry to the sweetly hollow homophonic music of the ARS ANTIQUA, with particular reference to the opaque works of the great master of the NOTRE DAME SCHOOL of Paris, PEROTIN.

For many years Reich deliberately avoided programmatic references in his titles, preferring to define them by names of instruments or numbers of musical parts. Recent works such as *The 4 Sections* for orchestra and *Electric Counterpoint* for guitar and tape continue this pattern. But other recent works suggest his interest in programmatic and historical connections, as in *Different Trains* for string quartet and tape (1988), which concerns the Holocaust and is partly MUSIQUE CONCRÈTE, and the multimedia stagework *The Cave* (1989–93).

Among other recent compositions are *Nagoya Marimbas* for two marimbas (1994), *City Life* for 17 performers with concrète urban sounds from two sampling keyboards (1994), and *Proverb* for three sopranos, two tenors, two vibraphones, and four SYNTHESIZERS (1995–96).

Reichardt, Johann Friedrich. *See* GOETHE, JOHANN WOLFGANG VON.

PEOPLE IN MUSIC

Reiner, Fritz, eminent Hungarian-born American conductor; b. Budapest, Dec. 19, 1888; d. N.Y., Nov. 15, 1963. Reiner studied piano and composition at the Royal Academy of Music in Budapest. He concurrently took courses in law.

Reiner was conductor of the Volksoper in Budapest from 1911 to 1914 and of the Court (later State) Opera in Dresden from 1914 to 1921. He also conducted in Hamburg, Berlin, Vienna, Rome, and Barcelona. In 1922 he was engaged as music director of the Cincinnati Symphony Orchestra, and in 1928 he was naturalized as a U.S. citizen. In 1931 he became a professor of conducting at the Curtis Institute of Music in Philadelphia, numbering among his students LEONARD BERNSTEIN and LUKAS FOSS.

In 1936–37 Reiner made guest appearances at London's Covent Garden. Between 1935 and 1938, he was guest conductor at the San Francisco Opera, and from 1938 to 1948 he was music director of the Pittsburgh Symphony Orchestra. He then was a conductor at the Metropolitan Opera in N.Y. until 1953.

Reiner achieved the peak of his success as a conductor with the Chicago Symphony Orchestra, serving as music director from 1953 to 1962, and bringing it to the point of impeccably fine performance in both CLASSICAL and modern music. His striving for perfection created for him the reputation of a ruthless master of the orchestra. He was given to explosions of temper; however, musicians and critics agreed that his high standards helped transform the Chicago Symphony into a first-rate orchestra.

Fritz Reiner (seated) *goes over a score with a young assistant. (Library of Congress/Corbis)*

Reinhardt, Django (Jean Baptiste), Belgian jazz guitarist; b. Liberchies, Jan. 23, 1910; d. Fontainebleau, May 16, 1953. Reinhardt began his career in Paris in 1922. He gained recognition through his recordings with the singer Jean Sablon and the violinist Stephane Grappelli. In 1934 he formed the Quintette du Hot Club de France with Grappelli. The group was unique in featuring three guitarists (Reinhardt played lead, with the other two supplying a chunky rhythmic accompaniment), bass, and violin. After World War II, he toured the U.S., appearing with Duke Ellington in N.Y.

Reinhardt was an innovative figure in the early JAZZ movement in Europe. His lightning-fast picked melody lines transformed the guitar from an accompaniment to lead instrument. In later years he utilized electrical amplification.

rejdowak. Bohemian ballroom dance in TERNARY time; later popular in Europe as the REDOWA.

Relâche. "Instantaneous ballet" by ERIK SATIE, 1924, first produced in Paris.

PEOPLE IN MUSIC

At the premiere the curtain bore the inscription in huge letters: "Erik Satie est le plus grand musicien du monde" (Erik Satie is the greatest musician in the world), adding that those who disagreed were invited to leave the hall.

related keys. Those KEYS with the first degree of relationship with the main key, whose TRIADS are contained within the available DIATONIC degrees of the main key. Thus, E minor is related to C major, D major, G major, and B minor, because E minor appears in these keys as the MEDIANT, SUPERTONIC, SUBMEDIANT, and SUBDOMINANT, respectively.
See also RELATIVE KEY.

relative key. A NATURAL MINOR KEY is relative to that MAJOR key the TONIC of which lies a MINOR THIRD above its own. A major key is relative to that natural minor key the tonic of which lies a minor third below its own. As a result, the two keys share key signatures, i.e., G major is the relative of E minor, sharing a signature of one sharp (F♯).

relative pitch. Ability to name an INTERVAL, or the exact second note, after hearing an interval and being given the identity of the first note. This ability can be learned, unlike PERFECT PITCH, which is an innate talent.

R.E.M. (Vocals: [John] Michael Stipe, b. Decatur, Ga., Jan. 4, 1960; Guitar/mandolin: Peter [Lawrence] Buck, b. Berkeley, Calif., Dec. 6, 1956; Bass/keyboards/vocals: Michael [Edward] Mills, b. Orange, Calif., Dec. 17, 1958; Drums/vocals: Bill Berry [born William Thomas Berry], b. Duluth, Minn., July 31, 1958; Berry left the group in 1997.) Popular American alternative ROCK band, which takes its name from "Rapid Eye Movement," an allusion to a stage of sleep. They were formed in Athens, Georgia in 1980 by four University of Georgia students. A year later, they released independently the single *Radio Free Europe*, gaining them a contract with I.R.S. Records. An EP and LP followed in rapid succession.

The group toured Europe in 1983 and continued to record, building a reputation among critics and alternative music listeners. They became known for their dense sound,

FRÉDÉRIC CHOPIN'S Preludes, op.28, are ordered by the CIRCLE OF FIFTHS, further arranged by alternating a major key with its relative minor (C major, A minor, G major, E minor, etc.).

PEOPLE IN MUSIC

One is tempted to translate the word reservata as "reserved," in the sense of being exclusive, describing a style of composition appreciated only by expert musicians. An alternative explanation of the term is "reservation," indicating a restricted use of ornamentation.

resolution. The progression of a DISSONANCE, whether a simple INTERVAL or a CHORD, to a CONSONANCE. Generally, SEMITONE motion is a controlling factor, whether moving from LEADING TONE to TONIC or from SUBDOMINANT to MEDIANT (in the DOMINANT-SEVENTH CHORD). Augmented intervals tend to resolve by expansion, while diminished intervals resolve by contraction.

Direct resolution, immediate progression from the dissonance to the consonance; *indirect* (or *delayed, deferred, retarded*) *resolution,* one passing through some intermediate dissonance(s) before reaching the final restful consonance.

resonance. The resounding of upper HARMONICS over the FUNDAMENTAL. *Resonance-box,* a hollow resonant body like that of the VIOLIN or ZITHER. *See also* RESONATOR.

Resonancias. Orchestral work by CARLOS CHÁVEZ, 1964, first conducted by the composer in Mexico City. Thematic elements are reflected by resonance, forming new melodic patterns.

resonator. Any object that amplifies sound. The SOUNDBOARD of the grand PIANO is a resonator of the strings. The hollow bodies of CHORDOPHONES serve the same purpose, because caverns are natural resonators.

MUSICAL INSTRUMENT

The elimination of unwelcome resonance is the most vexing and least predictable part of a proper architectural plan in constructing a concert hall. Orchestral players usually dampen their instruments to preclude "sympathetic vibrations," in which a particular pitch played on an instrument produces a sudden increase in loudness out of keeping with the rest of the notes. Is this the real meaning of that hoary cliché "Beware of bad vibes"?

Respect. The 1965 composition and recording by OTIS REDDING that became a major hit when it was covered two years

later by ARETHA FRANKLIN, who turned it into a women's liberation anthem.

Respighi, Ottorino, eminent Italian composer; b. Bologna, July 9, 1879; d. Rome, April 18, 1936. Respighi studied violin and composition at Bologna's Liceo Musicale from 1891 to 1900.

In 1900 Respighi went to Russia and played first viola in the orchestra of the Imperial Opera in St. Petersburg. He took lessons there with NIKOLAI RIMSKY-KORSAKOV, which proved a decisive influence in Respighi's coloristic orchestration. From 1903 to 1908 he was active as a concert violinist, and he also played the viola in the Mugellini Quartet of Bologna.

In 1913 Respighi was engaged as a professor of composition at Rome's Liceo (later Conservatory) di Santa Cecilia. In 1924 he was appointed its director but resigned in 1926, retaining only a class in advanced composition. Subsequently, he devoted himself to composing and conducting. He was elected a member of the Italian Royal Academy in 1932. In 1925–26 and again in 1932 he made tours of the U.S. as a pianist and a conductor.

Resphigi's style of composition is a highly successful blend of songful melodies with full and rich harmonies; he was one of the best masters of modern Italian music in OR-CHESTRATION. His power of evocation of the Italian scene and his ability to sustain interest throughout the length of a composition is incontestable. Although he wrote several operas, he achieved his greatest success with two symphonic poems, LE FONTANE DI ROMA (1917) and I PINI DI ROMA (1924), each consisting of four tone paintings of the Roman landscape.

Respighi also wrote several arrangements, including *Antiche arie e danze per liuto* (1917, 1923, 1931) and musical syntheses of other composers' work. He was even more prolific as a composer of vocal music. He wrote nine operas, several songs and song cycles, and chamber music, including the Violin Sonata in B minor (1917) and *Quartetto dorico* for string quartet (1924).

Respighi's wife, Elsa Olivieri Sangiacomo (b. Rome, March 24, 1894; d. 1996), was his pupil. She composed a

A great innovation for the time was the insertion of a phonograph recording of a nightingale into the score of *I pini di Roma.*

fairy opera, *Fior di neve,* the symphonic poem *Serenata di maschere,* and numerous songs. She also finished her husband's opera *Lucrezia* in 1937.

response (respond; Fr. *réponse*). 1. RESPONSORY. 2. An answer, in CALL-AND-RESPONSE texture. 3. The musical reply, by the choir or congregation, to what is said or sung by the priest or officiant.

responsory (Lat. *reponsorium;* Fr. *répons*). 1. That PSALM, or part of one, sung in alternation between soloist and congregation, after the reading of lessons. The practice dates to at least the 11th century. The great responsories are found in the Matins and monastic Vespers, lesser responsories at other hours. POLYPHONIC settings were mostly in the form of MOTETS and continued to be composed up until the 18th century. 2. The GRADUAL. 3. A *respond;* that is, the first part of a responsory psalm, sung by the congregation.

rest (It. *pausa*). An interval of silence between two tones; hence, the sign indicating such a pause.   pah′oo-zǎh

Retablo de Maese Pedro, El (Master Peter's puppet show). Puppet opera by MANUEL DE FALLA, 1923, based on Cervantes's *Don Quixote,* first performed in Seville.

The Knight of the Woeful Countenance watches a puppet show in which a young damsel keeps being throttled by disasters. Finally Quixote can no longer bear it, and he demolishes the puppet theater.

The score demonstrates de Falla's skill at investing Spanish folksong material with sophisticated harmony.

retardation. 1. A holding back, decreasing in speed. 2. A SUSPENSION resolving upward.

retrograde. 1. Performing a melody backwards. A pedantic melodic device often encountered in POLYPHONIC works, much beloved by composers of puzzle CANONS, and usually prefaced by them with fanciful phrases such as *Vade retro Satanas* (Get Thee behind me, Satan, Mark 8:33), *Ubi alpha ibi omega* (Where alpha is, omega is too), *Canite more He-*

braeorum (Sing in the Hebrew manner [that is, from right to left]), and (the most famous designation) *cancrizans* (literally, walking like a crab).

In the Minuet of his Symphony No. 47, FRANZ JOSEPH HAYDN explicitly marked *al rovescio,* meaning it could be played backwards without any change of the original music. JOHANN SEBASTIAN BACH's *MUSICAL OFFERING (Das musikalisches Opfer)* has a two-part canon in which the original subject is sounded simultaneously with its retrograde form. LUDWIG VAN BEETHOVEN has a crab motion in the final fugue of his *HAMMERKLAVIER SONATA.*

A remarkable example of a very melodious and harmonious piece representing a combination of the original and its retrograde form is an anonymous canon, erroneously attributed to WOLFGANG AMADEUS MOZART. It is played by two violinists reading a page across the table from one another, so that the player opposite performs the tune beginning with the last note and ending with the first note of the vis-à-vis partner. The wonder of it is that the result is in perfect harmony, and that a sharp applies to two different notes in the opposite parts without creating an unresolved DISSONANCE.

2. One of three standard techniques in DODECAPHONIC MUSIC. After a century of neglect, the technique of retrograde motion staged a revival in the music of the 20th-century Vienna School. ARNOLD SCHOENBERG has a retrograde canon in No. 18 of *PIERROT LUNAIRE,* as does ALBAN BERG in the middle section of his opera *LULU.*

retrograde inversion. Playing a melody backwards and upside down. A standard technique in DODECAPHONIC MUSIC.

reveille (Fr. *réveil*). The military signal for (1) getting up in the morning and (2) the first military formation of the day. It is based on the second, third, and fourth notes of the harmonic series playable on a BUGLE.

rā-vä′ēu

rêverie (Fr.). A dreamy meditation, the title of many ROMANTIC pieces.

Revolution. A 1968 BEATLES song, first released as a hard-rocking single, then as a more subdued album track on the famous *White Album.* JOHN LENNON could not decide whether he should be counted out or in when it came to violent revolutionary activities, so he sang it both ways!

Revolutionary Étude. The popular name of FRÉDÉRIC CHOPIN's Piano Étude in C minor, op.10, no. 12, supposedly composed when Chopin heard the sad news of the occupation of Warsaw by the Russians. The stormy surging SCALES in the left hand lent credibility to this story.

revue. A generic term for theatrical spectacles in which singing, speaking, dancing, and entertainment of all types are combined into a package that has no pretense of a unified plot. Each sketch in a revue is self-sufficient. The genres vary from sentimental BALLADS and duets to satire on topical subjects, from classical dances to popular MARCHES.

Revues originated in France under the reign of the "bourgeois" king, Louis Philippe, in 1830. A "Revue de fin d'année" was actually a review of events during the year past. In the second half of the 19th century, such revues were called *varietés.*

The most brilliant and daring revue of the first quarter of the 20th century took place at the theater named Folies-Bergère (follies of the district of Bergère). In the 19th century, the boldest exhibition of the female body was the high-kicking *CANCAN,* which titillated tourists and provided purists with subjects for sermons on the decay of public morality.

The British had two types: the revues, which emphasized political satire, and the MUSIC HALL, which focused on social humor and sentimentality. In the U.S., the Las Vegas floor show comes closest in spirit to the classic revue.

Revueltas, Silvestre, remarkable Mexican composer; b. Santiago Papasquiaro, Dec. 31, 1899; d. Mexico City, Oct. 5, 1940. Revueltas began violin studies when he was 8 in Colima, then entered the Juárez Institute in Durango at age 12. After studying composition and violin in Mexico City from 1913 to 1916, he took courses at St. Edward College in Austin, Texas, from 1916 to 1918, and at the Chicago Musical College until 1920. He then returned to Chicago to study violin further from 1922 to 1926.

PEOPLE IN MUSIC

From 1926 to 1928 Revueltas was active as a violinist and conductor in Texas and Alabama. Then he was appointed assistant conductor of the Orquesta Sinfónica de México in 1929, and he began to compose. He remained with the Orquesta until 1935.

In 1937 Revueltas went to Spain, where he was active in the cultural affairs of the Loyalist government during the Civil War. His health was ruined by exertions and an irregular life-style, and he died of pneumonia in 1940. His remains were deposited in the Rotonda de los Hombres Ilustres in Mexico City on March 23, 1976, to the music of his *Redes* and the funeral march from LUDWIG VAN BEETHOVEN's *EROICA* Symphony.

Revueltas possessed an extraordinary natural talent and an intimate understanding of Mexican music. He succeeded in creating works of great originality, melodic charm, and rhythmic vitality.

rhapsody (from Grk. *rapto* + *ode,* woven song; Fr. *rapsodie*). In Homeric times, itinerant singers, called *rhapsodes* (song weavers), recited their odes at festivals and political events.

răhp-sŏh-dē′

The rhapsodic concept was revived toward the end of the 18th century, when Christian F. D. Schubart published a collection of songs entitled *Musicalische Rhapsodien.* By the 19th century the reincarnated rhapsody was an instrumental improvisation on FOLK SONGS or on MOTIVES taken from native music. Later, the meaning of rhapsody was expanded to include instrumental compositions without source material.

FRANZ LISZT wrote a series of piano works (later orchestrated) called *HUNGARIAN RHAPSODIES* (1851), and JOHANNES BRAHMS composed several untitled piano rhapsodies. Among other composers who wrote rhapsodies were ANTONÍN DVOŘÁK, ALEXANDER GLAZUNOV, MAURICE RAVEL, BÉLA BARTÓK, and GEORGES ENESCO.

Rhapsody in Blue. Symphonic piece for piano and orchestra by GEORGE GERSHWIN, composed in 1924 and first performed by him in N.Y.

Although titled "blues," the work incorporates elements of JAZZ—most notably SYNCOPATION—into an orchestral piece. The piece is both lyrical and dramatic, and its expan-

The famous opening CLARINET GLISSANDO (or slide) is one of the most well-known introductions in American music.

sive melody and pleasingly modernistic harmonies made it a landmark in American music.

Rhapsody in Rivets. Rhapsody No. 2 for piano and orchestra by GEORGE GERSHWIN, 1932, which he wrote for SERGE KOUSSEVITZKY and the Boston Symphony Orchestra. Gershwin was the piano soloist in the Boston premiere.

Rivets in the title (later discarded) refers to the rhythmic sound of the riveting being done by construction workers throughout the streets of N.Y. Besides jazzy rhythms there is also a RUMBA.

Rheingold, Das. Music drama by RICHARD WAGNER, composed during 1851–54. It was written to be the *Vorabend* (fore-evening) to the great tetralogy DER RING DES NIBELUNGEN. Wagner wrote his own lofty, poetic text for the work. It was premiered in Munich in 1869.

◀

A fallen sculpture of a man's head was a key image in the San Francisco Opera's 1990 production of Das Rheingold.

The maidens of the river Rhine guard a horde of gold, which in this case is not just a precious yellow metallic element but a magical substance. Whoever forges a ring out of the Rhine gold will be master of the world. The Nordic gods who mill around their castle in Valhalla are no less quarrelsome than the gods of Mt. Olympus and are beset as much as the Greeks by trouble with disobedient underlings. The dwarf Alberich of the Nibelung clan renounces love in order to obtain the gold, and from it he forges the baneful ring of the Nibelung. Wotan, the Nordic Jupiter, succeeds in obtaining the ring from the incautious Alberich, who then pronounces a curse upon it.

Meanwhile, Wotan has to contend with an annoying couple of giants, Fasolt and Fafner, who demand payment for their work in building Valhalla. Although Wotan offers them the goddess of youth, Freia, in partial payment, they demand the gold as well. Having obtained it, the giants quarrel among themselves and the more vicious of them, Fafner, slays the other.

Realizing that Valhalla must be protected against the giant foes, Wotan procreates nine Valkyries, the stallion-riding warrior maidens generously endowed with brass-plated bosoms. Their main task is to take the bodies of slain heroes to Valhalla where they can be restored to life and protect the stronghold. Wotan also begets human children, Siegmund and Sieglinde, who in time will beget Siegfried. Wotan's hope is that Siegfried, the ideal of a Nordic hero, will track down the giant Fafner, recapture the ring, and return it to the Rhine maidens.

A whole encyclopedia of LEITMOTIVS is unfolded in *Das Rheingold* and used in the remaining operas. Not only the gods, giants, and dwarfs are characterized by these leitmotivs, but also objects or ideas involved in the action: the ring itself, the curse imposed upon it, the magic helmet, or *Tarnhelm,* which can transform a person into any human or animal shape, and the sword Nothung, the Nordic equivalent of King Arthur's Excalibur.

Rhenish Symphony. ROBERT SCHUMANN's Third Symphony, 1851, in E-flat major. Exceptionally, it is in five movements, but the penultimate movement, descriptive of the Cologne Cathedral, may be regarded as an INTERMEZZO.

The title is justified because in this work Schumann intended to reflect life in the Rhine countryside. It was first performed, appropriately, in the Rhenish town of Düsseldorf.

rhythm (It. *ritmo;* Fr. *rythme;* Ger. *Rhythmus*). The measured movement of similar TONE-groups, that is, the effect produced by the systematic grouping of tones with reference to regularity both in their accentuation and in their succession as equal or unequal in time value. A rhythm is, therefore, a tone-group serving as a pattern for succeeding identical groups. Traditionally, it follows the prosody of verse.

Rhythm is the animating element of all music and constitutes the essential formative factor in MELODY. A melody divested of rhythm loses its recognizable meaning, while rhythm without melodic content may possess an independent existence. The interdependence of melody and rhythm is expressed in the term MELORHYTHM. Rhythm must be distinguished from METER, which is an expedient grouping of rhythmical units upon which the rhythm is superimposed. A metrical group can itself constitute a rhythm, but a rhythmic figure cannot form a metrical entity.

The simplest rhythm beyond the monotonous repetition of the same note value is an alternation of a long and a short note, corresponding to the trochee in poetry. The metrical arrangement of such a rhythmic figure may be $\frac{3}{16}$, $\frac{3}{8}$, or any multiples of these fractions.

In the 20th century there is a marked tendency among composers to write music without barlines, thus abolishing metrical groupings all together. In compositions of the avant-garde both meter and rhythm are often replaced by durations given in seconds or fractions of a second. In his book *New Musical Resources,* the American composer HENRY COWELL proposed new shapes of musical note values making subdivisions into any kind of rhythmic groupings possible.

St. Augustine already makes this distinction in his treatise *De musica* (fifth century A.D.): "Omne metrum rhythmus, non monis rhythmus etiam metrum est" (Every meter is rhythm, but not every rhythm is also meter).

rhythm and blues (R&B). A generic term developed by the music industry in the late 1940s to distinguish recordings in a popular style by African-American artists from their white counterparts.

Rhythm and blues was considered strictly black music by the majority, and segregated by record companies into divisions they called "race records" (for Columbia, Okeh; for Victor, Bluebird; other labels simply reserved specific series numbers). In the segregated world of the U.S., rhythm and blues was, in the conservative view, a crucial part of the "devil's formula" for destroying the morals of white teenagers. But white teenagers began to purchase these recordings, despite their parents' warnings. Gradually white musicians such as BILL HALEY and (later) ELVIS PRESLEY recorded many of the black musicians' material and were thus able to crack the color barrier musically, if not socially. Not all the white artists were appropriate for this task, and many of these so-called COVER VERSIONS are as limp as the originals are gut-wrenching. It is a historical truism that many rhythm-and-blues artists of the 1940s and early 1950s were kept from the success they deserved by segregation.

Slight changes in style led to the white equivalent of rhythm and blues, ROCK 'N' ROLL. This new variant not only brought the influence of country-western (CARL PERKINS, JERRY LEE LEWIS, and BUDDY HOLLY), but also opened the door to some African-American performers who could adapt their music to the new style (CHUCK BERRY, LITTLE RICHARD, and FATS DOMINO).

rhythm guitar. *See* GUITAR, RHYTHM.

rhythm section. PERCUSSION section in a JAZZ band consisting of PIANO, BASS, and DRUMS, supplying the main beat. If a guitar is used, it will function within this section at times.

ribs. The curved sides of the VIOLIN, connecting belly and back.

rē-châr-kăh′rĕh   **ricercar** (It. *ricercare, ricercata,* research, inquire). Instrumental composition of the 16th and 17th centuries generally characterized by imitative treatment of the theme(s). Ricercar is one of the most vaguely defined forms, encompassing elements of CANON, FUGUE, FANTASY, and early SONATA.

Early in the 16th century, *ricercar* retained a more or less literal meaning of "trying out." The musician might begin by tuning the LUTE and playing improvisatory ARPEGGIOS and melodic FIORITURAS as a sort of introduction to the principal section of the work. An Italian 16th-century theorist describes the ricercar as a sequence of *suoni licenziosi,* not in the sense of "licentious sounds" but of sounds arranged with a certain degree of license, to be played *senza arte* (without artifice, artlessly). VINCENZO GALILEI wrote about a musician who played "une bella ricercata con le dita" (a fine ricercar with his fingers) and then began to sing.

Originally, the ricercar was a prelude to a song, keyboard composition, or dance tune played on a lute, but within a century it assumed an independent significance comparable to a fugue and sonata, in a contrapuntal style far removed from its pristine "artlessness." It tended toward short themes closely imitated, resulting in a very strict manner in comparison with the later "free fugue."

The BAROQUE ricercar was little heard in the 19th century but was revived in the 20th century by several composers, among them IGOR STRAVINSKY, BOHUSLAV MARTINŮ, and GIAN FRANCESCO MALIPIERO, when the slogan "Back to Bach" became fashionable.

Rich, Buddy (Bernard), remarkable American jazz drummer and bandleader; b. N.Y., June 30, 1917; d. Los Angeles, April 2, 1987. Rich's parents were vaudeville performers who made him a part of their act before he was two. He was only four when he appeared as a drummer and tap dancer on Broadway, and he made his first tour of the U.S. and Australia at the age of six. He was leading his own stage band by the time he was 11.

In 1937 Rich joined the band of Joe Marsala. After working with Bunny Berigan, Harry James, ARTIE SHAW, and Benny Carter, he performed with TOMMY DORSEY (1939–42; 1944–45). He then led his own band until 1951. He again performed with James (1953–54; 1955–57; 1961–66) and Dorsey in 1954–55, and also led his own combo from 1957 to 1961. In 1966 he founded his own big band, with which he toured worldwide until it folded in 1974.

In subsequent years, Rich made appearances at his own N.Y. club, Buddy's Place, leading a small combo. During the last years of his life, he also toured with his own jazz-rock big band.

Rich was one of the outstanding SWING drummers of his time.

Richard Wagner: Venezia. An homage for piano by FRANZ LISZT, 1883, written when he learned of his son-in-law Wagner's death in Venice. Contrary to expectations, there are no quotations of Wagner's music, except for the use of aug-

When JOHANN SEBASTIAN BACH presented his *MUSICAL OFFERING* (1747) to Frederick the Great of Prussia, he chose the ricercar as the center of his work. His melodic theme was based on an acrostic in Latin, *Regis iussu cantio et reliqua canonica arte resoluta* (By the King's command the theme and additions resolved in canonic style.) The first letter of each word determined the note in the theme.

PEOPLE IN MUSIC

mented triads, vaguely reminiscent of the *Ride of the Valkyries.*

Richards (Richard), **Keith.** *See* ROLLING STONES, THE.

PEOPLE IN MUSIC

Richter, Sviatoslav (Teofilovich), outstanding Russian pianist; b. Zhitomir, March 20, 1915; d. Moscow, Aug. 1, 1997. Both of Richter's parents were pianists. The family moved to Odessa when he was a child. He was engaged as a piano accompanist at the Odessa Opera and developed exceptional skill in playing orchestral scores at sight. He made his formal debut as a concert artist at the Odessa House of Engineers in 1934.

In 1937 Richter entered the Moscow Conservatory as a student of Heinrich Neuhaus, graduating in 1947. He acquired a notable following even during his student years. In 1945 he made a stunning appearance at the All-Union Contest of Performances and was awarded its highest prize. In 1949 he received the Stalin Prize.

In subsequent years, Richter played throughout the Soviet Union and Eastern Europe. During the Russian tour of the Philadelphia Orchestra in 1958, Richter was soloist, playing SERGEI PROKOFIEV's Fifth Piano Concerto in Leningrad. He made several international concert tours, including visits to China in 1957 and the U.S. in 1960.

Both in Russia and abroad he earned a reputation as a piano virtuoso of formidable skill. He was especially praised for his impeccable sense of style, with every detail of the music rendered perfectly. His performances of the ROMANTIC repertoire brought him great renown, and he made notable excursions into the works of CLAUDE DEBUSSY, MAURICE RAVEL, and SERGEI PROKOFIEV as well. He gave the first performances of Prokofiev's Sixth, Seventh, and Ninth sonatas.

Rider Quartet. *See* RITTERQUARTETT.

Riders to the Sea. Opera by RALPH VAUGHAN WILLIAMS, 1937, based on the 1904 play by Irish playwright John Millington Synge, first performed in London. The drama is a lament on the fate of an Irishwoman who has lost all her sons at sea. Vaughan Williams enhances the depressing monotony of the story in his MONODIC setting, occasionally relieved by acrid DISSONANCES.

Rienzi (*Cola Rienzi, der letzte der Tribünen*). Opera by RICHARD WAGNER, 1842, produced in Dresden. The composer's LIBRETTO is based on the historical novel by Edward Bulwer-Lytton.

Rienzi is a member of a powerful Roman family in the 14th century. He is trying to restore Roman self-government but is caught up in the struggle between his and other leading families. In the opera, as in the novel and actual history, Rienzi, his sister, and a handful of his adherents perish in a fire at the Capitol.

This is one of Wagner's early operas written in the Italian style. Its OVERTURE, with its stirring trumpet calls, is occasionally performed in concert, but the opera is rarely performed in its entirety or staged.

Bulwer-Lytton also authored the line "It was a dark and stormy night." His remarkably bad writing style inspired an annual Bulwer-Lytton prize for horrendous prose.

riff. 1. A call-and-response refrain in JAZZ, consisting of sharply rhythmed brief turns often played by wind and percussion instruments as an interlude after a solo. 2. As per (1) but, in popular music, played on whatever instrument is chosen (keyboards and electric guitar are common), and often contained within a solo improvisation. 3. HOOK.

rigadoon (Fr. *rigaudon;* It. *rigodone*). A lively dance originating in the 17th century in southern France. Set in ALLA BREVE time, it usually opens on a quarter-note UPBEAT and contains a trio section and a number of reprises. The rigadoon was often part of the instrumental SUITES of the 17th and 18th centuries.

MAURICE RAVEL included a rigadoon in his piano suite *Le Tombeau de Couperin* (1920).

rē-goh-dŏhn

Rigoletto. Opera by GIUSEPPE VERDI, 1851, to a libretto based on Victor Hugo's play *Le Roi s'amuse* (The King pleases himself) first performed in Venice.

Rigoletto, a hunchbacked court jester, mocks an aggrieved father, Monterone, whose daughter was seduced by the evil Duke of Mantua. He is cursed by the victim of his insensitive raillery. Monterone's curse is prophetic, because

Rigoletto's own daughter, Gilda, is debauched in turn by the despicable rake. Incensed, Rigoletto hires an assassin to kill the Duke and deliver his body in a sack at the door of a tavern.

But when Rigoletto arrives there at midnight, he hears the Duke repeat his immortal and immoral misogynist aria *La donna è mobile*. Horrified, he opens the sack and finds his dying daughter, who had been stabbed when she disguised herself and voluntarily took the knife intended for the Duke, whom she still loves. "Maledizione!" he cries out, recalling the curse.

The opera is a perennial favorite, and the Duke's aria is sung by a myriad of TENORS in concert. There is also a magnificent vocal quartet.

FRANZ LISZT wrote a paraphrase for piano on the themes from *Rigoletto.*

PEOPLE IN MUSIC

Riley, Terry (Mitchell), significant American composer and performer; b. Colfax, Calif., June 24, 1935. From 1955 to 1957, Riley studied piano with Duane Hampton at San Francisco State College and composition with Seymour Shifrin and William Denny at the University of California at Berkeley, earning his master's degree in 1961.

Throughout the early 1960s Riley went to Europe, where he played piano and saxophone in cabarets in Paris and in Scandinavia. In 1967 he was a creative associate at the Center for Creative and Performing Arts at the State University of N.Y. in Buffalo. In 1970 he was initiated in San Francisco as a disciple of Pandit Pran Nath, the North Indian singer, and followed him to India. From 1971 to 1980 he was associate professor at Mills College in Oakland, California. In 1979 he held a Guggenheim fellowship. Throughout the 1980s and 1990s, he appeared frequently in improvised recitals as both a pianist and vocalist.

In his music, Riley uses the idea of varied repetition of melody and rhythms. His landmark *IN C* (1965) is in mobile form, played by members of an ensemble who proceed freely from one segment to another (totaling 53), along with an unrelenting high C OCTAVE. This piece launched the second wave of MINIMALISM.

Riley's titles suggest connections with the Beat Generation, non-Western religion, and a NEW AGE sensibility. Besides his improvised recitals, he has written pieces for conventional orchestra and string quartet, including *Salome Dances for Peace* for string quartet (1989), *The Jade Palace Orchestral Dances* for orchestra (1989), *June Buddhas,* concerto for chorus and orchestra (1991), and *4 Wöfli Sketches* for chamber ensemble (1992).

Riley has also written several innovative works for synthesizer, beginning with *Poppy Nogoods Phantom Band* (1966), a record album in which he played all the parts. He followed this with another landmark work, *A Rainbow in Curved Air* (1968). Since then, he has tended to combine synthesizers with other instruments, particularly the Indian SITAR and TABLĀ, composing a number of works for live performance.

Riley also composed the chamber opera the *Saint Adolf Ring* (1992) and the film scores *Les Yeux fermés* (1973) and *Le Secret de la vie* (1975).

Rimsky-Korsakov, Nikolai (Andreievich), great Russian composer and master of orchestration, member of the "Mighty 5"; b. Tikhvin, near Novgorod, March 18, 1844; d. Liubensk, near St. Petersburg, June 21, 1908. Rimsky-Korsakov was raised in the Russian countryside until he was 12 years old. At that time, he entered the Naval School in St. Petersburg, graduating in 1862.

PEOPLE IN MUSIC

Rimsky-Korsakov took piano lessons as a child with provincial teachers and, beginning around 1860, with a professional musician, Theodore Canille, who introduced him to MILY BALAKIREV. At this time, he also met CÉSAR CUI and ALEXANDER BORODIN. In 1862 he was sent on the clipper Almaz on a voyage that lasted two and a half years. Returning to Russia in the summer of 1865, he settled in St. Petersburg, where he remained most of his life.

During his travels, Rimsky-Korsakov maintained contact with Balakirev and continued to report to him the progress of his musical composition. He completed his First Symphony (the earliest significant work in this form by a Russian composer), and it was performed under Balakirev's direction at a concert of the Free Music School in St. Petersburg in 1865.

In 1871 Rimsky-Korsakov was engaged as a professor of composition and orchestration at the St. Petersburg Conservatory, even though he was aware of the inadequacy of his own technique. He remained on the faculty until his death, with the exception of a few months in 1905, when he was relieved of his duties because of his public support of rebellious students during the revolution of that year.

In 1873 Rimsky-Korsakov abandoned his naval career but was appointed to the post of inspector of the military orchestras of the Russian navy, until it was abolished in 1884. From 1883 to 1894 he was also assistant director of the Court Chapel and led the chorus and orchestra there. Although he was not a gifted conductor, he gave many performances of his own works. He made his debut at a charity concert for the victims of the Volga famine, in St. Petersburg in 1874, in a program that included the first performance of his Third Symphony.

From 1886 until 1900 Rimsky-Korsakov conducted the annual Russian Symphony concerts organized by the music publisher Belaieff. In June 1889 he conducted two concerts of Russian music at the World Exposition in Paris, and in 1890 and 1900 he conducted concerts of Russian music in Brussels. His last appearance abroad was in the spring of 1907, when he conducted in Paris two Russian historic concerts arranged by Serge Diaghilev. In the same year he was elected corresponding member of the French Academy, succeeding EDVARD GRIEG.

These activities, however, did not distract Rimsky-Korsakov from his central purpose as a national Russian composer. His name was grouped with those of Cui, Borodin, Balakirev, and MODEST MUSSORGSKY as the "Mighty 5." These five were recognized as the leading composers of their generation, and Rimsky-Korsakov maintained an intimate friendship with most of them. At Mussorgsky's death he collected and prepared his manuscripts for publication. He also revised Mussorgsky's *BORIS GODUNOV,* and it was in Rimsky-Korsakov's version that the opera became famous. He had decisive influence in the affairs of Belaieff and helped publish a great number of works by Russian composers of the St. Petersburg group.

Although he was far from being a revolutionary, Rimsky-Korsakov freely expressed his disgust at the bungling administration of Czarist Russia. The government censors wanted to cut some of Aleksandr Pushkin's lines in Rimsky-Korsakov's own last opera, THE GOLDEN COCKEREL (1906–07), but he refused to compromise. He died of a heart attack, with the situation unresolved. The opera was produced posthumously, with the censor's changes, and the original text was not restored until the revolution of 1917.

Rimsky-Korsakov was one of the greatest masters of Russian music. His source of inspiration was Mikhail Glinka's operatic style. He made use of both the purely Russian idiom and coloristic oriental melodic patterns. His symphonic suite SCHEHERAZADE (op.35, 1888) and *The Golden Cockerel* represent Russian orientalism at its best. In the purely Russian style, the opera SNOW MAIDEN (1880–81) and the *Russian Easter Overture* (op.36, 1888) are outstanding examples. The influence of RICHARD WAGNER and FRANZ LISZT on his music was small. Only in his opera THE LEGEND OF THE INVISIBLE CITY OF KITEZH (1903–05) are there recognizable echoes from *PARSIFAL*.

In the art of ORCHESTRATION, Rimsky-Korsakov had few equals. His treatment of instruments, in both solo passages and in ensemble, was imaginative. In his treatise on orchestration he selected only passages from his own works to demonstrate the principles of practical and effective application of registers and tone colors (unlike HECTOR BERLIOZ, who included the work of others in his groundbreaking book on the same subject).

Although generally a conservative who followed the academic rules, Rimsky-Korsakov experimented boldly with melodic progressions and ingenious harmonies that pointed toward modern usages. He especially favored the MAJOR SCALE with the lowered SUBMEDIANT and the OCTATONIC scale of alternating WHOLE TONES and SEMITONES (which Russian reference works called "Rimsky-Korsakov's scale"). In the score of his *Mlada* (1889–90) there is an ocarina part tuned in this scale. In *The Golden Cockerel* and *Kashchei the Immortal* (1902) he used DISSONANT harmonies in unusual superpositions. But he set for himself a definite limit in innovation and severely criticized RICHARD STRAUSS, CLAUDE DEBUSSY, and VINCENT D'INDY for their modernistic practices.

As an educator, Rimsky-Korsakov was of the greatest importance to the development and maintenance of the traditions of the Russian national school. Among his students were ALEXANDER GLAZUNOV, ANATOLI LIADOV, NICOLAS TCHEREPNIN, Maximilian Steinberg, MIKHAIL GNESSIN, and NIKOLAI MIASKOVSKY. IGOR STRAVINSKY studied privately with him from 1903.

In addition to works previously mentioned, Rimsky-Korsakov wrote many operas, orchestral works, including Overture on 3 Russian Themes, op.28 (first version, 1866; second version, 1879–80), Fantasia on Serbian Themes, op.6 (first version, 1867; second version, 1886–87), Symphony No. 2, op.9, *Antar* (first version, 1868; second version, 1875; third version, 1897), Symphony No. 3, op.32 (first version, 1866-73; second version, 1886), and Piano Concerto in C-sharp Minor, op.30 (1882–83). He also composed chamber works for string quartet (1875–99) and other instrumental combinations.

Rimsky-Korsakov wrote many choral works with orchestral accompaniment, as well as A CAPPELLA choruses. His piano works include character pieces, such as variations. He was also a prolific arranger and editor, including his edition of 100 Russian folk songs, op.24, from 1876. He orchestrated ALEXANDER DARGOMYZHSKY's posthumous opera *The Stone Guest* (1872) and Alexander Borodin's PRINCE IGOR (1890).

Rimsky-Korsakov's greatest task of musical reorganization was the preparation for publication and performance of Mussorgsky's works. He reharmonized the cycle *Songs and Dances of Death* and the symphonic picture NIGHT ON BALD MOUNTAIN (1886), orchestrated the opera KHOVANSHCHINA, and revised *Boris Godunov* (melody, harmony, and orchestration).

Two of Rimsky-Korsakov's relations were important Russian musicians. His son, Andrei (Nikolaievich) Rimsky-Korsakov (b. St. Petersburg, Oct. 17, 1878; d. there (Leningrad), May 23, 1940), studied philology. He devoted his energies to Russian music history. In 1915 he began the publication of an important magazine, *Musikalny Sovremennik* (The musical contemporary), but the revolutionary events of 1917 forced suspension of its publication. He edited books on his father and Mussorgsky. He was married to the composer Julia Weissberg.

Among his pedagogical works, the book on harmony published in 1884 was widely used in Russian music schools.

his retirement in 1983. Through his career, he earned numerous awards and honorary degrees.

The most profound influence on Rochberg's music was that of ARNOLD SCHOENBERG and ANTON WEBERN. Later in life, he turned to classical models, even resorting to overt quotations in his works of recognizable fragments from music by composers as mutually unrelated as HEINRICH SCHÜTZ, JOHANN SEBASTIAN BACH, GUSTAV MAHLER, and CHARLES IVES. He has at times tried to synthesize his pre-20th-century influences, at other times practiced COLLAGE or ASSEMBLAGE, or set one style against another within one work. For example, in his String Quartet No. 3 (1972), the different movements feature either strong ATONALITY, Bartókian rhythm, or a Brahmsian variation set.

Other works by Rochberg include the opera *The Confidence Man,* composed in 1982, and based on the story by Herman Melville, and the monodrama *Phaedra* for mezzo-soprano and orchestra, composed in 1974–75. His orchestral works include six symphonies, among other works. He wrote seven string quartets, two piano trios and other chamber works, as well as piano pieces and vocal works, both accompanied and unaccompanied.

rock. A term that covers a variety of popular American styles dating from the 1960s, each an outgrowth of the ROCK 'N' ROLL movement of the 1950s, itself a descendant of earlier black and white musical influences.

The rock era is generally said to have begun in 1964, when the BEATLES of Liverpool, England, arrived in America. Their early songs and covers represented a turn to textures dominated by electric guitars with percussive rhythmic support. Over the years, the Beatles's songwriters (especially JOHN LENNON and PAUL MCCARTNEY) found various syntheses of the elements that had gone into rock 'n' roll, adding others along the way and moving rock instrumentation into new territory.

On the other end of the spectrum were the ROLLING STONES, whose influences went further into RHYTHM-AND-BLUES style, harsher than what the Beatles had drawn from. This choice, plus the sexualized stance taken by Mick Jagger and Keith Richards in their songs, made the Beatles seem tame by comparison in terms of raw energy. Both groups contributed to a major change in popular music: where rock 'n' roll was strongly rooted in dance, rock grew increasingly into a listening and even concert music.

The U.S. also contributed its influences on rock. One such style predated the "British invasion" of the 1960s, namely the surfing music of the West Coast (Beach Boys, Jan and Dean) that combined DOO-WOP vocal harmonies with a rock 'n' roll beat. Another was an African-American development known as MOTOWN or SOUL, depending on whether the music was centered on Detroit or Memphis, respectively. Both drew on GOSPEL music and rhythm and blues. Motown also borrowed the girl-group sound for most of their artists. The Memphis sound brought more of the older blues singing style to its recordings, most of it done by solo artists or duets.

The term *rock,* seemingly an abbreviation for rock 'n' roll, gradually replaced the older name, as the music moved into nonblues harmonic patterns and made the electric guitar the primary lead melody instrument, replacing the saxophone. Soon, musical styles were given geographic names, sometimes as a marketing ploy. The most legitimate of these was the "San Francisco sound." This was associated with the hippie movement, drug experimentation, and antiwar protest. Group improvisation, often free-form and significantly increasing the length of a song, was another hallmark of the San Francisco style.

From there rock has flourished for 30 plus years, often challenged commercially and artistically: by DISCO in the 1970s and other dance music thereafter, by HIP-HOP and RAP in the 1980s, by soul in its balladic forms, and so on. But rock has shown a great capacity for reinventing itself when the creative juices are about to run dry: when the overblown art rock of the 1970s seemed destined to make rock a dinosaur, the NEW WAVE and PUNK movements came out of England, reinventing both the Beatles's and Rolling Stones's contributions.

Among the numerous subgenres that have grown out of 1960s rock are:

acid rock, a heavier form, developed in the California music scene in the later 1960s, with emphasis on FEEDBACK guitar solos and powerful amplification. Often, there are cryptic references to drugs such as LSD ("acid") in the lyrics

art rock, an odd mixture of rock instrumentation (with strong emphasis on keyboards) and classical orchestration or imitations thereof; the music can be original, in the style of a classical piece, or "borrowed" from actual works

blues rock, an especially British genre, taking both rural and urban blues into a rock context, with a strong dose of guitar (also keyboard and harmonica) improvisation

folk rock, putting folk songs or neotraditional songs into a rock context, much as the Byrds and BOB DYLAN did

hard rock, similar to acid rock, but with a higher dynamic level, thicker texture, and an unmistakable hook—the predecessor of *heavy metal* (also called *metal*), which pushes the envelope further by even greater concentration on the rhythm guitar, the lead guitar becoming buried in the thick texture and adding a theatrical element

jazz rock (also known as *fusion*), a mixture of the harmonic and melodic elements of JAZZ with the rhythm and instrumentation of rock, representing jazz's attempt to overcome commercial failure during the 1960s and rock's desire for fresh materials and respect

mellow rock (*soft rock*), rock's contribution to MOR (middle of the road), easy listening, and Muzak—it grew out of folk rock's merging with late rock 'n' roll balladry, with Carole King at the head of the pack

new wave, a late 1970s English revival of the lean sound of 1960s rock (in reaction to art rock and disco)

punk rock (*punk*), historically synchronous with new wave, but influential by the "garage bands" of the 1960s and hard rock—originally connected to British youth's social rage, but eventually becoming a fashion statement—the punk spirit survived into the 1990s with *grunge,* an Americanized variant with more depression than alienation.

Along the way, rock has at times borrowed from other styles (CLASSICAL, disco, REGGAE, hip-hop) without losing its essence. Musicians like FRANK ZAPPA have been able to play most rock styles and parody them with great skill.

The greatest mass demonstration of rock and perhaps the greatest manifestation of the attractive power of music in all history, was the Woodstock Festival in Bethel, N.Y., held in August 1969. The convergence of hundreds of thousands of people in one place was remarkable in and of itself. However, the fact that they were able to stay together peacefully, despite the shortages of food and water and the rain that turned the outdoor festival into a large field of mud, inspired awe among observers as well as the participants.

Woodstock stood in stark contrast to a concert held at the Altamount race track in California just months later. There, while the Rolling Stones played, a group of Hell's Angels beat an audience member to death. These two festivals have come to represent the creative versus the destructive aspects of rock.

rock ’n’ roll. A popular American style of the 1950s that emerged from the African-American popular style of RHYTHM AND BLUES. The term is probably related to various songs using double entendre, especially a slang expression for sex. A Cleveland DJ named Alan Freed is generally credited with popularizing the generic term *rock ’n’ roll.*

As opposed to the prevailing BALLAD style of the time, which featured singers with smooth orchestral background, rock ’n’ roll featured a percussively heavy reinforcement of the METER (beat) played by combos consisting, minimally, of piano, bass, drums, and guitars, often with a single saxophonist or small wind section. BLUES harmonic structures were common, but without the corresponding mood.

In 1956 the landscape of rock ’n’ roll was brightened by the rise of ELVIS PRESLEY. Presley took elements of R&B and country music and wed them into a style that was initially known as ROCKABILLY. However, it was Presley's magnetic

The term *rockabilly* was derived from *rock* wed to *hillbilly,* a common name for country music.

stage presence, including his famous "gyrating" hips, that made him a sensational star.

Elvis opened the door for many other performers, black and white. CARL PERKINS was an even purer practitioner of rockabilly, enjoying one enormous hit with his famous song *Blue Suede Shoes.* JERRY LEE LEWIS took Elvis's sexuality and pumped it up to the nth degree in songs like *Great Balls of Fire.* CHUCK BERRY was one of rock's first great guitarists and also a great songwriter. He cleverly aimed his songs directly at his teenage audience, addressing issues close to their hearts, including dating and driving cars. LITTLE RICHARD was one of rock's most flamboyant performers.

Rock 'n' roll suffered a temporary eclipse when it was discovered that DJ's accepted bribes from recording companies for pushing their rock records, a practice that became known as *PAYOLA.* But no scandal could stop the inexorable march of rock 'n' roll. In 1960 CHUBBY CHECKER and his innovative dance, the twist, added a new beat to rock 'n' roll. This introduced the era of the discotheque, a dance hall where records were played, which replaced the nightclub and its live entertainment.

In the late '50s and early '60s, rock seemed to run out of steam. Many of its early stars were either dead, discredited, or in exile (Elvis was in the Army from 1958 – 60). The record labels responded by fabricating "teen idols" to fill the void, including singers like Fabian and Frankie Avalon. It was not until 1964 with the "British Invasion" that a new generation of musicians revitalized rock 'n' roll and transformed it into ROCK.

(We're Gonna) Rock around the Clock. ROCK 'N' ROLL song by Max Freedman and Jimmy De Knight, 1953. It was made famous by BILL HALEY and his Comets in 1954 and even more so when it was used in the 1955 film *Blackboard Jungle.*

Rock of Ages. An 18th-century English HYMN by Thomas Hastings and Augustus Toplady, which has been a perennial favorite.

Rock-a-Bye Baby. Lullaby by a 15-year-old Effie Crockett, 1872. Other than the first line of text, the song is entirely her creation.

rococo *(*from Fr. *roc,* shell*).* An architectural term applied to a transitional era of composition current from about 1725 to 1775. Some musicologists use the terms GALANT STYLE or "early Classic."

In part, rococo served to lighten, even eliminate the "Gothic" contrapuntal textures of composers like JOHANN SEBASTIAN BACH, who was increasingly considered old-fashioned. It reemphasized MONODIC HOMOPHONY, while maintaining the pervasive ORNAMENTATION, character pieces, dance forms, and tonality of the BAROQUE. But it was a period of intense experimentation:

- at the formal level, as FRANZ JOSEPH HAYDN and others developed what was later called SONATA form

- at the expressive level, as C.P.E. BACH and others found that a sudden pause could have great effect

- and on other levels, such as DYNAMICS (the CRESCENDOS in the Mannheim school) and ORCHESTRATION (the formation of the modern orchestra, incorporating winds, even in concerted pieces)

One result, the question-and-answer phrase based on TONIC-DOMINANT-tonic harmonic motion, became the essence of CLASSIC music.

The transition from rococo to Classic is best seen in the difference in the music of WOLFGANG AMADEUS MOZART as an adolescent from that of Mozart the composer in his 20s.

Rodeo. Ballet by AARON COPLAND, 1942, premiered in N.Y. with choreography by Agnes de Mille. The scenario concerns the adventures of a cowgirl, following the archetypal plot of the strong woman who loses her independence in order to attract a man. Copland drew a four-part orchestral suite from it, emphasizing his recreations of traditional American western music.

Rodgers, Jimmie (James Charles), pioneering American country-music singer, guitarist, and songwriter; b. Meridian, Miss., Sept. 8, 1897; d. N.Y., May 26, 1933. Rodgers's father worked for the railroads maintaining the lines; his mother died from tuberculosis when Rodgers was quite young. He was primarily raised by an aunt, who was well educated and encouraged his interests in literature and music.

At the age of 12, Rodgers returned to living with his father in Meridian but soon was on his own. He began performing locally and joined a traveling tent show. After returning home once again, he began working on a crew under his father repairing railroad tracks. Between the mid-teens and 1920 he worked in a variety of positions—from trackman to flagman, brakeman, and baggage master—for different railroad lines.

In the early '20s Rodgers held a job as a truckdriver and began experimenting with accompanying himself on the guitar. Diagnosed in 1924 with tuberculosis, he nonetheless formed a trio with his in-laws and began performing regularly. Again working for the railroads, he moved first to Arizona and then to North Carolina, where he hosted a radio show. He was soon joined by a group called the Teneva Ramblers, with whom he began to tour.

In August 1927 Victor Records' executive Ralph Peer traveled to Bristol, Tennessee, seeking local talent to record. Rodgers and the Ramblers auditioned but soon quarreled over their billing; as a result Rodgers recorded as a solo act. His first record was only moderately successful, but his second, *Blue Yodel* (more commonly known as *T for Texas*), established his career. Rodgers incorporated a bluesy singing style with a simple guitar accompaniment, and his trademark "yodeled" refrains.

Through the late '20s Rodgers recorded and toured, becoming known as "the Singing Brakeman" and "America's Blue Yodeller." However, the strains of touring, writing material, and recording it wore on Rodgers's already frail health.

In 1930 the effects of the Depression led to a decrease in record sales. Rodgers was still performing but found he was not getting as much income. Meanwhile, he continued to record but increasingly was slowed by his illness. To ease his

At the same Bristol, Tennessee, recording session, Ralph Peer also "discovered" the CARTER FAMILY. The Carters and Jimmie Rodgers became RCA's most popular artists for many years.

pain, he became reliant on alcohol and pain killers, which only lessened his ability to perform.

In February 1933 Rodgers collapsed while performing in Texas. Concerned about his family, he asked to be rushed to N.Y. so he could record a few more records—guaranteeing them some income. Arriving there in May, he bravely made his last sessions and died there in May.

In 1961 Rodgers was the first performer to be placed in the Country Music Hall of Fame in Nashville, and in 1977 a U.S. postage stamp was issued to commemorate the 80th anniversary of his birth. He is duly recognized as the father of modern country music.

Rodgers, Richard (Charles), celebrated American composer of popular music; b. Hammels Station, Long Island, N.Y., June 28, 1902; d. N.Y., Dec. 30, 1979. Rodgers began piano lessons when he was six. He studied at Columbia University from 1919 to 1921 and at the Institute of Musical Art in N.Y. from 1921 to 1923, receiving instruction from Henry Krehbiel and Percy Goetschius.

Just before he entered Columbia, he was introduced to the lyricist LORENZ HART, and the two collaborated on university productions while also placing some songs in Broadway revues. In 1925 they had their big break when they scored the *Garrick Gaieties,* a huge commercial success that introduced the song *Manhattan.*

This success led to a string of musicals, including *Dearest Enemy* (1925), PEGGY-ANN (1926), and A CONNECTICUT YANKEE (1927, based on the Mark Twain novel). In 1930 the duo went to Hollywood, where they spent five years placing songs in a number of early film musicals, the best-remembered of which is *Blue Moon.*

In 1935 they returned to working on Broadway. A year later, they scored a huge hit with ON YOUR TOES, a musical featuring a famous ballet sequence called *Slaughter on 10th Avenue.* This was followed by THE BOYS FROM SYRACUSE in 1938 and, perhaps their most famous collaboration, PAL JOEY, in 1940. By this time, however, Hart was becoming increasingly difficult to work with, suffering from bouts of depression and alcoholism. He died in 1943, leaving Rodgers partnerless.

Meanwhile, in 1942 Rodgers had been approached by lyricist OSCAR HAMMERSTEIN II about creating a musical based on a stage play that told the story of the founding of the state of Oklahoma. The result was a classic of the American theater, the first true "book musical," *OKLAHOMA!* Besides its many hit songs—including the title song, *Oh What a Beautiful Morning,* and *Surrey with the Fringe on Top*—the musical told a coherent story, with the songs actually fitting into the action. This revolutionized Broadway musicals.

Rodgers and Hammerstein were Broadway's most creative duo through the '50s. They had a string of successes, beginning with *CAROUSEL* (1945), followed by *SOUTH PACIFIC* (1949), and *THE KING AND I* (1951). Their last great success was *THE SOUND OF MUSIC* (1959), which also produced numerous hits.

In 1960 Hammerstein died, leaving Rodgers partnerless again. Although Rodgers worked sporadically through the '60s and '70s with various partners, he never again had the success he had enjoyed in the '50s. He died in 1979.

Rodzinski, Artur, eminent Polish-born American conductor; b. Spalato, Dalmatia, Jan. 1, 1892; d. Boston, Nov. 27, 1958. He studied jurisprudence at the University of Vienna and at the same time took lessons in piano with Emil Sauer, composition with Franz Schreker, and conducting with Franz Schalk. He made his conducting debut in Lwów in 1920 and subsequently conducted at the Warsaw Opera. In 1926 he was appointed assistant conductor to LEOPOLD STOKOWSKI with the Philadelphia Orchestra. Concurrently, he was head of the opera and orchestra departments at the Curtis Institute of Music.

In 1929 Rodzinski was appointed conductor of the Los Angeles Philharmonic. After four seasons there, he was engaged as conductor of the Cleveland Orchestra, where he introduced the novel custom of presenting operas in concert form. On Jan. 31, 1935, he conducted the American premiere of DMITRI SHOSTAKOVICH's controversial opera *LADY MACBETH OF THE DISTRICT OF MTZENSK.* He became a naturalized American citizen in 1932.

In 1943 he received his most prestigious appointment, as conductor of the N.Y. Philharmonic, but his independent

PEOPLE IN MUSIC

character and temperamental ways of dealing with the management forced him to resign amid raging controversy in the

middle of his fourth season (Feb. 3, 1947). Almost immediately he was engaged as conductor of the Chicago Symphony Orchestra, but there, too, a conflict rapidly developed, and the management announced after a few months of the engagement that his contract would not be renewed, stating as a reason that his operatic ventures using the orchestra were too costly.

After these distressing American experiences, Rodzinski conducted mainly in Europe. In the autumn of 1958 he received an invitation to conduct at the Lyric Opera in Chicago, but after three performances of RICHARD WAGNER's *TRISTAN UND ISOLDE* (Nov. 1, 7, and 10), he was forced by a heart ailment to cancel his remaining appearances. He died in a Boston hospital.

Roland. Tragédie lyrique by JEAN-BAPTISTE LULLY, 1685, premiered in Paris. The libretto is drawn from the well-known Italian epic *Orlando furioso* by Ariosto, suggested by King Louis XIV himself. The central episode concerns the passion of Orlando, knight of Charlemagne, for a young woman who rejects his love. He finds consolation in his victorious battles.

This story is the subject of many other operas, including FRANZ JOSEPH HAYDN's *Orlando paladino* (1782).

PEOPLE IN MUSIC

Roldán, Amadeo, Cuban violinist, conductor, and composer; b. Paris (of Cuban parents), July 12, 1900; d. Havana, March 2, 1939. Roldán studied violin at the Madrid Conservatory with Fernández Bordas, graduating in 1916. He won the Sarasate Violin Prize, then studied composition with Conrado del Campo in Madrid and with Pedro Sanjuan.

In 1921 Roldán settled in Havana. In 1924 he became concertmaster of the Orquesta Filarmónica, being named its conductor in 1932. In the late 1920s and early 1930s he kept company with the members of Grupo de Avance, who sought to modernize Cuban artistic culture. He later became professor of composition at the Conservatory beginning in 1935.

In his works, he employed the MELORHYTHMS of Afro-Cuban popular music, particularly indigenous mestizo folk music (and folklore). His percussion works anticipated Edgard Varèse's *Ionisation*.

Rolling Stones, The, also called the Stones, long-lived English ROCK group, with the BEATLES, were the prime movers of the transition from ROCK 'N' ROLL to rock in the 1960s. (Vocals/harmonica/guitar: Mick [Michael Philip] Jagger, b. Dartford, Kent, July 26, 1944; Lead guitar/vocal: Keith Richards [Richard], b. Dartford, Kent, Dec. 18, 1943; Guitar/vocal: Brian Jones [born Lewis Brian Hopkins-Jones] b. Cheltenham, Feb. 28, 1942; d. London, July 3, 1969; Bass: Bill Wyman [born William Perks], b. Penge, S.E. London, Oct. 23, 1936; Drums: Charlie Watts, b. Neasden, N. London, June 2, 1941. Jones was replaced in 1969 by Michael "Mick" Taylor, b. Welwyn Garden City, Jan. 17, 1948; Taylor was replaced in 1974 by Ron Wood, b. Hillingdon, June 1, 1947; Bill Wyman was replaced in 1992 by Darryl Jones.) The group played the RHYTHM-AND-BLUES circuit in England until Andrew Loog Oldham (b. 1944) saw them and, like Brian Epstein with the Beatles, made the Stones ready for more general consumption, the scruffy answer to the sweet-faced Liverpudlians. Oldham demoted Stewart from full membership because of his overall appearance (much as Epstein had replaced Pete Best with RINGO STARR). The pianist played with the group on recordings and on tours, functioned as tour manager and became their trusted confidant.

With a recording contract the Stones combined their rhythm-and-blues covers (*Not Fade Away, It's All Over Now*)

PEOPLE IN MUSIC

with rock balladry (*Tell Me, Time Is on My Side*). By 1965 Jagger and Richards were collaborating on most of their material, which found its stylistic niche in sexually oriented rock (*The Last Time, Satisfaction*). While the Beatles continued to focus on love and relationships, the Stones's songs turned to sometimes bitter social commentary (*Get Off of My Cloud, 19th Nervous Breakdown, Mother's Little Helper, Have You Seen Your Mother Baby*) even as more usual commentary continued (*Paint It Black, Let's Spend the Night Together*).

Jagger and Richards solidified their outlaw image with the hard rock classic *Jumpin' Jack Flash* in 1968. The brilliant album *Beggars Banquet* followed, which included the songs *Sympathy for the Devil, Street Fighting Man, Salt of the Earth, No Expectations,* and others. This was Jones's last album, his positive musical contributions now outweighed by his drug addictions, alcoholism, overall bad health, and unreliability. He was gently forced out of the group and was found dead two months later, drowned in his own swimming pool. He was replaced by Mick Taylor, slide guitarist, formerly of John Mayall's Bluesbreakers, who stayed with the group until 1975.

Another brilliant album followed in 1969, *Let It Bleed.* It included *Gimme Shelter,* one of the Stones's most successful arrangements. However, the year ended with the fateful concert at Altamount, where a fan was killed by the Hell's Angels. For a while, it looked like the bad boy image of the Stones had caught up with them.

The '70s were not the best of times for the band (their retrospective album for this period was titled, aptly, *Suckin' in the '70s*). Richards was fighting his own heroin addiction and was often unavailable for recording or songwriting. Although the band produced the brilliant *Exile on Main Street* album in 1972, the band went into a slump. In 1975 Taylor left the group to be replaced by Ron Wood, who had previously played with Rod Stewart and the Small Faces.

The band began to show some life again toward the end of the decade, introducing the first of many comebacks. They had hits in the early '80s with *Emotional Rescue* and *Start Me Up*. But they then went into another period of creative stagnation, as Jagger pursued an abortive solo career and Richards, retaliating, formed his own group, the X-Pensive Winos.

In 1989 there was another remarkable comeback, this time with the *Steel Wheels* album and tour. Seemingly having settled old differences, the band played better than ever, and the new material bode well for the future. In 1992 bass player Bill Wyman finally retired. He has never been officially replaced, although Darryl Jones has filled his chair on tour and record.

The year 1994 saw the release of *Voodoo Lounge,* produced by Don Was. It marked a return to a harder sound and a simpler form of recording. It was followed by yet another successful tour, which produced a semilive, semiacoustic album. *Bridges to Bablyon* followed in 1997, a somewhat less-successful album, although it too spawned a monstrous world tour.

Rollins, "Sonny" (Theodore Walter), outstanding African-American jazz tenor saxophonist; b. N.Y., Sept. 7, 1929. Rollins played piano as a child and then took up saxophone in high school. In 1947 after graduation, he began playing in the N.Y. area. He fell in with the young players of BEBOP and began recording and performing with Bud Powell, Art Blakey, MILES DAVIS, and THELONIOUS MONK. In 1954 Rollins recorded with Davis, who featured three compositions by the young saxophonist. But, soon thereafter, he left the group to move to Chicago.

In Chicago, Rollins hooked up with Clifford Brown and MAX ROACH, who were leading their own quintet. He stayed with them for 18 months, before returning to N.Y. to make his first solo recordings. His 1956 record *Saxophone Colossus* is generally recognized as his first great solo work.

When ORNETTE COLEMAN arrived on the N.Y. scene in 1958, introducing FREE JAZZ, Rollins was at first disturbed by the new style. He took a self-imposed retirement for two years to reexamine his playing. When he reemerged in 1961, he was playing in a free style. He continued to record, play, and tour through the '60s in this new style but then took another break, from 1968 to 1971, to study and evaluate his playing.

PEOPLE IN MUSIC

Like many other jazz players, Rollins experimented with a jazz-rock fusion style in the '70s. And, like others, his work in this style was not too successful. Since the early '80s, he has taken an eclectic approach, playing in traditional BOP as well as more progressive and electric settings.

Roman Carnival, The (*Le Carnaval romain*). Concert OVERTURE by HECTOR BERLIOZ, 1844, first performed in Paris with the composer conducting. This is Berlioz's most successful overture. It is an arrangement of two episodes from his underrated but unsuccessful opera *Benvenuto Cellini* (1838). Since Cellini was a notorious high-liver, the overture is full of sensual joy.

Roman Festivals (*Feste romane*). SYMPHONIC POEM by OTTORINO RESPIGHI, 1929, first performed in N.Y.

Roman numerals. A system of enumeration used in music in three ways: (1) for the designation of instrumental parts (Flute I, Flute II, etc.); (2) in the analysis of harmonic progression, based on SCALE steps (I = TONIC, V = DOMINANT, etc.); and (3) as a method of enumerating works according to the composer's whim (i.e., LUCIANO BERIO's *Sequenza* series, KARLHEINZ STOCKHAUSEN's *Klavierstücke*).

romance. 1. Originally a type of Spanish poetic narrative, a ballad or popular tale in verse; later, Romance lyrical songs. The French and Russian romance is a short art song or LIED composed of several STANZAS. 2. (Ger., *Romanze*; It. *romanza*) Short instrumental pieces of sentimental or romantic cast, without specific form. *Romances sans paroles,* songs without words.

romancero (Sp.). Collections of ballads or romances (heroic tales), sung or recited by *juglares* (minstrels).

romanesca. A type of court dance that originated in the Roman countryside in Italy in the 16th century. It is structurally related to the FOLIA, with its persistent bass formation (TONIC, DOMINANT, SUBMEDIANT, MEDIANT) upon which there are embroidered melodies, either written out or improvised by singers.

Romantic era. In music history, the period from about 1815 to 1915, overlapping with late CLASSIC on one end and IMPRESSIONISM, EXPRESSIONISM, and PRIMITIVISM on the other.

The Romantic movement in music was closely allied with related movements in literature and art. Where the Classic composers had valued formal beauty, the Romantics emphasized self-expression. The Romantics believed form should arise organically out of the subject itself, rather than the subject being shoehorned into a preordained model. This led to a more free-form composition, with stormy moments of high emotion.

Some other key elements of the Romantic movement were:

- an interest in the common man and his expression (such as folk songs and folk tales)

- an emphasis on nature and natural beauty over the man-made

- an emphasis on nationalism and national identity

All of these elements would show up, in one way or another, in Romantic music.

In instrumental music, the SONATA form that had reached its highest development in the Classical era was replaced by more open-ended and larger forms. Symphonies grew bigger, along with the size of the orchestra itself. PROGRAM MUSIC—either based on a specific myth or story or to relate a specific emotion—became a favorite form. Smaller works tended to reflect specific moods, like FRÉDÉRIC CHOPIN's popular NOCTURNES.

In vocal music, there were similar developments. Poetry and music came together in a way they had never done before in the German LIED. Operas tended to emphasize stories of great passion, again drawn on folk tales or stories based on national history. The orchestra was brought to the foreground to paint the picture of the scene before the audience, and the chorus too was enlarged. RICHARD WAGNER's famous *RING* cycle was the natural culmination of these tendencies.

A growth in nationalism led to many more "schools" of composers, each drawing on the folk melodies and traditional rhythms of their homelands. FRANZ LISZT's famous *HUNGARIAN RHAPSODIES,* JEAN SIBELIUS's *FINLANDIA,* and even FELIX MENDELSSOHN's *SCOTCH SYMPHONY* are all examples of how this interest in expressing national identity was expressed musically. Mendelssohn's work is also an example of tone-painting in music; here he tries to evoke the Scottish countryside through his composition. This reflects the Romantic interest in nature as well as in nostalgia and memory.

As in many artistic movements, the Romantic movement began to suffer from its own excesses. Overblown works brimming with melodramatic emotions replaced the more heartfelt earlier compositions. A natural reaction to this was a return to the purity of Classical forms—which were seen in the NEOCLASSICAL movement of the 20th century.

Still, the fundamental tension between Classical and Romantic tendencies continues to be one of the driving forces behind the creation of new musical art. And, just as the early 20th-century composers turned their backs on the excesses of Romanticism, today we see a revival of Romantic interest in self-expression through a return to melody and harmony in music.

Romantic Symphony. Symphony No. 4 by ANTON BRUCKNER, 1874, in E-flat minor, first performed in Vienna (1888). The name is Bruckner's, and the work is one of his shortest symphonies. The themes are spacious, and the development rich and resonant. Like many Bruckner symphonies, the work went through major revisions.

Romany music. *See* GYPSY MUSIC.

Romeo and Juliet. Ballet by SERGEI PROKOFIEV, 1938, after William Shakespeare, first produced in Brno. It is the most engaging ballet by Prokofiev. He drew two orchestral suites from it.

cused of murder. He is cleared, and Rose-Marie's faith in him is vindicated. Includes the famous duet *Indian Love Call.*

Rosenberg, Hilding (Constantin), important Swedish composer and teacher; b. Bosjokloster, Ringsjon, Skane, June 21, 1892; d. Stockholm, May 19, 1985. Rosenberg studied piano and organ in his youth and then was active as an organist. He went to Stockholm in 1914 to study piano, then studied composition at the Stockholm Conservatory in 1915–16, where he later took a conducting course.

Rosenberg made trips abroad from 1920, then returned home to study composition and conducting. He was a RÉPÉTITEUR and assistant conductor at the Royal Opera in Stockholm from 1932 to 1934, and also appeared as a guest conductor in Scandinavia, leading performances of his own works. He likewise was active as a teacher, numbering Sven-Erik Bäck, Karl-Birger Blomdahl, and Ingvar Lidholm among his students. In 1948 he conducted his own works on a tour of the U.S.

Rosenberg was the foremost Swedish composer of his era. He greatly influenced Swedish music by his experimentation and stylistic diversity, which led to a masterful style marked by originality, superb craftsmanship, and refinement. A prolific composer, Rosenberg's works include nine operas, four ballets, five oratorios, four cantatas, eight numbered symphonies and other orchestra works, and concertos for various solo instruments. He also composed chamber music, numerous works for piano, vocal works, songs, incidental music to almost 50 plays, and film scores.

Rosenkavalier, Der. Opera by RICHARD STRAUSS, 1911, to a libretto by his most imaginative collaborator, Hugo von Hofmannsthal, first produced in Dresden.

The intricacy of the plot, with its many entanglements, lovers' quarrels, cross-dressing, and contrived mistaken identities, is in the most extravagant manner of the 18th-century farce. The action takes place in Vienna in WOLFGANG AMADEUS MOZART's time. The characters embroiled in the comedy are the *Feldmarschallin* (Marie Thérèse, the wife of the absent Feldmarschall), a young count (Octavian, the Rosenkavalier) whom she takes as a temporary lover, an ag-

The noted vocal team of Nelson Eddy and Jeanette Macdonald, who appeared in countless films, were famous for their duet version of *Indian Love Call.*

ing baron (Ochs), and a innocent young woman (Sophie), whom the baron proposes to marry.

The baron, who is the Feldmarschallin's cousin, surprises her in her bedroom when she is just completing a tryst with her young lover. To avoid his detection, she rushes Octavian into her dressing room. He reappears dressed in women's clothing as her maid, "Mariandel."

Ochs proposes to marry the young, well-to-do Sophie and is seeking a messenger to carry his proposal to her via a silver rose. All the while, he is also shamelessly flirting with "Miriandel." The Feldmarschallin recommends her kinsman "Count Rofrano" to be Ochs's love messenger—who is in fact Octavian/Miriandel.

Naturally, on delivering the proposal, Octavian and Sophie fall madly in love. Ochs arrives to pursue his intended, but she is repulsed by his ugly, aging body and manner. General mayhem ensues, as Sophie's father reacts in shock when Octavian announces that Sophie will not marry the baron. A duel is fought between the young man and the baron, resulting in a minor flesh wound to the old codger, who cries out in pain.

Octavian then hatches a plan to unmask the lusty baron. He has intermediaries arrange with Ochs to meet "Mariandel" at a country inn. Ochs attempts to seduce "her," but "she" rebuffs him. Meanwhile, Octavian has arranged for Sophie and her father to meet him at the inn—and they see the philandering ways of Ochs.

As general pandemonium again threatens to break out, the Marschallin arrives—DEUS EX MACHINA-like—the various subplots are explained, and the characters restored to their rightful places. The baron is cast away, the young lovers united, and the Marschallin and Sophie's father slip away arm-in-arm as well.

The music is almost Mozartean in its melodious involvement, with Viennese waltzes enlivening the score. After the morbid and somber scores of his earlier operas *SALOME* and *ELEKTRA*, Strauss proved that he could combine BEL CANTO with musical invention.

> As if this were not enough, the part of the Rosenkavalier is entrusted to a mezzo-soprano, so that when he/she changes his/her dress, the actress singing the role actually engages in double gender-swapping (as does the actress playing Cherubino in Mozart's *THE MARRIAGE OF FIGARO*).

PEOPLE IN MUSIC

Rosenthal, Moriz, famous Austrian pianist; b. Lemberg (now Lvov, Ukraine), Dec. 17, 1862; d. N.Y., Sept. 3, 1946.

Rosenthal studied piano at the Lemberg Conservatory with Karol Mikuli, a pupil of FRÉDÉRIC CHOPIN. In 1872, when he was ten, he played Chopin's Rondo in C for two pianos with his teacher in Lemberg.

The family moved to Vienna in 1875, and Rosenthal became the pupil of Rafael Joseffy, who was a virtuoso at the keyboard. FRANZ LISZT accepted Rosenthal as a student during his stay in Weimar and Rome from 1876 to 1878. After a hiatus of some years, during which Rosenthal studied philosophy at the University of Vienna, he returned to his concert career in 1884 and established for himself a reputation as one of the world's greatest virtuosos.

Beginning in 1888, Rosenthal made 12 tours of the U.S., where he became a permanent resident in 1938.

His wife, Hedwig Kanner-Rosenthal (b. Budapest, June 3, 1882; d. Asheville, N.C., Sept. 5, 1959), was a distinguished pianist and piano teacher.

Rosenthal was nicknamed the "little giant of the piano" because of his small stature and great pianist power.

Roslavetz, Nikolai (Andreievich), remarkable Russian composer; b. Suray, near Chernigov, Jan. 5, 1881; d. Moscow, Aug. 23, 1944. Roslavetz studied violin with his uncle in Kursk, then violin and composition at the Moscow Conservatory, graduating in 1912. He won the Silver Medal for his cantata *Heaven and Earth*, based on the poem by Lord Byron.

A composer of advanced tendencies, Roslavetz published in 1913 an ATONAL Violin Sonata, the first of its kind by a Russian composer. His Third String Quartet exhibits 12-TONE properties. He edited a short-lived journal, *Muzykalnaya Kultura*, in 1924, and became a leading figure in the modern movement in Russia.

With a change of Soviet cultural policy toward SOCIALIST REALISM and nationalism, Roslavetz was subjected to severe criticism in the press for continuing to compose in a modern style. To conciliate the authorities, he tried to write operettas. He then was given an opportunity to redeem himself by going to Tashkent to write ballets based on Uzbek folk songs, but he failed in all these pursuits.

After his death in 1944, interest in Roslavetz's earlier, more experimental works was rekindled abroad. A prolific composer, he wrote many orchestral and chamber works, works for piano, and vocal works.

PEOPLE IN MUSIC

PEOPLE IN MUSIC

Diana Ross and the Supremes, c. 1964. (Benson collection) ▶

Ross, Diana, African-American pop and soul singer; b. Detroit, March 26, 1944. She sang for social events in Detroit, then organized a female trio whose other members were her close contemporaries Florence Ballard and Mary Wilson, assuming the grandiose name of the Supremes, under which name the trio became the most successful of the 1960s MO-TOWN stable of artists. Ballard dropped out in 1967 and was replaced by Cindy Birdson, and the group was thenceforth called Diana Ross and the Supremes. Their many hits included *Come See about Me; Stop! In the Name of Love; Baby Love; You Can't Hurry Love;* and *I Hear a Symphony.* The Supremes, and Ross as their top singer, broke the curse of drugs and alcohol besetting so many pop singers by campaigning for virtue and love *sans* narcotics.

In 1969 Ross left the Supremes and started on a highly successful career as a solo singer, in cabarets, in nightclubs, on the radio, on television, in Las Vegas, on Broadway, and in the movies, where she starred in a film biography of BIL-LIE HOLIDAY, *Lady Sings the Blues* (1970), which produced a No. 1 soundtrack album. Her next film, *Mahogany* (1972) was less successful. As a soloist she hit the top of the charts with the antidrug number *Reach Out and Touch* and her signature song, *Ain't No Mountain High Enough.* She recorded the eponymous album *Diana! An Evening with Diana Ross,* a duet album with Marvin Gaye, the generic song *Why Do Fools Fall in Love,* and a duet with Li-onel Richie, *Endless Love.* Other solo hits include *Touch Me in the Morning, Do You Know Where You're Going* (from

Mahogany), *Love Hangover, Upside Down, I'm Coming Out, Muscles,* and *Missing You.*

Rossignol, Le. See NIGHTINGALE, THE.

Rossini, Gioacchino (Antonio), great Italian OPERA composer possessing an equal genius for shattering MELODRAMA in tragedy and for devastating humor in comedy; b. Pesaro, Feb. 29, 1792; d. Paris, Nov. 13, 1868. Rossini came from a musical family. His father was town trumpeter in Lugo and Pesaro and played brass instruments in provincial theaters, and his mother sang opera as *seconda donna.* When his parents traveled, he was usually boarded in Bologna.

After the family moved to Lugo, Rossini's father taught him to play the horn. He also studied singing with a local canon. Later the family moved to Bologna, where he studied singing, harpsichord, and theory and learned to play the violin and viola. Soon he acquired enough technical ability to serve as *maestro al cembalo* (keyboard master) in local churches and at occasional opera productions. He studied voice with the tenor Matteo Babbini.

In 1806 Rossini was accepted as a student at the Liceo Musicale in Bologna, where he studied singing and solfeggio, cello, piano, and counterpoint. He also began composing. On Aug. 11, 1808, his cantata *Il pianto d'Armonia sulla morte d'Orfeo* was performed at the Liceo Musicale in Bologna and received a prize. About the same time he

An 1867 caricature of Rossini that appeared in the journal, La Lune *(The moon). (Leonard de Selva/Corbis)*

wrote his first opera, *Demetrio e Polibio,* and in 1810 he was commissioned to write a work for the Teatro San Moisè in Venice. He submitted his opera *La cambiale di matrimonio,* which won considerable acclaim. In 1812, he obtained a commission from La Scala of Milan. The resulting work, *La pietra del paragone,* was a great success.

In 1813 Rossini produced three operas for Venice: *Il Signor Bruschino,* TANCREDI, and *L'Italiana in Algeri,* the last of which became a perennial favorite. Three more works rapidly followed, but they were unsuccessful.

By that time Rossini, still a very young man, had been approached by the famous impresario Barbaja, manager of the Teatro San Carlo and the Teatro Fondo in Naples, with an offer for an exclusive contract, under the terms of which Rossini was to supply two operas annually. The first opera Rossini wrote for him was *Elisabetta, regina d'Inghilterra,* produced there in 1815. The title role was entrusted to the famous Spanish soprano Isabella Colbran, also Barbaja's favorite mistress. An important innovation in the score was Rossini's use of *recitativo stromentato* in place of the usual *recitativo secco.*

Rossini now determined to try his skill in composing a full-scaled OPERA BUFFA, *IL BARBIERE DI SIVIGLIA,* based on the famous play by Beaumarchais. It was an audacious decision on Rossini's part, because an Italian opera on the same subject by Giovanni Paisiello (1740–1816), under the same name, was still playing with undiminished success. To avoid confusion, Rossini's opera on this subject was performed at the Teatro Argentina in Rome under a different title, *Almaviva, ossia L'inutile precauzione.*

Rossini was only 23 years old when he completed the score, which proved to be his greatest accomplishment. Rossini conducted its first performance in Rome in 1816. If contemporary reports and gossip can be trusted, the opening was marred by various stage accidents. The unruly Italian audience interrupted the spectacle with catcalls! However, the next performance scored a brilliant success. For later productions, Rossini used the title *Il Barbiere di Siviglia.*

Strangely enough, the operas he wrote immediately after *Il Barbiere* were not uniformly successful: *La Gazzetta,* produced in Naples in 1816, passed unnoticed, and the next opera, *Otello,* also produced in Naples in 1816, had initial success but was not retained in the repertoire after a few sporadic performances. There followed *La Cenerentola* and *La gazza ladra,* both from 1817, which fared much better. But the following seven operas, produced in Naples between 1817 and 1822, were soon forgotten. Only the famous Prayer in *Mosè in Egitto* saved the opera from oblivion.

The *prima donna assoluta* in all these operas was Colbran, who, after a long association with Barbaja, went to live with Rossini, who finally married her in 1822. This event, however, did not result in a break between the producer and composer. Barbaja even made arrangements for a festival of Rossini's works in Vienna at the Kärntnertortheater, of which he became a director. While in Vienna, Rossini met LUDWIG VAN BEETHOVEN. Returning to Italy, he produced a fairly successful mythological opera, SEMIRAMIDE (Venice, 1823), with Colbran in the title role.

Rossini then signed a contract for a season in London with Giovanni Benelli, director of the Italian opera at the King's Theatre. He arrived in London late in 1823 and was received by King George IV. He conducted several of his operas and was also a guest at the homes of the British nobility, where he played piano as an accompanist to singers, for very large fees.

In 1824 Rossini settled in Paris, where he became director of the Théâtre-Italien. For the coronation of King Charles X he composed *Il viaggio a Reims,* which was performed in Paris under his direction in 1825. He used parts of this *pièce d'occasion* in his opera LE COMTE ORY. In Paris he met GIACOMO MEYERBEER, with whom he established a friendship. After the expiration of his contract with the Théâtre-Italien, he was given the nominal titles of *Premier Compositeur du Roi* and *Inspecteur Général du Chant en France* at an annual salary of 25,000 francs. He was now free to compose for the Paris Opéra, where he produced several operas, including *Le Comte Ory* in 1828.

In 1829 Rossini obtained an agreement with the government of King Charles X guaranteeing him a lifetime annuity of 6,000 francs. In return, he promised to write more works for the Paris Opéra. Later that year, his GUILLAUME TELL was given its premiere at the Opéra. It became immensely popular.

But then—at the age of 37—Rossini stopped writing operas. The French revolution of July 1830, which dethroned King Charles X, invalidated his contract with the French government. Rossini sued the government of King Louis Philippe, the successor to the throne of Charles X, for the continuation of his annuity. The incipient litigation was settled in his favor in 1835.

In 1832 Rossini met Olympe Pélissier, who became his mistress, and in 1837 Rossini legally separated from Colbran. She died in 1845, and in 1846 Rossini married Pélissier. From 1836 to 1848 they lived in Bologna, where Rossini served as consultant to the Liceo Musicale. In 1848 they moved to Florence, and in 1855 he returned to Paris, where he remained for the rest of his life. His home in the suburb of Passy became the magnet of the artistic world. Rossini was a charming, affable, and gregarious host: he entertained lavishly, was a great gourmet, and invented recipes for Italian food that were enthusiastically adopted by French chefs. His wit was fabulous, and his sayings were eagerly reported in the French journals.

Rossini did not abandon composition entirely during his last years of life, despite illness and depression. In 1867 he wrote a *Petite messe solennelle,* and, as a token of gratitude to the government of the Second Empire, he composed a "hymn to Napoleon III and his valiant people," *Dieu tout puissant.* Of great interest are the numerous piano pieces, songs, and instrumental works that he called *Péchés de vieillesse* (Sins of old age, 1857–68), a collection containing over 150 pieces.

What were the reasons for Rossini's decision to stop writing operas? Rumors flew around Paris that he was unhappy about the cavalier treatment he received from the management of the Paris Opéra, and that he had spoken disdainfully of yielding the operatic field to "the Jews" (Meyerbeer and FROMENTAL HALÉVY), whose operas captivated the Paris audiences. The report does not ring true, because Rossini was friendly with Meyerbeer. Besides, he was not in the habit of complaining, and he enjoyed life too well.

There are three more plausible reasons for his failure to continue to compose:

percussion, with which he produced numerous recordings, including *Soul Menu* (1993), *A Lincoln Portrait* (1988), *Jade Tiger* (1984), and *A Walk in the Woods* (1985).

Rouse has become most widely known for his trilogy of operas, beginning with FAILING KANSAS (1994), inspired by Truman Capote's *In Cold Blood,* which explores his technique of COUNTERPOETRY (a rhythmically strict COUNTER-POINT of un-pitched/pitched and spoken/sung voices). Other works that explore this technique include *Living Inside Design* (1994; a collection of extended spoken songs) and *Autorequiem* (1994) for strings, percussion, and voice. The second in the trilogy is the critically acclaimed DENNIS CLEVELAND (1996),

Mikel Rouse.

the first talk-show opera. The third and final work is the in-progress *The End of Cinematics,* based upon four "retro-songs" and involving the use of real-time film.

Composers are usually elevated by terms applied to their work that manage to enter common musical parlance. Rouse has not one but two: the above-mentioned counterpoetry (of his own devising) and TOTALISM (coined by the N.Y. critic Kyle Gann). His other works include a suite of six piano pieces, *Two Paradoxes Resolved* (1989), *Copperhead* for electric quartet (N.Y., 1992), and *Quorum* (1984), the first piece of its kind for sequencer and used for Ulysses Dove's choreographic work *Vespers,* presented by the Alvin Ailey Dance American Theater in 1987.

PEOPLE IN MUSIC

Roussel, Albert (Charles Paul Marie), outstanding French composer; b. Tourcoing, Departement du Nord, April 5, 1869; d. Royan, Aug. 23, 1937. Orphaned as a child, Roussel was educated by his grandfather, mayor of his native town, and, after the grandfather's death, by his aunt. He studied academic subjects at the College Stanislas in Paris and then studied mathematics in preparation for entering the Naval Academy.

At the age of 18, Roussel began his training in the navy, and from 1889 to Aug. 1890 he was a member of the crew of the frigate *Iphigénie,* sailing to Indochina. This voyage was of great importance to Roussel, because it opened for him a world of Eastern culture and art, which became one of the chief sources of his musical inspiration. He later sailed on the cruiser *Devastation.* Roussel received a leave of absence for reasons of health and spent some time in Tunis. He then was stationed in Cherbourg and began to compose there. In 1893 he was sent once more to Indochina.

Roussel resigned from the navy in 1894 and went to Paris, where he began to study music seriously with Eugène Gigout. In 1898 he entered the Schola Cantorum in Paris as a pupil of VINCENT D'INDY. He continued this study until 1907, when he was already 38 years old. At the same time, he taught a class in COUNTERPOINT, which he conducted at the Schola Cantorum from 1902 to 1914. Among his students were ERIK SATIE and EDGARD VARÈSE.

In 1909 Roussel and his wife, Blanche Preisach-Roussel, undertook a voyage to India, where he became acquainted with the legend of the queen Padmavati, which he selected as a subject for his famous opera-ballet of the same name. His choral symphony *Les Evocations* from 1912 was also inspired by this tour. At the outbreak of World War I in 1914, Roussel applied for active service in the navy but was rejected and volunteered as an ambulance driver. After the Armistice of 1918, he settled in Normandy and devoted himself to composition. In the autumn of 1930 he visited the U.S.

Roussel began his work under the influence of French IMPRESSIONISM, with its dependence on exotic moods and poetic association. However, the sense of formal design asserted itself in his symphonic works. His *Suite en fa* from

1927 signalizes a transition toward NEOCLASSICISM. The thematic development is vigorous, and the rhythms are clearly delineated, despite some asymmetrical progressions. The orchestration, too, is in the CLASSIC tradition.

Roussel possessed a keen sense of the theater. He was capable of fine characterization of exotic or mythological subjects but also could depict humorous situations in lighter works. An experiment in a frankly modernistic manner is exemplified by his *Jazz dans la nuit* for voice and piano from 1928.

rovescio (*rovesciamento;* It., reverse). 1. Melodic INVERSION. A famous example is *Contrapuntus VI* in JOHANN SEBASTIAN BACH's *ART OF FUGUE (Die Kunst der Fuge)*. The 18th variation in SERGEI RACHMANINOFF's *Rhapsody on a Theme of Paganini* is a precise melodic inversion of the theme. Because the theme is encompassed by a MINOR TRIAD, its inversion becomes a melody in major. 2. Among some BAROQUE composers, the term *rovescio* (along with its cognates *riverso* and *rivolto*) refers to RETROGRADE (cancrizans) motion. The postlude of PAUL HINDEMITH's *LUDUS TONALIS* represents both inversion and retrograde movement (allowance being made for shifting ACCIDENTALS).

roh-věs'shoh

Row, Row, Row Your Boat. American ROUND of uncertain authorship, first published in 1852.

Rózsa, Miklós, brilliant Hungarian-American composer; b. Budapest, April 18, 1907; d. Los Angeles, July 27, 1995. Rózsa studied piano and composition in Leipzig with Hermann Grabner and musicology with Theodor Kroyer. In 1931 he settled in Paris, where he became successful as a composer, his works often performed in European music centers.

PEOPLE IN MUSIC

In 1935 he went to London, where he composed for films. In 1940 he emigrated to the U.S. and settled in Hollywood. He was on the staff of MGM from 1948 to 1962 and also taught at the University of Southern California in Los Angeles from 1945 to 1965.

Rózsa's orchestral and chamber music is written in the advanced modern style in vogue in Europe between the two world wars. NEOCLASSICAL in general content, it is strong in POLYPHONY and incisive rhythm. For his film music he employs a more Romantic and diffuse style, relying on a Wagnerian type of grandiloquence. He won Oscars for his film scores to *Spellbound* (1945), *A Double Life* (1947), and *Ben-Hur* (1959). Rózsa was more successful than most in balancing concert and film music careers, and both types of works continue to be performed.

roo-băh′tōh, tem′pōh

rubato, tempo (*rubato;* It., stolen time). Play with a free treatment of the MELODY; specifically, dwell on and (sometimes almost insensibly) prolong prominent melody tones or chords. This requires an equivalent subsequent acceleration of less prominent tones, which are thus "robbed" of a portion of their time value. The measure remains constant, and the accompaniment is not disrupted.

A different kind of total rubato, affecting an entire musical section, occurs in the performing practice of the ROMANTIC era.

PEOPLE IN MUSIC

Rubinstein, Anton (Grigorievich), renowned Russian pianist, conductor, composer, and teacher; b. Vykhvatinetz, Podolia, Nov. 28, 1829; d. Peterhof, near St. Petersburg, Nov. 20, 1894. Rubinstein was born into a family of Jewish merchants. Despite this fact, he was baptized in Berdichev in July of 1831. His mother gave him his first lessons in piano.

The family moved to Moscow, where Rubinstein's father opened a small pencil factory. A well-known Moscow piano teacher, Alexandre Villoing, was entrusted with Rubinstein's musical education and was in fact his only piano teacher. In 1839 Villoing took him to Paris, where Rubinstein played before FRÉDÉRIC CHOPIN and FRANZ LISZT. He remained there until 1841, then made a concert tour in the Netherlands, Germany, Austria, England, Norway, and Sweden, returning to Russia in 1843.

Because Anton's brother Nikolai showed a talent for composition, the brothers were taken in 1844 to Berlin, where, on GIACOMO MEYERBEER's recommendation, Anton studied composition with Siegfried Dehn. He returned to Russia in 1848 and settled in St. Petersburg. There he enjoyed the enlightened patronage of the Grand Duchess Helen and wrote three Russian operas in 1852–53. In 1854, with the assistance of the Grand Duchess, Rubinstein undertook another tour in western Europe. He found publishers in Berlin and gave concerts of his own works in London and Paris, exciting admiration as both composer and pianist. On his return in 1858, he was appointed court pianist and conductor of the court concerts.

Rubinstein assumed the direction of the Russian Musical Society in 1859, and in 1862 founded the Imperial Conservatory in St. Petersburg, remaining its director until 1867. For 20 years thereafter he held no official position. From 1867 until 1870 he gave concerts in Europe, winning fame as a pianist second only to Liszt. During the season of 1872–73 he made a triumphant American tour, playing in 215 concerts, for which he was paid lavishly. Rubinstein appeared as a soloist and jointly with the violinist Józef Wieniawski (to whom he was apparently not speaking at the time).

Returning to Europe, Rubinstein elaborated a cycle of historical concerts in programs ranging from JOHANN SEBASTIAN BACH to Chopin. He usually devoted the last concert of a cycle to Russian composers. In 1887 he resumed the directorship of the St. Petersburg Conservatory, resigning again in 1891, when he went to Dresden. He returned to Russia in 1894, the year of his death.

In 1890 he established the Rubinstein Prize, an international competition open to young men between 20 and 26 years of age. Two prizes of 5,000 francs each were offered, one for composition, one for piano. Competitions were held in St. Petersburg, Berlin, Vienna, and Paris every five years.

Rubinstein's role in Russian musical culture was of the greatest importance. He introduced European methods into education and established high standards of artistic performance. He was the first Russian musician who was equally prominent as composer and interpreter. According to contemporary reports, his playing possessed extraordinary power (his OCTAVE passages were famous) and insight, revealed particularly in his performance of LUDWIG VAN BEETHOVEN's sonatas.

Rubinstein's renown as a composer was scarcely less than that as a performer. His *Ocean Symphony* was one of the most frequently performed orchestral works in Europe and

Rubinstein produced a sensation by playing without a score, a novel practice at the time.

America, and his piano CONCERTOS were part of the standard repertoire. His pieces for piano solo *Melody in F, Romance,* and *Kamennoi Ostrow,* became perennial favorites.

After his death, Rubinstein's orchestral works all but vanished from concert programs, as did his operas (with the exception of *THE DEMON,* composed in 1871, which is still performed in Russia). However, his Piano Concerto No. 4 in D minor, is occasionally heard. Among his compositions are 28 operas and one ballet. He composed six symphonies, seven piano concertos and other orchestral works, and concert and programmatic OVERTURES. His chamber works include three violin SONATAS, five piano trios, ten string quartets, and works for other instruments. He also wrote numerous piano pieces, choral works, and songs.

His brother Nikolai Grigorievich (b. Moscow, June 14, 1835; d. Paris, March 23, 1881) was a prominent pianist, conductor, teacher, and composer. In 1859 he became head of the Moscow branch of the Russian Musical Society, which opened the Moscow Conservatory and which he directed until his death. Among his pupils were Sergei Taneyev, Alexander Siloti, and Emil Sauer.

PEOPLE IN MUSIC

Rubinstein, Arthur (Artur), celebrated Polish-born American pianist; b. Lodz, Jan. 28, 1887; d. Geneva, Dec. 20, 1982. Rubinstein was a product of a Jewish merchant family with many children, of whom he alone exhibited musical propensities. He became emotionally attached to the piano as soon as he saw and heard the instrument. At the age of 7, he played pieces by WOLFGANG AMADEUS MOZART, FRANZ SCHUBERT, and FELIX MENDELSSOHN at a charity concert in Lodz.

Rubinstein's first regular piano teacher was Adolf Prechner. He was later taken to Warsaw, where he had piano lessons with Alexander Roycki. He then went to Berlin in 1897 to study with Heinrich Barth and also received instruction in theory. In 1900 he appeared as soloist in Mozart's A Major Concerto, K.488, in Potsdam. He repeated this success that same year in Berlin under Joseph Joachim's direction, then toured in Germany and Poland.

After further studies with IGNACY PADEREWSKI in Switzerland in 1903, Rubinstein went to Paris, where he played with the Lamoureux Orchestra and met MAURICE RAVEL, PAUL DUKAS, and Jacques Thibaud. He also played the G-Minor Piano Concerto by CAMILLE SAINT-SAËNS in the presence of the composer, who was pleased by his performance.

The ultimate plum of artistic success came when Rubinstein received an American contract. He made his debut at CARNEGIE HALL in N.Y. in 1906, as soloist with the Philadelphia Orchestra in his favorite Saint-Saëns CONCERTO. His American tour was not altogether successful, and he returned to Europe for further study.

In 1915 he appeared as soloist with the London Symphony Orchestra. During the 1916–17 season he gave numerous recitals in Spain, a country in which he was to become extremely successful. From Spain he went to South America, where he also became a great favorite. He developed a flair for Spanish and Latin American music, and his renditions of the piano works of ISAAC ALBÉNIZ and MANUEL DE FALLA were models of authentic Hispanic modality. HEITOR VILLA-LOBOS dedicated to Rubinstein his *RUDE-POEMA,* regarded as one of the most difficult piano pieces ever written.

Symbolic of his cosmopolitan career was the fact that Rubinstein maintained apartments in N.Y., Beverly Hills, Paris, and Geneva. He was married to Aniela Mlynarska in 1932. Of his four children, one was born in Buenos Aires, one in Warsaw, and two in the U.S. In 1946 he became an American citizen.

In 1958 Rubinstein gave his first postwar concert in Poland, and in 1964 he played in Moscow, Leningrad, and Kiev. In Poland and in Russia he was received with tremendous emotional acclaim. But he forswore any appearances in Germany as a result of the Nazi extermination of members of his family during World War II. In 1976, at the age of 89, he gave his farewell recital in London.

Rubinstein was one of the finest interpreters of Chopin's music, to which his fiery temperament and poetic lyricism were particularly congenial. His style of playing tended toward bravura in CLASSICAL compositions, but he rarely indulged in mannerisms. His performances of Mozart, LUDWIG VAN BEETHOVEN, ROBERT SCHUMANN, and JOHANNES BRAHMS were particularly inspiring.

In Rubinstein's characteristic spirit of robust humor, he made jokes about the multitude of notes he claimed to have dropped but asserted that a worse transgression against music would be pedantic inflexibility in TEMPO and DYNAMICS. He was a *bon vivant,* an indefatigable host at parties, and a fluent, though not always grammatical, speaker in most European languages, including Russian and his native Polish.

In Hollywood, Rubinstein played on the sound tracks for the motion pictures *I've Always Loved You* (1946), *Song of Love* (1947), and *Night Song* (1947). He also appeared as a pianist, representing himself, in the films *Carnegie Hall* (1947) and *Of Men and Music* (1951). A film documentary entitled *Artur Rubinstein, Love of Life* was produced in 1975. A 90-minute television special, *Rubinstein at 90,* was broadcast to mark his entry into that nonagenarian age in 1977, in which he spoke philosophically about the inevitability of death.

Rubinstein was the recipient of numerous international honors: membership in the French Académie des Beaux Arts and the Légion d'honneur and the Order of Polonia Restituta of Poland, the Gold Medal of the Royal Philharmonic Society of London, and several honorary doctorates from American institutions of learning. He was a passionate supporter of Israel, which he visited several times. In 1974 an international piano competition bearing his name was inau-

Arthur Rubinstein in concert, c. 1950. (Corbis/Bettmann) ▶

gurated in Jerusalem. In 1976 he received the U.S. Medal of Freedom, presented by President Ford.

During the last years of his life, Rubinstein was afflicted with retinitis pigmentosa, which led to total blindness. But even then he never lost his *joie de vivre*. He once said that the slogan "wine, women, and song" as applied to him was 80 percent women and only 20 percent wine and song. He slid gently into death in his Geneva apartment, as in a pianissimo ending of a Chopin nocturne, ritardando, morendo...

Rubinstein had expressed a wish to be buried in Israel. His body was cremated in Switzerland, and his ashes were flown to Jerusalem to be interred in a separate emplacement at the cemetery, because Jewish law does not permit cremation.

Rudepoema. Piano piece by HEITOR VILLA-LOBOS, composed during 1921–26, and written for ARTHUR RUBINSTEIN. The title literally means "rude poem," in the sense of unrestrained savagery. It is technically so difficult that for many years only the greatest virtuosos could tackle it. Villa-Lobos subsequently orchestrated the piece, conducting its first performance in Rio de Janeiro, 1942.

Rudhyar, Dane (born Daniel Chennevière), French-American mystical visionary, painter, poet, and composer; b. Paris, March 23, 1895; d. San Francisco, Sept. 13, 1985. He changed his name in 1917 to Rudhyar, derived from an old Sanskrit word conveying the sense of dynamic action and the color red, astrologically related to the zodiacal sign of his birth and the planet Mars.

Rudhyar studied philosophy at the Sorbonne in Paris (baccalauréat, 1911) and took music courses at the Paris Conservatory. In composition he was largely self-taught. He also achieved a certain degree of proficiency as a pianist, developing a technique which he called "orchestral pianism." In Paris he attended the famous premiere of IGOR STRAVINSKY'S *THE RITE OF SPRING* in 1913. At the same time he joined the modern artistic circles.

In 1916 he went to America, becoming a naturalized citizen in 1926. His "dance poems" for orchestra, *Poèmes ironiques* and *Vision vegetale*, were performed at the Metropolitan Opera in N.Y. in 1917. In 1918 he visited Canada, where, in Montreal, he met the pianist Alfred Laliberté, who was closely associated with ALEXANDER SCRIABIN. Through him Rudhyar became acquainted with Scriabin's mystical ideas. He also published a collection of French poems, *Rapsodies,* in Toronto in 1918.

In 1920 Rudhyar went to Hollywood to write scenic music for *Pilgrimage Play, The Life of Christ,* and also to act the part of Christ in the prologue of the silent film version of *The Ten Commandments* produced by Cecil B. DeMille. In Hollywood he initiated the project of "Introfilms," depicting inner psychological states on the screen through a series of images, but it failed to receive support and was abandoned.

Between 1922 and 1930 Rudhyar lived in Hollywood and N.Y. He was one of the founding members of the International Composers Guild in N.Y. In 1922 his symphonic poem *Soul Fire* won the $1,000 prize of the Los Angeles Philharmonic. In 1928 his book *The Rebirth of Hindu Music* was published in Madras, India.

After 1930 Rudhyar devoted most of his time to astrology. His first book on the subject, *The Astrology of Personality* (1936), became a standard text in the field. Indeed, it was described by Paul Clancy, a pioneer in the publication of popular astrological magazines, as "the greatest step forward in astrology since the time of Ptolemy." A new development in Rudhyar's creative activities took place in 1938 when he began to paint, along nonrepresentational symbolist lines. The titles of his paintings (*Mystic Tiara, Cosmic Seeds, Soul and Ego, Avatar,* etc.) reflect mystical themes.

Rudhyar's preoccupation with astrology left him little time for music, but in the 1960s he undertook a radical revision of some early compositions and wrote several new ones. He was also active as a lecturer.

The natural medium for Rudhyar's musical expression was the piano. Indeed, his few symphonic works were mostly orchestrations of original piano compositions in which he built sonorous chordal formations supported by resonant PEDAL POINTS, occasionally verging on POLYTONALITY. A kinship with Scriabin's piano music was clearly felt, but Rudhyar's harmonic idiom was free from Scriabin's Wagnerian antecedents.

Despite his study of Eastern religions and music, Rudhyar did not make use of Eastern modalities. He called his creations "syntonic," built mostly on DISSONANT but euphonious HARMONY. He lived his last years in Palo Alto, California.

Rudolph, Archduke of Austria. *See* BEETHOVEN, LUDWIG VAN.

Rudolph the Red-Nosed Reindeer. Christmas ballad by Johnny Marks, 1949. The immediate appeal of the song led to its selling four million copies of sheet music and over six million records as sung by Gene Autry.

Ruggles, Carl (Charles Sprague), remarkable American composer; b. Marion, Mass., March 11, 1876; d. Bennington, Vt., Oct. 24, 1971. Ruggles learned to play violin as a child, then went to Boston, where he took violin lessons and studied theory. He later enrolled as a special student at Harvard University, where he attended composition classes of JOHN KNOWLES PAINE. Impressed with the widely assumed supremacy of the German school of composition (of which Paine was a notable representative), Ruggles changed his given name from Charles to Carl.

In 1907 Ruggles went to Minnesota, where he organized and conducted the Winona Symphony Orchestra from 1908 to 1912. In 1917 he went to N.Y., where he became active in the promotion of modern music. He was a member of the International Composers Guild and of the Pan American Association of Composers, and also taught composition at the University of Miami from 1938 to 1943.

Ruggles wrote relatively few works, which he constantly revised and rearranged, and mostly in small forms. He did not follow any particular modern method of composition but instinctively avoided needless repetition of thematic notes, which made his melodic progressions ATONAL. His use of DISSONANCES, at times quite strident, derived from the linear proceedings of chromatically inflected COUNTERPOINT. A certain similarity with the 12-TONE method of composition of ARNOLD SCHOENBERG resulted from this process, but Ruggles never adopted it explicitly.

Before Rudyhar's death, his wife asked him whom he expected to meet in the spiritual world. He replied, "Myself."

PEOPLE IN MUSIC

In his sources of inspiration, Ruggles reached for spiritual exaltation with mystic connotations, scaling the heights and plumbing the depths of musical expression. Such music could not attract large groups of listeners and repelled some critics, one of whom remarked that the title of Ruggles's *Sun-Treader* ought to be changed to "Latrine-Treader."

Unable and unwilling to withstand the prevailing musical mores, Ruggles removed himself from the musical scene. He went to live on his farm in Arlington, Vermont, and devoted himself mainly to his avocation, painting. His pictures, mostly in the manner of Abstract Expressionism, were occasionally exhibited in N.Y. galleries. In 1966, he moved to a nursing home in Bennington, where he died at the age of 95.

A striking revival of interest in Ruggles's music took place during the last years of his life. His name began to appear with increasing frequency on the programs of American orchestras and chamber music groups. His manuscripts were recovered and published, and virtually all of his compositions have been recorded.

Rule Britannia. Patriotic British song by THOMAS AUGUSTINE ARNE, 1740, published with the subtitle *celebrated ode in honour of Great Britain.*

rumba (rhumba). A syncopated Cuban dance in quadruple time, popular in the U.S. in the 1930s–50s, having acquired elements of SWING.

run. 1. A rapid SCALE passage. In vocal music, a run is usually sung to one syllable. *Run a division,* perform such a passage, i.e., a dividing up of a melodic phrase into a rapid COLORATURA passage. 2. A leak of air in the ORGAN windchest.

Rusalka (The nixie). Opera by ALEXANDER DARGOMYZHSKY, 1856, based on Pushkin's dramatic poem, first performed in St. Petersburg.

A miller's daughter is seduced and impregnated by a local prince who marries a lady of his own station. The wronged girl throws herself into the river Dnieper, thus becoming a Rusalka (nixie, a female water sprite). In her submarine existence, she continues to exercise profound emotional influence on the prince, who often comes to the river bank to evoke memories of his tragic love.

The Rusalka sends her daughter, who was born in the river, to the prince. She asks him to visit her mother, who is now queen of the waters. The prince follows his daughter and rejoins her in the river.

The opera is important for its use of natural inflections of Russian speech. It is a classic in Russia (and was extremely influential on the "Mighty 5") but almost never is performanced outside its home country.

Rusalka (The nixie). Opera by ANTONÍN DVOŘÁK, 1901, first performed in Prague. A nixie (see above entry) leaves her watery realm and falls in love with a human prince. Because of the disparity of their ranks, however, marriage is impossible. She returns to her lake, but the prince realize he really loves her. He follows her to the watery deep and expires in her arms.

The opera is very popular in the Czech lands and probably the most performed Dvořák opera in the non-Slavic world.

Ruslan and Ludmila. Opera by MIKHAIL GLINKA, 1842, first produced in St. Petersburg. The LIBRETTO follows Aleksandr Pushkin's fairy-tale of that name.

Ludmila, daughter of the Grand Duke of Kiev, is betrothed to the valiant Russian knight Ruslan. However, during the wedding feast she mysteriously vanishes as the scene is darkened and lightning and thunder rend the skies. The Grand Duke promises her hand to anyone who will find her. Two suitors, besides Ruslan, take part in the hunt, but Ruslan is helped by a benign magician. He discovers that Ludmila was abducted by the sinister magus Chernomor (the name means black mortifier), whose might resides in his long beard; this presents an obvious clue to the resolution of the problem. Ruslan is confronted with horrendous obstacles, most spectacularly a huge severed head guarding Chernomor (the part of the head is sung by a vocal quartet), but of course he regains his beloved in the end.

The score contains interesting harmonic innovations such as WHOLE-TONE SCALES. It also draws on traditional Russian folk melodies.

Russell, George (Allan), African-American jazz pianist, music theorist, teacher, and composer; b. Cincinnati, June 23, 1923. Russell took up the drums in his youth, then turned to composition, composing for Benny Carter, DIZZY GILLESPIE, EARL "FATHA" HINES, and others. His interest in a contemporary music combining BEBOP and 20th-century classical is spelled out in one of his early hits, *A Bird in Igor's Yard* (1949).

Russell developed a composition style based on using the MODES, then studied composition with Stefan Wolpe. After teaching at the Lenox (Massachusetts) School of Jazz in 1959–60, he became active as a pianist in his own sextet in 1960–61. From 1969 he also taught at the New England Conservatory of Music in Boston.

Russian bassoon (bassoon serpent). A SERPENT built with an upright brass bell, somewhat similar in appearance to a bassoon, including a mouthpiece on a CROOK. It was invented in the late 18th century and used in the 19th, especially in Russian military bands.

Russolo, Luigi. *See* FUTURISM.

Rysanek, Leonie, distinguished Austrian soprano; b. Vienna, Nov. 14, 1926; d. there, March 7, 1998. Rysanek studied at the Vienna Conservatory with Rudolf Grossmann, whom she later married. She made her debut as Agathe in *DER FREISCHÜTZ* in Innsbruck in 1949, then sang at Saarbrücken from 1950 to 1952.

Rysanek first attracted notice when she appeared as Sieglinde at the Bayreuth Festival in 1951. She became a member of the Bavarian State Opera in Munich in 1952, and went with it to London's Covent Garden in 1953, where she sang Danae in RICHARD STRAUSS'S LIEBE DER DANAE. In 1954 she joined the Vienna State Opera, and also sang in various other major European opera houses.

On Sept. 18, 1956, Rysanek made her U.S. debut as Senta at the San Francisco Opera. In 1959 she made a spectacular appearance at the Metropolitan Opera in N.Y., when she replaced MARIA CALLAS in the role of Lady Macbeth on short notice. She remained on the Metropolitan's roster until 1973 and then sang there again in 1975–76 and in subsequent seasons.

Rysanek received the Lotte Lehmann Ring from the Vienna State Opera in 1979. In 1984 she toured Japan with the Hamburg State Opera, and in 1988 she appeared in JENŮFA in San Francisco. She sang Kabanicha in KÁŤA KABANOVÁ in Los Angeles in 1988. In 1990 she appeared as Herodias at the Deutsche Oper in Berlin, and in 1992 she sang the Countess in THE QUEEN OF SPADES in Barcelona, a role she repeated for her farewell appearance at the Metropolitan Opera in Jan. 2, 1996.

Her younger sister Lotte Rysanek (b. Vienna, March 18, 1928) attained a fine reputation in Vienna as a lyric soprano.

Rzewski, Frederic (Anthony), American pianist, teacher, and avant-garde composer of Polish descent; b. Westfield, Mass., April 13, 1938. Rzewksi studied counterpoint with RANDALL THOMPSON and orchestration with WALTER PISTON at Harvard University, earning his bachelor of arts degree in 1958. He continued his studies with ROGER SESSIONS and MILTON BABBITT at Princeton University, taking his master's degree in 1960.

During 1960–61, Rzewksi received instruction from LUIGI DALLAPICCOLA in Florence on a Fulbright scholarship, and from ELLIOTT CARTER in Berlin on a Ford Foundation grant, from 1963 to 1965. With Alvin Curran and Richard Teitelbaum, he founded the M.E.V. (Musica Elettronica Viva) in Rome in 1966. He was active as a pianist in various avant-garde settings and also played concerts with the topless cellist Charlotte Moorman. In 1977 he became professor of composition at the Liège Conservatory.

Among Rzewksi's compositions are three dramatic works: *The Persians,* music theater (1985), *Chains,* 12 television operas (1986), and *The Triumph of Death,* stage oratorio (1987–88). He also composed *Una breve storia d'estate*

PEOPLE IN MUSIC

for three flutes and small orchestra (1983), several enduring instrumental works, including *Attica* and *Coming Together,* both for narrator and variable ensemble (1972), and *Crusoe* for four to 12 performers (1993).

Rzewksi's piano pieces include *The People United Will Never Be Defeated,* 36 variations on the Chilean song *El pueblo unidor jamás será vencido!* (1975), Piano Sonata (1991), and *De Profundis* (1992). Other works include *Impersonation,* an audio drama (1967), and the hard to categorize *Spacecraft* (his magnum opus, 1967, "a plan for spacecraft," published in *Source,* 3, 1968).

Sabre Dance. Excerpt from *GAYANÉ* by ARAM KHACHA-TURIAN, 1942. The most famous number from the ballet, its quasi-Oriental melody depicts a Caucasian military dance full of animal energy.

Sachs, Hans, famous German poet and MEISTERSINGER; b. Nuremberg, Nov. 5, 1494; d. there, Jan. 19, 1576. Sachs was educated at the Nuremberg grammar school from 1501 to 1509. After serving his apprenticeship from 1511 to 1516, he returned to Nuremberg as a master shoemaker in 1520.

Sachs joined the Meistersinger guild about 1509, where he received instruction from Linhard Nunnenbeck. Under Sachs, the guild was an active force in the Reformation movement from 1520. He wrote over 6,000 poetical works, ranging from Meisterlieder to dramatic pieces, as well as 13 *Meistertöne* (melodies to which texts can be fitted later on).

sackbut (Fr. *saqueboute*). 1. Early form of TROMBONE, dating back to 1000 A.D. 2. In the Bible, the translation of *sabbek,* a harplike instrument.

Sacre du printemps, Le. See RITE OF SPRING, THE.

sacred concerto (Ger. *geistliche Konzert;* It. *sacra symphonia*). An early BAROQUE religious genre, a predecessor of the CANTATA.

Composers such as the GABRIELIS (ANDREA and GIO-VANNI) and HEINRICH SCHÜTZ sought to incorporate the new CONCERTATO (concerted) style, with divided choruses and instrumental groups, into sacred contexts. Schütz was especially successful and prolific with the sacred concerto, and many other German Baroque composers contributed to the genre. Eventually, the development of set pieces (ARIA,

RECITATIVE, CHORUS) led to the cantatas of DIETRICH BUXTE-
HUDE and JOHANN SEBASTIAN BACH.

Sadko. Opera by NIKOLAI RIMSKY-KORSAKOV, 1898, first
produced in Moscow. The LIBRETTO is based on an ancient
Russian epic.

Sadko is a popular minstrel in Novgorod, the first capital
of Russia. He has dreams of selling wares abroad, which are
realized when a flock of swans on Lake Ilmen—in reality
the feathered daughters of the King of the Ocean—take
him to their abode on the bottom of the lake. He catches
magic goldfish that turn out to be made of real gold. He returns to Novgorod a rich man.

Sadko is a model of the Russian fairy-tale opera. The
Song of India, sung by a Hindu merchant visiting Novgorod,
is a perennial favorite on the concert stage.

The score of *Sadko* abounds in bold innovations. A chorus in $\frac{11}{4}$ meter was considered so difficult to perform that
Russian opera choristers devised a line of 11 syllables as an aid
to learning it: "Rim-sky-Kor-sa-kov-is-al-to-ge-ther-mad!"

PEOPLE IN MUSIC

Sadra, I Wayan, significant Indonesian composer, performer, and writer on music; b. Denpasar, Bali, Aug. 1,
1953. Sadra attended Konservatori Karawitan, where he specialized in traditional Balinese music, particularly *gender
wayang* (music for the Balinese shadow play). He graduated
in 1972. In 1973–74 he worked with the well-known experimental Indonesian choreographer Sardono W. Kusumo.

After touring with his group in Europe and the Middle
East, Sadra settled in Jakarta, where he studied painting. He
taught Balinese GAMELAN at Institute Kesenian Jakarta from
1975 to 1978, and at the Indonesian University from 1978
to 1980. Beginning in 1983, he taught experimental composition, Balinese gamelan, and music criticism at Sekolah
Tinggi Seni Indonesia Surakarta, where he earned a degree in
composition in 1988. He concurrently wrote new-music criticism for various Indonesian newspapers, including *Suara
Karya* and *Bali Post.*

Sadra appeared widely as a performer with traditional
Indonesian ensembles. In 1988 he was keynote speaker at
the national Pekan Komponis (Composers' Festival) in

Jakarta, and in 1989, he appeared in California at the Pacific Rim Festival. In 1990 he was a featured participant at Composer-to-Composer in Telluride, Colorado.

Along with the development of Indonesia's national identity has come an increase of national new-music festivals, increased interaction among artists from different regions, and a greater degree of individual freedom to create autonomous music, all of which have contributed to the emergence of a distinct Indonesian contemporary art music. Sadra is one of the outstanding young composers to emerge from this period, and his works have contributed much to the development of *musik kontemporer, komposisi,* and *kreasi baru* (new creations). He is also concerned with the social context of performance, considering audience development as important as the development of new works.

Sadra's compositions are often scored for unusual combinations of instruments. In an experimental piece performed at the Telluride Institute, raw eggs were thrown at a heated black panel; as the eggs cooked and sizzled, they provided both a visual and sonic element for the closing of the piece. He also proposed to the mayor of Solo, Central Java, a new work entitled *Sebuah Kota Yang Bermain Musik* (A city that plays music), wherein the entire population of the city would make sounds together for a specified five minutes. The proposal was not accepted, but Sadra hopes for its realization in the future.

Saga, En (A saga). SYMPHONIC POEM by JEAN SIBELIUS, 1893, first performed in Helsinki, with the composer conducting. With this work, Sibelius established his individual musical style. It is based on a MOTIVE in a MINOR MODE that reflects the Scandinavian spirit: introspective, strong, and persevering. The work is indeed a saga of Finland.

Sagittarius, Henricus. *See* SCHÜTZ, HEINRICH.

Sailor's Hornpipe. Traditional English dance tune, first printed in America as early as 1796.

St. Louis Blues. BLUES song by W. C. Handy, 1914. It stabilized the form of urban blues, anticipated in his previous success, *The Memphis Blues*. The sales of sheet music and recordings of *St. Louis Blues* leaped into millions.

PEOPLE IN MUSIC

Saint-Saëns, (Charles-) **Camille,** celebrated French composer; b. Paris, Oct. 9, 1835; d. Algiers, Dec. 16, 1921. Saint-Saëns's widowed mother sent him to his great-aunt, Charlotte Masson, who taught him piano. He proved exceptionally gifted and gave a performance in a Paris salon before he was five years old. At six he began to compose, and at seven he became a private pupil of Camille Stamaty. So rapid was his progress that he made his pianistic debut at the Salle Pleyel in 1846, playing a WOLFGANG AMADEUS MOZART concerto and a movement from LUDWIG VAN BEETHOVEN's C-minor concerto, with orchestra.

After studying harmony with Pierre Maleden, Saint-Saëns entered the Paris Conservatory, where his teachers were François Benoist (organ) and Fromental Halévy (composition). He won second prize for organ in 1849, and first in 1851. In 1852 he competed unsuccessfully for the Grand Prix de Rome and again in 1864, when he was already a composer of some stature. His *Ode à Sainte Cécile* for voice and orchestra was awarded the first prize of the Société Sainte-Cécile in 1852.

On Dec. 11, 1853, Saint-Saëns's first numbered symphony was performed. From 1853 to 1857 he was organist at the church of Saint-Merry in Paris. In 1857 he succeeded Louis Lefébure-Wély as organist at the Madeleine. He filled this important position with distinction and soon acquired a great reputation as an organ virtuoso and a master of improvisation. He resigned in 1876 and devoted himself mainly to composition and conducting. He also continued to appear as a pianist and organist.

From 1861 to 1865 Saint-Saëns taught piano at the École Niedermeyer, numbering among his pupils André Messager and GABRIEL FAURÉ. Saint-Saëns was one of the founders of the Société Nationale de Musique in 1871, established to encourage French composers, but withdrew in 1886 when VINCENT D'INDY proposed to include works by foreign composers in its programs.

In 1875 Saint-Saëns married Marie Truffot. Their two sons died in infancy, and they separated in 1881 but never

After hearing Saint-Saëns's first symphony, CHARLES GOUNOD wrote him a letter of praise containing a prophetic phrase regarding the *"obligation de devenir un grand maître"* (the obligation to become a great master).

divorced. Madame Saint-Saëns died in Bordeaux in 1950 at the age of 95.

In 1891 Saint-Saëns established a museum in Dieppe (his father's birthplace), to which he gave his manuscripts and his collection of paintings and other art objects. In 1907 he witnessed the unveiling of his own statue (by Marqueste) in the court foyer of the city's opera house.

Saint-Saëns received many honors. In 1868 he was made a Chevalier of the French Legion of Honor, in 1884 Officer, and in 1900 Grand Officer. In 1913 he received the Grand-Croix (the highest rank). In 1881 he was elected to the Institut de France. He was also a member of many foreign organizations and received an honorary doctorate of music degree at Cambridge University.

Saint-Saëns visited the U.S. for the first time in 1906. He was a representative of the French government at the Panama-Pacific Exposition in 1915 and conducted his choral work *Hail California,* written for the occasion, in San Francisco. In 1916, at the age of 81, he made his first tour of South America. He continued to appear in public as conductor of his own works almost to the time of his death. He took part as conductor and pianist in a festival of his works in Athens in May 1920. He played a program of his piano pieces at the Saint-Saëns Museum in Dieppe in 1921. For the winter he went to Algiers, where he died.

The position of Saint-Saëns in French music was very important. His abilities as a performer were extraordinary. He aroused the admiration of RICHARD WAGNER during the latter's stay in Paris in 1860–61 by playing at sight the entire scores of Wagner's operas. Curiously, Saint-Saëns achieved greater recognition in Germany than in France during the initial stages of his career. His most famous opera, SAMSON ET DALILA, was produced in Weimar in 1877 under the direction of Eduard Lassen, to whom the work was suggested by FRANZ LISZT. It was not performed in France until nearly 13 years later, in Rouen. He played his first and third piano concertos for the first time at the Gewandhaus in Leipzig.

Saint-Saëns was a master of orchestral writing, creating rich voicings and harmonies. He also excelled at writing in COUNTERPOINT. At the beginning of his career, these qualities were not yet fully exploited by French composers at the time, the French public preferring a lighter type of music. However, Saint-Saëns overcame this initial opposition and toward the end of his life was regarded as an embodiment of French traditionalism.

The shock of the German invasion of France in World War I made Saint-Saëns abandon his former predilection for German music, and he wrote virulent articles against German art. He was unalterably opposed to modern music and looked askance at CLAUDE DEBUSSY. He regarded later manifestations of musical modernism as outrages and was outspoken in his opinions.

That Saint-Saëns possessed a fine sense of musical characterization and true Gallic wit is demonstrated by his ingenious SUITE *CARNIVAL OF THE ANIMALS*. His most famous and favorite work, Saint-Saëns wrote it in 1886 but did not allow it to be published during his lifetime. It includes representation of human animals, a few choice musical parodies, and the beloved *The Swan*, famous as a cello piece and a dance. The work has been orchestrated (posthumously), and the American poet Ogden Nash composed some verses that are often performed with the work. He also published a book of elegant verse (1890).

Among Saint-Saëns's compositions are 13 operas, of which only two (*Samson et Dalila* and *Henry VIII*, Paris, 1883) are still performed, one ballet, incidental music to five plays, and a pioneering film score, *L'Assassinat du Duc de Guise,* composed in 1908. Saint-Saëns's current reputation rests primarily on his orchestral music, including five symphonies (especially No. 3, for organ and orchestra; c.1886), five piano concertos (all first performed with Saint-Saëns as soloist), three violin concertos, two cello concertos, many symphonic poems, orchestral suites, overtures, dances, rhapsodies, marches, and band music.

Saint-Saëns also composed chamber music for various ensembles, piano pieces, sacred vocal works, secular choral works, song cycles, and about 100 solo songs. He prepared cadenzas to Mozart's piano concertos K.482 and K.491, and to Beethoven's Fourth Piano Concerto and Violin Concerto, and various transcriptions and arrangements.

sainete (Sp., small farce). Spanish musical comedy popular in the 18th century. It was eventually displaced by the ZARZUELA.

Salieri, Antonio, famous Italian composer and teacher; b. Legnago, near Verona, Aug. 18, 1750; d. Vienna, May 7, 1825. Salieri studied violin and harpsichord with his brother, Francesco, then continued violin studies with the local organist, Giuseppe Simoni. He was orphaned in 1765 and subsequently was taken to Venice, where he studied THOROUGHBASS with Giovanni Pescetti, deputy maestro di cappella of San Marco, and singing with Ferdinando Pacini, a tenor there.

PEOPLE IN MUSIC

Florian Gassmann brought Salieri to Vienna in 1766 and provided for his musical training and a thorough education in the liberal arts. There he came into contact with Pietro Metastasio and CHRISTOPH WILLIBALD GLUCK, the latter becoming his patron and friend. Salieri's first known OPERA, *LA VESTALE* (not extant), was premiered in Vienna in 1768. His comic opera *Le Donne letterate* was successfully performed at the Burgtheater in 1770. The influence of Gluck is revealed in his first major production for the stage, *Armida,* from 1771.

Upon the death of Gassmann in 1774, Salieri was appointed his successor as court composer and conductor of the Italian Opera. After Gluck was unable to fulfill the commission for an opera to open the Teatro alla Scala in Milan, the authorities turned to Salieri, whose *L'Europa riconosciuta* inaugurated the great opera house in 1778. While in Italy he also composed operas for Venice and Rome. He then returned to Vienna, where he brought out his LUSTSPIEL, *Der Rauchfangkehrer,* in 1781.

With Gluck's encouragement, Salieri set his sights on Paris. In an effort to provide him with a respectful hearing, Gluck and the directors of the Paris Opéra advertised Salieri's *Les Danaïdes* in 1784 as a work from Gluck's pen. Following a number of performances, it was finally acknowledged as Salieri's creation.

Returning to Vienna, Salieri composed three more stage works, including the successful *La grotta di Trofonio* in 1785.

In 1786 Salieri wrote again for the Paris Opéra, unsuccessfully, but a year later his next French opera, TARARE, was a triumphant success. After Da Ponte revised and translated Beaumarchais's French LIBRETTO into Italian and Salieri thoroughly recomposed the score, it was given as *Axur, re d'Ormus* (Axur, king of Ormus) in Vienna in 1788, and subsequently performed throughout Europe to great acclaim.

Salieri was appointed court kapellmeister in Vienna in 1788, holding that position until 1824, although he did not conduct operatic performances after 1790. He continued to compose for the stage until 1804, his last major success being *Palmira, regina di Persia* (Palmira, queen of Persia) in 1795.

Salieri's influence on the musical life of Vienna was considerable. From 1788 to 1795 he was president of the Tonkünstler-Sozietät, the benevolent society for musicians founded in 1771. He was its vice president from 1795, and also a founder of the Gesellschaft der Musikfreunde. He was widely celebrated as a pedagogue, his pupils including LUDWIG VAN BEETHOVEN, JOHANN NEPOMUK HUMMEL, FRANZ SCHUBERT, Carl Czerny, and FRANZ LISZT. He received numerous honors, including the Gold Medallion and Chain of the City of Vienna. He was also made a Chevalier of the French Legion of Honor and a member of the French Institute.

But Salieri's eminence and positions in Vienna also earned him a reputation for intrigue. Many unfounded stories circulated about him, culminating in the fantastic tale that he poisoned WOLFGANG AMADEUS MOZART. This tale prompted Aleksandr Pushkin to write his drama *Mozart and Salieri,* which subsequently was set to music by NIKOLAI RIMSKY-KORSAKOV.

Salieri was a worthy representative of the traditional Italian school of operatic composition. He was a master of HARMONY and ORCHESTRATION. His many operas are noteworthy for their expressive melodic writing and sensitive vocal treatment. All the same, few held the stage for long, and all have disappeared from the active repertoire.

Salieri also composed numerous sacred works, secular works, including CANTATAS, choruses, and songs, and instrumental pieces.

A contemporary interpretation of the Mozart-Salieri rivalry, Peter Shaffer's play entitled *Amadeus,* was successfully produced on stage in London in 1979 and in N.Y. in 1980. It later obtained even wider circulation through the award-winning film version of 1984.

Salome. Opera by RICHARD STRAUSS, 1905, based on a German translation from the original French play by Oscar Wilde, first performed in Dresden.

The story, obliquely connected with the biblical narrative, is centered on Salome, stepdaughter of Herod, king of Judea. John the Baptist, imprisoned by Herod, is brought to the palace at Salome's request. She is fascinated by him, even though he curses her, and brazenly cries, "I want to kiss your mouth!"

Herod, who lusts after Salome, asks her to dance for him. She agrees on condition that he will fulfill any wish she desires, and she performs the provocative *Dance of the Seven Veils.* The reward she demands is the severed head of John the Baptist. Horrified, Herod tries to dissuade her from her monstrous intention but yields in the end. When the head is brought out on a platter, Salome mocks it: "You wouldn't let me kiss your mouth!" she cries, and kisses it passionately on the lips. Provoked beyond endurance by this act of depravity, Herod commands the guards to kill her.

The score is a masterpiece of stark realism, set to music of overwhelming power, ranging from exotic melodiousness to crashing DISSONANCE. The opera aroused unusually vehement opposition when it was staged at the Metropolitan Opera in N.Y. in 1907. The moralistic uproar in the public and press was such that the management was compelled to cancel further performances. It took two decades for the American public to accept it.

Strauss also wrote a French version (*Salomé*).

Salomon, Johann Peter. *See* HAYDN, FRANZ JOSEPH.

Salón México, El. Orchestral piece by AARON COPLAND, 1937, inspired by Mexican tunes. The title refers to a dance hall in Mexico City in which Copland heard a local group play Mexican popular music. The first performance of the work was given there, with CARLOS CHÁVEZ conducting. It became one of Copland's most popular works.

salon music. Music that flourished in Paris and Vienna in the 18th and 19th centuries. A salon is the drawing room in aristocratic mansions, and salon music therefore satisfying the need for light entertainment. Many composers and critics looked down their noses at this music designed to please the growing middle class.

FRANZ LISZT complained of the *"atmosphere lourde et mephitique des salons"* (dull and noxious atmosphere of the salons). During his Paris sojourn, the German poet Heinrich Heine voiced his despair at the universal proliferation of piano music "that one hears in every house, day and night," adding that "at the very moment of the writing of this report a couple of young ladies in the neighboring house are playing a *morceau* for two left hands."

FRÉDÉRIC CHOPIN was not averse to writing piano music designed for salon performances. ROBERT SCHUMANN described Chopin as the "vornehmste Salonkomponist" (most elegant salon composer), and his famous Waltz in A-flat major as a "Salonstück der nobelsten Art, aristokratisch durch und durch" (salon piece of the noblest art, aristocratic through and through). Lesser composers frankly entitled their works *Études de salon, Petites fleurs de salon,* etc.

Although salon music largely disappeared with the outbreak of World War I, social salons continued to be maintained by wealthy hostesses in Paris and other music capitals. For example, Countess de Polignac, the daughter of the American sewing machine manufacturer Singer, was married to a French aristocrat and began a series of musical matinees. She commissioned works by IGOR STRAVINSKY, MANUEL DE FALLA, and others for performance. Throughout the 1980s the American patroness Betty Freeman hosted musicales at her Beverly Hills home in California, providing much-needed exposure for her invited audiences to modern composers and trends.

salon orchestra. Orchestras organized for performances of light music in cafés, cabarets, and houses of the rich. The minimal ensemble was the piano trio. The so-called Vienna type of salon orchestra consisted of a seated violinist, a standing violinist, and cello, flute, and percussion. The Berlin salon ensemble added the clarinet, cornet, trombone, viola, and double bass, while the Paris salon orchestra usually employed piano, violin, cello, flute, cornet, and drums.

Special editions were published for these orchestras to enable them to play light OVERTURES or dance SUITES in so-called "theater arrangements." Cues were inserted in the piano parts to replace the missing instruments.

Although SALON MUSIC was deprecated for its low taste, the salon orchestra performed a positive educational role, providing classical and semiclassical music in workable arrangements.

Salonen, Esa-Pekka, Finnish conductor and composer; b. Helsinki, June 30, 1958. Salonen entered the Sibelius Academy in Helsinki as a horn pupil of Holgar Fransman in 1973, taking his diploma in 1977. He then studied composition with EINOJUHANI RAUTAVAARA and conducting with Jorma Panula. He subsequently studied with Franco Donatoni in Siena, attended the Darmstadt summer course, and finally received instruction from Niccolò Castiglioni in Milan in 1980–81.

After appearances as a horn soloist, Salonen took up conducting. He was a guest conductor throughout Scandinavia and later extended his activities to include Europe. In 1984 he made his U.S. debut as a guest conductor with the Los Angeles Philharmonic. He became principal conductor of the Swedish Radio Symphony Orchestra in Stockholm in 1984, and led it on a tour of the U.S. in 1987. He also served as principal guest conductor of the Oslo Philharmonic from 1984 and the Philharmonia Orchestra in London from 1985. In 1989 he was appointed music director of the Los Angeles Philharmonic, beginning his highly successful tenure in 1992.

In his music, Salonen employs fairly modern techniques while preserving the formal centrality of traditional TONALITY. His orchestral works include *Apokalyptische Phantasie* (Apocalyptic fantasy) for brass band and tape (1978), *Boutade* for violin, cello, piano, and orchestra (1979), *auf den ersten Blick und ohne zu wissen* (at first glance and without knowing, a quotation from Franz Kafka's *The Trial*) for alto saxophone and orchestra (1980–81), *Giro* (1981), and *Mimo II* (1992). His chamber pieces include the Cello Sonata (1976–77), Wind Quintet (1982), and *YTA 1* for flute (1982) and YTA 2 for piano (1985).

PEOPLE IN MUSIC

salsa (Sp., sauce). Modern Latin American dance in a raucous rhythmic manner. It originated in the Caribbean islands, most notably Cuba, with roots traceable to Africa. It emigrated to the U.S. with those fleeing Castro's 1959 revolution.

Salsa may have received its name because of its hot, peppery, and pervasive rhythm over a hypnotically repetitive melodic line. Its meter is invariably $\frac{4}{4}$, with quarter notes alternating with eighth notes in syncopated beats.

PEOPLE IN MUSIC

Salzedo (Salzédo), (León) **Carlos,** eminent French-born American harpist, pedagogue, and composer; b. Arcachon, France, April 6, 1885; d. Waterville, Maine, Aug. 17, 1961. Salzedo studied at the Bordeaux Conservatory from 1891 to 1894, winning first prize in piano. He then entered the Paris Conservatory, where his father, Gaston Salzédo, was a professor of singing. He studied piano with Charles de Bériot gaining first prize in 1901, and harp with Josef H. Hasselmans, also receiving first prize.

From 1901 to 1905 Salzedo began his career as a concert harpist, traveling all over Europe. He was solo harpist of the Association des Premiers Prix de Paris in Monte Carlo from 1905 to 1909. In 1909 he settled in N.Y. and was first harpist in the orchestra of the Metropolitan Opera from 1909 to 1913. In 1913 he formed the Trio de Lutèce (from Lutetia, the ancient name for Paris), with Georges Barrère (flute) and Paul Kéfer (cello).

In 1921 Salzedo was cofounder, with EDGARD VARÈSE, of the International Composers' Guild in N.Y., with the aim of promoting modern music. This organization presented many important new works. In the same year he founded a modern music magazine, *Eolian Review,* later renamed *Eolus* (discontinued in 1933). He became an American citizen in 1923.

Salzedo was elected president of the National Association of Harpists and also held teaching positions at the Institute of Musical Art in N.Y. and the Juilliard Graduate School of Music. In addition, he organized and headed the harp department at the Curtis Institute of Music in Philadelphia. In 1931 he established the Salzedo Harp Colony at

Camden, Maine, for teaching and performing during the summer months.

Salzedo introduced a number of special effects on the harp and published studies for his new techniques. He designed a "Salzedo Model" harp, capable of rendering novel sonorities (Eolian flux and chords, gushing chords, percussion, etc.).

Salzedo's compositions are rhythmically intricate and feature elaborate COUNTERPOINT, requiring a virtuoso technique. He composed for his instrument, including numerous solo pieces and transcriptions, harp ensembles, chamber works with and without voice, and a few CONCERTO and concerto-like works.

samba. Characteristic Brazilian dance marked by a rolling rhythm in $\frac{2}{4}$ time and vigorous syncopation. Samba has also become a generic description of any Brazilian dance in a fast tempo.

sampler. Electronic digital recorder capable of recording a sound or series of sounds and then storing them in the form of digital information.

Sampling, a modern studio technique in which small bits of earlier recordings are stored and then interwoven into a new work to varying degrees. This technique has been most fully developed in RAP.

Samson et Dalila. Opera by CAMILLE SAINT-SAËNS, 1877, first performed in Weimar to a German LIBRETTO.

It tells the biblical story of Delilah, the priestess of the Philistine temple. She entices the Hebrew warrior Samson and during his sleep cuts his hair, the source of his physical power. He is then blinded, chained, and taken to the Philistine temple in Gaza. There, summoning his strength which has returned, he breaks the pillars supporting the roof, bringing the temple down on himself and the worshippers.

On account of the restrictions regarding theatrical representation of biblical characters, the opera was not performed on the stage in France until 1892, and not in England until 1909.

MUSICAL INSTRUMENT

PEOPLE IN MUSIC

sānāyī (*shannāi;* Sansk.; Pers. *surnā*). A conical SHAWM of North India, made of wood, with finger holes and a wide bore. Sometimes the bell is metallic.

Sanctus. A section of the MASS ORDINARY. It comprises the *Sanctus, Benedictus,* and the *Osanna* (Hosanna).

sanjuanito. National dance of Ecuador, dedicated to St. John, in $\frac{2}{4}$ time.

Sankey, Ira D(avid), noted American evangelistic singer, gospel hymn composer, and hymnbook compiler; b. Edinburgh, Pa., Aug. 28, 1840; d. N.Y., Aug. 13, 1908. As a youth of 17, Sankey became choir leader in the Methodist Church of New Castle, Pennsylvania. He served for a year with the N.Y. 12th Infantry Regiment at the time of the Civil War.

In 1870 Sankey was a delegate to the YMCA convention at Indianapolis, where his forceful singing attracted the attention of the evangelist preacher Dwight L. Moody. He joined Moody as music director and remained at this post for some 30 years, until approaching blindness forced his retirement in 1903.

Of his many gospel tunes, the most popular has proved to be *The Ninety and Nine* (1874), which Sankey improvised at a moment's notice during a service in Edinburgh, Scotland. His chief publications were *Sacred Songs and Solos* (London, 1873) and six volumes of *Gospel Hymns and Sacred Songs* (1875–91). As president of the publishing firm Biglow & Main from 1895 to 1903, Sankey brought out numerous works, including many of his own. He is not to be confused with another gospel song writer, Ira Allan Sankey, a lesser light.

Santa Lucia. Neapolitan BALLAD by Teodor Cottrau, published in 1850. Like many others of its kind, its popularity has not abated.

santūr (Turk.; Arab., Pers. *santir;* Mod. Grk. *santouri*). Trapezoidal hammered DULCIMER, with 14 courses of four metal strings apiece and curved blade-shaped beaters. The instrument dates from the 15th century and may be the ancestor of the Chinese *yangqin.*

Sapho. Opera by CHARLES GOUNOD, 1851, first produced in Paris. The libretto describes in melodramatic terms the life of the Greek poetess who flourished on the island of Lesbos.

This was Gounod's first opera, and the score anticipates the gift of melody that became his second nature.

Sapho. Opera by JULES MASSENET, 1897, based on a story by Alphonse Daudet, first produced in Paris. The heroine poses as an artist's model. A young man from the country falls in love with her, but their differences are such that they eventually go their separate ways.

The score is not one of Massenet's best, but it is invariably pleasing in its melodious lilt and harmonious tilt.

saraband (*sarabande;* It. *sarabanda;* Fr. *sarabande;* Ger. *Sarabande*). A dance of Spanish or Middle Eastern origin, at first a dance song in 16th-century Hispanic countries. The origin of the word is conjectural, its roots variously traced to Arabia via Moorish Spain, to Mexico, or to Panama.

săh-rah-bahn′d

Ironically, one of the earliest mentions of the word *saraband* occurs in the ruling of the Spanish Inquisition in 1583 that forbade the performing of the saraband on penalty of fine and imprisonment, apparently due to its immoral and suggestive nature.

Half a century after its proscription in Spain, the saraband quietly slithered into France and even Elizabethan England, becoming a stately dance in triple time. It remained popular in the 17th and 18th centuries, with both fast and slow types developing.

The saraband became an integral part of the BAROQUE instrumental SUITE, found in works by JOHANN SEBASTIAN BACH, GEORGE FRIDERIC HANDEL, and other masters. The instrumental form usually has two eight-measure reprises, in slow tempo and triple time. Its place in the suite, as the slowest movement, is before the GIGUE, with an optional movement often interpolated.

MUSICAL INSTRUMENT

PEOPLE IN MUSIC

sārăngī (Sans.) Indian bowed CHORDOPHONE, with three or four playing strings and a number of SYMPATHETIC STRINGS below them. The instrument is played between the knees of a seated performer. Its bow is thick and short. Formerly a FOLK instrument, it now participates in the classical music of India.

Sarasate (y Navascuez), **Pablo** (Martin Meliton) **de,** celebrated Spanish violinist and composer; b. Pamplona, March 10, 1844; d. Biarritz, Sept. 20, 1908. Sarasate began violin study when he was five. After making his public debut at eight, he was granted a private scholarship to study in Madrid. With the assistance of Queen Isabella, he pursued studies at the Paris Conservatory from 1856, where he took first prize in violin and SOLFÈGE in 1857 and in harmony in 1859.

Sarasate launched his career as a virtuoso with a major concert tour when he was 15. In 1866 he acquired a Stradivarius violin. His playing was noted for its extraordinary beauty of tone, impeccable purity of INTONATION, perfection of technique, and grace of manner.

In the early years of his career, Sarasate's repertoire consisted almost exclusively of FANTASIES on operatic airs, most of which he arranged himself. He later turned to the masterpieces of the violin literature. His tours, extending through all of Europe, the Americas, South Africa, and Asia, were an uninterrupted succession of triumphs. He bequeathed to his native city the gifts that had been showered upon him by admirers throughout the world. The collection was placed in a special museum.

Among works written for Sarasate were MAX BRUCH's Second Concerto and *Scottish Fantasy,* ÉDOUARD LALO's Concerto and *Symphonie espagnole,* CAMILLE SAINT-SAËNS's first and third concertos and *Introduction et Rondo capriccioso,* and HENRYK WIENIAWSKI's second concerto. Sarasate's compositions, pleasing and effective, include *Zigeunerweisen* (1878), *Spanische Tänze* (four books, 1878–82), and *Carmen Fantasy* in four movements (1883).

sardana. Catalonian round dance in $\frac{6}{8}$ time, alternating rapid and slow sections. PABLO CASALS wrote an orchestral

Sardana (1926) that stylizes the authentic rhythm and melody.

Šárka. Symphonic poem by BEDŘICH SMETANA, 1877, premiered in Prague. *Šárka* was incorporated into Smetana's orchestral cycle *MÁ VLAST* (as No. 3).

sarōd. An unfretted, plucked, pear-shaped classical Indian LUTE. It has six metal playing strings (two of which may be paired) and 12 or more SYMPATHETIC STRINGS below them. Like the larger SITAR, it uses bulbous gourds for resonance and was once a bowed CHORDOPHONE (although now rare). Both instruments are played in a sitting position, but the sarōd is played like a Western lute or guitar, while the sitar is held nearly upright.

MUSICAL INSTRUMENT

sarrusphone. A brass WIND INSTRUMENT with a double reed, invented in 1863 by and named after the Parisian bandmaster Sarrus. Although a family of sarrusphones was manufactured, the bass alone survives, as a CONTRABASS instrument in military bands.

MUSICAL INSTRUMENT

Satie, Erik (Alfred-Leslie), celebrated French composer, originator of intentionally unindelible "furniture music," who elevated his eccentricities and verbal virtuosity to the plane of high art; b. Honfleur, May 17, 1866; d. Paris, July 1, 1925. Satie received his early training from a local organist, Vinot, who was a pupil of Louis Niedermeyer.

PEOPLE IN MUSIC

At 13, Satie went to Paris, where his father was a music publisher, and received instruction in harmony and in piano. However, his attendance at the Conservatory was only sporadic between 1879 and 1886. He played in various cabarets in Montmartre. In 1884 he published a piano piece that he numbered, with malice aforethought, op.62.

Satie's whimsical ways and Bohemian lifestyle attracted many artists and musicians, including CLAUDE DEBUSSY, whom he met in 1891. He joined the Rosicrucian Society in Paris in 1892 and began to produce short piano pieces with eccentric titles intended to ridicule modernistic fancies and classical pedantries alike. Debussy thought highly enough of him to orchestrate two numbers from his piano suite *Trois Gymnopédies* in 1888.

In 1898 Satie moved to Arcueil, a suburb of Paris. There he held court for poets, singers, dancers, and musicians, among whom he had ardent admirers. Satie was almost 40 when he decided to pursue serious studies at the Paris Schola Cantorum, taking courses in COUNTERPOINT, FUGUE, and ORCHESTRATION with VINCENT D'INDY and ALBERT ROUSSEL from 1905 to 1908. DARIUS MILHAUD, Henri Sauguet, and Roger Desormière organized a group, which they called only half-facetiously "École d'Arcueil," in honor of Satie as master and leader.

But Satie's eccentricities were not merely those of a Parisian poseur. Rather, they were part of his aesthetic creed, which he enunciated with boldness and total disregard for the establishment (he was once brought to court for sending an insulting letter to a music critic). Although he was dismissed by most serious musicians as an uneducated person who tried to conceal his ignorance of music with his criticisms, he exercised a profound influence on the young French composers of the first quarter of the 20th century.

Moreover, Satie's stature as an innovator in the modern idiom grew after his death, so that later AVANT-GARDE musicians, including JOHN CAGE, accepted him as the inspiration for their own experiments. Thus, environmental or "space" music could be traced back to Satie's *Musique d'ameublement* (furniture music, 1920; collaboration with Milhaud) in which players were stationed at different parts of a hall playing different pieces in different tempos.

When critics accused Satie of having no idea of form, he published TROIS MORCEAUX EN FORME DE POIRE (Three pieces in the form of a pear; for piano four-hands, 1903), the fruit being reproduced in color on the cover. Other pieces bore self-contradictory titles, such as *Heures séculaires et instantanées* (Eternal and instantaneous hours) and *Crépuscule matinal de midi* (Morning twilight at noon). Other titles were *Pièces froides* (Cold pieces), *Embryons desséchés* (Dried embryos), *Prélude en tapisserie* (Wallpaper prelude), *Trois véritables préludes flasques (pour un chien)* (Three real, limp preludes [for a dog]), etc.

Satie's humorous instruction in his piano piece *Vexations*—to play it 840 times in succession—was carried out literally in N.Y. in 1963, by a group of five pianists working in relays overnight, thus setting a world's record for duration of any musical composition.

In his ballet *Parade* (*ballet realiste*, 1917; collaboration with the poet Jean Cocteau, painter Pablo Picasso, choreographer Léonine Massine), Satie introduced JAZZ in Paris. His ballet *Relâche* (*ballet instananée*, 1924), featured an *"entr'acte cinématographique,"* i.e., a film was shown during the intermission as part of the production. At its first performance, the curtain bore the legend "Erik Satie is the greatest musician in the world; whoever disagrees with this notion will please leave the hall." While the composer may have designed this slogan with his tongue in both cheeks, the late 20th-century listener may well enjoy the absurd humor and commentary, rebellious attitude, strong harmonic sense, virtually total lack of romanticism, and popular origins of "le maître d'Arcueil."

Satie published a facetious autobiographical notice as *Mémoires d'un amnésique* (The memoirs of an amnesiac; 1912).

Savoyards. Members of the D'Oyly Carte Opera Company that produced comic operas of Gilbert and Sullivan at the Savoy Theatre in London (hence the term Savoy opera, which was not limited to Gilbert and Sullivan). The company produced operas until 1982, and was revived in 1988.

Sawallisch, Wolfgang, eminent German conductor; b. Munich, Aug. 26, 1923. Sawallisch began piano study when he was five, later pursuing private training in Munich before entering military service during World War II in 1942. He then completed his musical studies at the Munich Hochschule für Musik.

In 1947 Sawallisch became RÉPÉTITEUR at the Augsburg Oper, making his conducting debut there in 1950. He then was Generalmusikdirektor of the opera houses in Aachen from 1953 to 1958, Wiesbaden from 1958 to 1960, and Cologne from 1960 to 1963, and also conducted at the Bayreuth Festivals from 1957 to 1961.

From 1960 to 1970 Sawallisch was chief conductor of the Vienna Symphony Orchestra, making his first appearance in the U.S. with that ensemble in 1964. He also was Generalmusikdirektor of the Hamburg State Philharmonic from 1961 to 1973. From 1970 to 1980 he was chief conductor of the Orchestre de la Suisse Romande in Geneva, and from 1971 also Generalmusikdirektor of the Bavarian

PEOPLE IN MUSIC

State Opera in Munich, where he was named Staatsoperndi-rektor in 1982.

In 1990 Sawallisch was named music director of the Philadelphia Orchestra, effective with the 1993–94 season. He appeared as a guest conductor with a number of the world's major orchestras and opera houses.

A distinguished representative of the revered Austro-German tradition, Sawallisch earned great respect for his un-ostentatious performances. He also made appearances as a sensitive piano accompanist to leading singers of the day.

PEOPLE IN MUSIC

Sax, Adolphe (Antoine-Joseph), Belgian inventor of the SAXOPHONE; b. Dinant, Nov. 6, 1814; d. Paris, Feb. 4, 1894. Sax's father was the instrument maker Charles-Joseph Sax (b. Dinant-sur-Meuse, Feb. 1, 1791; d. Paris, Apr. 26, 1865). Adolphe acquired great skill from his early youth in constructing musical instruments. His practical and imaginative ideas led him to undertake improvements of the CLARINET and other wind instruments. He also studied the FLUTE and clarinet at the Brussels Conservatory.

In 1842 he went to Paris with a wind instrument of his invention, the saxophone, made of metal, with a single-reed mouthpiece and conical bore. He exhibited brass and wood-wind instruments at the Paris Exposition of 1844, winning a silver medal. His father joined him in Paris, and together they continued to manufacture new instruments. They evolved the saxhorn (improved over the KEY BUGLE and OPH-ICLEIDE by replacing the keys with a VALVE mechanism) and the saxotromba, a hybrid instrument producing a tone mid-way between the BUGLE and the TRUMPET.

Conservative critics and rival instrument makers ridiculed Sax's innovations, but HECTOR BERLIOZ and others warmly supported him. His instruments were gradually adopted by French military bands. Sax won a gold medal at the Paris Industrial Exposition of 1849. Financially, however, he was unsuccessful, and he was compelled to declare bankruptcy in 1856 and again in 1873.

Sax taught saxophone at the Paris Conservatory from 1858 to 1871, and also published a method for the instrument. He exhibited his instruments in London in 1862 and, five years later, received the Grand Prix in Paris for his improved instruments. Although Wieprecht, Červeny, and others disputed the originality and priority of his inventions, legal decisions gave the rights to Sax. The saxophone became a standard instrument, and many serious composers made use of it in their scores.

saxophone (sax; It. *sassofono*). A metal wind instrument family patented 1846 by ADOLPHE SAX, having a CLARINET mouthpiece with single reed, the KEY MECHANISM and FINGERING also resembling those of the clarinet. It has a mellow, penetrating tone of veiled quality.

In the latter part of the 19th century, the saxophone became a standard instrument, and many serious composers made use of it in their scores. The instrument fell out of popularity after Sax's death in 1894, but about 1918 a spectacular revival of the saxophone took place, when it was adopted in JAZZ bands. Its popularity became worldwide, and numerous methods were published and special schools established. Saxophone virtuosos appeared, for whom many composers wrote concertos.

MUSICAL INSTRUMENT

◄

Modern saxophone. (Benson collection)

The first great jazz saxophonist was Sidney Bechet. The most famous, perhaps, of all time was BEBOP master CHARLIE PARKER.

The saxophone remains a popular band instrument, an essential part of most jazz ensembles, and a relatively infrequent but timbrally significant contributor to classical music.

scabellum (Lat.; Grk. *kroupalon, kroupezion*). Wooden foot clapper, attached like a sandal, used to keep time for music, dancing, or public games.

Scala, La. *Teatro alla Scala,* the most famous Italian opera house, founded in 1778 in Milan.

Although it is popularly imagined that the theater owes its name to the spectacular ladder leading to its doors (*scala* being Italian for ladder), the theater was actually named after Regina della Scala, the wife of the Duke Visconti of Milan. A whole galaxy of Italian composers—GIOACCHINO ROSSINI, GAETANO DONIZETTI, VINCENZO BELLINI, GIUSEPPE VERDI, and GIACOMO PUCCINI—had their operas premiered at La Scala, and great conductors, including ARTURO TOSCANINI, presided over many performances.

In 1943 La Scala was almost entirely destroyed by an Allied air attack on the city. It was rebuilt in 1946 with the financial assistance of musicians and music lovers worldwide, and was reopened in May 1946, with Toscanini conducting. The restoration was remarkably faithful.

The Teatro alla Scalla has six tiers, four of which are taken over by 146 boxes lined with elegant multicolored fabrics, with lighting provided by a sumptuous chandelier. In 1955 it engendered *La Piccola Scala,* suitable for performances of CHAMBER OPERA and modern BALLET.

scale(s) (It. *scala,* ladder; Ger. *Leiter, Tonleiter*). 1. In the tubes of wind instruments (especially ORGAN pipes), the ratio between width of bore and length. 2. The COMPASS of a voice or instrument; also, the series of TONES producible on a wind instrument. 3. A series of tones that form (a) any MAJOR or MINOR key (DIATONIC scale); (b) the CHROMATIC scale of successive steps in SEMITONES; or (c) any predetermined series of tones within a modal or tonal system.

The American pedagogue Percy Goetschius played the C-major scale for his students and asked them a rhetorical question, "Who invented this scale?" and answered it himself, "God!" Then he played the WHOLE-TONE scale and asked again, "Who invented this scale?" And he announced disdainfully, "Monsieur Debussy!" CLAUDE DEBUSSY did not invent the whole-tone scale, but he made ample use of it, as did many other composers of his time.

Other scales, built on QUARTER-TONE progressions, engaged the attention of composers: the GYPSY SCALE, the PENTATONIC SCALE suitable for quasi-Eastern melismas, and the OCTATONIC scale of alternating whole tones and semitones, used by NIKOLAI RIMSKY-KORSAKOV, FRANZ LISZT, PIOTR ILYICH TCHAIKOVSKY, IGOR STRAVINSKY, and many others.

Many other composers have created their own scales. FERRUCCIO BUSONI experimented with possible scales of seven notes and stated that he had invented 113 different scales of various INTERVALLIC structures. The first to examine and classify scales based on the symmetrical division of the octave was the theorist and composer Alois Hába in his book *Neue Harmonielehre* (1927). Joseph Schillinger undertook a thorough codification of all possible scales having any number of notes from 2 to 12, working on the problem mathematically.

Progressions of large intervals (thirds, fourths, fifths, etc.) cannot be properly described as scales, without contradicting the etymology of the word (which implies stepwise motion). But helixlike constructions, involving spiraling chromatics, may well be called scales. Quarter-tone scales and other microtonal progressions also belong in this category.

Scaramouche. Suite by DARIUS MILHAUD, 1937, for two pianos, first performed in Paris. Scaramouche is a standard character of Italian COMMEDIA DELL'ARTE (Scamarella).

Scarf Dance. *See* PAS DES ECHARPES.

Scarlatti, (Pietro) **Alessandro** (Gaspare), important Italian composer, father of (Giuseppe) DOMENICO SCARLATTI; b. Palermo, May 2, 1660; d. Naples, Oct. 22, 1725. Nothing is known about Scarlatti's musical training. When he was 12, he went with his two sisters to Rome, where he found patrons who enabled him to pursue a career in music. His

In his *Thesaurus of Scales and Melodic Patterns,* NICOLAS SLONIMSKY tabulated some 2,000 scales within the multiple octave range.

PEOPLE IN MUSIC

first known OPERA, *Gli equivoci nel sembiante,* was performed there in 1679.

By 1680 Scarlatti was maestro di cappella to Queen Christina of Sweden, whose palace in Rome served as an important center for the arts. He also found patrons in two cardinals, Benedetto Pamphili and Pietro Ottoboni, and served as maestro di cappella at S. Gerolamo della Carita.

From 1684 to 1702 Scarlatti was maestro di cappella to the Viceroy at Naples. During these years he composed prolifically, bringing out numerous operas, SERENATAS, ORATORIOS, and CANTATAS. In addition, he served as director of the Teatro San Bartolomeo, where he conducted many of his works. His fame as a composer for the theater soon spread, and many of his works were performed in leading music centers of Italy. One of his most popular operas, *Il Pirro e Demetrio* from 1694, was even performed in London. His only confirmed teaching position dates from this period, when he served for two months in the spring of 1689 on the faculty of the Conservatorio di Santa Maria di Loreto.

Tiring of his exhaustive labors, Scarlatti was granted a leave of absence and set out for Florence in June 1702. Prince Ferdinando de' Medici had been one of his patrons for some years in Florence, and Scarlatti hoped he could find permanent employment there. When this did not materialize, he settled in Rome and became assistant maestro di cappella at S. Maria Maggiore in 1703, being promoted to maestro di cappella in 1707. One of his finest operas, *Il Mitridate Eupatore,* was performed in Venice in 1707. Since the Roman theaters had been closed in 1700, he devoted much of his time to composing serenatas, cantatas, and oratorios.

In late 1708 Scarlatti was again appointed maestro di cappella to the Viceroy at Naples. His most celebrated opera from these years, *Il Tigrane,* was given in Naples in 1715. In 1718 Scarlatti's only full-fledged comic opera, IL TRIONFO DELL'ONORE (The triumph of honor), was performed there. Scarlatti's interest in purely instrumental music dates from this period, and he composed a number of conservative orchestra and chamber music pieces.

Having again obtained a leave of absence from his duties, Scarlatti went to Rome to oversee the premiere of his opera *Telemaco* in 1718. His last known opera, *La Griselda,* was given there in 1721. From 1722 until his death, he lived in retirement in Naples, producing only a handful of works.

Scarlatti was the foremost Neapolitan composer of the late BAROQUE era in Italy. He composed 58 operas (between 1679–1721), 27 serenatas (c.1680–1723), 36 oratorios, PASSIONS, and other sacred pieces (1679–1720), over 600 secular cantatas, MASSES and mass movements, MOTETS, and MADRIGALS. His instrumental music includes 12 *sinfonie di concerto grosso,* keyboard TOCCATAS, trio sonatas, SUITES, etc. He also produced some pedagogical manuals.

Scarlatti, (Giuseppe) **Domenico,** famous Italian composer, harpsichordist, and teacher, son of (Pietro) ALESSANDRO (Gaspare) SCAR-

Domenico Scarlatti. (New York Public Library)

LATTI; b. Naples, Oct. 26, 1685; d. Madrid, July 23, 1757. Nothing is known about Scarlatti's musical training. In 1701 he was appointed organist and composer at the Royal Chapel in Naples, where his father was maestro di cappella. The two were granted a leave of absence in June 1702, and they went to Florence. Later that year Domenico returned to Naples without his father and resumed his duties. His first opera, *Ottavia ristituita al trono,* was performed in Naples in 1703. He was sent to Venice by his father in 1705, but nothing is known of his activities there.

In 1708 Scarlatti went to Rome, where he entered the service of Queen Maria Casimira of Poland. In her service until 1714, he composed a number of operas and several other works for her private palace theater. He became assistant to Tommaso Bai, the maestro di cappella at the Vatican, in 1713. Upon Bai's death the next year, he was appointed his successor. He also became maestro di cappella to the Portuguese ambassador to the Holy See in 1714. During his years in Rome he met ARCANGELO CORELLI and GEORGE FRIDERIC HANDEL.

An unconfirmed story tells that Scarlatti and Handel engaged in a friendly contest, Scarlatti being judged the superior on the harpsichord and Handel on the organ.

Scarlatti resigned his positions in 1719. By 1724 he was in Lisbon, where he took up the post of mestre at the patriarchal chapel. His duties included teaching the Infanta Maria Barbara, daughter of King John V, and the King's younger brother, Don Antonio.

In 1728 Maria Barbara married the Spanish Crown Prince Fernando and moved to Madrid. Scarlatti accompanied her, remaining in Madrid for the rest of his life. In 1724 he visited Rome, where he met Johann Joaquim Quantz, the great flute virtuoso. In 1725 he saw his father for the last time in Naples, and in 1728 he was back in Rome, where he married Maria Caterina Gentili. He returned to Spain soon after.

In 1738 Scarlatti was made a Knight of the Order of Santiago. When Maria Barbara became queen in 1746, he was appointed her maestro de camera. His last years were spent quietly in Madrid. From 1752 until 1756 ANTONIO SOLER studied with him. So closely did Scarlatti become associated with Spain that his name eventually appeared as Domingo Escarlatti.

Scarlatti composed over 500 single-movement SONATAS for solo keyboard. Although these works were long believed to have been written for the HARPSICHORD, the fact that Maria Barbara used pianos in her residences suggests that some of these works were written for that instrument as well. At least three were written for the organ. It is clear by the key pairings and shared melodic material that many of the sonatas were meant to be performed in pairs.

Scarlatti's sonatas reveal his gifts as one of the foremost composers in the "free style" (a HOMOPHONIC style with graceful ORNAMENTATION, in contrast to the formal contrapuntal style). He also obtained striking effects by the frequent crossing of hands, tones repeated by rapidly changing fingers, and other effects achievable only on the keyboards.

During Scarlatti's lifetime three collections of his keyboard works were published (London, 1738; London, 1739; Paris, 1742–46). The sonatas were variously called "essercizi per gravicembalo," "suites de pièces pour le clavecin," and "pièces pour le clavecin." Alessandro Longo, RALPH KIRKPATRICK, and Giorgio Pestelli prepared chronological catalogues, although none can be proven definitive. Scarlatti also composed 17 orchestral SINFONIAS, 15 operas, some with collaborators, one ORATORIO, nine secular CANTATAS and SERENATAS, numerous ARIAS, and sacred vocal music.

Scarlatti's nephew, Giuseppe Scarlatti (b. Naples, c.1718; d. Vienna, Aug. 17, 1777), composed operas.

scat (singing). A style of JAZZ vocal performance. A singer improvises using nonsense syllables, often quite rapidly, but always with a strong rhythmic pulse and often in imitation of the sounds produced by instruments.

The technique originated in the 1920s, with LOUIS ARMSTRONG as its major proponent. Later, ELLA FITZGERALD made the technique her trademark, and many other singers in the BEBOP and subsequent traditions carried it forward.

Singer BOBBY MCFERRIN has taken elements of scat to new heights, incorporating all kinds of instrumental and vocal sounds into his performances.

Scelsi, Giacinto (born Conte Giacinto Scelsi di Valva), remarkable Italian composer; b. La Spezia, Jan. 8, 1905; d. Rome, Aug. 9, 1988. Scelsi was descended from a noble family. He received initial training in harmony when he was a teenager.

After studies with Egon Koehler in Geneva, Scelsi completed his formal training with Walter Klein in Vienna in 1935–36, where he became interested in ARNOLD SCHOENBERG's method of writing music outside the bounds of traditional TONALITY. At the same time, he became deeply immersed in the study of the musical philosophy of the East, in which SCALES and RHYTHMS are perceived as having a direct relation to human emotions. Scelsi's works began to have considerable performances in Italy and elsewhere, most particularly in the U.S.

A curious development arose after his death, when an Italian musician named Vieri Tosatti published a sensational article in the *Giornale della Musica,* declaring "I was Giac-

PEOPLE IN MUSIC

into Scelsi." He claimed that Scelsi sent him thematic sections of unfinished compositions, usually in the 12-TONE system, for development and completion, using him as a ghostwriter. Scelsi sent so many such "improvisations" to Tosatti that the latter had two other musicians to serve as secondary "ghosts," who, in turn, confirmed their participation in this peculiar transaction.

The matter finally got to the court of public opinion, where it was decided that the works were genuine compositions by Scelsi, who improvised them on his electric piano, and that they were merely edited for better effect by secondary arrangers.

scena (from Grk., stage). In opera, an accompanied dramatic solo, consisting of ARIOSO and RECITATIVE passages. It helps carry forward the story and often ends with an ARIA.

shâ′năh

scenario. A concise script outlining the contents of a play, OPERA, BALLET, or other performance work, with an indication of the participating characters/performers.

scene (Fr. *tableau;* Ger. *Auftritt*). Usually, a part of an ACT, e.g., an OPERA may contain three acts and seven SCENES, which are distributed among the three acts. Sometimes a composer subdivides an opera into scenes without specifying the number of acts, e.g., SERGEI PROKOFIEV's *WAR AND PEACE* and MODEST MUSSORGSKY's *BORIS GODUNOV.*

PEOPLE IN MUSIC

Schaeffer, Pierre, French acoustician, composer, and novelist; b. Nancy, Aug. 14, 1910. Working in a radio studio in Paris, Schaeffer came up with the idea of arranging a musical montage of random sounds, including outside NOISES. In 1948 he formulated the theory of MUSIQUE CONCRÈTE, which was to define such random assemblages of sounds.

When magnetic tape was perfected, Schaeffer made use of it by speeding up or slowing down the tape's movement. This changed the PITCH and dynamics of the recorded material and modified the nature of the instrumental timbre. He made several collages of elements of "concrete music," among them *Concert de bruits* (1948; with Pierre Henry) *Symphonie pour un homme seul* (1950), and an experimental opera, *Orphée 53* (1953). He incorporated his findings and ideas in the book *A la recherche d'une musique concrète* (In search of concrete music; 1952) and *Traité des objets sonores* (Treatise on sonorous objects; 1966).

Eventually, Schaeffer abandoned his acoustical experimentations and turned to literature. He published both fictional and quasiscientific novels, among them *Le Gardien de volcan* (The guardian of the volcano; 1969), *Excusez-moi si je meurs* (Excuse me if I kill; 1981), and *Prélude, Chorale et Fugue* (Prelude, chorale, and fugue; 1983).

Schafer, R(aymond) **Murray,** Canadian composer and educator; b. Sarnia, Ontario, July 18, 1933. Schafer studied at the Royal Conservatory of Music of Toronto from 1952 to 1955. He went to Vienna in 1956 and then on to England, where he was active with the BBC from 1956 to 1961.

Returning to Canada in 1961, Schafer served as artist-in-residence at Memorial University from 1963 to 1965 and taught at Simon Fraser University from 1965 to 1975. In 1974 he held a Guggenheim fellowship. He was active with the World Soundscape project from 1972. In 1987 he received the Glenn Gould Award.

Schafer's compositions often took familiar thematic material and distorted, varied, or in some other way changed it. A good example is his satire/tribute for orchestra and tape, *The Son of Heldenleben,* written in 1968. In this work, Schafer systematically distorted the thematic materials of RICHARD STRAUSS'S *EIN HELDENLEBEN,* retaining the essential motivic substance of the original score.

Schafer is best known for his experimental use of language and performance environments, although in later years he composed for more traditional ensembles. Among such later compositions are *Gitanjali* for soprano and small orchestra (1990) and *The Darkly Splendid Earth: The Lonely Traveller* for violin and orchestra (1991). He is also an active and innovative educator and author.

Schafer's best-known book is *The Tuning of the World,* in which he discusses his theories of composition and performance.

Schandeflöte (Ger., flute of shame). A heavy vertical FLUTE made of iron. It was hung on a tight ring around the neck of a town fifer in medieval Germany as punishment for the crime of playing too many wrong notes.

MUSICAL INSTRUMENT

A sign was placed on the fifer's jacket spelling out the extent of his inharmonious conduct so that he could receive the full brunt of public disgrace. Theories that this symbol replaced the wearing of a red-lettered "S" (for *Schande* or shame) around the fifer's neck cannot be verified.

Schauspieldirektor, Der. *See* IMPRESARIO, THE.

Schauspielmusik (Ger.). *See* THEATER MUSIC.

Scheherazade. Symphonic SUITE by NIKOLAI RIMSKY-KORSAKOV, 1888, based on *The Thousand and One Nights,* first performed in St. Petersburg. The connecting link within the suite is a brief violin solo representing the narrative of the Sultan's most resourceful wife. She saves herself from the Sultan's customary execution of each of his wives after the wedding night by telling him exciting tales.

The work is brilliantly orchestrated. Eastern-like melodies and timbres are cleverly worked into the score. The work has often been choreographed as a BALLET.

PEOPLE IN MUSIC

Schenker, Heinrich, outstanding Austrian music theorist; b. Wisniowczyki, Galicia, June 19, 1868; d. Vienna, Jan. 13, 1935. Schenker studied law at the University of Vienna, earning his degree in 1890, while also taking courses with ANTON BRUCKNER at the Vienna Conservatory. Schenker composed some songs and piano pieces, which JOHANNES BRAHMS liked sufficiently to recommend them to his publisher. For a while Schenker served as accompanist of the baritone Johannes Messchaert.

Around 1900 Schenker returned to Vienna and devoted himself entirely to theoretical research. He tried to derive the basic laws of musical composition from a thorough analysis of the standard masterworks. This gave birth to what is called in music theory courses SCHENKERIAN ANALYSIS. A complex system, it has a strong, loyal, but small, following among music theoreticians.

Schenkerian analysis (Schenkerianism). A theory of musical analysis evolved over several decades by HEINRICH SCHENKER. It derives its principle from the natural series of

OVERTONES. The continuum of these overtones is defined as *Klang* (clang), that is, a cumulative sound. The linear distribution of this Klang is the fundamental line (*Urlinie*), governing the melodic design. The bass line is named fundamental arpeggio (*Grundbrechung*).

The process of analysis is in several stages. The actual composition is defined as foreground (*Vorgrund*), its partial REDUCTION is middle ground (*Mittelgrund*), and its final schematization—the background (*Hintergrund*)—constitutes the fundamental structure (*Ursatz*), representing the summation of the *Urlinie* and the *Grundbrechung*. These successive stages are obtained by a series of motions (*Züge*).

Because the harmonic series is the basic source of the *Ursatz,* the Schenkerian system is based on the TONIC MAJOR TRIAD, with the SUBDOMINANT and DOMINANT triads derived from it, and with minor triads having a secondary role.

In his original historical exposition, Schenker covers the common practice period from JOHANN SEBASTIAN BACH to JOHANNES BRAHMS (RICHARD WAGNER is omitted). Analysis of CHROMATIC harmony is made by even further adjustments.

Following this system, it is possible to analyze even modern works (Schenker once analyzed a piece of IGOR STRAVINSKY to point out the composer's "errors"). However, the limitations of the Schenker system becomes increasingly evident with each successive step toward ATONALITY. The system is completely useless when applied to CHANCE compositions.

Scherzi, Gli. One of several nicknames for the FRANZ JOSEPH HAYDN quartets op.33 (Nos. 37–42, 1781). The MINUETS in them are marked either *scherzo* or *scherzando*, i.e., to be played faster than the usual minuet tempo.

The same group of quartets is known as *Jungfernquartette* (Maiden quartets) because the title page of the first edition represented a young female. They are also known as the *Russian Quartets* because they were dedicated to a Russian grandduke.

scherzo (It., joke; Ger. *Scherz*). 1. A vivacious movement in the late CLASSIC and ROMANTIC symphony, with strongly marked rhythms and sharp, unexpected contrasts in both rhythm and harmony.

skâr′tsōh

While in most late Classic symphonies the scherzo was placed in the position formerly occupied by the minuet (i.e., the third movement), LUDWIG VAN BEETHOVEN shifted it to the second movement in his Ninth Symphony.

In the second half of the 18th century, the term *scherzo* was standardized as an instrumental composition in $\frac{3}{4}$ or $\frac{3}{8}$ time in a rapid tempo. (Occasionally, duple-meter scherzos were composed.) Structurally, scherzo was a modification of the ternary Classic MINUET. In the 19th century, it usually replaced the Classic minuet in SONATAS, CHAMBER MUSIC, and SYMPHONIES. Like the minuet, the scherzo contains a contrasting middle part, the TRIO (because these were first written for three instruments only).

2. In the ROMANTIC era, an instrumental piece of a light, piquant, and humorous character. FRÉDÉRIC CHOPIN elevated it to a form of prime importance; his four piano scherzos are extended, virtuosic compositions, while retaining their ternary form. PAUL DUKAS called *THE SORCERER'S APPRENTICE* a scherzo, and IGOR STRAVINSKY wrote an orchestral work entitled *Scherzo fantastique,* inspired by German poet Otto Maeterlinck's half-literary, half-scientific essay *Les Abeilles* (The bees).

3. In the 16th century, a vocal composition in a light manner, although titles such as *Scherzi sacri* (sacred scherzos) are also found.

Scherzo à la russe. Orchestral work by IGOR STRAVINSKY, 1944, for JAZZ big band. Stravinsky conducted an orchestral arrangement in San Francisco, 1946. The piece is a sophisticated POTPOURRI of Russian FOLKlike motives.

Scherzo Fantastique. Orchestral work by IGOR STRAVINSKY, 1909, premiered in St. Petersburg.

The composition was inspired by Otto Maeterlinck's essay *Les Abeilles* (The bees). Each section of the score corresponds to a beehive event: birth of the queen, nuptial flight, swarming, etc. The publishers quoted from the book in the score, and Maeterlinck, a hot-tempered poet, promptly sued Stravinsky for copyright infringement.

Fifty years later, in one of his conversation books with Robert Craft, Stravinsky denied ever intending to use the Maeterlinck book as a programmatic source. However, his own 1907 letter to NIKOLAI RIMSKY-KORSAKOV plainly contradicts this.

Schickele, Peter, American composer and musical humorist, better known as P. D. Q. Bach; b. Ames, Iowa, July 17, 1935. Schickele was educated at Swarthmore College, earning a bachelor of arts degree in 1957. He studied composition with ROY HARRIS in Pittsburgh in 1954, DARIUS

PEOPLE IN MUSIC

MILHAUD at the Aspen School of Music in 1959, and VIN-CENT PERSICHETTI and William Bergsma at the Juilliard School of Music in N.Y., where he took his master's degree in 1960.

After serving as composer-in-residence to Los Angeles public schools in 1960–61, Schickele taught at Swarthmore in 1961–62 and Juilliard after that.

Schickele rocketed to fame at N.Y.'s Town Hall in 1965, in the rollicking role of the roly-poly character P. D. Q. Bach, the mythical composer of such wonderful travesties as:

The Civilian Barber (a SUITE from an "unrediscovered opera")

Gross Concerto for Divers Flutes (featuring a Nose Flute and a Wiener Whistle, both eaten during the performance)

Concerto for piano vs. orchestra

The Seasonings

Pervertimento for Bagpipes Bicycles & Balloons

No-No Nonette

Missa Hilarious

Sanka Cantata

The Abduction of Figaro

Schickele published *The Definitive Biography of P. D. Q. Bach (1807–1742?)* in 1976.

In 1967 Schickele organized a chamber-rock-jazz trio known as Open Window, which frequently presented his own compositions, including orchestral works, vocal pieces (including rounds), film and television scores, and chamber music. He hosts a weekly radio show, *Schickele Mix,* which redefines music appreciation.

Schifrin, Lalo (Boris), Argentine-American pianist, conductor, and composer; b. Buenos Aires, June 21, 1932. Schifrin studied music at home with his father, the concertmaster of the Teatro Colón orchestra. He subsequently studied harmony with Juan Carlos Paz.

PEOPLE IN MUSIC

Schifrin won a scholarship to the Paris Conservatory in 1950, where he studied with Charles Koechlin and OLIVIER MESSIAEN. Schifrin became interested in JAZZ and represented Argentina at the International Jazz Festival in Paris in 1955. Returning to Buenos Aires, he formed his own jazz band, adopting the BEBOP style.

In 1958 Schifrin went to N.Y. as arranger for XAVIER CUGAT, then was pianist with DIZZY GILLESPIE's band from 1960 to 1962. He composed several works for Gillespie, including *Manteca, Con Alma,* and *Tunisian Fantasy,* based on Gillespie's *Night in Tunisia.* In 1963 he wrote a ballet, *Jazz Faust.* He also experimented with applying the jazz idiom to religious texts, as, for instance, in his *Jazz Suite on Mass Texts* in 1965.

In 1964 Schifrin went to Hollywood, where he rapidly became a popular composer for films and television. Among his scores are *The Liquidator* (1966), *Cool Hand Luke* (1967), *The Fox* (1967), *The Four Musketeers* (1973), *Voyage of the Damned* (1975), *The Amityville Horror* (1978), *The Sting II* (1983), and *Bad Medicine* (1985). He achieved his greatest popular success with the theme for the television series *Mission: Impossible* (1966–73), in 5/4 time, for which he received two Grammy Awards. The theme was revised in the motion picture based on the series in 1997.

Schifrin has continued to compose for classical orchestras while pursuing his career in film and television. Among his more recent compositions are Guitar Concerto (1984), *Songs of the Aztec* for soloist and orchestra (Teotihuacan, Mexico, 1988), and two piano concertos, including No. 2, *Concerto of the Americas* (Washington, D.C., 1992). In 1988 he became music director of the newly organized Paris Philharmonic.

Schikaneder, Emanuel (Johannes Joseph). *See* MAGIC FLUTE, THE.

Schillinger, Joseph (Moiseievich), Russian-born American music theorist and composer; b. Kharkov, Aug. 31, 1895; d. N.Y., March 23, 1943. Schillinger studied at the St. Petersburg Conservatory with NIKOLAI TCHEREPNIN and Joseph Wihtol. He was active as a teacher, conductor, and administrator in Kharkov from 1918 to 1922, and Moscow

PEOPLE IN MUSIC

and Leningrad from 1922 and 1928, before emigrating to the U.S. in 1928. He became a naturalized American citizen in 1936.

Schillinger settled in N.Y. as a teacher of music, mathematics, and art history. He developed and taught his own system of composition based on rigid mathematical principles. He taught at the New School for Social Research, N.Y. University, Columbia University Teachers College, and privately.

While he composed several orchestral works, Schillinger is best remembered for his magnum opus, the treatise entitled *The Schillinger System of Musical Composition* (two volumes, N.Y., 1941; fourth edition, 1946). It has influenced several generations of composers.

Schillinger was sought out as a teacher by many composers and performers in both the classical and JAZZ worlds, including TOMMY DORSEY, VERNON DUKE, GEORGE GERSHWIN, BENNY GOODMAN, OSCAR LEVANT, and GLENN MILLER.

Schindler, Anton Felix. *See* BEETHOVEN, LUDWIG VAN.

Schluß (Ger., conclusion). The indication of the final section (subsection, phrase) of a composition. The last movement of a large work is sometimes referred to as *Schlußsatz* (concluding part). The Schluß in a simple chant may be limited to two notes, the *penultima vox* (next-to-last voice) and *ultima vox* (last voice), to use the terminology of medieval Latin treatises.

An ideal Schluß in CLASSIC music is provided by WOLF-GANG AMADEUS MOZART's Symphony No. 39 in E-flat major. It concludes with a simple restatement of the principal THEME, suggesting a signature in Gothic characters. One of the most extended Schlüsse is that of the Second Symphony of JEAN SIBELIUS. It consists of a seemingly unending succession of ascending scales. The most abrupt Schluß occurs with the C-major chord at the end of SERGEI PROKOFIEV's *March* from the opera LOVE FOR THREE ORANGES.

By definition, the Schluß must be a UNISON or a CONCORD, but FRÉDÉRIC CHOPIN and ROBERT SCHUMANN sometimes end an individual piece of a cycle on an unresolved DOMINANT-SEVENTH CHORD. The final chord in GUSTAV MAHLER's grand symphony DAS LIED VON DER ERDE is a DISCORD. In ATONAL writing, a dissonant ending is almost expected, unless it happens to be a single tone lost in mid-air, *pianissimo*.

shlooss

Toward the middle of the 20th century, several composers, among them KARL-HEINZ STOCKHAUSEN, EARLE BROWN, and JOHN CAGE, composed works without an ascertainable Schluß, wherein any moment of a composition may be either beginning or end.

PEOPLE IN MUSIC

Schnabel, Artur, celebrated Austrian-born American pianist and pedagogue; b. Lipnik, April 17, 1882; d. Axenstein, Switzerland, Aug. 15, 1951. Schnabel made his debut at eight years of age, then studied with Theodor Leschetizky in Vienna from 1891 to 1897.

Schnabel went to Berlin in 1900, where, five years later, he married the contralto Therese Behr, with whom he frequently appeared in recitals. He also played in recitals with leading musicians of the day. He likewise gave solo recitals in Europe and the U.S., presenting acclaimed cycles of LUDWIG VAN BEETHOVEN's sonatas. He taught at the Berlin Hochschule für Musik from 1925 to 1933.

After the rise of the Nazi regime in 1933, Schnabel left Germany and settled in Switzerland. He taught master classes at Lake Como and recorded the first complete set of the Beethoven sonatas. With the outbreak of World War II in 1939, he went to the U.S., becoming a naturalized citizen in 1944. After teaching at the University of Michigan from 1940 to 1945, he returned to Switzerland.

Schnabel was one of the greatest pianists and teachers in the history of keyboard playing. He concentrated upon the masterworks of the Austro-German repertoire. He gave these pieces an intelligent, straightforward interpretation, avoiding any uncalled-for embellishments. He was renowned for his performances of Beethoven and FRANZ SCHUBERT and prepared an edition of the Beethoven piano sonatas.

Schnabel was also a composer. In his works, he pursued an uncompromisingly modern style, thriving on DISSONANCE and creating melodic patterns along ATONAL lines. He wrote three symphonies and other works for orchestra, chamber pieces including five string quartets and a piano quintet, many solo pieces for piano, and songs. His writings include *Reflections on Music* (1933) and *Music and the Line of Most Resistance* (1942).

Schnabel's son, Karl Ulrich Schnabel (b. Berlin, Aug. 6, 1909), is a pianist, teacher, and composer. He studied with Leonid Kreutzer (piano) and Paul Juon (composition) at the Prussian State Academy of Music in Berlin (1922–26). After making his debut in Berlin in 1926, he toured in Europe. From 1935 to 1940 he made duo appearances with his father. On Feb. 23, 1937, he made his U.S. debut in N.Y., where he settled in 1939. With his wife, Helen (née Fogel) Schnabel, he toured extensively in duo recitals from 1940 to her death in 1974. From 1980 he appeared in duo recitals with Joan Rowland. In addition to his many tours around the globe, he devoted much time to teaching. He is the author of *Modern Technique of the Pedal* (N.Y., 1950) and also composed several pieces for piano four-hands.

Schnaderhüpfel (Ger. dialect). Song of the Bavarian Alps in $\frac{3}{4}$ time. It usually consists of symmetric STANZAS with a harmonic scheme of alternating TONIC and DOMINANT harmonies.

Schnittke, Alfred (Garrievich), prominent Russian composer of German descent; b. Engels, near Saratov, Nov. 24, 1934; d. Hamburg, Aug. 3, 1998. Schnittke studied piano in Vienna from 1946 to 1948, where his father was a correspondent of a German-language Soviet newspaper. He then took courses in composition and in instrumentation at the Moscow Conservatory from 1953 to 1958. After serving on its faculty from 1962 to 1972, he devoted himself fully to composition.

PEOPLE IN MUSIC

Schnittke made many trips abroad. In 1981 he was a guest lecturer at the Vienna Hochschule für Musik und Darstellende Kunst. That same year, he was elected a member of the West German Akademie der Kunste. However, his health began to fail in the mid-'80s. In 1985 he survived a serious heart attack, and in 1988 and again in 1991 he suffered debilitating strokes. He died in 1998.

After writing in a traditional manner, Schnittke became acutely interested in the new Western techniques, particularly in SERIALISM and "sonorism," in which changes in DYNAMICS become an organizing force in composition. Soon he became known as one of the boldest experimenters in contemporary composition in Russia and also developed an international reputation. Schnittke also wrote many pieces that take a postmodern look at NEOCLASSICISM and neo-BAROQUE music.

Among Schnittke's works are a significant number of orchestral pieces, including four violin concertos, eight symphonies, and six concerti grossi, for various instruments. He also wrote many descriptively titled orchestral works, including ...*pianissimo*... (1967–68), *In memoriam* (1972–78), *(K)ein Sommernachstraum* ([Not] a midsummer night's dream, 1985), and *Five Fragments on Pictures by Hieronymus Bosch* (1994).

Schnittke wrote many chamber works and pieces for piano, including *Dedication to Stravinsky, Prokofiev, and Shostakovich* for piano six-hands (1979) and two piano sonatas (1987–88; 1990). He also composed many vocal pieces, including *Seid nüchtern und wachet...,* a cantata for four soloists, chorus, and orchestra. It was based on a version of the Faust legend published in 1587 under the title *Historia von D. Johann Fausten* and commissioned by the Vienna Choral Academy to celebrate its 125th anniversary (first performed as *Faust Cantata,* Vienna, June 19, 1983).

Schoeck, Othmar, eminent Swiss pianist, conductor, and composer; b. Brunnen, Sept. 1, 1886; d. Zurich, March 8, 1957. Schoeck was the son of the painter Alfred Schoeck. He went to Zurich, where he took courses at the Industrial College before pursuing musical training at the Zurich Conservatory beginning in 1905. After further studies with MAX REGER in Leipzig in 1907–08, he returned to Zurich. He worked at first conducting various choral groups, and then was conductor of the St. Gallen symphony concerts from 1917 to 1944.

Schoeck was one of the most significant Swiss composers of his era. He won his greatest renown as a masterful composer of songs, of which he wrote about 400, and he wrote several operas. He was also highly regarded as a piano accompanist and conductor. Among his many honors were an honorary doctorate from the University of Zurich, awarded in 1928, first composer's prize of the Schweizerische Tonkünstlerverein, in 1945, and Grand Cross of Merit and Order of Merit of the Federal Republic of Germany, in 1956. In 1959 the Othmar Schoeck Gesellschaft was founded to promote performance of his works.

Schoenberg (Schönberg), **Arnold** (Franz Walter), outstanding Austrian-born American composer and theorist whose new method of musical organization in 12 different tones

PEOPLE IN MUSIC

related only to one another profoundly influenced the entire development of modern techniques of composition; b. Vienna, Sept. 13, 1874; d. Los Angeles, July 13, 1951. Schoenberg studied at the Realschule in Vienna. He learned to play the cello and also became proficient on the violin. His father died when Schoenberg was 16, at which time he took a job as a bank clerk to earn a living. An additional source of income was arranging popular songs and orchestrating operetta scores.

◄ *Arnold Schoenberg, c. 1940. (New York Public Library)*

Schoenberg's first original work was a group of three piano pieces, which he wrote in 1894. It was also about that time that he began to take lessons in COUNTERPOINT from Alexander von Zemlinsky, whose sister Mathilde Schoenberg married in 1901. He also played cello in Zemlinsky's instrumental group, Polyhymnia. In 1897 Schoenberg wrote an unnumbered string quartet, in D major, which was performed in public a year later in Vienna. About the same time, he wrote two songs with piano accompaniment, which he designated as op.1.

In 1899 Schoenberg wrote his first true masterpiece, *VERKLÄRTE NACHT,* set for string sextet. It was first performed in Vienna by the Rose Quartet and members of the Vienna Philharmonic in 1902. It is a fine work, deeply filled with the spirit of ROMANTIC poetry, with its harmonic style stemming from RICHARD WAGNER's works.

**Arnold Schoenberg
time line**

1874 ▸ Born

1894 ▸ Begins composition lessons with Alexander von Zemlinsky

1899 ▸ Composes *VERKLÄRTE NACHT*

1901 ▸ Marries Zemlinsky's sister, Mathilde, and lives for two years in Berlin, where he launches the artistic cabaret "Überbrettl" and teaches at the Stern Conservatory

1904 ▸ Back in Vienna, with Zemlinsky he organizes the Vereinigung Schaffender Tonkünstler where, in 1907, his *KAMMERSYMPHONIE,* op.9, is performed with members of the Rose Quartet and the Vienna Philharmonic

1908 ▸ Composes his Second String Quartet, his last work (with one late exception) to carry a definite key signature

1909 ▸ Composes his first atonal composition, the piano piece, op.11, no.1

1910 ▸ Appointed to the faculty of the Vienna Academy

1911 Completes work on his influential theoretical text, *Harmonielehre*

1912 Brings out his *5 Orchesterstücke* in London and composes the melodrama *PIERROT LUNAIRE,* op.21

1913 The long-awaited first complete performance of *Gurre-Lieder* is given by the Vienna Philharmonic, conducted by Franz Schreker

1918 Organizes the Society for Private Musical Performances

1924 Articulates his "method of composing with 12 different notes related entirely to one another," exemplified in its integral form in his Piano Suite, op.25

1925 Becomes professor of a master class at the Prussian Academy of Arts in Berlin

1932 Completes the first two acts of his *Moses und Aron*

1933 The German Ministry of Education dismisses him from his post at the Prussian Academy of Arts in Berlin because he is Jewish. In response, he reconverts to Judaism, a faith he had abandoned for Lutheranism in 1898, and emigrates to the U.S.

1935–36 Joins the faculties at the University of Southern California and the University California, Los Angeles

About 1900, Schoenberg was engaged as conductor of several amateur choral groups in Vienna and its suburbs, a position that increased his interest in vocal music. He then began work on a choral composition, *Gurre-Lieder,* of monumental proportions, to the translated text of a poem by the Danish writer Jens Peter Jacobsen. For grandeur and opulence of orchestral sonority, it surpassed even the most formidable creations of GUSTAV MAHLER or RICHARD STRAUSS. He completed the first two parts of it in the spring of 1901, but the composition of the remaining section was delayed by ten years. It was not until 1913 that Franz Schreker was able to arrange its complete performance with the Vienna Philharmonic and its choral forces.

In 1901 Schoenberg moved to Berlin, where he launched an artistic cabaret called *Überbrettl.* He composed a theme song for it with trumpet OBBLIGATO and conducted several shows. He met Strauss, who helped him to obtain the Liszt Stipendium and a position as a teacher at the Stern Conservatory. Schoenberg returned to Vienna in 1903 and became friendly with Mahler, who became a strong supporter of his activities. Mahler's power in Vienna was then at its height, and he was able to help Schoenberg's career as a composer.

In 1904 Schoenberg organized with Zemlinsky the Vereinigung Schaffender Tonkünstler for the purpose of encouraging performances of new music. Under its auspices he conducted the first performance of his symphonic poem *Pelléas und Mélisande* in 1905. There followed a performance in 1907 of Schoenberg's KAMMERSYMPHONIE, op.9, with the participation of the Rose Quartet and the wind instrumentalists of the Vienna Philharmonic. The work was received poorly by critics and the audience, because of its departure from traditional TONAL HARMONY. It featured chords built on FOURTHS and nominal DISSONANCES used without immediate resolution.

Schoenberg's reputation as an independent musical thinker attracted to him such progressive-minded young musicians as ALBAN BERG, ANTON WEBERN, and EGON WELLESZ, who followed Schoenberg in their own development. Schoenberg's Second String Quartet, composed in 1908, which included a soprano solo, was his last work that carried a definite KEY SIGNATURE.

In 1909 Schoenberg completed his piano piece op.11, no. 1, which became the first ATONAL musical composition. In 1910 he was appointed to the faculty of the Vienna Academy of Music, and, a year later, he completed his important theory book *Harmonielehre,* dedicated to the memory of Mahler. It is based on a traditional description of CHORDS and PROGRESSIONS, but also points the way toward possible new musical developments, including fractional tones and melodies formed by change of timbre on the same note. That same year, Schoenberg went again to Berlin, where he became an instructor at the Stern Conservatory and taught composition privately.

In 1912 Schoenberg brought out a work that attracted a great deal of attention: *5 Orchesterstücke* (5 orchestral pieces) which was performed for the first time not in Germany or Austria, but in London, under the direction of Sir Henry Wood. The critical reception was that of incomprehension, with a considerable measure of curiosity. The score was indeed revolutionary in nature, each movement representing an experiment in musical organization.

In the same year, Schoenberg produced another innovative work, a song cycle with instrumental accompaniment. It was entitled *PIERROT LUNAIRE,* op.21, consisting of 21 MELODRAMAS to German texts translated from verses by the Belgian poet Albert Giraud. Here Schoenberg introduced SPRECHSTIMME, with a gliding speech-song replacing precise PITCH. Later that year, the work was given, after some 40 rehearsals, in Berlin. The critics were unanimous in their condemnation of it.

Meanwhile, Schoenberg made appearances as conductor of his works in various European cities (Amsterdam, 1911; St. Petersburg, 1912; London, 1914). During World War I he was sporadically enlisted in military service. After the Armistice, he settled in Mödling, near Vienna. Discouraged by his inability to secure performances for himself and his associates, he organized in Vienna, in 1918, the Verein für Musikalische Privataufführungen (Society for private musical performances). Critics were not allowed to attend any of these concerts, and any vocal expression of approval or disapproval was forbidden. The organization disbanded in 1922.

1941	Becomes a naturalized American citizen
1947	Receives the Award of Merit for Distinguished Achievements from the National Institute of Arts and Letters
1947	Composes *A SURVIVOR FROM WARSAW,* op.46
1951	Dies

Verklärte Nacht remains Schoenberg's most frequently performed composition, known principally through its arrangement for string orchestra.

Schoenberg's use of Sprechstimme in *Pierrot Lunaire* was not the first appearance of this technique. ENGELBERT HUMPERDINCK had used it in his incidental music to E. Rosmer's play *KÖNIGSKINDER* in 1897.

In 1924 Schoenberg's creative evolution reached the point at which he found it necessary to establish a new governing principle of tonal relationship. He called it the "method of composing with 12 different notes related entirely to one another." This method was used in his music as early as 1914, and is used partially in his *5 Klavierstücke,* op.23, and in his *Serenade,* op.24.

TWELVE-TONE COMPOSITION was employed for the first time in its integral form in Schoenberg's Piano Suite, op.25, of 1924. In it, thematic material is based on a group of 12 different notes arrayed in a certain prearranged order. Such a TONE ROW was henceforth Schoenberg's mainspring of thematic invention, with DEVELOPMENT provided by the devices of INVERSION, RETROGRADE, and RETROGRADE INVERSION of the basic series. Allowing for TRANSPOSITION, 48 forms were obtainable in all, with COUNTERPOINT and HARMONY, as well as melody, derived from the basic tone row. Immediate repetition of thematic notes was admitted, and the realm of rhythm remained free.

As with most historic innovations, the 12-tone technique was not the immaculate conception of Schoenberg's alone but was, rather, a logical development of many currents of musical thought.

In 1925 Schoenberg was appointed professor of a master class at the Prussian Academy of Arts in Berlin. With the advent of the Nazi regime in 1933, the German Ministry of Education dismissed him from his post because he was a Jew. As a matter of record, Schoenberg had abandoned his Jewish faith in Vienna in 1898 and in a spirit of political accommodation converted to Lutheranism. Some 35 years later, horrified by the hideous persecution of Jews at the hands of the Nazis, he was moved to return to his ancestral faith and was reconverted to Judaism in Paris in 1933. With the rebirth of his Jewish consciousness, he turned to specific Jewish themes in works such as *A SURVIVOR FROM WARSAW* (op.46, 1947) and *MOSES UND ARON* (acts I–II, 1930–32; act III not composed).

Although Schoenberg was well known in the musical world, he had difficulty obtaining a teaching position. He finally accepted the invitation of Joseph Malkin, founder of the Malkin Conservatory of Boston, to join its faculty. He

harfe (The magic harp) was heard at the Theater an der Wien. This score's overture eventually became popular as the overture to *Rosamunde,* even though it was not written for that play, which was not produced until three years later.

Although Schubert still had difficulties earning a living, he formed a circle of influential friends in Vienna and appeared as a pianist at private gatherings. Sometimes he sang his songs, accompanying himself at the keyboard. He was also able to publish some of his songs.

A mystery is attached to Schubert's most famous work, begun in 1822, the Symphony in B minor, the UNFINISHED SYMPHONY. Only two movements are known to exist, with portions of the third movement, a SCHERZO, remaining in sketches. What prevented him from finishing it? Speculations are as many as they are worthless, particularly because he was usually careful in completing a work before embarking on another composition. He completed another symphony after the so-called "unfinished" one—the *Great Symphony* in C major (1825–26).

In 1823 Schubert completed his masterly song cycle DIE SCHÖNE MÜLLERIN, and in 1824 he once again spent the summer as a private tutor in Count Esterházy's employ. In 1827 he wrote another remarkable song cycle, DIE WINTERREISE. In the spring of 1828, he presented in Vienna a public concert of his works. In that year, which proved to be his last, Schubert wrote such masterpieces as the piano sonatas in C minor, A major, and B-flat major, the String Quintet in C major, and the two books of songs posthumously named the SCHWANENGESANG (Swansong).

Schubert's health was frail, and he moved to the lodgings of his brother Ferdinand. On the afternoon of Nov. 19, 1828, Schubert died, at the age of 31. The actual cause of his death is unknown.

Schubert is often described as the creator of the genre of the German lieder. However, CARL FRIEDRICH ZELTER and JOHANN FRIEDRICH REICHHARDT wrote strophic lieder a generation before him. What Schubert truly created was an incomparably beautiful flowering of lieder typifying the era of German ROMANTIC sentiment. His songs conveyed deeply felt emotions, ranging from peaceful joy to enlightened melancholy, from philosophic meditation to throbbing

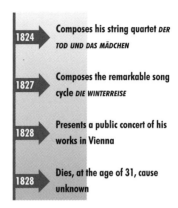

1824	Composes his string quartet DER TOD UND DAS MÄDCHEN
1827	Composes the remarkable song cycle DIE WINTERREISE
1828	Presents a public concert of his works in Vienna
1828	Dies, at the age of 31, cause unknown

From Schubert's sketches, it is possible to follow his method of composition: he would write the melody first, indicate the harmony, and then write out the song in full. He would often revise the finished song many times.

drama. The poems he selected for his settings were expressive of these types of emotions.

In a sense, Schubert's MOMENTS MUSICAUX, impromptus, and other piano works are songs without texts. On several occasions he used musical material from his songs for instrumental works. For example, the great WANDERER FANTASIA for piano, was based on his song DER WANDERER. The *Trout Quintet (Die Forelle)* for piano and strings features a set of variations on Schubert's song of the same name. His String Quartet in D minor includes a set of variations on his song *Der Tod und das Mädchen* in its second movement.

Besides his songs, Schubert excelled at short instrumental forms. He was not given to large theater works and ORATORIOS, and his operas were unsuccessful or unperformed. He wrote seven MASSES, including a *Deutsche Messe,* but most of his religious music was in single movements and composed before 1821. Even his extended works in SONATA FORM are not conceived on a grand scale but constructed according to the symmetry of RECAPITULATIONS.

Much confusion exists in the numbering of Schubert's symphonies, the last being listed in most catalogues as No. 9. The missing uncounted symphony is No. 7, which exists as a full draft, in four movements, of which the first 110 bars are fully scored. Several completions have been made, the most recent cleverly constructed by Brian Newbould, in 1977. The *Unfinished Symphony* is No. 8.

There remains the "Gmunden" or "Gastein" Symphony, so named because Schubert was supposed to have written it in Gastein, in the Tirol, in 1825. It was long regarded as irretrievably lost but was eventually identified with Symphony No. 9, the "Great" (D.944, 1825). Incredibly, as late as 1978 there came to light in a somehow overlooked pile of music in the archives of the Vienna Stadtsbibliothek a sketch of still another Schubert symphony, composed during the last months of his life. This insubstantial but magically tempting waft of Schubert's genius was completed by Newbould, and it is numbered as his 10th.

The recognition of Schubert's greatness was astonishingly slow. Fully 40 years elapsed before the discovery of the manuscript of the "Unfinished" Symphony. Posthumous performances were the rule for his symphony premieres, and the publication of his symphonies was exceedingly tardy. ROBERT SCHUMANN, ever sensitive to great talent, was eager to salute the kindred genius in Schubert's symphonies. But it took half a century for Schubert to become firmly established in music history as one of the great "Sch's" (with FRÉDÉRIC CHOPIN and DMITRI SHOSTAKOVICH phonetically included).

Among the great number of compositions left by Schubert are numerous stage works, including operas, SINGSPIELE, incidental music, and melodramas, many unfinished or in sketch form. In addition to his symphonies, Schubert wrote eight concert and theatrical overtures (1812?–19), including two "in Italian style"; and three short pieces for violin and orchestra (1816–1817). Besides his religious vocal works and lieder, Schubert also composed secular choruses, almost entirely for men's voices and in German.

Schubert's works for piano include 18 sonatas, many of which are unfinished to varying degrees (1815–28), fantasies, impromptus—including 6 *Moments musicals* [*sic*] (D.780, 1823–28)—fugues, variations, and other shorter works. Schubert was perhaps the greatest composer of works for piano four-hands, including fantasies (among them the *Grande sonate*, D.48, 1813), sonatas (including the *Grand duo*, D.812, 1824), marches (including the famous *Marches militaires*, D.733, 1818), and polonaises. He also composed various dances for piano, including waltzes, minuets with trios, deutsche Ländler, ecossaises, GALOPS, and a COTILLION.

Among Schubert's chamber pieces are 16 string quartets, including *Der Tod und das Mädchen* (D.810, 1824), four piano trios, and other ensemble and solo works.

Schubert's brother Ferdinand (Lukas) Schubert (b. Lichtenthal, near Vienna, Oct. 18, 1794; d. Vienna, Feb. 26, 1859) was a composer and teacher. He was devoted to his brother and took charge of his manuscripts after his death. He wrote two Singspiels and much sacred music, including four Masses and a REQUIEM.

Schuller, Gunther (Alexander), significant American composer, conductor, and music educator; b. N.Y., Nov. 22, 1925. Schuller came from a musical family. His paternal grandfather was a bandmaster in Germany before emigrat-

The standard Schubert catalogue was compiled by Otto Erich Deutsch. "D. numbers" are used to group Schubert's works, just as "K. numbers," named for Ludwig Ritter von Köchel, are used to identify those of WOLFGANG AMADEUS MOZART.

PEOPLE IN MUSIC

ing to America, and his father was a violinist with the N.Y. Philharmonic. Young Gunther was sent to Germany as a child for thorough academic training.

Returning to N.Y., Schuller studied at the St. Thomas Choir School from 1938 to 1944, and also received private instruction in theory, flute, and horn. He played in the N.Y. City Ballet orchestra in 1943, then was first horn in the Cincinnati Symphony orchestra from 1943 to 1945 and the Metropolitan Opera orchestra in N.Y. from 1945 to 1949. At the same time he became fascinated with JAZZ. He played the horn in a combo conducted by MILES DAVIS, and also began to compose jazz pieces.

Schuller taught at the Manhattan School of Music in N.Y. from 1950 to 1963, Yale University School of Music from 1964 to 1967, and New England Conservatory of Music in Boston, where he greatly distinguished himself as president from 1967 to 1977. He was also active at the Berkshire Music Center at Tanglewood, Massachusetts, in various capacities, from teaching composition to serving as its director, between 1963 to 1984.

Schuller has been active as a music publisher as well as writing several textbooks. His best-known book is the very valuable study *Early Jazz: Its Roots and Musical Development,* which was published in 1968.

In his multiple activities, Schuller forged a link between serious music and jazz, popularizing the style of COOL JAZZ. In 1957 he launched the slogan THIRD STREAM to designate the combination of classical forms with improvisatory elements of jazz. In many such works he worked in close cooperation with John Lewis of the Modern Jazz Quartet.

As part of his investigation into the roots of jazz Schuller became interested in early RAGTIME and formed, in 1972, the New England Conservatory Ragtime Ensemble. Its recordings of SCOTT JOPLIN's piano rags in original small-band arrangements were instrumental in bringing about the "ragtime revival."

In Schuller's own works he has used modern composition methods, even when his general style was dominated by jazz. Good examples of this musical fusion are his operas *The Visitation* (1966), *The Fisherman and His Wife,* children's opera (1970), and *A Question of Taste* (1989). Among his many orchestral works are CONCERTOS for horn, piano, violin, trumpet, saxophone, viola, and organ.

Schuller also composed many chamber pieces, *Sonata/Fantasia* for piano, written in 1993. His vocal works include *Poems of Time and Eternity* for chorus and nine instruments from 1972, and *Thou Art the Son of God,* cantata for chorus and chamber ensemble, composed in 1987.

Schuller has received many honors and awards in his long career, including many honorary doctor of music degrees. In 1967 he was elected to membership in the National Institute of Arts and Letters and in 1980 to the American Academy and Institute of Arts and Letters. In 1989 he received the William Schuman Award of Columbia University. In 1991 he was awarded a MacArthur Foundation grant.

Schuman, William (Howard), eminent American composer, music educator, and administrator; b. N.Y., Aug. 4, 1910; d. there, Feb. 15, 1992. Schuman began composing at 16, turning out a number of popular songs. He also played in JAZZ groups.

PEOPLE IN MUSIC

From 1928 to 1930, Schuman took courses at N.Y. University's School of Commerce, before turning decisively to music. He completed his musical education at N.Y.'s Juilliard School in 1932–33, and at Teachers College of Columbia University, earning his bachelor of science degree in 1935 and his master's two years later. He also studied conducting at the Salzburg Mozarteum during the summer of 1935, and composition with ROY HARRIS from 1936 to 1938.

Schuman came to the attention of the Boston Symphony Orchestra's conductor SERGE KOUSSEVITZKY, who conducted the premieres of Schuman's AMERICAN FESTIVAL OVERTURE in 1939, Third Symphony in 1941 (which received the first N.Y. Music Critics' Circle Award), *A Free Song* in 1943 (which received the first Pulitzer Prize in music), and the *Symphony for Strings,* also in 1943. ARTHUR RODZINSKI conducted the premiere of Schuman's Fourth Symphony in 1942.

Schuman taught at Sarah Lawrence College from 1935–45. He then served as director of the music publishing firm G. Schirmer, Inc., until 1952, while also working as president of the Juilliard School of Music until 1962, where he acquired a notable reputation as a music educator. He subsequently was president of Lincoln Center for the Performing Arts in N.Y. from 1962 to 1969.

Schuman was the recipient of numerous honors. He held two Guggenheim fellowships (1939–41), was elected a member of the National Institute of Arts and Letters (1946) and the American Academy of Arts and Letters (1973), was awarded the gold medal of the American Academy and Institute of Arts and Letters (1982), won a second, special Pulitzer Prize (1985), and received the National Medal of Arts (1987). Columbia University established the William Schuman Award in 1981, a prize of $50,000 given to a composer for lifetime achievement. Fittingly, Schuman was its first recipient.

Schuman's music is characterized by great emotional tension, maintained by powerful unbalanced rhythms. The contrapuntal structures in his works reach a great degree of complexity and allow for DISSONANCE without, however, losing the essential TONAL references. In several of his works he employs American MELORHYTHMS, but his general style of composition transcends national borders.

Among Schuman's important works are the opera THE MIGHTY CASEY (1951–53), several ballet scores, ten symphonies (1936–76), a piano concerto (1938), *American Festival Overture* (1939), and various other orchestral works, including the beautiful *New England Triptych* (1956). He composed five string quartets (1936–88), other chamber works, and piano pieces. Schuman also composed vocal works with various accompaniments,

Schumann, Clara (Josephine) **Wieck,** famous German pianist, teacher, and composer, wife of ROBERT (Alexander) SCHUMANN; b. Leipzig, Sept. 13, 1819; d. Frankfurt am Main, May 20, 1896. Clara was only five when she began training with her father (Johann Gottlob) Friedrich Wieck (1785–1873), a leading music teacher. She made her debut at the Leipzig Gewandhaus in 1828, where she gave her first complete recital in 1830. Her father then took her on her first major concert tour in 1831–32, which included a visit to Paris.

Upon her return to Leipzig, Clara pursued additional piano training as well as studies in voice, violin, instrumentation, score reading, COUNTERPOINT, and composition. She also published several works for piano. In 1838 she was named k.k. Kammervirtuosin (chamber virtuoso) to the Austrian court.

Robert Schumann entered Clara's life in 1830 when he became a lodger in the Wieck home. In 1837 he asked her to marry him, a request that set off a battle between the couple and Clara's father. The issue was only settled after the couple went to court, and they were finally married in 1840. They went to Dresden and then to Düsseldorf in 1850. In spite of her responsibilities in rearing a large family, Clara continued to pursue a concert career. She also became active as a teacher, serving on the faculty of the Leipzig Conservatory and teaching privately.

After her husband's death in 1856, Clara went to Berlin in 1857. After a sojourn in Baden-Baden from 1863 to 1873, she lived intermittently in Berlin until 1878. Throughout these years she toured widely as a pianist, making regular appearances in England beginning 1856 and a tour of Russia in 1864. In 1878 she settled in Frankfurt as a teacher at the Hoch Conservatory, a position she retained with distinction until 1892. She made her last public appearance in 1891.

As a pianist, Clara was a masterly and authoritative interpreter of her husband's compositions. Later she became an equally admirable interpreter of JOHANNES BRAHMS, her lifelong friend. She was completely free of all mannerisms and impressed her audiences chiefly by the earnestness of her regard for the music she played. A remarkable teacher, she attracted students from many countries.

As a composer, Clara revealed a genuine talent, especially in her numerous character pieces for piano. She wrote a piano concerto (1836), piano trio (1847), piano concertino (1847), three romances for violin and piano (1853), and some songs. She also wrote cadenzas to LUDWIG VAN BEETHOVEN's concertos in C minor and G major. She also edited the first comprehensive edition of Schumann's works and some of his early correspondence.

Robert Schumann made use of Clara's melodies in several of his works.

Schumann, Robert (Alexander), German composer of great imaginative power, whose music expressed the deepest spirit of the ROMANTIC era, husband of CLARA (Josephine) Wieck SCHUMANN; b. Zwickau, June 8, 1810; d. Endenich, near Bonn, July 29, 1856. Schumann was the fifth and youngest child of a Saxon bookseller, who encouraged his musical inclinations. At the age of ten he began taking piano lessons from J. G. Kuntzsch, organist at the Zwickau Marienkirche.

Robert Schumann, c. 1845. (New York Public Library) ▶

In 1828 Schumann enrolled at the University of Leipzig as a student of law, although he gave more attention to philosophical lectures than to law. In Leipzig he became a piano student of Friedrich Wieck, his future father-in-law. In 1829 he went to Heidelberg, where he applied himself seriously to music. In 1830 he returned to Leipzig and lodged in Wieck's home. He also took a course in composition with Heinrich Dorn.

Schumann's family life was not a happy one. His father died at the age of 53 of a nervous disease not completely diagnosed, and his sister Emily committed suicide at the age of 19. Of his three brothers, only one reached late middle age. Schumann's idols, the writers and poets Novalis, Kleist, Byron, Lenau, and Hölderin, all died young and in tragic circumstances. He hoped to start his music study with CARL MARIA VON WEBER, who also died unexpectedly.

Schumann wrote plays and poems in the Romantic tradition and at the same time practiced piano in the hope of becoming a virtuoso. He never succeeded in this ambition. Ironically, it was his beloved bride, Clara, who became a fa-

Robert Schumann time line

1810 — Born

1828 — Enrolls as a law student at the University of Leipzig, where he studies piano with Friedrich Wieck, his future father-in-law

1831 — Completes his piano piece, *PAPILLONS*, op.2

1833 — First signs of mental depression, anxiety, and instability

1834 — Begins publication of the progressive journal *Neue Zeitschrift für Musik*, making literary contributions under various pseudonyms

1835 — Completes his famous piano piece *Carnaval*, op.9

1837 — Completes his brilliant piano pieces, *Phantasiestücke*, op.12

mous concert pianist, and Schumann himself was often introduced to the public at large as merely her husband.

Schumann's own piano study was halted when he developed an ailment in the index and middle fingers of his right hand. He tried all the fashionable remedies of the period. In addition, he used a mechanical device to lift the middle finger of his right hand, but it only caused him harm. His damaged fingers exempted him from military service; the medical certificate issued in 1842 stated that the index and middle fingers of his right hand were so affected that he was unable to pull the trigger of a rifle.

Schumann was a handsome man and liked the company of young ladies. He also enjoyed beer, wine, and strong cigars. This was in sharp contrast with his inner turmoil. As a youth, he confided to his diary a fear of madness. He had auditory hallucinations that caused insomnia, and he also suffered from acrophobia. When he was 23, he noted sudden onsets of inexpressible angst, momentary loss of consciousness, and difficulty in breathing. He called his sickness a pervasive melancholy, a popular malaise of the time. He thought of killing himself.

What maintained Schumann's spirits was his great love for Clara Wieck, nine years his junior, to whom he did not hesitate to confess his psychological distress. Her father must have surmised the unstable character of Schumann and resisted Clara's becoming engaged to him. The young couple went to court to overcome Wieck's objections and were finally married in 1840, the day before Clara turned 21. In 1843, when Schumann and Clara already had two daughters, Wieck approached him with an offer of reconciliation. Schumann gladly accepted the offer, but the relationship remained formal.

Whatever inner torment disturbed Schumann's mind, it did not affect the flowering of his genius as a composer. As a young man he wrote music full of natural beauty, harmonious and melodious in its flow. His compositions are remarkably free from the somber and dramatic qualities that characterize the music of LUDWIG VAN BEETHOVEN and his Romantic followers.

The life and music of Schumann represent the flowering of German ROMANTICISM, with its drama, ecstasies, and ulti-

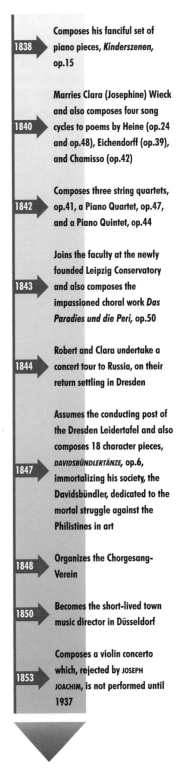

1838 Composes his fanciful set of piano pieces, *Kinderszenen,* op.15

1840 Marries Clara (Josephine) Wieck and also composes four song cycles to poems by Heine (op.24 and op.48), Eichendorff (op.39), and Chamisso (op.42)

1842 Composes three string quartets, op.41, a Piano Quartet, op.47, and a Piano Quintet, op.44

1843 Joins the faculty at the newly founded Leipzig Conservatory and also composes the impassioned choral work *Das Paradies und die Peri,* op.50

1844 Robert and Clara undertake a concert tour to Russia, on their return settling in Dresden

1847 Assumes the conducting post of the Dresden Leidertafel and also composes 18 character pieces, *DAVIDSBÜNDLERTÄNZE,* op.6, immortalizing his society, the Davidsbündler, dedicated to the mortal struggle against the Philistines in art

1848 Organizes the Chorgesang-Verein

1850 Becomes the short-lived town music director in Düsseldorf

1853 Composes a violin concerto which, rejected by JOSEPH JOACHIM, is not performed until 1937

1854 Feeling suicidal, at his own request he enters a sanatorium at Endenich, near Bonn, where he remains to the end of his life

1855 Visited by JOHANNES BRAHMS, with whom he plays piano four-hands

1856 Dies

mate tragedy. The great difference between CLASSIC and Romantic music lies in the fusion of personal events with musical production. FRANZ JOSEPH HAYDN wrote innumerable symphonies and countless string quartets, but his life was free of disturbances and dreamlike visions. Schumann's works, on the other hand, were rich and varied in musical flora, with each of his pieces an expression of his passing mood. His life followed the catalogue of his works. He lived in musical fantasies, until his mental world became a fantasy itself.

One of the most extraordinary features of Schumann's artistic imagination was his fanciful way of personifying his friends and intimates through musical acronyms. His platonic love for Ernestine von Fricken, of the little town of Asch in Bohemia, inspired him to use the notes A–E♭(E♯)–C–B♮(H) or A♭(A♯)–C–B(H). Both spelled Asch and were used as themes for his most famous piano pieces, *PAPILLONS,* op.2 (1829–31) and *Carnaval: Scènes mignonnes sur quartre notes,* op.9 (1833–35). The latter piece features sections named *Chiarina* (Schumann's nickname for Clara) and *Chopin.* Incidentally, it was Ernestine's adoptive father, an amateur flutist, who gave Schumann the theme for his remarkable set of variations for piano titled *Études symphoniques.* His op.1 was a set of variations on the notes A–B–E–G–G, which spelled the name of Countess Meta von Abegg, to whom he was also poetically attached.

As Schumann's talent for music grew and he became recognized as an important composer, he continued his literary activities. In 1834 he cofounded a progressive journal, *Neue Zeitschrift für Musik,* in which he militated against the empty mannerisms of fashionable salon music. He wrote essays, signing them with the imaginary names of Florestan, Eusebius, or Meister Raro. Eusebius was the name of three Christian saints. Etymologically, it is a Greek compound, *eu + sebiai,* good worship. Florestan is "one in a state of flowering," while Raro, which means "rare," could be formed from the juxtaposition of Schumann's and Clara's names: Cla**raro**bert.

As early as 1831, Schumann, in the guise of Eusebius, hailed the genius of FRÉDÉRIC CHOPIN in an article containing the famous invocation "Hut ab, ihr Herren, ein Genie!" (Hats off, gentlemen, a genius!) The article appeared in the

Allgemeine Musikalische Zeitung, signed only by his initials. In an editorial note, he was identified merely as a young student of Professor Wieck. But the winged phrase became a favorite quotation of biographers of both Chopin and Schumann, cited as Schumann's discovery of Chopin's talent. Actually, Chopin was a few months older than Schumann and had already started on a brilliant concert career, while Schumann was an unknown.

Another fanciful invention of Schumann was the formation of an intimate company of friends, which he named *Davidsbündler,* dedicated to the mortal struggle against Philistines in art and to the passionate support of all that was new and imaginative. He immortalized this society in his brilliant piano work DAVIDSBÜNDLERTÄNZE, 18 character pieces, op.6 (1837).

Another characteristically Romantic trait was Schumann's attachment to nocturnal moods, nature scenes, and fantasies. The titles of his piano pieces are typical: *Nachtstücke,* op.23 (1839), *Waldszenen,* op.82 (1848–49), and *Fantasiestücke,* op.12 (1832?–37), the last including the poetic *Warum?* and the explosive *Aufschwung.* A child at heart himself, he created in his 1838 piano set of exquisite miniatures, *Kinderszenen* (Scenes from childhood), op.15, a marvelous musical nursery that included the beautifully sentimental dream piece TRÄUMEREI.

Parallel with his piano works, Schumann produced some of his finest lieder, including the song cycles to poems by Heine (op.24, 1840) and Eichendorff (op.39, 1840), Chamisso (*Frauenliebe und -Leben,* op.42, 1840), and *Dichterliebe,* again to Heine's words (op.48, 1840). In 1841, in only four days, he sketched out his First Symphony, in B-flat major, born, as he himself said, in a single "fiery hour." He named it the SPRING SYMPHONY. It was followed in rapid succession the following year by three string quartets (op.41), Piano Quintet (op.44), and Piano Quartet (op.47). To the same period belongs also his impassioned choral work *Das Paradies und die Peri,* op.50 (1843). Three more symphonies followed within the next decade, and also a piano concerto, a masterpiece of a coalition between the percussive gaiety of the solo part and songful paragraphs in the orchestra. An arresting HOCKETUS occurs in the finale, in which duple meters come into striking conflict with the triple rhythm of the solo part.

In 1843 Schumann was asked by FELIX MENDELSSOHN to join him as a teacher of piano, composition, and score reading at the newly founded Conservatory in Leipzig. In 1844 he and Clara undertook a concert tour to Russia, and in the autumn of 1844 they moved to Dresden, remaining there until 1850. To this period belong his great C-major Symphony (1846), the Piano Trio (1847), and the opera GENOVEVA (1848). In 1847 he assumed the conducting post of the Liedertafel and in 1848 organized the Chorgesang-Verein in Dresden.

In 1850 Schumann became town music director in Düsseldorf, but his disturbed condition began to manifest itself in such alarming ways that he had to resign, though he continued to compose. In 1853 he completed a violin concerto. JOSEPH JOACHIM, in whose care Schumann left the work, thought it not worthy of his genius, and ruled that it should not be performed until the centennial of Schumann's death. In the 1930s an eccentric Hungarian violinist, Jelly d'Aranyi, declared that Schumann's ghost had appeared before her at a seance, revealed to her the place where the manuscript was kept (which was no secret, anyway), and urged her to perform it. She was cheated out of the prize, however, and the concerto was first performed by another violinist in Berlin, in late 1937. Aranyi had to be satisfied with giving its first British performance.

Schumann's condition continued to deteriorate. In February 1854 he threw himself into the Rhine but was rescued. A month later, he was placed, at his own request, in a sanatorium at Endenich, near Bonn, remaining there until the end of his life. Strangely, he did not want to see Clara, and there were months when he did not even inquire about her and the children. But JOHANNES BRAHMS was a welcome visitor, and Schumann enjoyed his company during his not infrequent periods of lucidity. In February 1855 Brahms played piano four-hands with him. Schumann made a notation in his diary, "Visit from Brahms. A genius."

The common assumption that Schumann's illness was syphilitic in origin cannot be proven, but cumulative symptoms and clearly observed sudden changes of moods point to this disease. He also was plagued by tinnitus, a painful single tone ringing in his ears. (The syphilitic BEDŘICH SMETANA also suffered from tinnitus, and incorporated it into a string quartet.)

Schumann had seven children. Three daughters lived to very old age, but one son suffered from mental disease.

Schuppanzigh, Ignaz. *See* BEETHOVEN, LUDWIG VAN.

Schütz, Heinrich (Henrich), also called Henricus Sagittarius, great German composer; b. Kostritz, Oct. 8, 1585; d. Dresden, Nov. 6, 1672. Schütz was born into a prosperous family of innkeepers. In 1590 the family settled in Weissenfels, where his father became burgomaster. He was trained by Heinrich Colander, the town organist.

PEOPLE IN MUSIC

In 1599 Schütz became a choirboy in the court chapel of Landgrave Moritz of Hessen-Kassel. In Kassel he pursued academic studies with Georg Otto, the court Kapellmeister. In 1608 he entered the University of Marburg to study law. An opportunity to continue his musical education came in 1609 when Landgrave Moritz offered to send him to Venice to take lessons with the renowned master GIOVANNI GABRIELI. Under Gabrieli's tutelage, he received thorough training in composition and also learned to play the organ. In 1611 he brought out a book of five-voice MADRIGALS, which he dedicated to his benefactor. After Gabrieli's death in 1612, Schütz returned to Kassel, serving as second organist at the court chapel.

In 1615 the Elector invited Schütz to Dresden as Saxon Kapellmeister, where Michael Praetorius was also working. In 1616 Landgrave Moritz asked the Elector to allow Schütz to return to Kassel, but the Elector declined. In 1617 Schütz assumed fully his duties as Saxon Kapellmeister, being granted an annual salary of 400 florins. In 1619 he published his first collection of sacred music, the *Psalmen Davids sampt etlichen Moteten und Concerten*. Also in 1619 he married Magdalena Wildeck, daughter of a court official in Dresden. They had two daughters. His wife died on Sept. 6, 1625, and Schütz remained a widower for the rest of his life.

During a court visit to Torgau, Schütz produced the first German opera, *Dafne*, set to a translation and adaptation of the libretto for JACOPO PERI's opera of the same name. It was presented at Hartenfels Castle on April 13, 1627, to celebrate the wedding of Princess Sophia Eleonora of Saxony to Landgrave Georg II of Hesse-Darmstadt.

In 1628 Schütz was granted a leave of absence and went to Italy. There he had an occasion to study the new operatic style of CLAUDIO MONTEVERDI, which he adopted in his *Symphoniae sacrae* (published in Venice, in 1629).

Schütz returned to his post in Dresden in 1629. When Saxony entered the 30 Years' War in 1631, conditions at the Dresden court chapel became difficult. In 1633 he accepted an invitation to go to Copenhagen, where he obtained the post of Kapellmeister to King Christian IV. In June 1634 he returned to Dresden. His *Musicalische Exequien,* composed for the funeral of Prince Heinrich Posthumus, appeared in 1636. He also published two volumes of *Kleine geistliche Concerte* (1636 and 1639).

Schütz composed the music for the opera-ballet *Orpheus und Euridice,* performed in Dresden in 1638 to celebrate the marriage of Prince Johann Georg of Saxony and Princess Magdalena Sybilla of Brandenburg. In late 1639 Schütz obtained another leave of absence to serve as Kapellmeister to Georg of Calenberg, who resided in Hildesheim.

After a year's stay in Dresden, in 1641–42, Schütz set out once more for Copenhagen, where he again served as Kapellmeister until April 1644. Returning to Germany, he lived mostly in Braunschweig in 1644–45 and was active at the court of nearby Wolfenbüttel. In 1645 he returned to Dresden; the Elector declined his request for retirement but allowed him to live a part of each year in Weissenfels.

Schütz continued to compose industriously. The second book of his *Symphoniae sacrae* appeared in 1647, followed by his *Geistliche Chor-Musik* (Sacred choral music) a year later. In succeeding years, he repeatedly asked to be pensioned, but his requests were ignored. Finally, when Johann Georg II became Elector in 1657, Schütz was allowed to retire on a pension with the title of chief Kapellmeister. His Passions on St. Luke, St. John, and St. Matthew all date from these last years, as does his *Christmas Oratorio* (1664). About 1670 he returned to Dresden to settle his affairs and await his end, which came peacefully in 1672, in his 87th year.

The importance of Schütz in music history resides in his astute adaptation of the new Italian styles to German music. His work was the direct or indirect inspiration for most German BAROQUE composers. He was extraordinarily productive, but not all of his works survived. The majority of his extant compositions are vocal works of a sacred nature.

Schwanengesang (Swansong). A posthumous collection of LIEDER by FRANZ SCHUBERT, 1828, published in Vienna. Most of the settings are of poems by Rellstab and Heine. However, there is no evidence that Schubert intended to compose a cycle on this basis. He often set one poet's work for a certain period of time before moving on.

Schwartz, Arthur, American composer of popular music; b. N.Y., Nov. 25, 1900; d. Kintnersville, Penn., Sept. 3, 1984. In the early '20s, Schwartz studied English at N.Y. University and literature at Columbia University, where he subsequently took a degree in law. He taught himself to play the piano and began writing songs while still in college. After practicing law from 1924 to 1928, he turned to music.

With the lyricist Howard Dietz, Schwartz began a successful collaboration on works for the N.Y. musical stage, such as the revues *Three's a Crowd* (1930; includes *Something to Remember You By*), *The Band Wagon* (includes *Dancing in the Dark;* the film version of 1953 includes *That's Entertainment*), and *Flying Colors* (1932; includes *Louisiana Hayride*). They also collaborated on the musicals *Revenge with Music* (1934; includes the songs *If There Is Someone Lovelier Than You* and *You and the Night and the Music*) and *Between the Devil* (1937; includes *I See Your Face before Me*).

With Dorothy Fields, Schwartz wrote the musicals *Stars in Your Eyes* (1939), *A Tree Grows in Brooklyn* (1951), and *By the Beautiful Sea* (1954). Again with Dietz, he produced the revue *Inside U.S.* (1948) and the musicals *The Gay Life* (1961) and *Jennie* (1963). Between 1936 and 1955 he also wrote for films.

Schwartz, Stephen. *See* GODSPELL.

Schwarzkopf, (Olga Maria) **Elisabeth** (Friederike), celebrated German soprano; b. Jarotschin, near Posen, Dec. 9,

PEOPLE IN MUSIC

Schwartz's 1930s-era hit *What A Wonderful World* has recently been revived in a reissued recording by JAZZ trumpeter LOUIS ARMSTRONG.

PEOPLE IN MUSIC

Elisabeth Schwarzkopf, photographed in 1956. (Hulton-Deutsch Collection/Corbis) ▶

Schwarzkopf joined the Nazi Party in 1940. After the war, the Allied forces excused her involvement.

1915. Schwarzkopf studied at the Berlin Hochschule für Musik, making her operatic debut as a Flower Maiden in RICHARD WAGNER'S *PARSIFAL* at the Berlin Städtische Oper in 1938. She then studied with Maria Ivogün while continuing on its roster, appearing in more important roles from 1941.

In 1942 Schwarzkopf made her debut as a LIEDER artist in Vienna and also sang for the first time at the State Opera there as Zerbinetta, remaining on its roster until the Nazis closed the theater in 1944.

In 1946 Schwarzkopf rejoined the Vienna State Opera and appeared as Donna Elvira during its visit to London's Covent Garden in 1947. Subsequently, she sang at Covent Garden regularly until 1951. In 1947 she made her first appearance at the Salzburg Festival as Susanna. She also sang regularly at Milan's La Scala from 1948 to 1963. WILHELM FURTWÄNGLER invited her to sing in his performance of LUDWIG VAN BEETHOVEN'S Ninth Symphony at the reopening celebrations of the Bayreuth Festival in 1951. That same year, she created the role of Anne Trulove in IGOR STRAVINSKY'S *THE RAKE'S PROGRESS* in Venice.

In 1953 Schwarzkopf gave her first recital at N.Y.'s Carnegie Hall, and in 1955 she made her U.S. operatic debut as the Marschallin with the San Francisco Opera. In 1964 she made her belated Metropolitan Opera debut in N.Y. in the same role, continuing on its roster until 1966. In 1975 she made a farewell tour of the U.S. as a concert singer.

Also in 1953, Schwarzkopf married Walter Legge (b. London, June 1, 1906; d. St. Jean, Cap Ferrat, March 22, 1979), an influential English recording executive, orchestral manager, and writer on music. In addition to her acclaimed Mozart and Strauss roles, she was also admired in Viennese operetta. As an interpreter of lieder, she was incomparable.

Schweitzer, Albert, famous Alsatian theologian, philosopher, medical missionary, organist, and music scholar; b. Kaysersberg, Jan. 14, 1875; d. Lambarene, Gabon, Sept. 4, 1965. Schweitzer studied piano as a child with his father, a Lutheran pastor, then began organ studies at age eight, his principal mentors being Eugen Münch in Mulhouse, Ernst Münch in Strasbourg, and Charles Widor in Paris.

PEOPLE IN MUSIC

Schweitzer pursued training in philosophy (Ph.D., 1899) and theology (Ph.D., 1900) at the University of Strasbourg. During this same period, he studied music theory with Gustav Jacobsthal in Strasbourg and in piano from Isidor Philipp and Marie Jaëll in Paris. In 1896 he became organist of the Bach Concerts in Strasbourg. He also joined the faculty of the University there in 1902, where he completed his full medical course (M.D., 1912). He concurrently was organist of the Bach Society in Paris (1905–13).

In 1913 Schweitzer went to Lambarene in the Gabon province of French Equatorial Africa and set up a jungle hospital, which subsequently occupied most of his time and energy. However, he continued to pursue music, theology, and philosophy, making occasional concert tours as an organist in Europe to raise funds for his hospital work. In 1952 he was awarded the Nobel Peace Prize, the only professional musician to hold this prestigious award. His philosophical and theological writings established his reputation as one of the foremost thinkers of his time.

In the field of music Schweitzer distinguished himself as the author of one of the most important books on JOHANN SEBASTIAN BACH. This work greatly influenced the interpretation of Bach's music.

scoop. Vocal TONES arrived at by a rough and imprecise PORTAMENTO from a lower tone, instead of a firm attack.

scop (Old Eng.). Ancient English BARD.

skōhr-dăh-too′răh

scordatura (from It. *discordatura,* mistuning). Retuning an instrument for greater ease of playing certain notes or for achieving a timbral effect. The practice arose in the 16th century to facilitate the playing of the LUTE in different keys.

Scordatura received its highest development in early BAROQUE music, with composers ingeniously changing the tuning of string instruments to enable them to play easily in keys of several sharps or flats. A pioneer of scordatura was HEINRICH VON BIBER, whose *Mystery Sonatas* for violin are systematically arranged in scordatura so that the violin becomes in effect a transposing instrument, with each string having its own transposition. Under such conditions not only the notes themselves but the INTERVALS between them become altered. ANTONIO VIVALDI also applied scordatura in his concertos.

An anonymous string quartet misattributed to Benjamin Franklin uses different scordaturas for different instruments in different movements. Thus, a quartet of absolute amateurs, playing on open strings only, can perform a fairly intricate contrapuntal work.

With the progress of instrumental techniques and construction, scordatura lost its *raison d'être,* but modern composers occasionally apply it to secure a fundamental harmony in a minor key by tuning down a semitone the two lower strings of a violin, viola, or cello.

In the coda of PIOTR ILYICH TCHAIKOVSKY's *Pathétique Symphony,* the melodic line descends to F♯ but the violins playing the passage have to stop at their lowest note, G, and the final F♯ has to be taken over by other instruments. To avoid this frustrating sense of incompleteness, the conductor

LEOPOLD STOKOWSKI instructed the violinists to tune down the open G string to F♯, a procedure that can be classified as scordatura.

score (Fr. *partition;* Ger. *Partitur;* It. *partitura*). A systematic notation of music for several instruments or voices in which the individual parts are placed one below another. Exact vertical alignment of all parts symbolizes simultaneity, so that the music can be read in its totality.

A *full* or *orchestra score* lists all instruments, with the woodwinds on top, brass instruments in the middle, and the strings on the bottom. Percussion and keyboard (except basso continuo) are placed between the brass and the strings. In CONCERTOS, the solo parts are placed immediately above the string section, as are the vocal parts and choruses in operas, ORATORIOS, and other vocal works.

The first page of a full score must list all instruments as a sort of inventory, with instruments in the high range placed above those of the lower range (within each instrumental family). Thus, the bottom line of a score is occupied by the double-bass part. In order to save space, the STAVES of instruments that have rests on a particular page in the score are omitted, and only the active parts are printed. As a rule, first and second flutes and other paired instruments share the same staff in the orchestra score, although it is often necessary to split individual string sections into several staves when they play different lines.

The task of the conductor, in surveying these musical masses under his or her command, is further complicated by the fact that clarinets, the English horn, saxophones, French horns, and most trumpets are transposing instruments. Some 20th-century composers, notably SERGEI PROKOFIEV, wrote the parts of transposing instruments in the key of C, so that the conductor does not have to be confused by the look of the score, gazing at a clarinet part with one sharp in the key signature while the strings have one flat.

In chamber music with piano participation, the piano part is placed invariably below the other instruments, which in turn are disposed according to their relative PITCH. Thus, in a string quartet the first violin is placed on top, then the second violin, the viola, and at the bottom, the cello.

Close or *compressed score,* short score; *open score,* orchestral score; *organ score,* like a piano score, with a third staff for pedal bass; *piano score,* piano arrangement of an orchestral score, the words of any leading vocal parts being inserted above the music, often without their notes; *short score,* any abridged arrangement or skeleton transcript; also a four-part vocal score on two staves; *supplementary score,* one appended to the body of the score when all parts cannot be written on one page; *vocal score,* that of an A CAPPELLA composition, or one in which the vocal parts are written out in full, usually on separate staves, the piano accompaniment, arranged or compressed from the full score, on two staves below.

scoring. *See* INSTRUMENTATION; ORCHESTRATION.

Scotch Bagpipe Melody. Traditional Scottish melody in $\frac{6}{8}$ time, first published in 1609 with the text *Have I Ridden upon My Gray Nag.*

Scotch snap or **catch.** The rhythmic motive ♪ ♩. found in many Scottish airs. This "inverted dotting" on the beat is also characteristic of STRATHSPEY and other Scottish dances.

Mendelssohn dedicated the *Scotch Symphony* to Queen Victoria.

Scotch Symphony. FELIX MENDELSSOHN's Third Symphony, 1842, op.56, in A minor, first performed in Leipzig. As in most of Mendelssohn's symphonies, it is in four movements. The most Scottish in character is the second movement (*Vivace*), which is filled with Scottish modalities.

PEOPLE IN MUSIC

Scotto, Renata, famous Italian soprano; b. Savona, Feb. 24, 1933. Scotto began her music study in Savona at age 14 and at 16 went to Milan for further vocal training. She made her debut as Violetta in Savona in 1952. After winning a national vocal competition in 1953, she made her formal debut as Violetta at Milan's Teatro Nuovo.

Scotto then joined Milan's La Scala, where she sang secondary roles until being called upon to replace MARIA CALLAS as Amina during the company's visit to the Edinburgh Festival in 1957. She made her U.S. debut at the Chicago Lyric Opera in 1960, as Mimi, a role she also chose for her Metropolitan Opera debut in N.Y. five years later. She scored a brilliant success in this role in the Metropolitan Opera production of LA BOHÈME in the *Live from Lincoln Center* telecast on PBS in 1977.

Thereafter, Scotto was a stellar figure in the U.S. opera scene and also toured widely as a recitalist. In later years she was active as an opera director, producing MADAMA BUTTER-FLY at the Metropolitan Opera in 1986. She sang her final performance there as Cio-Cio-San in 1987. In 1995 she sang the Marshallin at the Spoleto Festival U.S.A. in Charleston, South Carolina. Among her other fine roles were Lucia, Gilda, Elena in I VESPRI SICILIANI, Norma, Manon Lescaut, Luisa Miller, Francesca da Rimini, and Elizabeth of Valois.

Scratch Orchestra. An organization founded in 1969 by CORNELIUS CARDEW, an outgrowth of his Scratch Music concept. He defined the orchestra as "a large number of enthusiasts pooling their resources (not primarily musical) and assembling for action." He further declared that:

> the word *music* and its derivatives are not understood to refer exclusively to sound. Each member of the orchestra is provided with a notebook (or a scratchbook) in which he notates a number of accompaniments performable continuously for indefinite periods. . . . Scratch Music can be entitled Scratch Overture, Scratch Interlude, or Scratch Finale, depending on its position in the concert.

The highlight of the Scratch Orchestra history was its 1972 performance of Cardew's *The Great Learning* (after Confucius, in Ezra Pound's translation). He later repudiated the work, saying that "a revolution is not a dinner party, but an insurrection, an act of violence by which one class overthrows another."

Scriabin, Alexander (Nikolaievich), remarkable Russian composer whose solitary genius had no predecessors and left no disciples; b. Moscow, Jan. 6, 1872 (Russian Orthodox Christmas); d. there, April 27, 1915. Scriabin's father was a lawyer, and his mother, Lyubov Petrovna (née Shchetinina),

PEOPLE IN MUSIC

a talented pianist who had studied at the St. Petersburg Conservatory. His mother died of tuberculosis when he was an infant, and his father remarried and spent the rest of his life in diplomatic service abroad.

Scriabin was reared by an aunt, who gave him initial instruction in music, including piano. At 11 he began regular piano lessons with Georgi Conus, and at 16 he became a pupil of Nikolai Zverev. In 1885 he began the study of theory with Sergei Taneyev, continuing his studies with him when he entered the Moscow Conservatory in 1888. He also received instruction in piano with Vasili Safonov. He practiced assiduously but never became a virtuoso. At his piano recitals, he performed mostly his own works.

Graduating with a gold medal from Safonov's class, Scriabin remained at the Moscow Conservatory to study FUGUE with Anton Arensky but failed to pass the required test and never received a diploma for composition. Upon leaving the Conservatory in 1892, he launched a career as a concert pianist. By that time he had already written several piano pieces in the manner of FRÉDÉRIC CHOPIN. The publisher Jurgenson brought out his opp. 1, 2, 3, 5, and 7 in 1893. In 1894 Belaieff became his publisher and champion, financing his first European tour in 1895.

In 1896 Scriabin gave a concert of his own music in Paris. Returning to Russia, he completed his first major work, a piano concerto, and was soloist in its first performance in Odessa in 1897. In the same year, he married the pianist Vera Isakovich. They spent some time abroad, and in early 1898 they gave a joint recital in Paris in a program of Scriabin's works.

From 1898 to 1903 Scriabin taught piano at the Moscow Conservatory. His first orchestral work, *Reverie,* was conducted in Moscow by Safonov in 1899, who also conducted the first performance of Scriabin's First Symphony two years later. Scriabin's Second Symphony was brought out by Anatoli Liadov in St. Petersburg in 1902. After the death of Belaieff in 1904, Scriabin received an annual grant of 2,400 rubles from the wealthy Moscow merchant Morosov and went to Switzerland, where he began work on his Third Symphony, *Le Poème divin* (The divine poem). It had its first performance in Paris in 1905, under the direction of

ARTHUR NIKISCH. At that time Scriabin separated from Vera and established a household with Tatiana Schloezer, sister of the music critic Boris de Schloezer, who subsequently became Scriabin's close friend and biographer.

In late 1906 Scriabin appeared as a soloist with the Russian Symphony Society, conducted by Modest Altschuler, in N.Y. He also gave recitals of his works there and in other U.S. music centers.

Tatiana joined him in N.Y. in January 1907, but they were warned by friends that, because Scriabin had never obtained a legal divorce from Isakovich, they could run into trouble with the authorities. There was no evidence that any charges were actually contemplated, but to safeguard themselves against any problems, they went to Paris in March 1907. Altschuler continued to champion Scriabin's music, and in 1908 he gave the world premiere with his Russian Symphony Orchestra of Scriabin's great work LE POÈME DE L'EXTASE (Poem of ecstasy). The first Russian performance followed in St. Petersburg a year later.

In the spring of 1908 Scriabin met SERGE KOUSSEVITZKY, who became one of his most ardent supporters, both as a conductor and as a publisher. He gave Scriabin a five-year contract with his newly established publishing firm Éditions Russes, with a generous guarantee of 5,000 rubles annually. In the summer of 1910 Koussevitzky engaged Scriabin as soloist on a tour in a chartered steamer down the Volga River, with stopovers and concerts at all cities and towns of any size along the route.

Scriabin wrote for Koussevitzky his most ambitious work, PROMETHÉE, subtitled *Le Poème du feu* (Prometheus, the poem of fire). It had an important piano part, which the composer performed at its premiere in Moscow in 1911. The score also included a color keyboard (*clavier à lumière*, or in Italian, *luce*) intended to project changing colors on a screen. At that time, Scriabin was deeply interested in the relation of musical frequencies to the color spectrum. The construction of such a color organ was, however, entirely unfeasible at the time, and the premiere of the work was given without it.

The unique collaboration between Scriabin and Koussevitzky came to an unfortunate end soon after the production

A performance with colored lights projected on a screen was attempted by Altschuler at Carnegie Hall in N.Y. in 1915, but it was a total failure. (Subsequent attempts have ranged from utter failures to near approximations.)

of *Promethée*. A disagreement over finances, and a clash of two mighty egos, led them to part. Scriabin left Koussevitzky's publishing firm, and in 1912 signed a contract with Jurgenson, who guaranteed him 6,000 rubles annually.

In 1914 Scriabin visited London and was soloist in his piano concerto and *Promethée* at a concert led by Sir Henry Wood. He also gave a recital of his own works. His last public appearance was in a recital in Petrograd in April 1915. Upon his return to Moscow, an abscess developed in his lip, leading to blood poisoning. He died after a few days' illness.

In his time, Scriabin was the Russian composer who most separated himself from the realm of national music. He created works of great originality derived from his inner tonal world. He was a genuine innovator in harmony. At first his music showed the influences of other composers (Chopin, FRANZ LISZT, and RICHARD WAGNER). Scriabin gradually evolved his own MELODIC and HARMONIC style, marked by extreme CHROMATICISM. In his piano piece *Désir*, op.57, composed in 1908, the threshold of POLYTONALITY and ATONALITY is reached. The KEY SIGNATURE is eliminated in his subsequent works, with chromatic alterations and compound APPOGGIATURAS creating a harmonic web of such complexity that all distinction between CONSONANCE and DISSONANCE vanishes.

Building chords by fourths rather than by thirds, Scriabin constructed his MYSTIC CHORD, the harmonic foundation of *Promethée*. In his Piano Sonata No. 7 (1913), he introduces a chordal structure of 25 notes (D♭–F♭–G–A–C, repeated in five octaves), which was dubbed "a five-story chord." These harmonic extensions were associated in Scriabin's mind with mystical doctrines. He aspired to a universal art in which the impressions of the senses projecting all human senses, tactile, olfactory, gustatory, as well as aural and visual.

The titles of most of Scriabin's later works were the expressions of such mystic strivings: *Le Poème divin, Le Poème de l'extase, VERS LA FLAMME* (1914). His 11 piano sonatas (including the Sonata-Fantasy, op.19, 1892–97; the *Messe blanche*, op.64, 1911; and the *Messe noire*, op.68, 1913) revealed a similar state of constant yearning, with tempestuous melodic lines in rising and falling waves of richly compounded harmonies.

Scriabin made plans for the writing of a *MYSTERIUM* to accomplish a wedding of all the sensory experiences, but only the text of a preliminary poem (*L'Acte préalable*) was completed at his death. Scriabin dreamed of having the *Mysterium* performed as a sacred action in the Himalayas, and actually made plans for going to India. But the outbreak of World War I in 1914 put an end to this project.

Scriabin's fragmentary sketches for *L'Acte préalable* for his *Mysterium* were arranged in 1973 by the Russian musician Alexander Nemtin, who supplemented this material with excerpts from Scriabin's eighth Piano Sonata, *Guirlandes,* and the Preludes, op.74. The resulting synthetic score was performed in Moscow in 1973 under the title *Universe.* A species of color keyboard was used at the performance, projecting colors according to Scriabin's musical spectrum.

In addition to the works mentioned above, Scriabin wrote many other piano works in Chopinesque genres, including MAZURKAS, NOCTURNES, IMPROMPTUS, ÉTUDES, and PRELUDES. He also composed several "poems," piano character pieces with unstated lyrical associations.

Scriabin was the most poetic (not to say extravagant) composer in the use of expression marks. His marks attempt to communicate to the performer what Scriabin felt about the music as he composed it. This, in turn, was to inspire the performer to experience these feelings and therefore inspire similar ones in the listener. Unlike ERIK SATIE's ironic comments on the score, Scriabin's are absolutely serious. Among his many unique instructions are:

Avec entraînement et ivresse. With impetuosity and inebriated abandon (*Le Poème divin*).

Avec un intense désir. With an intense desire (PROMETHEUS).

Avec une douce ivresse. With tender inebriation (Tenth Piano Sonata).

Avec une douceur de plus en plus caressante et empoisonnée. With a tenderness ever more caressing and venomous (Ninth Piano Sonata).

Avec une ivresse debordante. With overflowing inebriation (Third Piano Sonata).

Avec une joie débordante. With an overflowing joy (Seventh Piano Sonata).

Avec une passion naissante. With a nascent passion (*Poème-nocturne*, op.61, 1911).

Brumeux. Misty; an indistinct, unspoken quality.

Comme des éclairs. Like lightning flashes (Seventh Piano Sonata).

Comme un rêve. Like a dream (*Poème-nocturne*).

Comme un cri. Like a cry (*Préludes*).

Comme un murmure confus. Like an indistinct murmur (*Poème-nocturne*).

Comme une ombre mouvante. Like a moving shadow (*Poème-nocturne*).

Con lumionosità. With luminosity (Fifth Piano Sonata).

Dans un vertige. Vertiginously; in a state of dizziness (*Prometheus*).

De plus en plus lumineux et flamboyant. Ever more luminously and flamboyantly.

Ecroulement formidable. A terrible catastrophe (*Le Poème divin*).

Effondrement subit. A sudden collapse (Sixth Piano Sonata).

Épouvante surgit, L', elle se mêle à la danse délirante. Terror rises and joins in the delirious dance.

Flot lumineux. Luminous stream (*Prometheus*).

Haletant. Out of breath (Tenth Piano Sonata).

Pâmé. Faintly, as if in a fainting spell (*Le Poème divin*).

Presque en délire. Almost delirious.

Rêve prend forme, Le. The dream takes shape (Sixth Piano Sonata).

Riso ironico (It.). Ironic laughter (*Poème satanique*).

Tout devient charme et douceur. All becomes enchantment and fragrance.

Scriabin's three children with Tatiana Schloezer were legitimized at his death. His son Julian, an exceptionally gifted boy, drowned accidentally at age 11 in the Dnieper River at Kiev in 1919. Julian's two piano preludes, written in the style of the last works of his father, were published in a Scriabin memorial volume in Moscow in 1940.

Scriabin's daughter Maria Scriabine (b. Moscow, Jan. 30, 1911) is a music aesthetician, scholar, and composer. In 1927 she settled in Paris, where she studied theory with René Leibowitz. In 1950 she joined the Radiodiffusion Française and worked with electronics. Her compositions include a *Suite radiophonique* (1951), a ballet, *Bayalett* (1952), and some chamber music. She wrote several books on modern music and also wrote a biography of her father.

Scruggs, Earl (Eugene), American country-music singer and banjo player; b. Flint Hill, N.C., Jan. 6, 1924. Scruggs began playing banjo as a child. He was influenced by other North Carolina musicians, who had developed a new way of picking the banjo, using three fingers of the picking hand rather than two. He was already playing at the age of six in a family band with his brothers.

At the age of 15, Scruggs began playing with a local group called the Carolina Wildcats over the radio. During World War II, he worked in a textile mill. Toward the end of the war, he was hired by country musician "Long" John Miller to play in his band; when the band broke up, he found himself in Nashville, where mandolinist BILL MONROE was looking for a new banjo player to join his group.

Monroe's group also included a young guitar player and vocalist named Lester Flatt. Flatt's smooth vocals and Scruggs's new style of playing the banjo made Monroe's group, the Blue Grass Boys, an immediate hit.

In 1948 Scruggs and Flatt left Monroe because of his autocratic leadership style. They formed their own band, The Foggy Mountain Boys. A year later, they recorded the classic bluegrass banjo instrumental, *Foggy Mountain Breakdown.*

PEOPLE IN MUSIC

In 1967 *Foggy Mountain Breakdown* was used as the theme song for the film *Bonnie and Clyde.*

The band signed with Columbia Records in 1950 and five years later were made members of the GRAND OLE OPRY radio program. That same year, they launched their first syndicated television program.

In the early '60s, Flatt and Scruggs were discovered by a new generation of bluegrass fans and FOLK revival musicians. They were hired to perform *The Ballad of Jed Clampett,* the theme song for the television comedy series *The Beverly Hillbillies,* and even made a few appearances on the show. The 1967 film soundtrack for *Bonnie and Clyde* further popularized the group.

However, Flatt and Scruggs were soon arguing over the direction of the band: Flatt preferred more traditional material, while Scruggs wanted to branch out. They dissolved their partnership in 1969, and Scruggs formed his own group, the Earl Scruggs Revue, featuring his sons Randy and Gary. The group had some success in the folk-rock style through the mid-'70s.

Scruggs went into semiretirement in the early '80s. He performs only occasionally and rarely gives interviews.

Sculthorpe, Peter (Joshua), eminent Australian composer; b. Launceston, Tasmania, April 29, 1929. Sculthorpe studied at the University of Melbourne Conservatorium of Music, taking his bachelor's degree in 1950. He then took courses at Oxford University from 1958 to 1960.

Returning to Australia, Sculthorpe became a lecturer in music at the University of Sydney in 1963 and a reader in 1969. He also was composer-in-residence at Yale University while on a Harkness Fellowship from 1965 to 1967, and a visiting professor of music at the University of Sussex in 1971–72. In 1977 he was made an Officer of the Order of the British Empire. He has also received many other awards and honorary degrees.

Sculthorpe has looked to Asia, in particular Japan, Indonesia, and Tibet, for both literary and musical inspiration. As a result, his music often combines European EXPRESSIONISM with native sounds. He has also been influenced by the physical environment of Australia, as in *Sun Music I–IV* for orchestra (1965–67), and in his utilization of birdcalls and insect sounds. Other important orchestral works include a

PEOPLE IN MUSIC

Piano Concerto (1983), and two SONATAS for strings (1983, 1988). He has also written many chamber works, including 11 string quartets (1947–90), many works for and with piano, and numerous vocal settings.

Scythian Suite. Orchestral work by SERGEI PROKOFIEV, 1916, first performed in Petrograd with the composer conducting. This, the first important orchestral score by Prokofiev, has the subtitle of *Ala and Lolli,* the names of Scythian gods. The finale describes the sunrise in sonorous displays of B-flat major.

Prokofiev was very conscious of the importance of the sun. He even circulated a questionnaire among his friends, inquiring simply, "What is your opinion of the sun?"

Sea Symphony, A. The First Symphony of RALPH VAUGHAN WILLIAMS, 1910, for vocal soloists, chorus, and orchestra, to texts from Walt Whitman. Its four movements are entitled *A Song for All Seas All Ships, On the Beach at Night Alone, The Waves,* and *The Explorers.* Vaughan Williams conducted its first performance at the Leeds Festival.

season (It. *stagione*). Scheduled performances for an operatic or concert music organization over a specific time period up to one calendar year.

Seasons, The *(Die Jahreszeiten).* Secular ORATORIO by FRANZ JOSEPH HAYDN, 1801, to a libretto by van Swieten. The work is based on an English poem by J. Thomson. It was then translated into German and premiered at the Schwarzenburg Palace, Vienna.

Sechter, Simon. *See* SCHUBERT, FRANZ (PETER).

second. 1. *See* INTERVAL. 2. The ALTO part or voice. 3. Performing a part lower in PITCH than the first, as second bass, second violins. 4. Lower in PITCH, as second string. 5. Higher; as second line of staff.

seconda prattica (It., second practice). A concept promoted by CLAUDIO MONTEVERDI in his *Scherzi musicali* (1607), also called *stile moderno;* as distinguished from PRIMA PRATTICA (*stile antico*).

sĕh-kōhn′dăh prăh′tē-kah

The seconda prattica is characterized by MONODIC settings in which the emphasis is placed on clear articulation of text and simplicity of harmonic accompaniment. This principle is enunciated in the succinct axiom "The words must be the master of music, and not its servant." In many ways, seconda prattica anticipates the reforms of CHRISTOPH WILLIBALD GLUCK and later composers.

Secret of Suzanne, The. *See* SEGRETO DI SUSANNA, IL.

section. 1. A short division (one or more periods) of a composition, having distinct rhythmic and harmonic boundaries; specifically, half a phrase. 2. In JAZZ big bands, the division into musically determined families: the *melody* (clarinets, saxophones, trumpets, trombones) and *rhythm* sections (piano, guitar, double bass, percussion). Sometimes the last group is subdivided into *harmony* (piano and other keyboards, guitar, etc.) and *rhythm* sections (double bass, percussion).

secular music. Music other than that intended for worship and devotional purposes.

See You Later, Alligator. Song by Robert Guidry. It was made popular by BILL HALEY and the Comets in the 1955 film musical *Rock Around the Clock*.

Seeger, Pete(r), noted American folk singer, songwriter, and political activist, son of Charles (Louis) Seeger; b. Patterson, N.Y., May 3, 1919. Seeger's father was a musicologist and composer who had a strong interest in FOLK MUSIC. Seeger studied sociology at Harvard University before turning to folk music.

PEOPLE IN MUSIC

Taking up the BANJO, Seeger became active as a traveling musician. Through folklorist ALAN LOMAX, he met WOODY GUTHRIE, a singer/songwriter from Oklahoma, who he encouraged to move to N.Y. With Guthrie, Lee Hays, and Millard Lampell, he organized the Almanac Singers in 1941 and subsequently appeared before union and political audiences. He then joined the WEAVERS in 1949, with which he became well known thanks to their No. 1 hit recording of Leadbelly's *Goodnight Irene.*

In the early '50s, the Weavers found it increasingly difficult to get work because of their political activities. Seeger himself was targeted by the House Committee on Un-American Activities, which cited him for contempt of Congress in 1956 because he refused to "name names"—i.e., give the Committee the names of fellow "Communists" and left-leaning associates.

In spite of being blacklisted, Seeger pursued his career and his commitment to various causes. A leading figure in the folk-song revival of the late 1950s, he won notable success with his songs *Where Have All the Flowers Gone?* and *If I Had a Hammer.* In all, he wrote over 100 songs, many of which became popular via his many tours through the U.S. and abroad.

In the 1960s, Seeger was an important figure in both the Civil Rights movement and the anti-Vietnam war protests. He encouraged young singer/songwriters like BOB DYLAN and JOAN BAEZ in their early careers.

In the late '60s, Seeger became interested in ecological issues, particularly the pollution of the Hudson River valley where he lived. He had a replica of an 18th-century sloop (a type of sailboat) built, named it the Clearwater, and began sailing up and down the river, giving fund-raising concerts along the way.

Seeger continues to perform, although he has been in semiretirement since the early '90s.

Seeger, Ruth Crawford. *See* CRAWFORD (SEEGER), RUTH PORTER.

segno (It.). A sign. *Al segno,* to the sign; *dal segno* (*D.S.,* from the sign), directions to the performer to turn back and repeat from the place marked by the sign 𝄋 to the word *Fine,* or to a double-bar with a FERMATA (⌢); *segno di silenzio,* silence; a pause.

sān′yōh

Segovia, Andrés, Marquis of Salobreia, great Spanish guitarist and teacher; b. Linares, near Jaen, Feb. 21, 1893; d. Madrid, June 2, 1987. Segovia took up guitar at a very

PEOPLE IN MUSIC

early age. However, his parents opposed his choice of instrument and saw to it that he received lessons in piano and cello instead, but to no avail.

While taking courses at the Granada Institute of Music, Segovia sought out a guitar teacher. Finding none, he taught himself, later studying briefly with Miguel Llobet. He made his formal debut in Granada at the age of 16, then played in Madrid in 1912, at the Paris Conservatory in 1915, and in Barcelona in 1916. He toured South America in 1919. He made his formal Paris debut in 1924 in a program that included a work written especially for him by ALBERT ROUSSEL, entitled simply *Segovia.*

Segovia made his U.S. debut at N.Y.'s Town Hall in 1928, then toured all over the world, arousing admiration for his technique and artistry. He did much to reinstate the guitar as a concert instrument capable of great expression. He made many transcriptions for the guitar, including one of JOHANN SEBASTIAN BACH's Chaconnes from the Partita No. 2 for violin. He also commissioned several composers to write works for him, including Manuel Ponce, Joaquín Turina, MARIO CASTELNUOVO-TEDESCO, HEITOR VILLA-LOBOS, and Alexander Tansman.

Segovia continued to give concerts at an advanced age. He made appearances in 1984 in celebration of the 75th anniversary of his professional debut. He received many honors and awards during his long career. King Juan Carlos of Spain made him Marquis of Salobreia in 1981, the same year the Segovia International Guitar Competition was founded in his honor. In 1985 he was awarded the Gold Medal of the Royal Philharmonic Society of London.

sĕh′gwĕh

segue (It., follow). 1. A copyist's indication at a page bottom of a player's part that the player is to continue through to the next page, without stopping. *Segue l'aria,* the aria follows. 2. SIMILE.

sā-gē-dē′yăh

The famous *Seguidilla* in GEORGES BIZET'S *CARMEN* is a stylization of the dance.

seguidilla (Sp.). A Spanish song and dance in triple meter, some types being leisurely, others lively. The style is usually set in a MINOR KEY, accompanied by GUITAR, voice, and, at times, CASTANETS. The structure often alternates between guitar solos and ensemble. *See also* MARINERA.

Seitensatz (Ger., side section). The second section (theme group) in the EXPOSITION of SONATA FORM, as contrasted with HAUPTSATZ, the first (main) section.

Semele. Secular ORATORIO by GEORGE FRIDERIC HANDEL, 1744, first performed in London.

Semele is loved by Jupiter, which upsets Jupiter's wife, Juno. She urges Semele to ask Jupiter to reveal himself in the full splendor of his divine presence, aware that no mortal could survive the radiance of such a manifestation. Semele requests it, but Jupiter tries to avoid doing it. When Semele insists, Jupiter reveals himself and Semele is destroyed.

The tenor aria *Wheree'er You Walk* is a recital favorite.

Semiramide. Opera by GIOACCHINO ROSSINI, 1823, first produced in Venice.

Semiramide is the Queen of Babylon. She conspires with her lover to kill the king. This done, she takes another lover, a young barbarian, but to her horror discovers that he is her own son by a previous union. When her first lover attacks her son, she intercepts his dagger and dies. Thereupon, her son slays her first lover and by hereditary rights becomes king.

A number of other composers wrote operas on this subject, among them Nicola Porpora, CHRISTOPH WILLIBALD GLUCK, ANTONIO SALIERI, DOMENICO CIMAROSA, GIACOMO MEYERBEER, and in the 20th century OTTORINO RESPIGHI.

The opera is seldom performed, but the OVERTURE is a concert favorite.

semiseria (It.). BAROQUE and CLASSIC OPERA SERIA with a happy ending, sometimes including comic and parodic elements.

semitone (Lat. *semitonus*). *See* NOTATION; INTERVAL.

Semper Fidelis. March by JOHN PHILLIP SOUSA, 1886, dedicated to the U.S. Marine Corps.

Semper paratus. Song by Francis Saltus von Boskerck, 1928. A captain of the U.S. Coast Guard, he published it, and it has become the official march of the Coast Guard.

Send in the Clowns. Song by STEPHEN SONDHEIM, 1973, from the musical *A LITTLE NIGHT MUSIC.* The song, a philosophical look at youth and aging, is the composer's best-known song. A recording of it won a Grammy Award in 1976.

sentence. A passage of symmetrical rhythmic form, generally not over 16 MEASURES long, and usually ending with a full TONIC CADENCE.

September Song. BALLAD by KURT WEILL, 1938, from the musical *Knickerbocker Holiday.* As rendered by Walter Huston, it became a hit.

MAURICE RAVEL'S *Introduction and Allegro* is a septet with the unusual scoring of harp, flute, clarinet, and string quartet.

septet (Ger. *Septett;* Fr. *septuor;* It. *settimino*). A concerted composition for seven voices or instruments. In the latter case, wind and string instruments are usually mixed in with a piano part (e.g., septets by LUDWIG VAN BEETHOVEN, IGOR STRAVINSKY).

sequence (1) (from Lat. *sequentia*). In GREGORIAN CHANT, a freely composed, wide-ranging chant category (also called *prose*) with syllabic texts, popular for about three centuries starting in c.850 A.D. A couplet form was common, with two lines of text per melodic line, followed by a different couplet melody. Gradually, the texts rhymed and scanned and grew increasingly strophic. For many centuries, sequences were composed to fill the needs of the liturgical calendar and were incorporated into the PROPRIUM. But the 16th-century COUNCIL OF TRENT eliminated all but five sequences from the chant books (*Victimae Paschali, Lauda Sion, Veni sancte spiritus,* STABAT MATER, *Dies irae*), many of which were set by later composers.

sequence (2). The repetition, at different PITCH levels and at least twice in succession, of a melodic MOTIVE. This is an extremely fruitful technical device that was used almost universally in BAROQUE music. In a sequence, a thematic phrase is imitated in the same voice a degree higher or lower, without altering its rhythmic pattern. In its simplest form, a sequence contains two segments, connoting the TONIC and the DOMINANT harmonies effectively.

Examples of such sequences are found by the thousands in classical works. The theme of WOLFGANG AMADEUS MOZART's A-major piano sonata (K.331) is typical. The opening notes of LUDWIG VAN BEETHOVEN's Fifth Symphony and the subsequent phrase also constitute such a tonic-dominant sequence.

As with fugal answers, sequences are considered TONAL if they move along a given KEY. They are *real* if they are true as to the precise interval and thus represent a MODULATION.

sequencer. An electronic device that is used to record melodic and rhythm patterns for playback. These can then be looped (repeated) or hooked together to form complete compositions.

serenade (from It. *serenata,* evening song; Ger. *Nachtmusik, Ständchen*). 1. From the 16th century, a song traditionally performed by a lover before the beloved's window. It was habitually accompanied on the LUTE or GUITAR and performed at day's end. A serenade is a favorite device in OPERA. Eventually, any song or instrumental piece in this amorous style. *See also* AUBADE.

2. From the mid-18th century, a multimovement piece of instrumental entertainment music, practically synonymous with DIVERTIMENTO. An instrumental serenade is usually scored for small ensemble, designed for open-air performance or festival occasions. WOLFGANG AMADEUS MOZART wrote his HAFFNER *Serenade* for a wedding in the family of the Burgomaster of Salzburg.

In the 19th century, the title *serenade* was often attached to a multimovement instrumental work (e.g., those by JOHANNES BRAHMS).

Sérénade d'Arlequin. Excerpt, 1900, by Riccardo Drigo (1846–1930), from the BALLET *Les Millions d'Arlequin (Arlekinada)*. A cello solo much loved by its performers.

Serenade for String Orchestra. Multimovement work by PIOTR ILYICH TCHAIKOVSKY, 1882, first performed in Mos-

The longest tonal sequence occurs toward the end of PIOTR ILYICH TCHAIKOVSKY's overture to the opera *EUGENE ONEGIN*, which contains eight segments and descends fully two octaves by consecutive degrees.

An example of a mock serenade is that of Mephistopheles in CHARLES GOUNOD's *FAUST*.

cow. A work of symphonic proportions, Tchaikovsky said that in it he paid his debt to WOLFGANG AMADEUS MOZART, and deliberately imitated Mozart's manner. But the music has more of the spirit of the BAROQUE, and its Finale makes use of the Russian song *Under the Green Apple Tree*. When Tchaikovsky thought he imitated somebody, he invariably composed most like himself.

Sérénade mélancolique. Concert piece by PIOTR ILYICH TCHAIKOVSKY, 1876, for violin and orchestra, first performed in Moscow. It is a short lyric elegy in the melancholy key of B-flat minor, in the manner of a NOCTURNE. It is a favorite with violinists worldwide.

serenata (It.; from Lat. *serenus,* serene). 1. A species of dramatic CANTATA in vogue during the 18th century. 2. An instrumental composition midway between a SUITE and a SYMPHONY, but freer in form than either, having five, six, or more MOVEMENTS, and in chamber music style. 3. *See* SERENADE.

sĕh-rĕh-nah´tăh

serialism. A method of composition in which thematic units are arranged in an ordered SET.

TONAL serialism was introduced by ARNOLD SCHOEN-BERG in 1924, as the culmination of a long period of experiments with ATONAL CHROMATIC patterns. Schoenberg's method deals only with the 12 different notes of the chromatic scale. Total serialism organizes different INTERVALS, rhythmic values, DYNAMICS, and all other musical values in independent sets. Even the placement of performers in a concert hall could be determined by arranging them as a set.

The mathematical term *set,* for a TONE ROW, was introduced by MILTON BABBITT in 1946. He experimented with techniques of tonal, rhythmic, and intervallic sets. George Perle proposed the term "set complex" to designate 48 different forms generated by a fundamental 12-tone series. In all these sets the magic number 12 plays a preponderant role. In the general concept of serialism, sets may contain any number of PITCHES, in any scale, including nontempered intervals.

See also DODECAPHONY.

Serkin, Peter (Adolf), outstanding American pianist, son of RUDOLF SERKIN; b. N.Y., July 24, 1947. At age 11 Serkin enrolled at the Curtis Institute of Music in Philadelphia, where he studied with Mieczyslaw Horszowski, Lee Luvisi, and his father. He graduated in 1964. He made his debut as a soloist with Alexander Schneider and a chamber orchestra at the Marlboro (Vermont) Music Festival in 1958. He later studied there with the flutist Marcel Moyse and also received additional piano training from Karl Ulrich Schnabel.

Serkin made his N.Y. debut as a soloist with Alexander Schneider and his chamber orchestra in 1959. His N.Y. recital debut followed in 1965. He continued to tour as a recitalist through the '70s.

In 1973 he formed the group Tashi ("good fortune" in Tibetan) with clarinetist RICHARD STOLTZMAN, violinist Ida Kavafian, and cellist Fred Sherry. The group toured extensively, giving performances of contemporary music in particular.

After leaving the group in 1980, Serkin began to appear again as a soloist and recitalist. He acquired a distinguished reputation as an interpreter of both traditional and contemporary scores. He also made appearances as a fortepianist.

In 1983 Serkin was awarded the Premio of the Accademia Musicale Chigiana in Siena. In 1992 he joined the faculty of the Curtis Institute of Music in Philadelphia.

Serkin, Rudolf, eminent Austrian-born American pianist and teacher of Russian descent, father of PETER (Adolf) SERKIN; b. Eger, March 28, 1903; d. Guilford, Vt., May 8, 1991. Serkin studied piano with Richard Robert and composition with Joseph Marx and ARNOLD SCHOENBERG in Vienna. He made his debut as a soloist with the Vienna Symphony Orchestra at age 12.

Serkin's career began in earnest with his Berlin appearance with the Busch chamber orchestra in 1920. Thereafter, he performed frequently in joint recitals with Adolf Busch, whose daughter he married in 1935. He made his U.S. debut in a recital with Busch at the Coolidge Festival in Washington, D.C., in 1933. He then made a critically acclaimed appearance as a soloist with ARTURO TOSCANINI and the N.Y. Philharmonic in 1936.

PEOPLE IN MUSIC

PEOPLE IN MUSIC

In 1939 Serkin became a naturalized U.S. citizen. After World War II, he pursued an international career. He appeared as a soloist with major orchestras, gave recitals in leading music centers, and played in numerous chamber music settings. In 1939 he was appointed head of the piano department at the Curtis Institute of Music in Philadelphia. He was its director from 1968 to 1976.

In 1950 Serkin helped to establish the Marlboro (Vermont) Music Festival and school and subsequently served as its artistic director. In 1985 he celebrated his 70th anniversary as a concert artist.

Serkin received numerous awards and honorary degrees. He was awarded the Presidential Medal of Freedom in 1963 and in 1988 the National Medal of Arts. The authority and faithfulness of his interpretations of the Viennese classics placed him among the masters of the 20th century.

MUSICAL
INSTRUMENT

---

serpent. A bass wind instrument invented by Canon Edme Guillaume of Auxerre in 1590. It was indeed constructed in the shape of a snake, consisting of several pieces of wood bound together by a leather covering. KEYS were added later.

Its original use was to double ecclesiastical chanting. But, despite its ungainly appearance and a considerable difficulty in handling, by the 18th century the serpent had come to provide the deep bass in military bands, in support of the BASSOON. The serpent was also known as a *Russian bassoon* because it was regularly used in Russian military bands.

The serpent was still used as a band instrument in the first half of the 19th century, but HECTOR BERLIOZ derided it as a laughable monstrosity in his famous book on orchestration. This damnation was the serpent's last hiss—by the 20th century, it could be found only in a few village churches.

The serpent has played a small role in the EARLY MUSIC revival.

Serva Padrona, La (The maid as mistress). OPERA BUFFA by GIOVANNI BATTISTA PERGOLESI, 1733, as an INTERMEZZO to his opera *Il Prigionier superbo* (The proud prisoner), first performed in Naples.

The opera itself is forgotten, but the INTERMEZZO became a *cause célèbre* in the thundering polemical exchange between the advocates of Italian and French opera after its performance in Paris in 1752. Amazingly, JEAN-JACQUES ROUSSEAU sided with the Italian concept of operatic universalism cultivating BEL CANTO. He later reversed his position.

The plot, a typical 18th-century farce, involves a scheming servant girl ("la serva") who sets her sights on her middle-aged master. To prove that she is desirable to men of higher rank, she convinces his valet to wear the uniform of an army captain and pretend to be in love with her. The master is impressed and decides to marry her himself, and she thus becomes "la padrona," the mistress of the house.

service. A religious gathering, including all of the musical material—hymns, psalms, organ music—that is played during it. In the Catholic church, services are usually named for the time of day in which they are performed.

Sessions, Roger (Huntington), eminent American composer and teacher; b. Brooklyn, Dec. 28, 1896; d. Princeton, N.J., March 16, 1985. Sessions studied at Harvard University, taking his bachelor's degree in 1915. He then took a course in composition with HORATIO PARKER at the Yale School of Music, earning a master's two years later.

After graduation, Sessions took private lessons with ERNST BLOCH in Cleveland and N.Y., an association of great importance to him. His early works were strongly influenced by Bloch's rhapsodic style and rich harmonic idiom verging on POLYTONALITY. From 1917 to 1921 Sessions taught music theory at Smith College, then was appointed to the faculty of the Cleveland Institute of Music, first as assistant to Bloch, then as head of the department from 1921 to 1925.

Sessions lived mostly in Europe from 1926 to 1933, supporting himself on two Guggenheim fellowships (1926, 1927), an American Academy in Rome fellowship (1928), and a Carnegie Foundation grant (1931). From 1928 to 1931 he also was active with AARON COPLAND in presenting the Copland-Sessions Concerts of contemporary music in N.Y.

PEOPLE IN MUSIC

From 1933 to 1953, Sessions taught at a number of colleges, including Princeton University (1935–44) and the University of California, Berkeley (1944–53). In 1953 he returned to Princeton as Conant Professor of Music and, in 1959, as codirector of the Columbia-Princeton Electronic Music Center in N.Y. He subsequently taught at the Juilliard School of Music in N.Y. from 1965 to 1985.

In 1974 Sessions received a special citation of the Pulitzer Award Committee "for his life's work as a distinguished American composer." In 1982 he was awarded a second Pulitzer Prize for his Concerto for Orchestra.

In his compositions, Sessions evolved a remarkably compact POLYPHONIC style, rich in unresolvable DISSONANCES and textural density, and yet filled with true lyricism. In his later works, he adopted a method of SERIAL COMPOSITION. The music of Sessions was decidedly in advance of his time. The difficulty of his style, for both performers and listeners, creates a paradoxical situation in which he is recognized as a leading composer of his time, while actual performances of his works are infrequent.

set. A term adopted from mathematical set theory to denote a grouping of PITCH classes or other musical elements. Normally it refers to a 12-NOTE set containing all pitch classes within the EQUAL TEMPERED SYSTEM but may also refer to elements indicating DURATION, time points, and/or DYNAMIC levels. Also called a *series*.

set piece. In music, a separate movement or readily identifiable portion of an opera, etc., formal in structure and cohesive in idiom (as a FINALE).

Seven Deadly Sins, The *(Die sieben Todsünden).* Ballet in song by KURT WEILL, 1933, for soprano, dancer, male vocal quartet, and orchestra, with text by Bertolt Brecht, premiered in Paris. This was the last collaboration of Brecht and Weill.

The character Anna is portrayed by both the soprano and dancer. She comments on the nature of the seven deadly sins in the 20th century. The male quartet serves as a kind of chorus, providing further ironic commentary on how we view sin in today's world.

1776. Musical by Sherman Edward, 1969. This is one of very few historically based musicals that have succeeded in the theater despite lofty content.

The play portrays the spring and summer of 1776 in Philadelphia, with a grand climax on the 4th of July. Adams, Franklin, Washington, and Jefferson duly appear onstage. The work is remarkably true to history, and there is even a discussion of the details of the text of the Declaration of Independence.

Among the songs are *Cool Considerate Men, Sit Down John, Riddle Twiddle and Resolve,* and *Molasses and Rum.*

seventh (Fr. *septième;* Ger. *Septime;* It. *settimo*). *See* INTERVAL. *Seventh chord,* one "of the seventh," composed of a root with its third, fifth, and seventh, and seventh.

Seventh Symphony. Symphony by GUSTAV MAHLER, 1908, in five movements, premiered in Prague with the composer conducting. Longer than his Fifth Symphony (*The Giant*), the Seventh has both pessimistic and optimistic passages.

Seventy-Six Trombones. Marching song by MEREDITH WILLSON, 1957, from the musical *THE MUSIC MAN.* It became a tremendous hit.

Sext. One of the Little Hours of the Office of the Roman Catholic LITURGY. Originally, it was the fifth hour in the daily cycle, but since the 1972 liturgical reform, it is the third (after Lauds and Terce). In either case, it is the service associated with noontime.

sextet (It. *sestet, sestetto;* Ger. *Sextett;* Fr. *sextour*). A concerted composition for six voices or instruments. Most works for string sextet call for pairs of violins, violas, and cellos (LUIGI BOCCHERINI, JOHANNES BRAHMS, ANTONÍN DVOŘÁK, ARNOLD SCHOENBERG). LUDWIG VAN BEETHOVEN wrote a mixed sextet and a wind sextet.

The most famous vocal sextet is in GAETANO DONIZETTI's *LUCIA DI LAMMERMOOR.*

sextuplet (It. *sestole, sestolet;* Ger. *Sextole;* Fr. *sextolet*). A group of six equal notes to be performed in the time of four like notes in the established rhythm. In the *true* sextuplet, the first, third, and fifth notes are accented, while the *false* sextuplet is simply a double TRIPLET.

shading. 1. In the interpretation of a composition, the combination and alternation of any or all the varying degrees of tone power between FORTISSIMO and PIANISSIMO, for obtaining artistic effect. 2. The placing of anything so near the top of an ORGAN pipe as to affect the vibrating column of air within.

shakuhachi. A Japanese end-blown notched FLUTE, made of lacquered bamboo, that came from China at the end of the first millennium A.D. It has been associated with Japanese priests since the 16th century, and has not survived in its home country. Compositions for shaku-hachi are typically programmatic and contemplative in character.

shamisen (samisen). A Japanese long-necked plucked lute, held upright in a seated position. It has three strings running over a slender neck, from a pegbox to an ivory or wood (now plastic) bridge. There are three standard tunings and variants, allowing the playing of as many open PITCHES as possible, depending on the function of the shamisen in the musical context. It is played with a large plectrum. The original form of this CHORDOPHONE, the *jamisen,* came from China c.1400.

shank. *See* CROOK.

Shankar, Ravi, famous Indian sitarist and composer; b. Benares, April 7, 1920. Shankar was trained by his brother, Uday Shankar (b. Udaipur, Rajasthan, Dec. 8, 1900; d. Calcutta, Sep. 29, 1977), a dancer and choreographer of international renown.

Ravi began his career as a musician and a dancer, often touring with his brother's troupe. He then engaged in serious study of the sitar, in time becoming a great virtuoso. As a consequence of the growing infatuation with oriental arts in Western countries in the 1960s, he suddenly became popular, and his concerts were greeted with reverential awe by youthful multitudes. This popularity increased a thousandfold when GEORGE HARRISON of the BEATLES took lessons from him.

As a composer, Shankar distinguished himself by several film scores, including the famous *Pather Panchali* trilogy. He also wrote the film scores for *Kabulliwallah* and *Anuradha*. For the Tagore centenary he wrote a ballet, *Samanya Kshati,* based on Tagore's poem of the same name. It was produced in New Delhi in 1961.

Shankar wrote two concertos for sitar and orchestra (1970, 1976) and collaborated with YEHUDI MENUHIN and PHILIP GLASS, among others. His efforts to introduce Indian music to the rest of the world have often met with disapproval by Indians who believe that the tradition of apprenticeship and oral learning should not be disturbed.

Shannāi. *See* SĀNĀYĪ.

shanty (*chantey, chanty;* from Fr. *chanter,* sing). A characteristic song of the English working class in centuries past. Most commonly, the *sea shanty,* a sailor's work song designed to facilitate the difficult gang labor aboard ship.

Shapey, Ralph, American conductor, teacher, and composer; b. Philadelphia, March 12, 1921. Shapey studied violin with Emanuel Zeitlin and composition with STEFAN WOLPE. He served as assistant conductor of the Philadelphia National Youth Administration Symphony Orchestra from 1938 to 1947.

In 1954 Shapey founded and became music director of the Contemporary Chamber Players of the University of Chicago, with which he presented new works. In 1963–64 he taught at the University of Pennsylvania and then was made professor of music at the University of Chicago in 1964, where he remained for several decades. After serving as Distinguished Professor of Music at the AARON COPLAND School of Music at Queens College of the City University of N.Y. (1985–86), he resumed his duties at the University of Chicago, retiring as professor emeritus in 1991.

Disappointed by repeated rejections of his works by performers and publishers, Shapey announced in 1969 that he would no longer submit his works to anyone for performance or publication. However, in 1976 he had a change of heart and once more gave his blessing to the performance and publication of his works. In 1982 Shapey became a MacArthur Fellow and in 1989 was elected a member of the American Academy and Institute of Arts and Letters.

On Nov. 21, 1991, he conducted the premiere of his *Concerto Fantastique* with the Chicago Symphony Orchestra. In 1992 the judges of the Pulitzer Prize in music awarded him its prize for this score, but then the Pulitzer Prize board rejected its own judges' decision and denied Shapey the honor. The ensuing scandal did little to enhance the reputation of the Pulitzer Prize in music. In 1994 Shapey was elected a member of the American Academy of Arts and Sciences.

Shapey follows NEOCLASSICAL models in his compositions. However, he uses SERIAL techniques and freely interjects jarring DISSONANCES into his works, making his pieces difficult for some critics and members of the public to understand.

Among his orchestral works are Symphony No. 1 (1952), *Invocation,* concerto for violin and orchestra (1958), *Rituals* (1959), Double Concerto for violin, cello, and orchestra (1983), and SYMPHONIE CONCERTANTE (1985). His chamber pieces include nine string quartets (1946–95), Chamber Symphony for ten instruments (1962), *Concertante I* for trumpet and ten performers (1984) and *II* for alto saxophone and 14 performers (1987), *Dinosaur Annex* for violin and vibraphone marimba (1993), *Constellations for*

Bang on a Can All-Stars for chamber ensemble (1993), and *Evocation IV* for violin, cello, piano, and percussion (1994).

Shapey also composed a variety of vocal works, including *Song of Songs* for soprano, chamber orchestra, and tape: *I* (1979), *II* (1980), and *III* (1980), *In Memoriam Paul Fromm* for soprano, baritone, and nine performers (1987), and *Centennial Celebration* for four vocal soloists and 12 instrumentalists (1991).

sharp (adjective). 1. Of tones or instruments, too high in PITCH. 2. Of INTERVALS, MAJOR or AUGMENTED. 3. Of KEYS, having a sharp or sharps in the signature. 4. Of ORGAN stops, shrill. 5. Of digitals, the black keys, or any white key a SEMITONE above another white key (i.e., F and C).

sharp (noun; Ger. *Cross*). The character ♯, which raises the PITCH of the note immediately following it by a SEMITONE; the *double sharp* ✕ raises the note by two semitones.

Sharp, Cecil (James), English folk music collector and editor; b. London, Nov. 22, 1859; d. there, June 23, 1924. He studied mathematics and music at Uppingham and Clare College, Cambridge. In 1882 he settled in Adelaide, Australia, where he worked in a bank and practiced law. In 1889 he resigned from the legal profession and took up a musical career.

He was assistant organist of the Adelaide Cathedral and codirector of the Adelaide College of Music. In 1892 Sharp returned to England, where he was music instructor of Ludgrove School (1893–1910) and principal of the Hampstead Conservatory (1895–1905). At the same time, he became deeply interested in English folk songs. He published a *Book of British Songs for Home and School* (1902), then proceeded to make a systematic survey of English villages with the aim of collecting authentic specimens of English songs. In 1911 he established the English Folk Dance Society and also was director of the School of Folk Song and Dance at Stratford-upon-Avon.

During World War I Sharp was in the U.S. collecting folk music in the Appalachian Mountains, with a view to establishing their English origin. In 1923 he received the de-

PEOPLE IN MUSIC

A traditional ballad singer, one of many photographs in the collection of the English Folk Dance and Song Society. (Vaughan Williams Memorial Library, EFDSS) ▶

gree of M.M. *honoris causa* from the University of Cambridge. In 1930 the "Cecil Sharp House" was opened in London as headquarters of the English Folk Dance Society (amalgamated with the Folk Song Society in 1932).

Among his important writings (all published in London) are *English Folk-Song: Some Conclusions* (1907; 2nd edition, 1936; 4th edition, 1965, by M. Karpeles), *Folk-Singing in Schools* (1912), *Folk-Dancing in Elementary and Secondary Schools* (1912), and, with A. Oppe, *The Dance: An Historical Survey of Dancing in Europe* (1924). He also published many significant folk-song editions.

In old American slang, two bits equaled a quarter, not that any U.S. coinage of a "bit" ever existed.

Shave and a Haircut. Words sung to a musical refrain so well known that it can be recognized simply by tapping out its rhythm. There are many forms of this piece of doggerel, e.g., "Bum di-de-de-dum bum, that's it"; "Shave and a haircut, bay rum"; and "Shave and a haircut, two bits."

PEOPLE IN MUSIC

Shaw, Artie (born Arthur Jacob Arshawsky), outstanding American JAZZ clarinetist, bandleader, composer, and arranger; b. N.Y., May 23, 1910. Shaw was brought up in New Haven, Connecticut, where he became an alto saxophonist in Johnny Cavallaro's dance band when he was 15. He took up the clarinet at 16 and then worked as music director and arranger for the Austin Wylie Orchestra in Cleveland until 1929. He subsequently toured as a tenor saxophonist with Irving Aaronson's band, going with it to N.Y., where he played in Harlem and found a mentor in Willie "the Lion" Smith.

After a stint as a freelance studio musician from 1931 to 1935, Shaw formed a sophisticated band that stirred excitement with its rendition of his *Interlude in B-flat* in N.Y. in 1936. In 1937 he organized a SWING band that won enormous success with the hit recording of COLE PORTER's *Begin the Beguine* in 1938.

In 1940 Shaw went to Hollywood, where he produced the hit recording *Frenesi*. He toured again with his own big band, from which he drew members of the Gramercy 5, a group with which he was active on and off from 1940 until its last recording session in 1954. In the interim, he led several big bands, winning his greatest acclaim with his recording of *Little Jazz* in 1945.

Shaw's interest in the classical repertoire for his instrument led him to appear as a soloist with various orchestras. He also performed at N.Y.'s CARNEGIE HALL.

Shaw retired from music-making in the mid-'50s, and spent much of the '60s living in Spain and writing. He came out of retirement in 1983 to lead another band and has performed sporadically since then.

Shaw is a remarkable clarinetist, his superb playing perhaps best revealed in his recording *Concerto for Clarinet* in 1940. He was married eight times, numbering among his wives the film stars Lana Turner and Ava Gardner.

shawm (Fr. *chalemie;* Ger. *Schalmei;* It. *piffaro;* bass shawm: Fr. *bombarde;* Ger. *Pommern*). An early form of OBOE with a harsh, nasal sound.

Brought into Europe in the 12th century, the shawm remained popular until the 17th century, when the oboe superseded it. The shawm's shape was like that of a BASSOON. It was made of a long piece of wood with a curved metal bell. From the 16th century there were open-reed and reed-capped types. At the height of its popularity there were shawms of all sizes, providing a range from bass to high soprano.

MUSICAL
INSTRUMENT

Shéhérazade. Song cycle by MAURICE RAVEL, 1904, for voice and orchestra, to a text by Tristan Klingsor, first performed in Paris. The music is filled with an impressionistic quasi-oriental flavor.

sheng (Chin.). A Chinese FREE-REED MOUTH ORGAN, the earliest known example of this instrument type (mentioned in c.1100 B.C.). The traditional shape is described as a phoenix, involving a mouthpiece, wind chest, and around 17 bamboo pipes pointing upwards. Four of these are dummy pipes, to provide symmetry. Each pipe has a small finger hole that must be closed in order to sound. *See also* SHŌ.

shepherd's bell (Ger. *Herdenglocke*). An Alpine bell hung over a sheep's neck to help locate the herd. WOLFGANG AMADEUS MOZART and GUSTAV MAHLER included the instrument in some scores.

shepherd's horn. A generic name for a lip-vibrated wind instrument of ancient origin, originally made of animal horn or tusk. The instrument was used functionally to communicate, call animals, or to perform magical or religious rituals.

Shifrin, Seymour, American composer and teacher; b. N.Y., Feb. 28, 1926; d. Boston, Sept. 26, 1979. After studies at N.Y.'s High School of Music and Art, Shifrin received private instruction from WILLIAM SCHUMAN from 1942 to 1945. He continued his training at Columbia University, where he completed his graduate study in composition with Otto Luening in 1949. He then pursued additional training with DARIUS MILHAUD in Paris on a Fulbright scholarship (1951–52).

Shifrin held two Guggenheim fellowships (1956, 1960). He taught at Columbia University (1949–50), City College of the City University of N.Y. (1950–51), the University of California, Berkeley (1952–66), and Brandeis University (1966–79).

Shifrin wrote music drawing on the CHROMATIC SCALE, with finely crafted contrapuntal lines often resulting in sharp DISSONANCE. He wrote orchestral works, chamber music, including five string quartets, and many other works for or-

---

MUSICAL INSTRUMENT

Like the HARMONICA, the sheng can create different PITCHES by having the player inhale and exhale.

MUSICAL INSTRUMENT

MUSICAL INSTRUMENT

PEOPLE IN MUSIC

chestra and vocalists. His best-known work is 1964's *Satires of Circumstance* for mezzosoprano, flute, clarinet, violin, cello, double bass, and piano (1964).

shift. In playing the violin, etc., a change by the left hand from the FIRST POSITION. The second position is called the *half-shift,* the third the *whole shift,* and the fourth the *double shift.* When out of the first position, the player is *on the shift,* and *shifting up* or *down,* as the case may be.

shimmy. An African-American foxtrot of the 1920s, emphasizing movement of the upper torso, in quick RAGTIME rhythm.

shō. A Japanese FREE-REED MOUTH ORGAN, with continuous sound production possible through both inhalation and exhalation. It is closely related to the SHENG.

MUSICAL INSTRUMENT

◄

Japanese shō player. (Benson collection)

MUSICAL INSTRUMENT

shofar. An ancient Jewish ritual TRUMPET, made from a ram's horn. It is blown only at the beginning of the Jewish New Year.

Shore, Dinah (Frances Rose), popular singer and talk-show host, b. Winchester, Tenn., March 1, 1917; d. Los Angeles, Calif., Feb. 24, 1994. Shore first performed as a teenager on Nashville radio, then went to N.Y. She took her new first name from the hit pop song *DINAH.*

Shore was hired as the vocalist for Cuban bandleader XAVIER CUGAT, making her first hit recordings in the early

PEOPLE IN MUSIC

'40s. She had over 80 chart hits through her solo career, primarily in the '50s. Her sweet voice and squeaky-clean image made her a natural for similar material, including the treacly hit *Buttons and Bows*.

Shore was best-known in the '60s, '70s, and '80s as a television personality.

PEOPLE IN MUSIC

Short, Bobby (Robert Waltrip), African-American singer and pianist of popular music; b. Danville, Ill., Sept. 15, 1926. He was self-taught in music. He appeared in vaudeville as a child. In 1937, Short went to N.Y., where he began his career as a highly successful nightclub entertainer. He also appeared in Los Angeles, London, and Paris with equal success.

Short ultimately garnered a reputation as the leading café singer of his time. He has had a regular engagement at N.Y.'s Cafe Carlyle for many years.

short octave. The lowest OCTAVE in early keyboard instruments that omitted the CHROMATIC tones and used the black keys to sound notes usually assigned to the white keys, with only B♭ keeping its proper position.

The rationale for the omission of chromatic tones except for B♭ was that chromatics were used very seldom in the deep bass register in keyboard compositions of the BAROQUE period. There were also advantages. Thanks to the short octave, organists or harpsichordists could play chords in widely spread positions because the stretch of the short octave was only five white keys. In his E minor Toccata for harpsichord, JOHANN SEBASTIAN BACH has a difficult interval of the tenth in the bass. But in the short octave it would require the stretch of only one octave.

The retention of the B♭ in the short octave is explained by the great frequency of that note in scales, dating back to the Middle Ages.

PEOPLE IN MUSIC

Shostakovich, Dmitri (Dmitrievich), preeminent Russian composer of the Soviet generation, whose style and idiom of composition largely defined the nature of new Russian music; b. St. Petersburg, Sept. 25, 1906; d. Moscow, Aug. 9, 1975. Shostakovich was a member of a cultured Russian family. His father was an engineer employed in the government office of weights and measures, and his mother was a professional pianist.

Shostakovich grew up during the most difficult period of Russian revolutionary history, when famine and disease decimated the population of Petrograd. Of frail physique, he suffered from malnutrition. ALEXANDER GLAZUNOV, the director of the Petrograd Conservatory, appealed personally to the Commissar of Education, to grant an increased food ration for Shostakovich, which was essential for his physical survival.

At the age of nine, Shostakovich began piano lessons with his mother. In 1919 he entered the Petrograd Conservatory, where he studied piano and composition, taking degrees in 1923 and 1925 in each subject, respectively. As a graduation piece he submitted his First Symphony, written at the age of 18. It was first performed by the Leningrad Philharmonic in 1926, under the direction of Nicolai Malko, and subsequently became one of Shostakovich's most popular works. He pursued postgraduate work in composition until 1930.

Shostakovich's Second Symphony was composed for the tenth anniversary of the Soviet Revolution in 1927. It carried the subtitle *Dedication to October* and ended with a rousing choral finale. Nonetheless, it was less successful than his first symphony, despite its revolutionary sentiment.

Shostakovich next wrote a satirical opera, THE NOSE, after Gogol's whimsical story, in which he revealed his flair for musical satire. The score featured a variety of modernistic devices and included an interlude written for percussion instruments only. *The Nose* was produced in Leningrad in 1930, with considerable popular acclaim. It was attacked, however, by official theater critics as a product of "bourgeois decadence" and was quickly withdrawn from the stage. Somewhat in the same satirical style was his ballet *The Golden Age* from 1930. It included a celebrated DISSONANT POLKA, satirizing the current disarmament conference in Geneva. That same year, Shostakovich's Third Symphony, subtitled *May First* was performed in Leningrad. It had a choral finale saluting the International Workers' Day. Despite its explicit revolutionary content, it failed to earn the approval of Soviet spokesmen, who dismissed the work as nothing more than a formal gesture of proletarian solidarity.

Shostakovich's next work was to precipitate a crisis in his career, as well as in Soviet music in general: an OPERA based on a short story by the 19th-century Russian writer Leskov, entitled *LADY MACBETH OF THE DISTRICT OF MTZENSK.* The book depicted adultery, murder, and suicide in a merchant home under the Czars. It was produced in Leningrad in 1934, and was hailed by most Soviet musicians as a work comparable to the best productions of Western modern opera. But both the staging and the music ran counter to growing Soviet puritanism. After its Moscow production, *Pravda,* the official organ of the Communist party, published an article accusing Shostakovich of creating a "bedlam of noise." The brutality of this assault dismayed Shostakovich. He vowed to compose in a more acceptable manner in the future.

Shostakovich's next stage production was a ballet, *The Limpid Brook,* portraying pastoral scenes on a Soviet collective farm. In this work he tempered his dissonant style, and the subject seemed eminently fitting for the Soviet theater. But it, too, was condemned in *Pravda,* this time for an insufficiently dignified treatment of Soviet life.

Having been rebuked twice for two radically different theater works, Shostakovich abandoned all attempts to write for the stage and returned to purely instrumental composition. But as though pursued by vengeful fate, he again suffered a painful reverse. His Fourth Symphony (1935–36) was rehearsed by the Leningrad Philharmonic but withdrawn before the performance when representatives of the government and even the orchestral musicians themselves sharply criticized the piece.

Shostakovich's rehabilitation finally came with the production of his Fifth Symphony in Leningrad in 1937, a work of rhapsodic grandeur, culminating in a powerful climax. It was hailed as a model of true Soviet art, classical in formal design, lucid in harmonic idiom, and optimistic in its message.

The height of Shostakovich's fame was achieved in his Seventh Symphony. He began its composition during the siege of Leningrad by the Nazis in the autumn of 1941. He served in the fire brigade during the air raids, then flew from Leningrad to the temporary Soviet capital in Kuibishev, on the Volga, where he completed the score, performed there in 1942. Its symphonic development is realistic in the extreme. The theme of the Nazis, in mechanical march time, rises to monstrous loudness, only to be overcome and reduced to a pathetic drum dribble by a victorious Russian song. The work became a musical symbol of the Russian struggle against the overwhelmingly superior Nazi war machine. It was subtitled *LENINGRAD SYMPHONY* and was performed during the war by virtually every orchestra in the Allied countries.

After the tremendous emotional appeal of the *Leningrad Symphony*, the Eighth Symphony, written in 1943, had lesser impact. The Ninth, Tenth, and Eleventh Symphonies followed (1945, 1953, 1957) without attracting much notice. The Twelfth Symphony (1960 – 61), dedicated to the memory of Lenin, aroused a little more interest.

But it was left for his Thirteenth Symphony, premiered in 1962, to create a controversy that seemed to be Shostakovich's peculiar destiny. Its vocal first movement for solo bass and male chorus was a setting of words by the Soviet poet Evtushenko. It expressed the horror of the massacre of Jews by the Nazis during their occupation of the city of Kiev and contained a warning against residual anti-Semitism in Soviet Russia. This met with unexpected criticism by the chairman of the Communist party, Nikita Khrushchev. He complained about the exclusive attention in Evtushenko's poem to Jewish victims, and his failure to mention the Ukrainians and other nationals who were also slaughtered. The text of the poem was altered to meet these objections, but the Thirteenth Symphony never gained wide acceptance.

There followed the remarkable Fourteenth Symphony from 1969, in 11 sections, scored for voices and orchestra, to words by García Lorca, Apollinaire, Rilke, and the Russian poet Küchelbecker. Shostakovich's Fifteenth Symphony, his last, performed in Moscow under the direction of his son Maxim in 1972, demonstrated his undying spirit of innovation. The score is set in the key of C major, but it contains a 12-TONE passage and literal allusions to motives from

GIOACCHINO ROSSINI's *WILLIAM TELL* overture and the Fate motif from RICHARD WAGNER's *DIE WALKÜRE.*

Shostakovich's adoption, however limited, of themes built on 12 different notes—a procedure that he himself had condemned as antimusical—is interesting both from the psychological and sociological standpoint. He experimented with these techniques in several other works, but his first explicit use of a 12-tone subject occurred in his twelfth string quartet from 1968.

One by one, Shostakovich's early works, originally condemned as unacceptable to Soviet reality, were returned to the stage and concert hall. The objectionable Fourth and Thirteenth Symphonies were published and recorded, and the operas *The Nose* and *Lady Macbeth of the District of Mtzensk* (revised and renamed *Katerina Izmailova,* after the name of the heroine) had several successful revivals.

Shostakovich excelled in instrumental music. Besides the 15 symphonies, he wrote 15 string quartets, various concertos, 24 preludes for piano (op.34, 1932–33), 24 preludes and fugues for piano (op.87, 1950–51), two piano sonatas, and several short piano pieces. He also wrote choral works and song cycles.

What is remarkable about Shostakovich is the unfailing consistency of his compositional style. His entire oeuvre, from his first work to his last (147 opus numbers), proclaims a personal article of faith. His idiom is unmistakably of the 20th century, making free use of dissonant harmonies and intricate contrapuntal designs, yet never abandoning inherent tonality. He invariably reaches a tonal climax in his works, often in a triumphal triadic declaration. Most of his works carry key signatures, and his metrical structure is governed by a unifying rhythmic pulse.

Shostakovich was equally eloquent in dramatic and lyric utterances. He had no fear of prolonging his slow movements in relentless dynamic rise and fall, and the cumulative power of his rapid movements is overwhelming. While the symphonies have given Shostakovich great visibility in the concert hall, the string quartets are more personal and more indicative of his compositional moods. Yet, through all the ups and downs of his career, he never changed his musical

Another personal quirk of Shostakovich's was the use in some of his scores of a personal monogram, D–S–C–H (for D, E♯, C, H in German notation, i.e., D, E♭, C, B). In this way, he added a personal musical signature to these works.

language in its fundamental modalities. When the flow of his music met obstacles, whether technical or external, he solved them without changing the main direction.

Shostakovich's continual worries about the unpredictable Stalin and his henchmen have made the composer a textbook study of survival under the worst of political circumstances. At one period of his life (the years between 1945 and Stalin's death in 1953), he wrote compositions that he simply put away until the dust cleared.

His honors, both domestic and foreign, were many. He visited the U.S. as a delegate to the World Peace Conference in 1949, as a member of a group of Soviet musicians in 1959, and to receive an honorary D.F.A. degree from Northwestern University in 1973.

shout. 1. An African-American audience response involving footstamping, handclapping, singing drones, and interjecting shrill vocal commentary between phrases of GOSPEL music. 2. A genre of STRIDE piano piece, first composed in the 1920s. The most famous example is James P. Johnsons's *Carolina Shout* (1925).

Show Boat. Musical by JEROME KERN and OSCAR HAMMERSTEIN II, 1927, based on the novel by Edna Ferber.

The story concerns a Mississippi showboat that carries a versatile assortment of passengers. The captain's daughter Magnolia falls in love with a gambler named Gaylord Ravenal, whom she marries despite her father's disapproval. Distressed by Gaylord's gambling, Magnolia leaves him and joins a Chicago nightclub as a singer, and she becomes very successful. Many years later, Gaylord returns and Magnolia takes him back.

This work took the Broadway musical to new heights of topicality (dealing with the issues of race relationships) and musical integrity, producing a truly unified work, immediately hailed by critics as a classic of American musical theater. PAUL ROBESON established his national reputation with his performance of OL' MAN RIVER. Other songs include *Can't Help Lovin' Dat Man, Make Believe, Why Do I Love You?, Bill,* and *You Are Love.*

GEORGE GERSHWIN visited the Georgia Sea Islands and heard a native group of singers perform a religious "shout." This inspired one of the most famous moments in his *PORGY AND BESS.*

shuffle. A syncopated dance with a dragging, sliding step, meant to appear somewhat random and confused.

Shuffle Along. Musical by EUBIE BLAKE and Noble Sissle, 1921, one of the first Broadway shows written by and starring African-American performers. The insubstantial plot deals with a mayoral election in a small town. Its considerable success was due in no small part to songs such as *Everything Reminds Me of You*, *If You've Never Been Vamped*, *I'm Just Wild about Harry*, and *Love Will Find a Way*.

Shuffle Off to Buffalo. Song by Harry Warren, 1933. It became a hit in the movie musical *42nd Street*.

Sibelius, Jean (actually, Johan Julius Christian), great Finnish composer; b. Hämeenlinna, Dec. 8, 1865; d. Järvenpää, Sept. 20, 1957. Sibelius was the son of an army surgeon and from early childhood showed a natural aYnity for music. At the age of nine he began to study piano, then took violin lessons with a local bandmaster. He learned to play violin well enough to take part in amateur performances of chamber music.

In 1885, Sibelius enrolled at the University of Helsingfors (Helsinki) to study law but abandoned it after the first semester. In the fall of 1885 he entered the Helsingfors Con-

PEOPLE IN MUSIC

The family name stems from a Finnish peasant named Sibbe, traced back to the late 17th century. The Latin noun ending was commonly added among educated classes in Scandinavia.

Bust of Jean Sibelius at the Sibelius Memorial in Helsinki, Finland. (Dave Bartruff/Corbis)

▶

servatory, where he studied violin. He also took courses in composition with Martin Wegelius.

In 1889 Sibelius's second string quartet was performed in public. It produced a sufficiently favorable impression to obtain for him a government stipend for further study in Berlin, where he took lessons in COUNTERPOINT and FUGUE with Albert Becker. Later he proceeded to Vienna for additional musical training and became a student of Johann Nepomuk Fuchs and KARL GOLDMARK in 1890–91. In 1892 he married Aino Järnefelt.

From then on, Sibelius's destiny as a national Finnish composer was determined. The music he wrote was inspired by native legends, with the great Finnish epic *Kalevala* a prime source of inspiration. Later that year, his symphonic poem *Kullervo,* scored for soloists, chorus, and orchestra, was first performed in Helsingfors. There followed one of his most remarkable works, the symphonic poem entitled simply EN SAGA. In it he displayed to the full his genius for VARIATION forms, based on a cumulative growth of a basic THEME with effective contrapuntal embellishments.

From 1892 to 1900 Sibelius taught theory and composition at the Helsingfors Conservatory. In 1897 the Finnish Senate granted him an annual stipend of 3,000 marks. In 1899 he conducted in Helsingfors the premiere of his First Symphony and subsequently conducted the first performances of all of his symphonies, except for the fifth.

In 1900 the Helsingfors Philharmonic gave the first performance of Sibelius's most celebrated and most profoundly moving patriotic work, FINLANDIA. Its melody soon became identified among Finnish patriots with the aspiration for national independence, so that the Russian Czarist government (then in control of Finland) went to the extreme of forbidding its performances during periods of political unrest. In 1901 Sibelius was invited to conduct his works at the annual festival of the Allgemeiner Deutscher Tonkünstlerverein at Heidelberg. In 1904 he settled in his country home at Järvenpää, where he remained for the rest of his life.

In 1913 Sibelius accepted a commission from the American music patron Carl Stoeckel, to be performed at the 28th annual Festival at Norfolk, Connecticut. For it he contributed a symphonic legend, *Aalotaret* (Nymphs of the ocean; later revised as *The Oceanides*). He took his only sea voyage to America to conduct its premiere in 1914, on which occasion he received an honorary doctor of music degree from Yale University.

Returning to Finland just before the outbreak of World War I, Sibelius withdrew into seclusion but continued to work. He made his last public appearance in Stockholm, conducting the premiere of his Seventh Symphony in 1924. He wrote a few more works thereafter, including a score for Shakespeare's *The Tempest* and a symphonic poem, TAPIOLA. He virtually ceased to compose after 1927.

At various times, rumors were circulated that Sibelius had completed his Eighth Symphony, but nothing was forthcoming from Järvenpää. One persistent story was that Sibelius himself decided to burn his incomplete works. Although willing to receive journalists and reporters, he avoided answering questions about his music. He lived out the remainder of his very long life in retirement, absorbed in family interests.

Only once was Sibelius's peaceful life gravely disrupted, when the Russian army invaded Finland in 1940. Sibelius sent an anguished appeal to America to save his country, which by the perverse fate of world politics became allied with Nazi Germany. But after World War II Sibelius cordially received a delegation of Soviet composers who made a reverential pilgrimage to his rural retreat.

Honors were showered upon him. Festivals of his music became annual events in Helsinki, and in 1939 the Helsinki Conservatory was renamed the Sibelius Academy. A postage stamp bearing his likeness was issued by the Finnish government on his 80th birthday, and special publications—biographical, bibliographical, and photographic—were published in Finland. Artistically, too, Sibelius attained the status of greatness rarely given to a living musician; several important contemporary composers acknowledged their debt of inspiration to him, RALPH VAUGHAN WILLIAMS among them.

Sibelius was the last great representative of 19th-century nationalistic ROMANTICISM. He stayed aloof from modern developments, but was not uninterested in reading scores and listening to performances on the radio of works by such composers as ARNOLD SCHOENBERG, SERGEI PROKOFIEV, BÉLA BARTÓK, and DMITRI SHOSTAKOVICH.

The music of Sibelius also marked a culmination of the growth of national Finnish art. Like his predecessors, he was schooled in the Germanic tradition, and his early works reflect German lyricism and dramatic thought. He opened a new era in Finnish music when he abandoned formal conventions and began to write music that seemed formless and diffuse but actually followed a powerful line of development by variation and repetition. A parallel with LUDWIG VAN BEETHOVEN's late works has frequently been drawn.

The thematic material employed by Sibelius is not modeled directly on known Finnish FOLK songs. Rather, he re-created the characteristic melodic patterns of folk music. The prevailing mood is somber, even tragic, with a certain elemental sweep and grandeur.

Sibelius's instrumentation is highly individual, with long songful solo passages and with protracted transitions that are treated as integral parts of the music. His genius found its most eloquent expression in his symphonies and symphonic poems. He wrote only a moderate amount of chamber music, much of it in his earlier years. His only OPERA, *The Maid in the Tower* (1896), to a text in Swedish, was never published. He wrote some incidental music for the stage, including the celebrated *Valse triste,* written in 1903 for *Kuolema,* a play by his brother-in-law Arvid Järnefelt.

In addition to the pieces mentioned above, Sibelius's works include incidental music for the theater; seven symphonies (1899; 1902; 1904–7; 1911; 1915; 1923; 1924) and symphonic poems and other orchestral works; chamber works, including string quartets (1885; 1889; 1890; 1909, *Voces intimae*) and various other combinations; over 25 piano works (1893–1929); organ pieces; numerous choral works, and 95 songs (1891–1917).

Sibila. A verse preceding Christmas MASS as celebrated on the islands of Majorca and Sardinia. It consists of the prophecies of the Apocalypse and is usually sung in Catalan ("Jesucrist, Rei universal . . .").

Sicilian Vespers, The *(I Vespri Siciliani).* Opera by GIUSEPPE VERDI, 1855, first produced in Paris at the Grande Exposition under the French title *Les Vêpres siciliennes.*

The subject was not the most politic choice for a French audience, because it dealt with the expulsion of the French from Sicily in the 13th century. The Vespers of the title are the church bells rung by a patriotic Sicilian noblewoman as a signal for the expected uprising. The opera ends in a massacre of the French.

Not a major Verdi opera, but it has remained surprisingly popular in the world's opera houses.

sē-chē-lē-ah′nǎh **siciliana, -o** (It.; Fr. *sicilienne*). A pastoral dance in moderate tempo and $\frac{6}{8}$ or $\frac{12}{8}$ time, frequently in a minor key; it somewhat resembles a BARCAROLLE. The characteristic rhythm is ♪. ♪ ♪.

In its classical form it is often orchestrated with flutes and oboes and included in the BAROQUE SUITE. Its origins are not clearly understood.

Alla siciliana, arias in this style, with frequent use of the NEAPOLITAN SIXTH chord.

side drum (U.K.). *See* SNARE DRUM.

sidemen. Members of a JAZZ or popular group accompanying a soloist.

Sidewalks of New York, The. Song by James W. Blake and Charles B. Lawlor, 1894. Originally performed in vaudeville, it became the unofficial N.Y. anthem, lustily intoned by the hoarse voices of candidates for political office. Alfred Smith adopted it for his presidential campaign in 1928, and N.Y.'s colorful if corrupt mayor James Walker loved it.

The song is also known by the first line of its chorus, *East Side West Side.*

Siège de Corinthe, Le (The siege of Corinth). Opera by GIOACCHINO ROSSINI, 1826, first performed in Paris. The story deals with a daughter of the governor of Corinth. She refuses to submit to the commander of the Turkish army, who offers to end the siege of city if she will sleep with him. She dies with her father in the city ruins.

Because the first production of the opera happened to take place during the uprising against the Ottoman rulers by Greek nationalists, to whom the French were highly sympathetic, it won a particularly warm reception. Actually, the score was a revision of an opera on a similar subject that was first produced in Naples, 1820, under the title *Maometto II.*

Siegfried. Music drama by RICHARD WAGNER, the third part of the tetralogy *Der Ring des Nibelungen,* first produced in 1876 as part of the inaugural Bayreuth Festival.

Siegfried is the incestuous child of Siegmund and Sieglinde, children of Wotan. He is guarded by the Nibelung dwarf Mime. Wotan predicts that a hero will emerge who will make the mighty sword with which to kill the murderous giant Fafner, magically transformed into a dragon. Siegfried fulfills Wotan's prophecy, forges the sword, and slays Fafner. Inadvertently, he touches the hot gore of the slain dragon and, putting his finger to his lips, he suddenly becomes aware that he can understand the language of the birds.

Siegfried also reads the mind of Mime and realizes that he plots his death. He kills the malevolent dwarf and goes forth to his next adventure, to rescue Brünnhilde. She is the disobedient Valkyrie who was punished by Wotan for trying to help Siegmund and placed on a rock surrounded by a ring of fire. Siegfried reaches her as she lies in deep sleep and puts the fateful ring of the Nibelung, now in his possession, on her finger. He then awakens her with a kiss.

The score contains some of the most gorgeous episodes in Wagner's massive *Ring,* the scene with the birds being particularly poetic.

Siegfried Idyll. Work by RICHARD WAGNER, 1870, for small orchestra. It was composed and conducted by Wagner in his home on Lake Lucerne as a surprise for the birthday of his wife, Cosima, on Christmas Day, celebrating the birth of their son, Siegfried. In the manuscript the work is titled simply *Symphonie.*

In this work, Wagner made use of several leading motives from his opera SIEGFRIED.

PEOPLE IN MUSIC

Sierra, Roberto, Puerto Rican composer; b. Vega Baja, Oct. 9, 1953. Sierra began training at the Puerto Rico Conservatory of Music and at the University of Puerto Rico, graduating in 1976. He then pursued studies in London at the Royal College of Music and the University from 1976 to 1978, at the Institute of Sonology in Utrecht during 1978, and with modern experimental composer GYÖRGY LIGETI at the Hamburg Hochschule für Musik from 1979 to 1982.

Sierra was assistant director (1983–85) and director (1985–86) of the cultural activities department at the University of Puerto Rico, then dean of studies (1986–87) and chancellor (from 1987) at the Puerto Rico Conservatory of Music. From 1989 to 1992 he was composer-in-residence of the Milwaukee Symphony Orchestra. In 1992 he became an assistant professor at Cornell University.

Among Sierra's notable works are *El Mensajero de Plata,* a chamber opera written in 1984, and *El Contemplado,* a ballet score from 1987. His orchestral works include *Concierto Caribe* for flute and orchestra (1995), a violin concerto called *Evocaciones* (1994), *Ritmo* (1995), and *Saludo* (1995). He also composed chamber pieces, including string and wind quintets and works for solo clarinet, and keyboard works. His vocal works include *Bayoán,* oratorio for soprano, baritone, and orchestra composed in 1991, and *entre terceras* for two synthesizers and computer from 1988.

sight reading. An ability to read unfamiliar music with ease. In singing it is synonymous with SOLFÈGE.

Before the system of NOTATION was firmly established, sight reading included a great deal of IMPROVISATION within the given METER and KEY. Choirboys were trained to sing MENSURAL music by sight. But the real challenge to professional musicians came in the 19th century, when to read at sight a difficult piece of piano music required a superior ability to coordinate melody, harmony, and rhythm.

All professional instrumentalists and vocalists must be able to read at sight as a matter of routine, but there are some extraordinary musicians who can play complicated works with great precision and fluency at sight. Piano accompanists are routinely expected to play their parts and follow the soloist without rehearsal. For them, playing *a prima vista* or *à livre ouvert* (Fr., at the open book) is a necessity in a practical concert career when little time is available for rehearsal. Accompanists for popular songs at auditions should know the standard repertoire well enough to play in any key requested.

signal horn. A BUGLE.

signature tune. A brief musical phrase that becomes associated with a popular band on the radio, played at the beginning and/or at the end of a program or performance.

signature, key. In modern NOTATION, the ACCIDENTALS (SHARPS or FLATS) that predetermine the TONALITY or tonalities to be used.

signature, time. In modern NOTATION, a numerical indication of the numbers of BEATS in a MEASURE.

silence. Literally, the absence of sound. In the 20th century, introduced as a viable element of music.

The most ambitious composition using the effect of total silence is *4' 33"* by JOHN CAGE, scored for any combination of instruments and subdivided into three movements during which no intentional sounds are produced. It was "unheard" for the first time at Woodstock, N.Y., in 1952, with David Tudor at the piano.

Silence. A seminal text by JOHN CAGE, his first, written in 1961 while he was a fellow at the Center for Advanced Studies at Wesleyan University in Middletown, Connecticut. Embodying ideas essential to any understanding of Cage himself, *Silence* quickly became a classic text in 20th-century musical aesthetics.

Silent Night (Stille Nacht, heilige Nacht). Christmas song by Franz Gruber, composed on Christmas Eve, 1818. It is the most popular Christmas song in Germany, England, and the U.S.

Silk Stockings. Musical by COLE PORTER, 1955, based on the film *Ninotchka.* The heroine is a young Soviet woman

The longest notated silence is the five-bar rest in the score of THE SORCERER'S APPRENTICE by PAUL DUKAS. GYÖRGY LIGETI composed a work consisting entirely of a quarter-note rest.

who is sent to Paris on a cultural mission but becomes involved in the bourgeois ways of life and love. She is spirited back to Russia by three grim Soviet commissars, but her American lover eventually brings her back to Paris.

The anti-Soviet jokes involve a U.S.S.R. agent who, when told that SERGEI PROKOFIEV has died, is puzzled: "I didn't even know he was arrested." The agent carries with him the book *Who's Still Who.* The best anti-Soviet song is *Siberia,* but *All of You* is also memorable.

PEOPLE IN MUSIC

Sills, Beverly (born Belle Miriam Silverman), celebrated American soprano and operatic administrator; b. N.Y., May 25, 1929. Sills's father was an insurance salesman from Rumania and her mother a rather musical person from Odessa. At the age of three Beverly appeared on the radio with the nickname Bubbles, and won a prize at a Brooklyn contest as the most beautiful baby of 1932. From this auspicious beginning she performed in television, radio, film, and commercials.

Sills began formal vocal studies with Estelle Liebling when she was seven. She also studied piano with Paolo Gallico. In 1947 she made her operatic debut as Frasquita in *CARMEN* with the Philadelphia Civic Opera, then toured with several opera companies. She sang with the San Francisco (1953) and N.Y. City (1955) Operas, quickly establishing herself at the latter as one of its most valuable members.

Sills extended her repertoire to embrace modern American operas, including the title role of DOUGLAS MOORE's *THE BALLAD OF BABY DOE.* She also sang in the American premiere of LUIGI NONO's *INTOLLERANZA 1960.* She appeared at the Vienna State Opera and in Buenos Aires in 1967, at La Scala in Milan in 1969, and at Covent Garden in London and the Deutsche Oper in Berlin in 1970.

Sills made her first appearance with the Metropolitan Opera as Donna Anna in a concert production of *DON GIOVANNI* on July 8, 1966, at the Lewisohn Stadium in N.Y. Her formal debut with the Metropolitan took place at Lincoln Center in N.Y. as Pamira in *LE SIÈGE DE CORINTHE* in 1975.

At the height of her career, Sills received well-nigh universal praise, not only for the excellence of her voice and her virtuosity in BEL CANTO COLORATURA parts, but also for her intelligence and learning. She became general director of the N.Y. City Opera in 1979 and made her farewell performance as a singer in 1980.

During her tenure as director with the N.Y. City Opera, she both promoted American musicians and broadened the operatic repertoire. She retired in 1988. She also produced related television shows.

In her personal life, Sills suffered a double tragedy: one of her two children was born deaf, and the other mentally retarded. In 1972 she accepted the national chairmanship of the Mothers' March on Birth Defects.

Sills received honorary doctorates from Harvard University, N.Y. University, and the California Institute of the Arts. In 1971, she was the subject of a cover story in *Time.* In 1980 she was awarded the U.S. Presidential Medal of Freedom. In 1998 she was inducted into the National Women's Hall of Fame.

Sills's most notable roles included Cleopatra in GEORGE FRIDERIC HANDEL's *GIULIO CESARE,* Lucia, Elisabeth in *ROBERTO DEVEREUX,* Anna Bolena, Elvira in *I PURITANI,* and Maria Stuarda.

Simon, Paul, popular American singer, guitarist, and songwriter; b. Newark, N.J., Oct. 13, 1941. While in high school in N.Y., he got together with ART GARFUNKEL. As Tom and Jerry, they recorded Simon's ROCK 'N' ROLL song *Hey, Schoolgirl* in 1957, and appeared on Dick Clark's *American Bandstand* television show. Simon then studied English literature at Queens College at the City University of N.Y., and also was active as a promoter and songwriter for various N.Y. music publishers.

After appearing in N.Y. clubs, Simon teamed up with Garfunkel again in the early '60s. Now performing as Simon and Garfunkel, the two brought out the album *Wednesday Morning 3 A.M.* in 1964, which included the song *The Sounds of Silence.* Unknown to either performer, their record label added bass and drums to the song, and it became a hit single in 1965. In 1966 they brought out an album entitled *The Sound of Silence,* which secured their reputation. Among subsequent albums were *The Graduate* (1968; from the film of the same title; includes the hit song

PEOPLE IN MUSIC

Mrs. Robinson), *Bookends* (1968), and *Bridge over Troubled Water* (1970).

Personal differences led the duo to breakup in 1970. Simon followed with a varied solo career through the '70s. He became interested in Latin and other exotic musical rhythms, exhibited in his 1972 hit *Me and Julio down by the Schoolyard*, a playful reminiscence of growing up in N.Y. *Fifty Ways to Leave Your Lover* (1975) was his first No. 1 hit as a soloist. However, Simon's ambitions to extend his creativity into moviemaking, by writing and starring in the 1980 film *One Trick Pony*, was a disaster, leading to a re-evaluation of his career.

During the '80s, Simon struggled to regain his popularity. Then, in mid-decade, he heard some popular music from South Africa. Intrigued, he visited the country and began improvising with the musicians there. The result was the very successful and highly influential 1986 album, *Graceland*. It produced numerous hits and was a critical triumph for Simon.

Simon followed *Graceland* with another mix of traditional music and his own introspective lyrics on the 1990 album *Rhythms of the Saints*. This time, he collaborated with South American musicians. The sound was less buoyant than *Graceland*, but the album was a critical, if not commercial, success.

Simon once again tried his hand at combining drama and music. This time he collaborated with poet Derek Walcott on a Broadway musical, *The Capeman*. It was based on the troubled life of a teenage Puerto Rican gang leader in N.Y., Salvador "The Capeman" Agron. Agron, having been convicted in 1959 for the merciless killing of two teenage boys, was sentenced to death at the age of 16 (but eventually reprieved and freed). After a rocky period of development, the musical opened on Broadway in 1998. Although the music was widely praised, the show was criticized for its lack of dramatic impact and its subject matter, and it quickly closed.

Simon Boccanegra. Opera by GIUSEPPE VERDI, 1857, premiered in Venice. Boccanegra (black mouth) was a historical Doge of Genoa in the 14th century. In the opera, Boccanegra lives with the memory of a daughter he had by a Genoese noblewoman. The mistress is now deceased, and the child has disappeared.

Many years elapse, during which time Simon's daughter has been raised by her grandfather. Her romance with a young patrician is temporarily thwarted by a jealous rival. The true identities and relationships between grandfather, father, and daughter/granddaughter are disclosed in the last act. Before his death from poison, Boccanegra proclaims his daughter's lover as the new Doge.

Phillip Joll and Nuccia Focile in Simon Boccanegra, 1997. (Robbie Jack/Corbis)

The opera, although less significant than Verdi's masterpieces, nevertheless retains a hold on the major opera houses.

Simone, Nina (born Eunice Kathleen Waymon), African-American JAZZ singer, keyboardist, and composer; b. Tryon, N.C., Feb. 21, 1933. After completing her high school training, Simone's hometown residents raised the money to send her to the Juilliard School of Music in N.Y., where she studied piano and theory with Carl Friedberg. She then continued her studies with Vladimir Sokoloff at the Curtis Institute of Music in Philadelphia.

In 1954 Simone began singing at an Atlantic City, New Jersey, nightclub and subsequently devoted herself to popular music genres, appearing as a jazz, pop, and soul artist. In 1959 she had her first hit with a cover of *I Love You Porgy* from GEORGE GERSHWIN'S *PORGY AND BESS*.

PEOPLE IN MUSIC

Simone's early '60s hits had a more funky feeling, particularly the popular *I Put A Spell On You,* a cover of the Screamin' Jay Hawkins classic. She has always been more popular in Britain and France, and by the end of the decade settled in the latter country.

Simone continues to be active in Europe. She has also composed instrumental music and over 50 songs.

Sinatra, Frank (Francis Albert), phenomenally popular American singer and actor. b. Hoboken, N.J., Dec. 12, 1915, d. Los Angeles, May 14, 1998. Sinatra had no training as a singer and could not read music. After singing in a school glee club and on amateur radio shows, he appeared on N.Y. radio shows.

In 1939 Sinatra became a singer with the popular band lead by HARRY JAMES and then gained fame as a vocalist with TOMMY DORSEY from 1940 to 1942. Sinatra's popularity—particularly with young female fans—led him to embark on a solo career. His famous appearances at N.Y.'s Paramount Theater in the mid-'40s attracted mobs of teenagers, making him an instant star. He was invited to Hollywood, where he quickly appeared in a number of dramatic and musical films.

However, Sinatra's initial popularity was short-lived. He went through a dry period both in films and as a singer. In 1952 he revealed an unexpected dramatic talent as an actor, eliciting praise from astonished cinema critics and an Academy Award for his appearance in *From Here to Eternity.* Other successful films followed (*Guys and Dolls, The Manchurian Candidate*).

Along with his renewed success as an actor, Sinatra found new inspiration as a singer. He teamed up with arranger Nelson Riddle to produce a series of classic albums. Sinatra found new expressiveness in a series of recordings that showed him to be a master of the American popular song.

Also in the 1950s, Sinatra established himself as a leading performer in Las Vegas. His ability to "pack 'em in" at the casinos made him a regular attraction in town for decades. His successful association with the casino management led some to speculate about his friendship with mobsters, many of whom were intimately involved in the Vegas phenomenon.

PEOPLE IN MUSIC

Sinatra's press agents were quick to exploit the phenomenon, dubbing him "Swoonlight Sinatra."

Sinatra managed to make yet another comeback at the height of the ROCK 'N' ROLL era in 1967. He scored two hits: *Strangers in the Night* and *Something Stupid,* a duet with his daughter Nancy (who had her own hit at the time with the gutsy *These Boots Are Made for Walkin'*).

Sinatra continued to record and tour through the '70s, '80s, and into the '90s. However, his declining health led to his retirement in 1995. His death was mourned the world over.

sine tone (wave). The sound (and its visual correlate) of one pure FREQUENCY. The FLUTE is the acoustic instrument most able to produce this kind of sound wave.

sinfonia (It.). 1. A SYMPHONY, especially in the 18th century. 2. Within larger vocal works, an OVERTURE.

sin-fōh-nē′ăh

sinfonia concertante (It.). *See* SYMPHONIE CONCERTANTE.

sinfonietta (It., little symphony). A smaller-scale SYMPHONY, sometimes for chamber orchestra.

sin-fōh-nē-ĕt′ah

Singakademie. An historically important musical institution organized in Berlin in 1791 to present concerts of vocal music. In 1829 FELIX MENDELSSOHN conducted a performance there of JOHANN SEBASTIAN BACH's *St. Matthew Passion* that greatly contributed to the renewed appreciation of Bach's music.

singing. The repetitive emission of sound energy in a sequence of melodious TONES. It is the most natural vocal action of humans, birds, and some marine animals such as whales. When the witty Austrian tenor Leo Slezak was asked how early he began studying voice, he replied, "I vocalized the chromatic scale when I was six months of age."

The organ that produces the melodious sounds within a definite range is the voice box in the larynx. The impulse to sing (or to speak) is generated in the muscles of the diaphragm, which pushes air upwards into the lungs, and from there into the larynx and the vocal cords, which are set in periodical vibrations.

The ability of a trained singer to produce sounds of tonal purity and definite PITCH constitutes the art of singing. Because a singer needs no instrument outside his or her own body upon which to practice, voice training requires nothing more than the control of the vocal cords and the propulsion of air from the lungs. It is, however, no easy task.

The range of the singing voice is usually not more than 30 tones, but these tones can be modulated in an extraordinary versatility of tonal inflections and dynamic nuances. A professional singer is able to project the voice with great subtlety in degrees of power ranging from the faintest PIANISSIMO to thundering FORTISSIMO.

Because the Roman Catholic church frowned on women being heard in church (or any other public arena), prepubescent boys and specially trained male singers were required to perform the higher vocal parts. The barbarous practice of creating CASTRATO singers kept adult male voices artificially high for a lifetime, permitting the singing of male soprano and alto roles in opera and church. Fortunately the practice began to disappear as women gained the right to act in public, so that even by WOLFGANG AMADEUS MOZART's day the castrato was a rarity. The practice did continue in the Roman Catholic church until the mid-19th century, with the last castrato dying in the early 20th century.

During the so-called Golden Age of opera, the concept of proper singing was limited to the BEL CANTO of Italian singing, but even the gondoliers of Venice knew how to sing *O SOLE MIO* with the inflections of a Caruso. Italians and non-Italians strove for perfection in opera companies all over the world, from Italy to Russia, England, the U.S., and South America. But as late ROMANTIC vocal writing made new demands of range and endurance on singers, the bel canto ideal fell by the wayside, not to be revived until after the Second World War.

In works by AVANT-GARDE composers, singers are given parts requiring the production of all kinds of physiological sounds, such as howling, shrieking, hissing, grunting, moaning, buzzing, gurgling, chuckling, and coughing. There are even individuals who can sing upon both inhaling and exhaling (CIRCULAR BREATHING), so that it becomes possible to sustain a note indefinitely. Finally, there are those who can sing through the nose.

A widely used special technique is SPRECHSTIMME, which preserves the inflection upward or downward but does not require precise pitch.

Singin' in the Rain. Song by Nacio Herb Brown and Arthur Freed, 1929. It first appeared in the screen musical *Hollywood Revue.* JUDY GARLAND revived it successfully in another film musical, *Little Nellie Kelly* (1940).

The song most famously inspired the musical film *Singin' in the Rain* (which included many earlier Brown and Freed songs). In it, GENE KELLY and his umbrella did their unforgettable dance to the song.

Gene Kelly dancing in the famous rain scene in the film, Singin' in the Rain, *1952. (UPI/Corbis-Bettmann)*

single reed. A thin piece of wood, cane, or other material attached securely to an aperture at one end of a single-reed WOODWIND instrument. It provides the necessary vibration to start the flow of air through the instrument, supplied by the player through the MOUTHPIECE. The PITCH heard is determined by the FINGERING used.

MUSICAL INSTRUMENT

Singspiel (Ger.). From a literary viewpoint, a theatrical piece, usually lighthearted, with added musical numbers. The German Singspiel developed and was particularly popular in the 18th century (WOLFGANG AMADEUS MOZART wrote four of them, including *THE MAGIC FLUTE*).

From a musical viewpoint, the difference between the Singspiel and a full-fledged opera lies in the use of spoken

zing^k'shpēl

dialogue (as opposed to RECITATIVE), but this distinction became less pronounced when purely operatic works began admitting dialogue as part of the action. Many features of the Singspiel were adopted in German ROMANTIC opera.

PEOPLE IN MUSIC

Sissle, Noble (Lee), African-American singer, bandleader, lyricist, and composer; b. Indianapolis, July 10, 1889; d. Tampa, Dec. 17, 1975. Sissle became a singer in Edward Thomas's Male Quartet in 1908 and then in Hann's Jubilee Singers in 1912.

He subsequently attended DePauw University and Butler University. After conducting a hotel orchestra in Indianapolis, he sang with Bob Young's band in Baltimore in 1915, where he met pianist/composer EUBIE BLAKE. The two then worked with James Reese Europe's Society Orchestra in N.Y. Following service as a drum major in the 369th Regimental Infantry Band in France during World War I, Sissle returned to the U.S. and teamed up with Blake as a vaudeville duo in 1919.

After success with their musicals *SHUFFLE ALONG* in 1921 and *Chocolate Dandies* in 1924, they performed in Europe. Sissle remained there to work with his own band and as a solo performer from 1927 until returning to the U.S. to resume his association with Blake in 1933. They then produced the show *Shuffle Along of 1933*.

Sissle was subsequently active with his own bands, making regular appearances at Billy Rose's Diamond Horseshoe in N.Y. from 1938 to 1950. Later he operated his own nightclub, Noble's.

sistrum. An ancient Egyptian IDIOPHONE used in religious ritual, composed of a semicircular metal frame with crossbars overhung with tinkling rings.

MUSICAL
INSTRUMENT

sitar. A classical South Asian stringed instrument with a bowl-shaped body and metal frets, plucked with a PLECTRUM. Like the smaller SAROD, it uses bulbous gourds for resonance and was once a bowed CHORDOPHONE (now rare). Both instruments are played in a sitting position, but the sarod is played like a Western LUTE or GUITAR, while the sitar is held nearly upright.

Sitkovetsky, Dmitry. See DAVIDOVICH, BELLA.

(Sittin' On) The Dock of the Bay. Posthumous No. 1 pop hit for soul singer OTIS REDDING, coauthored with session guitarist Steve Cropper. Redding had died tragically in an airplane crash, along with his backup band, The Bar-Kays, shortly before the song hit the charts.

◀

Sitar player from Sri Lanka. (David Burckhalter)

Six Epigraphes antiques. Pieces for piano four-hands by CLAUDE DEBUSSY, 1917. The composer and Jean Roger-Ducasse premiered the work in Paris. The *Epigraphes* were later orchestrated by ERNEST ANSERMET. Debussy always felt an affinity with ancient Greek prosody, and these pieces are instances of his Grecian moods.

Six, Les. A group of younger French composers, first called *Les Nouveaux Jeunes* (The new youth) who formed a loose concert-giving alliance in the years just after World War I. Although dissimilar in musical personality and aesthetic, the composers (GEORGES AURIC, Louis Durey, ARTHUR HONEGGER, DARIUS MILHAUD, FRANCIS POULENC, and GERMAINE TAILLEFERRE) shared an anti-romantic attitude typical of the era. Les Six was sustained, at least in the public eye, by its connections to ERIK SATIE and Jean Cocteau who, as the apostles of this age of disenchantment, preached the new values of urban culture, with modern America as a model.

Most of Les Six wrote in a NEOCLASSICAL style and had resolutely unmonumental artistic goals. But Durey, an

PEOPLE IN MUSIC

avowed Communist, was the first to reject this lack of "seriousness." The five remaining members stayed around long enough to contribute incidental music to Cocteau's play *Les Mariés de la Tour Eiffel* in 1921. However, the group soon faded from the scene as individuals pursued their own destinies.

Sixteen Tons. MERLE HAGGARD song that became a No. 1, finger-snapping hit for TENNESSEE ERNIE FORD in 1955. It described the hard life and poor working conditions of Southern coal miners.

Skalkottas, Nikos (Nikolaos), greatly talented Greek composer; b. Chalkis, island of Euboea, March 8, 1904; d. Athens, Sept. 19, 1949. Skalkottas studied violin with his father and his uncle at the Athens Conservatory from 1914 to 1920. In 1921 he went to Berlin, where he continued his violin studies at the Hochschule für Musik until 1923, then took lessons in theory with Philipp Jarnach from 1925 to 1927.

But the greatest influence on Skalkottas's creative life was ARNOLD SCHOENBERG, with whom he studied in Berlin from 1927 to 1931. Skalkottas eagerly absorbed Schoenberg's instruction in the method of 12-TONE composition, but in his own music applied it in a very individual manner, without trying to imitate Schoenberg's style. In Berlin, Skalkottas also received some suggestions in free composition from KURT WEILL.

In the early '30s Skalkottas returned to Athens and earned his living by playing violin in local orchestras but continued to compose diligently, until his early death from a strangulated hernia. His music written between 1928 and 1938 reflects Schoenberg's style. Later works are tonally conceived, and several use traditional Greek MODES, set in the typical asymmetric meters of Balkan FOLK music.

After his death, a Skalkottas Society was formed in Athens to promote performances and publications of his works. About 110 scores of various genres are kept in the Skalkottas Archives in Athens, many of which received only posthumous premieres.

The song was satirized by Mickey Katz in *Sixteen Tons (of Kosher Salami)*.

PEOPLE IN MUSIC

Schoenberg, in his book *Style and Idea*, refers to Skalkottas as one of his most gifted students.

skiffle. A British popular music style, popular in the 1950s. These bands were formed around often homemade and easy-to-play instruments, such as washboard, kazoo, harmonica, and washtub bass. While its goal was a more acoustic, less electrified sound, many of the performers were JAZZ musicians and future rock 'n' rollers. Others became leaders of the 1960s "British invasion," such as the BEATLES.

skip. Melodic progression by an INTERVAL wider than a SECOND. A DISJUNCT progression.

skomorokhis (Russ.). MINSTRELS who provided entertainment for the Russian court and aristocracy up to the 18th century. They cultivated versatile talents as singers, actors, and acrobats.

Skriabin, Alexander (Nikolaievich). *See* SCRIABIN, ALEXANDER (NIKOLAIEVICH).

Skyscrapers. Ballet by JOHN ALDEN CARPENTER, 1926, first performed in N.Y. This was the first theatrical work inspired exclusively by the American urban landscape. Elements of JAZZ are much in evidence.

slap-bass. The manner of playing on the double bass by slapping the strings with the palm of the right hand for rhythmic effect. It is associated almost exclusively with JAZZ and funk styles.

Slatkin, Leonard (Edward), prominent American conductor; b. Los Angeles, Sept. 1, 1944. His father was Felix Slatkin (b. St. Louis, Dec. 22, 1915; d. Los Angeles, Feb. 8, 1963), a violinist and conductor who played with the St. Louis Symphony Orchestra from 1931 to 1937 and a founding member of the Hollywood String Quartet from 1947 to 1961.

Leonard studied violin, viola, piano, and conducting in his youth. After briefly attending Indiana University and Los Angeles City College, he studied with Walter Susskind at the Aspen Music School in 1964. He then studied conducting

PEOPLE IN MUSIC

with Jean Morel at the Juilliard School of Music in N.Y., earning his bachelor of music degree in 1968.

In 1968 Slatkin joined the St. Louis Symphony Orchestra as assistant conductor to Susskind and was successively named associate conductor in 1971, associate principal conductor in 1974, and principal guest conductor in 1975. He made his European debut in London as a guest conductor with the Royal Philharmonic in 1974.

Slatkin was music advisor of the New Orleans Philharmonic from 1977 to 1980, and also music director of the Minnesota Orchestra summer concerts beginning in 1979. In 1979 he became music director of the St. Louis Symphony Orchestra. He took it on a major European tour in 1985. In 1990 he also became music director of the Great Woods Performing Arts Center in Mansfield, Massachusetts, the summer home of the Pittsburgh Symphony Orchestra. A year later, he was given a similar position at the Blossom Music Center (Cuyahoga Falls, Ohio), the summer home of the Cleveland Orchestra.

Slatkin appeared widely as a guest conductor, both in North America and Europe, demonstrating particular affinity for works of the 19th and 20th centuries. In 1996 he became music director of the National Symphony Orchestra in Washington, D.C.

Dvořák also arranged them for two pianos.

Slavonic Dances. Two sets of orchestral dances by ANTONÍN DVOŘÁK, 1878 and 1886 (opp. 46 and 72). These dances are not mere transcriptions or inventions based on authentic Slavonic tunes but original creations in the manner of Slavic FOLK songs. The melodies employ Ukrainian, Serbian, Polish, and, of course, Czech rhythms.

Sleeping Beauty, The. Ballet by PIOTR ILYICH TCHAIKOVSKY, 1890, first performed in St. Petersburg. The scenario is taken from a classical fairy tale.

An evil fairy, scorned at the royal court, dooms a young princess to die when she comes of age. But a good fairy transforms the seeming death into a deep sleep, from which the princess awakens when a prince charming, providentially named Desire, kisses her.

The score is one of Tchaikovsky's most poetic creations. Particularly popular is the *Waltz.* A SUITE of five numbers was drawn from the score.

sleighbells. Small round bells traditionally attached to the harness of a horse drawing a sleigh. Now a similarly constructed IDIOPHONE (horse and sleigh not required).

Vulia Makhalina dancing in a 1993 production of Sleeping Beauty. *(Robbie Jack/Corbis)*

Some modern scores use sleighbells, including EDGARD VARÈSE's *Ionisation* and GUSTAV MAHLER's Fourth Symphony.

Sleigh Ride. Rollicking orchestral novelty by LEROY ANDERSON, 1950, which attained great success.

slendro. One of two GAMELAN scale types (the other is PELOG). Slendro is a family of PENTATONIC scales.

slide. 1. The movable U-shaped tube that fits inside the stationary tubing of the TROMBONE. By extending or shortening the composite tube, one lowers or raises the PITCH. 2. In the ORGAN, a SLIDER. 3. Three or four swiftly ascending or descending SCALE TONES. 4. On a VIOLIN bow, that part of the nut that slides along the stick. 5. Obsolete term for TRILL.

MUSICAL INSTRUMENT

slide horn, trombone, or **trumpet.** A brass instrument that uses a slide instead of KEYS or VALVES. In return, there is the *valve trombone* used in bands, where the slide is replaced by valves.

MUSICAL INSTRUMENT

Large, ornamental slit drums from Borneo. (Smithsonian Institution)

slider. A mechanism in the OR-GAN that admits air into different pipes. In this way, the player can control from the keyboard the number of pipes sounding for each note.

slit drum (Ger. *Schlitztrommel;* Fr. *tambour de bois*). A wooden tube of varying size used for centuries among the peoples of central Africa and Australia, often mistakenly called a DRUM or GONG.

The earliest examples were huge hollowed-out tree trunks placed over pits and stamped on. In later manifestations the trunk was hollowed out through a longitudinal slit, struck by beaters, and sometimes placed on a stand. It is similar to the *teponaztli* of South America.

Instruments have gradually grown smaller, even portable, and the number of slits has been increased to provide more PITCHES. Commercial versions for children's use are now commonplace. In some areas the slit drum has served as a method of communication: simple messages can be transmitted through rhythmic beats carrying the tidings of danger, joy, death, or war.

Slonimsky, Nicolas (actually, Nikolai Leonidovich), legendary Russian-born American musicologist; b. St. Petersburg, April 27, 1894; d. Los Angeles, Dec. 25, 1995. Slonimsky was given his first piano lesson in 1900 by his famous maternal aunt Isabelle Vengerova (b. Minsk, March 1, 1877; d. N.Y., Feb. 7, 1956). She later became a well-known piano teacher after settling in America.

Some modern composers, among them CARL ORFF and KARLHEINZ STOCKHAUSEN, have made use of slit drums in their compositions.

PEOPLE IN MUSIC

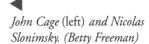
John Cage (left) *and Nicolas Slonimsky. (Betty Freeman)*

Slonimsky enrolled in the St. Petersburg Conservatory and studied harmony and orchestration with two pupils of NIKOLAI RIMSKY-KORSAKOV. He also tried unsuccessfully to engage in Russian journalism. After the Revolution he made his way south. He was a rehearsal pianist at the Kiev Opera, where he took composition lessons with RHEINHOLD GLIÈRE in 1919. In 1920 he was in Yalta, where he earned his living as a piano accompanist to displaced Russian singers and as an instructor at the dilapidated Yalta Conservatory.

Slonimsky then proceeded to Turkey, Bulgaria, and Paris, where he became secretary to the well-known Russian conductor SERGE KOUSSEVITZKY. In 1923 he went to the U.S. He became an opera coach at the Eastman School of Music in Rochester, N.Y., where he took an opportunity to study composition with the visiting professor Selim Palmgren, and conducting with ALBERT COATES. In 1925 he was again working for Koussevitzky in Paris and Boston, but was fired in 1927.

Slonimsky began writing music articles for the *Boston Evening Transcript* and the *Christian Science Monitor* and ran a monthly column of musical anecdotes of questionable authenticity in *Étude*. He taught theory at the Malkin Conservatory in Boston and at the Boston Conservatory. He also conducted the Pierian Sodality at Harvard University from 1927 to 1929 and the Apollo Chorus from 1928 to 1930.

In 1927 Slonimsky organized the Chamber Orchestra of Boston with the purpose of presenting modern works. With it he gave first performances of works by CHARLES IVES, EDGARD VARÈSE, HENRY COWELL, and others. He became a naturalized U.S. citizen in 1931. In 1931–32 he conducted special concerts of modern American, Cuban, and Mexican music in Paris, Berlin, and Budapest under the auspices of the Pan-American Association of Composers, producing a ripple of excitement. He repeated these programs at his engagements with the Los Angeles Philharmonic in 1932 and at the Hollywood Bowl in 1933. The poor audience reaction to the modern music he played at the Bowl led Slonimsky to abandon his conducting career.

From 1945 to 1947 he was by happenstance a lecturer in Slavonic languages and literatures at Harvard University (the head of the department had died of a heart attack). He also began his career as a compiler of music dictionaries in the '40s.

In 1962–63 Slonimsky traveled in Russia, Poland, Yugoslavia, Bulgaria, Rumania, Greece, and Israel under the auspices of the Office of Cultural Exchange at the U.S. State Department. Returning from his multinational travels, he taught variegated musical subjects at the University of California, Los Angeles, from 1964 to 1967.

As a composer Slonimsky cultivated miniature forms, usually with a gimmick: *Studies in Black and White* for piano (1928) in "mutually exclusive consonant counterpoint," a song cycle, *Gravestones,* to texts from tombstones in an old cemetery in Hancock, New Hampshire (1945), and *Minitudes,* a collection of 50 short piano pieces (1971–77). His orchestral work *My Toy Balloon* (1942), a set of variations on a Brazilian song, includes in the score 100 colored balloons to be exploded *fff* at the climax.

Slonimsky also conjured up a *Möbius Strip-Tease,* a perpetual vocal CANON notated on a Möbius band to be revolved around the singer's head. It had its first and last performance at the Arrière-Garde Coffee Concert at the University of California, Los Angeles, with the composer officiating at the piano, in 1965.

Among his vocal works, Slonimsky is best remembered for writing a series of mock-serious songs, using as his texts advertisements that appeared in the *Saturday Evening Post.* These included *Make This a Day of Pepsodent, No More Shiny Nose,* and *Children Cry for Castoria,* all composed in 1925.

More scholarly, though no less defiant of academic conventions, is his *Thesaurus of Scales and Melodic Patterns* published in 1947. It is an inventory of all conceivable and inconceivable tonal combinations, culminating in a mindboggling "grandmother chord" containing 12 different tones and 11 different INTERVALS. He also published *Music Since 1900,* a chronology of musical events (N.Y., 1937; fifth edition, 1994).

In addition, Slonimsky took over the vacated editorship (because of the predecessor's sudden death) of *Thompson's International Cyclopedia of Music and Musicians* (fourth–eighth editions, 1946–58). He accepted the editorship of the fifth through eighth editions of the prestigious *Baker's Biographical Dictionary of Musicians* (1958, 1978, 1984, 1991). He also wrote a collection of musical anecdotes, an early book on Latin American music, a general music dictionary, and an autobiography.

Slonimsky died at the venerable age of 101 years in 1995.

Slonimsky took pride in claiming to have written the first singing commercials—although his songs could hardly have been seriously used as advertising jingles.

slur. A curved line under or over two or more notes, signifying that they are to be played LEGATO.

In bowed string music the slur signifies a group to be played on one bow; in vocal music the slur unites notes to be sung in one breath; the notes so sung are also called a slur. In piano writing, a slur can indicate the extension of a musical PHRASE, often suggesting a slight CRESCENDO followed by a corresponding DIMINUENDO. *See also* TIE.

Slurred melody, one in which two or more tones are sung to one syllable; opposed to SYLLABIC MELODY.

Smetana, Bedřich, great Bohemian composer; b. Leitomischl, March 2, 1824; d. Prague, May 12, 1884. Smetana's talent manifested itself very early. Although his father had misgivings about music as a profession, he taught his son violin. Smetana also had piano lessons with a local teacher, making his first public appearance at the age of six.

After the family moved to Jindřichův Hradec in 1831, Smetana studied with the organist František Ikavec. He then continued his academic studies in Jihlava and Německý Brod, after which he entered the Classical Grammar School in Prague in 1839. He also had piano lessons with Jan Batka and led a string quartet for which he composed several works.

Bedřich Smetana. (New York Public Library)

Smetana's lack of application to his academic studies led his father to send him to the gymnasium in Plzeň, but he soon devoted himself to giving concerts and composing. He met a friend from his school days there, Kateřina Kolářová, whom he followed to Prague in 1843. He was accepted as a theory pupil of Kolářová's piano teacher, Josef Proksch, at the Music Institute. To pay for his lessons, Smetana was recommended by Bedřich Kittl, director of the Prague Conservatory, for the position of music teacher to the family of Count Leopold Thun. He took up his position in January 1844 and for three and a half years worked earnestly in the count's service. He also continued to compose.

Bent on making a name for himself as a concert pianist, Smetana left the count's service in the summer of 1847 and planned a tour of Bohemia. However, his only concert in Plzeň proved such a financial disaster that he returned to Prague, where he eked out a meager existence. He wrote to FRANZ LISZT, asking him to find a publisher for his op.1, the *6 Characteristic Pieces* for piano. Liszt was impressed with the score, accepted Smetana's dedication, and found a publisher. In 1848 Smetana established a successful piano school, and a year later he married Kolářová. In 1850 he became court pianist to the abdicated Emperor Ferdinand.

Smetana's reputation as a pianist grew, especially as an interpreter of FRÉDÉRIC CHOPIN, but his compositions made little impression. The death of his children and the poor health of his wife (who had tuberculosis) affected him deeply. He set out for Sweden in 1856, giving a number of successful piano recitals in Göteborg, where he remained. He soon opened his own school and became active as a choral conductor. His wife joined him in 1857, but the cold climate worsened her condition. When her health declined, they decided to return to Prague in 1859, but she died en route, in Dresden, on April 19. Stricken with grief, Smetana returned to Göteborg. Before his wife's death, he had composed the symphonic poems *Richard III* and *Valdštýnv tabor* (Wallenstein's camp). He now began work on a third, *Hakan Jarl.*

During Smetana's sojourn in Sweden, Austria granted political autonomy to Bohemia, and musicians and poets of the rising generation sought to establish an authentic Bohemian voice in the arts. Agitation arose for building a national theater in Prague. Although earlier attempts to write operas in a Bohemian vein had been made by such composers as František Škroup and Jiří Macourek, their works were undistinguished.

Smetana believed the time was ripe for him to make his mark in Prague, and he returned there in May 1861. However, when the Provisional Theater opened in late 1862, its administration proved sadly unimaginative. Smetana contented himself with the conductorship of the Hlahol Choral Society, teaching, and writing music criticism. In his articles he condemned the poor musical standards prevailing at the Provisional Theater. In 1862–63 he composed his first OPERA, *Braniboři v Čechách* (The Brandenburgers in Bohemia), conducting its successful premiere at the Provisional Theater in early 1866. His next opera, THE BARTERED BRIDE *(Prodaná nevěsta),* proved a failure at its premiere under his direction later that year, but eventually it was accorded a niche in the operatic repertoire at home and abroad.

Smetana became conductor of the Provisional Theater in 1866. He immediately set out to reform its administration and to raise its musical standards. For the cornerstone laying of the National Theater on May 16, 1868, he conducted the first performance of his tragic opera DALIBOR. It was criticized as an attempt to introduce elements of RICHARD WAGNER's style into the Bohemian national opera. In 1871, when there was talk of crowning Emperor Franz Josef as King of Bohemia, Smetana considered producing his opera *Libuše* for the festivities. No coronation took place, however, and the work was withheld.

Hoping for a popular success, Smetana composed the comic opera *Dvě vdovy* (The two widows) in 1874. Smetana's success, however, was short-lived. By the autumn of 1874 he was deaf and had to resign as conductor of the Provisional Theater. In spite of the bitter years to follow, marked by increasingly poor health, family problems, and financial hardship, he continued to compose. Between 1874 and 1879 he produced his six orchestral masterpieces collectively known as MÁ VLAST (My country).

From 1876 dates his famous String Quartet in E minor, subtitled *Z mého života* (From my life), which he described as a "remembrance of my life and the catastrophe of complete deafness." His opera *Hubička* (The kiss) was successfully premiered in Prague later that year. It was followed by the opera *Tajemství* (The secret), which was heard for the first time in fall 1878.

For the opening of the new National Theater in Prague on June 11, 1881, Smetana's opera *Libuše* was finally given its premiere performance. The ailing composer attended the opening night and was accorded sustained applause. His last opera, *Čertova stěna* (The devil's wall), was a failure at its first hearing in Prague in fall 1882.

By this time Smetana's health had been completely undermined by the ravages of syphilis, the cause of his deafness. His mind eventually gave way, and he was confined to an asylum. At his death in 1884 the nation was plunged into a state of mourning. The funeral cortège passed the National Theater as Smetana was carried to his final resting place in the Vyšehrad cemetery.

Smetana was the founder of the Czech national school of composition, and it was through his efforts that Czech national opera came of age. Although the national element is predominant in much of his music, a highly personal style of expression is found in his String Quartet No. 1 and in many of his piano pieces.

Outside his homeland, Smetana remains best known for THE BARTERED BRIDE, MÁ VLAST, and the his String Quartet No. 1. In addition, he contributed many works, mostly secular, to the well-established Czech choral tradition. He also composed a second string quartet (1882–83), a piano trio (1855), and numerous smaller-scale piano pieces.

Smiles. Song by Lee Robert, 1917, written to cheer up American soldiers in military camps. It sold over three million copies of sheet music and was added to numerous movie musicals as a theme song.

Smith, Bessie (Elizabeth), beloved African-American BLUES, JAZZ, and VAUDEVILLE singer, frequently and accurately billed as the "Empress of the Blues"; b. Chattanooga, Tenn., April 15, 1894; d. Clarksville, Miss., Sept. 26, 1937. Born into a wretchedly poor family, she joined Rainey's Rabbit Foot Minstrels (blues pioneer MA RAINEY was her teacher) in 1912 and developed a style of singing that rapidly brought her fame.

PEOPLE IN MUSIC

Smith's first record, *Down Hearted Blues,* sold 800,000 copies in 1923. In all, she made over 200 recordings through the early '30s. She also appeared in the film *St. Louis Blues* in 1929. Her last years were marred by alcoholism.

Although not as popular as she once was, Smith continued to tour through the '30s. She died from injuries sus-

Bessie Smith, c. 1923. (Benson Collection) ▶

tained in an automobile accident near Coahana, Mississippi, after performing. A great deal of controversy has surrounded her death; some say that she was refused admission to a nearby white hospital, and so bled to death. The documentary evidence is incomplete.

Smith was a large, impressive woman—5 feet 9 inches tall, and weighing over 200 pounds—with a powerful voice to match. The excellence of her voice, along with her natural expressive qualities and improvisatory abilities, combined to make her the consummate blues singer of her time.

Smith, Gregg, American conductor and composer; b. Chicago, Ill., Aug. 21, 1931. Smith studied composition with Leonard Stein, LUKAS FOSS, and Ray Moreman, and conducting with Fritz Zweig at the University of California, Los Angeles, earning his M.A. degree in 1956.

In 1955 in Los Angeles, Smith founded the Gregg Smith Singers, a chamber choir, with which he toured and recorded extensively. From 1970 he was active with them in N.Y. He also taught at Ithaca College, State University of N.Y. at Stony Brook, Peabody Conservatory of Music in Baltimore, Barnard College, and the Manhattan School of Music in N.Y.

Smith's repertoire extends from EARLY MUSIC to contemporary American scores. He composed much vocal music,

PEOPLE IN MUSIC

including two operas, choral works, songs, and pieces for chamber orchestra.

Smith, John Stafford. *See* STAR-SPANGLED BANNER, THE.

Smith, Kate (Kathryn Elizabeth) famous American singer of popular music; b. Greenville, Va., May 1, 1907; d. Raleigh, N.C., June 17, 1986. As a child, Smith sang in church socials and later for the troops in Army camps in the Washington, D.C., area during World War I.

Although she had no formal training, Smith landed a part in the musical *Honeymoon Lane* in Atlantic City, New Jersey, in 1926, and then appeared in it on Broadway. Subsequently, she sang in the Broadway musicals *Hit the Deck* in 1927 and *Flying High* three years later.

Smith began singing on her own radio show in 1931, opening her first broadcast with *When the Moon Comes over the Mountain,* which thereafter served as her theme song. In 1938 she introduced IRVING BERLIN'S *GOD BLESS AMERICA,* which she immortalized in innumerable subsequent performances.

Thanks to her enormous popularity, Smith raised more money for U.S. War Bonds during World War II than any other artist. She starred in her own television show (1950–55; 1960), and continued to make guest appearances until 1975. President Reagan awarded her the U.S. Medal of Freedom in 1982.

Smith was one of the most successful singers of popular music in her time. During her lengthy career, she made over 15,000 radio broadcasts, introducing over 1,000 songs. She also recorded nearly 3,000 songs.

PEOPLE IN MUSIC

Smith, Willie "the Lion" (William Henry Joseph Bonaparte Bertholoff), remarkable African-American JAZZ pianist and composer; b. Goshen, N.Y., Nov. 24, 1897; d. N.Y., April 18, 1973. Smith attended Howard University in Washington, D.C., and studied music privately with Hans Steinke. After serving in the U.S. Army in World War I, he settled in Harlem, where he established himself as one of the great STRIDE pianists.

PEOPLE IN MUSIC

DUKE ELLINGTON dedicated his *Portrait of a Lion* to Willie "The Lion" Smith.

He toured Europe several times, and Africa in 1949–50. His own compositions (*Fingerbuster, Echoes of Spring, Portrait of the Duke*) had an authenticity that described perfectly the atmosphere of Harlem jazz piano between the two world wars.

Smoke Gets in Your Eyes. Song by JEROME KERN, 1933, from the musical *Roberta.* It was tremendously successful and was incorporated in the film biography of Kern, *Till the Clouds Roll By* in 1946.

PEOPLE IN MUSIC

Smyth, (Dame) **Ethel** (Mary), eminent English composer; b. London, April 22, 1858; d. Woking, Surrey, May 8, 1944. Smyth studied with Carl Reinecke and Salomon Jadassohn at the Leipzig Conservatory in 1877 but soon turned to Heinrich von Herzogenberg for her principal training, following him to Berlin. Her String Quintet was performed in Leipzig in 1884. She returned to London in 1888, where she presented her orchestral Serenade and an overture, *Antony and Cleopatra,* both in 1890.

In 1893 Smyth's prestige as a serious composer rose considerably with the presentation of her MASS for solo voices, chorus, and orchestra at the Albert Hall. After that she devoted her energies to the theater. Her first opera, *Fantasio,* to her own libretto in German, after Alfred de Musset's play, was produced in Weimar in 1898. This was followed in 1902 by *Der Wald,* also to her own German LIBRETTO, first produced in Berlin. It was produced in London in the same year as *The Forest,* and in N.Y. by the Metropolitan Opera a year later.

Smyth's next opera, THE WRECKERS, was her most successful work. Written originally to a French libretto, *Les Naufrageurs,* it was first produced in a German version as *Strandrecht* in Leipzig in 1906. The composer herself translated it into English, and it was staged in London in 1909. The score was revised some years later and produced at Sadler's Wells, London, in 1939.

In addition to various operas, Smyth composed a concerto for violin, horn, and orchestra in 1927 and *The Prison* for soprano, bass chorus, and orchestra, in 1931. Among her other works are two string quartets (1884; 1902–12), Cello

Sonata (1887), Violin Sonata (1887), and two Trios for Violin, Oboe, and Piano (1927). Among her vocal works are many choral pieces, including *Hey Nonny No* for chorus and orchestra (1911) and *Sleepless Dreams* for chorus and orchestra (1912), and songs.

Smyth's music showed strong German characteristics, in the general style and in the treatment of dramatic situations on the stage. At the same time, she was a believer in English national music and its potentialities.

Smyth was a militant leader for women's suffrage in England, for which cause she wrote *The March of the Women* in 1911, the battle song of the suffragettes. After suffrage was granted, her role in the movement was officially acknowledged: in 1922 she was made a Dame Commander of the Order of the British Empire.

Smyth published a number of books in London, mostly autobiographical in nature. She also authored some humorous essays and reminiscences, published as *A Three-Legged Tour in Greece* (1927), *A Final Burning of Boats* (1928), *Female Pipings in Eden* (1934), *Beecham and Pharaoh* (1935), and *Inordinate (?) Affection* (1936).

snare drum (U.K., side drum; Ger. *Schnarrtrommel,* rattle drum; Fr. *caisse à timbre, caisse claire;* It. *cassa chiara*). A smaller cylindrical DRUM of wood or metal, across the lower head of which are stretched several gut strings or strands of metal wire (snares), whose rattling against the head reinforces and alters the tone. The upper head is struck alternately or simultaneously with two drumsticks. This is the most commonly used drum in symphonic bands and scores.

Snow Maiden, The (Snegurotchka). Opera by NIKOLAI RIMSKY-KORSAKOV, 1882, first produced in St. Petersburg. The Snow Maiden is the delicate offspring of incompatible parents, Frost and Spring. At the peril of her life she must not let warmth, physical or emotional, enter her heart.

A young villager is captivated by her icy beauty and follows her wherever she goes. Her mother warns her to keep away from the destructive rays of the sun as summer approaches. She ignores her warnings and melts away like spring snow.

MUSICAL INSTRUMENT

The opera is one of the most poetic productions of the Russian operatic stage, but it is rarely, if ever, staged elsewhere.

Sobre las Olas (Over the waves). Mexican WALTZ by Juventino Rosas, 1888. It became a perennial favorite all over the world.

socialist realism. The official aesthetic of the Soviet Union, which was adopted in 1932.

The former Soviet Union was the first modern state that attempted to regulate its art, literature, drama, and music according to explicitly defined ideological principles. Since the structure of the Soviet government was derived from the doctrine of the dictatorship of the proletariat (the working class), a Russian Association of Proletarian Musicians (RAPM) dictated proper musical forms suitable for the masses. It was disbanded by the Soviet government in 1932 after its failure to help in the creative formulation of mass music became evident.

In terms of music, socialist realism requires the retention of the TONAL system, broadly based on the MODES of Russian FOLK songs and of the other Republics of the Soviet Union. The socialist realists concentrated on the national development of operas and secular ORATORIOS, in which revolutionary ideals can be expressed verbally as well as musically. Patriotic subjects were particularly recommended, and a good overcoming evil scenario was strongly preferred. The *LENINGRAD SYMPHONY* of DMITRI SHOSTAKOVICH is a remarkable example, particularly so because it was written during continued retreats of the Soviet armies before the Nazis, and yet its finale predicts victory.

The party even went so far as to dictate compositions in major tonalities. Anatoly Lunacharsky, first Commissar of Education of the USSR, explained the political advantage of major keys by comparing them with the convictions of the Soviet party, while minor keys reflected the introvert pessimism of their enemies.

In the domain of rhythm, marching time was a natural medium for the optimistic attributes of socialist realism, but it was reserved for its proper position in the FINALE of a symphony or the final chorus of an opera. In this respect social-ist realism merely continued the old tradition of Russian music. Even such melancholy composers as PIOTR ILYICH TCHAIKOVSKY and SERGEI RACHMANINOFF excelled in tri-umphant march-time movements.

The Soviet government, like the Nazis in Germany, thought modern art was decadent, since it tended to empha-size individual expression over mass accessibility. For this reason, official composers like Shostakovich struggled throughout their careers to create worthy art that at the same time would be acceptable to the government.

With the collapse of the Soviet Union, the last major country promoting social realism is China. There, too, the results have been mixed. Operas have been composed in the traditional Chinese style based on uplifting stories of peasant workers, but have gained little lasting popularity. Attempts to add Chinese traditional musical instruments to Western-type orchestras have also been less than successful.

Socrate. Symphonic drama by ERIK SATIE, 1920, for high solo voices and instruments, premiered in Paris. The texts are French translations of excerpts from Plato's dialogues concerning his great teacher, including the description of Socrates's forced suicide.

soft pedal. The left PEDAL on the piano. It reduces and changes the sound by shifting the keyboard so that (1) only two of the three strings for each note (i.e., *course*) in the middle piano register are struck by the hammers; and (2) only one of the two strings of each course in the bass reg-ister are struck. In the 19th century the soft pedal could shift in two stages, with corresponding results.

LUDWIG VAN BEETHOVEN refers to this as *due corde* (two strings) and *una corda* (one string), with the full release of the pedal indicated by *tre corde* (three strings).

soggetto cavato (It., excavated subject). A curious form in which the subject is derived from the letters, syllables, or vowels in a name or other source. B-A-C-H is a typical mod-ern example.

Derived subjects have been used by several modern com-posers applying tonal equivalents for the entire alphabet. MARIO CASTELNUOVO-TEDESCO devised birthday greeting cards in which the name of the recipient was derived by ar-

sŏhd-jet′tōh kăh-văh′tōh

ranging several successive alphabets in English corresponding to the chromatic scale. This method generates melodic patterns at angular INTERVALS.

Soir, Le (The evening). FRANZ JOSEPH HAYDN's Symphony No. 8 in G Major (1761), a sequel to *LE MIDI* (Noontime), his Symphony No. 7. It is sometimes called *La Tempesta,* although the music is not too tempestuous. The evening mood is generally undisturbed.

PEOPLE IN MUSIC

Soler (Ramos), **Antonio** (Francisco Javier José), important Catalan composer and organist; b. Olot, Gerona (baptized), Dec. 3, 1729; d. El Escorial, near Madrid, Dec. 20, 1783. Soler entered the Montserrat monastery choir school in 1736, where his mentors were the maestro Benito Esteve and the organist Beninto Valls. About 1750 he was made maestro de capilla in Lérida, and in 1752 he was ordained a subdeacon.

Soler became a member of the Jeronymite monks in El Escorial in 1752, taking the habit, and then being professed in 1753. He was made maestro de capilla in 1757. He also pursued studies with José de Nebra and DOMENICO SCARLATTI.

Soler was a prolific composer of both sacred and secular vocal music, as well as instrumental music. Among his works are nine MASSES, five REQUIEMS, 60 PSALMS, 13 MAGNIFICATS, 14 litanies, 28 LAMENTATIONS, five MOTETS, and other sacred works. He also composed 132 villancicos (1752–78), 120 keyboard SONATAS, six quintets for string quartet and organ (1776), and *6 conciertos de dos órganos obligados,* liturgical organ pieces. He also wrote several books on music theory.

Soler, Vicente Martin y. *See MARRIAGE OF FIGARO, THE.*

sol-fa. 1. TONIC SOL-FA. 2. SOLMIZATION and the syllables sung in it.

solfège (Fr.; It. *solfeggio*). A vocal exercise either on one vowel, on the SOLMIZATION syllables (SOL-FA), or to words. The term has been expanded to include teachings in EAR TRAINING, vocalization, and a study of CLEFS, METERS, and rhythms.

sōhl-fezh′

solmization. A method of teaching the SCALES and INTER-VALS by syllables, the invention of which is ascribed to GUIDO D'AREZZO. It was based on the hexachord, or six-tone scale. The first six tones of the major scale (C, D, E, F, G, A) were named *Ut, Re, Mi, Fa, Sol, La.* The seventh syllable *Si,* for the leading tone, was added during the 17th century. About the same time, the name *Ut* for C was changed to *Do,* except in France.

solo (It., alone). A piece or passage for a single voice or instrument, or one in which one voice or instrument predominates. In orchestral scores, it marks a passage where one instrument takes a leading part. In a two-hand arrangement of a PIANO CONCERTO, solo marks the entrances of the solo piano.

soh'loh

solo quartet. 1. A quartet consisting of four singers (four solo voices). 2. A piece or passage in four parts for four singers. 3. A nonconcerted piece for four instruments, one of which has a leading part.

Solti, (Sir) **George** (real name, György Stern), eminent Hungarian-born English conductor; b. Budapest, Oct. 21, 1912; d. Antibes, Sept. 5, 1997. Solti began to study piano when he was six, making his first public appearance in Bu-dapest when he was 12. At 13 he enrolled there at the Franz Liszt Academy of Music, studying piano with ERNST DOHNÁNYI and briefly with BÉLA BARTÓK. He also took composition courses with ZOLTÁN KODÁLY. Solti graduated at the age of 18, and was engaged by

PEOPLE IN MUSIC

George Solti in rehearsal, 1963.
(Hulton-Deutsch Collection/
Corbis)

the Budapest Opera as a *repetiteur.* He also served as an assistant to BRUNO WALTER (1935) and ARTURO TOSCANINI (1936, 1937) at the Salzburg Festivals.

In 1938 Solti made a brilliant conducting debut at the Budapest Opera with WOLFGANG AMADEUS MOZART's *MARRIAGE OF FIGARO.* However, the wave of anti-Semitism in Hungary under the reactionary military rule forced him to leave Budapest (he was Jewish). In 1939 he went to Switzerland, where he was active mainly as a concert pianist. In 1942 he won the Concours International de Piano in Geneva, and, finally, in 1944, he was engaged to conduct concerts with the orchestra of the Swiss Radio.

In 1946 the American occupation authorities in Munich invited Solti to conduct LUDWIG VAN BEETHOVEN's *FIDELIO* at the Bavarian State Opera. His success there led to his appointment as its Generalmusikdirektor, a position he held from 1946 to 1952. In 1952 he became Generalmusikdirektor in Frankfurt, serving as director of the Opera and conductor of the Museumgesellschaft Concerts.

Solti made his U.S. debut with the San Francisco Opera, conducting RICHARD STRAUSS's *ELEKTRA* in 1953. He later conducted the Chicago Symphony Orchestra, N.Y. Philharmonic, and at the Metropolitan Opera in N.Y., where he made his first appearance in late 1960, with RICHARD WAGNER's *TANNHÄUSER.* He was then engaged as music director of the Los Angeles Philharmonic, but the appointment collapsed when the board of trustees refused to grant him full powers in musical and administrative policy.

In the meantime, he made his Covent Garden debut in London in 1959. In 1961 he assumed the post of music director of the Royal Opera House there, retaining it with great distinction until 1971. In 1969 he became music director of the Chicago Symphony Orchestra, in which capacity he achieved a triumph as an interpreter and orchestra builder, so that the "Chicago sound" became a synonym for excellence.

Under Solti's direction the Chicago Symphony Orchestra became one of the most celebrated orchestras in the world. He took it to Europe for the first time in 1971, eliciting glowing praise from critics and audiences. He subsequently led the ensemble on a number of acclaimed tours there and also took it to N.Y. for regular appearances at Carnegie Hall.

Solti held the additional posts of music advisor of the Paris Opéra from 1971 to 1973 and music director of the Orchestre de Paris from 1972 to 1975, which he took on a tour of China in 1974. He served as principal conductor and artistic director of the London Philharmonic from 1979 to 1983, after which he was accorded the title of conductor emeritus. During these years he retained his post with the Chicago Symphony.

In 1983 Solti conducted the RING cycle at the Bayreuth Festival, in commemoration of the 100th anniversary of the death of RICHARD WAGNER. Solti retained his prestigious position with the Chicago Symphony Orchestra until the close of the 100th anniversary season in 1990–91, and subsequently held the title of Laureate Conductor. In 1992–93 he served as artistic director of the Salzburg Festival. In 1993 he received the National Medal of Arts.

Solti was given numerous awards in his lifetime. In 1968 he was made an honorary Commander of the Order of the British Empire, and in 1971 he was named an honorary Knight Commander of the Order of the British Empire. In 1972 he became a British subject and was knighted.

Solti is generally acknowledged as a superlative interpreter of the symphonic and operatic repertoire. He is renowned for his performances of Wagner, GIUSEPPE VERDI, GUSTAV MAHLER, Strauss, and other ROMANTIC masters. He also conducted notable performances of Bartók, IGOR STRAVINSKY, ARNOLD SCHOENBERG, and other 20th-century composers.

Solti placed great demands on his musicians but won their allegiance through his quest for excellence. His recordings received innumerable awards, his international reputation being secured through his complete stereo recording of Wagner's *Ring* cycle (the first).

Solti won 30 Grammy awards for his recordings, more than any other musician.

Sombrero de tres picos, El (The three-cornered hat). Ballet by MANUEL DE FALLA, 1919, first performed in London by the Diaghilev Ballet.

The confusing story centers on the governor of a Spanish province who tries to seduce the comely wife of a local miller. He carelessly leaves the emblem of his authority, a Napoleonic three-cornered hat, on the premises. All kinds of nonsensical events ensue. The music sparkles with Spanish rhythms.

Some Enchanted Evening. Song by RICHARD RODGERS and OSCAR HAMMERSTEIN II, 1949, from their musical *SOUTH PA-CIFIC*.

Somebody Loves Me. An engaging song by GEORGE GERSH-WIN, 1924, written for that season's edition of the revue called *George White's Scandals*.

Some Day I'll Find You. Song by NOEL COWARD, 1930, which served as the theme song of his play *Private Lives*.

Something for the Boys. Musical by COLE PORTER, 1943.
    Three cousins (two female, one male) inherit a huge Texas ranch. One of the young women takes a liking to an airman at a nearby military base. She discovers that she can intercept radio messages in the carbon filling in her tooth. This inspires the commanding officer to install similar receiving sets in the teeth of his men.
    Among its funny songs is *When We're Home on the Range.*

son (Sp.). Generic name of indigenous songs of Cuba and neighboring islands, reflecting the influence of African rhythms and set usually in a strongly accented $\frac{2}{4}$ time. Like the zapateado (a Latin American dance in triple meter, characterized by heel stamping to emphasize the strong SYNCOPA-TION), the son allows great freedom with contrapuntal embellishments. It includes texts in couplet form on the subject of beauty and guitar accompaniment with *rasgueado* strumming.

sōh-nah′tăh   **sonata** (It.). An instrumental composition in three or four extended movements contrasted in THEME, TEMPO, and mood; usually for a solo instrument with accompaniment or chamber ensemble. *Sonata a tre,* TRIO SONATA.

sonata da camera (It.). Chamber sonata, for one or more solo instruments and BASSO CONTINUO. It includes several dance movements in the manner of a BAROQUE SUITE, often with a prefatory movement. As distinct from SONATA DA CHIESA.

sonata da chiesa (It.). Church sonata, not necessarily religious in connotation. It is a four-part work in alternating slow and fast movements. Compare to SONATA DA CAMERA.

sōh-nah′tăh dah kee-eh′sah

The sonata da chiesa was a favorite form of early BAROQUE composers, but it gradually vanished as an independent composition in the 18th century.

sonata form. A structure or procedure usually used for first movements of CLASSIC and ROMANTIC SYMPHONIES, SONATAS, and chamber works, although it may be used for other movements as well.

Sonata form fuses BINARY and TERNARY forms: from binary, sonata form took the division at the piece's halfway point, with its repeat signs; the second half's beginning in the DOMINANT or a key other than the TONIC; and the return to the tonic by piece's end; from the ternary, it took the tripartite form of the ABA structure and renamed the three parts EXPOSITION, DEVELOPMENT, and RECAPITULATION. The essential difference between the exposition and recapitulation is that while the exposition ends in a nontonic key, the recapitulation "repeats" the exposition but adjusts it harmonically so that it will end in the tonic.

Sonata form is also known as sonata-allegro form and *first-movement form.*

sonata-concerto form. A combination of SONATA FORM with the RITORNELLO procedure.

sonata-rondo form. A RONDO-form movement in at least seven sections, where the central episode (e.g., C in ABA-CABA) functions as a DEVELOPMENT section. And, while the initial B section emphasizes a key other than the TONIC, the repeat of B is adjusted or simply transposed into the tonic.

Sonatas and Interludes. JOHN CAGE's masterwork for PREPARED PIANO, 1946–48. It is comprised of 20 short pieces (16 sonatas and four interludes). They collectively express in music the theory of *rasa* and the (eight) permanent emotions of Indian philosophy, as described in Ananda Coomaraswamy's book *The Dance of Shiva.* The specific correlation of emotion to setting is never specified, but the work as a whole is an effective blend of musical tendencies from both East and West.

The work garnered Cage a grant from the Guggenheim Foundation and a $1,000 award from the National Academy of Arts and Letters for having "extended the boundaries of music." It was premiered on April 6, 1948, at Black Mountain, North Carolina.

sonatina (Fr. *sonatine;* Ger. *Sonatine*). A short SONATA in two or three (rarely four) movements, the first in an abbreviated SONATA FORM.

sōh-năh-tē′năh

PEOPLE IN MUSIC

Sondheim, Stephen (Joshua), brilliant American composer and lyricist; b. N.Y., March 22, 1930. Of an affluent family, Sondheim received his academic education in private schools. He composed a school musical at the age of 15. He then studied music at Williams College, where he wrote the book, lyrics, and music for a couple of college shows. He graduated magna cum laude in 1950. He then went to Princeton University, where he took lessons in modern composition with MILTON BABBITT.

Sondheim made his mark on Broadway when he wrote the lyrics for LEONARD BERNSTEIN's WEST SIDE STORY in 1957. His first success as a lyricist-composer came with the Broadway musical A FUNNY THING HAPPENED ON THE WAY TO THE FORUM in 1962, which received a Tony award. His next musical, *Anyone Can Whistle* in 1964, proved an interesting failure.

Company (1970), for which Sondheim wrote both lyrics and music, established him as a major and innovative composer and lyricist on Broadway. There followed *Follies* in 1971, for which he wrote 22 pastiche songs. It was named best musical by the N.Y. Drama Critics Circle. His next production, A LITTLE NIGHT MUSIC, with the nostalgic score harking back to the turn of the century, received a Tony, and its leading song, SEND IN THE CLOWNS, was awarded a Grammy in 1976.

In 1976 Sondheim produced *Pacific Overtures,* based on the story of the Western penetration into Japan in the 19th century. It was composed in a stylized Japanese manner, modeled after Kabuki theater. He also wrote the score to the musical *Sunday in the Park with George,* inspired by the painting by Georges Seurat entitled *Sunday Afternoon on the Island of La Grande Jatte,* which received the Pulitzer Prize for drama in 1985.

In 1987 Sondheim's musical *Into the Woods,* based on five Grimm fairytales, scored a popular success on Broadway. It was followed by the disturbing musical *Assassins* in 1990 and the operatically emotional *Passion* in 1994.

In 1992 Sondheim was selected to receive the National Medal of Arts, but he rejected the medal by stating that to accept it would be an act of hypocrisy in light of the controversy over censorship and funding of the NEA. After the inauguration of Bill Clinton as president in 1993, Sondheim accepted the award and was honored at the Kennedy Center in Washington, D.C.

Sonetti del Petrarca. Piano pieces by FRANZ LISZT, 1844–45. They were inspired by specific sonnets of Petrach (nos. 47, 104, 123) and included in the second volume of Lizst's ANNÉES DE PÈLERINAGE. Their execution requires that the pianist have the ability to play subtle shadings, particularly in DYNAMICS.

song. A short poem with a musical setting characterized by a structure in simple periods. There are FOLK songs (indigenous or traditional) and art songs (classical). The latter may be either in SONG FORM, STROPHIC FORM, or THROUGH-COMPOSED.

A song may be limited to a single burst of PITCHED sound, a manifestation of sexual attraction, or a savage war cry. It may be a succession of sounds, in MONOTONE or in varying pitch levels. RHYTHM is an integral part of a song even at the most primitive stage. This intrinsic union is expressed in the Spanish language by the term MELORHYTHM, in which melos (MELODY) carries a definite rhythmic line.

song-and-dance man. Colloquial term for a VAUDEVILLE performer who can sing and dance. Several great Broadway stars began their careers in this lowly capacity.

song form. A form of composition, either vocal or instrumental, which has three sections and two themes, the second (contrasting) theme occupying the second section.

Song of Norway. OPERETTA pastiche, based on the music of EDVARD GRIEG.

The plot is a distorted biography of Grieg in which he tries to persuade the parents of Nina Hagerup that his music has the seeds of commercial success. This he achieves by composing and playing excerpts from his piano concerto and instantaneously achieves fame and fortune. He also has personal squabbles with Nina, although they eventually marry, as they did in real life.

Apart from the piano concerto, several of Grieg's piano pieces, the *PEER GYNT* suite, and some songs are used in this work. There is also a ballet extravaganza called *Song of Norway.*

Songs without Words *(Lieder ohne Worte).* Cycles of piano pieces by FELIX MENDELSSOHN, 1829–45, in eight books. Most of the individual titles of these pieces, such as *Spring Song,* with its rapid passages, and the *Bee's Wedding,* with its buzzing CHROMATICS, are, however, the inventions of publishers. There are only three authentic titles given by Mendelssohn himself: *Gondola Song, Duetto,* and *Folksong.*

songspiel. A hybrid English-German designation of a modern satirical OPERA, CABARET, or VAUDEVILLE show that emerged in Germany between the two world wars. The English "song" had a narrowed meaning of "cabaret song" in German.

KURT WEILL's opera *AUFSTEIG UND FALL DER STADT MAHAGONNY* bears the designation Songspiel, which is authentic, and not a misprint for SINGSPIEL.

Sonnambula, La (The sleepwalker). Opera by VINCENZO BELLINI, 1831, first produced in Milan, 1831. The LIBRETTO is by Eugène Scribe, who had a genius for turning out librettos marked by total implausibility.

The somnambulist of the title is a young orphaned woman betrothed to a villager in Switzerland early in the

19th century. The marriage is nearly wrecked when she wanders in her sleep into the bedroom of a visiting nobleman, who is there to court the proprietess of the local tavern. Nobody believes that she wandered into the visitor's room in her sleep, but as they argue pro and con, she appears on the ledge of the house singing a sad ARIA. Her intended bridegroom is reassured of her fidelity.

The score is full of beautiful melodies, as befits the composer's name.

Sonnenquartette. FRANZ JOSEPH HAYDN's six string quartets, 1772, op.20. The sunny title has nothing to do with the music, but refers to the engraving of a rising sun on the cover of an early edition of the quartets.

sonnerie (Fr.). 1. An arrangement of bells in a tower; also, the signal played on those bells. 2. A TRUMPET or BUGLE signal for military or hunting purposes.

sonority (from Lat. *sonus,* sound; Fr. *sonorité*). *See* RESONANCE.

sonus (Lat.). General term for sound, however produced. *Sonus* denotes the physical aspect of sound, while *vox* describes a particular TONAL quality.

Sophisticated Lady. Song by DUKE ELLINGTON, 1933, first composed as an instrumental piece. It was later given lyrics and became one of Ellington's biggest hits.

sopila (*sopella, sopelo;* Croat.; It. *tororo*). An indigenous SHAWM of Croatia, with a short, wide DOUBLE REED. Sopilas are usually played in pairs of different-sized instruments, either in parallel THIRDS or SIXTHS. Occasionally, two melodies are played at once.

sopranino (It., little soprano). A very high (or highest) member of a particular instrument family, e.g., sopranino saxophone, sopranino clarinet (obsolete), and sopranino recorder (with a range similar to that of the PICCOLO).

MUSICAL
INSTRUMENT

In order to tighten the sopila's three joints, water is poured into the tube through the bell.

sōh-prah-nee′nōh

soprano (It.; from Lat. *superanus,* standing over; Ger. *Sopran*). 1. The highest class of the human voice; the *treble* voice. The normal compass of the soprano voice ranges from C^1 to A^2; solo voices often reach above C^3, some as high as C^4. Some vocal parts call for a boy soprano, meaning a natural voice of an preadolescent boy.

Coloratura soprano, a singer with an unusually high range and a strong affinity with BEL CANTO; *dramatic soprano, soprano drammatico, soprano giusto,* a singer capable of dynamic, dramatic, and tragic qualities; the expectation of a strong upper register is matched by an evenness of power throughout the range; *lyric soprano,* a singer distinguished by a poetic quality of phrasing in bel canto; *soprano leggiero,* a light soprano; *soprano sfogato,* a high soprano.

2. A high member of a particular instrument family, e.g., soprano saxophone, soprano recorder, soprano trumpet.

soprano string. The E string on the violin.

Sorcerer's Apprentice, The (*L'Apprenti sorcier*). Symphonic scherzo by PAUL DUKAS, 1897.

An apprentice to a sorcerer tries to make his cleaning chores easier while his master is away. Using magic spells, he gets the various brooms and mops going but does not know how to stop them. Everything goes haywire until the sorcerer returns, repairs the damage (magically, of course), and gives his young apprentice a verbal lashing he will not soon forget.

This is by far Dukas's best-known work, with its rather classicist approach to IMPRESSIONIST harmonies. It was to Dukas what *BOLÉRO* would be to MAURICE RAVEL: a great success and a bane to its composer in its eclipsing of virtually all his other works.

The Sorcerer's Apprentice was made famous in America by its inclusion in the Disney animated feature *Fantasia* (1940).

sordino (It.). 1. A string instrument MUTE; *con sordini,* with the mutes; *senza sordini,* without the mutes; *si levano i sordini,* take off the mutes. 2. Damper (of the piano); *senza sordini,* with damper pedal; so used by LUDWIG VAN BEETHOVEN, who wrote *con sordini* to express the release (raising) of the damper pedal, instead of ℞.

MUSICAL INSTRUMENT

Sordino is the rare masculine form referring to the trumpet mute.

sortita (It.). 1. A closing VOLUNTARY. 2. The first number sung by any leading character in an OPERA. An *aria di sortita* is, however, also an air at the conclusion of which the singer makes his or her exit.

sostenuto pedal. The middle piano PEDAL. It was invented in the 1860s and is now commonplace on grand pianos. It sustains (keeps lifted) dampers already raised by depressed KEYS, thus prolonging the TONES of strings affected. The effect is not unlike a PEDAL POINT or points.

MUSICAL
INSTRUMENT

soubrette (Fr., little kitten; from Prov. *soubret,* coy; It. *servetta*). In comic OPERA and OPERETTA, a maidservant or lady's maid or an ingenue of intriguing and coquettish character. The term is also applied to light roles of similar type.

Susanna in THE MARRIAGE OF FIGARO (*Le nozze di Figaro*) and Papagena in THE MAGIC FLUTE are typical soubrette roles. The coloratura soubrette is exemplified by Rosina in THE BARBER OF SEVILLE and Zerbinetta in ARIADNE AUF NAXOS.

Curiously, the term soubrette is used mostly in Germany. The French prefer a term in honor of a famous French singer, Louise Dugazon (1755–1821), who sang such roles—*jeune Dugazon.*

soul. A style of African-American RHYTHM AND BLUES popularized in the 1960s. A passionate, embellished singing style is typical. Soul singers draw on the vocal styles first introduced in GOSPEL music.

sound (It. *son*). A generic name for all audible sensations, produced by sound waves ranging from about 16 to 25,000 cycles per second (cps).

A pure TONE without any OVERTONES, such as is produced by the tuning fork, generates a sinusoidal sound wave. It can be schematically represented as a semicircle above a horizontal line followed by a similar semicircle below this line. Two such semicircles form one cycle of the sound wave.

The total number of cps is also called the frequency of vibrations (Hertz, abbreviated Hz) of the sound waves.

The PITCH of a sound is measured by the frequency of vibrations per second. Low sounds or pitches have low frequencies, while high pitches have high frequencies.

In addition to the primary sound, each sound wave also produces additional pitches that may be audible, called OVERTONES. The relative strength of the overtones produced by a musical instrument determines its TIMBRE or TONE COLOR. Middle C on the piano, on the violin, or on the flute has the same frequency of vibrations per second, but they all differ in timbre, a difference immediately recognizable by a musical ear. Sound waves created by each instrument are compounded with the sound waves of the overtones, and the resulting curve is no longer sinusoidal, but complex, having several peaks.

The loudness of a tone depends on the amplitude, or the swing, produced by the vibrations of a sounding body. The amplitude can be observed visually by plucking a string and letting it vibrate, producing a blur.

NOISE is a sound without a definite pitch. When the entire spectrum of tones and noises is produced together, the effect is called *white noise*.

sound effects. Simulations of natural or industrial sounds employed in radio, television, and motion picture productions. These may include such devices as a THUNDER MACHINE (RICHARD STRAUSS, *ALPINE SYMPHONY*) imitation of falling rain, galloping horses, the whirring of airplane propellers, etc.

With the invention of the SAMPLER and MIDI, the possibility of both imitation and creation of new effects has grown exponentially.

sound hole. A hole cut in the belly of a stringed instrument.

sound installation. A form of mixed media in which the visual (usually sculpture) and aural (sound of any kind) are combined. Two basic categories exist:

the noninteractive installation, where all elements are controlled by the creators or by random factors not under human control the interactive installation, where the spectator affects the sound by contact with the sculptural element or by interfering with electronic devices (such as breaking an invisible beam, adjusting controls, etc.).

Sound of Music, The. Musical by RICHARD RODGERS and OSCAR HAMMERSTEIN II, 1959. It was inspired by the true story of the von Trapp family who escaped from Nazi Austria and achieved international fame as a singing ensemble.

A candidate in an Austrian nunnery accepts the position as a governess to the seven children of a high-born widower. Inevitably, the governess falls in love with the widower, and they are married. The entire family then escapes Austria during one of their performances.

The Sound of Music has become one of the most durable and admired American musicals. The score includes the title song, *My Favorite Things, Climb Every Mountain, Edelweiss,* and *16 Going on 17.*

soundboard. Thin plate of wood placed below or behind the strings of various instruments to reinforce and prolong their tones; in the ORGAN, the cover of the windchest.

MUSICAL INSTRUMENT

sound post. In the VIOLIN, etc., the small cylindrical wooden prop set inside the body, between belly and back, just behind (nearly beneath) the treble foot of the bridge. It transfers the vibrations from the bridge into the body of the instrument.

MUSICAL INSTRUMENT

Sousa, John Philip, famous American bandmaster and composer; b. Washington, D.C., Nov. 6, 1854; d. Reading, Penn., March 6, 1932. Sousa was the son of a Portuguese father and a German mother. He studied violin and orchestration with John Esputa, Jr., and violin and harmony with George Felix Benkert in Washington, D.C. He also acquired considerable proficiency on wind instruments.

After playing in the Marine Band from 1868 to 1875, he was active in theater orchestras. In 1873 he published his first march, simply titled *Review.* In 1876 he was a violinist in the special orchestra in Philadelphia conducted by JACQUES OFFENBACH during his U.S. tour. In 1880 he was

PEOPLE IN MUSIC

John Philip Sousa, c. 1900.
(New York Public Library) ▶

appointed director of the Marine Band, which he led with distinction until 1892.

Sousa then organized his own band and gave successful concerts throughout the U.S. and Canada. He played at the Chicago World's Fair in 1893 and at the Paris Exposition in 1900. He also made four European tours (1900, 1901, 1903, and 1905), with increasing acclaim, and finally a world tour in 1910–11.

During World War I Sousa served as a lieutenant in the Naval Reserve. He continued his annual tours almost to the time of his death.

Sousa's flair for writing band music was extraordinary. The infectious rhythms of his military marches and the brilliance of his band arrangements earned him the nickname "The March King." Particularly celebrated is THE STARS AND STRIPES FOREVER, which became famous all over the world. In 1987 a bill was passed in the U.S. Congress and duly signed by President Reagan making it the official march of the U.S.

Sousa wrote dozens of marches. Some of the more notable are:

The Gladiator (1886; the first work to sell a million sheet-music copies)

The National Game (1925; written for the 50th anniversary of the National League of baseball)

The Pride of the Wolverines (1926)

The Royal Welch Fusiliers (No. 1, 1929; No. 2, 1930)

Sousa was instrumental in the development of the SOUSAPHONE, a special kind of tuba made specifically for marching bands.

Semper Fidelis (1888)

The Washington Post (1889)

In addition to the many marches, Sousa composed ten OPERETTAS, the most famous being *EL CAPITÁN,* composed in 1895. He also composed band SUITES, OVERTURES, descriptive pieces, instrumental solos, orchestral works, about 76 songs, BALLADS, and hymns, and many arrangements and transcriptions.

sousaphone. A spiral type of bass TUBA (helicon), coiled around the player, with a large bell turned forward. The sousaphone is named after JOHN PHILIP SOUSA, who was instrumental in its development and who used it in his bands.

MUSICAL
INSTRUMENT

South Pacific. Musical by RICHARD RODGERS and OSCAR HAMMERSTEIN II, 1949, based on James Michener's *Tales of the South Pacific.*

The central characters are Emile de Becque, a French plantation owner on a South Pacific island, and Nellie Forbush, a young U.S. Navy nurse. They meet after the Japanese attack on Pearl Harbor, when an American unit settles on the island. Emile and Nellie fall in love, but at first she is disturbed by his former union with a Polynesian woman. Nellie changes her mind, and she and Emile are reunited.

South Pacific was one of the greatest Broadway successes, second only to *Oklahoma!* It received the Pulitzer Prize. The love BALLAD *Some Enchanted Evening* became a classic of the American musical theater. The memorable score also includes *Bali Ha'i, I'm Gonna Wash That Man Right Outa My Hair, There is Nothin' Like a Dame, A Wonderful Guy, Younger Than Springtime,* and *Happy Talk.*

space. In the STAFF, the INTERVAL between two lines or LEDGER LINES.

space (or spatial) **music.** *See* SPATIAL DISTRIBUTION.

spatial distribution. The placement of musicians on the stage, long a matter of tradition, has assumed an unexpected significance in modern times. ELLIOTT CARTER specifies the exact position of the players in his string quartets. LUKAS FOSS, in his *Elytres* for 12 instruments, places the musicians at maximum distances available on the stage.

The use of directional loudspeakers in performances of ultramodern works is an electronic counterpart of spatial distribution. In German broadcasting studios, experiments have been made in distributing a 12-TONE ROW in SERIAL works among 12 electronic amplifiers placed in a clock-like circle, with each amplifier being assigned an individual note of the series.

spectrum. By analogy with the prismatic spectrum of primary colors, a totality of possible musical sounds can be described as a tonal spectrum.

Before the era of ELECTRONIC MUSIC, the colors of the auditory spectrum were limited to the available instruments of actual manufacture. With the aid of electronic generators it is possible to build a spectrum possessing an infinite capacity of instrumental colors.

Spiel (Ger.). Play; performance; game. *Spielen,* to play (as a verb). *Spielmann,* an itinerant musician of the Middle Ages.

The modern instrument that took up the name "spinet" has little in common with the venerable BAROQUE instrument, being simply a small upright piano.

spinet. A keyboard instrument of the HARPSICHORD family, closely related to the VIRGINAL. However, its shape is more like that of the modern grand piano. The spinet was popular during the 18th century and then abruptly disappeared.

Spinnenlied (Ger.). Spinning song; originally, a traditional work song. In classical music, the spinning wheel is often represented by a circulating OSTINATO around a PEDAL POINT. Goethe's *Gretchen am Spinnrade* (from FAUST part I) is a lyric that invites this kind of approach. FRANZ SCHUBERT's setting (1814) is the best-known and greatest one.

spin′toh

spinto (It., compelled, intense). A high operatic SOPRANO or TENOR role of a dramatic yet passive type (Madama Butterfly, Desdemona), as opposed to dramatic and lyric.

spiritual. A term related to the European spiritual song, composed in many languages and for many different forces.

The shortened term was then applied to religious songs cultivated by African-American slaves in the antebellum South. In reality, this music is a form of the American gospel HYMN, a term usually reserved for the music of white churches.

Spirituals became popular in the 19th century, thanks to touring groups of college choirs, beginning with the famous group out of Fisk College in Tennessee. Collections of these songs were published and became popular among parlor pianists. In the 20th century, many recitalists have included spirituals in their performances, along with the classical repertoire. Singers like MAHALIA JACKSON became famous for their interpretation of spirituals.

See GOSPEL.

Spohr, Louis (Ludewig, Ludwig), celebrated German violinist, composer, and conductor; b. Braunschweig, April 5, 1784; d. Kassel, Oct. 22, 1859. The Spohr family moved to Seesen in 1786. His father, a physician, played the flute, and his mother was an amateur singer and pianist. Spohr began violin lessons at the age of five. In 1791, he returned to Braunschweig, where he studied with organist Carl August Hartung and violinist Charles Louis Maucourt. He also composed several violin pieces.

PEOPLE IN MUSIC

Duke Carl Wilhelm Ferdinand admitted Spohr to the ducal orchestra and arranged for his further study with the violinist Franz Eck. In 1802 Eck took him on a tour to Russia, where he met MUZIO CLEMENTI and JOHN FIELD. He returned to Braunschweig in 1803 and resumed his post in the ducal orchestra. On his return, he met Pierre Rode, whose compositions and violin technique were major influences on Spohr.

In 1804 Spohr made his first official tour as a violinist to Hamburg (his first actual tour to Hamburg in 1799 proved a failure, and a second, early in 1804, was aborted when his Guarnerius violin was stolen). He also gave concerts in Berlin, Leipzig, and Dresden. In 1805 he became concertmaster in the ducal orchestra at Gotha.

In 1806 Spohr married the harpist Dorette (Dorothea) Scheidler (1787–1834). He wrote many works for violin and harp for them to perform together and also toured with her in Germany in 1807.

Spohr's reputation as a virtuoso established, he began writing compositions in every genre, all of which obtained excellent success. In 1812 he gave a series of concerts in Vienna and was acclaimed both as a composer and as a violinist. He was concertmaster in the orchestra of the Theater an der Wien until 1815. He then made a grand tour of Germany and Italy, where NICCOLÒ PAGANINI heard him in Venice. In 1816 Spohr's opera *FAUST*, skillfully employing many devices that foreshadowed developments in later German operas, was performed by CARL MARIA VON WEBER in Prague.

After a visit to Holland in 1817, Spohr became Kapellmeister of the Frankfurt Opera, where he produced one of his most popular operas, *Zemire und Azor*. In 1820 he and his wife visited England and appeared at several concerts of the London Philharmonic Society. This was the first of six visits to England, where he acquired an immense reputation. His works continued to be performed there long after his death.

On his return trip from England, Spohr presented concerts in Paris. His reception there, however, failed to match his London successes, and he proceeded to Dresden, where Weber recommended him for the Kapellmeister post at the court in Kassel. Attracted by the lifetime contract, Spohr accepted the post and settled there in 1822. A year later, he produced his operatic masterpiece, *JESSONDA*, which remained popular throughout the rest of the 19th century. Following this success were performances of his oratorio *Die letzten Dinge* (The last judgment; 1826) and his Fourth Symphony, *Die Weihe der Töne* (1832), both eliciting great praise.

Spohr's wife died in 1834, and in 1836 he married the pianist Marianne Pfeiffer. She was the sister of his friend Carl Pfeiffer, librettist of *Der Alchymist* (the alchemist; composed in 1830).

In 1837 Spohr began having difficulties with the Electoral Prince of Kassel. The Elector canceled a festival in Kassel and forbade Spohr from making a trip to Prague. The composer went there nevertheless to conduct *Der Berggeist* (1825); on his return, he visited WOLFGANG AMADEUS MOZART's widow and birthplace in Salzburg. He traveled to England in 1839 for the Norwich Festival but could not ob-

Spohr's *Violinschule* (Violin school), a set of 66 studies covering every aspect of his violin style, was published in 1831.

tain permission from the Prince to return for the performance of his *Der Fall Babylons* (The fall of Babylon) in 1842.

In 1841 Spohr took his wife's suggestion to use two orchestras for his Seventh Symphony in three parts, portraying the mundane and the divine. In 1843, in England, his success was so great that a special concert was given by royal command. It was the first time a reigning English monarch attended a Philharmonic Concert.

In 1844 Spohr received the silver medal from the Société des Concerts in Paris, and a festival honoring him was held in Braunschweig. In 1845 he received a golden wreath from the Berlin Royal Opera. In 1847 he visited England for the third time, then went to Frankfurt for the German National Assembly. In 1853 he appeared at the New Philharmonic Concerts in London.

Returning to Kassel, Spohr found himself in an increasingly difficult position because of his political views. The Elector of Hesse refused him further leaves of absence. Spohr ignored the ban, however, traveling to Switzerland and Italy. In the litigation that followed with the Kassel court, Spohr was ordered to forfeit part of his yearly income. He was retired from Kassel in 1857, on a pension despite his lifetime contract. Although he fractured his left arm in a fall in late 1857, he conducted *Jessonda* in Prague in July 1858. He conducted for the last time in Meiningen later that year.

Spohr's compositional style was characteristic of the transition period between the CLASSIC and ROMANTIC. He was technically a master. While some of his works demonstrate a spirit of bold experimentation (*The Historical Symphony*, no. 6; the Symphony No. 7 for two orchestras; the Concerto for String Quartet and Orchestra; the Nonet), he was an intransigent conservative. He admired LUDWIG VAN BEETHOVEN's early works but confessed total inability to understand those of his last period. He also failed to appreciate Weber.

It is remarkable, therefore, that Spohr was an early champion of RICHARD WAGNER. In Kassel he produced DER FLIEGENDE HOLLÄNDER (1843) and TANNHÄUSER (1853), despite strenuous court opposition. He was a highly esteemed teacher, numbering among his students Ferdinand David and Moritz Hauptmann.

Spohr never visited the U.S., despite the fact that his daughter lived in N.Y. and an invitation to hold a festival in his honor was issued.

In addition to the operas and oratorios mentioned above, Spohr wrote ten symphonies, 18 violin concertos (c.1799–1844), four clarinet concertos, two "concertantes" for two violins, two concertantes for harp and violin, and six concert overtures. His chamber works include 34 string quartets, seven string quintets, four "double quartets" for strings, 14 violin duets, five piano trios, and three sonatas for harp and violin.

PEOPLE IN MUSIC

Spontini, Gasparo (Luigi Pacifico) significant Italian opera composer; b. Majolati, Ancona, Nov. 14, 1774; d. there, Jan. 24, 1851. Spontini's father, a modest farmer, intended him for the church. He placed him in the care of an uncle, a priest at Jesi, who attempted to stifle the young man's musical aspirations. Spontini sought refuge at Monte San Vito with another relative, who not only found a competent music teacher for him, but settled the dispute with his family, so that, after a year, he was able to return to Jesi.

In 1793 Spontini entered the Conservatorio della Pietà de' Turchini in Naples, to study singing and composition. When he failed to obtain the position of maestrino there in 1795, he quit the Conservatorio without permission.

Spontini rapidly mastered the conventional Italian style of his time. Some of his church music performed in Naples came to the attention of a director of the Teatro della Pallacorda in Rome, who commissioned him to write an opera. This was *Li puntigli delle donne,* produced during Carnival in 1796. Over the next few years, he produced operas for Parma, Rome, and Venice before going to Paris in 1803.

After eking out an existence as a singing teacher, Spontini found a patron in the Empress Joséphine. He won appointment as composer of Joséphine's private music in 1805. For her he wrote several occasional pieces, including the CANTATA *L'eccelsa gara* in 1806, celebrating the battle of Austerlitz.

After a series of unsuccessful operas, Spontini was approached by the poet Étienne de Jouy to write the music to his LIBRETTO for *LA VESTALE*. Thanks to Joséphine's patronage, it was a triumphant success at its premiere in 1807, in spite of virulent opposition from some critics. Spontini's next opera, *Fernand Cortez* from 1809, failed to equal his previous success, although the second version, which debuted in 1817, won it a place in the repertoire.

In 1810 Spontini married Céleste Érard, daughter of Jean-Baptiste Érard, and accepted the post of director of the Théâtre-Italien. Although his artistic policies were successful, his personality clashed with those of his superiors, and he was dismissed in 1812.

In 1814 Spontini's opera *Pélage, ou Le Roi et la paix,* celebrating the Restoration, was successfully produced. A month later he was named director of Louis XVIII's private music and of the Théâtre-Italien, although soon after he sold his privilege to the latter to another Italian composer, Alfredo Catalani.

Having become a favorite of the Bourbons, Spontini was made a French citizen by the king in 1817 and was granted a pension in 1818. In spite of his favored position, his grand opera *Olimpie* proved a dismal failure at its premiere in 1819.

The next year, Spontini went to Berlin as Generalmusikdirektor, scoring an initial success with the revised version of *Olimpie* in 1821. However, his eminence quickly waned. He had been placed on an equal footing with the Intendant of the Royal Theater, and there were frequent misunderstandings and sharp clashes of authority. These problems were increased by Spontini's jealousies and dislikes, his overweening self-conceit, and his despotic temper.

Partly through intrigue, partly by reason of his own lack of self-control, Spontini was charged in criminal court in January 1841. That April, during a performance of DON GIO-VANNI that he was conducting, a riot ensued and Spontini was compelled to leave the hall in disgrace. In July he was sentenced to nine months in prison. Soon thereafter Spontini was dismissed as Generalmusikdirektor by the king, although he was allowed to retain his title and salary. In 1842 his sentence was upheld by an appeals court, but the king pardoned him that same month.

Spontini then went to Paris, where illness and growing deafness overtook him. In 1844 he was raised to papal nobility as the Conte di San Andrea. In 1850 he retired to his birthplace to die.

Spontini's importance to the lyric theater rests upon his effective blending of Italian and French elements in his serious operas, most notably *La Vestale* and *Fernand Cortez.* His influence on HECTOR BERLIOZ was particularly notable. He also composed songs, choral music, and instrumental pieces.

shpreh′shtim-meh

Sprechstimme (*Sprechgesang;* Ger., speech song). A type of inflected vocal delivery with PITCHES indicated only approximately on the STAFF. The singer follows the pitch contour without actually voicing any NOTES, and the effect is exaggerated speech.

It was popularized through its expressive use by ARNOLD SCHOENBERG in *PIERROT LUNAIRE* and later works. The method was used systematically for the first time in 1897 in the operatic melodrama *KÖNIGSKINDER* by ENGELBERT HUMPERDINCK. This technique is often used in contemporary opera and song cycles. Modern variants such as HARRY PARTCH's "intoning voice" and MIKEL ROUSE's "counterpoetry" are also found.

Spring Symphony. The First Symphony by ROBERT SCHUMANN, 1841, in B-flat major (op.38), premiered in Leipzig. Schumann, who titled the work, composed it during the winter, at the happiest time of his life, when he had just married his beloved Clara.

Spring Symphony. Work for voices and orchestra by BENJAMIN BRITTEN, 1949, premiered during the Holland Music Festival in Amsterdam. Unpretentiously arranged to words from English poems glorifying springtime, the piece ends with an allusion to the medieval English round *SUMER IS ICUMEN IN.*

springar. Traditional couple dance of Norway, in triple meter, usually accompanied by the HARDINGFELE.

Springsteen, Bruce, American rock singer, guitarist, and songwriter; b. Freehold, N.J., Sept. 23, 1949. Springsteen began playing in various rock groups in his native Asbury Park, New Jersey, as a teenager. Eventually, he formed the E Street Band with other local musicians and began playing in clubs on the Jersey shore.

PEOPLE IN MUSIC

Springsteen auditioned for the recording executive John Hammond in the early 1970s and was quickly signed to Columbia Records. After cutting a few albums, Springsteen hit it big in 1975 with the album *Born to Run,* which struck a sympathetic chord with disillusioned youth and soon made Springsteen a cult figure. The title song received a certified gold award.

Springsteen's upward rise was temporarily dampened by a dispute with his early management. This resulted in a three-year break until his next album was released. *Darkness on the Edge of Town* (1978), as the title suggests, presented a fairly bleak picture of life in America. In 1980 Springsteen produced the two-album set *The River,* telling a loosely linked story of Americans in search of meaning in their daily lives. Ironically, the pop-sounding song *Hungry Heart* from this collection became Springsteen's first top 10 hit.

Springsteen's career took another unusual turn when he issued the 1982 album *Nebraska.* This featured just Springsteen with minimal accompaniment on a series of FOLK-sounding songs. Critically acclaimed, it in no way forecast the tremendous success of the followup, *Born in the USA* (1984). Besides the title track, this album produced many top 10 hits, including *Dancing in the Dark, My Hometown,* and *Glory Days.* A very successful world tour followed.

Springsteen subsequently brought out the albums *Bruce Springsteen & the E-Street Band Live/1975–1985* (1985) and *Tunnel of Love* (1987), the latter winning him a Grammy Award. In 1988 he was active with the Amnesty International Human Rights Now! Tour.

In 1990 Springsteen ended his 16-year affiliation with the E-Street Band. He also moved to California, shocking his New Jersey-based fans. Springsteen's output has been uneven in the '90s, although he scored a major hit with the theme song from the movie *Philadelphia* in 1996. *The Ghost of Tom Joad,* also from 1996, featured more songs in a FOLK-oriented style, and Springsteen followed with an acoustic tour of small clubs.

In 1998 Springsteen released a large collection of outtakes and other previously unissued material called *Tracks,* as well as a book of the lyrics of his songs.

square dance. A parlor or country dance, such as a QUA-DRILLE, performed by several couples in a square formation.

SRO. *See* STANDING ROOM ONLY.

stäh′bäht mäh′tĕr

Stabat Mater (dolorosa, Lat.). A Latin SEQUENCE on the Crucifixion sung in the Roman Catholic LITURGY. It commemorates the seven sorrows of the Virgin and is used in several Divine Offices.

With its emotional appeal and liturgical acceptability by the 16th-century Council of Trent, this sequence has been set to music by composers such as JOSQUIN DES PREZ, GIOVANNI PIERLUIGI DA PALESTRINA, GIOVANNI BATTISTA PERGOLESI, FRANZ JOSEPH HAYDN, GIOACHINO ROSSINI, FRANZ SCHUBERT, GIUSEPPE VERDI, and ANTONÍN DVOŘÁK.

stähk-kah′tōh

staccato (It., detached). Play as a series of separate, disconnected notes, the opposite of LEGATO. On a string instrument, the bow does not leave the string, unlike *sautillé* (bounced). The effect is successful on most instruments. Played FORTE, the effect is *martellato,* and in PIANISSIMO and rapid tempo, it is sometimes described as *virtuoso staccato.*

Staccato mark, a dot (♩) or wedge-shaped stroke (♩) over a note, the former indicating a less abrupt staccato than the latter. *Mezzo-staccato* is indicated by dotted notes under or over a slur (♩♩).

Stade, Frederica von. *See* VON STADE, FREDERICA.

Stadler Quintet. Clarinet quintet by WOLFGANG AMADEUS MOZART, 1789, K.581. It was written for the virtuoso clarinetist Anton (Paul) Stadler (1753–1812).

For the plural, *staves* is preferred to *staffs.*

staff (stave). The five parallel lines used in modern PITCH NOTATION. PLAINCHANT used four lines, at most.

Staff notation, the staff and all musical signs connected with it; *grand* or *great staff,* one of 11 lines, with middle C occupying the (middle) sixth.

stalls (U.K.). In a theater, the front rows of the orchestra (seating) section.

Stand By Me. Ben E. King classic, a pop hit for him in both 1961 and 1984. Cover versions that also charted were cut by Spyder Turner (1967), JOHN LENNON (1975), and Mickey Gilley (1980).

Stand By Your Man. TAMMY WYNETTE country megahit of 1969 that set women's liberation back significantly. Also, the title of her autobiography.

standard. Usually used to describe an American popular song that has been recorded or covered so many times that it has become known universally. It is also used to describe the popular songs of the '30s and '40s by nostalgic critics who decry the quality of today's music.

standing ovation. Unanimous and tumultuous applause at the end of a particularly exciting musical performance. The audience is so transported by admiration for the performer(s) that the people are impelled to rise from their seats and clap their hands mightily and sometimes even rhythmically, joyously abandoning themselves to unrestrained vociferation and, in extreme cases, cries of joy. The spontaneity of such manifestations, however, is sometimes suspect. *See* CLAQUE.

Standing Room Only (SRO). An indication in some theaters that all seats for a particular performance are sold out. A few places may remain, however, where a hardy individual can watch the performance standing up behind the last row of seats.

stanza. A symmetric unit of a song text, of four or more lines. A unified section in and component of a LIED or other song type.

Stardust. Love BALLAD by HOAGY CARMICHAEL, 1929. The tune was written while Carmichael was reminiscing about a young woman he knew at the University of Indiana. The lyrics were added later. The song remains very popular.

Starr, Ringo (born Richard Starkey), English ROCK 'N' ROLL drummer and singer, member of the celebrated Liverpudlian

The country singer WILLIE NELSON made *Stardust* the title cut of his album of American standards that he recorded in the '70s.

PEOPLE IN MUSIC

group the BEATLES; b. Liverpool, July 7, 1940. His nickname originated from his ostentatious habit of wearing several rings on each of his fingers. As an adolescent he performed menial jobs as a messenger boy for British railways, a barman on a boat, etc. A sickly boy, he spent several years in hospitals to cure an effusion on the lung, but he played drums in ward bands. He spontaneously evolved a rhythmic technique of an overwhelming vitality.

Starr first played drums professionally with the Liverpool-based group, Rory Storm and the Hurricanes. In 1962 he joined the BEATLES, an association that continued until the dissolution of the group in 1970. After the Beatles disbanded, Starr had an often successful career as a performer and actor. Among his solo hits were *It Don't Come Easy* (1972) and *Back Off Boogaloo* (1973). He also had the distinction of being the only one of the Beatles to work with the other three after 1970.

Starr has made various "comebacks" through the '70s, '80s, and '90s. He currently tours with a floating group of musicians billed as his "All-Starr" band.

Stars and Stripes Forever. Rousingly patriotic march by JOHN PHILIP SOUSA, 1897, that became his best known work.

Star-Spangled Banner, The. The official U.S. national ANTHEM since 1931.

The tune is that of *To Anacreon in Heaven,* first published in London about 1780. Its composition is ascribed to John Stafford Smith (1750–1836), a scholar, organist, and composer. As a member of the Anacreontic Society, London, he wrote the song as a whimsical glorification of the Greek poet Anacreon, famous for his odes to love and wine.

The words are by Francis Scott Key (1779–1843), during the War of 1812 between the British and American forces. Key, a lawyer, wrote part of the text aboard a British ship (where he went to plead for the release of a Maryland physician) on the morning of Sept. 14, 1814. He was inspired by the sight of the American flag still waving at Fort McHenry near Baltimore despite the British bombardment of it on the previous night. Key later wrote additional verses, none of which are ever sung. The poem was printed in a

An anonymous author came up with these famous lyrics for Sousa's work: "Be kind to your web-footed friends. For a duck may be somebody's mother."

broadside under the title *Defence of Fort McHenry*, to the Smith tune.

Although *The Star-Spangled Banner* was a *de facto* national anthem in the 19th century and was used as such by the U.S. Army and Navy, it did not become the official American anthem until President Hoover signed the Senate bill to that effect.

The anthem has been used to symbolize America in numerous compositions, including GIACOMO PUCCINI's MADAMA BUTTERFLY and, more recently, Daniel Lentz's *A Crack in the Bell* for vocal soloist, three keyboards, and optional chamber orchestra (1986). A law exists in some American state statutes against the mutilation or disfigurement of the melody or harmony of the anthem. It was invoked by the Boston police to preclude a performance of IGOR STRAVINSKY's arrangement of the anthem at a Boston Symphony Orchestra concert in 1942.

The anthem's wide ranging melody—covering an octave and a fifth—makes it notoriously difficult to sing. Attempts to correct this problem by transposing the second half of the song to another key have been unsuccessful.

static music. Music that does not change over a long period of time, or changes very slowly so as to be almost imperceptible. It is particularly popular among AVANT-GARDE composers, or those who create special sound environments. Often, these composers follow Eastern philosophies that emphasize contemplation and relaxation through art.

Stayin' Alive. Disco hit of 1978 from the popular *Saturday Night Fever* film. It was performed in glorious FALSETTO by the BEE GEES.

steel band (drum). A type of ensemble developed spontaneously in Trinidad, with the instrumentation provided by steel oil barrels discarded by local oil companies. The players, called Panmen, select DRUM tops that are dented in such a way that each dent produces a different tone. By further manipulating these drum tops, a whole DIATONIC SCALE can be produced.

Natives who have absorbed the sounds of American and British popular music have learned to form whole orchestras of steel drum tops, performing in four-part harmony. The highest PITCH is called *ping-pong,* and the bass is called *boom.* The steel band is usually supplemented by several pairs of MARACAS and GUIROS. The songs are of the CALYPSO type, with topical texts.

Steiner, Max(imilian Raoul Walter), Austrian-born American composer; b. Vienna, May 10, 1888; d. Los Angeles, Dec. 28, 1971. Steiner studied at the Vienna Conservatory with Johann Nepomuk Fuchs and Hermann Grädener and also had some lessons from GUSTAV MAHLER. At the age of 14 he wrote an OPERETTA. In 1904 he went to England, and in 1911 he proceeded to Paris.

In 1914 Steiner settled in the U.S. After conducting musical shows in N.Y., he moved in 1929 to Hollywood, where he became a successful film composer. His music offers a blend of lush harmonies artfully derived from both PIOTR ILYICH TCHAIKOVSKY and RICHARD WAGNER, arranged in a manner marvelously suitable for the portrayal of psychological drama on the screen. Among his film scores, of which he wrote more than 200, are *King Kong* (1933), *The Charge of the Light Brigade* (1936), *Gone with the Wind* (1939), and *The Treasure of the Sierra Madre* (1948).

Steinway & Sons. Celebrated family of German-American piano manufacturers. The founder of the firm was Heinrich Engelhard Steinweg (b. Wolfshagen, Feb. 15, 1797; d. N.Y., Feb. 7, 1871; in 1864 he Anglicized his name to Henry E. Steinway). He learned cabinetmaking and organ building at Goslar and in 1818 entered the shop of an organ maker in Seesen, also becoming church organist there.

From about 1820 Steinway became interested in piano making and worked hard to establish a business of his own. He built his first piano in 1836. In 1839 he exhibited one grand and two square pianos at the Braunschweig State Fair, winning the gold medal.

The Revolution of 1848 caused Steinway to emigrate to America with his wife, two daughters, and four of his five sons: Charles (actually, Christian Karl Gottlieb; b. Seesen,

Jan. 4, 1829; d. there, March 31, 1865), Henry (actually, Johann Heinrich Engelhard; b. Seesen, Oct. 29, 1830; d. N.Y., March 11, 1865), William (actually, Johann Heinrich Wilhelm; b. Seesen, March 5, 1835; d. N.Y., Nov. 30, 1896), and (Georg August) Albert (b. Seesen, June 10, 1840; d. N.Y., May 14, 1877). The management of the German business at Seesen was left in charge of the eldest son, (Christian Friedrich) Theodore (b. Seesen, Nov. 6, 1825; d. Braunschweig, March 26, 1889).

The family arrived in N.Y. on June 29, 1850, and for about two years father and sons worked in various piano factories there. On March 5, 1853, they established the Steinway & Sons factory, with premises on Varick St. In 1854 they won a gold medal for a square piano at the Metropolitan Fair in Washington, D.C. Their remarkable prosperity dates from 1855, when they took first prize for a then-innovative square overstrung piano with cast-iron frame at the N.Y. Industrial Exhibition. In 1856 they made their first grand, and in 1862 their first upright. Among numerous honors subsequently received were first prize at London, 1862, first grand gold medal of honor for all styles at Paris, 1867 (by unanimous verdict), and diplomas for "highest degree of excellence in all styles" at Philadelphia, 1876.

In 1854 the family name (Steinweg) was legally changed to Steinway. In 1865, upon the death of his brothers Charles and Henry, Theodore gave up the Braunschweig business and became a full partner in N.Y. He built Steinway Hall on 14th Street, which, in addition to the offices and retail showrooms, housed a concert hall that became a leading center of N.Y. musical life. In 1925, headquarters were established in the Steinway Building on 57th St. Theodore was especially interested in the scientific aspects of piano construction and made a study of acoustical theories, which enabled him to introduce important improvements. He returned to Germany in 1870.

On May 17, 1876, the firm was incorporated and William was elected president. He opened a London branch in 1876 and established a European factory at Hamburg in 1880. That year he also bought 400 acres of land on Long Island Sound and established there the village of Steinway (now part of Long Island City), where since 1910 the entire manufacturing plant has been located. Control and active management of the business, now the largest of its kind in the world, has remained in the hands of the founder's descendants. Theodore E. Steinway (d. N.Y., April 8, 1957), grandson of Henry E. Steinway, was president from 1927. In 1955 he was succeeded by his son, Henry Steinway.

The firm was sold to CBS in 1972, although the Steinway family continued a close association. In 1988 Steinway & Sons celebrated its 135th anniversary with a special concert in N.Y. and the unveiling of its 500,000th piano.

stem. The vertical line attached to a NOTE head.

step. A melodic PROGRESSION of a SECOND; also, a degree. *Chromatic step,* progression of a CHROMATIC second; *diatonic step,* progression between neighboring tones of any DIATONIC scale; *half step,* step of a SEMITONE; *whole step,* step of a WHOLE TONE.

stereophonic (Grk., solid sound). A recording technique developed in the 1950s to produce an impression of listening to an actual concert performance by having the sounds come from two directions (i.e., from two speakers).

Stern, Isaac, outstanding Russian-born American violinist; b. Kremenetz, July 21, 1920. Stern was taken to the U.S. as an infant and was trained by his mother, a professional singer. He studied the violin at the San Francisco Conservatory from 1928 to 1931, then with Louis Persinger. He also studied with Naoum Blinder from 1932 to 1937.

In 1936 Stern made his orchestra debut as soloist in CAMILLE SAINT-SAËNS's Third Violin Concerto with the San Francisco Symphony Orchestra. His N.Y. debut followed a year later. After further training in San Francisco, he returned to N.Y. and gave a notably successful concert in 1939. Four years later, his CARNEGIE HALL debut there was a triumph.

In 1947 Stern toured Australia, and in 1948 he made his European debut at the Lucerne Festival. He subsequently appeared regularly with American and European orchestras, and in 1956 he made a spectacularly successful tour of Rus-

PEOPLE IN MUSIC

sia. In 1961 he organized a trio with the pianist Eugene Istomin and the cellist Leonard Rose, which toured widely until Rose's death in 1984.

Stern performed as a soloist from the '60s on, along with guest appearances with orchestras around the world. He also became a well-known commentator on classical music, appearing on several public television programs. He has been active in general cultural undertakings, and is an energetic worker for the cause of human rights. In 1986 he celebrated the 50th anniversary of his orchestra debut.

Stern received various honors. In 1979 he was made an Officer of the French Legion of Honor. In 1984 he received the Kennedy Center Honors Award. In 1987 he was given the Wolf Prize of Israel. Stern belongs to the galaxy of virtuoso performers to whom fame is a natural adjunct to talent and industry.

Steuermann, Edward (Eduard), eminent Polish-American pianist, pedagogue, and composer; b. Sambor, near Lemberg (now Lvov), June 18, 1892; d. N.Y., Nov. 11, 1964. Steuermann studied piano with FERRUCCIO BUSONI in Berlin in 1911–12, and theory with ARNOLD SCHOENBERG from 1912 to 1914. He also took some composition lessons with ENGELBERT HUMPERDINCK.

PEOPLE IN MUSIC

Returning to Poland, Steuermann taught at the Paderewski School in Lvov, and concurrently at the Jewish Conservatory in Krakow from 1932 to 1936. In 1936 he emigrated to the U.S. He taught piano at the Juilliard School of Music in N.Y. from 1952 to 1964, and also was on the faculty of the Philadelphia Conservatory from 1948 to 1963. He gave summer classes at the Mozarteum in Salzburg and in Darmstadt in the '50s and '60s.

As a concert pianist and soloist with major orchestras, Steuermann was an ardent champion of NEW MUSIC, particularly of Arnold Schoenberg. He gave the first performance of Schoenberg's Piano Concerto in 1944 and also made excellent arrangements for piano of Schoenberg's operatic and symphonic works, among them ERWARTUNG, DIE GLÜCKLICHE HAND, KAMMERSYMPHONIE No. 1, and the Piano Concerto. He received the Schoenberg Medal from the ISCM in 1952.

Although he did not follow Schoenberg's method of composition with consistency, Steuermann's music possesses an expressionistic tension that is characteristic of the Second Viennese School.

Steuermann's nephew, Michael (Andreas) Gielen (b. Dresden, July 20, 1927), is a noted conductor who also specializes in works of Schoenberg.

PEOPLE IN MUSIC

Still, William Grant, eminent African-American composer; b. Woodville, Miss., May 11, 1895; d. Los Angeles, Dec. 3, 1978. Still's father was bandmaster in Woodville. After his death when Still was in his infancy, his mother moved the family to Little Rock, Arkansas, where she became a high school teacher. He grew up in a home with cultured, middle-class values, and his stepfather encouraged his interest in music by taking him to operettas and buying him opera recordings; he was also given violin lessons.

Still attended Wilberforce College in preparation for a medical career but became involved in musical activities on campus. After dropping out of college, he worked with various groups, including W. C. Handy's band in 1916. Still then attended the Oberlin College Conservatory.

During World War I, Still played violin in the U.S. Army. Afterward he returned to work with Handy and became oboist in the *Shuffle Along* orchestra in 1921. He then studied composition with EDGARD VARÈSE and at the New England Conservatory of Music in Boston. He held a Guggenheim fellowship in 1934–35. He was awarded honorary doctorates by Howard University (1941), Oberlin College (1947), and Bates College (1954).

Determined to develop a symphonic type of African-American music, Still wrote the *Afro-American Symphony* in 1930. In his music he occasionally made use of actual FOLK songs, but mostly he invented his thematic materials.

Still's well-written music is not well enough known. It includes operas, ballets, and incidental music, as well as five symphonies. He also composed other orchestral and chamber works, choral works, songs—including *Songs of Separation* (1949) and *From the Hearts of Women* (1961)—piano pieces, works for band, and arrangements of spirituals.

Still's second wife was the writer Verna Arvey, who collaborated with him as librettist in his stage works.

stochastic (from Grk. *stochos,* target). A term, borrowed from probability theory, denoting a modern compositional process that is governed by rules of probability. The term was introduced into music by IANNIS XENAKIS to designate a CHANCE composition whose elements (melody, harmony, rhythm, etc.) are circumscribed by the structural parameters of the initial thematic statement. Stochastic procedures are in actual practice equivalent to controlled IMPROVISATION.

Stockflöte (Ger., cane flute). Vertical FLUTE or RECORDER inserted in the upper part of a walking stick. It was manufactured in the first half of the 19th century in Austria and attained popularity among poetically inclined walkers in the Vienna wood, hills, and environs.

Stockhausen, Karlheinz, outstanding German composer; b. Modrath, near Cologne, Aug. 22, 1928. Stockhausen was orphaned during World War II and was compelled to hold various jobs to support himself. All the same, he learned to play the piano, violin, and oboe, then studied piano and

MUSICAL INSTRUMENT

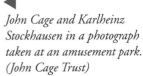

PEOPLE IN MUSIC

◀

John Cage and Karlheinz Stockhausen in a photograph taken at an amusement park. (John Cage Trust)

composition at the Cologne Staatliche Hochschule für Musik from 1947 to 1950. He also took courses in German philology, philosophy, and musicology at the University of Cologne.

After studies in Darmstadt in 1951, Stockhausen received instruction in composition from OLIVIER MESSIAEN in Paris in 1952. He subsequently studied communications theory and phonetics with Werner Meyer-Eppler at the University of Bonn from 1954 to 1956.

Beginning in 1953, Stockhausen was active at the ELECTRONIC MUSIC studio of the West German Radio in Cologne. He also was a lecturer at the Internationalen Ferienkürse für Musik in Darmstadt until 1974, and was founder-artistic director of the Cologne Kürse für Neue Musik from 1963 to 1968. He likewise served as professor of composition at the Cologne Hochschule für Musik from 1971 to 1977.

Stockhausen undertook energetic missionary activities in behalf of NEW MUSIC as a lecturer and master of ceremonies at AVANT-GARDE meetings all over the world. He made a lecture tour of Canadian and American universities in 1958, and in 1965 was a visiting professor of composition at the University of Pennsylvania and in 1966–67 at the University of California at Davis. In 1969 he gave highly successful public lectures in England that were very well attended.

Stockhausen was made a member of the Swedish Royal Academy (1970), Berlin Academy of Arts (1973), and American Academy and Institute of Arts and Letters (1979). He also was made a Commandeur dans l'Ordre des Arts et des Lettres of France (1985) and an honorary member of the Royal Academy of Music in London (1987).

In his early works, Stockhausen used the techniques of MUSIQUE CONCRÈTE as one ingredient in his personal style. His first works tended to have abrupt changes in instrumentation, accompanied by repetitive percussion patterns. He used highly complex COUNTERPOINT, allowing for much DISSONANCE, often set against a PEDAL-POINT or repeated tone.

Stockhausen perfected a system of constructivist composition in which the subjective choice of the performer determines when to perform certain themes. While this allows for CHANCE elements in each performance to occur, Stockhausen also included prerecorded materials that were preselected by him.

Performances of Stockhausen's works are often directed by himself, and are accompanied by screen projections and audience participation. He also specifies the architectural aspects of the auditoriums in which he gives his demonstrations.

Among his many notable compositions are:

Klavierstücke I–IV (1952–53), *V–X* (1954–55), and *XI* (1956)

Zeitmasse for five woodwinds (1955–56)

Gruppen for three orchestras (1955–57)

Gesang der Jünglinge, ELECTRONIC MUSIC after the Book of Daniel, scored for five groups of loudspeakers surrounding the audience (1956)

Kontakte for electronics (1959–60)

Momente for soprano, four choruses, and 13 instrumentalists (1962–64)

Sternklang, ambitious "park music" for five groups (1971)

Licht (Light), a projected cycle of seven operas, one for each day week of the week: *Dienstag* (Tuesday, 1977–91); *Donnerstag* (Thursday, 1978–80); *Samstag* (Saturday, 1981–83); *Montag* (Monday, 1985–88); and *Freitag* (Friday, 1996)

Stokowski, Leopold (Anthony), celebrated, spectacularly endowed, and magically communicative English-born American conductor; b. London (of a Polish father and an Irish mother), April 18, 1882; d. Nether Wallop, Hampshire, Sept. 13, 1977. Stokowski attended Queen's College, Oxford, and the Royal College of Music in London, where he studied organ, theory, and composition. At the age of 18 he obtained the post of organist at St. James, Piccadilly.

In 1905 Stokowski went to America and served as organist and choirmaster at St. Bartholomew's in N.Y. He be-

PEOPLE IN MUSIC

came a U.S. citizen in 1915. In 1909 he was engaged to conduct the Cincinnati Symphony Orchestra. Although his contract was for five years, he obtained a release in 1912 to accept an offer from the Philadelphia Orchestra, the beginning of a long and spectacular career as a symphony conductor. He led the Philadelphia Orchestra for 24 years as its sole conductor, bringing it to a degree of brilliance that rivaled the greatest orchestras in the world.

In 1931 Stokowski was officially designated by the board of directors of the Philadelphia Orchestra as music director, which gave him control over the choice of guest conductors and soloists. He conducted most of the repertoire without using a score, an impressive accomplishment at the time. After some years of leading the orchestra with a baton, he finally dispensed with it and shaped the music with only the fingers of his hands. He emphasized the colorful elements in the music, creating the famous "Philadelphia sound" in the strings and achieving a well-nigh BEL CANTO quality.

Tall and slender, with an aureole of blond hair, Stokowski's presented a striking contrast with his stocky, mustachioed German predecessors. He was the first conductor to attain the status of a star comparable to that of a motion picture actor. Abandoning the proverbial ivory tower in which most conductors dwelt, he actually made an appearance as a movie actor in the film *100 Men and a Girl*.

In 1940 he agreed to participate in the production of Walt Disney's celebrated film *Fantasia,* which featured both live performers and animated characters. Stokowski conducted the music and in one sequence engaged in a bantering colloquy with Mickey Mouse.

Stokowski was praised in superlative terms in the press, but not all music critics approved of his cavalier treatment of classic masterpieces. He altered orchestrations, he doubled some solo passages in the brass, and he occasionally introduced percussion instruments not provided in the score. He even cut individual bars that seemed to him devoid of musical action. Furthermore, Stokowski's own orchestral arrangements of JOHANN SEBASTIAN BACH raised the eyebrows of professional musicologists. Yet there is no denying the effectiveness of the sonority and the subtlety of color that he created by such means. Many great musicians hailed Stokow-

Stokowski changed the seating of the orchestra, placing violins to the left and cellos to the right.

ski's new orchestral sound. SERGEI RACHMANINOFF regarded the Philadelphia Orchestra under Stokowski, and later under EUGENE ORMANDY, as the greatest with which he had performed.

Stokowski boldly risked his popularity with Philadelphia audiences by introducing modern works. He conducted ARNOLD SCHOENBERG's music, culminating in the introduction of his formidable score GURRELIEDER in 1932. An even greater gesture of defiance was his world premiere of AMÉRIQUES by EDGARD VARÈSE in 1926, a score that opens with a siren and thrives on DISSONANCE. Stokowski made history by joining the forces of the Philadelphia Orchestra with the Philadelphia Grand Opera Company in the first American performance of ALBAN BERG's masterpiece WOZZECK (March 31, 1931). The opposition of some listeners became vocal. When audible commotion in the audience erupted during his performance of ANTON WEBERN's Symphony, he abruptly stopped conducting, walked off the stage, then returned only to begin the work all over again.

From his earliest years with the Philadelphia Orchestra Stokowski adopted the habit of addressing the audience, cautioning them to keep their peace during the performance of a modernistic score or reprimanding them for their lack of progressive views. Once he even took to task the prim Philadelphia ladies for bringing their knitting to the concert. In 1933 the board of directors took an unusual step in announcing that there would be no more "debatable music" performed by the orchestra, but Stokowski refused to heed this proclamation. Another eruption of discontent ensued when he programmed some Soviet music at a youth concert and trained the children to sing the INTERNATIONALE.

Interested in new electronic sound, Stokowski was the first to make use of the THEREMIN in the orchestra in order to enhance the sonorities of the bass section. He was also instrumental in introducing recordings.

In 1936 Stokowski resigned as music director of the Philadelphia Orchestra. He was succeeded by Ormandy but continued to conduct concerts as coconductor until 1938. From 1940 to 1942 he took a newly organized All-American Youth Orchestra on a tour in the U.S. and in South America. During the 1942–43 season he was associate conductor, with ARTURO TOSCANINI, of the NBC Symphony Orchestra. He shared the 1949–50 season with DMITRI MITROPOULOS as conductor of the N.Y. Philharmonic, and from 1955 to 1960 he conducted the Houston Symphony Orchestra.

In 1962 Stokowski organized in N.Y. the American Symphony Orchestra and led it until 1972. On April 26, 1965, at the age of 83, he conducted the orchestra in the first complete performance of the Fourth Symphony of CHARLES IVES. In 1973 he went to London, where he continued to make recordings and conduct occasional concerts; he also appeared in television interviews. He died in his sleep at the age of 95. Rumor had it that he had a contract signed for a gala performance on his 100th birthday in 1982.

Stokowski was married three times: his first wife was the pianist Olga Samaroff, whom he married in 1911 and divorced in 1923; his second wife was Evangeline Brewster Johnson, heiress to the Johnson and Johnson drug fortune; they were married in 1926 and divorced in 1937; his third marriage, to Gloria Vanderbilt, produced a ripple of prurient newspaper publicity because of the disparity in their ages (he was 63, she 21); they were married in 1945 and divorced in 1955.

Stoltzman, Richard (Leslie), outstanding American clarinetist; b. Omaha, July 12, 1942. Stoltzman began clarinet lessons when he was eight and gained experience playing in local JAZZ settings with his father, an alto saxophonist. He then studied mathematics and music at Ohio State University, earning a bachelor of music degree in 1964, and also studied clarinet with Robert Marcellus. After studies at Yale University for his master's degree, awarded in 1967, he completed his clarinet training with Harold Wright at the Marlboro Music School and with Kalman Opperman in N.Y. He then pursued postgraduate studies at Columbia University's Teachers College from 1967 to 1970.

Stoltzman played in many concerts at Marlboro. He cofounded the group Tashi ("good fortune" in Tibetan) with PETER SERKIN, Ida Kavafian, and Fred Sherry in 1973 and toured widely with the group. He likewise taught at the California Institute of the Arts from 1970 to 1975.

PEOPLE IN MUSIC

Stoltzman made his N.Y. solo recital debut in 1974. After receiving the Avery Fisher Prize in 1977, he pursued an international career as a virtuoso. He appeared as soloist with major orchestras, as a chamber music artist, and as a solo recitalist. In 1982 he became the first clarinetist ever to give a solo recital at N.Y.'s Carnegie Hall. In 1986 he received the Avery Fisher Artist Award, and in 1989 he made his debut at the London Promenade concerts as soloist in the Mozart Clarinet Concerto.

Stoltzman maintains an extensive repertoire, ranging from the classics to the AVANT-GARDE, and including popular music genres. He has also commissioned works and made his own transcriptions.

stomp. 1. A generic term for a beat pattern in AFRICAN MUSIC, in which a foot stomping on the ground is integral to the rhythm, often engendering a correspondingly obstinate melodic lilt. 2. An early JAZZ composition for dancing. The *Black Bottom Stomp* is a famous example.

Stomp. Theatrical presentation (1991), originally presented in London. The brainchild of Luke Cresswell and Steve McNicholas, it is built around a group of polished performers who create irresistibly rhythmic music and dance using commonplace objects (Zippo lighters, push brooms, newspapers, oil drums, etc.). There is no plot or dialog, with the highly regimented performance antics recalling the essential practices of both English VAUDEVILLE and the more rarified U.S. HAPPENING.

The work was enormously popular in London and Edinburgh and subsequently found a second home in N.Y., with a fresh-faced American cast. Critically lauded, *Stomp* has been seen by countless audiences throughout England and the U.S. To date, there are five distinct casts.

Stone, Carl, innovative American composer and performer; b. Los Angeles, Feb. 10, 1953. He studied with James Tenney and MORTON SUBOTNICK at the California Institute of the Arts in Valencia (B.F.A., 1975). He served as music director of KPFK Radio in Los Angeles (1978–81) and as di-

PEOPLE IN MUSIC

Carl Stone, c. 1995. ▶

rector of Meet the Composer/California (from 1981). In 1985 he was co–artistic director of the 7th New Music America Festival. Among his awards are an NEA grant (1981–82), tour support awards from the California Arts Council (1984–90), and annual ASCAP awards (from 1985). In 1989 he was funded by the Asian Cultural Council for a six-month residence in Japan. From 1992 to 1995 he served as president of the American Music Center.

Stone composes exclusively electroacoustic music, often employing natural sounds and occasional fragments of familiar pieces, as in his *Sonali* (1988, WOLFGANG AMADEUS MOZART'S *THE MAGIC FLUTE*); Hop Ken (1987, MODEST MUSSORGSKY'S *PICTURES AT AN EXHIBITION*); and Shing Kee (1986, recording of a Japanese pop star singing a FRANZ SCHUBERT LIED). He inscrutably manipulates his Macintosh computer in solo performances to create sensuous, playful, and often enigmatic real-time compositions.

Stone has performed extensively in the U.S., Canada, Europe, Asia, Australia, South America, and the Near East. Among choreographers who have used his music are Bill T. Jones, Ping Chong, and Blondell Cummings. His *Ruen Pair* (1993) was created as part of a (Paul Dresher) consortium commission from the Meet the Composer/*Reader's Digest* Fund. His untitled collaborative work with Kuniko Kisanuki for electronics and dancer (1995) was commissioned by the

Stone is also an ethnic food enthusiast (see J. Gold, "Carl Stone: Between Bytes," in *Los Angeles Times*, Aug. 19, 1990), naming many of his pieces after favorite restaurants.

Aichi-ken Cultural Center in Nagoya, Japan. In 1998 he received a residency fellowship to the Bellagio Center in Italy.

Stone Guest, The *(Kamennyi gost).* Opera by ALEXANDER DARGOMYZHSKY, 1872, after Pushkin's poem. The score was left unfinished at Dargomyzhsky's death and was completed by NIKOLAI RIMSKY-KORSAKOV and CÉSAR CUI. The first performance took place posthumously in St. Petersburg. Pushkin's story is based on the same story as Da Ponte's *DON GIOVANNI* libretto for WOLFGANG AMADEUS MOZART.

The stone guest of the title is the statue of the Commendatore slain by Don Juan. Not only does Juan try to seduce his widow, but he also invites the statue to supper. The marble handshake of the Stone Guest crushes Don Juan, and he falls dead.

The opera is important because of Dargomyzhsky's successful adaptation of the inflections of Russian speech.

Stookey, (Noël) **Paul.** *See* PETER, PAUL, AND MARY.

stop (1). One of numerous devices on the ORGAN console, each in the form of a knob. The player draws (pulls) a stop according to the desirable TONE COLOR or instrumental quality that is marked on each knob. That part of the mechanism in turn admits and stops (directs) the flow of wind to the grooves beneath the chosen pipe. Several stops can be drawn simultaneously to produce a stronger or more complex sound.

Rows of organ pipes of like character are arranged in graduated succession. These are called *speaking* or *sounding* stops, classified as *flue* (having flue pipes) and *reed* (having reed pipes) work.

Auxiliary stop, one to be drawn with some other stop(s), to reinforce the tone of the latter; *complete stop,* one having at least one pipe for each KEY of the MANUAL to which it belongs; *compound stop,* mixture stop; *divided stop,* the lower half of whose REGISTER is controlled by a different stop knob separate from the upper, and bearing a different name; *flue stop,* one composed of flue pipes; *foundation stop,* one of normal 8′ pitch; *half, incomplete,* or *imperfect stop,* one produc-

The expression "pull out all the stops" comes from the organ world—it means to go all out.

ing (about) half the TONES of the full SCALE of its manual; *mechanical stop,* one not having a set of pipes, but governing some mechanical device; *mixture stop,* one with two or more ranks of pipes, thus producing two or more tones for each key; *mutation stop,* one producing tones a MAJOR THIRD or PERFECT FIFTH (or a higher OCTAVE of either) above the 8′ stops; *partial stop,* half stop; *pedal stop,* a stop on the pedal; *reed stop,* one composed of reed pipes; *solo stop,* one adapted for the production of characteristic melodic effects, whether on the solo organ or not; *sounding* or *speaking stop,* one having pipes and producing musical tones.

stop (2). 1. On stringed instruments, the pressure of a finger on a string to vary the PITCH; a double stop is when two or more strings are so pressed and sounded simultaneously. 2. On WIND instruments with finger holes, the closing of a hole by finger or key to alter the pitch. 3. On instruments of the HORN family, the partial or total closing of the bell by inserting the hand.

stop time. A rhythmic device in JAZZ in which the group suddenly stops playing while one or more members play a solo. In older jazz, stop times were worked out in advance, while in later jazz, the soloist could improvise more freely and thus direct the return of the group, or the individual members might return gradually rather than all at once. The most effective use of stop time is in up-tempo music, but the CADENZA for the soloist before the piece ends is standard in all tempos.

Stormy Weather. BALLAD by HAROLD ARLEN, 1933, originally part of the *Cotton Club Parade* of 1933. Its melancholy, hypnotic power later found a platform in the 1943 film of the same name, as sung by LENA HORNE.

Stradivari (Latinized as Stradivarius), **Antonio,** celebrated Italian violin maker; b. probably in Cremona, 1644; d. probably there, Dec. 18, 1737. Stradivari was a pupil of NICCOLÒ AMATI in the early 1660s. His earliest known violin dates from 1666. He may have worked for Amati and others from 1666 before purchasing the house that contained his

SCOTT JOPLIN wrote a *Stop Time Rag* in which foot stomps are notated in the score, so that when the music stops the stomping continues—giving the effect of a soloist emerging from the full orchestra.

PEOPLE IN MUSIC

workshop from 1680. His finest instruments were made in the period from 1700 to 1725, but he worked to the year of his death. He made his last instrument at the age of 92. His cellos command even higher prices than the violins, and violas the highest of all, for he made very few of them.

Stradivari had 11 children, of whom Francesco (1671–1743) and Omobono (1679–1742) were his coworkers. Stradivari also made early-style viols, guitars, lutes, mandolins, etc.

strain. In general, a SONG, tune, air, or MELODY. Also, some well-defined passage in a piece. Technically, a period, sentence, or short division of a composition. A motive or theme.

strambotto (It., rustic song). A 16th-century vocal genre akin to the MADRIGAL and FROTTOLA, set to poetry with specific STANZA and rhyme schemes. Favored by Lord Byron, the strambotto is distinguished by simplicity, symmetry of phrase, and accessible harmony.

Strange Fruit. The song tells the story of a lynching in the South. It was first performed by the JAZZ singer BILLIE HOLIDAY, and it took a good deal of courage to perform it. She often closed her nightclub act with the song. Although often attributed to Holiday, it was actually written by Lewis Allen.

Strangers in the Night. A rare No. 1 pop hit for FRANK SINATRA in the '60s. This Kaempfert-Snyder-Singleton song (1966) was featured in the film *A Man Could Get Killed* and netted Sinatra a Grammy. It contains the well-known "doobie-doobie-doo" in the chorus.

stranka (strančica). Transverse wooden FLUTE of Croatia and Slavonia, with a cylindrical bore and five or six finger holes. It is associated with shepherds.

Straszny Dwóri. See HAUNTED CASTLE, THE.

Stratas, Teresa (real name, Anastasia Stratakis), outstanding Canadian soprano of Greek extraction; b. Toronto, May 26,

His label reads: "Antonius Stradivarius Cremonensis. Fecit Anno . . . (A x S)."

MUSICAL INSTRUMENT

PEOPLE IN MUSIC

1938. Stratas's father owned a restaurant in a town near Toronto, and she was allowed from early childhood to sing for customers. She also sang in concert with her brother, a violinist, and her sister, a pianist.

In 1954 Stratas entered the Royal Conservatory of Music of Toronto, where she studied voice with Irene Jessner. She graduated with an Artist Diploma in 1959, shortly after making her professional operatic debut with the Toronto Opera Festival as Mimi in *LA BOHÈME* on Oct. 13, 1958. In 1959 she was a cowinner of the Metropolitan Opera Auditions, which led to her formal debut with the company in N.Y. that year, as Poussette in *MANON*. She soon established herself as a singer of great versatility.

Stratas sang virtually all the standard SOPRANO parts, and demonstrated her particular mettle and fettle in the complete version of ALBAN BERG's *LULU*, which was given for the first time in Paris in 1979. In 1986 she appeared on Broadway in *Rags*. Also in N.Y., she created the role of Marie Antoinette in JOHN CORIGLIANO's *The Ghosts of Versailles* (Dec. 19, 1991). In 1992 she appeared as Mélisande in Chicago, and in 1994 she appeared again at the Metropolitan Opera in both *IL TABARRO* and *PAGLIACCI*. She won international acclaim for her dramatic portrayal of Violetta in Franco Zeffirelli's film version of *LA TRAVIATA* in 1983.

Stratas was made an Officer of the Order of Canada in 1972. A film portrait of her was made by Harry Rasky as *StrataSphere*. Her remarkable lyric voice made her interpretations of such roles as Cherubino, Zerlina, Lisa in THE QUEEN OF SPADES, Marguerite in *FAUST*, Micaëla, Liù, and KURT WEILL's Jenny in *AUFSTEIG UND FALL DER STADT MAHAGONNY* particularly memorable.

strath·spay′

strathspey (Scots, valley of the Spey river). A lively Scottish dance, somewhat slower than the REEL. It is also in $\frac{4}{4}$ time, progressing rhythmically as one 16th note followed by a dotted eighth (SCOTCH SNAP).

Strauss. Family of celebrated Austrian WALTZ composers and musicians:

1. **Johann** (Baptist) **Strauss** I, violinist, conductor, and composer, known as "Father of the Waltz"; b. Vienna,

PEOPLE IN MUSIC

March 14, 1804; d. there, Sept. 25, 1849. Johann was born into a humble Jewish family of Hungarian descent. Called "black Schani," he made a concerted effort to conceal his Jewish origins. His father was an innkeeper who apprenticed his son to a bookbinder, but Johann's musical talent revealed itself at an early age. After Strauss ran away, his parents consented to his becoming a musician.

At the age of 15 Johann became a violist in Michael Pamer's dance orchestra, where he found a friend in JOSEF LANNER. In 1819 he became a member of Lanner's small band, and later served as second conductor of Lanner's orchestra in 1824–25.

In 1825 Johann organized his own orchestra, which quickly became popular in Viennese inns. He composed his first waltz, *Täuberln-Walzer*, in 1826. His renown spread, and his orchestra increased rapidly in size and efficiency. From 1833 he undertook concert tours in Austria, and in 1834 was appointed bandmaster of the first Vienna militia regiment. His tours extended to Berlin in 1834, and to the Netherlands and Belgium in 1836. In 1837–38 he invaded Paris with a picked corps of 28 and had immense success both there and in London. In 1846 he was named k.k. (i.e., *kaiserlich und königlich,* imperial and royal) Hofballmusikdirektor.

After catching scarlet fever from one of his children, Johann died at the age of 45. Among his published waltzes, the *Lorelei-, Gabrielen-, Taglioni-, Cäcilien-, Victoria-, Kettenbrucken-,* and *Bajaderen-Walzer* are favorites. Also popular are *Elektrische Funken, Mephistos Höllenrufe,* and the *Donau-Lieder.* He also wrote 33 GALOPS, 14 POLKAS, 33 QUADRILLES, COTILLIONS, and CONTREDANSES, 23 MARCHES (including the *RADETZKY-MARSCH,* 1848), and nine potpourris.

Johann I had three sons who carried on the family musical tradition:

2. **Johann** (Baptist) **Strauss II,** greatly renowned violinist, conductor, and composer, known as the "Waltz King"; b. Vienna, Oct. 25, 1825; d. there, June 3, 1899. His father intended him for a business career, but his musical talent manifested itself when he was a mere child. At the age of six he wrote the first 36 bars of waltz music that later was published as *Erster Gedanke.* While he was still a child, his

A gilded statue of Johann Strauss II, in the Stadt park in Vienna. (Bob Krist/Corbis) ▶

Johann Strauss II time line

1825	Born
1831	Composes the first 36 bars of a waltz that later was published as *Erster Gedanke*
1842	Pursues violin training with Anton Kohlmann
1844	Makes his first public appearance as conductor of his own ensemble at Dommayer's Casino at Hietzing
1849	Upon the death of his father, Johann joins his father's band with his own
1856–86	Makes tours of Europe
1863–71	Serves as k.k. Hofballmusikdirektor in Vienna
1867	Composes the ever-popular ON THE BEAUTIFUL BLUE DANUBE waltz, one of nearly 500 dance pieces (498 opus numbers) produced in his lifetime
1872	Directs 14 "monster concerts" in Boston and four in N.Y.
1874	The perennially popular operetta DIE FLEDERMAUS is first staged at the Theater an der Wien

mother arranged for him to study secretly with Franz Amon, his father's concertmaster. After his father left the family in 1842, he pursued violin training with Anton Kohlmann. He also studied theory with Joseph Drechsler until 1844.

Johann made his first public appearance as conductor of his own ensemble at Dommayer's Casino at Hietzing in 1844. His success was instantaneous, and his new waltzes won wide popularity. Despite his father's objections to this rivalry in the family, Johann continued his concerts with increasing success.

After his father's death in 1849, Johann united his father's band with his own, subsequently making regular tours of Europe from 1856 to 1886. From 1863 to 1871 he was k.k. Hofballmusikdirektor in Vienna. In 1872 he accepted an invitation to visit the U.S. and directed 14 "monster concerts" in Boston and four in N.Y. He then turned to the theater.

Johann's finest OPERETTA is *DIE FLEDERMAUS* (The bat), which continues to hold the stage as one of the masterpieces of its genre. It was first staged at the Theater an der Wien in 1874, and within a few months was given in N.Y. Productions followed all over the world. It was performed in Paris with a new libretto as *La Tzigane* in 1877. The original version was finally presented there as *La Chauve-souris* in 1904. Also very successful was the operetta *DER ZIGEUNERBARON* (The gypsy baron), which premiered in 1885. All his operettas were first produced in Vienna, with the exception of

EINE NACHT IN VENEDIG (A night in venice) which premiered in Berlin in 1883.

Although Strauss composed extensively for the theater, his supreme achievement remains his dance music. He wrote almost 500 pieces (498 op. numbers). Of his waltzes the greatest popularity was achieved by ON THE BEAUTIFUL BLUE DANUBE (1867), whose main tune became one of the best known in all of music.

Other fine waltzes by Johann II include *Acceleration* (1860), *Morgenblätter* (1864), *Artist's Life* (1867), *Tales of the Vienna Woods* (1868), *Wine, Women, and Song* (1869), *Wiener Blut* (1873), *Where the Citrons Bloom* (1874), *Roses from the South* (1880), *Voices of Spring* (1883), and *Emperor* (1889).

Johann also composed numerous quadrilles, polkas, polka-mazurkas, marches, and galops, as well as several pieces in collaboration with his brothers.

3. **Josef Strauss,** conductor and composer; b. Vienna, Aug. 22, 1827; d. there, July 21, 1870. Josef studied theory with Franz Dolleschal and violin with Franz Anton. He was versatile and gifted, and, despite lifelong illnesses, wrote poetry, painted, and patented inventions.

Josef first appeared in public conducting in Vienna a set of his waltzes in 1853, and later appeared regularly as a conductor with his brother Johann's orchestra from 1856 to 1862. Their younger brother Eduard joined them in 1862, but Johann left the orchestra a year later, and Josef and Eduard continued to conduct the family orchestra.

Josef wrote 283 opus numbers, many of which reveal a composer of remarkable talent. Among his outstanding waltzes are *Perlen der Liebe* (1857), *5 Kleebald'ln* (1857), *Wiener Kinder* (1858), *Schwert und Leier* (1860), *Friedenspalmen* (1867), and *Aquarellen* (1869). He also composed polkas, quadrilles, marches, etc.

4. **Eduard Strauss,** conductor and composer; b. Vienna, March 15, 1835; d. there, Dec. 28, 1916. Eduard studied theory and composition with Gottfried Preyer and Simon Sechter, as well as violin and harp.

After playing harp in his brother Johann's orchestra, Eduard made his debut as a conductor and composer with it at the Wintergarten of the Dianabad-Saal in 1862. After Jo-

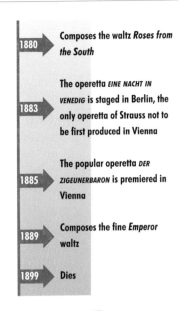

1880	Composes the waltz *Roses from the South*
1883	The operetta EINE NACHT IN VENEDIG is staged in Berlin, the only operetta of Strauss not to be first produced in Vienna
1885	The popular operetta DER ZIGEUNERBARON is premiered in Vienna
1889	Composes the fine *Emperor* waltz
1899	Dies

JOHANNES BRAHMS wrote on a lady's fan the opening measures of the famous *Blue Danube* waltz and underneath wrote: "Leider nicht von Brahms" (Alas, not by Brahms).

hann left the orchestra in 1863, Eduard and his brother Josef shared the conductorship of the orchestra until the latter's death in 1870.

From 1870 to 1878 Eduard was k.k. Hofballmusikdirektor, then made annual tours of Europe as a guest conductor, and also with his own orchestra. In 1890 and 1900–1901 he toured throughout the U.S., retiring in 1901.

Eduard wrote some 300 works, but they failed to rival the superior works of his brothers.

Strauss, Richard (Georg), great German composer and distinguished conductor, one of the most inventive music masters of the modern age; b. Munich, June 11, 1864; d. Garmisch-Partenkirchen, Sept. 8, 1949. Strauss's father was Franz (Joseph) Strauss (b. Parkstein, Feb. 26, 1822; d. Munich, May 31, 1905), a horn player and composer. Although a violent opponent of RICHARD WAGNER, Franz was valued highly by the master, who entrusted to him the solo horn passages at the premieres of *TRISTAN UND ISOLDE, DIE MEISTERSINGER VON NÜRNBERG,* and *PARSIFAL.*

Growing up in a musical environment, Richard studied piano as a child with August Tombo, harpist in the Court Orchestra. He then took violin lessons from Benno Walter, its concertmaster, and later received instruction from the court conductor, Friedrich Wilhelm Meyer.

According to his own account, Strauss began to improvise songs and piano pieces at an early age. Among his early works was the song *Weihnachtslied* (Christmas song), followed by a piano dance, *Schneiderpolka* (Tailor's polka). In 1881 his first orchestral work, Symphony in D Minor, was premiered in Munich under Hermann Levi. This was followed by the Symphony in F Minor, premiered by the N.Y. Philharmonic under Theodore Thomas in 1884.

Strauss also made progress as a performing musician. At 20, HANS VON BÜLOW engaged him as assistant conductor of his Meiningen Orchestra. About that time Strauss became associated with the poet and musician Alexander Ritter, who introduced him to the "music of the future," as it was commonly called, represented by orchestral works of FRANZ LISZT and operas by Wagner.

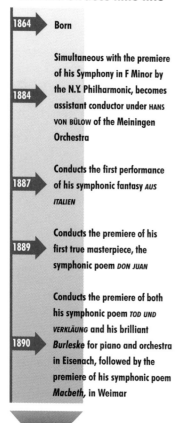

PEOPLE IN MUSIC

Richard Strauss time line

1864	Born
1884	Simultaneous with the premiere of his Symphony in F Minor by the N.Y. Philharmonic, becomes assistant conductor under HANS VON BÜLOW of the Meiningen Orchestra
1887	Conducts the first performance of his symphonic fantasy AUS ITALIEN
1889	Conducts the premiere of his first true masterpiece, the symphonic poem DON JUAN
1890	Conducts the premiere of both his symphonic poem TOD UND VERKLÄUNG and his brilliant Burleske for piano and orchestra in Eisenach, followed by the premiere of his symphonic poem Macbeth, in Weimar

In 1886 Strauss received an appointment as the third conductor of the Court Opera in Munich. In 1887 he conducted in Munich the first performance of his symphonic fantasy, AUS ITALIEN (From Italy). This was followed by the composition of his first true masterpiece, the symphonic poem DON JUAN (1888–89), in which he applied the thematic ideas of Liszt. He conducted its premiere in Weimar in 1889. It became the first of a series of his symphonic poems, all based on literary subjects.

Strauss's next symphonic poem of great significance was TOD UND VERKLÄRUNG (Death and transfiguration; 1888–89). In 1890, he conducted its premiere performance in Eisenach, on the same program with the premiere of his brilliant *Burleske* for piano and orchestra (1885–86), featuring EUGÈNE D'ALBERT as soloist. There followed the first performance of the symphonic poem *Macbeth* (1886–88; revised 1891), which Strauss conducted in Weimar that same year. In these works Strauss established himself as a master of PROGRAM MUSIC. He effectively adapted Wagner's system of LEITMOTIVS to the domain of symphonic music. His symphonic poems were interwoven with motives, each representing a relevant programmatic element.

Turning to stage music, Strauss wrote his first opera, *Guntram* (1892–93), for which he also composed the text. He conducted its premiere in Weimar on May 10, 1894, with the leading soprano role performed by Pauline de Ahna. They were married that September and remained together throughout their lives. She died on May 13, 1950, a few months after Strauss.

While active as a composer, Strauss did not neglect his conducting career. In 1894 he succeeded von Bülow as conductor of the Berlin Philharmonic, leading it for a season. Also in 1894 he became assistant conductor of the Munich Court Opera, and was promoted two years later to chief conductor. In 1896–97 he filled engagements as a guest conductor in European music centers. His works of the period included the sparkling TILL EULENSPIEGELS LUSTIGE STREICHE (Till Eulenspiegel's merry pranks), which premiered in 1895; ALSO SPRACH ZARATHUSTRA (Thus spake Zarathustra), a philosophical symphonic poem after Nietzsche, first performed in

1894 Conducts the premiere of his first stage work, *Guntram,* in Weimar, with the leading soprano role performed by Pauline de Ahna, whom Strauss marries later in the year

1894 Succeeds von Bülow as conductor of the Berlin Philharmonic and becomes assistant conductor of the Munich Court Opera

1895 The first performance of the sparkling TILL EULENSPIEGELS LUSTIGE STREICHE is given in Cologne

1896 ALSO SPRACH ZARATHUSTRA, tone poem after Nietzsche, is heard for the first time in Frankfurt am Main, Strauss conducting

1898 DON QUIXOTE, variations with cello solo, after Cervantes, is performed for the first time in Cologne, the same year that Strauss assumes the conductorship of the Berlin Royal Opera

1899 Conducts the first performance of his autobiographical symphonic poem, EIN HELDENLEBEN, in Frankfurt am Main

1901 His first successful opera, FEUERSNOT, is premiered in Dresden

1903 Appears at the Strauss Festival in London and receives an honorary doctor of philosophy degree from the University of Heidelberg

1904 Visits the U.S. for the first time, giving the premiere performance of his *SYMPHONIA DOMESTICA* at Carnegie Hall

1905 The dramatic opera *SALOME* is first staged in Dresden

1909 *ELEKTRA*, to a libretto by HUGO VON HOFMANNSTHAL, is premiered in Dresden

1911 The opéra-bouffe *DER ROSENKAVALIER* is first staged in Dresden

1914 Receives an honorary doctor of music degree from Oxford University

1915 *EINE ALPENSINFONIE* is premiered with the Dresden Court Orchestra, Strauss conducting

1917 Helps to found the Salzburg Festival, where he later appears as a conductor

1919 *DIE FRAU OHNE SCHATTEN* is premiered in Vienna, the same year Strauss assumes the post of codirector of the Vienna State Opera

1920 Tours with the Vienna Philharmonic in South America

1924–33 Produces three final operas for Dresden: *INTERMEZZO* (Nov. 4, 1924), *Die ägyptische Helena* (June 6, 1928), and *ARABELLA* (July 1, 1933)

1933–35 Serves as president of the newly organized Reichsmusikkammer

1896, with Strauss conducting; and *DON QUIXOTE,* variations with a cello solo, after Cervantes, from 1898.

In 1898 Strauss became a conductor at the Berlin Royal Opera, and ten years later he was made its Generalmusikdirektor, a position he held until 1918. He conducted the first performance of his extraordinary autobiographical symphonic poem *EIN HELDENLEBEN* (A hero's life) in Frankfurt am Main on March 3, 1899. There followed his first successful opera, *FEUERSNOT,* from 1901. In June 1903 Strauss was guest of honor at the Strauss Festival in London. That same year, the University of Heidelberg give him an honorary doctor of philosophy degree.

For his first visit to the U.S. in early 1904, Strauss presented the premiere performance of his *SYMPHONIA DOMESTICA* (Domestic symphony) at CARNEGIE HALL in N.Y. The score represented a day in the Strauss household, containing an interlude describing, quite literally, the feeding of the newly born baby. Some critics and audience members were shocked by its intimacy.

Next came Strauss's opera *SALOME,* to the German translation of Oscar Wilde's play. Ernst von Schuch led its premiere in Dresden on Dec. 9, 1905. *Salome* had its American premiere at the Metropolitan Opera in N.Y. on Jan. 22, 1907. The ghastly subject, involving intended incest, the famous dance of the seven veils, and decapitation, administered such a shock to the public and the press that the Metropolitan Opera took it off the repertoire after only two performances.

Scarcely less forceful was Strauss's next opera, *ELEKTRA,* to a libretto by the Austrian poet and dramatist HUGO VON HOFMANNSTHAL. In it, the horrors of matricide were depicted with extraordinary force in unabashedly DISSONANT harmonies. Schuch conducted its premiere in Dresden on Jan. 25, 1909.

Strauss then decided to prove to his admirers that he was quite able to write melodious operas to charm the musical ear. This he accomplished in his next production, also to a text of Hofmannsthal, *DER ROSENKAVALIER* (The knight of the rose) a delightful OPÉRA-BOUFFE in an endearing popular manner. Schuch conducted its premiere in Dresden on Jan. 26, 1911.

Turning once more to Greek mythology, Strauss wrote, with Hofmannsthal again as librettist, a short opera, *ARIADNE AUF NAXOS,* which he conducted for the first time in Stuttgart on Oct. 25, 1912. He later expanded it into a full-length work.

In June 1914 Strauss was awarded an honorary doctor of music degree from Oxford University. His next work was the formidable, and quite realistic, score *EINE ALPENSINFONIE* (Alpine symphony), depicting an ascent of the Alps. Strauss conducted its first performance with the Dresden Court Orchestra in Berlin on Oct. 28, 1915.

Then, again with Hofmannsthal as librettist, Strauss wrote the opera *DIE FRAU OHNE SCHATTEN* (The woman without a shadow; Vienna, Oct. 10, 1919). It has a complex plot, heavily endowed with symbolism.

In 1917 Strauss helped to organize the Salzburg Festival and appeared there in subsequent years as conductor. In 1919 he assumed the post of codirector with Franz Schalk of the Vienna State Opera, a position he held until 1924. In 1920 he took the Vienna Philharmonic on a tour of South America, and in 1921 he appeared as a guest conductor in the U.S.

For his next opera, *INTERMEZZO* (Dresden, Nov. 4, 1924), Strauss wrote his own libretto. Then, with Hofmannsthal once more, he wrote *Die ägyptische Helena* (The Egyptian Helen; Dresden, June 6, 1928). Their last collaboration was *ARABELLA* (Dresden, July 1, 1933).

When Hitler came to power in 1933, the Nazis were eager to persuade Strauss to join the party. Hitler even sent him a signed picture of himself with a flattering inscription, "To the great composer RICHARD STRAUSS, with sincere admiration." Strauss kept clear of formal association with the Führer and his cohorts, however. He agreed to serve as president of the newly organized Reichsmusikkammer on Nov. 15, 1933, but resigned from it on July 13, 1935, ostensibly for reasons of poor health.

Strauss entered into open conflict with the Nazis by asking Stefan Zweig, an Austrian Jew, to provide the LIBRETTO for his opera *DIE SCHWEIGSAME FRAU* (The silent woman). It was duly produced in Dresden on June 24, 1935, but then taken off the boards after a few performances. His political

1935 ▸ *DIE SCHWEIGSAME FRAU,* with a libretto by Stefan Zweig, an Austrian Jew, is produced in Dresden, thus putting Strauss into open conflict with the Nazis

1936 ▸ Despite ongoing difficulties with the Nazis authorities, Strauss composes the *Olympische Hymne* for the Berlin Olympic Games

1942 ▸ The last opera by Strauss performed during his lifetime, *CAPRICCIO,* is premiered in Munich, Strauss conducting

1943 ▸ Horn Concerto No. 2 is premiered in Salzburg

1944 ▸ *DIE LIEBE DER DANAE,* on a Greek theme, is given a public dress rehearsal in Salzburg

1945 ▸ Composes *METAMORPHOSEN* for string orchestra, mourning the disintegration of Germany

1945–47 ▸ Visits to Switzerland and London

1948 ▸ Is officially exonerated for all taint of Nazi collusion (June 8, 1948) and composes *VIER LETZTE LIEDER,* inspired by poems of Hesse and Eichendorff

1949 ▸ Returning to Germany, dies, at the age of 85

Eine Alpensinfonie employs a wind machine and THUNDER MACHINE in the orchestra to illustrate an alpine storm.

Von Bülow called Strauss "Richard the 2nd," i.e., the rightful heir of "Richard the 1st," Wagner.

difficulties grew even more disturbing when the Nazis found out that his daughter-in-law was Jewish. Despite these problems, Strauss agreed to write the *Olympische Hymne* for the Berlin Olympic Games in 1936.

On Nov. 5, 1936, Strauss was honored with the Gold Medal of the Royal Philharmonic Society in London. The next day he conducted the visiting Dresden State Opera in a performance of his *Ariadne auf Naxos* at Covent Garden.

For his next opera, Strauss chose Joseph Gregor as his librettist. They produced DAPHNE (Dresden, Oct. 15, 1938), which was once more based on Greek mythology. For their last collaboration, Strauss and Gregor produced the opera DIE LIEBE DER DANAE (The love of Danae), also on a Greek theme. Its public dress rehearsal was given in Salzburg on Aug. 16, 1944. By that time, however, most musical activity was ended by the war, so that the opera did not receive its official premiere until after Strauss's death.

The last opera by Strauss performed during his lifetime was CAPRICCIO (1940–41). Its libretto was prepared by the conductor Clemens Krauss, who led its premiere in Munich on Oct. 28, 1942. Another interesting work of this period was Strauss's Horn Concerto No. 2, first performed in Salzburg on Aug. 11, 1943.

During the last weeks of the war Strauss devoted himself to the composition of METAMORPHOSEN (1945), a work for string orchestra mourning the disintegration of Germany. It contained a symbolic quotation from the funeral march from LUDWIG VAN BEETHOVEN's EROICA SYMPHONY. He then completed another fine score, the Oboe Concerto (1945–46).

In 1945 Strauss went to Switzerland. Two years later he visited London for the Strauss Festival and also appeared as a conductor of his own works. Although official suspicion continued to linger regarding his relationship with the Nazi regime, he was officially exonerated of all taint on June 8, 1948. A last flame of creative inspiration brought forth the deeply moving VIER LETZTE LIEDER (Four last songs; 1948) for soprano and orchestra, inspired by poems of Hesse and Eichendorff. With this farewell, Strauss left Switzerland in 1949 and returned to his home in Germany, where he died at the age of 85.

Undeniably one of the finest master composers of modern times, Strauss remaining a ROMANTIC at heart. His genius is unquestioned as regards such early symphonic poems as *Don Juan* and *Also sprach Zarathustra*. Many of his operas have attained a permanent place in the repertoire, while his *Vier letzte Lieder* stand as a noble achievement of Romantic inspiration.

Stravinsky, Igor (Feedorovich), great Russian-born French, later American, composer, one of the supreme masters of 20th-century music, whose works exercised the most profound influence on the evolution of music; b. Oranienbaum, near St. Petersburg, June 17, 1882; d. N.Y., April 6, 1971. His father was Feodor (Ignatievich) Stravinsky (b. Noviy Dvor, near Rechitza, June 20, 1843; d. St. Petersburg, Dec. 4, 1902), one of the greatest Russian basses before FEODOR CHALIAPIN, distinguished not only for the power of his voice, but for his dramatic talent on the stage. He made 1,235 appearances in 64 operatic roles.

Igor was brought up in an artistic atmosphere, often attending opera rehearsals when his father sang, and acquiring an early love for the musical theater. He took piano lessons with Alexandra Snetkova and later with Leokadia Kashperova, who was a pupil of ANTON RUBINSTEIN.

It was not until much later, however, that Stravinsky began to study theory, first with Fyodor Akimenko and then with Vasili Kalafati from 1900 to 1903. His progress in composition was remarkably slow. He never entered a music school or a conservatory

PEOPLE IN MUSIC

◄

Igor Stravinsky, c. 1948. (New York Public Library)

Igor Stravinsky time line

1882 Born

1905 Begins lessons in orchestration with NIKOLAI RIMSKY-KORSAKOV

1906 Married for the first time, to Catherine Nosenko

1907 Composes the orchestral SCHERZO FANTASTIQUE, inspired by Maeterlinck's book La Vie des abeilles

1908 Composes the orchestral fantasy Fireworks for the wedding of Rimsky-Korsakov's daughter

1910 The first collaborative ballet for Serge Diaghilev and the Ballets Russes, THE FIREBIRD, is staged in Paris

1911 Settles in Paris (with frequent trips to Switzerland), where his second ballet for Diaghilev, PETROUCHKA, is premiered

1913 The revolutionary THE RITE OF SPRING is produced in Paris, with choreography by Vaslav Nijinsky

1914 Diaghilev produces Stravinsky's lyric fairy tale LE ROSSIGNOL, after Hans Christian Andersen

1918 Completes work on his ballet LES NOCES and also composes the musical stage play L'HISTOIRE DU SOLDAT

1920 The ballet PULCINELLA is premiered at the Paris Opéra

and never earned an academic degree. In 1901 he enrolled in the law school at St. Petersburg University and took courses there for eight semesters, without graduating. A fellow student was Vladimir Rimsky-Korsakov, a son of the composer NIKOLAI RIMSKY-KORSAKOV.

In the summer of 1902 Stravinsky traveled in Germany, where he befriended another son of Rimsky-Korsakov, Andrei, who was a student at the University of Heidelberg. He was introduced to Rimsky-Korsakov and became a regular guest at the latter's periodic gatherings in St. Petersburg. In 1903–04 he wrote a piano SONATA for the Russian pianist Nicolai Richter, who performed it at Rimsky-Korsakov's home.

In 1905 Stravinsky began taking regular lessons in orchestration with Rimsky-Korsakov, who taught him free of charge and under whose tutelage Stravinsky composed a Symphony in E-flat major. The second and third movements from it were performed in 1907, by the Court Orchestra in St. Petersburg, who gave its first complete performance a year later. There was little in this work that predicted Stravinsky's ultimate development as a master of form and orchestration. At the same concert, his *Le Faune et la bergère* (The faun and the shepherdess) for voice and orchestra had its first performance. This score revealed a certain influence of French IMPRESSIONISM.

To celebrate the marriage of Rimsky-Korsakov's daughter Nadezhda to the composer Maximilian Steinberg in 1908, Stravinsky wrote an orchestral fantasy entitled *Fireworks*. Rimsky-Korsakov died a few days after the wedding. Stravinsky deeply mourned his beloved teacher and wrote a *Chant funèbre* for wind instruments in his memory. It was first performed in St. Petersburg in 1909. There followed a *SCHERZO FANTASTIQUE* for orchestra, inspired by Maeterlinck's book *La Vie des abeilles* (Life of the bees), op.3 (1907). Stravinsky had at first planned a literal program of composition, illustrating events in the life of a beehive. Some years later, however, he denied any connection with Maeterlinck's book.

A signal change in Stravinsky's fortunes came when the famous impresario Serge Diaghilev commissioned him to write a work for the Paris season of his Ballets Russes. The result was the production of his first ballet masterpiece, THE FIREBIRD, staged by Diaghilev in Paris in 1910. Here he created music of extraordinary brilliance, steeped in the colors of Russian fairy tales. There are numerous striking effects in the score, such as a GLISSANDO of harmonics in the string instruments. The rhythmic drive is exhilarating, and the use of asymmetrical time signatures extremely effective. The harmonies are opulent, and the orchestration is biting. Stravinsky drew two orchestral SUITES from it.

Stravinsky's association with Diaghilev demanded his presence in Paris, which he made his home beginning in 1911, with frequent travels to Switzerland. His second ballet for Diaghilev was PETROUCHKA, produced in Paris in that year, with triumphant success. Not only was the ballet remarkably effective on the stage, but the score itself, arranged in two orchestral suites, was so new and original that it marked a turning point in 20th-century music. Spasmodically explosive rhythms, novel instrumental sonorities, with the use of the piano as an integral part of the orchestra, and bold harmonic innovations in employing two different KEYS simultaneously (C major and F-sharp major, the "*Petrouchka* chord") were greatly influential on modern European composers. CLAUDE DEBUSSY voiced his enchantment with the score, and young Stravinsky, still in his 20s, became a Paris celebrity.

Two years later, Stravinsky brought out a work of even greater revolutionary import, the ballet THE RITE OF SPRING (*Le Sacre du printemps;* Russian title *Vesna sviashchennaya,* The sacred spring), subtitled *Scenes of Pagan Russia.* It was produced by Diaghilev with his Ballets Russes in Paris in 1913, with choreography by the famous dancer Vaslav Nijinsky. The score marked a departure from all conventions of musical composition. While in *Petrouchka* the harmonies, though innovative and DISSONANT, could still be placed in the context of modern music, the score of *The Rite of Spring* contained such jarring dissonances as SCALES played at the INTERVALS of major sevenths and superpositions of minor upon major TRIADS with the common TONIC, chords treated as unified blocks of sound, and rapid metrical changes that seemingly defied performance. The score still stands as one of the most daring creations of the modern musical mind.

1922 Two short operas for Diaghilev, RENARD and MAVRA, are premiered in Paris

1925 Appears as piano soloist in the U.S. premiere of his neoclassical Piano Concerto, with the Boston Symphony Orchestra, under SERGE KOUSSEVITZKY

1927 The OPERA-ORATORIO OEDIPUS REX receives its first concert performance in Paris

1928 *Apollon Musagète,* pantomime for string orchestra, commissioned by the Elizabeth Sprague Coolidge Foundation, is first heard at the Library of Congress in Washington, D.C.

1929 *Capriccio* for piano and orchestra is first heard in Paris, with Stravinsky as soloist and ERNEST ANSERMET conducting

1930 Composes SYMPHONY OF PSALMS on the occasion of the 50th anniversary of the Boston Symphony Orchestra

1934 Obtains French citizenship and also composes the ballet *Perséphone* on a commission from the ballerina Ida Rubinstein

1937 *Jeu de cartes,* "ballet in three deals," is first performed at the Metropolitan Opera in N.Y.

1938 DUMBARTON OAKS, commissioned by Mr. and Mrs. Robert Woods Bliss, is first performed in Washington, D.C.

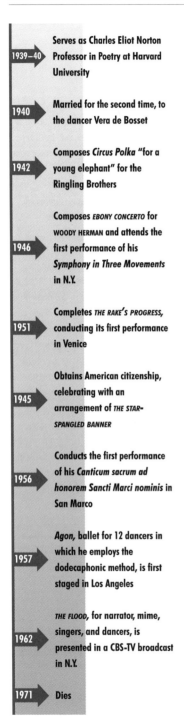

1939–40 Serves as Charles Eliot Norton Professor in Poetry at Harvard University

1940 Married for the second time, to the dancer Vera de Bosset

1942 Composes *Circus Polka* "for a young elephant" for the Ringling Brothers

1946 Composes EBONY CONCERTO for WOODY HERMAN and attends the first performance of his *Symphony in Three Movements* in N.Y.

1951 Completes THE RAKE'S PROGRESS, conducting its first performance in Venice

1945 Obtains American citizenship, celebrating with an arrangement of THE STAR-SPANGLED BANNER

1956 Conducts the first performance of his *Canticum sacrum ad honorem Sancti Marci nominis* in San Marco

1957 *Agon,* ballet for 12 dancers in which he employs the dodecaphonic method, is first staged in Los Angeles

1962 THE FLOOD, for narrator, mime, singers, and dancers, is presented in a CBS-TV broadcast in N.Y.

1971 Dies

To some of the audience at its first performance in Paris, Stravinsky's "barbaric" music was beyond endurance. The Paris critics exercised their verbal ingenuity in indignant commentary, one of them proposing that *Le Sacre du printemps* would be better titled *Le Massacre du printemps.* Nonetheless, in a few years, the work had become a popular concert piece.

In 1914 Diaghilev produced Stravinsky's lyric fairy tale *LE ROSSIGNOL,* after Hans Christian Andersen. Stravinsky had started composing the opera before *Petrouchka* and *The Rite of Spring.* The discords are not yet present, and other elements seem closer to *The Firebird* and the orientalisms of Rimsky-Korsakov's music all of which is appropriate to what is an exotic Eastern fantasy. From 1914 to 1918 Stravinsky worked on his ballet *LES NOCES* (The nuptials; Russian title *Svadebka,* Little wedding), evoking Russian peasant FOLK modalities. It was scored for an unusual ensemble of chorus, soloists, four pianos, and 17 percussion instruments.

The devastation of World War I led Stravinsky to conclude that the era of grandiose ROMANTIC music had become obsolete, and that a new spirit of musical economy was needed. As an illustration of such economy, he wrote the musical stage play *L'HISTOIRE DU SOLDAT* (The soldier's tale) scored for only seven players, with narrator, in 1918. About the same time he wrote a work for 11 instruments entitled *Ragtime,* inspired by the new American dance music.

Stravinsky continued his association with Diaghilev's Ballets Russes in writing the ballet *PULCINELLA* (Paris Opéra, 1920). It was based on themes once attributed to GIOVANNI BATTISTA PERGOLESI but now known to be by other 18th-century Italian composers. He also wrote for Diaghilev two short operas, *RENARD,* to a Russian fairy tale, and *MAVRA,* after Pushkin, both of which were premiered in Paris in 1922. These two works were the last in which he used Russian subjects, with the sole exception of an orchestral *Scherzo à la russe* from 22 years later.

Stravinsky had now entered a stylistic period usually designated as NEOCLASSICAL. The most significant works of this stage of his development were his Octet for wind instruments from 1923, and Piano Concerto (with wind instruments, double basses, and percussion; 1924), commissioned by SERGE KOUSSEVITZKY. In these works he abandoned the luxuriant instrumentation of his ballets and their aggressively dissonant harmonies. Instead, he used PANDIATONIC structures, firmly TONAL but starkly dissonant in their superposition of tonalities within the same principal key. Stravinsky's return to old forms, however, was not an act of ascetic renunciation but, rather, a grand experiment in reviving BAROQUE practices.

The Piano Concerto provided him with an opportunity to appear as soloist. Stravinsky was never a virtuoso pianist, but he was able to acquit himself satisfactorily. He played it with Koussevitzky in Paris and during his first American tour with the Boston Symphony Orchestra in 1925.

The Elizabeth Sprague Coolidge Foundation commissioned Stravinsky to write a pantomime for string orchestra. The result was *Apollon Musagète,* which was performed at the Library of Congress in Washington, D.C., in 1928. This score, serene and emotionally restrained, evokes the manner of JEAN-BAPTISTE LULLY's court ballets. Stravinsky continued to explore the resources of neo-Baroque writing in his Capriccio for piano and orchestra, which he performed as soloist, with ERNEST ANSERMET conducting, in Paris in 1929. This score is impressed by a spirit of hedonistic entertainment, reaclling the STYLE GALANT of the 18th century, yet it is unmistakably modern.

Stravinsky's well-nigh monastic renunciation of the grandiose edifice of glorious sound to which he himself had so abundantly contributed found expression in his OPERA-ORATORIO *OEDIPUS REX.* In order to emphasize its detachment from temporal aspects, he commissioned a Latin translation for the LIBRETTO, even though the original play was in Greek. Its music is deliberately hollow, with its dramatic points emphasized by ominous repetitive passages. Yet this very austerity of idiom makes *Oedipus Rex* a profoundly moving play. It had its first performance in 1927, with its stage premiere taking place in Vienna the following year.

A turn to religious writing occurred in Stravinsky's *SYMPHONY OF PSALMS,* written in 1930 for the 50th anniversary of the Boston Symphony Orchestra, and dedicated "to the glory of God." The work is scored for chorus and orchestra, omitting the violins and violas, thus emphasizing the lower instrumental REGISTERS and creating an austere sonority suitable to its solemn subject.

In 1931 Stravinsky wrote a violin concerto commissioned by Samuel Dushkin and performed by him in Berlin. On a commission from the ballerina Ida Rubinstein, he composed the ballet *Perséphone* in 1934. Here again he exercised his mastery of simplicity in formal design, melodic patterns, and contrapuntal structure.

For his American tour, Stravinsky wrote *Jeu de cartes* (Card game), a "ballet in three deals" to his own scenario depicting an imaginary game of poker (of which he was a devotee). He conducted its first performance at the Metropolitan Opera in N.Y. in 1937. His concerto for 16 instruments, DUMBARTON OAKS (named after the Washington, D.C., estate of Mr. and Mrs. Robert Woods Bliss, who commissioned the work), was first performed in Washington in the following year. In Europe it was played under the noncommittal title Concerto in E-flat.

With World War II engulfing Europe, Stravinsky sought permanent residence in America. He had acquired French citizenship in 1934, and in 1939 he applied for American citizenship. He and his wife became American citizens in late 1945. To celebrate this event he made an arrangement of THE STAR-SPANGLED BANNER, which contained a curious MODULATION into the SUBDOMINANT in the CODA. He conducted it with the Boston Symphony Orchestra in 1944. However, because of legal injunctions existing in the state of Massachusetts against intentional alteration of the national anthem, he was advised not to conduct his version at the second pair of concerts, and the standard version was substituted.

In 1939–40 Stravinsky was named Charles Eliot Norton lecturer at Harvard University. About the same time he accepted several private students, a pedagogical role not previously exercised.

Once he settled in the U.S., Stravinsky wrote in a wide range of styles for many different occasions. He accepted a commission from the Ringling Brothers to write *Circus Polka* "for a young elephant" in 1942, which he subsequently arranged for full orchestra. In 1946 he wrote EBONY CONCERTO for WOODY HERMAN's swing band. In 1951 he completed his opera *THE RAKE'S PROGRESS,* inspired by Hogarth's famous series of engravings, to a libretto by W. H. Auden and Chester Kallman. He conducted its world premiere in Venice that year, as part of the International Festival of Contemporary Music. The opera is an ingenious conglomeration of disparate elements, ranging from 18th-century British BALLADS to modern burlesque.

But whatever changes his music underwent during his long and productive career, Stravinsky remained a man of the theater at heart. In America he became associated with the brilliant Russian choreographer GEORGE BALANCHINE. Balanchine produced a number of ballets to Stravinsky's music, among them *Apollon Musagète, Violin Concerto, Symphony in three Movements* (1942–45; N.Y., 1946), *Scherzo à la russe, Pulcinella,* and *Agon,* a ballet for 12 Dancers (1954–57; Los Angeles, 1957).

It was in *Agon* that Stravinsky first used the DODECAPHONIC method of composition as developed by ARNOLD SCHOENBERG. *Agon* (Greek for competition) bears the subtitle *Ballet for 12 Tones.* This was despite the fact that Stravinsky had long criticized Schoenberg's methods, and the two men were never friends.

After Schoenberg's death, Stravinsky felt free to examine the essence of the 12-tone method. Stravinsky adopted dodecaphonic writing in its aspect of canonic COUNTERPOINT as developed by ANTON WEBERN. In this manner he wrote his *Canticum sacrum ad honorem Sancti Marci nominis,* which he conducted at San Marco in Venice in 1956. Another work written in a modified 12-tone technique is *THE FLOOD* (for narrator, mime, singers, and dancers), presented in a CBS-TV broadcast in N.Y. in 1962. Stravinsky died nine years later.

Stravinsky was married twice. His first wife, Catherine Nosenko, whom he married in 1906 and who bore him three children, died in 1939. The following year, Stravinsky married his longtime mistress, the dancer Vera de Bosset (b. St. Petersburg, Dec. 25, 1888; d. N.Y., Sept. 17, 1982), who was formerly married to the Russian painter Serge Sudeikin.

Few composers have escaped the powerful impact of Stravinsky's music. Ironically, it was his own country that had rejected him, partly because of the opposition of Soviet ideologues to modern music in general, and partly because of Stravinsky's open criticism of Soviet ways in art. But in 1962 he returned to Russia for a visit, and was welcomed as a prodigal son. As if by magic, his works began to appear on Russian concert programs, and Soviet music critics issued a number of laudatory studies of his works. Yet it is Stravinsky's early masterpieces, set in an attractive colorful style, that continue to enjoy favor with audiences and performers, while his more abstract scores are appreciated mainly by specialists.

In later years, Stravinsky was befriended by a musicologist named Robert Craft, who served as a kind of secretary-assistant to him. Craft duly recorded many conversations with the master and then published them in a series of highly successful books.

PEOPLE IN MUSIC

Strayhorn, Billy (William Thomas), African-American JAZZ pianist, composer, and arranger; b. Dayton, Ohio, Nov. 29, 1915; d. N.Y., May 31, 1967. Strayhorn studied music in Pittsburgh, joining DUKE ELLINGTON's band as lyricist and arranger in 1939. Many songs credited to Ellington (*Chelsea Bridge, Perfume Suite, Such Sweet Thunder, A Drum Is a Woman*) are in fact products of a both men, with Ellington suggesting the initial idea, mood, and character and Strayhorn doing the actual writing, often using Ellington's quasi-impressionistic techniques. Strayhorn's own acknowledged songs such as *Lush Life* and TAKE THE *"A" TRAIN* became JAZZ standards. He remained with the Ellington organization through his death in 1967.

street cries. Street vendors used to peddle their wares using melodious jingles, with each product having its own recognizable tune. Such street cries were common in France as early as the 13th century, and they were often incorporated in contemporary MOTETS. Street cries were also used by English composers of the early RENAISSANCE period. Particularly notable are those for fresh oysters and hot mutton. Newsboys often sold their papers in 19th-century London with a pleasant modal lift. A 20-century rendition of newsboys' calls can be heard in HARRY PARTCH's *San Francisco* (1943).

Even JOHANN SEBASTIAN BACH deigned to include the popular tune *Cabbage and Turnips* at the end of his great GOLDBERG VARIATIONS.

In the present century, LUCIANO BERIO's *Cries of London* (1973–74) is unusual. It is scored for eight voices, to authentic vending tunes. The tune urging customers to buy garlic is especially amusing.

In Cuba, Brazil, and Argentina, knife sharpeners and shoeshine boys open up a whole symphony of vendors' tunes at early tropical sunrise.

Street organs with reed pipes used to be a familiar sight and sound in Italy, with a monkey passing a hat for donations. A story is told that GIUSEPPE VERDI, annoyed by street organs playing the tune *La donna è mobile* from his RIGO-LETTO before his window, paid the street musicians to either stop playing or change their song.

Street Scene. Opera by KURT WEILL, 1947, based on a play by Elmer Rice, with lyrics by Langston Hughes, premiered in N.Y. The somber story involves the residents of a typically multiethnic N.Y. walk-up apartment building. In one family a frustrated housewife, Ann Maurrant, has been having an affair with a milkman, as her husband Frank has become hardened and angered by life. One day, while she and her lover are dallying in her apartment, he comes home, surprises them, and shoots them both dead. Of their two children, daughter Rose is the more affected. Although she has grown fond of Sam Kaplan, a Jewish student who would give up his religion for her, she realizes that her life is too full of burdens and uncertainties to make any commitment, and she leaves N.Y.

The work is probably the most ambitious attempt of Weill's to re-create his earlier style, integrating popular music with classical sonorities. In a very seamless show, a last-minute addition to the score, *Moon-Faced, Starry-Eyed* is the best-known number.

Streisand, Barbra (Barbara Joan), popular American singer and actress; b. N.Y., April 24, 1942. Raised in Brooklyn, Streisand dreamed of being a Broadway star. She studied acting for a short time in N.Y. and also sang in Greenwich Village clubs and performed in off-Broadway revues.

In late 1961 Streisand made her Broadway debut in *I Can Get It for You Wholesale,* receiving excellent reviews. It

PEOPLE IN MUSIC

led to a contract with Columbia Records. Her first album was surprisingly successful, making her the top-selling female vocalist in America and winning two Grammy awards.

Streisand next appeared in the Broadway musical FUNNY GIRL in 1964, based on the life of FANNY BRICE. The show produced the hit song *People,* which became a theme song for Streisand. She took the show to London in 1966, and two years later starred in the film version, for which she received an Academy Award.

Following this success, Streisand continued to appear in Hollywood features. In 1969 she appeared in the film version of HELLO, DOLLY! along with LOUIS ARMSTRONG. This was followed by more dramatic roles. She returned to a musical film in 1976 with the remake of *A Star Is Born.* It produced the hit song *Evergreen,* which she cowrote with PAUL WILLIAMS.

Streisand focused more on her recording career in the late '70s, earning hits by pairing herself with other stars. These duets included *You Don't Bring Me Flowers* with NEIL DIAMOND (1978); *Enough Is Enough,* a discofied hit with Donna Summer (1979); and *(I Am a) Woman in Love* with Barry Gibb of the BEE GEES (1980).

The '80s and early '90s were spent establishing her career as a director and filmmaker. Streisand returned to recording in 1993 with her album *Back to Broadway,* drawing on her original repertoire of pop songs. A year later, she had a successful two-night appearance at the new MGM Grand Hotel in Las Vegas, which with television and other rights netted her a reported twenty million dollars. She also gave four concerts that year in Great Britain.

Strepponi, Giuseppina (Clelia Maria Josepha). *See* VERDI, GIUSEPPE.

stretch. On a keyboard instrument, a wide INTERVAL or spread CHORD to be played by the fingers of one hand.

stret'tōh, -tăh   **stretto, -a** (It., straitened, narrowed; Fr. *strette*). A musical climax that usually occurs at the point when thematic and rhythmic elements have reached the point of saturation. A classic example is the FINALE of the second act in WOLFGANG

AMADEUS MOZART's *THE MARRIAGE OF FIGARO (Le nozze di Figaro)*, in *prestissimo* tempo.

A stretto at the end of an impassioned ARIA or a dramatic duet is virtually synonymous with a CABALETTA.

Particularly effective is a stretto in a FUGUE, in which the "narrowing" process is achieved by overlapping the parts of the SUBJECT and ANSWER, producing the effect of accelerated canonic IMITATION. This is particularly effective in the final fugal exposition.

strict style. A style of composition in which (most) DISSONANCES are regularly prepared and resolved.

stride piano. JAZZ piano style of the 1920s and 1930s. It retained elements of RAGTIME but had a freer, more swinging bass part. One great stride piano performer was FATS WALLER, in such songs as *I Would Do Anything for You.*

Strike up the Band. Musical by GEORGE GERSHWIN, 1929. This satirical musical tells the story of an American-Swiss war over the tariff on Swiss chocolate. The U.S. wins after discovering the Swiss yodeling code.

The title song is very popular, as is *The Man I Love*, which was cut from the play after the out-of-town tryouts. It was felt that the song held up the action.

The Man I Love had already been cut from *Lady, Be Good!* five years earlier.

string (Ger. *Saite;* It. *corda;* Fr. *corde*). A tone-producing cord. *First string*, the highest of a set; *open string*, one not stopped or shortened; *silver string*, one covered with silver wire; *soprano string*, the E string of the violin; *the strings*, the string group in the orchestra.

string(ed) instruments (Ger. *Streichinstrumente, Saiteninstrumente;* It. *strumenti a corda;* Fr. *instruments à cordes*). All instruments whose tones are produced by strings, whether struck, plucked, or bowed.

MUSICAL INSTRUMENT

A wise tradition reserves the term string instruments for members of the violin and related families in which the strings are brought into vibration primarily by bowing. String instruments manipulated by plucking, such as the LUTE, GUITAR, BALALAIKA, MANDOLIN, BANJO, and many

Eastern instruments, are usually included in a category of their own.

String instruments lend themselves to organization in any combination (even a duet for violin and double bass has been written), but the most common combinations, in addition to an unaccompanied string instrument, are STRING QUARTET, STRING TRIO, STRING QUINTET, and STRING ORCHESTRA.

string orchestra (Ger. *Streichorchester*). An orchestra comprised entirely of STRING(ED) INSTRUMENTS.

MUSICAL
INSTRUMENT

string piano. A traditional PIANO that is sounded by acting directly upon the strings, i.e., by strumming, bowing, plucking, hammering, etc.

string quartet (Ger. *Streichquartett;* Fr. *quatuor à cordes*). Historically, the most significant type of CHAMBER MUSIC. A string quartet consists of two violins, viola, and cello, providing a rich four-part harmony and an articulate interplay of contrapuntal forms, especially CANON and FUGUE. Opportunities for expressive and effective solo parts are many, with the solo instrument accompanied by the other three. Episodic duos and trios furnish another resource.

The traditional structure of a string quartet is that of SONATA FORM, consisting of four movements and usually including a minuet or a scherzo.

In the classic string quartet, the first violin is a natural leader. The SECOND violin is the leader's faithful partner, and the somewhat derogatory expression, "playing second

A modern string quartet in concert. (Benson collection) ▶

fiddle," suggests its subordinate function. The viola fills the harmony and emerges as an important member of the quartet usually in canonic passages. The cello holds the important duty of the bass voice, determining the harmony. Its sonorous ARPEGGIOS lend an almost orchestral quality to the ensemble. The employment of special effects such as PIZZICATO, and the availability of DOUBLE STOPS, contribute further to the ensemble's harmonic richness.

Claims for the priority of composing string quartets have been made for several composers of the 17th century. However, the first composer of stature to establish the string quartet as a distinctive musical form was FRANZ JOSEPH HAYDN, who wrote 83 of them.

WOLFGANG AMADEUS MOZART's string quartets brought the art to its highest flowering in the 18th century. His so-called *DISSONANZENQUARTETT* aroused a heated controversy because of its innovative use of DISSONANT harmonic combinations. LUDWIG VAN BEETHOVEN's last string quartets caused contemporary critics to state that they were the products of the composer's loss of hearing. As usual, he heard far better than the critics were ready to.

The taste for string quartets suffered a sharp decline in the modern era. CLAUDE DEBUSSY, MAURICE RAVEL, and IGOR STRAVINSKY wrote only a single string quartet each. ARNOLD SCHOENBERG and BÉLA BARTÓK revived it with considerable departures from tradition. Schoenberg even used a vocal solo in one of his. Russian composers continued to cultivate string quartets assiduously. DMITRI SHOSTAKOVICH wrote 15 of them.

LUIGI BOCCHERINI holds the record for writing string quartets. He wrote 102 of them.

string quintet. 1. A CHAMBER MUSIC ensemble with five string instruments, usually two violins, two violas, and cello.

2. A composition, usually multimovement, for this combination (or a close variant). The most prolific composer of string quintets was LUIGI BOCCHERINI, with 12. WOLFGANG AMADEUS MOZART wrote six, LUDWIG VAN BEETHOVEN wrote three, and FELIX MENDELSSOHN wrote two, as did JOHANNES BRAHMS. FRANZ SCHUBERT's great C-major quintet is scored for two violins, viola, and two cellos.

3. The string component of the orchestra, normally written in five parts (two violins, viola, cello, and double bass).

string trio. 1. An ensemble for three string instruments, usually violin, viola, and cello. 2. A composition, usually multimovement, for this combination (or a close variant). Historically, the string trio is an offshoot of the TRIO SONATA. FRANZ JOSEPH HAYDN wrote as many as 20 trios for two violins and cello, and WOLFGANG AMADEUS MOZART and LUDWIG VAN BEETHOVEN also contributed to the form.

strophe (Grk, turning). A rhythmic system composed of a repeated unit of two or more lines (REFRAIN). It provides a break in the continuity of a stanzaic song, leading to a new section, but preserving the unity of rhythm and musical setting. The strophe is often confused with the STANZA.

strophic bass. Repeated BASS in a SONG accompaniment, to which the melody varies freely. *Strophic composition, see* SONG.

PEOPLE IN MUSIC

The big hit song from *Annie* was the anthemic *Tomorrow!*

Strouse, Charles (Louis), American composer; b. N.Y., June 7, 1928. Strouse studied at the Eastman School of Music in Rochester, N.Y. He later took private lessons in composition with AARON COPLAND and NADIA BOULANGER, under whose guidance he wrote some ambitious instrumental music.

Strouse was mainly active as a composer for Broadway and films. With the lyricist Lee Adams (b. Mansfield, Ohio, Aug. 14, 1924), he wrote the musicals BYE BYE BIRDIE (1960) and *Applause* (1970), both of which won Tony awards. Other musicals include *Golden Boy* (1964), after a play by Clifford Odets, and *Annie* (1977).

Strouse also composed two children's operas, a piano concerto and other orchestral pieces, and a string quartet.

structure. The complete organization of a composition. While structure is often used as a synonym for FORM (in the sense of design), it can refer to elements such as HARMONY, COUNTERPOINT, MELODY, and RHYTHM. It can also refer to a specific style, such as DODECAPHONIC, TONAL, MOTIVIC, and symmetrical structures. In its adjectival form, it can identify structural conceptions, such as layering, variants, accentuation, groupings, symbolism, and perception.

strumento (stromento; It.). Instrument. *Strumenti a corda,* string instruments; *strumenti a fiato,* wind instruments; *strumenti da tasto,* keyboard instruments.

Student Prince (in Heidelberg), The. OPERETTA by SIG-MUND ROMBERG, 1924, premiered in N.Y. A royal prince, Karl Franz, enrolls in the University of Heidelberg. Incognito, he engages in a romance with a lovely German waitress named Kathie. When the news comes of his grandfather's death, the prince becomes king and is forced to abandon his waitress to marry a princess.

The score is full of sentimental songs and duets. Its choral drinking song becoming a particular favorite.

Studer, Cheryl, American soprano; b. Midland, Mich., Oct. 24, 1955. After training in Ohio and at the University of Tennessee, Studer studied voice with Hans Hotter at the Vienna Hochschule für Musik.

Studer appeared in concerts in the U.S. before singing at the Bavarian State Opera in Munich in 1980, then was a member of the Darmstadt Opera from 1983 to 1985. In 1984 she made her U.S. operatic debut as Micaëla at the Chicago Lyric Opera. From 1985 she sang at the Deutsche Oper in Berlin.

Studer made her Bayreuth Festival debut in 1985 as Elisabeth in *TANNHÄUSER,* then, in 1986, sang Pamina at her debut at the Paris Opéra. In 1987 she made her first appearance at London's Covent Garden as Elisabeth, and also sang at Milan's La Scala.

In 1988 Studer made her Metropolitan Opera debut in N.Y. as Micaëla and subsequently sang there with great success. In 1989 she made her first appearance at the Salzburg Festival as Chrysothemis. In 1990 she sang Elsa at the Vienna State Opera. She also appeared as Giuditta at the Vienna Volksoper in 1992. On May 4, 1994, she made her Carnegie Hall recital debut in N.Y. In 1996 she sang Beethoven's Leonora at the Salzburg Festival.

Studer has won particular distinction for her interpretation of roles in RICHARD STRAUSS's operas, including SALOME, the empress in *DIE FRAU OHNE SCHATTEN,* and Daphne.

PEOPLE IN MUSIC

Among her other admired roles are Donna Anna, Lucia, Aida, and Sieglinde.

shtoorm oont drahng′

Sturm und Drang (Ger., storm and stress). German literary term borrowed to describe a highly emotional MINOR-KEY style that emerged during the early CLASSIC period, particularly the 1770s and 1780s. It gave a glimpse of the extreme, non-Classic contrasts that would be a stylistic trademark of the ROMANTIC style of composition.

PEOPLE IN MUSIC

Styne, Jule (real name, Julius Kerwin Stein), English-born American composer of popular music; b. London, Dec. 31, 1905; d. N.Y., Sept. 20, 1994. Styne was taught piano by his parents. He was taken to the U.S. at the age of eight, appearing with the Chicago Symphony Orchestra as a child pianist. However, he did not pursue a concert career.

Styne won a scholarship to the Chicago College of Music at 13. After playing piano in JAZZ groups and dance bands, he went to Hollywood in 1940 and rapidly established himself as a successful song composer for films. He also was notably successful as a composer of Broadway musicals, which included *High Button Shoes* (1947), GENTLEMEN PREFER BLONDES (1949), *Bells Are Ringing* (1956), *Gypsy* (1959), *Do Re Mi* (1960; no relation to THE SOUND OF MUSIC), FUNNY GIRL, scenes from the life of the singer-comedienne FANNY BRICE (1964), *Hallelujah, Baby!* (April 26, 1967), and *Sugar* (1972).

stē-rē-enn′

styrienne (Fr.; It. *stiriana*). An instrumental or vocal AIR in slow movement and $\frac{2}{4}$ time. It is often set in a MINOR KEY, with a *Jodler* (yodel) after each verse.

subject. A melodic MOTIVE or PHRASE on which a COMPOSITION or MOVEMENT is founded; a THEME. In a FUGUE, the ANTECEDENT or DUX.

submediant. The third SCALE TONE below the TONIC; the sixth DEGREE.

subordinate chords. CHORDS not fundamental or principal. The TRIADS on the second, third, sixth, and seventh DEGREES, and all seventh chords but the dominant seventh.

Subotnick, Morton, American composer and teacher; b. Los Angeles, April 14, 1933. Subotnick studied at the University of Denver, earning his bachelor of arts degree in 1958, and with DARIUS MILHAUD and LEON KIRCHNER at Mills College in Oakland, California, where he completed his master's degree in 1960. He then was a fellow of the Institute for Advanced Musical Studies at Princeton University in 1959–60.

Subotnick taught at Mills College from 1959 to 1966, and then at N.Y. University until 1969. Beginning in 1969, he taught at the California Institute of the Arts, while he also held various visiting professorships and composer-in-residence positions. In 1979 he married Joan La Barbara.

His compositions run the gamut of AVANT-GARDE techniques, often with innovative use of electronics and electroacoustic devices. His *Silver Apples of the Moon* from 1967 became a classic. Subotnick has composed many additional pieces for orchestra and tape, with various instrumental soloists. He has also written pieces created solely on tape or electronically.

In 1995, working with programmer Mark Coniglio at the Institute for Studies in the Arts at Arizona State University in Tempe, Subotnick completed *Making Music,* an interactive CD-ROM composition program for children. His *All My Hummingbirds Have Alibis,* an "imaginary ballet" set to a series of Max Ernst's paintings for flute, cello, MIDI piano, MIDI mallets, and electronics (1991), was also later converted into a critically lauded CD-ROM.

substitution. 1. In contrapuntal progression, the RESOLUTION or PREPARATION of a DISSONANCE by substituting its higher or lower OCTAVE in some other part for the regular tone of resolution or preparation. 2. The use of alternate HARMONIES to fill a chord in a standard progression, e.g., the first INVERSION of the SUPERTONIC seventh chord instead of the SUBDOMINANT.

subtonic. The LEADING TONE (rarely used term).

suite. An instrumental genre designating a succession of MOVEMENTS not necessarily related to one another and unified only by the same KEY.

PEOPLE IN MUSIC

süē′t′

The most important of this category is the BAROQUE SUITE, composed primarily of dance forms. The standard selection and ordering of the movements is ALLEMANDE, COURANTE, SARABANDE, and GIGUE. Several optional movements, mostly derived from popular dances, are interpolated between the sarabande and gigue, notably a MINUET or GAVOTTE. Some suites end with a BOURRÉE.

JOHANN SEBASTIAN BACH expanded the length and content of his instrumental suites. Bach also wrote suites bearing the designation PARTITA.

Baroque HARPSICHORD composers, still contending with the problems of tuning in MEANTONE TEMPERAMENT, realized that it was best to construct suites in only one key so that a substantial work could be performed without constant retuning between pieces. FRANÇOIS COUPERIN and JEAN-PHILIPPE RAMEAU (who called their suites *ordres*) began to give their suite movements fanciful programmatic titles, and many of these pieces were far removed from the usual dance models.

The character of the suite was changed radically in the 19th century. While Bach, GEORGE FRIDERIC HANDEL, and other composers of the BAROQUE period followed the contrapuntal style of composition, composers of the later centuries regarded the suite mainly as an assemblage of variegated movements, often arranged from OPERAS, BALLETS, and theater music. Sometimes such suites became the only viable remnants of a score of incidental music, as for instance in *L'Arlésienne* (1872) of GEORGES BIZET or *PEER GYNT* (1888, 1891–92) of EDVARD GRIEG. PIOTR ILYICH TCHAIKOVSKY's *NUTCRACKER SUITE* is one of the most popular examples of the genre. The suite from *LULU* was the only music ALBAN BERG ever heard from his second opera.

NEOCLASSICAL composers of the second quarter of the 20th century, notably IGOR STRAVINSKY and PAUL HINDEMITH, made serious effort to revive the Baroque suite. Still other composers have used the term in its loosest sense—a collection of pieces or movements, often but not necessarily of a lighter character, for one instrument or ensemble, to be played consecutively.

Suite bergamasque. A set of four piano pieces by CLAUDE DEBUSSY, 1889–1905, in a hybrid form of the suite. Its

The meaning of the adjectives "English" and "French," applied (not by the composer) to 12 of Bach's keyboard suites, is unknown.

third movement is the famous *CLAIR DE LUNE*. Debussy took the title *Suite bergamasque* from the alliterative lines in Verlaine's poem entitled *Clair de lune,* "masques et bergamasques."

The term bergamasque is derived from a dance of Bergamo, Italy.

Suite provençale. Orchestral suite by DARIUS MILHAUD, 1937, based on dance melodies of Provence, first performed in Venice.

suling. Family of bamboo FLUTES in Indonesia and surrounding areas. They can be transverse, nose, whistle, or ring (end-blown) flutes, of various sizes, have anywhere from three to seven finger holes, known by various names, and used either as a solo instrument or in GAMELAN and more modern ensembles.

MUSICAL INSTRUMENT

Sullivan, (Sir) **Arthur** (Seymour), famous English composer and conductor, best known for his collaborations with the celebrated humorist (Sir) William Schwenck Gilbert; b. London, May 13, 1842; d. there, Nov. 22, 1900. His father, Thomas Sullivan, was bandmaster at the Royal Military College, Sandhurst, and later professor of brass instruments at the Royal Military School of Music, Kneller Hall. Young Arthur's musical inclinations were encouraged by his father, and in 1854 he became a chorister in the Chapel Royal, remaining there until 1858. In 1855 his sacred song *O Israel* was published.

PEOPLE IN MUSIC

In 1856 Sullivan received the first Mendelssohn Scholarship to the Royal Academy of Music in London. He then continued his training at the Leipzig Conservatory from 1858 to 1861, where he received instruction in COUNTERPOINT and FUGUE, COMPOSITION, piano, and CONDUCTING. He conducted his overture *Rosenfest* in Leipzig in 1860 and wrote a string quartet and music to *The Tempest,* which was performed there in 1861.

Sullivan's first major success was his CANTATA *Kenilworth,* which was premiered at the Birmingham Festival in 1864. That same year he visited Ireland and composed his *Irish Symphony.*

In 1866 Sullivan was appointed professor of composition at the Royal Academy of Music in London. About this time he formed a lifelong friendship with SIR GEORGE GROVE, the noted British musicologist. In 1867 they went on a memorable journey to Vienna in search of FRANZ SCHUBERT manuscripts, leading to the discovery of the SCORE of *Rosamunde.*

The year 1867 was also notable for the production of the first of those comic operas upon which Sullivan's fame chiefly rests, COX AND BOX (LIBRETTO by F. C. Burnand), which he composed in two weeks. Less successful were *The Contrabandista* (1867) and *Thespis* (1871), music lost. However, the latter is significant in that it inaugurated Sullivan's collaboration with Gilbert, the celebrated humorist. Gilbert became the librettist of all Sullivan's most successful comic operas, beginning with TRIAL BY JURY in 1875. They were produced by RICHARD D'OYLY CARTE, who formed a company expressly for the production of GILBERT AND SULLIVAN operas in 1876.

The first big success obtained by the famous team was *H.M.S. PINAFORE* in 1878, which had 700 consecutive performances in London and enjoyed an enormous vogue in "pirated" productions throughout the U.S. To protect their interests, Gilbert and Sullivan went to N.Y. in 1879 to give an authorized performance of *Pinafore,* and while there they also produced THE PIRATES OF PENZANCE (1879).

In 1881 came *Patience,* a satire on Oscar Wilde. In 1882 IOLANTHE began a run that lasted more than a year. This was followed by the comparatively unsuccessful *Princess Ida* in 1884, but then, a year later, came the universal favorite of all Gilbert and Sullivan operas, THE MIKADO. The list of these popular works is completed by RUDDIGORE (1887), THE YEOMEN OF THE GUARD (1888), and THE GONDOLIERS (1889).

After a quarrel and a reconciliation, the pair collaborated in two less popular works, *Utopia Limited* (1893) and *The Grand Duke* (1896). Sullivan's melodic inspiration and technical resourcefulness, united with the delicious humor of Gilbert's verses, raised light opera to a new height of artistic achievement, and his works in this field continue to delight countless hearers.

Sullivan was also active in other branches of musical life. He conducted numerous series of concerts, most notably those of the London Philharmonic Society from 1885 to 1887 and the Leeds Festivals from 1880 to 1898. He was principal of, and a professor of composition at, the National Training School for Music from 1876 to 1881.

Sullivan received numerous degrees and honors, including honorary doctorates of music from Cambridge (1876) and Oxford (1879) Universities. He was named Chevalier of the French Legion of Honor (1878) and was grand organist to the Freemasons (1887). He was knighted by Queen Victoria in 1883.

Parallel with his comic creations Sullivan composed many "serious" works, including the grand opera *Ivanhoe* (1891), which enjoyed a momentary vogue. Among his cantatas the most successful was *The Golden Legend,* after Longfellow, from 1886. His songs were highly popular in their day, and *The Lost Chord,* to words by Adelaide A. Proctor (1877), is still a favorite.

Among Sullivan's ORATORIOS, *The Light of the World* (1873) is the most memorable. Other stage works (all first performed in London) include *The Zoo* (1875), *The Sorcerer* (with a libretto by Gilbert; 1877), *Haddon Hall* (1892), and *The Beauty Stone* (1898).

Sullivan wrote the famous hymn *Onward, Christian Soldiers,* to words by Rev. Sabine Baring-Gould in 1871.

sum (summation) tone. A TONE resulting from the addition of the frequencies of two or more original tones forming a CONSONANT INTERVAL. A sum tone is much weaker than its opposite, the DIFFERENCE (DIFFERENTIAL) TONE, which is formed by the difference of the same original frequencies. Therefore, the sum tone is usually less disturbing to the player or listener.

Sumer is icumen in (Summer is coming in). The melody of the earliest known CANON. It was written for four voices, with the harmony formed by a double PEDAL POINT, or pedal (which is actually designated as *pes* [foot] in the original manuscript). It is of English origin, and its manuscript on parchment is preserved in the British Museum. The title above the music is *Rota* (ROUND). A controversy exists as to the date of its composition, with the estimate varying between 1250 and 1320.

Ezra Pound, in one of his sardonic moods, wrote a parody that begins, "Winter is icumen in / Lhude sing goddamm!"

The text of the canon is as follows:

Sumer is icumen in
Lhude sing cuccu!
Groweth sed and bloweth med,
And springth the wude nu
Sing cuccu!

Summer Morning's Dream *(Ein Sommermorgentraum).* The original subtitle of GUSTAV MAHLER's Third Symphony, 1896, as given in the original manuscript.

The work is in D minor (although the manuscript also indicates its being in the relative key of F major), in six movements, each romantically described as follows: "The summer arrives," "What the flowers tell me," "What the animals tell me," "What humanity tells me," "What the angels tell me" (accompanied by voices), and "What love tells me." Mahler conducted the first complete performance in Krefeld, 1902.

Summertime. The opening ARIA (after the Jasbo Brown Blues prologue) of GEORGE GERSHWIN's *PORGY AND BESS*, 1935, in which a woman sings a lullaby to her infant. In a work with many memorable moments, *Summertime* stands out as perhaps the most famous, and certainly the most covered by later artists.

PEOPLE IN MUSIC

Sun Ra (born Herman Blount), innovative African-American JAZZ pianist, electric keyboardist, bandleader, composer, and self-proclaimed extraterrestrial; b. Birmingham, Ala., May 1914; d. there, of a stroke, May 30, 1993. Sun Ra learned to play piano and first gained notice as a member of FLETCHER HENDERSON's orchestra in 1946–47. He then went to Chicago, where he became a prominent figure in the AVANT-GARDE JAZZ scene.

In 1956 Sun Ra founded his own band, which was variously known as Solar Arkestra, Intergalactic Myth-Science Arkestra, and Space Arkestra. Still later he was active in N.Y. and Philadelphia, and also toured throughout the U.S. and Europe.

Sun Ra combined electronics with the traditional instruments of a jazz band. Influenced by FREE JAZZ, he composed open-ended and lengthy compositions, often with titles referring to the spiritual or extraterrestrial worlds.

Sunny Boy. Sentimental BALLAD by RAY HENDERSON, 1925. It was made instantly famous in AL JOLSON's interpretation in the musical *The Singing Fool.*

Sun-Treader. Symphonic poem by CARL RUGGLES, 1926–31, inspired by a line from a poem by Robert Browning, "Sun-treader, light and life be thine forever."

The work features dissonant counterpoint in a modern style. Like most of Ruggles's works, the composer continued to revise it after its premiere in Paris, 1932.

šupeljka. Macedonian and Bulgarian end-blown shepherd's FLUTE. It has a cylindrical bore, six finger holes, and no mouthpiece.

MUSICAL INSTRUMENT

supertonic. The second DEGREE of a DIATONIC SCALE. In a major key, the supertonic triad is minor, while in a minor key, the supertonic triad is DIMINISHED. However, the first inversion of the supertonic triad, whether in major or minor, serves as a dignified substitute for the SUBDOMINANT triad in a CADENCE, because they have the same bass note.

In the NEAPOLITAN CADENCE, the first inversion of the lowered supertonic (e.g., in C major or C minor, F–A♭–D♭) has been a treasured cadential chord ever since its introduction in the 17th century. Its advantage is that it provides a resonant major tonal harmony in place of a weak minor modal harmony.

Suppé, Franz (von) (born Francesco Ezechiele Ermenegildo, Cavaliere Suppé-Demelli), famous Austrian composer; b. Spalato, Dalmatia (of Belgian descent), April 18, 1819; d. Vienna, May 21, 1895. At the age of 11 Suppé played the flute, and at 13 he wrote a MASS. He was sent by his father to study law at Padua. However, on his father's death, he went with his mother to Vienna in 1835, and continued serious

PEOPLE IN MUSIC

study at the Conservatory with Simon Sechter and Ignaz Seyfried.

Suppé conducted at theaters in Pressburg and Baden, then at Vienna's Theater an der Wien (1845–62), Kaitheater (1862–65), and Carltheater (1865–82). All the while, he wrote light OPERAS and other theater music of all degrees of levity, obtaining increasing success rivaling that of JACQUES OFFENBACH.

Suppé's music possesses the charm and gaiety of the Viennese genre but also contains elements of more vigorous popular rhythms. His most celebrated single work is the overture to *Dichter und Bauer* (Poet and peasant; 1846), which still retains a firm place in the light repertoire.

Suppé's total output comprises about 30 comic operas and operettas and 180 other stage pieces, most of which were brought out in Vienna. Other works include symphonies, concert overtures, a REQUIEM, three Masses, and other sacred works, choruses, dances, string quartets, and songs.

Supremes, The. *See* ROSS, DIANA.

Sur le Pont d'Avignon. French children's song, 1845, first published in a Parisian collection of nursery rhymes. The first line reads, "On the bridge of Avignon, they dance, they dance."

Surfin' Safari. First chart hit in 1962 for the BEACH BOYS, penned by group leaders Brian Wilson and Mike Love. It led the way to *Surfin' USA* (with a melody and guitar riff borrowed from CHUCK BERRY) and *Surfer Girl.*

Surprise Symphony. Symphony No. 94 by FRANZ JOSEPH HAYDN, 1792, in G major. It is the third of his 12 so-called *LONDON SYMPHONIES,* which he wrote for performance at the concerts conducted by the German violinist Johann Salomon in London.

The surprise is furnished by a sudden loud chord in the middle of the quiet opening theme of the slow second movement, a variation set. The anecdote is often told that Haydn put the loud chord in to wake up the English ladies who went to concerts for a refreshing nap, but when it was first performed, the papers failed to note such effect. One critic said that the loud chord suggested the discharge of a musket on a pastoral scene when a shepherdess lulled herself to sleep contemplating nature and a distant waterfall.

As if to disabuse people of such stories, German catalogues list the *Surprise Symphony* simply as *Paukenschlag (Drumstroke).*

surrealism. A word coined in 1903 by the French poet Guillaume Apollinaire in his fantastic play *Les Mamelles de Tirésias* (The breasts of Tiresias). Generally, it describes superrational experiences. Surrealism embraces the bizarre, unusual, and contradictory. It draws on the subconscious world of dreams and fantasy.

suspension (Ger. *Vorhalt*). A DISSONANCE caused by suspending (holding over) a TONE or tones of a CHORD while the other tones progress to a new HARMONY, thus creating a discord demanding RESOLUTION. Downward DIATONIC suspensions are by far more frequent than upward ones.

Süssmayr, Franz Xaver. *See* MOZART, WOLFGANG AMADEUS.

sustaining pedal. A misnomer for the SOSTENUTO PEDAL.

Sutherland, (Dame) **Joan,** celebrated Australian soprano; b. Sydney, Nov. 7, 1926. Sutherland first studied piano and voice with her mother. At 19, she commenced vocal training with John and Aida Dickens in Sydney, making her debut there as Dido in a concert performance in 1947. She then made her stage debut there in the title role of EUGENE GOOSENS's *Judith* in 1951, subsequently continuing her vocal studies with Clive Carey at the Royal College of Music in London. She also studied at the Opera School there.

Sutherland made her Covent Garden debut in London as the first Lady in *THE MAGIC FLUTE* in 1952. She attracted attention there when she created the role of Jenifer in MICHAEL TIPPETT's *The Midsummer Marriage* in 1955 and as Gilda two years later. She also appeared in the title role of *ALCINA* in the Handel Opera Society production in 1957. In the meantime, she married Richard Bonynge in 1954.

PEOPLE IN MUSIC

After making her North American debut as Donna Anna in Vancouver in 1958, Sutherland scored a triumph as Lucia at Covent Garden the next year. She then pursued a brilliant international career. She made her U.S. debut as Alcina in Dallas in 1960. Her Metropolitan Opera debut in N.Y. as Lucia in 1961 was greeted by extraordinary acclaim.

Sutherland continued to sing at the Metropolitan and other major opera houses on both sides of the Atlantic, and also took her own company to Australia in 1965 and 1974. During her husband's music directorship with the Australian Opera in Sydney from 1976 to 1986, she made stellar appearances with the company. In 1990 she made her operatic farewell in LES HUGUENOTS in Sydney.

Sutherland was universally acknowledged as one of the foremost interpreters of the BEL CANTO repertoire during her time. She particularly excelled in roles from operas by GIOACCHINO ROSSINI, VINCENZO BELLINI, and GAETANO DONIZETTI. She was also a fine Handelian.

In 1961 she was made a Commander of the Order of the British Empire and in 1979 was named a Dame Commander of the Order of the British Empire. In 1992 she was honored with the Order of Merit. Her autobiography appeared in 1997.

PEOPLE IN MUSIC

Suzuki, Shin'ichi, influential Japanese music educator and violin teacher; b. Nagoya, Oct. 18, 1898; d. Matsumoto, Jan. 26, 1996. He was the son of Masakichi Suzuki (1859–1944), a maker of string instruments and founder of the Suzuki Violin Seizo Company. He studied violin with Ko Ando in Tokyo and with Karl Klinger in Berlin from 1921 to 1928.

Upon his return to Japan, he formed the Suzuki Quartet with three of his brothers and also made appearances as a conductor with his own Tokyo String Orchestra. He became president of the Teikoku Music School in 1930 and subsequently devoted most of his time to education, especially the teaching of children (*see* SUZUKI METHOD).

In 1950 Suzuki organized the Saino Kyoiku Kenkyu-kai in Matsumoto, where he taught his method most successfully. In subsequent years his method was adopted for instruction on other instruments as well. He made many tours of the U.S. and Europe, where he lectured and demonstrated his method.

Suzuki method. A process of musical education based on repetition and strict regulation in training. It was founded by SHIN'ICHI SUZUKI, who maintained that any child, under proper conditions in a group environment, could achieve a high level of proficiency as a performer.

Although the program ranges through adolescence, it seems to be most successful with very young children, especially those between the ages of four and eight. They are taught to play the violin by imitating the physical movements and the visual placement of the fingers on the strings.

Suzuki students around the world progress through the same repertoire, so that they can easily play together at large meetings.

svirala (*sviralina;* Serb.). Generic term for indigenous FLUTE family instruments, also found in Croatia and Slavonia (*jedina*).

MUSICAL
INSTRUMENT

Swan Lake. Ballet by PIOTR ILYICH TCHAIKOVSKY, first performed in Moscow, March 4, 1877. The scenario is the heart of ROMANTICISM.

A young girl loved by a prince is changed into a swan by witchcraft. She can be saved only if he identifies her in the lake of swans. But he fails, selecting the wrong swan. His beloved perishes, and he jumps from the cliff into the water to his death.

The score contains some of Tchaikovsky's most romantic music, and a

◄

Margot Fonteyn in Swan Lake, *1951. (Hulton-Deutsch Collection/Corbis)*

popular instrumental SUITE has been drawn from it.

swan song. A last gasp or final effort made by an artist. The legend that swans sing beautifully at the approach of death is of ancient origin. Plato states that dying swans sing so sweetly because they know that they are about to return to the divine presence of Apollo to whom they are sacred. Another Greek writer reports that flocks of swans regularly descend on Apollo's temple during festive days and join the choir.

But the philosopher Lucian, skeptical as ever, made a journey to the swan breeding grounds in Italy. He inquired among the local peasants whether they ever heard a swan sing. He was told that swans only croak, cackle, and grunt in a most disagreeable manner. So-called *mute swans* maintained on royal preservations in Britain are not voiceless—they growl, hiss, and even trill. Despite these unpleasant characteristics, the swan, with its graceful long neck (18 vertebrae, as compared with the giraffe's seven) remains a symbol of poetic beauty.

GIOACCHINO ROSSINI was called the "Swan of Pesaro," his birthplace. Although he possessed a self-deprecating sense of humor, it never occurred to him how ambiguous this compliment really was. In his CARNIVAL OF THE ANIMALS, CAMILLE SAINT-SAËNS assigns his beautiful cello solo to the swan, and it inspired Anna Pavlova's famous dance creation *The Dying Swan.*

JEAN SIBELIUS wrote a symphonic poem entitled *The Swan of Tuonela,* with a mellifluously nasal English horn solo representing the dying swan song. A group of FRANZ SCHUBERT's posthumous songs was given the title SCHWANENGESANG by the publishers.

Yet no composer has dared to reproduce the true sound of the swan's song. Not even the bassoon in its lowest register is ugly enough to render justice to a dying swan's croaking.

In Hans Christian Andersen's tale *The Ugly Duckling,* a swan egg is deposited in a nest of ducks. After it is hatched, the young gray swan is an ugly duckling compared to its duck siblings, until one fine day it becomes a beautiful white swan. SERGEI PROKOFIEV wrote a poetic BALLAD for voice and piano based on this tale.

Swanee. Song by GEORGE GERSHWIN, 1919, included in *The Capitol Revue.* It was his first hit song, and his biggest commercial success. Some two million records and a million copies of sheet music were sold within a year of its release. It was popularized by entertainer AL JOLSON.

Swanee River. Common name for STEPHEN FOSTER'S *OLD FOLKS AT HOME.*

Sweelinck (real name, Swybbertszoon), **Jan Pieterszoon,** great Dutch organist, pedagogue, and composer; b. Deventer, May? 1562; d. Amsterdam, Oct. 16, 1621. Sweelinck was born into a musical family, his father, paternal grandfather, and uncle all being organists.

He went as a youth to Amsterdam, which was to be the center of his activities for the rest of his life. Jacob Buyck, pastor of the Oude Kerk, supervised his academic education. He most likely began his musical training under his father, then studied with Jan Willemszoon Lossy. Sweelinck is believed to have begun his career as an organist in 1577, although first mention of him is in 1580, as organist of the Oude Kerk, a position his father held until his death in 1573.

Sweelinck became a celebrated master of the keyboard, so excelling in the art of improvisation that he was called the "Orpheus of Amsterdam." He was also greatly renowned as a teacher, numbering among his pupils most of the founders of the so-called north German organ school. His most famous pupils were JACOB PRAETORIUS, Heinrich Scheidemann, Samuel and Gottfried Scheidt, and Paul Siefert.

The output of Sweelinck as a composer is now seen as the culmination of the great Dutch school of his time. Among his extant works are about 250 vocal pieces (33 chansons, 19 madrigals, 39 motets, and 153 Psalms) and some 70 keyboard works.

Sweelinck was the first to employ the PEDAL in a real fugal part, and originated the organ FUGUE built upon one theme with the gradual addition of counterthemes leading to a highly involved and ingenious FINALE—a form perfected by JOHANN SEBASTIAN BACH. In rhythmic and melodic freedom his vocal compositions show an advance over the earlier POLYPHONIC style, although they continued to feature complex COUNTERPOINT.

Sweelinck's son and pupil, Dirck Janszoon Sweelinck (b. Amsterdam [baptized], May 26, 1591; d. there, Sept. 16, 1652), was an organist, music editor, and composer who succeeded his father as organist at the Oude Kerk (from 1621), where he acquired a fine reputation as an improviser.

Sweet Adeline. Song by H. W. Armstrong, 1903. He named it in honor of the famous Italian prima donna ADELINA PATTI, who was giving one of her recurrent farewell concert tours in America at the time. It was once a staple of barbershop quartets.

Sweet Charity. Musical by CY COLEMAN, 1966. The central character is a hostess in a dance hall whose name is actually Charity. She is disappointed in men because one character steals her purse and throws her into the Central Park lake. Another puts her in the bedroom closet while he is making love to his regular date, and still another gets stuck with her in a stalled elevator and again in a parachute-jump ride at a carnival. Despite his increasing affection for her, he is unable to deal with her past and leaves her.

Includes *If My Friends Could See Me Now, Baby Dream Your Dream,* and *Big Spender.*

Sweet Rosie O'Grady. Song by Maude Nugent, 1896, published in N.Y. It is a typical Irish WALTZ, and it has been steadily successful through the years. There has been some controversy as to whether her husband, the songwriter William Jerome, was the actual composer.

swing. A smooth, sophisticated style of JAZZ playing, popular in the 1930s and early 1940s. Its distinctive characteristic was a trend away from small jazz groups, who improvised by musical instinct, toward a well-organized ensemble of professional instrumentalists. The main outline of MELODY and HARMONY was established during rehearsals, but improvisation was allowed in extended solos. The new style of performance required a larger band, so that the "swing era" became synonymous with the BIG-BAND era.

Swing music achieved its first great boom in 1935, largely through the jazz clarinet player BENNY GOODMAN, advertised as the "King of Swing." The jazz magazine *Down-beat* described swing in its issue of Jan. 1935 as "a musician's term for perfect rhythm." Its Nov. 1935 issue carried a glossary of "swing terms that cats use," in which swing was defined as "laying it in the groove."

Swing music is a natural product of the jazz era, which created a demand for larger bands and a greater volume of sound. The advent of swing music coincided with the development of the radio industry when, about 1930, millions could hear concerts broadcast into homes.

As the name indicates, swing symbolized an uninhibited celebration of the youthful spirit of the age. Big bands of the swing era were usually catapulted into syncopated action by a clarinetist, a trumpet soloist, or a saxophone player. The instrumentation of a big swing band derived from its jazz predecessor, with clarinet, saxophone, trumpet, trombone, percussion, and piano as its mainstays.

This metaphor, borrowed from the PHONOGRAPH industry, gave rise to the once popular adjective "groovy," in the sense of "cool," "bad," "out of sight," or just musically well executed.

Swing Low, Sweet Chariot. An African-American spiritual, first published in 1872. It is one of the most famous and poetic GOSPEL spirituals, with a PENTATONIC melody. It has been endlessly arranged and reinterpreted.

syllabic melody. One melody, each TONE of which is sung to a separate syllable.

syllable name. A syllable taken as the name of a note or tone, as *Do* for *C*.

symbolism. Describing compositions of the late 19th and early 20th centuries that, like their counterparts in the poetic and visual arts, are characterized by epigrammatic, sometimes oblique representations of emotions, topical themes, and events.

sympathetic strings. Strings stretched below or above the principal strings of LUTE and GAMBA family instruments to provide sympathetic RESONANCE and thus amplify the sounds of the melodic strings. These strings are generally not played upon. They are still found on CHORDOPHONES such as the HARDINGFELE of Norway and many of the classical Indian instruments.

MUSICAL INSTRUMENT

Some piano manufacturers add sympathetic strings above the strings in the treble to add resonance to the tinny sound of the upper range. These are called ALIQUOT STRINGS.

symphonia. In the Middle Ages, CONSONANCE, in contrast to DIAPHONIA, DISSONANCE. In BAROQUE music, the term was used indiscriminately for all genres of ensemble music, but eventually a SYMPHONY became crystallized as a specific form of orchestral composition.

symphonic. Resembling, or relating or pertaining to, a SYMPHONY. *Symphonic ode,* a symphonic composition combining chorus and orchestra; *symphonic band, see* BAND, SYMPHONIC.

symphonic poem (Ger. *Tonbild, Tondichtung*). An extended orchestral composition born in the 19th century. It follows in its development the thread of a story or the ideas of a poem, repeating and interweaving its themes appropriately. It has no fixed form, nor has it set divisions like those of a SYMPHONY.

Symphonie cévenole. See SYMPHONY ON A FRENCH MOUNTAIN THEME.

sahn-fōh′nē

symphonie concertante (Fr.; It. *sinfonia concertante*). An orchestral work that combines the formal elements of a SYMPHONY and a CONCERTO by including the use of soloists. WOLFGANG AMADEUS MOZART made good use of this form, in his works for violin and viola (K.364, 1779), two flutes, two oboe, and two bassoons (K.320, 1779), and other unfinished works.

In a sense, this genre is the CLASSIC equivalent of the CONCERTO GROSSO.

Symphonie fantastique. Program symphony by HECTOR BERLIOZ, 1830, premiered in Paris, the first of its kind.

Of all the compositions of the ROMANTIC age, the "Fantastic Symphony" by Berlioz is the most literal and also the most literary. The piece was inspired by a specific event in

Berlioz's life. He attended a Paris performance of *Hamlet* given by the Shakespearean Company of London, with Henrietta Smithson as Ophelia. He instantly became infatuated with her. He walked the streets of Paris in a state of fantastic obsession. He decided to express his passion/obsession in the language he knew best: music. In the work, Smithson is identified by a recurrent THEME.

Berlioz calls the repeated theme an IDÉE FIXE (a predecessor of the LEITMOTIV).

The symphony is premiered, but Smithson does not attend. Eventually they meet. They marry, but he speaks no English and she speaks no French. They are unhappy, and Berlioz leaves her. Smithson dies, the victim of an unusual early onset of senility. In a morbid coincidence, the Smithson theme turns out to have been adapted by Berlioz from an earlier work, his *March to the Gallows.*

Strangely, the printed score is dedicated not to his beloved Smithson, but to the "Czar of All the Russias," Nicolas I. Why? Berlioz, romantic soul that he was, also had proper regard for earthly necessities. During his concert tour to Russia in 1847, he was advised to seek imperial favor in the hope of obtaining a monetary reward. He duly put the name of the ruler on the opening page of his symphony, but there is no record of his receiving anything in return. The Czar was notoriously insensitive to art.

Rather than follow the formal subdivisions of a symphony, Berlioz integrated the music with the *idée fixe,* which appears in various guises through the movements. To point out the personal nature of the work he subtitled it *Épisode de la vie d'un artiste* (Episode in the life of an artist [namely, its composer]).

The five movements of the score are:

I. *Reveries, Passions* (SONATA FORM with slow introduction)

II. *A Ball* (fast WALTZ)

III. *Scene in the Fields* (spacious PASTORALE)

IV. *March to the Scaffold* (SCHERZO in DUPLE METER)

V. *Dream of a Witches' Sabbath* (FINALE, in which thematic transformation comes into full glory, including quotations of the DIES IRAE)

Berlioz supplied a literary program to the music: a "young musician of morbid sensibilities" takes opium to find relief from his lovesickness. It should be noted that Berlioz himself never smoked opium. However, this hallucinogenic drug was in vogue at the time and was the subject of several mystic novels and pseudoscientific essays.

Symphonie pathétique. The French name for PIOTR ILYICH TCHAIKOVSKY's Sixth Symphony.

symphony (from Grk. *syn* + *phōnē,* sounding together; Fr. *symphonie;* Ger. *Sinfonie;* It. *sinfonia*). An orchestral genre with distinct MOVEMENTS or divisions, each with its own THEME or themes (in the 19th and 20th centuries, sometimes shared). The symphony is the most significant and complex form of musical composition. In its CLASSIC form, it represents the supreme achievement of Western music.

A typical symphonic plan in the Classic period might be a four-movement work, organized as:

I. *Allegro* in the TONIC KEY (SONATA FORM, often with a slow introduction)

II. *Adagio* in a related key (choice of TERNARY, VARIATION, "sonata without development" forms)

III. MINUET or SCHERZO in the tonic key (in triple meter, with TRIO)

IV. *Allegro* or *Presto* in the tonic key (choice of sonata form, RONDO, sonata-rondo, variation forms)

The history of the symphony goes back 400 years. In the 17th century, the term SYMPHONIA was divested of its general meaning as a musical composition. Instead, it was applied exclusively to an instrumental ensemble without voices and was used for instrumental OVERTURES or INTERLUDES in early OPERAS.

In the first half of the 18th century, the instrumental SINFONIA was formally stabilized as a composition in three symmetric movements: Allegro, Andante, and Allegro. The opening Allegro was of the greatest evolutionary importance, because it followed the developing SONATA FORM. This form has clearly demarcated sections that became defined by theorists as EXPOSITION, DEVELOPMENT, and RECAPITULATION.

FRANZ JOSEPH HAYDN is commonly regarded as the "father of the symphony," but in fact several composers before Haydn's time wrote orchestral works that already comprised the formal elements of symphonic style. Particularly important among these predecessors were the musicians of the MANNHEIM SCHOOL, who in their performances emphasized contrasts of style, TEMPO, and instrumental combinations. Furthermore, they introduced the DYNAMIC elements of CRESCENDO and DIMINUENDO while preserving the contrasts of FORTE and PIANO.

The era of the Classic symphony began in the second half of the 18th century. Its most illustrious representatives were WOLFGANG AMADEUS MOZART and Haydn. Most Classic symphonies added a dance movement, usually a Minuet, to the three-part form. Despite the versatility of the symphonic form, its structure was essentially uniform.

A revolutionary change in the history of symphonic form occurred in the 19th century. The form of a symphony became individualized; like opera, it was no longer manufactured in large quantities, according to a prescribed formula. Symphonies acquired individual personalities, with the *EROICA SYMPHONY* of LUDWIG VAN BEETHOVEN being a famous example. In his Ninth Symphony, Beethoven added a chorus, an extraordinary innovation at the time.

Often symphonies of the ROMANTIC period were autobiographical. HECTOR BERLIOZ wrote a grandly programmatic orchestral work, *SYMPHONIE FANTASTIQUE,* as a musical confession of his love for an English Shakespearean actress. The ten symphonies of GUSTAV MAHLER are Romantic revelations of the most intense character. FRANZ LISZT selected two literary epics, Dante's *Divina Commedia* and Goethe's *Faust,* as inspirations for his symphonies.

Several composers who proclaimed themselves fervent NATIONALISTS wrote symphonies in a traditional Romantic style. Among the greatest was JEAN SIBELIUS, who assigned national Finnish subjects for his SYMPHONIC POEMS, but whose seven symphonies bear no programmatic subtitles.

The champion symphonist in Russia was NIKOLAI MIAS-KOVSKY, who wrote no less than 27.

For some reason, CLAUDE DEBUSSY and MAURICE RAVEL were never tempted to write symphonies. It is only in the 20th century that modern French composers, particularly DARIUS MILHAUD and ARTHUR HONEGGER, contributed to the genre.

The Russians remain faithful to the traditional symphonic form. PIOTR ILYICH TCHAIKOVSKY wrote six, ALEXANDER SCRIABIN and SERGEI RACHMANINOFF each wrote three, and DMITRI SHOSTAKOVICH wrote 15, several of which include vocal forces.

Strangely, Germany and Austria, the countries which created and maintained the art of symphonic composition, showed a decline of symphonic production in the 20th century. Perhaps the fact that RICHARD WAGNER, the most potent influence in post-Classic Germany, devoted his energies totally to the musical theater (his youthful symphony was not published until many years after his death), drew German composers away from symphonic composition. RICHARD STRAUSS wrote two, *SYMPHONIA DOMESTICA* and *ALPINE SYMPHONY*, but they are panoramic, symphonic in name only. PAUL HINDEMITH was not a Wagnerian, but rather a modern follower of MAX REGER. However, neither he nor Reger wrote symphonies in the traditional manner.

The three great composers of the modern Vienna school, ARNOLD SCHOENBERG, ALBAN BERG, and ANTON WEBERN, abstained from composing works of truly symphonic dimensions. IGOR STRAVINSKY, who began his career as a follower of NIKOLAI RIMSKY-KORSAKOV's pictorial symphonism, wrote several symphonies, but they were closer to the pre-Classic type of sinfonia than to the traditional Classic or Romantic type.

Ever since Haydn's symphonic journeys to London, England was a willing receptacle of German musical style. In the 20th century, EDWARD ELGAR wrote two grand symphonies and RALPH VAUGHAN WILLIAMS nine, some of them highly modern in idiom. BENJAMIN BRITTEN, generally regarded as the most remarkable English composer of the 20th century, never felt the symphonic urge. His works in symphonic form approach the manner of orchestral suites.

The Danish composer CARL NIELSEN wrote six symphonies, with somewhat programmatic content expressed in such subtitles as *Expansive* and *Inextinguishable*. The most

prolific Italian composer of symphonies was GIAN FRAN-
CESCO MALIPIERO, who wrote at least ten, several equipped
with suggestive subtitles.

In the U.S., among composers who pursued the symphonic career steadfastly through the years are ROY HARRIS,
who wrote 14, and WALTER PISTON, WILLIAM SCHUMAN,
DAVID DIAMOND, and VINCENT PERSICHETTI, who wrote eight
symphonies each. Of AARON COPLAND's symphonic works,
the most significant is his Third Symphony, which incidentally includes his famous *Fanfare for the Common Man.*

The main structure of a symphony during the two centuries of its formulation has not radically changed. The
lively scherzo replaced the mannered minuet. The four traditional movements were often compressed into one. The general tendency early in the 20th century was to reduce the orchestra to the bare bones of the BAROQUE sinfonia. In his
SYMPHONY OF PSALMS, Stravinsky eliminates the violins altogether in order to conjure desired austerity.

The piano, not a symphonic instrument *per se* and not
used in the symphonies of Schumann, FELIX MENDELSSOHN,
Tchaikovsky, JOHANNES BRAHMS, or any other composer of
the Romantic century regardless of individual style, became
a welcome guest in the symphonies of the 20th century, with
an obvious intent to provide sharp articulation and precise
rhythm. Shostakovich wrote an important piano part in his
First Symphony. Mahler used SLEIGHBELLS in his symphonies, but he did so in order to re-create the atmosphere
of the countryside, serving as dainty embellishments rather
than modernistic decorations.

Symphony for Organ and Orchestra.

Symphonic work by
AARON COPLAND, 1925, first performed in N.Y. with Copland's teacher NADIA BOULANGER as soloist. WALTER DAM-
ROSCH conducted. He somewhat humorously declared to
the audience that a youth who could write such music at the
age of 24 would be capable of murder a few years later.

Symphony in Three Movements.

Orchestral work by IGOR
STRAVINSKY, 1946, first premiered in N.Y., the composer
conducting. The work demonstrates the possibilities of con-
tinually evolving symphonic form.

A unique American sym-
phony is the Fourth Sym-
phony of CHARLES IVES, which
consists of four movements
written at different times and
in widely different styles.

Symphony of a Thousand. An unofficial nickname for the Eighth Symphony by GUSTAV MAHLER, 1906–07, in E-flat major. The title is justifiable by the work's forces: a huge ensemble with vocal soloists, two mixed choruses, and boys' chorus, as well as a battery of percussion instruments. It was first performed in Munich, 1910, the last symphony of Mahler's that he heard.

While Mahler never approved of the nickname, he wrote extravagantly about the significance of the work: "In this symphony the whole universe begins to sound in musical tones; it is no longer human voices, but planets and suns that are in motion here."

The *Symphony of a Thousand* is in effect an ORATORIO. It consists of two lengthy choral sections, the first based on the medieval Pentecostal hymn *Veni, Creator Spiritus,* and the second a rendition of a philosophical part of Goethe's *Faust.*

Symphony of Psalms *(Symphonie des Psaumes).* Work by IGOR STRAVINSKY, 1930, for chorus and orchestra, dedicated "to the glory of God on the occasion of the 50th anniversary of the Boston Symphony Orchestra." Because of a postponement of the Boston performance, its actual world premiere was given in Brussels; the Boston Symphony Orchestra performance followed one week later.

The text is in Latin, as it was in Stravinsky's OPERA-ORATORIO *OEDIPUS REX* of 1927. By using an ancient language, Stravinsky again intended to emphasize the timeless character of the subject. Unlike the opera, the psalms are set to perhaps the most serene music the composer ever wrote.

Symphony on a French Mountain Theme. Symphony No. 1 by VINCENT D'INDY, 1887, with piano OBLIGGATO, premiered in Paris. The work is also called the *Symphonie cévenole,* named after Cévennes, a mountain region in southern France.

symploche. A rhetorical musical device in which the beginning of a musical PHRASE serves also as its ending. A highly artistic example is the initial phrase of the ending to WOLFGANG AMADEUS MOZART's Symphony No. 39 in E-flat Major, K.543.

synaesthesia. Color associations with certain sounds or tonalities. It is said that Issac Newton chose to divide the visible spectrum into seven distinct colors by analogy with the seven degrees of the DIATONIC SCALE. Individual musicians differed greatly in associating a sound with a certain color.

The most common association between tonality and color is that of C major and whiteness. It is particularly strong for pianists for the obvious reason that the C-major scale is played on white keys. However, ALEXANDER SCRIABIN, who had a very strong feeling for color associations, correlated C major with red. F-sharp major should be associated with black, because it comprises all five black keys of the piano keyboard. However, Scriabin associated it with bright blue and NIKOLAI RIMSKY-KORSAKOV with dull green.

Any attempt to objectivize color associations is doomed to failure if for no other reason than the arbitrary assignment of a certain frequency to a given note. Standard PITCH has risen nearly a SEMITONE in the last century, so that the color of C would now be associated with C-sharp in relation to the old standards.

The most ambitious attempt to incorporate light into a musical composition was the inclusion of a projected COLOR ORGAN in Scriabin's score *PROMETHEUS*, in which the changes of instrumental coloration were to be accompanied by changing lighting in the concert hall.

synchrony. Metric or rhythmic synchrony is an inclusive term, of which POLYMETER and POLYRHYTHM are specific instances. Synchronization demands absolutely precise simultaneity of sets of mutually primary numbers of notes within a given unit of time, i.e., 3:2, 5:3, 11:4, etc.

TRIPLETS and QUINTUPLETS are of course common in free CADENZAS since FRÉDÉRIC CHOPIN's time. (There is a consistent use of four beats against three in Chopin's *Fantaisie-Impromptu*.) Beyond this, it is impossible for human players to achieve perfect synchrony.

In the 20th century, there have been some interesting machines created to play complex rhythms. The composer HENRY COWELL and the Russian inventor Leon Theremin invented the RHYMICON in the mid-'30s to play two rhythms against each other. The composer CONLOW NANCARROW created complex polyrhythms by hand punching piano rolls. These would then be played by a PLAYER PIANO, achieving complexities no human pianist could perform. And of course in the last two decades, SYNTHESIZERS—particularly DRUM MACHINES—have been created that can play multiple rhythms simultaneously with machine-like precision.

Synchrony. Orchestral work by HENRY COWELL, 1931, first performed in Paris. As the title suggests, this is an essay in orchestral synchronization. Cowell's novel technique of TONE CLUSTERS is prominently used.

MUSICAL
INSTRUMENT

synclavier. Digital SYNTHESIZER, developed in 1976. It features a piano-like KEYBOARD with the full capabilities of a digital synthesizer.

Syncopated Clock, The. Orchestral novelty by LEROY ANDERSON, composed in 1950. The piece describes musically an old-fashioned clock that goes haywire.

syncopation (from Grk. *syncope,* clash between disparate elements; missed heartbeat). One of the most powerful sources of rhythmic diversification.

In music, SYNCOPATION typically takes three forms:

- an ACCENT on a normally unaccented beat or part of a beat;

- a continuation of a note "over the BAR" so as to avoid striking a note on a normally accented beat; or

- the conflict of unequal rhythms in two or more parts.

In MENSURAL NOTATION, syncopation was used to make changes in the main stress. The consequence of such rhythmic displacement was the generation of a discordant tonal combination that had to be resolved into a consonance.

In contrapuntal theory, syncopation is classified as the fourth SPECIES of counterpoint. Syncopated notes were initially marked as auxiliary ornaments and were often written in small notes placed before the principal note. SUSPENSIONS and APPOGGIATURAS furnish the characteristic elements of dissonant syncopation. In works of the ROMANTIC era, syncopation served to enhance emotional stress in the composition.

Syncopation is the spice of music in dance forms. In triple meter, Viennese WALTZES create an effect of syncopation by stressing the third beat of the measure, while the MAZURKA tends to accent the second. In quadruple meter, MARCHES emphasize the main beat but supply syncopation in smaller rhythmic divisions against a regular beat. RAGTIME developed the march form into a highly syncopated melodic style. JAZZ gradually eliminated the need for emphasis of the regular beat, thus elevating syncopation into a TEXTURE.

Popular music in the U.S. since World War II has vacillated between a return to uniform rhythms with an accent on the strong beats of the measure (ROCK 'N' ROLL, MOTOWN, DISCO) and various degrees of syncopation, sometimes quite subtle (ROCK, FUNK, NEW WAVE), sometimes less so (REGGAE, GRUNGE).

synthesizer. A class of electronic devices that make possible the creation of any sound via electronic synthesis.

Like the personal computer, modern synthesizers are self-contained units that can be operated with a minimum of accessories. This is in contrast to the first ELECTRONIC MUSIC synthesizers, composed of several modules that could take up an entire wall or even room in the early years, i.e., Robert Moog's modules of 1964.

Unlimited musical horizons opened to electronic music with the introduction of synthesizers, which are capable of

MUSICAL
INSTRUMENT

◀

Keyboard synthesizer. (Yamaha Corp.)

producing any frequency with the utmost precision and distributing the relative strength of the OVERTONES so as to create any desired instrumental TIMBRE. While synthesizers through the 1960s were driven analogically (i.e., with dials approximating the desired parameters), the addition of computers to the process permitted digital synthesis, using the powerful mathematical capabilities of computers to control all sonic parameters.

The world of synthesizers has been enhanced by a common computer language called MIDI (musical instrument digital interface). This allows synthesizers to "talk" to other electronic modules, including SAMPLERS (which can record natural sounds for further enhancement) and SEQUENCERS (which can record entire compositions or sequences of notes and rhythms).

Syrian chant. Christian HYMNODY in use in early communities in Syria. It was derived originally from the churches of Antioch, traditionally considered the oldest Christian churches. There are Orthodox, non-Orthodox, and re-unified rites (the latter, with the Roman Catholic church), with similar rites influenced by Gypsy, Arab, and other non-Western music. Among related liturgies are the Assyrian and Maronite.

According to myth, Syrinx was a nymph beloved by the Greek god Pan; she was changed into a reed to escape his pursuit.

syrinx. Ancient Greek PANPIPES made of a set of reeds (usually seven) of varying sizes, and therefore PITCHES.

Syrinx. Piece for solo flute by CLAUDE DEBUSSY, 1913, named after the Greek nymph. Theorists have discovered that this work was the model for EDGARD VARÈSE's own solo flute work, *Density 21.5.*

system. Generally referring to compositional practices based on the systematic treatment of some organizing aspect(s) of music.

Szell, George (actually, György), greatly distinguished Hungarian-born American conductor; b. Budapest, June 7, 1897; d. Cleveland, July 30, 1970. Szell's family moved to

PEOPLE IN MUSIC

Vienna when he was a small child. He studied piano with Richard Robert and composition with Eusebius Mandyczewski, and also composition in Prague with J. B. Foerster. He played a WOLFGANG AMADEUS MOZART piano concerto with the Vienna Symphony Orchestra when he was ten years old, and the orchestra also performed an OVERTURE of his own composition.

At the age of 17, Szell led the Berlin Philharmonic in an ambitious program that included a symphonic work of his own. In 1915 he was engaged as an assistant conductor at the Royal Opera of Berlin. He then conducted OPERA orchestras in several German towns from 1917 to 1924.

From 1924 to 1929, Szell held the position of first conductor at the Berlin State Opera, then conducted in Prague and Vienna. He made his U.S. debut as guest conductor of the St. Louis Symphony Orchestra in 1930. In 1937 he was appointed conductor of the Scottish Orchestra in Glasgow. He was also a regular conductor with the Residentie Orkest in The Hague from 1937 to 1939. He then conducted in Australia.

At the outbreak of war in Europe in 1939 Szell was in America, which was to become his adoptive country by naturalization in 1946. His American conducting engagements included appearances with the Los Angeles Philharmonic, NBC Symphony, Chicago Symphony, Detroit Symphony, and Boston Symphony. In 1942 he was appointed a conductor of the Metropolitan Opera in N.Y., where he received high praise for his interpretation of RICHARD WAGNER's music dramas. He remained on its roster until 1946. He also conducted performances with the N.Y. Philharmonic in 1944 – 45.

In 1946 Szell was appointed conductor of the Cleveland Orchestra, a post which he held for 24 years. Under his guidance, the Cleveland Orchestra rose to the heights of symphonic excellence, taking its place in the foremost rank of world orchestras. He was also music advisor and senior guest conductor of the N.Y. Philharmonic from 1969 until his death.

Szell was a stern disciplinarian, demanding the utmost from his musicians to achieve perfect performances, but he was also willing to labor tirelessly at his task. He was particularly renowned for his authoritative and exemplary performances of the Viennese classics, but he was also capable of outstanding interpretations of 20th-century masterworks.

PEOPLE IN MUSIC

Szeryng, Henryk, celebrated Polish-born Mexican violinist and pedagogue; b. Zelazowa Wola, Sept. 22, 1918; d. Kassel, March 3, 1988. Szeryng began piano and harmony training with his mother when he was five, and at age seven turned to the violin, receiving instruction from Maurice Frenkel. After further studies with Carl Flesch in Berlin from 1929 to 1932, he went to Paris to continue his training with Jacques Thibaud at the Conservatory, graduating with a premier prix in 1937.

In 1933 Szeryng made his formal debut as soloist in the Concerto by JOHANNES BRAHMS, with the Warsaw Philharmonic. With the outbreak of World War II in 1939, he became official translator to the Polish prime minister Wladyslaw Sikorski's government-in-exile in London. He later was made personal government liaison officer. In 1941 he accompanied the prime minister to Latin America to find a home for some 4,000 Polish refugees. The refugees were taken in by Mexico, and Szeryng, in gratitude, settled there himself, becoming a naturalized citizen in 1946.

Throughout World War II Szeryng appeared in some 300 concerts for the Allies. After the war he pursued a brilliant international career and was active as a teacher. In 1970 he was made Mexico's special advisor to UNESCO in Paris. He celebrated the 50th anniversary of his debut with a grand tour of Europe and the U.S. in 1983.

A cosmopolitan fluent in seven languages, a humanitarian, and a violinist of extraordinary gifts, Szeryng became renowned as a musician's musician by combining virtuoso technique with a probing discernment of the highest order.

Szigeti, Joseph, eminent Hungarian-born American violinist; b. Budapest, Sept. 5, 1892; d. Lucerne, Feb. 19, 1973. Szigeti began studies at a local music school. While still a child, he was placed in the advanced class of Jenó Hubay at the Budapest Academy of Music. He then made his debut in

Berlin at age 13. He made his first appearance in London when he was 15 and subsequently toured England in concerts with FERRUCCIO BUSONI. He then settled in Switzerland in 1913, where he was a professor at the Geneva Conservatory from 1917 to 1925.

Szigeti made an auspicious U.S. debut playing the Violin Concerto by LUDWIG VAN BEETHOVEN with LEOPOLD STOKOWSKI and the Philadelphia Orchestra, at N.Y.'s Carnegie Hall in 1925. Thereafter, he toured the U.S. regularly while continuing to appear in Europe. With the outbreak of World War II, Szigeti went to the U.S. in 1940, becoming a naturalized citizen in 1951. After the end of the war he resumed his international career. He settled again in Switzerland in 1960 and gave master classes.

Szigeti was an artist of rare intellect and integrity. He avoided the role of the virtuoso, placing himself totally at the service of music. In addition to the standard repertoire, he championed the music of many 20th-century composers. He wrote several books of memoirs and on pedagogy.

Szigeti's son-in-law, Nikita Magaloff (b. St. Petersburg, Feb. 21, 1912) is a pianist noted for his lyric-dramatic interpretations of FRÉDÉRIC CHOPIN, with lapidary attention to detail.

Szymanowski, Karol (Maciej), eminent Polish composer; b. Timoshovka, Ukraine, Oct. 6, 1882; d. Lausanne, March 28, 1937. The son of a cultured landowner, Szymanowski grew up in a musical environment. He began to play piano and compose very early in life. His first teacher was Gustav Neuhaus in Elizavetgrad.

PEOPLE IN MUSIC

In 1901 Szymanowski went to Warsaw, where he studied harmony, COUNTERPOINT, and composition until 1904. With Gregor Fitelberg, Ludomir Rózycki, and Apolinary Szeluto, he founded the Young Polish Composer's Publishing Company in Berlin, which was underwritten by Prince Wladyslaw Lubomirski. The composers also became known as Young Poland in Music, publishing new works and sponsoring performances for some six years. Among the works the group published was Szymanowski's op.1, nine Piano Preludes in 1906.

Szymanowski was greatly influenced by German ROMAN-TICISM, and his first major orchestral works reveal the impact of RICHARD WAGNER and RICHARD STRAUSS. His First Symphony was premiered in Warsaw on March 26, 1909. He was dissatisfied with the score, however, and withdrew it from further performance. In 1911 he completed his Second Symphony, which demonstrated a stylistic change from German dominance to Russian influences, paralleling the harmonic evolution of ALEXANDER SCRIABIN. It was played for the first time in Warsaw on April 7, 1911.

After a Viennese sojourn in 1911–12 and a trip to North Africa in 1914, he lived in Timoshovka until 1917, where he wrote his Third Symphony. He appeared in concert with the violinist Paul Kochánski in Moscow and St. Petersburg, giving first performances of his violin works. It was for Kochánski that he composed his violin triptych, *Mythes* (*La Fontaine d'Aréthuse* in this cycle is one of his best-known compositions). About this time, his music underwent a new change in style, veering toward French IMPRESSIONISM. During the Russian Revolution of 1917, the family estate at Timoshovka was ruined, and Szymanowski lost most of his possessions.

From 1917 to 1919 Szymanowski lived in Elizavetgrad, where he continued to compose industriously, despite the turmoil of the civil war. After a brief stay in Bydgoszcz, he went to Warsaw in 1920. In 1920–21 he toured the U.S. in concerts with Kochánski and Artur Rubinstein. Returning to Warsaw, he gradually established himself as one of Poland's most important composers.

Szymanowski's international renown was considerable. His works were often performed in Europe, figuring prominently at ISCM festivals. He was director of the Warsaw Conservatory from 1927 to 1929 and reorganized the system of teaching along more liberal lines. He was rector of its successor, the Warsaw Academy of Music from 1930 to 1932.

His *STABAT MATER* (1925–26) produced a profound impression. His ballet-pantomime *Harnasie* (1923–31), based on the life and music of the Tatra mountain dwellers, demonstrated his ability to treat national subjects in an original, highly effective manner.

Popular Performers

"Popular music" is a general name given to any musical style that appeals to a broad audience. Today, pop stars come from all musical genres—from classical to folk to rock and rap—and also come from all around the world. The popularity of music is a testimony to its continuing importance, despite the changes in our lives that have occurred over the last decades.

The great African–American JAZZ TRUMPET player LOUIS ARMSTRONG was one of this century's most beloved performers. Born in New Orleans and raised in an orphanage, Armstrong originally played the CORNET before moving to Chicago on the invitation of his mentor, Joe "King" Oliver. He switched to the trumpet in the mid–'20s and made a series of recordings that revolutionized jazz playing. Later in life, Armstrong was equally beloved as a vocalist and film star. This photograph taken in 1960 perfectly captures his personality. (*Corbis/Hulton-Deutsch Collection*)

Another great JAZZ TRUMPET player was JOHN BIRKS "DIZZY" GILLESPIE. Gillespie was one of the prime movers in the post-World War II BEBOP movement. Along with SAXOPHONE player CHARLIE PARKER, he created this high-energy music that revolutionized jazz. Like LOUIS ARMSTRONG, Gillespie was a great showman; his puffed–up cheeks and distinctive bent trumpet were two of his trademarks. There are many stories told about how Gillespie came to play his bent horn; it is said that he was at a party where someone sat on his trumpet, bending the horn of the instrument up. This photograph was taken at a jazz festival in the early 1980s. (*Corbis/Derick A. Thomas*)

DID YOU KNOW???

- Dizzy Gillespie created the image of the "beatnik" by wearing a goatee and a beret.
- Gillespie sang his song "Salt Peanuts" with President Jimmy Carter, who was a peanut farmer.
- Gillespie was one of the first jazz musicians to introduce Latin rhythms in his music.

The great classical CONDUCTOR LEONARD BERNSTEIN burst on the concert scene in the late '40s when he was an assistant conductor with the New York Philharmonic. He went on to write a number of important popular and classical works, including the SCORE for the well–loved musical WEST SIDE STORY. Through his "Young People's Concerts," he introduced classical music to a new audience of listeners. This photograph, taken in 1984 at New York's CARNEGIE HALL, shows the passion that he brought to his conducting. (*Corbis/Robert Maass*)

No performer has done more to popularize OPERA today than LUCIANO PAVAROTTI. Like the great Italian opera singers of the past, such as ENRICO CARUSO, Pavarotti has performed the great opera ARIAS for a large, popular audience. Pavarotti has teamed with two other great TENORS, PLACIDO DOMINGO and JOSÉ CARRERAS, to form the "Three Tenors," performing at several sold–out shows around the world. This photograph was taken in Italy at a performance in 1979. (*Corbis/David Lees*)

Although classical music is not as popular today as it was a century ago, there are still performers who manage to draw large audiences through their artistry. One of them is the English–born LUTE player, JULIAN BREAM. He also represents a growing trend to revive earlier instruments, so that the music of the period can be played on the instrument for which it was composed. Bream has done much to popularize both the lute and classical GUITAR. (*Corbis/Hulton-Deutsch Collection*)

Beginning in the 1950s, a new form of popular music swept America and the world: ROCK AND ROLL. In the 1960s and 1970s, many of the most progressive rock bands came from England, in an assault on the American pop charts known as "The British Invasion." One of the most influential of the late '60s–early '70s bands was LED ZEPPELIN, a BLUES–based group that were one of the creators of the style of rock known as "heavy metal." Lead singer Robert Plant was a powerful singer and had a magnetic stage presence, as this photograph from 1971 reveals. (*Corbis/Neal Preston*)

One of the greatest popular singers/song-writers and PIANO players of our era is ELTON JOHN. John was one of the most flamboyant performers of the '70s and '80s, well–remembered for his catchy pop songs and his outlandish stage costumes. In recent years, he's toned down his act somewhat, but remains a gifted song-writer, as his work for Disney's *Lion King* showed. Here he is in performance in 1995. (*Corbis/Tim Mosenfelder*)

One of the pioneers of rock and roll was Elias McDaniel, better known as BO DIDDLEY. His song of the same name was a major hit in the mid-'50s, and introduced a Caribbean-flavored RHYTHM, known as the "Bo Diddley beat." Diddley continues to perform to today, and is shown here in 1986 holding his famous "square–bodied" electric guitar. The body shape is purely for show; it has no effect on the instrument's sound. (*Corbis/Neal Preston*)

In this day when the term "DIVA" is applied to any female pop singer, there are still a few performers who have the true magnetism to earn that name. One of them is the great TINA TURNER, a popular RHYTHM AND BLUES (R&B) singer since the 1960s. She began her career singing with her then–husband, GUITARIST Ike Turner, but has since the 1970s forged a solo career as a singer, actress, and model. Her legendary, high–energy dancing is captured in this photograph taken in the mid–1980s. (*Corbis/Henry Diltz*)

In the early '80s, a new musical form subsequently known as grunge burst on the scene. One of the bands that launched this new sound was the Seattle–based group NIRVANA. Their lead singer, Kurt Cobain, was a talented guitarist and songwriter, but also a deeply troubled person. This photo was taken in 1992 and captures his personality. (*Corbis/S.I.N.*)

One of the most popular musical styles of the '80s and '90s is RAP, which mixes rhymed lyrics with a heavily rhythmic accompaniment. Originally dominated by men, rap has produced lately many female stars who have become equally talented. One of the most popular female groups is the trio Salt 'n' Pepa, shown here performing at Woodstock II in 1994. (*Corbis/Neal Preston*)

Another musical style that has enjoyed renewed popularity over the last two decades is COUNTRY music. In fact, many country performers combine elements of ROCK, pop, and even R&B musics in their performances. One of the most progressive of the new country stars is singer Shania Twain, who has expanded the RHYTHMS, subject matter, and even dress styles of country performance. She is shown here in a 1998 concert. (*Corbis/James Lance*)

In 1932 Szymanowski appeared as soloist in the first performance of his Fourth Symphony, *SYMPHONIE CONCERTANTE* for piano and orchestra, at Poznan, and repeated his performances in Paris, London, and Brussels. In April 1936, greatly weakened by chronic tuberculosis, he attended a performance of his *Harnasie* at the Paris Opéra. He spent his last days in a sanatorium in Lausanne.

T

MUSICAL
INSTRUMENT

tablā. One of a pair of single-headed South Asian drums (the second, smaller drum is the *bāmyā*) featured in North Indian classical music; also, its collective name.

Tablā (left) *and bāmyā drums.
(K. Han/Northern Illinois U.)*

The body, made of clay, wood, or metal, is roughly hourglass shaped. The head and body are laced with zigzagging thongs to secure the wooden tuning dowels (changing the head tension as TIMPANI do). Tuning and TIMBRE are also affected by special black tuning paste placed on the heads of both drums, according to individual preference. The drum pair is played while sitting.

In the performance of a RAGA, after a melodic improvisation, the drummer enters with a TALA (rhythmic pattern).

tablature (from Lat. *tabula,* board; It. *intavolatura;* Ger. *Tablatur*). 1. Visual musical NOTATION by which pitches are indicated by their actual locations on the KEYBOARD, fingerboard, or other playing area. Letters, numbers, or other systems are used instead of staff notation.

TABLATURE was used for keyboard (14th–17th centuries), LUTE (16th–mid-17th centuries), and GUITAR (mid-16th–mid-18th centuries) music. A simplified tablature is still used in sheet music for plucked string instruments, recorder music (16th century), and vocal music (e.g., TONIC SOL-FA). As PERCUSSION music evolved from occasional timpani strokes to a timbral cornucopia, composers adopted the conventional staff, single lines, or other means to indicate the instrument to be played (where pitch is secondary).

2. Rules and regulations for the poetry and song of the MEISTERSINGER.

tableau (Fr.). Scene, in the theatrical sense.

tabor. Small shallow DRUM of the border region between France and Spain. It is held with a strap over the shoulder and played with only one hand, enabling the playing of a FIFE or pipe with the other simultaneously. It was first reported in the 12th century.

Tabourot, Jehan. *See* ARBEAU, THOINOT.

tacet (Lat., it is silent). In orchestral parts, the sign indicating a MOVEMENT in which the instrument in question is not used.

tactus (Lat., beat, stroke). In medieval theory, a standard beat, including DOWNBEAT and UPBEAT (Lat. *positio* and *elevatio;* Grk. *thesis* and *arsis*). The duration of a complete tactus was almost uniformly one second.

Tafelklavier (Ger., table keyboard). Square piano, constructed similarly to the CLAVICHORD and specifically adapted for hammer action. The French square piano (*piano carré*) was first manufactured in 1742. It became very popular in England and the U.S. before yielding to the upright piano.

Tafelmusik (Ger., table music; Fr. *musique de table*). Musical entertainment for banquets and similar festive occasions. Respectable composers contributed to the genre, e.g., Georg Philipp Telemann with his instrumental SUITES.

HARRY PARTCH, who built his own instruments in nontraditional tunings and shapes, created tablatures particular to each instrument.

tă′fel-klăh-vēr

MUSICAL INSTRUMENT

tăh′fel-moo-zik

There is a witty spoof on Tafelmusik in the finale of the second act of WOLFGANG AMADEUS MOZART'S opera *Don Giovanni*, where a band plays selections from various operas, including one of Mozart's own.

The French composer MICHELE-RICHARD DELALANDE published in 1703 a collection of "symphonies qui se jouent ordinairement au souper du Roy" (symphonies that are ordinarily played at the King's supper). While this sort of music was disdained in the 19th century, hedonistic composers of the 20th revived it gleefully. In its more extreme manifestations it serves as background to other activities, in the form of live musicians, recordings, or MUZAK.

Tagelied (Ger., day song). Poem of farewell made popular by the MINNESINGERS. They are usually songs of partings between lovers, sung at sunrise. RICHARD WAGNER has a Tagelied in the second act of *Tristan und Isolde*, warning against imminent danger.

In France and other Latin countries, the Tagelied is known as *alba* or *aubade*, a "morning" or "dawn" song.

MUSICAL INSTRUMENT

taiko (*daiko*; Jap.). Generic term for Japanese barrel DRUMS, played with sticks.

tailgate. Hot JAZZ style featuring sliding TROMBONE effects. It was derived from New Orleans parade bands, carried by horse wagons. The trombonist sat in the open tailgate facing backwards, so that the slide tubing could be extended when needed without hitting the other players!

PEOPLE IN MUSIC

Jean Cocteau compared Germaine Tailleferre to a young French woman painter, Marie Laurencin, saying that Tailleferre's music was to the ear what the painter's pastels were to the eye.

Tailleferre (born Taillefesse), (Marcelle) **Germaine,** b. Parc-St.-Maur, near Paris, Apr. 19, 1892; d. Paris, Nov. 7, 1983. Tailleferre studied harmony, SOLFÈGE, and accompaniment at the Paris Conservatory, taking several prizes for excellence. She also had informal lessons with MAURICE RAVEL.

Tailleferre received recognition as the only female member of the group of French composers known as LES SIX (the others were ARTHUR HONEGGER, DARIUS MILHAUD, FRANCIS POULENC, GEORGES AURIC, and LOUIS DUREY). Her style of composition was NEOCLASSICAL. Indeed, most of her works possess a fragile charm of unaffected *joie de jouer la musique* (joy of playing music).

Tailleferre was married to an American author, Ralph Barton, in 1926, but soon divorced him and married a French lawyer, Jean Lageat. She visited the U.S. in 1927 and again in 1942.

Tailleferre composed six operas, an OPERETTA, a BALLET, CONCERTOS for PIANO, duo pianos, HARP, and other orchestral works. Her chamber music includes *Image* for piano, flute, clarinet, string quartet, and celesta (1918), SONATAS and other works for violin, clarinet, and flute, solo sonatas for clarinet and harp, a string quartet (1917–19), and a piano trio (1978). Tailleferre also composed piano works and distinguished vocal music, including *Chansons françaises* for voice and instruments (1930), *Cantate du Narcisse* for voice and orchestra (1937), and *Concerto des vaines paroles* for baritone and orchestra (1956).

Takahashi, Aki, innovative Japanese pianist, sister of YUJI TAKAHASHI; b. Kakamura, Sept. 6, 1944. She studied first with her mother, then with Yutaka Ito, (Miss) Ray Lev, and George Vásárhelyi at the Tokyo Univ. of the Arts (M.A., 1969). Her European debut followed in 1972.

While acknowledged for her classical musicianship, Takahashi is particularly lauded for her imaginative interpretations of contemporary works. Among the composers who have written works for her are JOHN CAGE, FREDERIC RZEWSKI, YOJI YUASA, and MORTON FELDMAN. Her recording career is also distinguished. Her *Aki Takahashi Piano Space* (20 works, including those by LUCIANO BERIO, PIERRE BOULEZ, Cage, KARLHEINZ STOCKHAUSEN, ANTON WEBERN, et al.) earned her the Merit Prize at the Japan Art Festival in 1973. Her series of SATIE concerts performed in Tokyo (1975–77) heralded the so-called "Satie Boom" in Japan and resulted in her editing and recording the composer's complete piano works.

Other noteworthy recordings include *Triadic Memories* (Feldman), *Planetary Folklore* (MAMORU FUJIEDA), *Eonta* (IANNIS XENAKIS), and *L'Histoire de Babar* (FRANCIS POULENC). Her *Hyper Beatles* (1990) features arrangements of BEATLES songs by internationally recognized composers.

In addition to performing throughout Europe, Japan, and the U.S., Takahashi has also devoted time to teaching. She was artist-in-residence at the State University of N.Y. at

PEOPLE IN MUSIC

Buffalo (1980–81) and a guest professor at the California Institute of the Arts in Valencia (1984). She received the 1st Kenzo Nakajima prize (1982) and the 1st Kyoto Music Award (1986). In 1983 she became director of the "New Ears" concert series in Yokohama.

PEOPLE IN MUSIC

Takahashi, Yuji, Japanese composer and pianist, brother of AKI TAKAHASHI; b. Tokyo, Sept. 21, 1938. He studied composition with Shibata and Ogura at the Toho School of Music in Tokyo (1954–58) and also trained in electronics with KARLHEINZ STOCKHAUSEN (1963–65). He also studied computer music in N.Y. and attended summer courses at the Berkshire Music Center at Tanglewood (1966–68). He was a member of the Center for Creative and Performing Arts at the State University of N.Y. in Buffalo (1968–69).

In his music, Takahashi follows stochastic procedures as practiced by IANNIS XENAKIS. Like his sister, he also has acquired considerable renown as a pianist in programs of avant-garde music. Among his works are *Chromamorphe I* for violin, double bass, flute, trumpet, horn, trombone, and VIBRAPHONE (1963) and *II* for piano (1964); *Bridges I* for electric HARPSICHORD or piano, amplified cello, bass drum, and CASTANETS (1967) and *II* for two oboes, two clarinets, two trumpets, and three violas (1968); *Prajna Paramita* for four voices, each in one of four instrumental ensembles (1969); *Michi-Yuki* for chorus, two percussionists, and electric cello (1971); *Tadori* for TAPE (1972); *Kwanju, May 1980* for piano (1980); and *Kafka* for KEYBOARDS, saxophone, three singers, and live electronics (1990).

Take Me Out to the Ball Game. Song by Albert von Tilzer, 1908, introduced by him in VAUDEVILLE. It became the unofficial anthem of American baseball.

The composer himself never attended a game until some 20 years after writing the song.

Take the A Train. Jazz piece by BILLY STRAYHORN, 1941, written for DUKE ELLINGTON, who adopted it as his signature tune. The A train is a West Side N.Y. subway line that runs express to 125th Street, the center of Harlem's cultural life.

Takemitsu, Tōru, prominent Japanese composer; b. Tokyo, Oct. 8, 1930; d. there Feb. 20, 1996. Takemitsu studied composition privately with Yasuji Kiyose. In 1951 he organized the Tokyo Jikken Kobo (Experimental Workshop), with the aim of creating new music that would combine traditional Japanese modalities with modern composition techniques. In 1970 he designed the Space Theater for Expo '70 in Osaka.

PEOPLE IN MUSIC

Takemitsu was a visiting professor at Yale University during 1975, served as regent lecturer at the University of California, San Diego, in 1981, lectured at Harvard, Boston, and Yale Universities, and was composer-in-residence of the Colorado Music Festival, all during 1983. In 1984 he was composer-in-residence at the Aldeburgh Festival. He received numerous honors, including honorary memberships in the Akademie der Künste of the German Democratic Republic in 1979 and the American Academy and Institute of Arts and Letters in 1984. In 1985 he received the Ordre des Arts et des Lettres of the French government.

Takemitsu's music combines Eastern and Western musical characteristics. From the East, short MOTIVES are played out as floating dramas, subtle and exotic, through which he seeks "to achieve a sound as intense as silence." From the West, he has used virtually every conceivable technique developed by European and American modernists.

Among films for which Takemitsu provided scores is the celebrated *Woman in the Dunes* from 1964.

Takemitsu has composed orchestral works, string quartets, keyboards, and vocal works. Some of his works, such as *Autumn* for BIWA, SHAKUHACHI, and orchestra (1973) and *Ceremonial* for SHO and orchestra (1992), incorporate traditional Japanese instruments. In 1994 he won the Grawemeyer Award from the University of Louisville for his *Fantasma/Cantos* for clarinet and orchestra.

Tal, Josef (born Joseph Gruenthal, Pinne), prominent German-born Israeli composer, pianist, and pedagogue; b. Pinne, near Posen, Sept. 18, 1910. Tal took courses with PAUL HINDEMITH, CURT SACHS, and others at the Berlin Staatliche Hochschule für Musik from 1928 to 1930.

PEOPLE IN MUSIC

In 1934 Tal emigrated to Palestine, settling in Jerusalem as a teacher of piano and composition at the Conservatory two years later. When it became the Israel Academy of Music, he served as its director from 1948 to 1952. Beginning in 1950, he also lectured at the Hebrew University, where he headed the musicology department from 1965 to 1970 and then served as a professor, beginning in 1971.

Tal directed the Israel Center of Electronic Music from 1961, and appeared as pianist and conductor with the Israel Philharmonic and European orchestras. He was awarded the State of Israel Prize in 1971 and made an honorary member of the West Berlin Academy of Arts. In 1975 he received the Arts Prize of the City of Berlin and in 1982 became a fellow of its Institute for Advanced Studies.

A true musical intellectual, Tal applies in his music a variety of techniques. Patriotic Jewish themes often appear in his productions. He composed ten operas and dramatic scenes, among them *Ashmedai,* with electronics, in 1968. He also composed orchestral works, including four SYMPHONIES, three piano CONCERTOS, and concertos for viola, cello, violin and cello, flute, duo piano, and clarinet. His chamber music works include sonatas for violin, oboe, and viola, three string QUARTETS, a WOODWIND quintet, piano trio, and piano quartet. He has also written numerous keyboard works and vocal and choral works.

An active electronic composer, Tal often composes entire works or accompaniments on tape. These include five dance pieces, piano concertos Nos. 4–6 (1962, 1964, 1970), HARPSICHORD concerto (1964), HARP concerto (1971), and *Frequencies 440–462: Hommage à Boris Blacher* (1972).

tala. In Indian classical music, the system of cyclical rhythmic organization maintained by the pair of drums known collectively as TABLĀ.

The concept of tala is similar to Western METER. However, it differs in that the number of beats in one complete cycle (*tal*) can be 16 or more, and the cycle can last far longer than a measure. The tala system is taught by using vocalized syllables and hand gestures that can be incorporated into the performance itself.

tăh-lā-ŭ **talea** (Lat.). *See* ISORHYTHM.

Tales of Hoffmann, The. Opera by JACQUES OFFENBACH, 1881, based on stories of the German fabulist E.T.A. Hoffmann, premiered in Paris.

Hoffmann himself is the focus of the opera, telling the stories of his three great loves: a lithe mechanical puppet, a blithe Venetian courtesan, and a tubercular German maiden. In an ideal production not only does Hoffmann appear in all three acts (plus prologue and epilogue), but the characters representing the forces of evil, the servant, and in some productions the three beloveds are each acted by one singer.

Offenbach died before completing the ORCHESTRATION for the score, which was finished by French composer ERNEST GUIRARD for its posthumous premiere. The second act contains the famous *Barcarolle*.

Talking Heads. *See* BYRNE, DAVID.

tambour militaire (Fr.). Small side DRUM used in military bands. It has no definite pitch, but produces a dry, well-articulated sound in the general TENOR REGISTER.

As a rhythmic instrument it is used in SYMPHONIES, opera, and even CHAMBER MUSIC. Some examples:

tahn-bŏŏr-mē-lē-tarh′

MUSICAL INSTRUMENT

CARL NIELSEN gives the tambour militaire an important part in his Fifth Symphony, instructing the player to beat the drum loudly in its own rhythm "as if trying to stop the rest of the orchestra."

A military drum solo introduces the execution by hanging of Till Eulenspiegel in the work of the same title by RICHARD STRAUSS.

Edgard Varèse gives the military drum the leading "tenor" part in his *Ionisation*.

JEAN-PHILIPPE RAMEAU wrote a piece for CLAVECIN entitled *Tambourin*, with imitations of the characteristic rhythms of the instrument.

tambourin (Fr., small drum). 1. Cylindrical DRUM covered with skin on both ends, possibly of Arab origin. 2. Old dance in southern France accompanied by a PIPE and tambourin.

MUSICAL INSTRUMENT

tambourine (Fr. *tambour de basque*; It. *tamburino, tamburo basco*; Ger. *Schellentrommel*; Port. *pandeiro*; Sp. *pandero*). Popular instrument of Spanish origin, consisting of a single drumhead bordered by a shallow wooden ring with a number of metallic jingles. It can be played in a variety of ways:

MUSICAL INSTRUMENT

shaking, thumping, plunking, clicking, and striking against the knee or opposing hand. The sound produced by the drumhead is dry and short, with little resonance or reverberation.

The tambourine is regularly used to accompany Spanish dances, notably FLAMENCO. This association is put to good use by GEORGES BIZET (*CARMEN*), NIKOLAI RIMSKY-KORSAKOV (*Capriccio Espagnol*), CLAUDE DEBUSSY (*Ibéria*), and MAURICE RAVEL (*Rapsodie espagnole*).

A tambourine of biblical times, the *timbrel,* was furnished with several pairs of bronze jingles, which women shook to attract male attention. One surviving specimen, unearthed in Babylon and dating back to c.2700 B.C., has ten pairs of bronze jingles and is beautifully ornamented with precious stones.

> ♫
>
> In the Bible, Miriam, sister of Moses, played a timbrel during the exodus from Egypt.

MUSICAL INSTRUMENT

tambura (*tamboura, tampura*). Long-necked Indian LUTE, played while seated and held vertically. It has a gourd resonator and four strings tuned to the PITCH of the instruments or voice that it accompanies as a DRONE.

The tambura's strings are gently plucked in a slow OSTINATO unrelated to the other players' tempo. It represents a Hindu conception of universal harmony and therefore a perfection that the soloists can never hope to attain. Even the tambura's special role has been lost to the modern era, because it is often replaced by a HARMONIUM (which is also blamed for the loss of small pitch subtleties in Indian music).

MUSICAL INSTRUMENT

tamburo di legno (It., wooden drum). Generic term for a resonant wooden box used as an IDIOPHONE.

MUSICAL INSTRUMENT

tamburo scordato (It., drum without strings). Small DRUM without snares.

MUSICAL INSTRUMENT

tam-tam. 1. Large Eastern unpitched GONG, suspended from a stand and struck with a felt-covered stick. It spread through Europe in the 18th century.

The tam-tam is often associated with tragic situations. Because of this association, many classical composers have used it for atmospheric effect in their works:

FRANÇOIS-JOSEPH GOSSEC includes it in the funeral march in *Mirabeau* (1791).

PIOTR ILYICH TCHAIKOVSKY expresses the inexorability of fate in the *Pathétique Symphony* with it.

RICHARD STRAUSS uses it for funereal effect in *Death and Transfiguration.*

However, despite this common association with death or fate, the tam-tam functioned in courts, temples, and elsewhere to give signals and for other uses as well.

The tam-tam is not a true gong, such as those found in the Indonesian GAMELAN orchestras. Those gongs have raised hubs in the middle, upon which the instrument is struck and dampened by stick, and which are factors in its tuning. The tam-tam has a white-noise sound, with no particular place to be struck, and a much slower, more unpredictable decay.

Tan, Margaret Leng, significant Singaporean-American pianist; b. Penang, Malaysia, Dec. 12, 1945. She was educated in Singapore. At 16, she went to N.Y., where she studied with Adele Marcus at the Juilliard School, becoming the first woman to graduate with the D.Mus. Degree in 1971.

PEOPLE IN MUSIC

Tan specializes in new Asian and American music, evolving a highly individual approach to performance wherein sound, choreography, and theater assume equal significance. She has worked closely with such composers as JOHN CAGE, ALVIN LUCIER, WILLIAM DUCKWORTH, LOIS V VIERK, and SOMEI SATOH. She became particularly known for her interpretive command of the works of Cage, giving performances through Europe, the U.S., and Asia. She also appeared in PBS American Masters documentaries on Cage (1990) and Jasper Johns (1989). During the 1990–91 season, she presented retrospective performances of Cage's music in conjunction with retrospective exhibitions of Johns's paintings at the Walker Art Center in Minneapolis, the Whitney Museum of American Art in N.Y., the Hayward Gallery in London, and the Center for Fine Arts in Miami.

In 1984 she received an NEA Arts Solo Recitalist award and in 1988 an Asian Cultural Council grant for contemporary music research in Japan. In 1987 she appeared with the Brooklyn Philharmonic, and in 1991 she made her debut with the N.Y. Philharmonic. Among her critically acclaimed recordings are *Litania: Margaret Leng Tan Plays Somei Satoh* (1988), *Sonic Encounters: The New Piano* (1989; with works by Cage, ALAN HOVHANESS, GEORGE CRUMB, Satoh, and GE GAN-RU), and *Daughters of the Lonesome Isle* (1994). From 1993 she developed a repertory for the toy piano through commissions and transcriptions. Tan is also a regular contributor to *Piano Today*. She currently resides in Brooklyn, N.Y., with two dogs, three Steinways, and nine toy pianos.

MUSICAL INSTRUMENT

tanbūr (Pers., Turk.). Long-necked Near Eastern LUTE with a small pear-shaped body, a fretted neck, and a variable number of metal strings.

This tragic story is also the subject of CLAUDIO MONTEVERDI's dramatic madrigal *Il combattimento di Tancredi e Clorinda*, from 1624.

Tancredi. Opera by GIOACCHINO ROSSINI, 1813, premiered in Venice. The story deals with Tancred, a crusader who took part in the siege of Jerusalem. He is emotionally torn between two loves: a devoted Syrian girl and a Persian woman warrior, Clorinda, whom he loves profoundly. But, when he encounters Clorinda wearing her full armor, he mistakes her for a masculine enemy and fatally wounds her.

PEOPLE IN MUSIC

Tan Dun, significant Chinese composer; b. Si Mao, central Hunan Province, Aug. 18, 1957. While working among peasants during the Chinese Cultural Revolution, Tan Dun began collecting folk songs. After playing VIOLA in the Beijing Opera orchestra in 1976–77, he entered the recently reopened Central Conservatory in Beijing in 1978 to study composition, obtaining both B.A. and M.A. degrees.

In 1983 Tan Dun's String Quartet won a prize in Dresden, the first international music prize won by a Chinese composer since 1949. However, his interest in Western compositional styles led to a six-month ban on performances or broadcasts of his music soon thereafter.

In 1986 Tan Dun settled in N.Y., where he accepted a fellowship at Columbia University and studied with Chou Wen-Chung, Mario Davidovsky, and George Edwards.

Tan Dun's early works are romantic and florid, while after 1982 they reveal a progressing advancement of dissonance and sophistication, while retaining Chinese contexts. Among his works are *9 Songs,* a ritual opera for 20 singers/performers (1989). He has written several orchestral works, including *Li Sao,* a symphony (1979–80), Piano Concerto (1983), *Symphony in 2 Movements* (1985), *On Taoism* (1985), *Death and Fire: Dialogue with Paul Klee* (1991–92), and *Yi,* a cello concerto (1993–94).

Among Tan Dun's chamber pieces are two works for string quartet, *Feng Ya Song* (1982) and *8 Colors* (1986–88), and *Lament: Autumn Wind* for any six instruments, any voice, and conductor (1993). His piano compositions include *CAGE* (1993), in honor of JOHN CAGE, whom he greatly admired.

Taneyev, Sergei (Ivanovich), greatly significant Russian composer and pedagogue; b. Vladimir district, Nov. 25, 1856; d. Dyudkovo, Zvenigorodsk district, June 19, 1915. Taneyev began taking piano lessons at age five and entered the Moscow Conservatory at age nine. He studied theory with Nikolai Hubert and composition with PIOTR ILYICH TCHAIKOVSKY, who became a lifelong friend. Nicolas Rubinstein became his piano mentor in 1871.

Taneyev made his formal debut as pianist in the JOHANNES BRAHMS D-minor Concerto in Moscow in 1875. That same year, he played the Moscow premiere of the Tchaikovsky First Concerto, to the composer's complete satisfaction. He subsequently played the solo part in all of Tchaikovsky's works for piano and ORCHESTRA.

Taneyev graduated from the Conservatory as the first student to win the gold medal in both performance and composition in 1875. In 1876 he toured his homeland with violinist LEOPOLD AUER and also succeeded Tchaikovsky as professor of harmony and ORCHESTRATION at the Moscow Conservatory. In 1881, after Rubinstein's death, Taneyev took over the piano classes and also succeeded Hubert as composition professor. Taneyev served as the Conservatory's director from 1885 to 1889 and then taught COUNTERPOINT there until 1905.

Taneyev was a first-class pianist, but his compositions are rarely heard outside Russia. His compositional style represents a compromise between Russian melodies and Germanic contrapuntal writing.

In 1998 Tan Dun received the Grawemeyer Award from the University of Louisville for his opera *Marco Polo.*

PEOPLE IN MUSIC

The mastery revealed in Taneyev's symphonies and quartets is unquestionable. His most ambitious work was the operatic trilogy *Oresteia,* after Aeschylus, in three parts: *Agamemnon, Choëphorai,* and *Eumenides,* produced in St. Petersburg in 1895. His orchestral works include four symphonies, composed between 1873 and 1897, and a piano concerto written in 1876.

Among Taneyev's chamber works are ten string quartets (1874–1911), a violin SONATA, two string trios, two string quintets, piano quartet, piano quintet, and trio for violin, VIOLA, and tenor viola. Taneyev also composed piano pieces, choral works, and songs.

tango. The most celebrated dance of Argentina, danced by a couple and characterized by strongly marked SYNCOPATION.

The tango has the characteristics of the HABANERA. Both are in $\frac{2}{4}$ time with a dotted rhythmical figure in the accompaniment, and the first section is set in a MINOR KEY, the second in MAJOR. In the accompaniment the guitar and bandonion (a type of ACCORDION) are the primary melodic and harmonic instruments, supported by piano, double bass, saxophone, and PERCUSSION. A vocal part may be added.

Actress Betty Blythe dancing the tango in 1925. (Hulton-Deutsch Collection/Corbis) ▶

The tango developed as entertainment in the red-light districts of Buenos Aires in the last decades of the 19th century. It quickly became popular in the ballrooms of the U.S.

and Europe in the years just prior to World War I. At that time, its frank sexuality shocked the guardians of morality. Protests were voiced by clergy and government authorities, so that the Argentine ambassador to France found it necessary to state that the tango was the product of bordellos and was never tolerated in decent society. Fortunately for tango lovers, the concept of "decent society" has evolved a great deal, to the point that this once indecent dance is regularly performed on the legitimate stage.

The music of ASTOR PIAZZOLLA, who did for tango what FRÉDÉRIC CHOPIN did for the WALTZ, is valued by classical and popular music audiences alike.

tango-milonga. Dance song fusing the older rural MILONGA with the modern urban TANGO.

Tannhäuser. Opera by RICHARD WAGNER, 1845, to his own LIBRETTO, first produced in Dresden. Wagner described the score as a *Handlung* (action). The complete title is *Tannhäuser und der Sangerkrieg auf dem Wartburg.* Tannhäuser (b. c.1205; d. c.1270) was a real, historical figure, a German MINNESINGER, who led a wandering life in the 13th century and participated in a crusade.

In Wagner's opera, Tannhäuser is lured to Venusberg, a mountain in central Germany in whose caves, according to medieval legends, the Goddess Venus herself holds court. But he yearns to return to his own world and to his beloved Elisabeth. He joins a group of pilgrims in the valley of the Wartburg, which includes his friend Wolfram (also an historical figure).

A singing contest is held in the castle, and Tannhäuser shocks the assembly with his song in praise of Venus. He is expelled from the Wartburg and joins the pilgrims on their journey to Rome, where he hopes to obtain absolution from the Pope. Wolfram sings a song appealing to the evening star (that is, Venus) for protection of Elisabeth.

Having failed to obtain forgiveness in Rome, Tannhäuser returns home and encounters a funeral procession; it is that of Elisabeth. He collapses before her coffin and dies. He achieves redemption when the papal staff, brought back from Rome by the pilgrims, sprouts leaves.

The opera marks a turning point in music history as an artistic affirmation of the ROMANTIC LIED.

PEOPLE IN MUSIC

Tansman, Alexandre, Polish-born French pianist, conductor, and composer; b. Lodz, June 12, 1897; d. Paris, Nov. 15, 1986. Tansman studied at the Lodz Conservatory from 1902 to 1914 and also pursued training in law and philosophy at the University of Warsaw. He also received instruction in COUNTERPOINT, FORM, and COMPOSITION from Piotr Rytel in Warsaw.

In 1919 Tansman went to Paris, where he appeared as soloist in his own works in 1920. In 1927 he appeared as a soloist with the Boston Symphony Orchestra and then performed throughout Europe, Canada, and Palestine. He later took up conducting, making a tour of the Far East in 1932–33.

After the occupation of Paris by the Germans in 1940, Tansman made his way to the U.S. He lived in Hollywood, where he wrote music for films. He returned to Paris in 1946.

Tansman's music is distinguished by a considerable melodic gift and spirited rhythms. His harmony is often BITONAL, and there are impressionistic traits that reflect Parisian influence. He composed six operas, six ballets, seven symphonies, and other orchestral works. His compositions for piano include 20 *pieces faciles polonaises* (easy Polish pieces) from 1924, five SONATAS, MAZURKAS and other Polish dances, *Sonatine transatlantique* from 1930, and *Pour les enfants* (For the children), in four albums.

> ♫
> Tansman also wrote a monograph on IGOR STRAVINSKY, which was published in 1948.

tantric chants. Ritual singing of Hindu or Buddhist sects. This chanting is designed to attain purification of soul and body, when combined with body exercises such as yoga. The text is fashioned from the mystic syllables of the sacred mantras, and the symbols are inspired by the diagrams of the ritual mandalas.

Some Tibetan Buddhist chants last for over seven hours.

tăhnts-hâl-lĕ **Tanzhalle** (Ger.). Dance hall; a place of entertainment that flourished in Germany (especially Berlin) in the beginning of the 20th century.

tap dance. A type of American dance in which distinct rhythmic patterns are produced by the tapping of the performer's feet on the floor. Tap dancing developed out of traditional African-American dances, along with the influence of Irish step dancing.

Typical tap shoes have metal plates on the soles to enhance the sound. Tap dancing in wooden shoes was called buck-and-wing dancing, while in "soft-shoe" dancing the performer uses sliding and shuffling on the floor. Dancing pairs would trade rhythmically complex RIFFS with one another in a call-and-response manner. The best dancers could also work with timbral contrasts. Tap dance was popular in VAUDEVILLE, REVUES, MUSICALS, and film.

Tap dancing entered the concert hall with MORTON GOULD's four-movement Concerto for Tap Dancer and Orchestra (1952).

tape recording. A method involving a lacquered, extremely thin, magnetized plastic tape. The magnetic particles are encoded with sound signals through a *recording head*. These signals are then reproduced on a tape recorder or player with the appropriate pickup (*playback head*).

The direct predecessor of tape recording was *wire recording,* which was developed in Nazi Germany. A great number of musical performances were recorded, with the theoretically unlimited length of wire permitting far longer uninterrupted recordings than 78-rpm-disc recording could make.

The fragility of the wire led Nazi engineers to seek another medium for recording, and they began to develop what would later be called recording tape. The tape was wound on plastic wheel-shaped reels, protecting it from breakage or wear. Unrecorded tape was fed through the recording heads to an empty reel, much as film is passed through a projector. These machines came to be called reel-to-reel recorders. When the Allies overran Germany in 1945, they found early versions of the new tape-recording machine and brought them back to the U.S. for further development.

As a home medium, reel-to-reel tape began to give way to the long-playing record in the 1950s, although prerecorded tapes continued to be made into the early 1960s. Other tape media evolved: the *8-track,* on which the narrow tape is wound as a loop and runs continuously, except for switching from one "program" to the next (four programs, each in stereo, hence eight-track).

The 8-track's period of popularity was brief, because the *cassette* was developed in the 1970s. This involves even narrower tape in a miniature reel-to-reel format, on which both sides are recorded in stereo (hence its early name *four-track*). It can play longer than the 8-track, is more convenient to store, can be used for home recording (unlike the 8-track), and has developed sound comparable to that of most long-playing records.

As a studio medium, the reel-to-reel tape recorder was the principal means of recording music from the late 1940s to the 1980s. Reel-to-reel tape could range in width from ¼″ to 2″ (and larger) and could record several simultaneous tracks (channels) with different instruments, voices, effects, etc. This allowed each to be recorded with relatively little acoustic interference and then *mixed* and *equalized* (combined and balanced) to produce a final product. *Editing* allows for correcting errors by cutting and splicing desirable passages. One can also record over undesirable passages on individual channels while saving others. Multitrack recording allows for *overdubbing,* where one performer can add layers onto a single recording, to the point where a single person is the sole (or nearly sole) performer on a richly textured album.

While reel-to-reel tape is still used, it has largely been replaced by *digital recording.* Using computers, music is recorded as a constant numerical sampling of information, stored on a hard drive or tape (*DAT*). Because the information is stored digitally, it can be precisely edited and processed in many ways.

MUSICAL INSTRUMENT

tar (Pers.). Long-necked Persian LUTE, also played in Central Asia. It is generally made from one piece of hollowed-out wood, which is covered with a skin head. It has movable FRETS and from two and five strings, played with a PLECTRUM.

tăh-rähn-tel′läh

tarantella (It.; Ger. *Tarantelle*). Southern Italian dance in $\frac{6}{8}$ time. Its rate of speed gradually increases as the piece progresses, and the MODE alternates between major and minor.

Also, an instrumental piece in $\frac{3}{8}$ or $\frac{6}{8}$ time, in a very rapid tempo and bold and brilliant style. The tarantella, named after the city of Taranto, was especially popular in the 19th century.

According to legend, the playing of the tarantella cured tarantism, an uncontrollable impulse to dance supposedly caused by the bite of the tarantula spider. However, medical investigations of persons bitten by this creature have revealed no such choreographic symptoms.

Ta-Ra-Ra-Boom-De-Re. Nonsense march song of uncertain authorship, which first was published in 1891, with the DOWNBEAT on "boom." In addition to its own popularity, the song is well suited to lyrical parody.

Taras Bulba. Orchestral RHAPSODY by LEOŠ JANÁČEK, 1915–18, based on Gogol's novel, first performed in Brno, 1921.

The three movements depict the struggle of the Cossacks against Polish domination in the 15th century, involving Bulba and his two sons. The younger son, who betrays his land for the sake of a Polish girl, is taken prisoner by Bulba, who despite his anguish executes him. The elder son is caught by the Polish army and executed, as is Bulba.

tárogató. Traditional Hungarian REED instrument made of wood with a conical bore.

First mentioned in the 13th century, the tárogató apparently was brought by Arabs to southeastern Europe in the trading process. At the time it was something like a SHAWM, with a covered MOUTHPIECE and without finger holes. By the 19th century the DOUBLE REED was reduced to a single one, the mouthpiece became clarinetlike (although still partly covered), and the fingering was altered to resemble a saxophone's.

Tartini, Giuseppe, famous Italian violinist, teacher, music theorist, and composer; b. Pirano, Istria, Apr. 8, 1692; d. Padua, Feb. 26, 1770. Tartini's parents prepared him for a monastic life by entrusting his education to clerics in Pirano and Capodistria, where he received VIOLIN instruction. In 1708 he renounced the cloister but remained a nominal candidate for the priesthood.

MUSICAL INSTRUMENT

The tárogató has been known as the "national Hungarian instrument" since the Rákóczy rebellion in the 18th century.

PEOPLE IN MUSIC

Giuseppe Tartini. (New York Public Library)

In 1709 Tartini enrolled at the University of Padua as a law student. At the age of 19, he secretly agreed to wed the 21-year-old Elisabetta Premazore, a protégée of the powerful Paduan Cardinal Cornaro. The Cardinal vengefully brought a charge of kidnapping against him.

Tartini had to take refuge from prosecution at the monastery of the Friars Minor Conventual in Assisi, where he joined the opera orchestra. He was pardoned by the Paduan authorities in 1715, then lived in Venice and Padua, being made *primo violino e capo di concerto* at the basilica of S. Antonio in Padua in 1721.

Allowed to travel, Tartini acquired a distinguished reputation. From 1723 to 1726 he served as chamber musician to Count Kinsky in Prague. He then returned to Padua, where he organized a music school in 1728, numbering among his students Pietro Nardini and Gaetano Pugnani.

Tartini subsequently enjoyed a career as a violinist, making numerous concert tours in Italy. He retained his post at S. Antonio and also remained active at his school until at least 1767. In 1768 he suffered a mild stroke, which effectively ended his career.

Tartini's style of playing, particularly his bowing, became a model for other violinists. Among his compositions, the most famous is the violin SONATA in G minor known under the nickname *The Devil's Trill* (Trillo del diavolo; after 1744). The trill appears in its last movement.

Tartini supposedly had a dream in which the devil appeared to him. A master fiddler, the demon showed him how to play the famous trill that Tartini placed in his sonata.

Tartini was a prolific composer of violin music, including roughly 135 CONCERTOS, the same number of SONATAS with BASSO CONTINUO, 30 sonatas for solo violin or with basso continuo ad libitum, and 18 sonatas for two violins and bass continuo. Other works include concertos, 40 trio sonatas, four sonatas a quattro, and religious music. Many of these works were published during his lifetime.

Although Tartini lacked scientific training, he made several acoustical discoveries, most importantly the sum (SUMMATION) and difference (DIFFERENTIAL) tones. He observed these effects in 1714 and wrote various treatises about them. The difference tone became known also as a TARTINI TONE, or *terzo suono.* Violinists are aware of interferences from difference tones and the less audible sum tones, and they correct them by making a slight alteration of tuning.

Tartini tones. DIFFERENCE (DIFFERENTIAL) TONES produced by playing DOUBLE-STOPS in perfect nontempered TUNING. They were first discovered and described by GIUSEPPE TARTINI.

Taruskin, Richard, influential American musicologist and music critic; b. N.Y., April 2, 1945. He was educated at Columbia University, where he took his Ph.D. in historical musicology (1975). He also held a Fulbright-Hayes traveling fellowship that enabled him to conduct research in Moscow (1971–72). In 1975 he became an assistant professor at Columbia University, serving as an associate professor from 1981 to 1987. In 1985 he was a visiting professor at the University of Pennsylvania and in 1987 was the Hanes-Willis visiting professor at the Univ. of North Carolina at Chapel Hill. In 1986 he was made an associate professor at the University of California, Berkeley, becoming a professor there in 1989. He held a Guggenheim fellowship in 1986, in 1987 he was awarded the Dent Medal of England, and in 1989 he received the ASCAP-Deems Taylor Award.

Taruskin contributed many valuable articles on Russian music and composers to *The New Grove Dictionary of Opera* (1992) as well as to scholarly journals. His respected published works include *Opera and Drama in Russia* (Ann Arbor, 1981; new edition, 1994), *Mussorgsky: Eight Essays and*

PEOPLE IN MUSIC

an *Epilog* (Princeton, N.J., 1993), *Stravinsky and the Russian Traditions: A Biography of the Works through* Mavra (two volumes, Berkeley and Los Angeles, 1995), and *Text and Act: Essays on Music and Performance* (N.Y., 1995).

tăh-stē-â′răh –

tastiera per luce (It., keyboard of light). Color organ envisioned by ALEXANDER SCRIABIN. It was to be included in his orchestral work *PROMETHÉE*.

PEOPLE IN MUSIC

Tate, Jeffrey, talented English conductor; b. Salisbury, Apr. 28, 1943. Although a victim of spina bifida, Tate pursued studies at Cambridge University and St. Thomas's Medical School. He also attended the London Opera Centre in 1970–71. He was subsequently a member of the music staff at the Royal Opera, Covent Garden, from 1971 to 1977, and he served as assistant conductor at Bayreuth from 1976 to 1980.

Tate made his formal debut conducting *CARMEN* at the Göteborg Opera in 1978, and his debut at the Metropolitan Opera in N.Y. in 1980, conducting *LULU*. His debut at Covent Garden followed, with *LA CLEMENZA DI TITO* in 1982. He has performed as guest conductor at major OPERA companies around the world. He made his first appearance with the English Chamber Orchestra in 1983. In 1985 he was named its principal conductor, leading it on tours abroad, including one to the U.S. in 1988. In 1990 he was made a Commander of the Order of the British Empire.

In 1986 Tate became principal conductor at Covent Garden, and from 1991 to 1994 he served as chief conductor of the Rotterdam Philharmonic. In 1997 he was appointed principal conductor of the Minnesota Orchestra's Viennese Sommerfest. His extensive operatic and concert repertoire encompasses works from the CLASSICAL period to the 20th century.

A stylized tattoo occurs in GEORGES BIZET'S *CARMEN:* the infatuated Don José refuses to return to the barracks, with tragic consequences.

tattoo (It.; from Lat. *tactus*). 1. BEAT. 2. Military signals in a rapid rhythm used to summon soldiers back to the barracks.

Tatum, Art(hur), noted African-American JAZZ pianist; b. Toledo, Ohio, Oct. 13, 1910; d. Los Angeles, Nov. 5, 1956. Tatum was blind in one eye and had limited vision in the other. He attended a school for the blind in Columbus, Ohio. He learned to read Braille music notation and at 16 began to play in nightclubs. While playing in the Toledo area, the blues singer Adelaide Hall heard him and hired him to be her accompanist on the road.

Hall took Tatum to N.Y. in 1932 as part of her touring group. He made his first solo recordings there that year. He then spent some time working in Chicago and Cleveland, before returning to N.Y. in 1937, where he began a successful career in clubs, on records, and on radio. He made a spectacular tour of England in 1938, then pursued his career in N.Y. and Los Angeles.

Tatum organized his own trio in 1943, with bassist Slam Stewart and guitarist Tiny Grimes. He appeared in the film *The Fabulous Dorseys* in 1947.

Tatum's career got a significant boost in the 1950s when he was signed by producer Norman Granz. Granz recorded Tatum in a solo and small-group setting for his Verve label and kept these recordings in print long after the pianist's death. This helped keep his playing alive.

Tatum's art as a jazz improviser was captured on more than 600 recordings. He brought STRIDE piano playing to a point of perfection. He achieved small miracles with ornamental figures in the melody, while throwing effortless cascades of notes across the keyboard with an imagination as fast as his fingers. He also had a knack for improvising variations on popular classical pieces.

It is said that when FATS WALLER was in the audience at a Harlem club and heard that Tatum was playing, Fats commented "God is in the house tonight."

Tauber, Richard, eminent Austrian-born English tenor; b. Linz, May 16, 1891; d. London, Jan. 8, 1948. He was the illegitimate son of the actor Richard Anton Tauber, and his mother was a SOUBRETTE singer. He was christened Richard Denemy after his mother's maiden name, but he sometimes used the last name Seiffert, his mother's married name. He took courses at the Hoch Conservatory in Frankfurt am Main and studied voice with Carl Beines in Freiburg.

Tauber made his debut at Chemnitz as Tamino (in WOLFGANG AMADEUS MOZART's *THE MAGIC FLUTE*) in 1913 with such success that he was engaged in the same year at the Dresden Court Opera. He made his first appearance at the Berlin Royal Opera as RICHARD STRAUSS's Bacchus in

PEOPLE IN MUSIC

1915, and later he won particular success in Munich and Salzburg for his roles in Mozart's operas.

Around 1925 Tauber turned to lighter roles, winning remarkable success in the operettas of FRANZ LÉHAR. He made his U.S. debut in a 1931 N.Y. recital. In 1938 he settled in England, where he appeared as Tamino and Belmonte at London's Covent Garden. In 1940 he became a British subject.

Tauber wrote an operetta, *Old Chelsea,* taking the leading role at its premiere in London in 1943. He made his last American appearance at CARNEGIE HALL in N.Y. in 1947. He died a year later.

Tavener, John (Kenneth), English organist, pedagogue, and mystic religious composer; b. London, Jan. 28, 1944. Tavener studied with Lennox Berkeley at the Royal Academy of Music in London from 1961 to 1965 and privately with David Lumsdaine from 1965 to 1967. Beginning in 1960, he was organist at St. John's, Kensington, and he also taught composition at Trinity College of Music in London from 1969.

While he was influenced by medieval hymns and Indian mysticism, Tavener's compositions used SERIALISM and electronic sound generation. His early works— *The Cappemakers,* a dramatic CANTATA from 1964; *Cain and Abel,* dramatic cantata for soloists and chamber orchestra, staged in 1966; and *The Whale,* his best-known early work, a dramatic cantata for narrator, soloists, chorus, and orchestra, also from 1966—were free COLLAGES of styles. His conversion to Eastern Orthodox Christianity affected both his materials and his style.

Among his recent works are the operas *Eis Thanaton* (1986) and *Mary of Egypt* (1990–91), the orchestral works *The Repentant Thief* for clarinet, PERCUSSION, TIMPANI, and strings (1990), *Eternal Memory* for cello and ensemble (1992), and *Theophany* (1994), and various chamber pieces, including *Threnos* for cello (1990) and *The Last Sleep of the Virgin* for string quartet and handbells (1991). His late vocal compositions, a medium in which he excels, include *We Shall See Him As He Is* for SOPRANO, TENOR, CHORUS, organ, two trumpets, TIMPANI, and strings (1991–92), *The*

PEOPLE IN MUSIC

Child Lived for soprano and ensemble (1992), *Hymns of Paradise* for BASS, chorus, and strings (1992–93), and *The Apocalypse* for soprano, MEZZOSOPRANO, tenor, COUNTERTENOR, bass, chorus, children's chorus, and orchestra (1993–94).

Taylor, Cecil (Percival), African-American jazz pianist and composer; b. N.Y., Mar. 15, 1933. Taylor began PIANO lessons at age five and was improvising and composing by age eight. He later studied PERCUSSION. He studied harmony and COMPOSITION at the N.Y. College of Music and later studied composition at the New England Conservatory of Music in Boston. He also immersed himself in the Boston JAZZ scene. He then worked with his own combos in N.Y. Taylor first appeared at the Newport Jazz Festival in 1957.

In the early '60s, Taylor became famous as a pianist specializing in FREE JAZZ. He made his first tour of Europe in 1962, then played in jazz centers on both sides of the Atlantic. His music by this time was ATONAL, and totally free in rhythm as well. He had difficulty making ends meet playing this radical music and resorted to taking odd jobs including working as a dishwasher to support himself.

In the early '70s, Taylor worked as a jazz educator, teaching at the University of Wisconsin and at Rutgers University in New Jersey. He performed at N.Y.'s CARNEGIE HALL in 1977.

By the early '80s, Taylor was recording prolifically as both soloist and bandleader, but much of his output was on small European labels. (European audiences have always related better to avant-garde jazz than American ones.) He has since performed with both big bands and small trio settings, continuing to follow his own path as a composer and performer. A fan of dance, he has also written scores for Mikhail Baryshnikov and other choreographers.

Taylor, James, sweet-voiced American singer-songwriter; b. Boston, Mass., Mar. 12, 1948. Taylor was reared in Chapel Hill, North Carolina, the son of a college professor. He attended boarding school outside of Boston, where he suffered a nervous breakdown. By summer 1966 he was discharged from the mental hospital and living in N.Y., where

PEOPLE IN MUSIC

PEOPLE IN MUSIC

he formed a rock band called the Flying Machine with guitarist Danny "Kootch" Kortchmar. The band played local clubs and made some recordings that went unissued until Taylor achieved fame on his own. They disbanded in 1967.

The year 1968 found Taylor in London, where a demo tape ended up in the hands of PAUL MCCARTNEY and producer Peter Asher, then scouting for talent for the BEATLES' new Apple label. Taylor recorded one album for the label, but with the Beatles' empire crumbling amidst intergroup strife, the recording went nowhere. He returned to the U.S. in 1969 and signed with Warner Brothers Records. Still working with Asher, he produced the landmark *Sweet Baby James* album, which included the hits *Fire and Rain, Country Roads,* and the title cut.

Taylor's soft folk-rock sound gained him an immediate following, and he enjoyed continuing success through most of the '70s with his own material and covers of earlier hits. A stormy marriage to fellow singer CARLY SIMON brought Taylor much media attention from the mid-'70s through the early '80s. The '80s and '90s have seen him become primarily a touring artist. His recordings continue to chart on occasion. Exceptional is *New Moon Shine* (1991), which was phenomenally successful, as well as *Hourglass* (1997), featuring the songs *Little More Time With You* and *Enough To Be On Your Way.*

Taylor's brothers and sister have also recorded, including Livingston (b. 1950, Chapel Hill, N.C.), who performs in a more soft-pop vein than his brother. His biggest hit was *Lost in the Love of You.*

PEOPLE IN MUSIC

Tchaikovsky, Piotr Ilyich, greatly popular Russian composer; b. Votkinsk, Viatka district, May 7, 1840; d. St. Petersburg, Nov. 6, 1893. The son of a mining inspector at a plant in the Urals, Tchaikovsky was given a good education from both his French governess and his music teacher. When he was ten the family moved to St. Petersburg and he was sent to law school, from which he graduated at 19, becoming a government clerk. While at school he studied music with Gavriil Yakimovich Lomakin but did not display exceptional talent as a pianist or composer.

At 21 Tchaikovsky was accepted into a musical institute, newly established by Anton Rubinstein, which would become the St. Petersburg Conservatory. He studied with Nikolai Zaremba (harmony and COUNTERPOINT) and Rubinstein (COMPOSITION). He graduated in 1865, winning a silver medal for his CANTATA set to Schiller's *Hymn to Joy.* In 1866 he became professor of harmony at the Moscow Conservatory.

As if to compensate for a late start in his profession, Tchaikovsky began to compose with great application. His early works (a programmatic SYMPHONY subtitled *Winter Dreams,* some OVERTURES and small pieces for STRING QUARTET) reveal little individuality. With his SYMPHONIC POEM *Fatum* in 1868 came the first statement of his mature style: highly subjective, preferring MINOR MODES filled with nostalgic longing, and alive with keen rhythms.

In 1869 Tchaikovsky undertook the composition of his OVERTURE-FANTASY *Romeo and Juliet.* Not content with what he had written, he profited from advice from Mily Balakirev, whom he met in St. Petersburg. He revised the work in 1870, but this version proved equally unsatisfactory. He laid the composition aside and did not complete it until 1880. In its final form it became one of his most successful works.

The Belgian SOPRANO Desirée Artot, a member of an opera troupe visiting St. Petersburg in 1868, took great interest in Tchaikovsky, and he was moved by her attention. For a few months he seriously contemplated marrying her, and so notified his father (his mother had died of cholera when he was 14 years old). But this proved to be a passing infatuation on her part, for soon she married the Spanish singer Mariano Padilla y Ramos. Tchaikovsky did not seem terribly disturbed by this turn of events. Throughout his career Tchaikovsky never allowed psychological turmoil to interfere with his work.

Besides teaching and composing, Tchaikovsky contributed music criticism to Moscow newspapers from 1868 to 1874. Altogether he made 26 trips abroad (Paris, Berlin, Vienna, N.Y.). He visited the first Bayreuth Festival in 1876, reporting his impressions for the Moscow daily *Russkyie Vedomosti.* His closest friends were members of his own family,

Tchaikovsky time line

1840	Born
1859	Graduates from law school in St. Petersburg
1861	Enters ANTON RUBINSTEIN's newly established music institute
1865	Wins a silver medal upon graduation for his cantata *Hymn to Joy*
1866–78	Serves as professor of harmony at the Moscow Conservatory
1868	Composes his first mature composition, the symphonic poem *Fatum,* and also flirts with the idea of marriage to the opera singer Desirée Artot
1868–74	Writes music criticism for various Moscow newspapers
1869	Begins work on the overture-fantasy *Romeo and Juliet,* not completed until 1880
1875	His Piano Concerto No. 1 receives its world premiere in Boston, under Hans von Bülow
1876	Visits the first Bayreuth Festival and also composes the ballet *SWAN LAKE*
1877	Contracts a short-lived marriage with a conservatory student, Antonina Milyukova
1877–78	Spends time in Italy, Switzerland, Paris, and Vienna, composing his Fourth Symphony, dedicated to his patron, Nadezhda von Meck

1878 Composes the opera *EVGENY ONEGIN*

1888 Composes his Symphony No. 5

1889 Composes the ballet *THE SLEEPING BEAUTY*

1890 Composes his second important opera, *THE QUEEN OF SPADES,* after Pushkin

1891 Makes his only trip to America, appearing in N.Y., Baltimore, and Philadelphia

1892 Makes a concert tour in Russia and completes work on the celebrated ballet *THE NUTCRACKER*

1893 Symphony No. 6, op. 74, the *PATHÉTIQUE,* is first performed in St. Petersburg, just eight days before his death

1893 Dies (under circumstances that are still mysterious)

his brothers—particularly Modest (b. Alapaevsk, Perm district, May 13, 1850; d. Moscow, Jan. 15, 1916), a playwright, librettist for two of his brother's operas, and his future biographer—and his married sister Alexandra Davidov, at whose estate, Kamenka, he spent most of his summers. The correspondence with them, all of which was preserved and eventually published, throws a true light on Tchaikovsky's character and life. His other close friends were his publisher, Jurgenson, Nikolai Rubinstein, and several other musicians.

The most extraordinary of his friendships was with Nadezhda von Meck (b. Znamenskoye, near Smolensk, Feb. 10, 1831; d. Wiesbaden, Jan. 13, 1894), a wealthy widow whom he never met but who played a hugely important role in his life. Through the violinist JOSEPH KOTEK she learned about Tchaikovsky's financial difficulties. She commissioned works from him at large fees, then arranged to pay him an annuity of 6,000 rubles. For more than 13 years they corresponded voluminously, even when living in the same city (Moscow, Florence). On several occasions she hinted that she would not be averse to a personal meeting, but Tchaikovsky invariably declined, under the pretext that one should not see one's guardian angel in the flesh. On his part this correspondence had to remain within the circumscribed domain of art, personal philosophy, and reporting of daily events, without touching on his personal struggles.

In 1877 Tchaikovsky contracted marriage with a conservatory student, Antonina Milyukova, who had declared her love for him. This was an act of defiance of his own nature, because Tchaikovsky was a homosexual. He made no secret of this in the correspondence with his brother Modest, who was also a homosexual. He thought that by flaunting a wife he could allay the already rife rumors about his sexual preference.

However, when Milyukova tried to consummate the marriage on their wedding night, the result was disastrous, and Tchaikovsky fled. He attempted suicide by walking into the Moskva River, hoping to catch pneumonia, but he suffered nothing more than simple discomfort. He then went to St. Petersburg to seek the advice of his brother Anatol, a lawyer, who made suitable arrangements with Milyukova for a separation. (They never divorced, and she died in an insane asylum in 1917.) Von Meck, to whom Tchaikovsky wrote candidly of this disaster (without revealing its true cause), made an immediate offer of further financial assistance, which he gratefully accepted.

Tchaikovsky spent several months in 1877–78 in Italy, Switzerland, Paris, and Vienna, during which period he completed one of his greatest works, the Fourth Symphony, dedicated to von Meck. It was premiered in Moscow in 1878, but Tchaikovsky did not cut short his sojourn abroad to attend the performance.

Tchaikovsky resigned from the Moscow Conservatory in the autumn of 1878. From that time forward, he dedicated himself entirely to composition. The continued subsidy from von Meck allowed him to forget money matters. Early in 1878 he completed his most successful opera, *Evgeny Onegin* ("lyric scenes" after Pushkin). It was first produced in Moscow by a Conservatory ensemble in 1879 and gained success only gradually. The first performance at the Imperial Opera in St. Petersburg did not take place until 1884.

Tchaikovsky's natural state of mind was still morbid depression, but each new work sustained his faith in his destiny as a composer, despite many disheartening reversals. His Piano Concerto No. 1, rejected by Nikolai Rubinstein as unplayable, was given its world premiere in Boston in 1875—played by Hans von Bülow—and afterward was performed throughout the world by many famous pianists, including Rubinstein. The Violin Concerto, criticized by LEOPOLD AUER (to whom the score was originally dedicated) and attacked by EDUARD HANSLICK with sarcasm and virulence at its world premiere in Vienna in 1881, survived all detractors to become one of the most celebrated pieces in the violin repertory.

Early in 1890 Tchaikovsky wrote his second important opera, *The Queen of Spades* (also based on Pushkin), which was produced at the Imperial Opera in St. Petersburg that year. His ballets *SWAN LAKE* in 1876 and *THE SLEEPING BEAUTY* in 1889 became famous. But at the peak of his career he suffered a severe psychological blow: von Meck notified him of the ending of her subsidy and abruptly terminated their correspondence. He could now well afford the loss of the money, but his pride was deeply hurt by the manner in which she had acted. A plausible explanation is that her grown children had found out the truth about Tchaikovsky's homosexuality (which in those times was a crime as well as a sin) and that she was shocked by his duplicity in misrepresenting his reluctance to meet her.

It is indicative of Tchaikovsky's inner strength that even the desertion of one whom he regarded as his staunchest friend did not affect his ability to work. In 1891 he undertook his only voyage to America. He was received with honors as a celebrated composer and led four concerts of his works in N.Y. (including the inaugural concert of CARNEGIE HALL) and one each in Baltimore and Philadelphia. He did not linger in the U.S., however, and returned to St. Petersburg in a few weeks. Early in 1892 he made a concert tour as a conductor in Russia, then proceeded to Warsaw and Germany. In the meantime he had purchased a house in the town of Klin, not far from Moscow, where he wrote his last symphony, the PATHÉTIQUE.

Despite the perfection of his technique, Tchaikovsky did not arrive at the desired form and substance of this work at once, and he discarded his original sketch. The title *Pathétique* was suggested to him by Modest. The score was dedicated to his nephew, Vladimir Davidov. Its music is the final testament of Tchaikovsky's life and an epitome of his fatalistic philosophy. In the first movement the trombones are given the theme of the Russian service for the dead. Remarkably, the score of one of his most lighthearted works, THE NUTCRACKER, from 1891–92, was composed simultaneously with the early sketches for the *Pathétique*.

Tchaikovsky was in good spirits when he went to St. Petersburg to conduct the premiere of the *Pathétique* (which was but moderately successful) in 1893. A cholera epidemic was then raging there, and the population was warned against drinking unboiled water. Tchaikovsky apparently ignored this warning and showed the symptoms of cholera soon afterward. Nothing could be done to save him.

Almost immediately after his death, a rumor spread that Tchaikovsky had committed suicide. Some years later an émigré Russian musicologist published a story of a homosexual scandal involving a Russian nobleman's nephew. According to this story, a private tribunal was held and offered Tchaikovsky a choice between honorable suicide or disgrace and possible Siberian exile. Choosing the former option, Tchaikovsky was supplied with arsenic. However, this is no solid evidence that Tchaikovsky committed suicide.

As a composer Tchaikovsky stands apart from the militant national movement of the "Mighty Five." The Russian element is, of course, very strong in his music, and upon occasion he made use of Russian folk songs. But this national spirit is instinctive rather than consciously cultivated. Tchaikovsky's music was frankly sentimental, and his supreme gift of melody, which none of his Russian contemporaries could match, secured for him a lasting popularity among performers and audiences. Tchaikovsky's influence was profound on the Moscow group of composers, of whom ANTON ARENSKY and SERGE RACHMANINOFF were the most talented.

Tchaikovsky wrote successfully in every genre. He composed 11 operas, the three ballets mentioned above (and their SUITES), two piano concerti, and six numbered symphonies: No. 1, op.13, *Winter Dreams* (1866–74); No. 2, op.17, *Little Russian* or *Ukrainian* (1872–80); No. 3, op.29, *Polish* (1875); No. 4, op.36 (1877–79); No. 5, op.64 (1888); and No. 6, op.74, *Pathétique* (1893). Other orchestral works include the *Manfred* Symphony, op.58 (1886); *Burya* (The Tempest), symphonic fantasia, op.18 (1873), *Sérénade mélancolique* for violin and orchestra, op.26 (1876); *Variations on a Rococo Theme* for cello and orchestra, op.33 (1877); Violin Concerto, op.35 (1878; Vienna, 1881); *Italian Capriccio,* op.45 (1880); *Mozartiana* (1887); *Hamlet,* fantasy overture, op.67 (1888); and *Voyevoda,* symphonic ballad, op.78 (1891).

Among Tchaikovsky's chamber works are three STRING QUARTETS (1871, 1874, 1876); Piano Trio, op.50 (1882); and *Souvenir de Florence* for string sextet, op.70 (1890–92). For piano he composed two sonatas, opp. 80 (1865) and 37 (1878); *Les Quatre Saisons,* 12 character pieces for each month of the year (1875–76), and *Dumka: Russian Rustic Scene,* op.59 (1886). He also composed *Liturgy of St. John Chrysostom* for unaccompanied chorus, op.41 (1878); *Vesper Service* for unaccompanied chorus, op.52 (1881–82); and about 100 songs.

In Russia the truth of Tchaikovsky's homosexuality was totally suppressed. Any references to it in his diary and letters were removed.

Te Deum. Song of praise in the Roman Catholic LITURGY, sung in Matins on Sunday and feast days. It is generally referred to as an Ambrosian HYMN, although St. Ambrose was not the author. Text analysis dates it to before the 4th century.

In chant it sets 30 verses strophically, with a reciting formula for the body of the text, and later an alternating performance style, in which choral POLYPHONY alternates with CHANT or organ interludes.

The Te Deum is essentially a hymn of thanksgiving, salutation, or commemoration, and thus it is one of the most popular religious texts for polyphonic setting, with ORGANUM examples dating to the 10th century. Composers who have set this text include GILLES BINCHOIS, ORLANDO LASSUS, JEAN-BAPTISTE LULLY, HENRY PURCELL (in English), GEORGE FRIDERIC HANDEL (two, both in English) and both MICHAEL and FRANZ JOSEPH HAYDN. Handel wrote a *Te Deum for the Peace of Utrecht,* and Hector Berlioz contributed one for the Paris Exposition of 1855.

Later settings are by MAX BRUCKNER (1885), ANTONÍN DVOŘÁK (1896), GIUSEPPE VERDI (1898), RALPH VAUGHAN WILLIAMS (1928), BENJAMIN BRITTEN (1935), ZOLTÁN KODÁLY (celebrating 25 years of Hungarian independence, 1936), and WILLIAM WALTON (in English, 1953).

Te Deum Symphony. ANTON BRUCKNER's Ninth Symphony, whose finale he never completed. Before his death he suggested that his Te Deum might be used instead. It was first performed in this version in Vienna in 1903 but is usually played as a three-movement work. There have been recent attempts to compose an appropriate finale from his sketches.

Te Kanawa, (Dame) **Kiri,** brilliant New Zealand soprano; b. Gisborne, Mar. 6, 1944. Her father was a Maori tribesman who traced his ancestry to the legendary warrior Te Kanawa, and her mother was Irish.

Te Kanawa attended Catholic schools in Auckland and was coached in singing by a nun. She was sent to Melbourne to compete in a radio show. She also won first prize in a contest sponsored by the newspaper *Melbourne Sun.* In 1966 she received a grant for study in London.

PEOPLE IN MUSIC

Te Kanawa made her operatic debut at the Camden Festival in 1969, in GIOACCHINO ROSSINI'S *LA DONNA DEL LAGO*. She made her first appearance at London's Covent Garden in a minor role that same year, then as the Countess in WOLF-GANG AMADEUS MOZART'S *THE MARRIAGE OF FIGARO* in 1971. She made her U.S. debut in the same role with the Santa Fe Opera in 1971. It became one of her most brilliant interpretations, and she sang it again with the San Francisco Opera in 1972.

In 1974 Te Kanawa was called upon to substitute at a few hours' notice for the ailing TERESA STRATAS as Desdemona at the Metropolitan Opera in N.Y. It was a triumphant achievement, winning her unanimous praise. She also sang in a film version of *The Marriage of Figaro.* In 1977 she appeared as Pamina at the Paris Opéra, and later that year she took the role of Rosalinde in a Covent Garden production of *DIE FLEDERMAUS,* televised to the U.S. In 1981 she sang at the royal wedding of Prince Charles and Lady Diana Spencer in London, also televised around the globe. In 1990 she sang Strauss's Countess at the San Francisco Opera, and in 1991 she sang in the premiere of PAUL MCCARTNEY'S *Liverpool Oratorio* in London. In 1992 she appeared as Mozart's Countess at the Metropolitan Opera, returning there in 1997 in that role.

Te Kanawa excels equally as a subtle and artistic interpreter of lyric Mozart roles and in dramatic representations of Verdi's operas. Among other distinguished roles were the Marschallin and Arabella. She also won renown as a concert artist. In later years she expanded her repertoire to include popular fare, including songs by COLE PORTER and LEONARD BERNSTEIN'S *West Side Story.* Hailed as a *PRIMA DONNA assoluta,* she pursued one of the most successful international operatic and concert careers of her day. She was made an Officer of the Order of the British Empire in 1973, then a Dame Commander in 1982.

Tea for Two. Song by VINCENT YOUMANS and IRVING CAESAR, 1924, from the extremely popular musical *No, No, Nanette.* In 1958 an imitation-Latin cha-cha version rekindled its popularity. Before that, DMITRI SHOSTAKOVICH made a salon orchestra arrangement of it as *Tahiti Trot* in 1927.

teatro (It.). Theater. *Teatro lirico,* opera house.

Tebaldi, Renata, celebrated Italian soprano; b. Pesaro, Feb. 1, 1922. Tebaldi's mother, a nurse, took her to Langhirano after the breakup of her marriage to a philandering cellist. Renata was stricken with polio when she was three but survived. After initial vocal training, she studied at the Parma Conservatory from 1937 to 1940 and at the Pesaro Conservatory from 1940 to 1943.

PEOPLE IN MUSIC

Tebaldi made her operatic debut as Elena in ARRIGO BOITO's *MEFISTOFELE* in 1944. In 1946 ARTURO TOSCANINI chose her to sing in the reopening concert at La Scala in Milan, and she subsequently became one of its leading sopranos.

She made her first appearance in England in 1950 with the visiting La Scala company at London's Covent Garden as Desdemona. In 1950 she also sang Aida with the San Francisco Opera. In 1955 Tebaldi made her Metropolitan Opera debut in N.Y. as Desdemona, continuing there until 1973. She then toured Russia in 1975 and 1976.

Tebaldi's repertoire was almost exclusively Italian, and she excelled in both lyric and dramatic roles, being particularly successful as Violetta, Tosca, Mimi, and Madame Butterfly. She also sang Eva in RICHARD WAGNER's *DIE MEISTERSINGER VON NÜRNBERG.* On Nov. 3, 1958, she was the subject of a cover story in *Time* magazine. C. Casanova wrote her authorized biography as *Renata Tebaldi: The Voice of an Angel* (Dallas, 1995).

tek′nik, tek-nēk′

technic, technique. All that relates to the purely mechanical part of an instrumental or vocal performance. Mechanical training, skill, and dexterity.

Teen Angel. No. 1 hit for Mark Dinning in 1960, composed by Jean and Red Surray. A really syrupy ballad.

Teenager in Love, A. Dion and the Belmonts scored big in 1959 with this Pomus-Schuman confection out of N.Y.'s Brill Building.

PEOPLE IN MUSIC

Telemann, Georg Philipp, significant German composer; b. Magdeburg, Mar. 14, 1681; d. Hamburg, June 25, 1767.

Telemann received academic training at a local school, learning to play KEYBOARD instruments and the violin and acquiring knowledge of music theory. He subsequently attended the Gymnasium Andreanum in Hildesheim, where he became active in student performances of German CANTATAS.

In 1701 Telemann entered the University of Leipzig as a law student. A year later, he organized a collegium musicum there, and then was appointed music director of the Leipzig Opera, where he used the services of his fellow student singers and instrumentalists. In 1705 he went to Sorau as Kapellmeister to the court of Count Erdmann II of Promnitz. In 1708 he was appointed Konzertmeister to the court orchestra in Eisenach, and later was named Kapellmeister.

In 1709 Telemann married Louise Eberlin, a musician's daughter, but she died two years later in childbirth. In 1712 Telemann was appointed music director of the city of Frankfurt. There he wrote a quantity of sacred and secular music for public concerts given by the Frauenstein Society, which he directed. In 1714 he married Maria Katharina Textor, daughter of a local town clerk. They had eight sons and two daughters, of whom only a few survived infancy.

In 1721 Telemann received the post of music director of five churches in Hamburg, which became the center of his activities as composer and music administrator. In 1722 he was appointed music director of the Hamburg Opera, a post he held until 1738. During his tenure he wrote a number of operas for production there and also staged works by GEORGE FRIDERIC HANDEL and REINHARD KEISER. In 1737–38 he visited France. His eyesight began to fail as he grew older: the same infirmity from which JOHANN SEBASTIAN BACH and Handel suffered.

Extraordinarily prolific, Telemann mastered both the German and Italian styles of composition prevalent in his day. While he never approached the greatness of Bach or Handel, he nevertheless became an exemplar of the German BAROQUE at its grandest development. More than his two great contemporaries, Telemann bridged the gap into the ROCOCO and early CLASSIC styles.

Telemann's works include 35 operas, many of them German INTERMEZZOS, notably *Der gedültige Socrates* (Hamburg, 1721) and *Pimpinone, oder Die ungleiche Heyrath* (Hamburg, 1725); seven ORATORIOS, the best known being *Der Tag des Gerichts* (1762); over 1,250 cantatas, including four major sacred collections; and 46 PASSIONS, MASSES, PSALMS, and MOTETS.

In the instrumental realm Telemann's greatest collection was the *Musique de table* from 1733, containing three orchestral SUITES, three CONCERTOS, three QUARTETS, three TRIOS, and three SONATAS. His prodigious orchestral output comprises numerous overtures, concertos, sonatas, quartets, quintets, etc.

His grandson Georg Michael Telemann (b. Plön, Apr. 20, 1748; d. Riga, Mar. 4, 1831) was a composer and writer on music, reared and trained in music by his grandfather in Hamburg. He served as Kantor and teacher from 1773 to 1828, at the cathedral school in Riga, where he oversaw performances of many of his grandfather's works in his own editions.

Telmányi, Emil. *See* NIELSEN, CARL (AUGUST).

temperament. A calculated alteration of the acoustical values of musical INTERVALS to make possible the division of the perfect OCTAVE into 12 equal SEMITONES. Purely tuned tones of very nearly the same pitch, like C♯ and D♭, are made to sound identical by tempering them (i.e., slightly raising or lowering the pitch). When applied to all the tones of an instrument (as the piano), this system is called EQUAL TEMPERAMENT. When only the keys most used are so tuned (as was practiced formerly), the system is called UNEQUAL TEMPERAMENT or *meantone tuning*.

temple blocks. *See* CHINESE BLOCKS.

tem′pŏh **tempo** (It.; Fr. *temps*). Rate of speed, movement; time, measure.

Two systems of tempo indications (marks) have developed since the BAROQUE period. The earlier type, still very much in use, indicates tempo verbally. The most common indications are in Italian: *largo, adagio, moderato, andante, allegro, allegretto, presto,* and *prestissimo.* These terms are often qualified by additional words of caution such as *ma non troppo* or *poco.*

The first attempt to put precise meaning into these vague Italian modifiers was made by JOHANN JOAQUIM QUANTZ, who defined the natural speed measure as the human heartbeat, at 80 beats per minute. Taking $\frac{4}{4}$ as the basic meter, he assigned the exact duration of the pulse-beat to a half note in allegro, to a quarter note in allegretto, and to an eighth note in adagio.

The second system came with the invention in the early 19th century of the METRONOME, a mathematical measurement of the tempo. Theoretically this would standardize tempo terminology. LUDWIG VAN BEETHOVEN, the first major composer to make systematic use of the metronome, set down the "scientific" tempo for several of his works, even marking early works retrospectively. However, most modern interpreters found Beethoven's instructions unacceptable, blaming a "faulty" metronome. For example, Beethoven set the metronome mark for the *Marcia funèbre* from his *Eroica* Symphony at 80 eighth notes per minute, but most conductors prefer a slower tempo. Actual timing of ARTURO TOSCANINI's 1935 performance scored only 52 eighth notes a minute, 35 percent slower than what Beethoven apparently intended.

Many modern composers, particularly IGOR STRAVINSKY, abandoned traditional tempo marks entirely and replaced them by the precise metronome number. Because he insisted on precision in the performance of his works and abhorred ROMANTIC aberrations, his metronome marks were "final."

The rediscovery of recordings of great artists of the past disclosed a shocking departure from tempo markings indicated by the composer. The sentimental leanings among German musicians and theorists of the latter half of the 18th century led to constant shifts of tempo and dynamics—an astonishing practice contradicting the modern idea of the precise and ordered execution of classical works. Even Leopold Mozart commented favorably on the device of "stolen time," anticipating the ROMANTIC RUBATO so despised by modern interpreters. However, the tendency in the mid-20th century as regards tempo was generally in the direction of precision.

But toward the last third of the 20th century a curious counterreaction set in. Critics and the general public began to complain about the metronomic monotony of modern performers. An unscientific nostalgia spread through the music world. As in the preceding century, "personality" was hailed as superior to overzealous fidelity to the page. Even composers themselves welcomed flexible tempos affected by celebrated interpreters to vitalize the spirit of the music.

Some compromise between musical permissiveness and pedantry seems inevitable. Perhaps these words of Wanda Landowska can serve as a guide: "One must approach classical music as a well-mannered guest. One need not be too obsequious or reverential to the hostess, but one must not put one's feet on the table at meals."

A tempo, return to preceding tempo; *in tempo,* same as *a tempo; in tempo misurato,* in strict time (after a passage marked *tempo a piacere*); *l'istesso tempo,* or *lo stesso tempo,* the same tempo, despite a rhythmic change; *sempre in tempo,* always at the same tempo; *senza tempo,* same as *tempo a piacere; tempo a piacere,* play at will in terms of tempo; *tempo ad libitum,* metrically free; *tempo com(m)odo,* at a comfortable, convenient tempo; *tempo di Ballo, Minuetto, Valse,* etc., in the movement of a ballet, minuet, waltz, etc.; *tempo giusto,* at a proper, appropriate tempo; *tempo primo,* at the original pace; *tempo rubato, see* RUBATO.

tempo mark. Word or phrase indicating the rate of speed at which a piece should be performed. Thus, "Adagio (M.M. = 56)" signifies a tranquil movement in which a quarter note has the duration of one click of a metronome set at 56 (i.e., 56 beats per minute).

Temptations, The. Popular Motown vocal group of the 1960s. (Core group: Eddie Kendricks, b. Birmingham, Ala., Dec. 17, 1939; d. there, Oct. 5, 1992; David Ruffin, b. Meridian, Miss., Jan. 18, 1941, d. Philadelphia, Penn., June 1, 1991; Otis Williams [born Otis Miles], b. Texarkana, Tex., Oct. 30, 1941; Melvin Franklin [born David English], b. Montgomery, Ala., Oct. 12, 1942; d. Los Angeles, Feb. 23, 1995; Paul Williams, b. Birmingham, Ala., July 2, 1939; d. [suicide] Detroit, Mich., Aug. 17, 1973.) One of the best

PEOPLE IN MUSIC

of the Motown groups, the Temptations were noted for their fleet-footed choreography and double-lead vocals, provided by Kendricks and Ruffin.

Formed out of two Detroit ensembles of the late 1950s, the Primes and the Distants, the Temptations were signed to Motown in 1960 when they were known as the Elgins. They changed their name a year later, then scored their first hit with *Dream Come Home* in 1962. In 1963 Ruffin joined the group and the classic lineup was in place.

Joining with producer-songwriter Smokey Robinson, the group started 1964 with a major hit, *The Way You Do the Things You Do.* The classic *My Girl* followed, along with a number of other hits, including *Ain't Too Proud to Beg, I Know I'm Losin' You,* and *I Wish It Would Rain.* In 1968 Ruffin left the group. With a new producer in place, Norman Whitfield, they scored with several more hits, including *Psychedelic Shack* and *Papa Was a Rolling Stone.* However, Kendricks left the group in 1971, ending in the classic period for the group. He enjoyed a modest solo career, while the group itself continued to score minor hits.

Over the next two decades the group performed with changing rosters, with Kendricks and Ruffin occasionally rejoining them. They also paired with white soulsters Daryl Hall and John Oates for a 1985 concert and album to celebrate the newly refurbished Apollo Theater in N.Y. However, in 1991 Ruffin died of a drug overdose, and a year later Kendricks succumbed to lung cancer.

tempus (Lat.). *See* NOTATION.

Ten Cents a Dance. Song by RICHARD RODGERS and LORENZ HART, 1930, from the musical *Simple Simon.* This Depression-era classic is the sorrowful narrative of a young woman working as a "taxi dancer."

Tender Land, The. Opera by AARON COPLAND, 1954, first performed in N.Y. The tender land of the title is the American Midwest.

A young harvest worker has a summer romance with a farm girl, but he is indecisive about elopement and mar-

A "taxi dancer" was a rented partner—for a meager 10 cents—on the dance floor, just as a taxicab was a rented vehicle to take a passenger to a destination.

riage. Eventually he leaves the farm. Her love is more profound, and she sets out in search of him.

The score represents Copland's modern lyricism at its best.

tenebrae (Lat., darkness). Roman Catholic LITURGY for Holy Week, specifically the MATINS and LAUDS of Holy Thursday, Good Friday, and Holy Saturday. The name derives from the ritual of blowing out a candle after each PSALM until all are extinguished. The text includes excerpts from the Lamentations of Jeremiah. Settings include works by CARLO GESUALDO, ORLANDO LASSUS, GIOVANNI PIERLUIGI DA PALESTRINA, TOMÁS LUIS DE VICTORIA, FRANÇOIS COUPERIN, and IGOR STRAVINSKY.

Tennessee Waltz. Song by Redd Stewart and Pee Wee King, 1948, which was a hit for PATTI PAGE, among others. It captured the essence of the state of Tennessee well enough that the assembly there voted it the official state song in 1965.

Tenney, James (Carl), highly influential American pianist, conductor, teacher, and composer; b. Silver City, N.Mex., Aug. 10, 1934. From 1952 to 1954, Tenney studied engineering at the University of Denver before devoting himself to music. He studied piano with Edward Steuermann at the Juilliard School of Music in N.Y. in 1954–55 and piano and composition at Bennington (Vermont) College, where he earned his B.A. degree in 1958. He worked with KENNETH GABURO, LEJAREN HILLER, and HARRY PARTCH at the University of Illinois, where he took his masters degree in 1961. He was also associated with CHOU WEN-CHUNG, CARL RUGGLES, and EDGARD VARÈSE from 1955 to 1965.

Tenney performed with the STEVE REICH and PHILIP GLASS ensembles, while concurrently conducting research at the Bell Laboratories (with Max Mathews; 1961–64), Yale University (1964–66), and the Polytechnic Institute of Brooklyn (1966–70). He taught at the California Institute of the Arts (1970–75), University of California, Santa Cruz (1975–76), and York University in Toronto (from 1976).

As both performer and scholar, Tenney is a prominent advocate and theorist of contemporary music. He is a noted authority on CHARLES IVES and CONLON NANCARROW. Tenney's compositions include:

Quiet Fan for Erik Satie (1970) and *Clang* (1972) for orchestra

Quintext for string quartet and double bass (1972)

In the Aeolian Mode for prepared piano and variable ensemble (1973)

Spectral Canon for Conlon Nancarrow for player piano (1974)

Saxony for saxophone and tape delay (1978)

3 Indigenous Songs for mixed quintet (1979)

Glissade for viola, cello, double bass, and tape delay (1982)

Koan for string quartet (1984)

Rune for percussion ensemble (1988)

Critical Band for ensemble (1988)

Cognate Canons for string quartet and two percussionists (1995)

Among Tenney's pioneering works on tape or for computer are *Collage No. 1: Blue Suede* (1961), *Stochastic Quartet: String Quartet* for computer or strings (1963), *Fabric for Che* (1967), and *For Ann (rising)* (1969). He also composed a number of vocal and theater works.

tenor (from Lat. *tenere,* hold; It. *tenore*). 1. Highest and most expressive male voice.

The term derives from the fact that the CANTUS FIRMUS in early vocal POLYPHONY was given to a voice called the tenor, whose function was to "hold" the melody while other voices moved contrapuntally in relation to it. The voice part gradually became independent of its original function and came to refer simply to the voice range.

From the beginning of operatic history, tenors enjoyed great social and financial success as well as adulation. But they were also traditionally regarded as being mentally deficient (an Italian joke lists the degrees of comparison as "stupido, stupidissimo, tenore"). Although ENRICO CARUSO never learned to read music, he could hardly be called "stupido." Another nonstupid tenor was LEO SLEZAK (1873–1946), who possessed a Viennese kind of *Witz,* often at the expense of his fellow singers.

The ordinary tenor range is two OCTAVES, from the C below middle C to the C above (c⁰–c²). The tenor part is usually notated in the treble clef (from middle C), sounding an octave lower. Some singers in the BEL CANTO era could go higher in FALSETTO, i.e. Giovanni Battista Rubini (1794–1854), who regularly hit f². In some opera scores the tenor part is indicated by a combined tenor and treble CLEF.

The mark of distinction for great tenors is their ability to hold high C for a long time, often ignoring the musical and harmonic reasons to let go. Old film prints of opera ARIAS show tenors running up to the footlights during a highly dramatic duet to project a high C into the audience and then retreating to join a waiting SOPRANO.

Categories include the *dramatic tenor* (It. *tenore di forza*), with a full and powerful quality and a range from c to b¹ (Rodolpho in *LA BOHÈME,* Manrico in *IL TROVATORE*), *heroic tenor* (Ger. *Heldentenor*), with a strong sonority throughout the range (Siegfried in the *RING,* Otello), and *lyric tenor* (It. *tenore di grazia*), sweeter and less powerful, with a range from c² (or c#²; Gounod's Faust and Almaviva in *THE BARBER OF SEVILLE*).

2. A prefix to the names of instruments with a similar pitch relationship to other members of the same family, as *tenor trombone, tenor tuba, tenor violin.*

tenor C. Small c:

tenor clef. *See* CLEF(s).

tenor drum (Ger. RÜHRTROMMEL; It. *tamburo rullante*). Side drum, without snares. It is larger and therefore deeper sounding than a military drum, also of indefinite pitch.

tenor saxophone. Saxophone in B-flat, transposing down a whole tone. Its range is $B\flat_0-f^2$. It is commonly found in JAZZ ensembles, although a nontransposing "melody" tenor saxophone in C is still used in marching and wind bands.

tenor violin (Fr. *taille de violon;* Ger. *Tenorgeige*). Generic term for large violas, first made in the 16th century, with the bottom string G_0 an octave below the violin g^0. It resembles the bass VIOLA DA BRACCIO. It is also called *tenor-viola, violon-ténor, viola tenore, Oktavgeige,* and *controviolino.*

tenth (Lat. *decima*). *See* INTERVAL.

Tenth Symphony. Unfinished work by GUSTAV MAHLER, 1910–11. Two movements are more or less complete, the *Adagio* and *Purgatorio,* and were first performed posthumously in Vienna, in 1924. In them, Mahler's style reaches the ultimate of complexity for his time, making use of extremely DISSONANT combinations of tones.

The British musician Deryck Cooke (1919–76) completed the symphony, making use of some of Mahler's sketches and fragments. His first of three performing versions received the approval of Alma Mahler Werfel, the composer's widow, and was given its premiere in London in 1964.

Mahler's handwritten inscriptions in the manuscript point toward serious mental turbulence: "Madness possesses me! Devil, come and seize me, the cursed one!"

teponaxtli. Mexican SLIT DRUM, traditionally made out of a hollowed-out tree trunk and played with sticks.

Tequila. Funky instrumental hit for the Champs in 1958.

terce. In both the old and revised Roman Catholic LITURGY, the daily Canonical Hour celebrated at 9 A.M.

Terfel, Bryn, outstanding Welsh BASS-BARITONE; b. Pantglas, Nov. 9, 1965. He was a student of Arthur Reckless and Rudolf Piernay at the Guildhall School of Music in London (1984–89), winning the Kathleen Ferrier Memorial Scholarship (1988) and the Gold Medal (1989). After winning the Lieder Prize at the Cardiff Singer of the World Competi-

tion in 1989, he made his operatic debut as Guglielmo with the Welsh National Opera in Cardiff in 1990. In 1991 he sang Mozart's Figaro at his first appearance with the English National Opera in London, which role he also sang that same year at his U.S. debut in Santa Fe.

In 1992 Terfel appeared for the first time at the Salzburg Festival as the Spirit Messenger in *DIE FRAU OHNE SCHATTEN*. That same year he also made his Salzburg Festival debut as Jochanaan and his first appearance at London's Covent Garden as Masetto. In 1993 he made his debut with the Lyric Opera of Chicago as Donner and at the Vienna State Opera as Mozart's Figaro. He also appeared as Verdi's Ford with the Welsh National Opera. In 1994 he returned to the Vienna State Opera as Offenbach's four villains, at Covent Garden as Mozart's Figaro, and at the Salzburg Festival as Leporello. In 1994 he made an impressive appearance in the closing night gala concert of the 100th anniversary season of the London Promenade Concerts as soloist with Andrew Davis and the BBC Symphony Orchestra.

Terfel's highly acclaimed Metropolitan Opera debut in N.Y. followed on Oct. 19, 1994, as Mozart's Figaro. On Oct. 24, 1994, he made his N.Y. recital debut at Alice Tully Hall. In 1995 he returned to the Lyric Opera of Chicago and at the Metropolitan Opera as Leporello. Terfel has also won a wide following for his concert engagements, in a repertoire ranging from Bach to Walton.

ternary. Composed of, or progressing by, threes. *Ternary form,* ABA form, such as the MINUET and TRIO; DA CAPO form; *ternary measure,* simple triple time.

terraced dynamics (Ger. *Terrasendynamik*). Primarily BAROQUE style of dynamic changes by a direct transition from one degree of loudness to another as from *piano* to *mezzoforte,* from *mezzopiano* to *fortissimo,* etc., without intervening CRESCENDO or DECRESCENDO. The term was introduced by FERRUCCIO BUSONI.

Terraced dynamics were in common usage in the Baroque perhaps because of the inability of the CEMBALO to graduate the sound with a distinct change from *piano* to *forte* or vice-versa. In the Elizabethan period explicit indications such as *lowd, lowder, softer,* etc. were in use. LUDWIG VAN BEETHOVEN favored terraced dynamics in the form of a *subito piano* after a *forte.* During his NEOCLASSICAL period, IGOR STRAVINSKY began to cultivate terraced dynamics almost exclusively, to signify his return to Baroque usage.

Terry, Clark, African-American JAZZ trumpet and flügelhorn player and scat singer; b. St. Louis, Dec. 14, 1920. Terry worked with CHARLIE BARNET in 1947 and Count Basie from 1948 to 1951. He then joined DUKE ELLINGTON's band in 1951, enjoying a richly rewarding eight-year association. During his collaborations with OSCAR PETERSON, he evolved his trademark "mumbles" style of scat singing (named for the hit song of the same name). He described this style as sounding like an old man storytelling while drifting into incoherence. He also evolved a style of musical monologue made up of wittily juggled fragments of musical thought.

Terry played in the orchestra of Johnny Carson's *Tonight Show* until it relocated to Los Angeles, and also taught at various jazz clinics. During the '70s, Terry switched to playing primarily the flügelhorn.

Terry spent much of the '70s and '80s touring both the U.S. and Europe. In 1990 he was appointed director for the new Thelonious Monk Institute of Jazz at Duke University in Chapel Hill, North Carolina.

PEOPLE IN MUSIC

terzo suono (It., third tone). *See* DIFFERENCE (DIFFERENTIAL) TONE (TARTINI TONE).

tār-tsŏh sŏŏ-ô-nŏh

tessitura (It., texture). Use of high or low REGISTER in a given vocal range. If high notes are preponderant, the tessitura is said to be high, as in most COLORATURA SOPRANO parts; if low notes are especially frequent, as in BASS parts of some Russian songs, the tessitura is said to be low. In English a vocal part can "lie" high or low.

tes-sē-too′răh

tetrachord. 1. INTERVAL of a PERFECT FOURTH. 2. The four SCALE-TONES contained in a perfect fourth. In ancient Greek scales the tetrachord was treated invariably as a descending progression. However, the MEDIEVAL tetrachord was counted upward, an ascent retained in subsequent centuries. As a result the names of the MODES that developed from CONJUNCT or DISJUNCT tetrachords forming an entire DIATONIC SCALE were different from the Greek modes.

The musical quality of the tetrachord was determined by the placement of the SEMITONE in the diatonic progressions. Thus the PHRYGIAN tetrachord was formed by the placement of the semitone between the first and the second degrees. In the AEOLIAN and DORIAN tetrachords the semitone was between the second and third degrees, while in the IONIAN and MIXOLYDIAN modes it lies between the third and fourth degrees. The LYDIAN tetrachord is formed by WHOLE TONES only.

3. A set of four PITCH classes, usually associated with a 12-NOTE SET.

tetralogy. Thematically connected series of four stage works or ORATORIOS.

Tetrazzini, Luisa (actually, **Luigia**), celebrated Italian soprano; b. Florence, June 28, 1871; d. Milan, April 28, 1940. She learned the words and music of several operas by listening to her sister, the SOPRANO Eva Tetrazzini (b. Milan, March 1862; d. Salsomaggiore, Oct. 27, 1938), then studied at the Liceo Musicale in Florence. She made her operatic debut as Inez in *L'Africaine* in Florence (1890), after which she sang in Europe and traveled with various companies in South America. In 1904 she made her U.S. debut at the Tivoli Opera House in San Francisco. Her London debut at Covent Garden as Violetta followed in 1907. She was then engaged by OSCAR HAMMERSTEIN to sing with his Manhattan Opera House in N.Y., where she sang Violetta on Jan. 15, 1908. She remained with the company until it closed in 1910, subsequently appearing for a single season at the Metropolitan Opera (1911–12), making her debut there on Dec. 27, 1911, as Lucia.

After singing at the Chicago Grand Opera (1911–13), Tetrazzini toured as a concert artist. She made the first broadcast on British radio in 1925. Her last appearance in America was in N.Y. in 1931. She then taught in Milan.

Tetrazzini's fame was worldwide, and her name became a household word, glorified even in food, as in Turkey Tetrazzini. She published *My Life of Song* (London, 1921) and *How to Sing* (N.Y., 1923). See also C. Gattley's *Luisa Tetrazzini: The Florentine Nightingale* (Portland, Oregon, 1995).

Teutscher (Tanz). *See* DEUTSCHER TANZ.

text-sound composition. Medium that began in the dadaist movement of the first quarter of the 20th century and was revived, making use of RECORDING TAPE and other electronic devices, in the second half of the 20th century.

Text-sound works emphasize the sonorous element independent from the meaning, if any, of the words recited. Such compositions may hark back to prehuman cries through ritualistic incantation or else may project into an absurd future with the aid of COMPUTERS, SYNTHESIZERS, and stereophonic sound engineering. The medium evolved among modern poets, sound engineers, and Swedish composers, and was picked up by American composers. Among the first group the best-known work is the *Ursonate* of artist KURT SCHWITTERS, created between 1922 and 1932. Among the latter group the works of CHARLES AMIRKHANIAN achieved, in his own execution, a degree of true virtuosity.

texture. The musical parameter concerning the number and relationships of individual parts or lines in a piece. In essence, a vertical analysis of a work's external components. The most commonly described textures are MONOPHONIC, HOMOPHONIC, POLYPHONIC, and HETEROPHONIC.

Thaïs. Opera by JULES MASSENET, 1894, first performed in Paris, to a LIBRETTO drawn from the ironic novel by Anatole France.

A monk in Egypt is horrified by the depravity of the courtesan Thaïs and dreams of converting her. He succeeds rather well. He conducts Thaïs through the desert, where they reach the convent and she takes her vow as the bride of Christ. But the monk himself undergoes a reversal and now craves not her spirit but her flesh. To exorcise the obsession he beats himself violently but in vain. Meanwhile Thaïs attains spiritual perfection and dies a true Christian.

The instrumental solo *Méditation* from the score is a perennial favorite.

Thanks for the Memory. Song, 1938, by Ralph Rainger (1901–42), which later became the theme song of comedian Bob Hope.

That Old Black Magic. Song by HAROLD ARLEN, 1942, from the screen musical *Star-Spangled Banner.*

That'll Be the Day. The first No. 1 hit for BUDDY HOLLY and the Crickets, written by Holly and producer Norman Petty, released in 1957. It was revived by LINDA RONSTADT in 1976.

theater orchestra. Small, flexible ensemble for which arrangements are made. Separate instrumental parts are cued into other parts to be used when a particular instrument is not available. For example, an English horn solo might be cued into a clarinet or even a violin part. The piano part represents the harmonic skeleton of a theater arrangement.

theater set. A suite of instrumental pieces for small orchestra, a term often used by CHARLES IVES. *Theater set* is akin to *orchestral set.*

thematic catalogue. An inventory of works by an individual composer arranged according to genre (operas, symphonies, chamber music, solo works) or chronologically (including opus number) and supplemented by INCIPITS. Such catalogues may be compiled by the composers themselves, their publishers, or subsequent scholars.

FRANZ JOSEPH HAYDN entrusted his copyist with the job of compiling a thematic catalogue of those works "which I can recall at present, from the age of 18 until my 73rd year of life." The Haydn catalogue contains errors of both omission and commission. WOLFGANG AMADEUS MOZART also began cataloguing his compositions, but a complete thematic catalogue of his works was first put together by a botanist named LUDWIG KÖCHEL, who had a passion for inventories.

Thematic catalogues now exist for a majority of important composers and a minority of unimportant ones. Some extensive catalogues include information about the prove-nance of the manuscripts, details concerning various editions, etc.

thematic composition. Any compositional method based on the CONTRAPUNTAL treatment or development of one or more THEMES. *See also* CANON, INVENTION, FUGUE, SONATA FORM.

theme (Ger. *Thema;* It. *tema*). An extended and rounded-off melodic SUBJECT with accompaniment, in period FORM, proposed as groundwork for elaborate DEVELOPMENT and VARIATION.

theme and variations (Fr. *theme varié;* Ger. *Thema und Variationen;* It. *tema con variazioni*). A musical form and/or genre, in existence since the 16th century, in which a principal THEME is clearly and explicitly stated at the beginning and then followed by a number of VARIATIONs based on that theme. The pattern of development over the course of such a work is freely chosen, although the CLASSIC period evolved a remarkably consistent structure, particularly in music written for amateurs.

Theme and Variations: The Four Temperaments. A work for string orchestra and piano by PAUL HINDEMITH, 1940, depicting the four medieval humors: melancholic, sanguine, phlegmatic, and choleric. Although it was originally composed as a BALLET, its first performance as such took place two years after its concert premiere, in Boston, with LUKAS FOSS as soloist.

Theodorakis, Mikis (Michael George), Greek composer; b. Chios, July 29, 1925. Theodorakis studied at the Athens Conservatory. During the German occupation of his homeland during World War II, he was active in the resistance. After the liberation he joined the left wing but was arrested and deported during the civil war.

In 1953 Theodorakis went to went to Paris and studied with OLIVIER MESSIAEN, soon after which he began to compose. After returning to Greece in 1961 he resumed his political activity and served as a member of Parliament during

PEOPLE IN MUSIC

1963. Having joined the Communist party, he was arrested after the military coup in 1967 and incarcerated. During this period he wrote the music for the film *Z*, dealing with the police murder of Socialist politician Gregory Lambrakis in Salonika. Both the film and music were greatly acclaimed in Europe and America, and his fate became a cause célèbre. Yielding to international pressure, the military Greek government freed him in 1970.

In 1972 Theodorakis quit the Communist party and was active in the United Left. Returning to the Communist Party he served in Parliament in 1981 and again in 1985 – 86 before quitting it once more. In 1989 he became an ambassador of conservatism in Greece, going so far as to enter the legislative race on the New Democracy ticket. With 416 like-minded painters, writers, musicians, singers, and actors, Theodorakis signed his name to a manifesto condemning the divisive policies of the former Socialist government of Andreas Papandreou. He also ended four years of musical silence by appearing on an Athens stage before a crowd of 70,000 people, singing songs of protest and love in the name of national unity.

Theodorakis's works are usually programmatically inspired, whether instrumental or vocal, and his favorite subjects are Greek mythology and personal liberation. He wrote a ballet-opera, a BALLET (*Antigone*, 1959), and the film score for Kazantzakis's *Zorba the Greek*.

MUSICAL INSTRUMENT

President Wilson himself once sang *There's a Long, Long Trail* at a White House dinner.

---

theorbo. Large, double-necked ARCHLUTE with one set of strings for the melody and another for the bass.

theory. Systematic study of basic musical principles, particularly as related to composition and analysis.

There's a Long, Long Trail. Western ballad by Zo (Alonzo) Elliott, 1913, written while he was a student at Yale University. Shortly afterward he went to England, where he had the piece published. Eventually it became a standard song of World War I.

There's No Business Like Show Business. Rollicking song by IRVING BERLIN, 1946, from the musical *ANNIE GET YOUR*

GUN. It became a wry but celebratory hymn to commercial American theater, especially among theatrical people themselves.

Theremin (thereminovox). An early ELECTRONIC melody instrument invented by LEON THEREMIN. Its PITCH and DYNAMICS are controlled by moving the hands around two metal poles. These poles are electrically charged, and it is the disruption of the electric field—by the hand movement of the player—that makes the instrument's pitch or loudness change.

Although initially a serious instrument, the Theremin has become best known from its use in countless B-grade 1950s-era horror movies. Its whining, eerie sound was also heard in the theme music to the popular science fiction television show *Star Trek.*

Theremin, Leon (born Lev Termen), Russian inventor of the electronic instrument that bears his name; b. St. Petersburg, Aug. 15, 1896; d. Moscow, Nov. 3, 1993. Theremin studied physics and astronomy at the University of St. Petersburg, as well as cello and music theory. He then continued his studies in physics at the Petrograd Physico-Technical Institute.

In 1919 Theremin became director of its Laboratory of Electrical Oscillators. A year later, he gave a demonstration there of his *aetherophone,* which was the prototype of the *thereminovox* (THEREMIN). He also gave a special demonstration for Lenin, who was convinced that the electrification of Russia would ensure the success of communism.

In 1927 Theremin demonstrated his new instruments in Germany, France, and the U.S., where in 1928 he obtained a patent for the Theremin. In 1930 he presented a concert at CARNEGIE HALL in N.Y. with an ensemble of ten of his instruments, also introducing a space-controlled synthesis of color and music. In 1932 in the same hall, he introduced the first electrical symphony orchestra, conducted by ALBERT STOESSEL and including theremin fingerboard and KEYBOARD instruments. Among his American students from the 1930s, the best-known was Clara Rockmore, who became a celebrated soloist on the instrument. Theremin also invented

MUSICAL
INSTRUMENT

The most unique use of a Theremin in popular music was as an accompanying instrument in the BEACH BOYS's 1967 hit *GOOD VIBRATIONS.*

PEOPLE IN MUSIC

Leon Theremin in New York, c. 1935. (UPI/Corbis-Bettmann)

the *rhythmicon,* capable of playing different rhythms simultaneously or separately (introduced by HENRY COWELL), and an automatic musical instrument for playing directly from specially written musical scores (constructed for PERCY GRAINGER).

With the theorist Joseph Schillinger, Theremin established an acoustical laboratory in N.Y. He also formed numerous scientific and artistic associations, among them Albert Einstein, himself an amateur violinist. Einstein was fascinated by the relationships between music, color, and geometric and stereometric figures, and Theremin provided him a work space in his laboratory. He also experimented with orchestral conductor LEOPOLD STOKOWSKI, who tried to increase the dynamics of the double basses by adding a Theremin to the Philadelphia Orchestra. These experiments had to be abandoned, however, when the players complained of side effects including muscle cramps, which they attributed to the soundwaves produced by the Theremin!

In 1938 Theremin returned to Russia. It is not known whether he returned voluntarily or not. In any case, he soon had difficulties with the Soviet government, which was suspicious of his foreign contacts. He was detained for a period, and speculations and rumors abounded as to his possible fate. Whatever else may have happened, he worked steadily in electronic research for the Soviet government, continuing his experiments with sound as a sideline. Upon his retirement from his work in electronics he became a professor of acoustics at the University of Moscow in 1964.

With the advent of more liberal policies in the USSR, Theremin was able to travel abroad, appearing in Paris and Stockholm in 1989. His return visit to the U.S. was documented in the film *The Electronic Odyssey of Leon Theremin* in 1993.

These Boots Are Made for Walkin'. The No. 1, protofeminist hit for Nancy Sinatra in 1966, penned by producer Lee Hazelwood.

thesis (Grk., letting down). Originally the strong BEAT in Greek prosody and therefore musical theory. It is now the unaccented beat, having exchanged meanings with ARSIS.

Thibaud, Jacques, celebrated French violinist; b. Bordeaux, Sept. 27, 1880; d. Sept. 1, 1953. Thibaud began his training with his father and made his debut at age eight in Bordeaux. At age 13 he entered the Paris Conservatory as a pupil of MARTIN MARSICK, graduating with the *premier prix* in 1896.

Obliged to earn his living, Thibaud played at the Café Rouge, where he was heard by the conductor ÉDOUARD COLONNE, who offered him a position in his orchestra. In 1898 he made his debut as a soloist (with Colonne) with such success that he was engaged for 54 concerts in Paris in the same season. He subsequently appeared in all the musical centers of Europe, and from 1903 visited America numerous times.

With his two brothers, a pianist and a cellist, Thibaud formed a trio, which had some success. But this was discontinued when he joined ALFRED CORTOT and PABLO CASALS in a famous ensemble, with which he performed from 1930 to 1935. With Marguerite Long he founded the renowned Long-Thibaud competition in 1943. Thibaud was killed in an airplane crash near Mt. Cemet, in the French Alps, en route to French Indochina, in 1953.

Thibaud's playing was notable for its warmth of expressive tone and fine dynamics. His interpretations of LUDWIG VAN BEETHOVEN ranked very high, but he was particularly authoritative in French music.

There were rumors in the West that Theremin had been kidnapped by the KGB and forced to work on secret electronic spying devices.

PEOPLE IN MUSIC

third (Ger. *Terz;* It. *terza*). *See* INTERVAL.

Third Stream. A combining of COOL JAZZ and classical techniques associated with the 1950s. The term itself was first used by GUNTHER SCHULLER at a lecture at the Berkshire Music Center in Tanglewood, Massachusetts, in 1957. If the first stream is classical, and the second stream is JAZZ, Third Stream is their final union. The compositions of Schuller and JOHN LEWIS were the most popular ones in this style. Lewis's group, the Modern Jazz Quartet, was a primary proponent of third-stream music.

Third Symphony. PIOTR ILYICH TCHAIKOVSKY's symphony in D major, first performed in Moscow, 1875. The work is unusual in having five movements. The "added" second movement, marked *alla tedesca,* is an homage to ROBERT SCHUMANN.

This Is the Army. Revue by IRVING BERLIN, 1942. This patriotic revue was produced shortly after America's entry into World War II. It sported the hit song *Oh! How I Hate to Get Up in the Morning,* derived from Berlin's World War I days.

PEOPLE IN MUSIC

Thomas, (Charles Louis) **Ambroise,** noted French composer and teacher; b. Metz, Aug. 5, 1811; d. Paris, Feb. 12, 1896. Thomas entered the Paris Conservatory in 1828, where he studied piano and harmony and accompaniment. He also later studied composition with Jean François Le Sueur at the Conservatory, where he won the Grand Prix de Rome with his CANTATA *Hermann et Ketty* in 1832.

After three years in Italy and a visit to Vienna, Thomas returned to Paris and applied himself with great energy to the composition of operas. In 1851 he was elected to the Académie, and in 1856 he became a professor of composition at the Paris Conservatory. In 1871 he became director there. In 1845 he was made a Chevalier of the Légion d'honneur, being the first composer to receive its Grand Croix in 1894.

As a composer of melodious French operas, Thomas was second only to CHARLES GOUNOD. His masterpiece was *Mignon,* which was staged in Paris in 1866. This opera was long a mainstay of the operatic repertory the world over, with nearly 2,000 performances in less than 100 years at the Opéra-Comique alone. Equally successful was his Shakespearean opera *Hamlet* from 1868.

Thomas wrote 17 *opéras-comique* and three operas, three ballets, orchestral music, chamber works, keyboard music, and secular and sacred vocal works, including a REQUIEM and *Messe solennelle*.

Thomas, Michael Tilson, greatly talented American conductor; b. Los Angeles, Dec. 21, 1944. A grandson of Boris and Bessie Thomashefsky, founders of the Yiddish Theater in N.Y., Thomas was brought up in a culturally sophisticated atmosphere. He studied at the University of Southern California, where he received instruction in composition with INGOLF DAHL. He also studied with the pianist JOHN CROWN and the harpsichordist ALICE EHLERS, concurrently taking courses in chemistry.

PEOPLE IN MUSIC

Thomas acquired conducting skills by practical work with the Young Musicians Foundation Debut Orchestra, which he led from 1963 to 1967. He served as pianist in the master classes of JASCHA HEIFETZ and GREGOR PIATIGORSKY at the University of Southern California in Los Angeles. He also conducted at the Monday Evening Concerts, giving first performances of works by IGOR STRAVINSKY, AARON COPLAND, PIERRE BOULEZ, and KARLHEINZ STOCKHAUSEN.

In 1966 Thomas attended master classes at the Bayreuth Festival. In 1967 he was assistant conductor to Boulez at the Ojai Festival, where he conducted again in 1968, 1969, and 1973. As a conducting fellow at Berkshire Music Center at Tanglewood in 1968, he won the Koussevitzky Prize. The crowning point of his early career was his appointment in 1969 as assistant conductor of the Boston Symphony Orchestra, the youngest person ever to receive such a distinction with that great ensemble. He was spectacularly catapulted into public notice that same year when he was called upon to conduct the second part of the N.Y. concert of the Boston Symphony Orchestra, substituting for its music director, WILLIAM STEINBERG, who was suddenly taken ill.

In 1970 Thomas was appointed associate conductor of the Boston Symphony Orchestra, and then was a principal guest conductor there with COLIN DAVIS from 1972 to 1974. From 1971 to 1979 he served as music director of the Buffalo Philharmonic Orchestra. He also served as music director of the N.Y. Philharmonic Young People's Concerts from 1971 to 1976. He was principal guest conductor of the Los Angeles Philharmonic Orchestra from 1981 to 1985.

From 1986 to 1989 Thomas was music director of the Great Woods Performing Arts Center in Mansfield, Massachusetts, the summer home of the Pittsburgh Symphony Orchestra. From 1987 he served as artistic advisor of the New World Symphony Orchestra in Miami, and in 1988 he became principal conductor of the London Symphony Orchestra. In 1993 he was named music director designate of the San Francisco Symphony, and in 1995 he stepped down from his position with the London Symphony Orchestra to take up his duties in San Francisco, although he remained a principal guest conductor in London. In 1993 he received the Alice M. Ditson Award for his services to American music. From 1994 he also served as music director of the Ojai (California) Festival.

Thomas's repertoire is exhaustive, ranging from the earliest masters to the avant-garde, with a special interest in American music. He is also an excellent pianist and a charismatic public speaker.

PEOPLE IN MUSIC

Thomas, Theodore (Christian Friedrich), renowned German-American conductor; b. Esens, East Friesland, Oct. 11, 1835; d. Chicago, Jan. 4, 1905. Taught by his father, a violinist, Thomas played publicly at age six. In 1845 the family emigrated to N.Y., where he soon began to play for dances and weddings and in theaters, helping to support his family.

In 1851 Thomas made a concert tour as a soloist, and in 1853 he joined Jullien's Orchestra on its visit to N.Y., later touring the country with JENNY LIND and other popular performers. He became a member of the N.Y. Philharmonic Society in 1854.

With the pianist WILLIAM MASON, Thomas founded a series of monthly matinee chamber concerts at N.Y.'s Dodworth Hall in 1855, which remained a vital force until it was disbanded in 1869. He first gained notice as a conductor when he led a performance of *La favorite* at the N.Y.

Academy of Music in 1859. In 1862 he led his first orchestra concerts at N.Y.'s Irving Hall, which became known as the Symphonic Soirées in 1864. They were continued at Steinway Hall from 1872 to 1878. In 1865 Thomas began a series of summer concerts in Terrace Garden, relocating them in 1868 to Central Park Garden.

The influence of these enterprises on local musical culture was enormous, and Thomas's programs attained European celebrity. The first tour with the Theodore Thomas Orchestra was made in 1869, and in subsequent years he led it on many tours of the U.S. and Canada.

In 1873 Thomas established the famous Cincinnati Biennial May Festival, which he conducted until his death. He also founded the Cincinnati College of Music, which he served as president and director from 1878 to 1880, having given up his own N.Y. orchestra and conductorship of the N.Y. Philharmonic Society to accept this post.

After resigning his position in Cincinnati in 1880, Thomas returned to N.Y., where he immediately reorganized his orchestra. He was also reelected conductor of the Philharmonic Society Orchestra and the Brooklyn Philharmonic Orchestra (having been its conductor in 1862–63, 1866–68, and 1873–78). Besides conducting these orchestras, he was at different times director of several choruses. From 1885 to 1887 he was conductor and artistic director of the American Opera Company.

In 1891 Thomas settled permanently in Chicago as conductor of the Chicago Orchestra. In recognition of his distinguished services, a permanent home, Orchestra Hall, was built there by popular subscription. It was formally opened in late 1904 with a series of festival concerts, the last directed by him. After his death the name of the orchestra was changed to the Theodore Thomas Orchestra in 1906. It became the Chicago Symphony Orchestra in 1912.

The influence of Thomas upon the musical development of the U.S. has been strong and lasting. An ardent champion of RICHARD WAGNER, FRANZ LISZT, and JOHANNES BRAHMS, he also gave first performances in America of works by PIOTR ILYICH TCHAIKOVSKY, ANTONÍN DVOŘÁK, ANTON RUBINSTEIN, ANTON BRUCKNER, RUBIN GOLDMARK, CAMILLE SAINT-SAËNS, SIR FREDERIC COWEN, SIR CHARLES VILLIERS STANFORD,

JOACHIM RAFF, and RICHARD STRAUSS. He likewise programmed many works by American composers.

PEOPLE IN MUSIC

Thompson, Randall, eminent American composer and pedagogue; b. N.Y., Apr. 21, 1899; d. Boston, July 9, 1984. Thompson was a member of an intellectual New England family. He studied at the Lawrenceville School in New Jersey, where his father was an English teacher, and began singing lessons and received rudimentary music training from the school's organist Francis Cuyler Van Dyck. When Van Dyck died, Thompson took over his organ duties in the school.

Upon graduation, Thompson went to Harvard University, taking his bachelor's degree in 1920 and his master's two years later. He also had private lessons in N.Y. with ERNST BLOCH in 1920–21. In 1922 he submitted his orchestral prelude *Pierrot and Cothurnus,* inspired by the poetic drama *Aria da Capo* by Edna St. Vincent Millay, for the American Prix de Rome, and received a grant for residence in Rome. He conducted it there at the Accademia di Santa Cecilia in 1923. Encouraged by its reception, he proceeded to compose industriously, for piano, voices, and orchestra.

Thompson returned to the U.S. in 1925. From 1927 to 1929 he taught at Wellesley College, and again from 1936 to 1937. In 1929 he was appointed a lecturer in music at Harvard University, and in 1929–30 he held a Guggenheim fellowship. His First Symphony had its premiere in Rochester, N.Y. in 1930, with HOWARD HANSON conducting. Two years later, Hanson conducted the first performance of Thompson's Second Symphony, destined to become one of the most successful symphonies by an American composer. It enjoyed repeated performances in the U.S. and Europe. Audiences found the work distinctly American in substance, with the unusual element of JAZZ rhythms in the score.

Equally American and appealing, although for entirely different reasons, was Thompson's CHORAL work *Americana.* He used as texts for this work selections from H. L. Mencken's satirical column in his journal *The American Mercury.* Another piece of Americana followed in 1936, the nostalgic *Peaceable Kingdom* for A CAPPELLA chorus, inspired by the painting of the same name by Edward Hicks. For it,

Thompson set biblical texts from the prophets. Another a cappella work, deeply religious in nature, was the Alleluia from 1940, which became a perennial favorite in the choral literature. It was first performed at Tanglewood, Massachusetts, at the inaugural session of the Berkshire Music Center that year.

In 1942 Thompson composed his most celebrated choral work, *The Testament of Freedom,* to words of Thomas Jefferson, which was first performed with piano accompaniment at the University of Virginia in 1943 (an orchestral version was presented by the Boston Symphony Orchestra two years later). With this work Thompson firmly established his reputation as one of the finest composers of choral music in America.

But Thompson did not limit himself to choral music. His first String Quartet in D Minor from 1941 was praised, as was his first opera, *Solomon and Balkis,* after Kipling's *The Butterfly That Stamped,* a parody on BAROQUE usages, broadcast over CBS in 1942.

In 1949 Thompson wrote his Third Symphony, presented in that year at the Festival of Contemporary American Music at Columbia University in N.Y. Subsequent works included the ballet *Jabberwocky* (1951); an orchestral piece, *A Trip to Nahant* (1954); Requiem (1958); another opera, *The Nativity According to St. Luke* (1961); *The Passion According to St. Luke* (1965); *The Place of the Blest,* a cantata (1969); and *A Concord Cantata* (1975). He also composed incidental music, chamber works including a second string quartet in 1967, secular and sacred vocal works, and solo songs.

During all this time Thompson did not neglect his educational activities. After teaching at the University of California at Berkeley, the Curtis Institute of Music in Philadelphia (serving as director from 1939 to 1941), the School of Fine Arts at the University of Virginia, and Princeton University, Thompson spent 17 years at Harvard University, where he retired as professor emeritus. He received numerous awards and honors.

In his compositions Thompson preserved and cultivated the melodious poetry of American speech, set in crystalline TONAL harmonies.

Thomson, Virgil (Garnett), many-faceted American composer of great originality and music critic of singular brilliance; b. Kansas City, Mo., Nov. 25, 1896; d. N.Y., Sept. 30, 1989. Thomson began piano lessons at age 12 with local teachers. He received organ instruction and played in local churches, and also took courses at a local junior college.

In 1920 Thomson entered Harvard University, where he studied orchestration with E. B. Hill and became assistant and accompanist to A.T. Davison, conductor of its Glee Club. He also studied piano with H. Gebhard and organ with W. Goodrich in Boston. In 1921 he went with the Glee Club to Europe, where he remained on a John Knowles Paine Traveling Fellowship to study organ and COUNTERPOINT with NADIA BOULANGER. Returning to Harvard in 1922, he was made organist and choirmaster at King's College. After graduating in 1923, he went to N.Y. to study conducting and counterpoint at the Juilliard Graduate School.

In 1925 Thomson returned to Paris, which remained his base until 1940. He established friendly contacts with groups of musicians, writers, and painters, including Gertrude Stein, an association that was particularly significant in the development of his aesthetic ideas. In his music he refused to follow any one modern theory, instead embracing the notion of popular universality. This allowed him to use the techniques of all ages and all degrees of simplicity or complexity, from simple TRIADIC harmonies to 12-TONE intricacies.

Thomson's most famous composition is the opera *4 Saints in 3 Acts,* to a LIBRETTO by Stein, in which the deliberate confusion wrought by the author (there are actually four acts and more than a dozen saints, some of them in duplicate) and the composer's solemn, hymnlike treatment, create a hilarious modern OPERA BUFFA. It was first introduced at Hartford, Connecticut, in 1934, characteristically announced as being under the auspices of the "Society of Friends and Enemies of Modern Music," a group that Thomson directed from 1934 to 1937. The work became an American classic, with constant revivals staged in America and Europe. Also well known are his two other operas, *The Mother of Us All,* also to a libretto by Stein, on the life of the American suffragette Susan B. Anthony (N.Y., May 7, 1947), and *Lord Byron* (1961–68; N.Y., April 13, 1972).

In 1940 Thomson returned to the U.S. to become music critic of the *New York Herald-Tribune*. Far from being routine journalism, Thomson's music reviews are minor masterpieces of literary brilliance and critical acumen. He resigned in 1954 to concentrate on composition and conducting.

Thomson received the Pulitzer Prize in music in 1948 for his score to the motion picture *Louisiana Story*. He also received the Légion d'Honneur in 1947, and in 1948 he was elected to the National Institute of Arts and Letters and in 1959 to the American Academy of Arts and Letters. In 1982 he received an honorary doctor of music degree from Harvard University. In 1983 he was awarded the Kennedy Center Honor for lifetime achievement. He received the Medal of Arts in 1988.

thoroughbass. *See* BASSO CONTINUO.

Three Blind Mice. This perennial popular children's song is probably the earliest printed nonreligious tune in music history. It was published in 1609 as a ROUND for three voices and is still sung in English-speaking countries.

Three Places in New England. Orchestral set by CHARLES IVES, 1903–14. The three places are the St. Gaudens Memorial in Boston Common, Putnam's Camp in Redding, Connecticut, and the Housatonic River at Stockbridge.

The work, one of the most important in American music, evokes memories of the Civil War; characteristically Ives quotes fragments of popular American hymns and ballads. The score itself represents a fantastic web of POLYTONAL and POLYRHYTHMIC combinations.

In 1930 Ives reduced the original score for performance by a chamber orchestra at the request of NICOLAS SLONIMSKY, who conducted its first performance in N.Y. in 1931, with his Chamber Orchestra of Boston. This REDUCTION became the standard of all subsequent performances until the rediscovery of the original score for large orchestra, published posthumously about 1980.

Three-Page Sonata. Piano piece by CHARLES IVES, 1905. It is so entitled for the obvious reason that the manuscript has only three pages. Ives marked at the point of RECAPITULATION: "Back to 1st Theme—all nice Sonatas must have 1st Theme."

Threepenny Opera, The. See *Dreigroschenoper, Die.*

three-step. The ordinary (Vienna) WALTZ.

Threni. CANTATA by IGOR STRAVINSKY, 1958, for solo voices, chorus, and orchestra, to the Latin text of the Lamentations of Jeremiah. As in *Canticum sacrum* and (to some extent) *Agon,* Stravinsky employed in this score some SERIAL devices. *Threni* (tears) was first performed in Venice.

threnody (from Grk. *thrēnōdia,* lamentation). Poem or musical work expressing grief for the dead. The classical *threnos* was organized in RITORNELLO form, a chorus alternating with solo passages.

Threnody in Memory of the Victims of Hiroshima. SYMPHONIC POEM by KRZYSZTOF PENDERECKI, 1959–66, for 52 solo strings. Compositional interest in MICROTONAL clusters and fluctuating blocks of sound arose in the 1950s, and this work made these techniques internationally known. It is a programmatic work that portrays the city of Hiroshima before, during, and after the dropping of the first atomic bomb in 1945. While the piece is a cornucopia of effects (the sound portrait of the airplane Enola Gay is particularly unnerving), its overall elegiac quality is most overwhelming.

through-composed (Ger. *durchkomponiert*). Attribute of a song with each STANZA written to a different accompaniment, or composed in a developmental, quasi-symphonic manner. As opposed to STROPHIC.

thrush. Old slang for a female singer, especially of popular songs, named after a COLORATURA triller among songbirds.

MUSICAL
INSTRUMENT

thunder machine (Ger. *Donnermaschine*). Device used to imitate thunder by rotating a barrel with pebbles inside, first used by RICHARD STRAUSS in his *Alpine Symphony* of 1915. There are few instances of its subsequent use, except for special effects in silent movie orchestras.

tibia (Lat.). The Greek AULOS, an ancient vertical flute. *Tibicen,* a flute player.

MUSICAL
INSTRUMENT

tie. A curved line joining two notes of like PITCH, to be sounded as one note equal to their combined TIME VALUE. *Tied notes:* 1. Notes joined by a tie. 2. Notes whose hooks (flags) are attached by one or more thick strokes (beams).

Tie a Yellow Ribbon 'Round the Ole Oak Tree. Annoying ditty recorded by Tony Orlando and Dawn, written in a pseudo-1920s style by Irwin Levine and L. Russell Brown. It was a No. 1 hit on its release in 1973. Later, when Americans were held hostage in Iran, yellow ribbons began appearing in remembrance of them. This practice has continued during other times of national strife.

tiento (from Sp. *tentar,* search). Iberian musical form popular in the late RENAISSANCE and early BAROQUE, comparable to the Italian solo RICERCAR. The tiento is less elaborate but developmentally freer. It was especially popular with composers of VIHUELA and keyboard music.

tierce de Picardi (Fr.). *See* PICARDY THIRD.

t'yĕrs duh pē-kar'dē

Till Eulenspiegel's Merry Pranks (*Till Eulenspiegels lustige Streiche*). SYMPHONIC POEM by RICHARD STRAUSS, 1895, first performed in Cologne. The title bears an amplifying tag line, *nach alter Schelmenweise* (After Old Rogues' Tales).

Till Eulenspiegel is a hero of many medieval folk tales who is blamed for a variety of practical jokes. In the score he is finally caught and pays the supreme penalty on the gallows. His angular mischievous MOTIVE is cut off at the drumstroke marking his hanging. This is followed by an epilogue repeating his original lyrical tune.

The surname *Eulenspiegel* means "owl glasses."

tăn-băhl'

MUSICAL
INSTRUMENT

timbales. Pair of pitched, single-headed cylindrical drums of shallow diameter, their plastic heads tuned by tension screws. Timbales are mostly associated with Latin American dance music but can be found in modern classical scores, sometimes in lieu of TIMPANI, although their sonority is far less substantial.

tăn′br **timbre** (Fr.). 1. TONE COLOR. 2. Small bell. *Jeu de timbres,* GLOCKENSPIEL.

timbrel (Hebr.). *See* TAMBOURINE.

time. The division of the MEASURE into equal fractional parts of a whole, thus regulating the ACCENTS and rhythmic flow of music. It is indicated by the TIME SIGNATURE.

There are two major classes of time: DUPLE and TRIPLE. In *duple time* the number of beats per measure is divisible by two; in *triple time,* by three. There are also two subclasses, COMPOUND DUPLE TIME and COMPOUND TRIPLE TIME. In the former, each of the two beats contains a dotted note (or its equivalent) wholly divisible by three; in the latter not only is each beat divisible by three, but the number of beats in each measure is divisible by three.

time signature (Ger. *Taktzeichen*). The indication of the number of a specific NOTE VALUE in a MEASURE. This sign is always found at the beginning of the composition and at any point within the piece that the number of notes or the note value used changes.

Thus, $\frac{4}{4}$ indicates four beats (the first number, or numerator) at a quarter note per beat (the second number, or denominator). The actual sign is written as a vertical fraction without dividing line. The denominator is always a multiple of two (2, 4, 8, 16, etc.), as are the note values themselves.

Although some traditional associations exist, the time signature does not determine TEMPO, which requires a verbal or metronomic indication. For example, many CLASSIC slow movements are written in extremely rapid values (at least 16th notes, sometimes 32nd, 64th, or even 128th notes). This probably saves paper but also conveys a visual sense of unusually long phrases.

Some alternate time signatures—c and C—are remnants of MENSURAL notation, when the first signature meant *tempus imperfectum* and the second referred to a proportional diminution further explicated by a figure. When used today, these symbols are called *common time* ($\frac{4}{4}$) and *cut time* ($\frac{2}{4}$), respectively. There are two principal classes of time: DUPLE and TRIPLE (see TIME).

time-bracket notation. A type of highly flexible NOTATION developed by JOHN CAGE in his mature works (NUMBER PIECES) wherein time lengths are left largely to the discretion of the performer.

In the following example the performer is instructed to (1) begin playing the excerpt at any time between the first pair of bracketed times, and to (2) end playing the excerpt at any time between the second pair of bracketed times:

[00′00″– 00′15″] [00′30″– 01′00″]

While fully notated, no two performances of such a work can ever sound exactly the same.

Times They Are A-Changin', The. Quintessential social-protest song of the '60s, written by BOB DYLAN in 1963.

timpani (It., kettledrums, sometimes spelled *tympani;* Fr. *timbale, timballe;* Ger. *Pauken*). A large orchestral drum consisting of a hollow brass or copper hemisphere (the kettle) resting on a tripod. The top of the drum was originally covered with a treated animal hide. The head is now made of

tim′păh-nē

MUSICAL
INSTRUMENT

◀

Timpani. (The Selmer Company)

vellum stretched by means of an iron ring and tightened by a set of screws or by cords and braces. The instrument dates to the 6th century as a shallow *bowl drum* in the Middle East, arriving in Europe in the late Middle Ages.

The timpani are the only standard MEMBRANOPHONES in the orchestra capable of producing a definite PITCH. Originally the drums were played in pairs, the larger yielding any tone from F_0 to c^0, and the smaller from $B\flat_0$ to f^0. Its music is now written at actual pitch. In CLASSIC symphonies and overtures the timpani are usually played in pairs, tuned to the main TONIC and DOMINANT.

In the older instruments the screws around the rim increase or relax the tension of the membrane so that the pitch can be regulated accordingly. Modern timpani are equipped with pedals that can change the pitch with greater precision. These developments led to a genuinely CHROMATIC type of instrument.

In the 19th century the number of timpani in the orchestra increased. RICHARD WAGNER's *RING* requires four. HECTOR BERLIOZ, in his passion for grandiosity, scored the Tuba Mirum in his *Grande Messe des Morts* for 16. Uncommon TUNING is found in LUDWIG VAN BEETHOVEN's symphonies. Particularly remarkable is the tuning in an octave F to F in the SCHERZO of his Ninth Symphony, where it is applied antiphonally. A foreboding OSTINATO on a solo timpano bridges the transition from the scherzo to the finale in his Fifth Symphony.

The indication *timpani coperti* (covered) is synonymous with *timpani sordi* (muted), an effect achieved by covering the head with a piece of fabric.

Modern composers are apt to write timpani parts requiring acrobatic virtuosity in manipulating several instruments, playing on the rim, producing a terraced GLISSANDO with the chromatic pedals, retuning while performing a rapid TRILL, etc. Solo timpani occur in many modern works, and there are even timpani concertos. Alexander Tcherepnin composed a Sonatina for timpani and piano. JOHN VINCENT's *Symphonic Poem after Descartes* opens with a timpani solo in the rhythm of the Cartesian maxim *Cogito ergo sum* (I think therefore I am). The American composer and percussion virtuoso WILLIAM KRAFT composed a Timpani Concerto which was premiered in Indianapolis in 1984.

tin ear. Lack of musicality or appropriate responsiveness to music.

Tin Pan Alley. Colorful name for an area along Broadway in N.Y. where popular songwriters worked in great numbers, hoping to produce the latest hit or successful musical.

The term dates from the beginning of the century. The district moved geographically with the times, following the theaters' move uptown. Beginning around Union Square (14th Street), it moved first to 28th Street and then, after World War I, to the Brill Building (50th Street, also central to the advertising world).

The term has come to be associated with anything connected with the commercial and assembly-line elements of popular song as late as the 1960s.

tin whistle. Small, high-pitched, end-blown WHISTLE FLUTE, made of metal. It is also called *pennywhistle*. It is used as a traditional melody instrument, notably in the Irish-Scottish-British islands.

MUSICAL INSTRUMENT

tinnitus. Sustained pressure on the auditory nerve, causing a persistent ringing in the cochlea in the inner ear. Some believe it is caused by prolonged exposure to loud noise.

Some famous musicians who have suffered from the disease include:

> ROBERT SCHUMANN, who experienced it during the final stages of his mental illness (he heard a relentless drone on high A♭).

> BEDŘICH SMETANA, who suffered a similar aural disturbance, but the note he heard was high E, and he too eventually went insane. He introduced this sustained note in the violin part at the end of his First String Quartet, significantly entitled *From My Life*.

> PETE TOWNSHEND of the WHO, whose suffering from this disease led him to abandon touring with an electric ROCK group.

Some auditory specialists have speculated that teenagers who listen to music through headphones for long periods of time, at great volume, may be at risk of developing this disease.

**MUSICAL
INSTRUMENT**

PEOPLE IN MUSIC

---

tintinnabulum (Lat.). Since antiquity, a single or set of graduated bells. Also, the hammer it is struck with, or the clapper found in later exemplars.

Tiomkin, Dimitri, Uktainian-born American composer of film music; b. Poltava, May 10, 1894; d. London, Nov. 11, 1979. Tiomkin studied COMPOSITION with ALEXANDER GLAZUNOV and piano with FELIX BLUMENFELD and ISABELLE VENGEROVA at the St. Petersburg Conservatory.

In 1921 Tiomkin went to Berlin, where he studied with FERRUCCIO BUSONI and EGON PETRI. He was soloist in FRANZ LISZT's First Piano Concerto with the Berlin Philharmonic in 1924, the same year he gave concerts with Michael Khariton in Paris. He appeared in VAUDEVILLE in the U.S. in 1925, becoming a citizen in 1937. In 1938 he made his conducting debut with the Los Angeles Philharmonic. He later conducted his music with various U.S. orchestras. He married Albertina Rasch, a ballerina, for whose troupe he wrote music.

From 1930 to 1970 Tiomkin wrote over 150 film scores, including several for the U.S. War Department. His film music betrayed his strong Russian ROMANTIC background, tempered with American JAZZ. He received many honorary degrees and awards, including three Oscars for best score (*High Noon,* 1952; *The High and the Mighty,* 1954; *The Old Man and the Sea,* 1958) and a Golden Globe.

típico. Generic term for Latin American traditional music.

tiple (from Lat. *triplum,* treble). Generic term for several high-pitched instruments: the *guitarillo* of the Canary Islands; a small Spanish guitar (also called *timple*); the Cuban BANDURRIA, a small plucked instrument of medieval Spanish origin; and the treble *chirimía,* a Catalan SHAWM.

Tipperary. British song with uncertain authorship, c.1912. It was long associated with World War I, but it may have originally referred to the endless spate of colonial wars in which Great Britain was involved. It is believed that a music hall performer named Jack Judge helped compose the song.

Tippett, (Sir) **Michael** (Kemp), greatly renowned English composer; b. London, Jan. 2, 1905; d. there, Jan. 8, 1998. His family was of Cornish descent, and Tippett never refrained from proclaiming his pride of Celtic ancestry. He was equally emphatic in the liberal beliefs of his family. His father was a freethinker who ran a successful hotel business. His mother was a suffragette who once served a prison term. Her last name was Kemp, which Tippett eventually adopted as his own middle name.

Michael Tippett (seated at piano) with conductor Adrian Boult, 1958. (Hulton-Deutsch Collection/Corbis)

Tippett took piano lessons as a child and sang in his school chorus but showed no exceptional merit as a performer. He studied in London at the Royal College of Music from 1923 to 1928, where his teachers in COMPOSITION were Charles Wood and C.H. Kitson. He also took piano lessons there with Aubin Raymar, attended courses in CONDUCTING with ADRIAN BOULT and MALCOLM SARGENT and studied COUNTERPOINT and FUGUE with R.O. Morris from 1930 to 1932.

Tippett subsequently held several positions as a teacher and conductor. From 1933 to 1940 he led the South London Orchestra at Morley College, where he also served as director of music until 1951.

Tippett dissented from the social status quo from the outset. He openly proclaimed extremely liberal political views, atheism, and pacifism. His best-known work, the oratorio *A Child of Our Time* (1939–41), was inspired by the case of Henschel Grynspan, a 17-year-old refugee Jew who responded to his parents' persecution by assassinating a member of the Paris German embassy in 1938 (this act led to a major Nazi drive against the Jews).

Tippett's powerful, personal, and symbolic response to this event became the model for later compositions, particularly the eclectic yet archetypal use of African-American spirituals. As a conscientious objector he refused to serve even in a noncombatant capacity in the British military forces. For this he was sentenced to prison for three months during 1943. He served his term in a Surrey County jail with the suggestive name Wormwood Scrubs.

Because he was willing to stand for his beliefs (others simply left Britain until the war ended), Tippett never lost the respect of the community. In 1951 he initiated a series of broadcasts for the BBC, and from 1969 to 1974 he directed the Bath Festival. He received high honors from the British government: in 1959 he was named a Commander of the Order of the British Empire, in 1966 he was knighted, and in 1979 he was made a Companion of Honour.

Tippett visited the U.S. in 1965, and thereafter was a frequent guest in America. His symphonic works were performed by major American orchestras, often under his baton.

Tippett's works have a grandeur of ROMANTIC inspiration that sets them apart from most other contemporary music. He has created singing, flowing melodies, free from sentimentality. He excelled in large-scale vocal and instrumental forms. Tippett was a master of modern forms, evolving from a contrapuntal NEOCLASSICISM in the 1930s to heights of DISSONANT COUNTERPOINT without losing a basic sense of KEY SIGNATURE.

A man of great general culture, Tippett possessed a fine literary gift and an interest in Jungian psychology. He wrote his own LIBRETTOS. His compositions include seven operas (among them *The Midsummer Marriage,* 1946–52, *King Priam,* 1958–61; *The Knot Garden,* 1966–69, with the first appearance of openly gay operatic characters; *The Ice Break,* 1973–76, and *New Year,* 1986–88); four numbered symphonies (1945; 1956–57; with soprano, 1970–72; 1977); concertos for double string orchestra (1938–39), piano (1953–55; 1956), orchestra (1963), and violin, viola, and cello (1980); and *Water out of Sunlight* for strings (1988).

Tippett also did not shun special effects. Three times in his Fourth Symphony he injects episodes of heavy glottal aspiration meant to suggest the human life cycle.

His chamber works include five string quartets (1935–91), five piano SONATAS (1938–84), Sonata for Four Horns (1955), *The Blue Guitar* for guitar (1983), and *Prelude Autumn* for oboe and piano (1991). He also composed keyboard pieces, as well as vocal works for groups and soloists.

tirata (It.; Fr. *tirade, coulade*). Ornamental scalar passage or ARPEGGIO improvised to fill gaps between MELODY NOTES.

A tirata spanning the INTERVAL of an OCTAVE was a *tirata perfecta,* that of a fourth or fifth, a *tirata mezza;* and that of an interval greater than an octave, a *tirata aucta* (augmented).

Titan Symphony. GUSTAV MAHLER's original name for his First Symphony, 1883–88. Mahler later disavowed the association and also removed from the five-movement work its second movement (called *Blumine*). It was only put back in place for "completist" performances starting in the 1960s.

The composer treated the four-movement work as a SYMPHONIC POEM in two parts, the first being described by Mahler as *From the Days of Youth* and the second as *Commediate umana* (human drama, as opposed to Dante's *Divina commedia*). The main subject corresponds to the melody of the second song of Mahler's cycle *Lieder eines fahrenden Gesellen* (Songs of a Wayfarer, 1883–85), while the third movement is an eerie funeral march. The symphony was first performed in Budapest, 1889.

titles. In classical music, titles of compositions usually describe the form and content of the work. Such genres and forms as SYMPHONY, SONATA, PRELUDE, CANTATA, and OPERA may have been changeable through the centuries of their evolution. Thus *sinfonia* meant any instrumental composition or an orchestral interlude in an opera. Only in the 18th century did it acquire the meaning of a symphony in the modern sense of the word.

But the advent of ROMANTIC music made the problem of suitable titles acute. Time and again composers would assign a programmatic title to a work, only to repudiate it at a later time for fear that the music would be interpreted as ancillary to the story implied. What can be more programmatically explicit than LUDWIG VAN BEETHOVEN's *Pastoral* Symphony, with its realistic storm and three bird calls? Yet on second thought Beethoven carefully marked the score *Mehr Ausdruck der Empfindung als Malerei* (more an expression of feeling than [a] depiction).

GUSTAV MAHLER's overheated Romantic imagination prompted him to give all kinds of specific titles not only to most of his symphonies but also to individual movements. Later, however, he denied any such programmatic implications. So emphatic was he in his renunciation that when he was questioned about the meaning of one of his symphonies at a banquet he raised his glass as if for a toast and exclaimed, "Pereat den Programmen!" (Down with programs!).

Such repudiations are particularly baffling when a literary work lies at the foundation of a composition. HECTOR BERLIOZ boldly transplanted his early overture *Les Francs-juges* into the *Symphonie fantastique,* where it became a *March to the Scaffold.* To unify it with the rest of the symphony he inserted a couple of bars of the IDÉE FIXE, the common theme of the work. He did even better: in order to save the labor of recopying the old overture, he pasted the idée fixe onto the old manuscript, replacing a bar of rests.

A fascinating instance of a composer's decision to affix new programmatic titles is illustrated by ARNOLD SCHOENBERG's *Five Orchestral Pieces* of 1909. In the original they bore abstract titles without programmatic content. But 40 years later, yielding to his publisher's suggestion that he "humanize" the titles, he agreed to change the title of the third piece, *The Changing Chord,* to *Summer Morning by the Lake.*

ALEXANDER SCRIABIN's work titles are often mystical, and he was often willing to entertain suggestions from his close intellectual associates. It was his brother-in-law, Boris de Schloezer, who suggested that the opening motive of his Third Symphony, *Le Poème divin,* is a proclamation of self-assertion: "I am!" This notation appears in the final manuscript and published score. And it was Modest Tchaikovsky, the brother of the composer, who suggested the name *PATHÉTIQUE* for his Sixth Symphony.

To what lengths will a composer go to hide an initial programmatic intent? IGOR STRAVINSKY's *Scherzo Fantastique*

> FELIX MENDELSSOHN'S *FINGAL'S CAVE,* inspired by his visit to northern Scotland in 1829, was originally entitled *The Solitary Island.*

from 1909 was inspired by Maurice Maeterlinck's half-literary, half-scientific essay *Les Abeilles* (The bees). Each section of the score corresponds to a beehive event: birth of the queen, nuptial flight, swarming, etc. The publishers quoted from the book in the score, and Maeterlinck, a hot-tempered poet, promptly sued Stravinsky for infringement of copyright. Fifty years later, Stravinsky denied ever intending to use the Maeterlinck book as a programmatic source. But his own 1907 letter to NIKOLAI RIMSKY-KORSAKOV, not to mention the score itself, plainly contradicts this!

To Anacreon in Heaven. Song by J.S. Stafford, first published in London, c.1780. The original lyrics were a whimsical glorification of the Greek poet Anacreon, famous for his odes to love and wine. The melody was adapted to the poem *The Star-Spangled Banner* by Francis Scott Key (first part written 1814) sometime later in the 19th century. It has been the official U.S. national anthem since 1931.

To Know Him Is to Love Him. A 1958 hit for the Teddy Bears, written by a group member, Phil Spector. Spector later enjoyed a successful career as the creator of "teen symphonies" for groups like the Ronettes. The title comes from Spector's father's tombstone.

toccata (from It. *toccare,* strike, touch; *toccatina,* short toccata). A virtuoso KEYBOARD composition exploiting the articulation possible with these instruments: free and bold in style, consisting of runs and passages alternating with fugal or contrapuntal work, with a flowing, animated, and rapid movement.

    tŏhk-kah′täh

In the 16th century the term was understood widely to mean a PRELUDE or an IMPROVISATION before the composition proper, particularly in organ playing. In the 17th century the toccata assumed a more precise definition as a keyboard composition in a rapid tempo, in steady rhythm (in the works of GIROLAMO FRESCOBALDI, JOHANN JAKOB FROBERGER, JAN PIETERSZOON SWEELINCK, ANTONIO SCARLATTI, and JOHANN SEBASTIAN BACH). In the 19th and 20th centuries, ROBERT SCHUMANN, CHARLES WIDOR, LOUIS VIERNE, CLAUDE DEBUSSY, MAURICE RAVEL, SERGEI PROKO-

FIEV, FERRUCCIO BUSONI, and MAX REGER wrote toccatas marked by brilliant technical display.

tŏhk-kah′tŏh

toccato (It.). In the 17th century, the bass line of a trumpet FANFARE, often "touched" (played) on the TIMPANI.

PEOPLE IN MUSIC

Toch, Ernst, eminent Austrian-born American composer and teacher; b. Vienna, Dec. 7, 1887; d. Los Angeles, Oct. 1, 1964. Toch's father was a Jewish dealer in unprocessed leather, and there were no other musicians in the family. Toch began playing piano in his grandmother's pawnshop. He learned notation from a local violinist and copied WOLFGANG AMADEUS MOZART's string quartets for practice. Using them as models, he began composing chamber music. At age 17, his Sixth String Quartet, op.12 (1905), was performed by the famous Rosé Quartet in Vienna. From 1906 to 1909 he studied medicine at the University of Vienna.

In 1909 Toch won the prestigious Mozart Prize and a scholarship to study at the Frankfurt Conservatory. In 1910 he was awarded the Mendelssohn Prize. He also won the Austrian State Prize four times in a row. In 1913 he was appointed instructor in piano at the Hochschule für Musik in Mannheim. From 1914 to 1918 he served in the Austrian army. After the Armistice he returned to Mannheim, resumed his career, and became active in the modern movement. He soon attained, along with PAUL HINDEMITH, ERNST KRENEK, and others, a prominent position in the new German school of composition. He also completed his education at the University of Heidelberg, earning his Ph.D. in 1921.

In 1929 Toch moved to Berlin, establishing himself as pianist, composer, and pedagogue. In 1932 he made an American tour as a pianist playing his own works. He returned to Berlin, but with the advent of the Nazi regime he was forced to leave Germany in 1933. He went to Paris, then to London, and in 1935 he emigrated to the U.S. He gave music lectures at the New School for Social Research in N.Y. In 1936 he moved to Hollywood, where he wrote music for films. He became an American citizen in 1940.

In 1940–41 Toch taught composition at the University of Southern California. He then taught privately, numbering among his many students ANDRÉ PREVIN. From 1950 until his death Toch traveled frequently and lived in Vienna, Zurich, the MacDowell Colony in New Hampshire, and Santa Monica, California.

Toch's music is rooted in the tradition of the German and Austrian ROMANTIC movement of the 19th century, but his study of the classics made him aware of the importance of formal logic in thematic development. His early works consist mostly of chamber music and solo piano pieces. During his German period he wrote several pieces for the stage in the light manner of sophisticated entertainment. He also composed effective piano works of a virtuosic quality, which enjoyed considerable popularity among pianists of the time.

Toch possessed a fine wit and sense of exploration. His *Geographical Fugue* for speaking chorus (1930), articulating in syllabic counterpoint the names of exotic places, became a classic of its genre.

It was not until 1950 that Toch wrote his first full-fledged symphony, but from then on until his death of stomach cancer he composed fully seven symphonies, plus sinfoniettas for wind and string orchestra. He was greatly interested in new techniques; the theme of his last String Quartet (No. 13, 1953) is based on a 12-TONE ROW. In the score of his Third Symphony he introduced an optional instrument, the *hisser*, a tank of carbon dioxide that produced a hissing sound through a valve.

Toch's other works include three operas, notably *Die Prinzessin auf der Erbse* (The princess and the pea; Baden-Baden, 1927), works for orchestra, chamber works including 13 string quartets, piano pieces, and vocal works.

Among the honors Toch received were the Pulitzer Prize in music for his Third Symphony (1956), membership in the National Institute of Arts and Letters (1957), and the Cross of Honor for Sciences and Art from the Austrian government (1963). An Ernst Toch Archive was founded at the University of California, Los Angeles, in 1966, serving as a depository for his manuscripts.

Tod und Verklärung. See DEATH AND TRANSFIGURATION.

Todesgesang (*Todeslied;* Ger.). A DIRGE, or a musical composition commemorating the dead.

tŏh′des-gĕ-sang^k
tŏh′des-lēt

In 1920 several French composers contributed pieces to a collection entitled *Tombeau de Debussy.*

tombeau (Fr., gravestone). An instrumental composition dedicated to the memory of a dignitary or friend.

A musical tombeau may also be found under other guises: *planctus* or *lachrymae* (Lat.), *dirge, threnody, elegy, dump,* or *tears* (Eng.), *déploration* or *apothéose* (Fr.), and *lamento* (It.). The same function of reverential remembrance is expressed by the term *homage,* as in *Hommage à Rameau* by CLAUDE DEBUSSY and *Homage to Ives* by AARON COPLAND.

Tombeau de Couperin, Le. Piano SUITE by MAURICE RAVEL, 1914–17, with four of its six movements orchestrated and presented in Paris, 1920. A tribute to FRANÇOIS COUPERIN, the work uses BAROQUE SUITE movements. It is a relatively early example of NEOCLASSICISM.

MUSICAL
INSTRUMENT

tom-tom. Generic term for African, Asian, or Latin American indigenous drums, of high but (usually) indefinite PITCH. The instrument(s) may be played with hands or sticks. In addition to their use in traditional music they are found in JAZZ, popular, and dance bands, and PERCUSSION-oriented scores.

tohn

Ton (Ger.). TONE; KEY; MODE; PITCH; DIATONIC SCALE.
Tonart, key (tonality); *Tonbild* (tonal picture), SYMPHONIC POEM; *Tondichtung* (tonal poetry); symphonic poem (preferred by RICHARD STRAUSS); *Tondichter,* composer (ROMANTIC era).

tŏh-nah′tăh

tonada (Sp.). A Spanish SONG or dance song, in $\frac{3}{4}$, $\frac{6}{8}$, or both, also adopted in Latin America. Several tonadas have been written by classical composers. Its Portuguese equivalent is *toada.*

tŏh-nah-dē′ya

tonadilla (Sp.). A Spanish theater piece of a light character with folk MELORHYTHMS. It was originally a SONG (little

TONADA) placed in the interludes of spoken plays. It is an 18th-century predecessor of the ZARZUELA.

tonal. Pertaining to TONES, or to a tone, MODE, or KEY. *Tonal imitation,* imitation within the key of a composition (nonmodulating imitation).

tonal answer. An answer to the SUBJECT in a FUGUE, in which the TONIC is answered by the DOMINANT and the dominant is answered by the tonic, thus altering the intervallic content of the THEME.

tonal aura. A coloristic effect, such as that created by playing below the BRIDGE of stringed instruments, fluttertongue on the flute, GLISSANDO on the French horn, or particularly unsettling rumblings in the bass trombone.

ARNOLD SCHOENBERG's score *Begleitungsmusik zu einer Lichtspielszene* contains striking instances of musical aura, beginning with the sections marked *Threatening Danger* and *Fear* and culminating in the finale, *Catastrophe.*

tonality. A cumulative concept that embraces all pertinent elements of tonal structure, including melodic and harmonic elements that determine the collective tonal relations, i.e., a basic loyalty to a tonal center. The term itself is relatively new, having originated in France about 1820, but it was universally adopted.

Tonality does not require continuous allegiance. That is, a piece may MODULATE widely from the outset and travel far from the original KEY, and yet adhere to the sense of tonality as long as it follows the tonal structure. The guardian of tonality is the KEY SIGNATURE, and no matter how many times this signature is changed during a given composition, the sense of tonality remains as long as each individual section is cast in a definite key.

The opposite of tonality is ATONALITY.

tonarium. Catalogue of medieval CHANTS, usually organized according to the principal eight TONES of Gregorian chant, including ANTIPHONS, COMMUNIONS, INTROITS, and RESPONSORIES.

tone. 1. Definite PITCH, as opposed to pitchless NOISE. 2. WHOLE TONE; MAJOR SECOND. *Half tone,* MINOR or CHROMATIC second; SEMITONE. 3. TIMBRE; TONE QUALITY.

tone clusters. A row of adjacent tones played at once. These clusters are usually played on the piano. Small tone clusters can be performed on the piano KEYBOARD with fists or the palm of the hand. Extensive tone clusters of two octaves or more require the entire forearm, from fists to elbow.

The technique was first demonstrated publicly by HENRY COWELL at the San Francisco Music Club in 1912 on the day after his 15th birthday. The term itself was invented by Cowell six years later. He applied them systematically in many of his compositions, such as *Amiable Conversations* for piano, in which DIATONIC clusters are used in the right hand on white keys and PENTATONIC clusters are used in the left hand on the black keys. Cowell notated tone clusters with a thick black line on a stem for rapid notes or a white-note rod attached to a stem for half-notes.

The idea of a cluster is not entirely new. Composers of BATTAGLIA applied them using the palm of the hand, mostly in the bass, to imitate a cannon shot. A curious piano piece called *Alpine Storm* by the German-American composer George Kunkel (1840–1923) specifies the use of the left palm to simulate the effect of thunder. (The work is dedicated "to my son, Ludwig van Beethoven Kunkel.")

Independently of Cowell, CHARLES IVES employed tone clusters to illustrate the "celestial railroad" in the *Hawthorne* movement of his *Concord Sonata,* produced by gently pressing a wooden plank down on the keys in the treble to create sympathetic vibrations. BÉLA BARTÓK used tone clusters to be played by the palm in his Second Piano Concerto, a device borrowed expressly from Cowell, with his permission.

tone color (TIMBRE; Ger. *Klangfarben*). An often subjective description of musical sound quality, using adjectives such as penetrating, dry, nasal, liquid, etc. The peculiar tone color of a musical instrument or human voice depends on the relative strength of harmonics produced by the fundamental tone. The same PITCH produced on one instrument differs as much from one produced on another instrument as the tone color of the voice of one person differs from that of another.

The tone color of the flute is perceived as the purest of all instrument-generated tones because its distribution of harmonics approaches a sine wave. The clarinet, on the other hand, generates a harmonic series characterized by odd-numbered harmonics. The oboe owes its penetrating sound to harmonics of practically the same mutual strength. The harmonics of STRING instruments are also abundant in all registers.

ANTON WEBERN introduced the idea of a scale of tone colors, so that a succession of identical pitches on different instruments would form a scale he called the *Klangfarbe scale*.

tone poem. *See* SYMPHONIC POEM.

tone quality. *See* TONE COLOR.

tone row (Ger. REIHE). The fundamental subject in a 12-TONE composition.

tongue. 1.(*noun*) Reed. 2. To use the tongue in producing, modifying, or interrupting the output of most wind instruments. *See* TONGUING.

tonguing. Production of tone effects on WIND instruments with the aid of the tongue.

Single tonguing, effect obtained by the repeated tongue thrust to the position of the nearly inaudible consonant *t* or *d*; *double tonguing*, that obtained by the repetition of *t k*; *triple tonguing*, that obtained by *t k t*; etc.

tonic. The first NOTE (KEYNOTE) of a SCALE.

Tonic accent, in CHANT, unaccompanied cantillation, and in recitation, a prosodic stress on a long vowel or a syllable on a higher PITCH; *tonic chord*, the triad on the keynote; *tonic pedal*, PEDAL POINT on the keynote; *tonic section*, a complete sentence or longer passage in the opening key of a composition, with a CADENCE in that key before the piece proceeds.

tonic sol-fa (Ger. *Tonika-do*). A method of teaching vocal music, invented by Sarah Ann Glover of Norwich, England, about 1812. It is based on the MOVABLE DO system and uses the syllables Doh, Ray, Me, Fah, Soh, and Lah, adapted from the GUIDONIAN ALPHABET (with Te added for the leading tone).

This system, widely accepted in English-speaking countries, has the unfortunate consequence of divorcing the absolute sound from its adopted name. In all Latin countries and Russia, the FIXED DO method is used. In that system, Do is immovable and always designates the sound of PITCH class C.

Tonight We Love. Song, 1941, borrowed directly and unscrupulously from PIOTR ILYICH TCHAIKOVSKY's First Piano Concerto.

Tonmalerei (Ger., tone painting). Musical depiction or illustration. The realization of programmatic ideas in sound.

tono (*tuono;* It.). 1. TONE, PITCH. 2. WHOLE TONE. 3. KEY; MODE. *Primo tono, secondo tono,* etc., designations of ecclesiastical modes.

tonus (1) (Lat.). Chant RECITATION.
Tonus ad introitum, INTROIT reciting TONE; *tonus psalmorum,* PSALM reciting tone.

tonus (2). In the Middle Ages, a MODE. In the 16th century, a system of 12 modes, comprising six AUTHENTIC and six PLAGAL. The DORIAN MODE became the commonly accepted prototype and was called *primus tonus;* its plagal derivative, the Hypodorian, the *secundus tonus.* The PHRYGIAN MODE was called *tertius tonus,* and so forth. The complete theory of the tonus was expounded upon by Henricus Glareanus in his treatise *Dodecachordon* (12 modes), of 1547. The 11th tonus, IONIAN, is equivalent to the modern C-MAJOR scale.

Gioseffo Zarlino reordered the modes in his *Istitutioni harmoniche* published in 1558. He placed the Ionian mode at the head of the list, thus anticipating the coronation of the C-major scale as the fundamental tonal progression of

Someone in Hollywood published a song in response to the success of *Tonight We Love* entitled *Everybody's Making Money but Tchaikovsky.*

modern times. To fill out the DIATONIC scale the LOCRIAN and LYDIAN modes were added later, with the range from B to B and F to F, respectively.

tonus peregrinus (Lat., wandering mode). An irregular PSALM tone whose RECITATION NOTE changes in mid-chant. It is associated with Psalm 113, *In exitu Israel de Aegypto,* hence the name (referring to pilgrims). The wandering MODE is first mentioned as the "9th mode" in the 10th century.

torch song. American slang for a ballad of lovelorn lamentation, usually sung by a female singer with heart-wrenching CADENZAS. Musically, this is a song of the BLUES, if rarely in true blues MODE. (Many TIN PAN ALLEY blues have as little to do with BESSIE SMITH as *Alexander's Ragtime Band* has to do with SCOTT JOPLIN.)

Torch songs evolved in the SWING ERA as an outgrowth of urban blues. Pop singers like CARLY SIMON and LINDA RONSTADT helped revive interest in these songs in the '70s and '80s.

Toreador Song. The popular designation of Escamillo's entrance song in GEORGES BIZET's *CARMEN,* 1875. Alas, there is no such word as toreador in Spanish. A bullfighter is a *torero,* and the correct term for the man who actually kills the bull in the ring is *matador.*

Torke, Michael, American composer and pianist; b. Milwaukee, Sept. 22, 1961. Torke studied composition with Joseph Schwantner and piano at the Eastman School of Music in Rochester, N.Y., graduating in 1984. He then completed composition studies with Martin Bresnick and Jacob Druckman at the Yale University School of Music in 1984–85. Torke won the Prix de Rome and held a residency at the American Academy in Rome in 1986.

Torke's output reveals an effective blend of serious music, JAZZ, and ROCK elements. He is best known for his "color works":

The Yellow Pages for flute, clarinet, violin, cello, and piano (1984)

The name "torch song" is taken from the expression "to carry a torch," i.e., to care deeply for someone unattainable.

PEOPLE IN MUSIC

Ecstatic Orange, ballet for orchestra (1985)

Bright Blue Music for orchestra (1985)

Verdant Music for orchestra (1985)

Purple for orchestra (1987)

Black & White, ballet (1988)

Copper for brass quintet and orchestra (1988)

Ash for orchestra or chamber orchestra (1989)

Slate, ballet for concertante group and orchestra (1989)

Rush for piano and winds (1989)

Chalk for string quartet (1992)

Torke's other works include *Vanada* for brass, keyboards, and percussion (1984), *Adjustable Wrench* for chamber ensemble (1987), Saxophone Concerto (1993), and *Nylon* for guitar and chamber orchestra (1994). He also composed a television opera, *King of Hearts* (1993).

PEOPLE IN MUSIC

Tormé (born Torme), **Mel**(vin Howard), much beloved American singer and composer of popular music; b. Chicago, Sept. 13, 1925; d. Beverly Hills, June 5, 1999. At age four, Torme began singing with the Coon-Sanders band at a Chicago restaurant. He studied piano and drums, then sang with various bands and acted in radio soap operas from 1934 to 1940. After touring as a singer, drummer, and arranger with the Chico Marx band in 1942–43, he appeared in films and with his own vocal swing ensemble, the Mel-Tones.

Following World War II army service, Tormé launched a prominent career as a pop and jazz vocalist, performing in nightclubs, on radio and television, and on recordings. He won two successive Grammy Awards for best male jazz vocalist for his albums *An Evening with George Shearing and Mel Tormé* (1983) and *Top Drawer* (also with Shearing, 1984). He also appeared as soloist and conductor with several symphony orchestras, including San Francisco and Dallas.

In 1980 Mayor Tom Bradley proclaimed Mel Tormé Week in Los Angeles in commemoration of his 50th anniversary in show business. Among his more than 300 songs, *The Christmas Song* (1946) has become a holiday favorite.

Tormis, Veljo, Estonian composer; b. Kuusalu near Tallinn, Aug. 7, 1930. Tormis studied organ and choral conducting at the Tallinn Music Institute from 1943 to 1951, organ and composition at the Tallinn Conservatory during 1951, and composition with Vissarion Shebalin at the Moscow Conservatory from 1951 to 1956. He taught at the Tallinn Music Institute and consulted for the Estonian Composers' Union.

Tormis is an expert in Estonian folk music, which he often draws upon for his choral music. He has also drawn upon the traditional music of other Finno-Ugrian nations. His works range from simple, highly serious incantations to humorous parodies full of variety and buffoonery. Unaccompanied choral music dominates his output, the best-known work being *Forgotten Peoples*.

Tosca. Opera by GIACOMO PUCCINI, 1900, first produced in Rome. The LIBRETTO is derived from a semihistorical drama by Sardou.

The action takes place during the turbulent events in Rome in the summer of 1800. Napoleon's army advances into Italy and is greeted by Italian patriots as liberators from the oppressive Austrian rule.

Tosca is a famous opera singer. Her lover, the painter Cavaradossi, shelters a political refugee and becomes the target of persecution by the sinister chief of the Roman police, Scarpia. Captivated by Tosca's generous feminine endowments, Scarpia suggests she sleep with him in return for Cavaradossi's release from prison. In desperation she agrees to submit to him, whereupon Scarpia issues an order for a pretended execution of Cavaradossi, using blank cartridges. He ominously adds to his command that they follow "the case of Palmieri."

Confident of her lover's escape, Tosca stabs Scarpia to death after their love-making. But Scarpia has outwitted Tosca: "the case of Palmieri" was a code message to the soldiers to make the pretended execution real. Cavaradossi falls at the stake. After the soldiers are gone Tosca rushes to him,

PEOPLE IN MUSIC

but he does not rise. Distraught, she hurls herself to her death from the prison's parapet.

The score introduces many bold harmonic innovations: consecutive TRIADS, unresolved DISSONANCES, and WHOLE-TONE SCALES. At the same time, the exquisite art of Italian BEL CANTO is beautifully maintained. Tosca's lament at the cruelty of fate (*Vissi d'arte*) and Cavaradossi's moving CA-VATINA are among the finest ARIAS in the operatic repertory.

PEOPLE IN MUSIC

Toscanini, Arturo, great Italian conductor; b. Parma, Mar. 25, 1867; d. N.Y., Jan. 16, 1957. Toscanini entered the Parma Conservatory at age nine, graduating in 1885 as winner of the first prize for cello. He received the Barbacini Prize as the outstanding graduate of his class.

In 1886 Toscanini was engaged as cellist for the Italian opera in Rio de Janeiro. One night he was unexpectedly called upon to substitute for the regular conductor, when the latter left the podium at the end of the introduction after the public hissed him. The opera was AIDA, and Toscanini led it without difficulty. He was rewarded by an ovation and an engagement to lead the rest of the season.

Returning to Italy, he was engaged to conduct opera at the Teatro Carignano in Turin, making his debut there in late 1886, and later conducting the Municipal Orchestra there. Although still very young he quickly established a fine reputation. From 1887 to 1896 he conducted opera in the major Italian theaters. In 1892 he led the premiere of PAGLI-ACCI in Milan, and in 1896 the premiere of LA BOHÈME in Turin. He also conducted the first performances by an Italian opera company of GOTTERDÄMMERUNG in 1895 and SIEGFRIED in 1899. He made his debut as a symphony conductor in 1896, with the orchestra of the Teatro Regio in Turin.

In 1898 the impresario Giulio Gatti-Casazza engaged him as chief conductor for La Scala, Milan, where he remained until 1903, and again from 1906 to 1908. In the interim he led opera in Buenos Aires. When Giulio Gatti-Casazza became general manager of the Metropolitan Opera in 1908, he invited Toscanini to be principal conductor. Toscanini's debut in N.Y. was with *Aida*. While at the Metropolitan Toscanini conducted GIUSEPPE VERDI's *Requiem* in

1909, and two world premieres, GIACOMO PUCCINI's *The Girl of the Golden West* in 1910 and UMBERTO GIORDANO's *Madame Sans-Gêne* in 1915. He also gave the American premieres of CHRISTOPH WILLIBALD GLUCK's *ARMIDE* in 1910, ERMANNO WOLF-FERRARI's *LE DONNE CURIOSE* in 1912, and MODEST MUSSORGSKY's *BORIS GODUNOV* in 1913. Later that year he gave his first orchestral concert in N.Y., leading LUDWIG VAN BEETHOVEN's Ninth Symphony.

In 1915 Toscanini returned to Italy, and during the 1920–21 season took the La Scala Orchestra on a tour of the U.S. and Canada. From 1921 to 1929 he was artistic director of La Scala, where he conducted the posthumous premiere of ARRIGO BOITO's opera *NERONE,* which he helped complete for performance in 1924. In 1926–27 he was a guest conductor of the N.Y. Philharmonic, returning in this capacity through the 1928–29 season. Toscanini then was associate conductor with Willem Mengelberg in 1929–30, and subsequently was the Philharmonic's conductor from 1930 to 1936.

Toscanini took the N.Y. Philharmonic on a tour of Europe in 1930 and 1931, in both years also conducting in Bayreuth. Deeply touched by the plight of the Jews in Germany, he refused to conduct there. He also acceded to the request of the violinist BRONISLAW HUBERMAN, founder of the Palestine Symphony Orchestra, to conduct the inaugural concert of that orchestra at Tel Aviv in 1936. During this period he also filled summer engagements at the Salzburg Festivals (1934–37) and conducted in London (1935; 1937–39).

In 1937 Toscanini became music director of the NBC Symphony Orchestra, a radio orchestra organized especially for him. He conducted his first broadcast on Christmas that year in N.Y. He took it on a tour of South America in 1940, and on a major tour of the U.S. in 1950. He continued to lead the NBC Symphony Orchestra until the end of his career, conducting his last concert at N.Y.'s CARNEGIE HALL in 1954, 10 days after his 87th birthday. He then sent a doleful letter of resignation to NBC, explaining the impossibility of further appearances (apparently he suffered a memory lapse during that concert). He died a few weeks before his 90th birthday.

A lawsuit was brought against Toscanini in Milan when he accidentally injured the concertmaster with a broken violin bow.

Toscanini was one of the most celebrated masters of the baton in conducting history. Undemonstrative in his handling of the orchestra, he possessed an amazing energy and power of command. He demanded absolute perfection, erupting in violence when he was unable to obtain from the orchestra what he wanted.

Despite the occasional insults to his musicians, Toscanini was affectionately known to them as "The Maestro" who could do no wrong. His ability to communicate to singers and players was extraordinary, and even the most celebrated opera stars and instrumentalists never dared to question his authority.

Owing to extreme nearsightedness, Toscanini committed all scores to memory. His repertoire embraced virtually all of CLASSIC and ROMANTIC music, his performances of Italian operas, RICHARD WAGNER's music dramas, Ludwig van Beethoven's symphonies, and modern Italian works being especially inspiring. Among the moderns, he led works by RICHARD STRAUSS, CLAUDE DEBUSSY, MAURICE RAVEL, SERGEI PROKOFIEV, and IGOR STRAVINSKY, and among Americans, SAMUEL BARBER, whose *Adagio for Strings* he made famous. He also had his favorite Italian composers (ALFREDO CATALANI, GIUSEPPE MARTUCCI), whose music he fondly fostered.

Toscanini was a lifelong believer in democracy. In addition to refusing to conduct in Germany under the Nazis, he militantly opposed Fascism in Italy. But he never abandoned his Italian citizenship, despite long years of residence in America. In 1987 his family presented his valuable private archive to the N.Y. Public Library.

Tostquartette. A collective name for 12 quartets by FRANZ JOSEPH HAYDN, 1788 – 90, opp. 54, 55, and 64. They were dedicated to the amateur violinist and industrialist Johann Tost of Vienna. The fifth (op.55, no. 2) is nicknamed the *Razor Quartet.*

total music. A form of performance art in which the once autonomous art of music is again allied with other arts.

In modern times, music lost this intimate connection with either the sciences or liberal arts. It maintained its proud independence until the middle of the 20th century, when the avant-garde brought music out of isolation into the world of MIXED MEDIA. The slogan "total music" was launched, and the once exclusive art became (at various HAPPENINGS) an action to be performed on equal terms with conversation, consumption of food, sex, and sleep.

Performing musicians willingly surrendered their physical separation from the audience, inviting the collaboration of the public onstage. Formal attire that placed musicians on a higher plane was abandoned. Since nudity became permissible in the theater, musicians followed suit, notably CHARLOTTE MOORMAN.

Totenlied (Ger.). *See* TODESGESANG.

Totentanz (Ger., dance of death). A morbid but widespread image cultivated during the Middle Ages in poetry, painting, drama, and music. It evoked the image of death dancing with its prospective victim. Even in songs of youth, expectation of death was often the subject, as in *Gaudeamus igitur,* warning the young to enjoy life before "nos habebit humus" (the earth has us).

Other pieces with connection to the Totentanz image are the final confrontation between Don Giovanni and the Commendatore in WOLFGANG AMADEUS MOZART's opera, FRANZ SCHUBERT's Lied *Der Tod und das Mädchen* (Death and the Maiden), CAMILLE SAINT-SAËNS's *Danse macabre,* SERGEI RACHMANINOFF's *Rhapsody on a Theme by Paganini,* and the many settings of Federico García Lorca's poetry, including those by GEORGE CRUMB.

Among the many works that quote the DIES IRAE chant (from the Roman Catholic Requiem) is FRANZ LISZT's *Totentanz.*

Totentanz (*Danse macabre*). Work for piano and orchestra by FRANZ LISZT, 1865, first performed in the Hague.

Liszt was inspired by the frescos in the cemetery of the town of Pisa, which represent Death mowing down indiscriminately both the rich and the poor, the old and the young. Throughout the composition the ominous strains of the DIES IRAE chant are heard.

touch. 1. The method of applying the fingers to the keys of KEYBOARD instruments. 2. The amount and kind of resistance overcome by the fingers in depressing the keys of a keyboard instrument, as a *heavy, light,* or *elastic* touch.

toosh   **touche** (Fr.). FINGERBOARD. *Sur la touche,* in string playing, bow on or near the fingerboard.

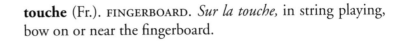

PEOPLE IN MUSIC

Tower, Joan (Peabody), American composer of instrumental music, pianist, and teacher; b. New Rochelle, N.Y., Sept. 6, 1938. Tower took courses in COMPOSITION with Henry Brant and Louis Calabro and studied piano at Bennington (Vermont) College, earning her B.A. degree in 1961. She completed her training with OTTO LUENING, JACK BEESON, and VLADIMIR USSACHEVSKY at Columbia University, earning a master's degree in 1964 and a doctorate in 1978.

In N.Y. in 1969, Tower cofounded the Da Capo Chamber Players, which became known for its promotion of contemporary music. She served as its pianist until 1984 and wrote many works for it. She taught at Bard College in Annandale-on-Hudson from 1972 and was composer-in-residence of the St. Louis Symphony Orchestra from 1985 to 1987. In 1976 she held a Guggenheim fellowship, and in 1974, 1975, 1980, and 1984 she held NEA fellowships. She also received a Koussevitzky Foundation grant in 1982 and an award from the American Academy and Institute of Arts and Letters in 1983. In 1986 she received the lucrative and prestigious Grawemeyer Award for her orchestral work *Silver Ladders.*

Tower practices different approaches to composition, but her central mode combines post-DEBUSSY harmonic sensitivity with a Stravinskyian rhythmic freedom and drive, often producing evocative and witty pictures of nature. Among her other orchestral works are *Sequoia* (1981), *Island Rhythms* (1989), concertos for clarinet, flute, piano, and violin (1985–91), Concerto for Orchestra (1991), and Concerto for Chamber Orchestra (1994).

Tower's chamber pieces include *Breakfast Rhythms I and II* for clarinet, flute, violin, cello, piano, and PERCUSSION (1974–75), *Black Topaz* for piano, flute, clarinet, trumpet, trombone, and two percussion (1976), *Petroushkates* for flute, clarinet, violin, cello, and piano (1980), *Snow Dreams* for flute and guitar (1983), *Island Premiere* for WIND quintet (1989; also for oboe and string quintet and for string quartet and string orchestra), *Elegy* for trombone and string quartet (1993), and Clarinet Quintet (1995). Tower has also composed many piano works.

Townshend, Pete(r Dennis Blandford). *See* WHO, THE.

Toy Symphony (*Kindersymphonie*). Toy symphonies ostensibly written for children to perform were popular in the 18th century. The most famous of these was for a century and a half attributed to FRANZ JOSEPH HAYDN, but thanks to the labors of persistent musicologists it was found to be a movement in an instrumental suite by LEOPOLD MOZART.

The toys in the orchestra are a RATTLE, a TRIANGLE, and several SQUEAKERS, to imitate the cuckoo, the quail, and the nightingale.

toye. Short piece for the VIRGINAL composed during the 16th and 17th centuries.

tract (Lat. *tractus,* extension). A psalmodic or other biblical chant replacing the ALLELUIA in the High Mass during penitential seasons (Lent) in the Roman Catholic LITURGY.

tragédie lyrique (Fr.). BAROQUE and CLASSIC French operas on classical subjects. The primary representatives of the genre are JEAN-BAPTISTE LULLY and JEAN-PHILIPPE RAMEAU, although CHRISTOPH WILLIBALD GLUCK also contributed to it during his Paris sojourn.

In the ROMANTIC era, *drame lyrique* superseded the tragédie lyrique, as classical subjects became rare in French opera.

Tragic Overture. Symphonic OVERTURE by JOHANNES BRAHMS, 1880, first performed in Vienna. This is one of two such works by the composer, the other being the *Academic Festival Overture.*

The *Tragic Overture* is in D minor, a TONALITY often having solemn and tragic connotations in ROMANTIC music. The tragic element can easily be heard in the ominously sounding beats of the TIMPANI and in the mighty blasts of the trombones. But there is a spirit of pastoral serenity in the second THEME and its DEVELOPMENT. Indeed, the overture is a diptych of contrasting moods.

Tragic Symphony. GUSTAV MAHLER's Sixth Symphony, 1903 – 05, in A minor. The tragic element is supplied in the orchestration by the inclusion of a large variety of PERCUSSION instruments, among them a hammer, whose blows seem to symbolize the end of hope. The nickname is not the composer's; the work is in four parts and was first performed in Essen, Germany, in 1906.

Trail of the Lonesome Pine, The. Ballad by Harry Carroll, 1913, describing the nostalgic beauty of the Blue Ridge Mountains in Virginia. It was often mistaken for an authentic FOLK SONG.

Tramp, Tramp, Tramp, or The Prisoner's Hope. Civil War ballad by George Frederick Root, 1864. It describes the anguish of a Union soldier taken prisoner by the Confederate Army.

PEOPLE IN MUSIC

Trampler, Walter, eminent German-American violist and pedagogue; b. Munich, Aug. 25, 1915; d. Port Joli, Nova Scotia, Sept. 27, 1997. Trampler received early music training from his father, and later enrolled at the Munich State Academy of Music. He made his debut as a violinist in Munich in 1933 and as a violist in Berlin in 1935.

From 1935 to 1938 Trampler served as first violist in the Deutschlandsender Orchestra, and then he emigrated to America. From 1947 to 1955 he was in the New Music String Quartet. He also made appearances with the Yale, Emerson, Budapest, Juilliard, and Guarneri quartets and with the Beaux Arts Trio. From 1969 he was a member of the Chamber Music Society of Lincoln Center.

Trampler taught at the Juilliard School of Music in N.Y. from 1962 to 1972, the Peabody Conservatory of Music in Baltimore from 1968 to 1970, the Yale School of Music from 1970 to 1972, Boston University from 1982 to 1995, and the Mannes College of Music in N.Y. from 1993 until his death in 1997.

One of the foremost viola masters, Trampler appeared as a soloist with leading orchestras of North America and Europe. He premiered works by several composers, including HANS WERNER HENZE, LUCIANO BERIO, and VINCENT PERSICHETTI.

transcendental. The piano style of FRANZ LISZT and his followers. It was so called because it surpasses the playing of former pianists and exceeds the limits of the piano by imitating the orchestra.

Transcendental études. *See* ÉTUDES D'EXÉCUTION TRANSCENDANTE.

transcription. The ARRANGEMENT or adaptation of a piece for some voice or instrument other than that for which it was originally intended.

Transfigured Night. *See* VERKLÄRTE NACHT.

transient. Passing, not principal, intermediate. *Transient chord,* an intermediate CHORD foreign both to the original KEY and the one that is reached; opposite of *pivot chord; transient modulation,* temporary MODULATION, followed by a return to the original key.

transition. 1. MODULATION, especially one that is TRANSIENT. 2. In TONIC SOL-FA, a modulation without change of MODE.

transpose. Perform or write out a composition in a KEY different from the original.

transposing instruments. 1. Instruments whose natural SCALE is always written in C major, regardless of CONCERT PITCH. Thus, for a clarinet in B♭, a written C-major scale will sound like the instrument's natural scale of B-flat major. To get the concert (sounding) scale of C major the music will have to be written in D major. 2. Instruments having some device by which the action or strings can be shifted so that tones are produced that are higher or lower than when they are in the normal position. IRVING BERLIN had a piano of this type, because he could only play in the natural key of F-sharp.

transposition (Ger. *Versetzung*) 1. Performance or NOTATION of a composition in a KEY higher or lower than the original, in order to adjust to the range of an individual's vocal range or a more convenient and more effective TONALITY in an instrumental work.

Most transpositions are made in song anthologies, usually from the original setting for a high voice to a lower range. Any singer can transpose a tune without training, but piano accompanists have to be talented to transpose a piece at sight.

2. One of three standard techniques in SERIAL composition (RETROGRADE, INVERSION, transposition).

MUSICAL INSTRUMENT

transverse flute (Fr. *flûte traversière;* Ger. *Traversflöte;* It. *flauto traverso*). The generic name for the CROSS FLUTE, held perpendicularly to the nose and across the lips, as opposed to the vertical flute (e.g., RECORDER).

MUSICAL INSTRUMENT

traps (trap set). Colloquial term for the JAZZ drum set.

traquenard (Fr.). Fast GALOP in $\frac{4}{4}$ time with dotted rhythms, found in BAROQUE instrumental SUITES.

trow'er-

Trauermarsch (Ger.). Funeral MARCH. *Trauermusik,* funeral music.

Träumerei. A quintessentially ROMANTIC piano piece by ROBERT SCHUMANN, 1838, from his cycle of 14 character pieces entitled *Kinderszenen* (Scenes from childhood), op.15. The piece is in the Romantic key of F major, with hints of related major and minor keys.

MUSICAL INSTRUMENT

Trautonium. Electronic musical instrument introduced in 1930 by the German electrical engineer Friedrich Trautwein (1888–1956). Paul Hindemith composed for it.

Travers, Mary. *See* PETER, PAUL AND MARY.

travesty. *See* TROUSER ROLE.

Traviata, La. Opera by GIUSEPPE VERDI, 1853, first performed in Venice. The LIBRETTO is drawn from the French play *La Dame aux camellias* by Alexandre Dumas fils. The title is nearly untranslatable. While some choose "The Wayward One," this eliminates the important point that the heroine was not wanton by nature. Perhaps a more accurate if unwieldy translation is "The woman diverted from the righteous way" or "The woman led astray."

La Traviata is Violetta, a courtesan. She meets a dashing gentleman, Alfredo, who proclaims his ardent love for her. They take lodgings together near Paris as an unwed couple. Alfredo's father Germont is dismayed by his son's misalliance and begs Violetta to let him go. She complies and contrives a way to end her affair with Alfredo.

After a period of anger, Alfredo learns Violetta is ill. He rushes to her side, finding her dying of consumption. After some bittersweet vocalizing and lots of guilt on Alfredo and Germont's part, Violetta dies in her lover's arms.

La Traviata is one of the most tuneful of Verdi's operas. There is a famous scene of drinking a toast, the BRINDISI *Libiamo,* as well as many poignant ARIAS and DUETS. The subject of the opera shocked the sensibilities of some mid-19th-century operagoers. The London papers expressed outrage that "the ladies of the aristocracy" should be allowed to attend the production "to see an innocent young lady impersonate the heroine of an infamous French novel who varies her prostitution by a frantic passion." But *La Traviata* survived, an unusually contemporary opera for its composer. Only *Stiffelio* (1850) takes place in Verdi's historical present. It was the major inspiration for VERISMO in general and GIACOMO PUCCINI's operas especially.

tre (It.). Three. *A tre,* for three voices or instruments; *a tre voci,* for (in) three parts or voices; *tre corde,* release piano soft pedal completely.

trā

treble. Voice of SOPRANO range, often sung by boys. Also of instruments, as in the *treble viol* or *treble recorder.*

trecento. Italian designation for the 1300s (14th century), its art, literature, and music. Specifically, it refers to the period of POLYPHONIC music from c.1325 into the early 15th century. The style is characterized by new forms of secular music setting vernacular texts. The most important forms of the trecento are the MADRIGAL and CACCIA, the best-known composers being Francesco Landini and Jacopo da Bologna.

Treemonisha. Opera, 1911, by SCOTT JOPLIN. It describes the life of an abandoned black baby girl found under a tree by a compassionate woman named Monisha and therefore christened Monisha of the Tree, or Treemonisha. It was performed in concert form in 1915, two years before Joplin's death.

Treemonisha did not receive its first stage performance until May 23, 1975, in Houston, orchestrated and conducted by GUNTHER SCHULLER.

Trees. Semiclassical song by Oscar Rasbach (1888–1975) to Joyce Kilmer's poem, which concludes that only God can make a tree. This song was once enormously popular on the concert circuit.

PEOPLE IN MUSIC

Treigle, Norman, remarkable American BASS-BARITONE; b. New Orleans, Mar. 6, 1927; d. there, Feb. 16, 1975. Treigle sang in a church choir as a child. Upon graduation from high school in 1943 he served in the Navy. After two years in service he returned to New Orleans and studied voice with Elizabeth Wood.

Treigle made his debut in 1947 with the New Orleans Opera as Lodovico in *OTELLO.* He then joined the N.Y. City Opera, making his debut in 1953 as Colline in *LA BOHÈME.* He remained with the company for 20 years, establishing himself as a favorite with the public. Among his successful roles were Figaro in *THE MARRIAGE OF FIGARO,* Don Giovanni, BOITO's Mefistofele, and Boris Godunov. He also sang in modern operas, including leading parts in the world premieres of three operas by CARLISLE FLOYD. Treigle's other contemporary roles included the title role in LUIGI DALLAPICCOLA's *THE PRISONER* and that of the grandfather in AARON COPLAND's *THE TENDER LAND.*

Treigle's untimely death, from an overdose of sleeping pills, deprived the American opera scene of one of its finest talents.

tremolo (It., quivering, fluttering). A popular EMBELLISH-MENT consisting of a repeated alternation of two notes in rapid TEMPO, once regarded as a powerful device to produce dramatic tension. However, tremolo is not synonymous with VIBRATO. In singing, a tremulous, somewhat unsteady tone is used; on bowed instruments the effect is produced by the very rapid alternation of down-bow and up-bow, written:

In his preface to the dramatic madrigal *Il combattimento di Tancredi e Clorinda,* CLAUDIO MONTEVERDI describes the tremolo as the most expressive dynamic device of the *STILE CONCITATO,* illustrating as it does Tancred's unwitting fatal wounding of his beloved, Clorinda. The use of the tremolo for dramatic effect reached its greatest popularity in the 19th century, particularly in opera. Later it degenerated into melodramatic effect and soon vanished from serious composition altogether, except for comical effects.

trâ′mŏh-lŏh

trepak. A Russian dance in fast DUPLE time.

trĕh-pahk′

triad. A CHORD consisting of three distinct PITCHes. If TONAL, a chord consisting of a given tone (the ROOT), a note a MAJOR or MINOR THIRD above the root, and the note a PERFECT, DIMINISHED, or AUGMENTED FIFTH above the root, within the chosen SCALE.

Modern theory recognizes four types of triads:

A *major triad,* consisting of a major third superimposed by a minor (i.e., a perfect fifth above the root)

A *minor triad,* consisting of a minor third superimposed by a major (also a perfect fifth above the root)

A *diminished triad,* consisting of two minor thirds, one on top of the other (i.e., a diminished fifth above the root)

An *augmented triad,* consisting of two major thirds, one on top of the other (i.e., an augmented fifth above the root)

The major and minor triads are fundamental to the determination of a key. The diminished triad is regarded as a DISCORD, since it contains a diminished fifth. The augmented triad is also a discord, because it contains an augmented fifth, even though the augmented fifth is enharmonically equivalent to a minor sixth.

In the 20th century some musicians attempted to deprive the triads of their specific connotations as consisting of two thirds and extended the notion of a triad to any chord containing three notes, even if chromatically congested or widely dispersed. Analogously, a group of two notes was described as a DYAD.

triadic modulation. A common way to change KEYS in the middle of a piece. In brief, a triad that belongs to both current and future keys is used as a PIVOT CHORD and the change is accomplished by a kind of TONAL overlapping or SEGUE. In some cases only one note of the pivot chord need be shared by both keys. *See also* MODULATION.

MUSICAL
INSTRUMENT

triangle. Steel rod bent into triangular shape, with one corner left slightly open. It is struck with a metal wand.

trichord. Set of three PITCH classes, usually a segment of a 12-NOTE SET. *Trichord piano,* instrument with three unison strings per TONE throughout the greater part of its compass.

tricinium (Lat.). In 16th-century Germany, a three-part vocal piece, as opposed to the more usual piece for four (or more) parts. Collections of secular, sacred, and instrumental tricinia were published, primarily for didactic purposes.

tricotet. A type of melody improvised, sung, danced, and played on instruments by medieval minstrels, completely free in form, rhythm, and character. French BAROQUE composers gave the name to fanciful sections of instrumental SUITES.

trill (Ger. *Triller;* It. *trillo;* Fr. *trille*). A melodic embellishment consisting of the even and rapid alternation of two tones a MAJOR or MINOR SECOND apart. The lower tone is the *principal note* (the one being ornamented), the higher tone the *auxiliary note* (the ornamenting one).

The practice of trilling was cultivated in France in the 17th century and was sometimes picturesquely described as *tremblement,* translated into English as *shake.*

A graphic symbol for a trill is a wavy line, sometimes extending according to the duration desired. The abbreviation *tr* is also used.

In modern instrumental writing, the trill invariably begins on the principal note, but in the BAROQUE period the trill often began on the auxiliary note. Interpretation of trill performance practice can differ from scholar to scholar and from source to source. Vocal trilling now seems to emerge from the VIBRATO technique in constant use by opera singers.

Trilletta, a short trill; *trillo caprino,* GOAT'S TRILL.

Trimpin, (Gerhard), German-born inventor, practitioner, and builder of soundsculpture and computerized acoustical instruments; b. Istein bei Lörrach, Basel, Nov. 26, 1951. Professionally, Trimpin is known by only his surname. His early music training emphasized WIND instruments, but recurrent lip infections forced a turn to electromechanical engineering, which he studied from 1966 to 1973. In 1979 he received a degree from the University of Berlin in social pedagogy, and later taught at the Sweelinck Conservatory in Amsterdam from 1985 to 1987, where he also conducted research in music and acoustic sound technologies.

PEOPLE IN MUSIC

From 1976 to 1979 Trimpin was active with Berlin's Theater Zentrifuge. In 1979 Trimpin settled in Seattle, where he resides in a workshop-laboratory filled with many unusual sound-producing objects. He produced set designs for San Quentin Drama Workshop, and designed four Bowed Cymbals for Ton de Leeuw's *Resonances* from 1987. For the 1986 New Music Festival in Middelburg he designed a percussive installation of 96 suspended Dutch wooden shoes, *Klompen.* A similar installation followed in 1987, *Floating Klompen,* for the Jan van Eyck Art Academy in Maastricht, subsequently seen at the San Francisco Exploratorium in 1990. From 1988 he collaborated in Mexico

City with CONLON NANCARROW, whose PIANOLA ROLLS he transcribed to computer disk.

Trimpin originated his own composition, *Circumference* for specially adapted instruments, which was first seen at the New Music America Festival in N.Y. in 1989. Other works include *Three Ply* (1984), *Ringo* (1985), *The Cocktail Party Effect* (1990), *Messing Around* (1990), *PHFFFT* (1991) *Contraption 1PP71512* (1991), and *D.R.A.M.A.ohno* (1993).

In 1995 Trimpin created a lavish installation of sounding fabrics, *Singing Textiles*, for Switzerland's Museum Technorama. After a long string of awards from various philanthropic agencies, Trimpin was awarded the lucrative and prestigious McArthur Award (the so-called "Genius" grant that gives the winner a large sum of money with which to do what he or she will) in 1997.

trē'ōh

Mixed trios are also found, such as those for piano, clarinet, and cello written by WOLFGANG AMADEUS MOZART and ARAM KATCHATURIAN.

trio (It.). 1. A generic term for a composition employing three instruments or (less often) three vocal parts. The so-called piano trio is scored for violin, cello, and piano. A trio set for violin, viola, and cello is usually called a string trio. LUDWIG VAN BEETHOVEN wrote five such works. FRANZ JOSEPH HAYDN wrote a number of trios for two violins and cello and more than 100 BARYTON trios. Examples of the piano trio include those of Beethoven, ROBERT SCHUMANN, FELIX MENDELSSOHN, JOHANNES BRAHMS, and PIOTR ILYICH TCHAIKOVSKY.

2. In MINUETS, MARCHES, and RAGTIME, a second dance or march, after which the first is repeated, sometimes in a different key. In the BAROQUE, it was also known as an ALTERNATIVO. The term *trio* is often used for the central (second) section of a CLASSIC or ROMANTIC SYMPHONY.

The terms minuet and SCHERZO are relics of the Baroque era, when these sections might actually be written for three instruments, such as two oboes and bassoon, or two horns and bassoon (cf. the finale of JOHANN SEBASTIAN BACH's *Brandenburg Concerto No. 1*).

trio sonata. Important BAROQUE CHAMBER MUSIC genre, written in three parts, the two upper (melody) parts supported by a BASSO CONTINUO part performed by two instruments. Hence the contradiction of seeing four persons perform a "sound piece for three"!

The upper parts were usually played by violins, flutes, and/or oboes, while the lower parts by cello or bassoon playing the bass line and HARPSICHORD, the latter supplying the harmonic skeleton of the work.

In pre-CLASSIC music the upper parts were often taken over by VIOLS and/or CORNETTOS, and the lower parts by a VIOLA DA GAMBA and harpsichord.

There are specimens of trio sonatas written for a considerably larger ensemble, but even in such cases the texture is in three principal parts. To emphasize this peculiarity the composer often added the words *a tre*.

The trio sonata borrows from other genres structurally: the SONATA DA CHIESA, with its slow-fast-slow-fast arrangement, and the SONATA DA CAMERA, with its SUITE-like dance movements.

GEORGE FRIDERIC HANDEL wrote 28 trio sonatas, including six scored for two oboes and bass, and ANTONIO VIVALDI wrote 12. JOHANN SEBASTIAN BACH's most famous trio sonata is in his *Musikalisches Opfer* (The musical offering) which he wrote for Frederick the Great.

Toward the middle of the 18th century, trio sonatas evolved into piano trios (violin, cello, piano). In these works, the piano part not only filled in the harmony but had an independent role melodically and contrapuntally, thus replacing one of the melody parts.

Trip to Chinatown, A. Musical farce by Percy Gaunt, 1893. The thin plot recounts a couple's trip to San Francisco's Chinatown. The songs in the original score were very popular, including *The Bowery* and *Reuben, Reuben*. Many new songs were added into the show during its run, including CHARLES HARRIS's classic *After the Ball*.

triple concerto. Concerto for three solo instruments and orchestra.

triple dot. Three dots placed to the right of a note head, augmenting its duration by ½ + ½(½) + ½(½)(½) its value, each subsequent dot adding half the value of the preceding dot. Thus, a half note with a triple dot equals ½ + ¼ + ⅛ + ¹⁄₁₆ = ¹⁵⁄₁₆ (of a whole note).

Triple dots are rare, because such durations can more easily be translated into tied notes.

triple time. Meter containing three units, as in $\frac{3}{4}$ or $\frac{3}{8}$.

triplet (Fr. *triolet;* Ger. *Triole;* It. *terzina*). A group of three equal notes to be performed in the time of two notes of like value in the established tempo.

The most common, the eighth-note triplet, is written:

If quarter-note or half-note triplets are called for, a square bracket must be used, as follows:

triplum (Lat.). The second added VOICE in medieval ORGANUM, resulting in a three-part texture of CANTUS FIRMUS (tenor), DUPLUM, and triplum (the highest). The term is also used for medieval compositions in three voices without a cantus firmus.

Tristan chord. A designation for the CHORD comprising F–B–D♯–G♯, which occurs in the second measure of the prelude to RICHARD WAGNER's *TRISTAN UND ISOLDE*. To resolve, the upper voice ascends chromatically (G♯–A–A♯–B), the alto and bass descend chromatically (D♯–D♭; F–E), and the tenor drops a minor third down (B–G♯). Thus the DOMINANT-SEVENTH chord of the key of A is formed, establishing the Tristanesque connection with the opening note of the piece, A. This chord and its ambiguous resolution are fundamental to melodic and harmonic transformations of the principal LEITMOTIVs of the entire score. So unusual was it for the music of the 19th century that Wagnerophiles built a whole mystique about it in the theory of CHROMATIC HARMONY.

Tristan und Isolde. Opera by RICHARD WAGNER, 1865, to his own LIBRETTO, first performed in Munich. The story is derived from an ancient Cornish legend.

King Mark of Cornwall sends his nephew Tristan to fetch his chosen bride Isolde, a princess of Ireland. During a sea voyage, Isolde falls in love with Tristan so deeply that only death can save her from disgrace. She asks her lady attendant to give her poison, but she prepares a love potion instead. After drinking it both Tristan and Isolde become consumed with passion.

Isolde marries Mark but continues to have secret meetings with Tristan; their love duet is surpassingly moving. Tristan, wounded by the King's henchman, is taken to his castle in Brittany. Isolde comes to visit him; a shepherd plays a tune on his wooden trumpet which is a signal that Isolde's ship is approaching. Tristan, still bleeding from his wound, rushes to meet her and expires lovingly. The concluding scene is Isolde's own *Liebestod* (love death), expressing a mystical belief that the deepest light of love can be fulfilled only in the deepest night of death.

Wagner's system of LEITMOTIVS reaches its greatest height of expression in this work. Wagner's annotators have painstakingly compiled the themes of love, death, day and night, love potion, and of soul states such as fidelity, suspicion, exaltation, impatience, and malediction.

Tristan und Isolde is couched in a highly chromaticized idiom. For some modernists, the PRELUDE to *Tristan und Isolde* is a prophetic vision of ATONALITY. ALBAN BERG inserted its opening measures in his atonal (and love-subsumed) *Lyric Suite*. On the other hand, CLAUDE DEBUSSY, whose attitude toward Wagner was ambivalent, made fun of the prelude in his whimsical *Golliwog's Cakewalk*.

Wagner chose to give the name Isolde to his illegitimate daughter born to him and Cosima von Bülow in April 1865. During this time, Cosima's husband, Hans von Bülow, was conducting the strenuous rehearsals of *Tristan und Isolde*.

Tristano, Lennie (Leonard Joseph), famous American JAZZ pianist and teacher; b. Chicago, Mar. 19, 1919; d. N.Y., Nov. 18, 1978. Tristano became blind in childhood but did not allow this handicap to deflect him from a study of music. He attended the American Conservatory of Music in Chicago, earning his bachelor's degree in music in 1943.

The Vienna Opera House accepted *Tristan und Isolde* for performance, but after 53 rehearsals the production was canceled.

PEOPLE IN MUSIC

After performing in Chicago clubs, Tristano settled in N.Y. in 1946, forming his own sextet a year later. He became famous as one of the leaders of the COOL JAZZ school, emphasizing thoughtful improvisation over emotional playing. Tristano ran a jazz school from 1951 to 1956 and then taught privately. He also made occasional appearances as a performer, touring Europe in 1965 and the U.S. in 1968. He was a master at piano improvisations.

For some reason, Tristano fell out of the public eye after this. Although he lived until 1978, he rarely recorded or performed during his last decade of his life.

tritone. INTERVAL of the AUGMENTED FOURTH, containing three consecutive WHOLE TONES, as F to B or D to G♯. It is sometimes notated as a DIMINISHED FIFTH (F to C♭; D to A♭).

Medieval theorists described the tritone as the DIABOLUS IN MUSICA (devil in music). They rejected melodic progressions using it from church music wherever possible. While the ecclesiastical MODES had the potential for melodic tritones, *MUSICA FICTA* were employed automatically to avoid this interval.

In German schools in JOHANN SEBASTIAN BACH's time a music student who inadvertently made use of the tritone was punished in class by a blow on the knuckles of the hand. Nonetheless, one of Bach's chorales begins with three whole tones in succession, to the words, "O schwerer Gang" (Oh, difficult step). This may be a play on the meaning of the words—because a tritone would have been viewed as a "difficult step."

The tritone was championed by modern composers because it is unacceptable in traditional music theory. In turning away from TONIC-DOMINANT harmonies, many composers looked to the tritone as a new method of created harmonic parts. Tritones were also well-suited to 12-TONE composition.

MUSICAL
INSTRUMENT

triumph cornet. Military CORNET in B♭ with an especially brilliant tone. It was invented by Vaclav Červeny in 1862.

tro′kē

trochee. In prosody, a foot consisting of one long (accented) and one short (unaccented) beat. In music, a trochaic METER corresponds to a leisurely WALTZ without an accented UP-BEAT.

Trois morceaux en forme de poir (Three pieces in the shape of a pear). A set of pieces for piano, four hands, by ERIK SATIE, 1903. It was written as a rebuttal to CLAUDE DEBUSSY'S reproach that Satie's music lacked form. A color picture of a pear appeared on the title page of the published edition. Of course, there are more than three pieces!

Trois véritables préludes flasques (pour un chien) (Three truly flabby preludes for a dog). A piano SUITE by ERIK SATIE, 1912, in which the title almost overwhelms the music. The adjective *flabby* is truly ill-suited. Perhaps Satie wanted a nonsensical rhyme for the alliterative "masques et bergamasques" from Paul Verlaine's *Clair de lune,* so beloved of the French avant-garde. Or perhaps the dog just liked preludes prepared in such a manner.

trojnice. Croatian triple flute, with one DRONE (left tube) and two playing tubes (melody on the right, secondary part in the middle).

MUSICAL INSTRUMENT

Trolley Song, The. Song by Hugh Martin, 1944, for the musical film *Meet Me in St. Louis.* It features an imitation of the jangling sound of the trolley car.

tromba marina (It., marine trumpet; Ger. *Trumscheit;* Fr. *trompette marine*). A bowed MONOCHORD with a single string stretched over a very long and narrow wooden box. The string was touched rather than stopped by the thumb, resulting in a long series of HARMONICS.

trŏm-băh-mah-rī′năh

MUSICAL INSTRUMENT

The tromba marina dates from at least the 12th century and may once have been plucked rather than bowed. At one point, there was a second string added (even more on occasion), but by the BAROQUE period it was once again a monochord. During this period the body achieved a slightly more angular shape, with a flared bottom and thinner neck. More spectacularly, instruments were built to reach six or seven feet in height.

The increased size amplified its tendency to buzz, and some makers invented devices to curb it. A variant added sympathetic brass strings for greater RESONANCE.

For many centuries the tromba marina was useful in acoustic experiments with harmonics. But it was also popular with street musicians. It seems to have become obsolete by the CLASSIC period, although acoustically minded builders have experimented with the concept in recent years.

The seemingly absurd name for this bowed monochord is explained in part by its playing of the harmonic series, just as the natural trumpet did. But "marina" remains a mystery, with no convincing explanation yet.

Supposedly the instrument was used in convents, hence the alternative name *Nonnengeige* (Ger., nun's fiddle).

MUSICAL INSTRUMENT

trombone (from It. *tromba* + *one,* big trumpet; Ger. *Posaune*). The TENOR instrument of the BRASS group, pitched below the trumpet and horn and above the (bass) tuba.

The trombone is the only standard orchestral instrument that utilizes a sliding tube (i.e., slide) to change its PITCH. The trombonist draws the slide in or out, which changes the size of the tube that air travels through to produce notes. The more extended the slide, the larger the tube and therefore the lower the note. The opposite effect is produced by drawing the slide in toward the player. Hence the instrument's colloquial name of slide trombone. Like other brass instruments, manipulation of the lips replaces the

Modern trombones and trumpets. (Benson Collection) ▶

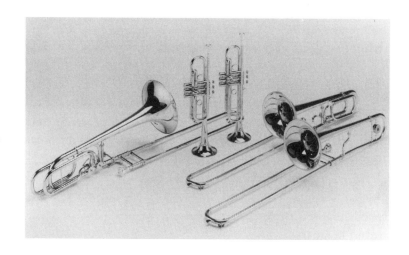

reeds of WOODWIND instruments and determines the harmonic being used at any one time to generate the pitch.

The trombone is one of the oldest Western brass instruments, dating to the early RENAISSANCE, when it was known as the SACKBUT. A *trombetta* (It., small trumpet) is mentioned in Dante's *Divina commedia*.

The trombone has developed strong associations with things apocalyptic or hellish. No orchestral instrument can sound the DIES IRAE more ominously. The trombone announces in doom-laden tones the entrance of the Commendatore's statue in WOLFGANG AMADEUS MOZART'S *DON GIOVANNI*, summoning the protagonist to his own last supper. But the trombone can also sound in triumph. Ludwig van Beethoven reserves the appearance of the trombone in his Fifth Symphony for the glorious finale.

The range of the tenor trombone (Ger. *Tenorposaune*), the one most often used in the orchestra, is from E below the bass clef to C an octave above middle C (E_0 to c^2). The alto trombone is tuned a perfect fifth above, the bass trombone a fourth lower. There is also a double trombone in B♭/F, in effect a tenor with an "F attachment" to shift to the bass range.

trompe de chasse (Fr.). Natural HORN used for hunting calls.

troparion. Byzantine HYMN in its simplest form, usually inserted between VERSES of PSALMS. The genre later evolved into the KONTAKION.

trope (from Grk. *trópos,* turn [of speech]). In medieval CHANT LITURGY, a musical insertion into any established piece from the ORDINARY, PROPRIUM, or DIVINE OFFICE. Originally the term applied to rhetorical figures of speech which Quintilian defined as "verbi vel sermonis a propria significatione in aliam mutatio" (a change from the proper meaning of a word into another).

Initially tropes took the form of MELISMAS, sometimes of great length. Later these melismas had words fitted to them, creating the texted trope (e.g., the Kyrie *orbis factor*). Other tropes were dramatic in tone, leading to the liturgical drama

MUSICAL
INSTRUMENT

(e.g., the Easter trope *Quem queritis,* dating to at least the 10th century).

In time the music of the tropes annexed all kinds of material, even secular tunes. This growth of unorthodox tropes and the supposed melismatic pollution of GREGORIAN CHANT caused the Council of Trent (1545–63) to ban all such usages, allowing only those melodic figures that had become firmly ingrained into traditional chants.

troubadour (from Old Prov. *trobador, tropator,* trope composer; It. *trovatore*). The generic name for poet-musicians and singers who roamed the areas of southern France, northern Spain, and northwestern Italy in the 11th through 13th centuries. The art of the troubadours gradually penetrated into northern France, where a performer became known as a TROUVÈRE. In Germany he was known as a MINNESINGER.

The troubadours originated many types of popular French songs, such as the ALBA, AUBADE, PASTOURELLE, and PASTORELA. A considerable number of their MONOPHONIC STROPHIC songs have been preserved, with their lack of rhythmic NOTATION leading to decades of discussion and dispute.

Trouble in Tahiti. Opera by LEONARD BERNSTEIN, 1952, first produced at Brandeis University in Waltham, Massachusetts.

The composer's own LIBRETTO describes a disgruntled wife, constantly squabbling with her uncongenial husband. She proposes that they go to a movie about a quarreling couple on the Pacific island of Tahiti as a form of therapy. The plan succeeds, and they live happily . . . for a few months.

The score features Bernstein's customary JAZZ-inflected TONALITY. The entire opera was incorporated into the revised *A Quiet Place* of 1984.

trouser role (travesty; U.K., breeches-part; Ger. *Hosenrolle*). In opera, a part sung by a female singer performing the role of a younger man or boy. Famous examples include

Siebel in FAUST

Cherubino in THE MARRIAGE OF FIGARO

Octavian in *DER ROSENKAVALIER*

Prince Orlovsky in *DIE FLEDERMAUS*

In the roles of Cherubino and Octavian, the young man (who is portrayed by a woman) puts on maidservant's clothing to disguise himself from an overbearing nobleman. This intentional double confusion—a woman portraying a man portraying a woman—was well appreciated by audiences of the day.

Trout Quintet (*Forelle-Quintett*). Piano quintet by FRANZ SCHUBERT, 1819, in A major, with violin, viola, cello, and double bass. The fourth movement is a set of variations on Schubert's song *Die Forelle* (The trout, 1819).

trouvère. A class of poet-musicians and singers who flourished during the 12th and 13th centuries in northern France. The songs of the trouvères created a profusion of literary and musical forms, known collectively as *chansons de geste* (songs of deeds). They also cultivated the forms RONDEAU, BALLADE, VIRELAIS, MOTET, and the instrumental ESTAMPE.

Thousands of these texts have been preserved in medieval *chansonniers* (songbooks). Fortunately many of the melodies have also been preserved. However, like the TROUBADOUR songs, no rhythmic notation is found in the manuscripts, thereby opening the way for discussion and dispute.

The word *trouvère* is probably derived from the French verb *trouver* (to find).

Trovatore, Il (The troubadour). Opera by GIUSEPPE VERDI, 1853, first produced in Rome. In a genre known for its absurd storylines, *Il Trovatore* probably takes the prize for the most ludicrous LIBRETTO in the history of opera. But the score contains some of Verdi's finest inventions, among them the celebrated *Anvil Chorus*.

The troubadour Manrico leads the rebellion against the King of Aragon, whose army is commanded by Manrico's brother, the Conte di Luna. However, the brothers are not aware that they are kith and kin. To complicate matters further, they love the same woman, Leonora. (She chooses Manrico.)

Enter a mysterious Gypsy woman named Azucena who tells Manrico the dreadful story that her own mother was burnt as a witch, so she decided to steal and slay the baby brother of di Luna. She informs Manrico that the baby killed was actually her own. (She doesn't mention that the other was saved, and that Manrico was that baby.)

Azucena is arrested as a spy and condemned to die the same fiery death as her mother. Manrico, who believes Azucena to be his mother, tries to save her life, but is captured by di Luna. Leonora begs di Luna to release him, and the unspeakable Count agrees, provided she give herself to him. She submits, but takes a slow working poison to escape her unwelcome lover. She goes to the tower where Manrico is kept and brings him the message of his freedom. The poison begins to work, and she dies in his arms.

At that moment di Luna arrives and orders Manrico executed after all. Just before she dies, Azucena reveals to di Luna that he has just executed his *own* brother, and she dies avenged.

PEOPLE IN MUSIC

Troyanos, Tatiana, brilliant American mezzosoprano; b. N.Y., Sept. 12, 1938; d. there, Aug. 21, 1993. She studied at the Juilliard School of Music in N.Y. (graduated 1963) and with Hans Heinz. On April 25, 1963, she made her operatic debut as Hippolyta in *A Midsummer Night's Dream* at the N.Y. City Opera. In 1965 she made her first appearance at the Hamburg State Opera as Preziosilla, remaining on its roster until 1975, winning distinction for such roles as Elisetta, Dorabella, and Baba. She also created the role of Jeanne in THE DEVILS OF LOUDUN there in 1969. In 1966 she sang for the first time at the Aix-en-Provence Festival as Strauss's Composer. In 1969 she made her debut at London's Covent Garden and at the Salzburg Festival as Octavian. In 1971 she sang Ariodante in the first operatic production given at the Kennedy Center in Washington, D.C., the same year she made her debut at the Chicago Lyric Opera as Charlotte. In 1975 she sang VINCENZO BELLINI's Romeo in Boston.

On March 8, 1976, she made a memorable debut at the Metropolitan Opera in N.Y. as Octavian. In subsequent years she was one of its leading members, in 1992 creating the role of Queen Isabella in PHILIP GLASS's *THE VOYAGE*. Her death from cancer deprived the Metropolitan Opera of the extraordinary gifts of one of America's finest singers.

Troyens, Les (The Trojans). Grand opera by HECTOR BERLIOZ, 1856–60, after the *Aeneid* of Virgil. The complete SCORE was so long that, at FRANZ LISZT's suggestion, Berlioz split it into two parts. Only the second part, *Les Troyens à Carthage,* was performed during his lifetime, in Paris in 1863. The first part, entitled *Le Prise de Troie,* was produced posthumously in Karlsruhe, Germany, in 1890. While there were performances of both parts together with major cuts thereafter, the first uncut complete performance occurred no sooner than 1969.

The LIBRETTO begins with the last days of Troy and ends with the suicide of Dido, the Queen of Carthage, after her abandonment by Aeneas. As so often happens with Berlioz's vocal works, the best known excerpt from *Les Troyens* is orchestral, namely, the *Royal Hunt and Storm* in the second part, when Dido and Aeneas avoid a downpour by sheltering in a cave. The rest is mythology.

trumpet (Ger. *Trompete;* Fr. *trompette;* It. *tromba*). A BRASS instrument with cupped mouthpiece and small bell, its tone brilliant, penetrating, and of great carrying power. At present the trumpet is a CHROMATIC, transposing instrument in B♭ (standard or SOPRANO trumpet) or other FUNDAMENTALS, as well as upper-register trumpets (sopranino, piccolo). The sounding range of the B-flat trumpet is e^0 to bb^2 (written $f\#^0$ to c^3).

MUSICAL INSTRUMENT

In one form or another, the trumpet is one of the most ancient of human instruments. Its principle, creating sound by blowing into a hollow object without the use of reeds, was achieved in trumpets made of conch shells, bamboo, cane, wood, bark, and ultimately metal.

From its introduction in the 14th century through the mid-19th century, the trumpet was limited to natural harmonic tones. It had to be manually tuned to the KEY of the work in which it was used. In order to effect a MODULATION to a lower key, the player had to insert extra tubing (a CROOK) into the instrument. To modulate to a higher key, the tubing had to be shortened.

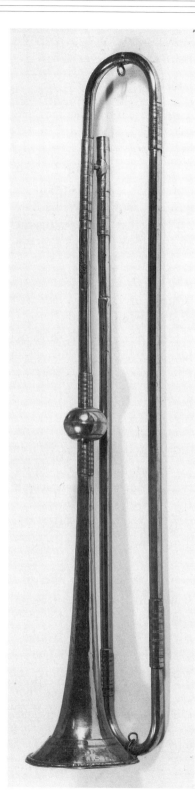

Early trumpet without keys (valves) showing a replaceable crook or extra tubing. (Smithsonian Institution) ▶

The alto trumpet in F is used in many scores by French composers, among them *España* by Emmanuel Chabrier.

It was not until the 19th century that efficient trumpet keys (VALVES) were invented that made it possible to play an entire CHROMATIC scale. As a result of this late discovery, the trumpet parts in the works of WOLFGANG AMADEUS MOZART, FRANZ JOSEPH HAYDN, and even LUDWIG VAN BEETHOVEN utilized mainly the TONIC and DOMINANT of the principal key.

The standard type of trumpet was stabilized in the second half of the 19th century as a transposing instrument in B-flat, which sounds a major second below the written note. In Germany, Russia, England, and the Netherlands the B-flat trumpet is used almost exclusively (in Germany it is, of course, in B). French and American composers increasingly used a trumpet in C, a nontransposing instrument.

The trumpet plays a very important role in JAZZ. It is the lead melody instrument in many jazz groups. Originally, jazz players favored the CORNET; LOUIS ARMSTRONG began his career playing that instrument. However, by the mid-'20s it was replaced by the louder and more versatile trumpet. Famous jazz trumpeters include Armstrong, DIZZY GILLESPIE, and WYNTON MARSALIS.

The most common dramatic use of the trumpet is that of a military summons. In LUDWIG VAN BEETHOVEN's *FIDELIO,* the trumpet announces the arrival of the new governor, who is to establish justice. In GEORGES BIZET's *CARMEN* the trumpet summons Don José to the barracks. In innumerable marches, operatic and orchestral, the trumpet sets the marching time for soldiers. But the trumpet can also be meditative and even philosophical, particularly when muted, as in *The Unanswered Question* by CHARLES IVES.

Trumpet Voluntary. A celebrated MARCH long and mistakenly attributed to HENRY PURCELL but actually written by Jeremiah Clarke (b. London, c.1673; d. there, suicide, Dec. 1, 1707), a younger contemporary of Purcell with an even briefer lifespan. The original title was *The Prince of Denmark's March,* originally a HARPSICHORD piece (by 1700). It was then scored for wind band with many a flourish, to glorify the arrival in England of Prince George of Denmark, consort of Queen Anne.

tuba. 1. Brass instrument in the BASS range of the orchestra, where it supplies a harmonic foundation for the trumpets and trombones above it. It replaced the SERPENT and OPHICLÉIDE. It has a wide conical bore, cupped mouthpiece, and flared bell held upright. It can have between three and six VALVES.

In the 19th century there were three sizes—tenor, bass, and double-bass—the last an OCTAVE below the tenor tuba, now obsolete (replaced by the BARITONE). The so-called WAGNER TUBA is smaller than the standard variety and more mellifluous. In two sizes, they were specially designed for the music dramas performed at the Bayreuth Festival, thus they were known as Bayreuth tubas.

2. Straight trumpet of the Romans.

3. In the organ, a reed STOP (*tuba mirabilis*) on a heavy pressure of wind, of very powerful and thrilling tone.

tubaphone. A GLOCKENSPIEL in which the metal bars are replaced by metal pipes, with a sound approaching that of a

MUSICAL
INSTRUMENT

MUSICAL
INSTRUMENT

XYLOPHONE. It is used in ARAM KHACHATURIAN's *Sabre Dance* (from *Ganayeh*).

Tubb, Ernest (Dale), American country-music singer, guitarist, and songwriter; b. near Crisp, Tex., Feb. 9, 1914; d. Nashville, Tenn., Sept. 6, 1984. Following in the path of JIMMIE RODGERS, Tubb became a leading figure in the development of the "Western swing" or HONKY-TONK style of COUNTRY MUSIC. His recording of *Walking the Floor over You* in 1941 established his reputation, and from 1942 he made regular appearances on the GRAND OLE OPRY radio program in Nashville. During World War II, Tubb worked out of Hollywood, appearing in a couple of B-grade Western films.

Tubb made his most influential recordings and radio appearances in the late '40s and early '50s with his band, the Texas Troubadours. The group was unusual for a country outfit of the day because they prominently featured electric guitar as the lead instrument. In 1947 Tubb opened his famous record shop in Nashville, which became the host of a midnight radio show following the *Grand Ole Opry*'s broadcast.

Tubb's '60s recordings suffered from the same kind of heavy-handed strings and choruses that marred many Nashville products of that era. In 1965 he was elected to the Country Music Hall of Fame. Although Tubb continued to perform until his death in 1984, his recording career virtually ended in 1970.

His son, Justin (b. 1935, San Antonio, Tex.) also was a country star and member of the *Grand Ole Opry* since 1955. He is most famous as the author of the song *Lonesome 7-7203*, a 1963 hit for Hawkshaw Hawkins.

Tubin, Eduard, Estonian-born Swedish composer and conductor; b. Kallaste, near Tartu, June 18, 1905; d. Stockholm, Nov. 17, 1982. Tubin studied with A. Kapp at the Tartu Conservatory and later with ZOLTÁN KODÁLY in Budapest. From 1931 to 1944 he conducted the Vanemuine Theater Orchestra in Tartu. He then settled in Stockholm in 1944, becoming a naturalized citizen in 1961. In 1982 he was elected to the Royal Swedish Academy of Music. He was at work on his 11th Symphony at the time of his death.

Tubin is best known for his SYMPHONIES (1934; *Legendary,* 1937; 1942; *Lyrical,* 1943; 1946; 1954; 1958; 1966; *Sinfonia semplice,* 1969; 1973), two CONCERTOS for violin, double bass, BALALAIKA, and the piano concertino, SONATAS (with piano) for violin (two), saxophone, viola, and flute, sonata for solo violin, two operas, a BALLET, and the *Requiem for Fallen Soldiers* for alto, male chorus, solo trumpet, PERCUSSION, and organ in 1979.

tubular chimes (Ger. *Röhrenglocken*). Metal bells made of long, hollow cylindrical tubes, arranged like a KEYBOARD and suspended from a frame. They are also called chimes, orchestral bells, or tubular bells.

The PITCH is more definite than that of the church bells it sometimes imitates (HECTOR BERLIOZ, *Symphonie fantastique*). Many modern scores use it, including EDGARD VARÈSE'S *IONISATION.*

MUSICAL INSTRUMENT

Tucker, Richard (born Reuben Ticker), brilliant American tenor; b. N.Y., Aug. 28, 1913; d. Kalamazoo, Mich., Jan. 8, 1975. Tucker sang in a synagogue choir in N.Y. as a child. He studied voice with Paul Althouse and subsequently sang on radio. His first public appearance in opera was as Alfredo in *LA TRAVIATA* in 1943 with the Salmaggi Company in N.Y.

Tucker made his Metropolitan Opera debut in N.Y. as Enzo in *LA GIOCONDA* in 1945, remaining on its roster until his death, specializing in the Italian TENOR repertoire. In 1947 he made his European debut at the Verona Arena as Enzo (Maria Callas made her Italian debut as Gioconda in the same performance). Tucker also sang at Covent Garden in London, La Scala in Milan, Vienna, and other major music centers abroad.

Tucker died while on a concert tour. He was the brother-in-law of the American tenor JAN PEERCE.

PEOPLE IN MUSIC

Tucker (born Abuza), **Sophie,** ribald popular Russian-born American entertainer; b. in Russia, Jan. 13, 1884; d. N.Y., Feb. 9, 1966. Tucker was taken to the U.S. in infancy. She began her career as a singer in her father's restaurant in Hartford, Connecticut, then sang in burlesque, VAUDEVILLE, and English MUSIC HALLS. She gained fame during the World

PEOPLE IN MUSIC

Tucker was particularly well known for the rendition of her theme song, *Some of These Days.*

PEOPLE IN MUSIC

War I era and remained a popular entertainer for 60 years, continuing her professional appearances in nightclubs, in films, and on radio and television.

Tuckwell, Barry (Emmanuel), noted Australian horn player and conductor; b. Melbourne, Mar. 5, 1931. Tuckwell was taught piano by his father and violin by his older brother, and was a chorister and organist at St. Andrew's Cathedral in Sydney.

At age 13 Tuckwell began studying the horn with Alan Mann at the Sydney Conservatory. Making rapid progress, he played in the Sydney Symphony Orchestra from 1947 to 1950. He then went to England, where he received valuable advice on horn technique from DENNIS BRAIN. He also gathered ideas about horn sound from listening to recordings by JAZZ trombonist TOMMY DORSEY.

Tuckwell filled positions as assistant first horn with the Halle Orchestra in Manchester from 1951 to 1953, the Scottish National Orchestra in 1953–54, and, as first horn, with the Bournemouth Symphony Orchestra in 1954–55. He then served for 13 years—until 1968—as first horn with the London Symphony Orchestra.

Tuckwell subsequently launched a solo career, achieving recognition as one of the foremost virtuosos on the instrument. In the academic field he compiled a horn method and edited horn literature. Several modern composers wrote works for him: Thea Musgrave (a CONCERTO requiring QUARTER TONES), RICHARD RODNEY BENNETT (*Actaeon*), IAIN HAMILTON (*Voyage*), ALAN HODDINOTT (a concerto), and DON BANKS (a concerto).

Tuckwell also pursued a conducting career, making guest appearances in Australia, Europe, and the U.S. He was conductor of the Tasmanian Symphony Orchestra from 1980 to 1983, and was also music director of the newly founded Maryland Symphony Orchestra in Hagerstown from 1982 to 1998. In 1965 he was made an Officer of the Order of the British Empire. In 1996 he became a naturalized American citizen.

PEOPLE IN MUSIC

Tudor, David (Eugene), brilliant American pianist and composer of live ELECTRONIC MUSIC; b. Philadelphia, Jan.

20, 1926; d. Tomkins Cove, N.Y., Aug. 13, 1996. At age 11 Tudor heard an organ work by OLIVIER MESSIAEN, marking the beginning of his devotion to the music of his time. He studied piano with J. Marin and I. W. Rademacher, organ and theory with H. William Hawke, and composition and analysis with STEPAN WOLPE.

Tudor's role as a pioneer performer of new music was established when he gave the U.S. premiere of PIERRE BOULEZ's Second Piano Sonata in N.Y. in 1950. About that time, he began a close association with JOHN CAGE, whose works he performed throughout the world. He evolved imaginative and virtuosic solutions to the challenges of AVANT-GARDE works through a rigorous preparation process, distilling compositions that incorporated some degree of IN-DETERMINACY into more conventional NOTATION for performance through the refining apparatus of measurements, calculations, conversion tables, and intricate computations.

When performing *5 Piano Pieces for David Tudor* by Sylvano Bussotti, Tudor put on thick, leather gloves to play the tone clusters.

After mastering the problems unique to avant-garde music, Tudor moved gradually into live electronic music. He became affiliated with the Merce Cunningham Dance Company in 1953, for which he produced numerous SCORES, including *Rain Forest I* (1968), *Toneburst* (1974), *Forest Speech* (1976), *Weatherings* (1978), *Phonemes* (1981), *Sextet for 7* (1982), *Fragments* (1984), *Webwork* (1987), *Five Stone Wind* (with Cage and TAKEHISA KOSUGI; 1988), and *Virtual Focus* (1990).

David Tudor (left) *and John Cage in Japan, testing a ritual bell. (John Cage Trust)*

Tudor taught at Black Mountain College from 1951 to 1953, and taught piano and new music performance as well at the Internationale Ferienkürse für Neue Musik at Darmstadt during the years 1956, 1958–59, and 1961. He also gave courses in live electronic music at the State University of N.Y. at Buffalo in 1965–66, the University of California at Davis in 1967, Mills College in Oakland, California, in 1967–68, and the National Institute of Design in Ahmedabad, India, in 1969.

In 1968 Tudor was selected as one of four core artists for the design and construction of the Pepsico Pavilion at Expo '70 in Osaka. Among his other collaborators were Lowell Cross, Marcel and Teeny Duchamp, Gordon Mumma, Anthony Martin, Molly Davies, and Jackie Matisse.

Tudor suffered a number of strokes in his later years, which rendered him blind at the end of his life. His cremated remains, along with those of Cage, were scattered within the community in which both once lived, the Gatehill Co-Op in Stony Point, N.Y.

tune. An AIR, MELODY. A term chiefly applied to short, simple pieces or familiar melodies. Its colloquial applications are practically boundless.

tuning (Fr. *action d'accorder;* Ger. *Stimmung*). 1. The process of bringing an instrument into tune with itself or with other instruments. By universal convention, orchestral tuning begins with the oboe giving an A of the middle OCTAVE, in most orchestras pitched at 440 cycles per second. The rest of the orchestral instruments adjust themselves to this PITCH.

In piano tuning, it is necessary to reconcile the difference between the tempered PERFECT FIFTH and FOURTH with the just INTERVALS based on the OVERTONE SERIES. Piano fifths and fourths have to be altered to make twelve fifths identical to seven octaves. The piano tuner arrives at this equation by making sure that tempered fifths produce about 47 BEATS a minute, made audible by the slight increase and decrease of the loudness of the principal tone.

2. The *accordatura* of a stringed instrument.

Tuning cone, hollow cone of metal for tuning metal flue pipes in the organ; *tuning crook,* CROOK; *tuning hammer,* hand wrench for tuning pianos; *tuning horn,* tuning cone; *tuning key,* tuning hammer; *tuning slide,* sliding U-shaped section of the tube in certain BRASS instruments, used to adjust pitch subtly to other instruments.

tuning fork (Fr. *diapason;* Ger. *Stimmgabel;* It. *corista*). A two-pronged metal fork yielding one fixed TONE, usually A above middle C (a¹; most commonly 440 cycles per second). By varying the thickness or the length of each prong, tuning forks can be manufactured to play various PITCHES.

tupan. Double-headed cylindrical drum of the South Slavic region, with the heads tuned a fifth apart. It is carried on straps over the body of the player, who strikes it with a drumstick in the right hand and a switch (whip) in the left hand, either together or in alternation.

MUSICAL
INSTRUMENT

Turandot. Opera by GIACOMO PUCCINI, 1926, left unfinished at his death and first performed incomplete at the Metropolitan Opera in N.Y. by ARTURO TOSCANINI. Toscanini stated on completion of the (incomplete) performance: "At this point, the master lay down his pen, and died." The next day, the work was performed with FRANCO ALFANO's ending using Puccini's thematic material, and it is in this form that *Turandot* is usually performed.

The SCORE is remarkable in many respects: in it Puccini attempted bold experimentation, approaching POLYTONALITY and ATONALITY. Because Turandot is a Chinese princess, Puccini made use of PENTATONIC SCALES supposedly based on East Asian FOLK SCALES.

The LIBRETTO is based on an 18th-century play by Carlo Gozzi. Princess Turandot announces that she will marry only a man wise enough to solve three riddles proposed by her, the price of failure being death. Her palace begins to look like a mortuary, as one after another contender fails the quiz.

But she meets her match in the person of Calaf, an exiled prince of Tatary, a Mongol group at war with China. He solves all her riddles, ludicrous as they are, and she begs him to release her from the obligation to marry. He agrees if she can guess his own name by the next morning.

FERRUCCIO BUSONI had previously written an opera based on the same play in 1917, although his version was less successful.

The only person who knows his name is Liù, a Tatar slave girl who has followed Calaf and loves him secretly. She is tortured on Turandot's order and stabs herself to death to avoid the disclosure. After Calaf gives her a clue in the form of an embrace, Turandot guesses that his name is Love. This realization makes it possible for her to marry him, and the opera concludes with a sumptuous oriental celebration.

Puccini's last completed music was the death of Liù. He spent many months trying to complete the opera, but the love duet and transformation of Turandot proved impossible for him to compose.

PEOPLE IN MUSIC

Turina (y Perez), **Joaquín,** prominent Spanish composer; b. Seville, Dec. 9, 1882; d. Madrid, Jan. 14, 1949. Turina studied with local teachers, then entered the Madrid Conservatory as a piano student of José Tragó. In 1905 he went to Paris to study composition with VINCENT D'INDY at the Schola Cantorum and piano with MORITZ MOSZKOWSKI. At ISAAC ALBÉNIZ's urging he turned to Spanish FOLK MUSIC for inspiration.

Returning to Madrid in 1914, Turina composed two characteristically Spanish symphonic works, *La procesión del Rocío* and *Sinfonía sevillana,* combining ROMANTIC and IMPRESSIONIST elements in an individual manner. The same effective combination is found in his chamber music of Spanish inspiration (*Escena andaluza, La oración del torero*) and piano music (*Sonata romántica, Mujeres españolas*). He also wrote five operas and incidental music for the theater.

In 1930 Turina was appointed a professor of composition at the Madrid Conservatory. He also founded the general music commission of the Ministry of Education, serving as its commissioner in 1941.

MUSICAL INSTRUMENT

Turken-Trommel (Ger.). Turkish drum; obsolete for bass drum.

Turkey in the Straw. American square dance tune identical to that of the song *Zip Coon,* published in N.Y., 1834. It was probably a variant of an Irish HORNPIPE, a popular dance style early in the 19th century.

turkey trot. African-American "animal step" dance popular in the early 20th century. Others include the grizzly bear, bunny hug, chicken flip, horse trot, and (naturally) the fox-trot.

Turkish March. Piece by LUDWIG VAN BEETHOVEN, 1812, from the incidental music to *The Ruins of Athens.* Its Turkish quality is nothing more than a rhythmic march in $\frac{2}{4}$ time.

Turkish music. *See* JANIZARY MUSIC.

Turm-musik (Ger.). Tower music, played on brass instruments by *Stadtpfeifer* in the turret of the town hall to announce the hour.

Turn of the Screw, The. Opera by BENJAMIN BRITTEN, 1954, after the psychological novel of Henry James, first produced in Venice.

A governess is placed in charge of a young boy and girl, in a dismal house in the English countryside. Two former servants, now dead, seem to exercise a mysterious hold on the children's minds. The governess herself entertains a neurotic belief in the strange posthumous influence. In questioning the boy she brings him to break his alliance with the ghosts; but in the process his heart gives way and he dies.

The opera, like the novel, leaves the mystery of reality and superstition unsolved. The score is expressionistic, and there is a modified application of DODECAPHONIC techniques. The thematic "screw" is turned in 15 INTERLUDES (VARIATIONS on the opening thematic fourth) connecting the opera's eight scenes. The composer makes superb use of a chamber orchestra.

Turn, Turn, Turn. A 1965 FOLK-ROCK hit for the BYRDS. It was written by PETE SEEGER, who drew his lyrics from the Book of Ecclesiastes.

Turner, Joseph Vernon, aka "Big Joe," African-American BLUES singer; b. Kansas City, Mo., May 18, 1911; d. Englewood, California, Nov. 24, 1985. Turner first worked as a

PEOPLE IN MUSIC

singing bartender in local nightclubs. In the late '20s and early '30s, he toured with several of the well-known Kansas City JAZZ bands, including COUNT BASIE's orchestra. In the mid-'30s, he became associated with the BOOGIE-WOOGIE pianist PETE JOHNSON. In 1938 they appeared together at CARNEGIE HALL in N.Y.

After moving to California, Turner sang with DUKE ELLINGTON's band. In 1945 he and Johnson began appearing at their own club in Los Angeles. He later toured the U.S. and Europe.

In the late '40s, Turner began recording in the JUMP style that was then very popular. Turner's 1954 recording of *Shake, Rattle, and Roll* helped create the ROCK 'N' ROLL craze which swept the nation in the 1950s. He followed with similar hits through the late '50s.

Turner fell out of the spotlight from the early '60s through the early '70s. He then returned as a singer of Kansas City–styled blues and jazz. He became a familiar figure on the jazz circuit, touring the U.S. and Europe and recording prolifically.

Turner, Tina (born Anna Mae Bullock), pulsating African-American soul and rock singer and actress; b. Brownsville, Tenn., Nov. 26, 1939. Bullock joined Ike Turner (b. Clarksdale, Miss., Nov. 5, 1931) and his band, the Kings of Rhythm, in St. Louis in 1956; he gave her the new name of "Tina." After they were married in 1958, they toured as the Ike and Tina Turner Revue, accompanied by a female dance-and-vocal trio, the Ikettes.

Tina made an explosive impact as a sexually provocative and intense singer, belting out such numbers as *I've Been Lovin' You Too Long* and *River Deep, Mountain High* (1966).

A 1969 tour of the U.S. with the ROLLING STONES catapulted the Revue onto center stage. They won a Grammy Award for their recording of PROUD MARY in 1971. While continuing to make appearances with her husband, Tina made the solo albums *Let Me Touch Your Hand* (1972) and *Tina Turns the Country On* (1974). In 1975 she appeared as the Acid Queen in the rock-opera film *Tommy,* and that year brought out the album *Acid Queen.*

PEOPLE IN MUSIC

After years of marital abuse, Tina left Ike in 1976 and obtained a divorce two years later. She then pursued a solo career as a ROCK-AND-SOUL songstress. After a few failures she produced the tremendously successful album *Private Dancer* in 1984. That same year she won four Grammy Awards, with *What's Love Got to Do with It?* being honored as best song and best record of the year. In 1985 she starred (opposite heartthrob Mel Gibson) in the film *Mad Max beyond Thunderdome.*

Tina's follow-up albums include *Break Every Rule* (1986) and *Foreign Affair* (1989). In the '90s, she has continued to perform and record. However, she has enjoyed greater success in Europe than at home. Her autobiography, also titled *What's Love Got to Do with It?*, was made into a successful film in 1993.

Tusch (Ger.; Eng. obs., *tuck, tucket*). A complimentary FAN-FARE played by orchestral musicians for an honored conductor or soloist.

toosh

tutti (It.). Indication in an orchestral or choral score that the entire orchestra or CHORUS is to enter. It is usually placed after an extended solo passage.

too'tē

Tutti Frutti. LITTLE RICHARD's joyous 1956 ode, whose cryptic lyrics were written in the studio when the producer deemed the original version too obscene to record. Perhaps the defining song of early rock, it was covered in white-bread style by Pat Boone later that year.

twelfth. *See* INTERVAL.

twelve-note composition. *See* DODECAPHONY.

twelve-tone music (Ger. *zwölftonmusik*). Historically significant method of musical organization, born in 1923 and most profoundly developed by ARNOLD SCHOENBERG. In this system, all 12 notes of the CHROMATIC scale are ordered and treated without concern for their TONAL and/or harmonic functions. In effect, all 12-tone themes are composed of the 12 different tones of the chromatic scale.

Schoenberg's own definition, which he regarded as the only correct one, is "the method of composition with 12 tones related only to one another."

The concept of 12-tone music was later incorporated in the generic category of SERIALISM, in which not only intervals but also dynamics and instrumental timbres can be organized in a series.

24 Violins of the King. *See* VINGT-QUATRE VIOLONS DU ROI.

Twilight of the Gods. *See* GÖTTERDÄMMERUNG.

Twinkle, Twinkle, Little Star. A melody that first appeared in the middle of the 18th century, probably derived from a French FOLK SONG. The French text, *Ah, Vous dirai-je, maman,* is the earliest known version of the song. In an 1834 American collection, *The Schoolmaster,* the tune is set to the alphabet and popularized in this form in Russia and other countries.

The familiar English words were written by a Londoner named Jane Taylor and published in an 1806 collection, *Rhymes for the Nursery.*

WOLFGANG AMADEUS MOZART wrote a set of piano variations on the melody of *Twinkle, Twinkle* during one of his sojourns in Paris.

Twist, The. Song by HANK BALLARD, 1959, that helped launch the dance craze of the same name in 1960, as sung by CHUBBY CHECKER. Ballard wrote the song and recorded it first. But when he failed to show up to a live broadcast of Dick Clark's *American Bandstand* television show, Checker substituted and began his march to fame, with a No. 1 record and other hits.

Twist and Shout. The Isley Brother's R&B rave-up of 1962, cashing in on the popular dance. This song was covered by the BEATLES two years later and became a major pop hit.

Two Guitars. Russian gypsy song of uncertain origin, published in 1912. In subsequent editions it was preceded by an ingenious introduction for violin PIZZICATO. The text comments on the melancholy two-guitar melody that evokes sadness in the soul of the listener.

PEOPLE IN MUSIC

Tye, Christopher, English organist and composer; b. c.1505; d. c.1572. In 1536 Tye received his music degree from Cambridge, and in 1537 he was appointed lay clerk at

King's College there. In 1543 he became Magister choristarum at Ely Cathedral, and in 1545 he received a doctorate in music degree from the University of Cambridge.

After becoming a deacon and a priest in 1560, Tye left Ely Cathedral in 1561. He held livings at Doddington-cum-Marche in the Isle of Ely, beginning in 1561, at Wilbraham Parva from 1564 to 1567, and Newton-cum-capella from 1564 to 1570.

Tye's son-in-law was Robert White (Whyte; b. c.1538; d. London, Nov. 1574), best known for settings of the Lamentations and instrumental fantasias.

Tye described himself as a gentleman of the King's Chapel on the title page of his only published work, *The Actes of the Apostles, translated into Englyshe metre to synge and also to play upon the Lute,* which was published in London in 1553. The HYMN tunes *Windsor* and *Winchester Old* are adaptations from this collection.

Tye was an important composer of English church music, leaving MASSES, SERVICES, MOTETS, and ANTHEMS. He was an active composer of VIOL consort music, notably his numerous IN NOMINE FANTASIAS.

tympani. *See* TIMPANI.

Typewriter, The. Popular novelty instrumental by LEROY ANDERSON, 1950. The score includes a part for the old-fashioned mechanical typewriter, with its clanging bell announcing the end of a line.

Tyranny, Blue Gene (real name, Robert Nathan Sheff), American keyboardist and composer; b. San Antonio, Jan. 1, 1945. He studied piano and composition privately (1957–62), winning a BMI Student Composers award for his *Piano Sonata on Expanding Thoughts* in 1961. From 1962 to 1968 he was active in the ONCE Group in Ann Arbor, Michigan, helping to establish its reputation for mixed media and cross-cultural performance. He also taught KEYBOARD and JAZZ COMPOSITION at Mills College in Oakland, California (1971–81).

Tyranny made numerous recordings and performed with Laurie Anderson and Peter Gordon. He collaborated on

PEOPLE IN MUSIC

Robert Ashley's *Perfect Lives (Private Parts)* (1976 – 83) and also wrote scores for dance, theater, film, and video. A 1975 fire destroyed about half of his early scores, many of which he is currently reconstructing. He is also an important proponent of integrating jazz and ROCK elements into concert music. The range of imagination and genre evidenced by his catalog is remarkable.

Among Tyranny's "procedural" works are *How to Make Music from the Sounds of Your Daily Life* (1967; realized on tape as *Country Boy Country Dog*), *How To Do It* (1973; intentionally incomplete), *The More He Sings, The More He Cries, The Better He Feels . . . Tango* (1984; realized for TAPE and piano; orchestrated 1985), and *Extreme Realizations Just before Sunset (Mobile)* (1987; realized for piano, tape, and computer). Other recent works include *The Forecaster* for orchestra and electronics (1988 – 89), *The Great Seal (Transmigration)* for piano duo (1990), *My Language Is Me (Millennium)* for voice and electronics (1990), and *Vocal Responses during Transformation* for voices and live electronics (1990).

tĕ-rŏh-l'yen′

tyrolienne (Fr.). A Tyrolian dance or dance song, based on the local equivalent of the LÄNDLER. A modern round dance in $\frac{3}{4}$ time and easy movement, with a characteristic dotted rhythm on the third beat. A peculiar feature of the dance song is the use of the YODEL, especially in the refrain.

GIOACCHINO ROSSINI wrote a tyrolienne for his WILLIAM TELL.

Tzigane. A RHAPSODY for violin and orchestra by MAURICE RAVEL, 1924, written for the Hungarian violinist JELLY D'ARANYI. Originally Ravel wrote it for violin and LUTHEAL, in which version it was first performed in London, 1924, with Ravel at the lutheal.

U

Uchida, Mitsuko, talented Japanese pianist; b. Tokyo, Dec. 20, 1948. Uchida began training in childhood in her native city, and at the age of 12 became a pupil of Richard Hauser at the Vienna Academy of Music. In 1968 she won the Beethoven Competition and in 1970 received second prize at the Chopin Competition in Warsaw.

In 1982 she won particular notice in London and Tokyo for her performances of the complete piano sonatas of WOLF-GANG AMADEUS MOZART, and during the 1985–86 season she appeared as soloist-conductor in all the piano concertos of Mozart with the English Chamber Orchestra in London. In 1987 she made her N.Y. recital debut, and in 1989 she was soloist in Mozart's Piano Concerto, K.271, in Salzburg.

Uchida's repertoire also includes works by CLAUDE DE-BUSSY, ARNOLD SCHOENBERG, and BÉLA BARTÓK.

'ud (*oud*). Arab LUTE, known since the 7th century. It has gone through numerous subtle changes in construction and numbers of strings (always in pairs), but it has retained a fretless fingerboard. The instrument is plucked with a PLEC-TRUM, and like modern guitars, tortoiseshell or a similar material is glued to the body near the SOUND HOLES to prevent damage from the pick.

The 'ud came to Spain during the Moorish occupation, and its introduction paved the way for the development of the European lute, VIHUELA, and guitar. It left with the Moors at the time of their expulsion.

The original 'ud had a pear-shaped body, whereas more modern instruments have an almond-shaped one. The modern 'ud comes in various sizes and has a shorter neck than the European lute, with four to six pairs of strings and three sound holes.

MUSICAL
INSTRUMENT

ukulele (Hawaiian, flea; U.K., ukelele). Popular small guitarlike instrument with four strings.

The instrument was originally imported by Portuguese sailors into Hawaii in the 1870s and found its way to the continental U.S. in the early 20th century. It proved very popular, in part because the use of TABLATURE allowed players who were unable to read music to learn quickly. Popular music of all kinds employed the instrument, and it could be heard in VAUDEVILLE, musicals, and films. Its popularity died out after World War II, but it could be heard in unusual settings, for example, as the accompanying instrument to the unusual vocal stylings of Tiny Tim (Herbert Khaury), who revived an endless number of TIN PAN ALLEY songs.

Ullmann, Viktor, Austrian composer; b. Teschen, Jan. 1, 1898; d. Oct. 17, 1944. He studied composition with AR-NOLD SCHOENBERG in Vienna and quarter-tone composition at the Prague Conservatory from 1935 to 1937. He was active as an accompanist and conductor at the New German Theater in Prague.

Ullmann wrote music in the EXPRESSIONISTIC manner, without renouncing latent tonality. In 1942 he was arrested by the Nazis and sent to the concentration camp in Theresienstadt (Terezín). There he composed a one-act opera, *Der Kaiser von Atlantis,* in 1943, depicting a tyrannical monarch who outlaws death but later begs for its return to relieve humanity of its suffering. The manuscript was preserved, and the work was performed for the first time on Dec. 16, 1975, in Amsterdam. His opera *Der zerbrochene Krug* of 1941 was premiered in Weimar on May 17, 1996.

Of the many composers at Theresienstadt, Ullmann was the most prolific, composing three piano sonatas, a string quartet, and many songs and choruses. He was part of the Nazi plan to present a "model camp" to the International Red Cross. As such, it flourished under its false guise for a few years until the Nazis decided to end the musical activities and make way for new prisoners. The Theresienstadt prisoners were taken to Auschwitz, one of the death factories in the Nazi arsenal. Most were exterminated, including Ullmann.

Other composers who perished at Auschwitz in 1944 were Pavel Haas (b. Brno, 1899; a student of LEOS JANÁČEK),

Hans Krása (b. Prague, 1899; composer of the children's opera *Brundibár,* performed 55 times at Theresienstadt), and Zikmund Schul (b. Kassel, 1916, student of Hába). Another active composer, Gideon Klein (b. Přerov, 1919), wrote chamber and vocal music at Auschwitz. He died at Fürtengrube in late January 1945.

una corda (It., one string; abbrev. *U.C.*). An indication directing the player to use the SOFT PEDAL. This pedal moves the entire KEYBOARD, and with it the hammers, slightly to the right so that the hammers strike only one string instead of two or three. When the composer wishes to restore full sonority, the indication is TRE CORDE (three strings).

oo-nǎh kôr′dǎh

LUDWIG VAN BEETHOVEN was the first to use these terms systemically in his piano works.

Unanswered Question, The. Chamber orchestra work by CHARLES IVES, 1908, sometimes subtitled *A Cosmic Landscape.* A solo trumpet propounds the "unanswered question" in an ATONAL setting, echoed in confusion by WOODWINDS, supported ethereally by STRINGS. The SCORE is remarkable because its components are written at different TEMPOS in different METERS. The work was not performed until nearly 50 years after its composition, at which point it became an instant classic.

***Unfinished* Symphony.** Symphony No. 8 by FRANZ SCHUBERT, 1822, set in the melancholy key of B minor. A profoundly ROMANTIC semi-symphony, it has but two complete movements. Despite its fragmentary condition, the symphony became Schubert's most famous orchestral work. The manuscript also contains a few measures of the SCHERZO (third movement).

While Schubert never intended it to remain unfinished, there is a mystery as to why it was left incomplete. Schubert intended the work to be a token of acknowledgment of his election as an honorary member to the musical societies in Linz and Graz in 1822, when he was 25 years old. The manuscript eventually wound up in the cluttered Viennese room of Anselm Hüttenbrenner, a friend of the composer's. It received its first performance 37 years after Schubert's untimely death at the age of 31.

On Schubert's death centennial in 1928, an international competition was held for the completion of the *Unfinished* Symphony. However, worldwide protests against this desecration of a musical monument changed the requirements to a work in the spirit of the master. The prize was given to the Sixth Symphony of Kurt Atterberg, who declared afterwards that his score was a deliberate imitation of the style of the judges of the competition. In recent years, completions have been made of the scherzo, but the total lack of sketches for the finale render any attempt to perform the "entire work" completely absurd.

unison (sounded as 1; It. *unisono*). 1. A TONE of the same PITCH as a given tone; also, a higher or lower OCTAVE of the given tone. Some texts use the term *prime*. 2. Performing the same exact pitches on a POLYPHONIC instrument or with two or more voices and/or MONOPHONIC instruments. The description is often applied to playing octaves or even double octaves. 3. In the piano, a group of two or three strings tuned to the same pitch and struck by one hammer; a string in such a group is called a *unison string*.

universal harmony. *See* HARMONY OF THE SPHERES.

***Universe* Symphony.** An unfinished project of CHARLES IVES for which he made sketches from 1911 to 1918. The work was intended (in his words) to be a "contemplation in tones of the mysterious creation of the earth and firmament, the evolution of all life in nature, in humanity, to the Divine." At least two attempts at completion have been made and performed.

unvocal. 1. Not suitable for singing. 2. Not vibrating with TONE. *Unvocal air* is breath escaping with a more or less audible sigh or hiss, due to unskillful management of the voice.

upbeat (Ger. *Auftakt*). 1. The raising of the hand in beating time. 2. The last part of a MEASURE, specifically just before the DOWNBEAT.

upright piano. A piano with its strings arranged cross-wise (diagonally) along the vertical soundboard, as distinguished from a GRAND PIANO, in which the strings and the soundboard are horizontal. The hammers are made to recoil by a spring. The upright piano became popular in the 19th century partly for economy of space and partly because of the proliferation of amateur pianists in middle-class society in Europe and the U.S.

Upshaw, Dawn, American soprano; b. Nashville, Tenn., July 17, 1960. Upshaw studied at Illinois Wesleyan University, earning her B.A. degree in 1982. She then pursued vocal training with Ellen Faull at the Manhattan School of Music in N.Y., where she received her M.A. degree two years later. She also attended courses given by Jan DeGaetani at the Aspen (Colorado) Music School.

In 1984 Upshaw won the Young Concert Artists auditions and entered the Metropolitan Opera's young artists development program. The next year, she was co-winner of the Naumburg Competition in N.Y. After appearing in minor roles at the Metropolitan Opera in N.Y., she displayed her vocal gifts in such major roles as GAETANO DONIZETTI's Adina and WOLFGANG AMADEUS MOZART's Despina in 1988. She also pursued a notably successful career as a soloist with major orchestras and as a recitalist. In 1990 she sang Pamina in a concert performance of Mozart's *Die Zauberflöte* at the London Promenade Concerts, and in 1992 she appeared as the Angel in OLIVIER MESSIAEN's *St. François d'Assise* at the Salzburg Festival. In 1995 she sang STRAUSS's Sophie in Houston, in 1996 GEORGE FRIDERIC HANDEL's Theodora at the Glyndebourne Festival, and in 1997 IGOR STRAVINSKY's Anne Trulove at the Metropolitan Opera.

Upshaw's remarkable concert repertoire ranges from early music to the most difficult avant-garde scores. In recent years she has added American popular song to her repertoire.

Urtext (Ger.). Ideally, an edited SCORE that claims to present the most authentic version of a musical work. The concept emerged in the early 20th century among German scholars, who reacted against the freestyle approach to editing that

MUSICAL INSTRUMENT

Some upright pianos are called SPINETS.

PEOPLE IN MUSIC

prevailed in the 19th century. The Urtext attempts to present the original manuscript as set down on paper by the composer.

Before the Urtext, editors treated the classics in a rather cavalier fashion, freely altering the notes and harmonies. JOHANN SEBASTIAN BACH has been the favorite object of their unwelcome tamperings. There is the notorious case of an editor's adding a bar to furnish a transitional CHROMATIC harmony in the C major Prelude from the first book of *The Well-Tempered Clavier*. This bowdlerization was taken up by other editors, with the result that Bach's version had to be "rediscovered."

Editions of LUDWIG VAN BEETHOVEN's piano sonatas by Hans von Bülow and others handle the Urtext with little respect. On the other end of the spectrum, however, overly worshipful editors do not dare to correct even the most obvious of errors. Surely Beethoven's omission of an essential E♭ in the traditional chordal passage of the final section of the *Appassionata* cannot be treated as sacrosanct in publishing the work, but it is quite proper to publish a facsimile with proper documentation.

Yet one can never be sure, in editing modern works, whether seeming errors were not intentional. A copyist tried to "correct" some "wrong" notes in a manuscript of CHARLES IVES, who notated in the margin: "Do not correct; the wrong notes are right." On the other hand, when a respectful copyist questioned a misplaced accidental in the proofs of NIKOLAI RIMSKY-KORSAKOV's symphonic work, the great master retorted on the margin: "Of course it is an error. I am not some person like Debussy or Richard Strauss to write wrong notes deliberately."

But what if the composer changes his or her own Urtext? One has to decide whether to honor the composer's original authentic Urtext or to accept his or her later revision.

Ussachevsky, Vladimir (Alexis), innovative Russian-born American composer; b. Hailar, Manchuria, Nov. 3, 1911; d. N.Y., Jan. 2, 1990. Ussachevsky's parents settled in Manchuria shortly after the Russo-Japanese War of 1905. His father was an officer of the Russian army, and his mother was a professional pianist.

PEOPLE IN MUSIC

In 1930 Ussachevsky moved to the U.S. and settled in California, where he took private piano lessons with Clarence Mader. From 1931 to 1933 he attended Pasadena Junior College, and in 1933 he received a scholarship to study at Pomona College, earning his B.A. degree in 1935. He then enrolled in the Eastman School of Music in Rochester, N.Y., in the composition classes of Howard Hanson, Bernard Rogers, and Edward Royce, earning his M.A. degree in 1936 and his Ph.D. three years later. He also had some instruction with Burrill Phillips.

In 1942, as an American citizen, Ussachevsky was drafted into the U.S. Army. Thanks to his fluency in Russian, his knowledge of English and French, and the ability to communicate in rudimentary Chinese, he was engaged in the Intelligence Division. He subsequently served as a research analyst at the War Department in Washington, D.C.

Ussachevsky then pursued postdoctoral work with OTTO LUENING at Columbia University, joining its faculty in 1947 and serving as a professor of music there from 1964 to 1980. In 1959 Ussachevsky was one of the founders of the Columbia–Princeton Electronic Music Center. He was active as a lecturer at various exhibitions of electronic sounds, and also traveled frequently to Russia and in China to present his music. He held two Guggenheim fellowships (1957, 1960), and in 1973 was elected to membership in the National Institute of Arts and Letters. After leaving Columbia, he was a faculty member at the University of Utah until 1985.

Ussachevsky's early works were influenced by Russian church music, in the tradition of PIOTR ILYICH TCHAIKOVSKY and SERGEI RACHMANINOFF. A distinct change came in 1951, when he became interested in ELECTRONIC MUSIC. To this period belong his works *Transposition, Reverberation, Experiment, Composition* and *Underwater Valse,* which make use of electronic sound. In 1952 LEOPOLD STOKOWSKI conducted in N.Y. the first performance of Ussachevsky's *Sonic Contours,* in which a piano part was metamorphosed with the aid of various electronic devices. About that time he began a fruitful partnership with Luening, with whom he composed *Incantation* for TAPE RECORDER, which was broadcast in 1953.

Luening and Ussachevsky then conceived the idea of combining electronic tape sounds with conventional instruments played by musicians. The result was *Rhapsodic Variations,* first performed in N.Y. in 1954. The work anticipated by a few months the composition of the important SCORE *Déserts* by EDGARD VARÈSE, which effectively combined electronic sound with other instruments.

The next work by Ussachevsky and Luening was *A Poem in Cycles and Bells* for tape recorder and orchestra, first performed by the Los Angeles Philharmonic in 1954. In 1956 Ussachevsky and Luening provided taped background for Shakespeare's *King Lear,* produced by Orson Welles, at the N.Y. City Center, and for Margaret Webster's production of *Back to Methuselah* for the N.Y. Theater Guild in 1958.

In 1960 LEONARD BERNSTEIN conducted the N.Y. Philharmonic in a commissioned work by Ussachevsky and Luening entitled *Concerted Piece* for tape recorder and orchestra. They also provided the electronic score for the documentary *The Incredible Voyage,* broadcast over the CBS television network in 1965. Among works that Ussachevsky wrote for electronic sound on his own were *A Piece* for tape recorder in 1956 and *Studies in Sound, Plus* in 1959.

In 1968 Ussachevsky began experimenting with a computer-assisted SYNTHESIZER. One of the works resulting from these experiments, *Conflict* (1971), is intended to represent the mystical struggle between two ancient deities.

In addition to purely electronic works and his collaborations with Luening, Ussachevsky composed several works for tape and ACOUSTIC instruments and/or voice. Among his incidental works for tape are *To Catch a Thief* (sound effects for the film; 1954), *The Boy Who Saw Through* (film; 1959), *No Exit* (film; 1962), and *Mourning Becomes Electra* (sound effects for the opera by M.D. Levy). He also composed conventional orchestral, chamber, and vocal pieces.

Ut. The first of the solmization syllables, the opening syllable of the HYMN *Ut queant laxis* (That they might be relaxed . . .) assigned by Guido d'Arezzo, to correspond with the TONIC of the MODE. Because *Ut* lacks a vowel at the end and is therefore difficult to sing, it was changed to DO(H), except in French nomenclature, where *Ut* is retained as the note C. *Ut* is the only syllable in Guido's hymn that constitutes an entire word (the rest of the lines begin with the initial vocables of the words).

Utrecht Te Deum. HYMN by GEORGE FRIDERIC HANDEL, 1713. It was written on the occasion of peace concluded in Utrecht, Holland, marking the end of the war of the Spanish succession.

It was first performed with another sacred work, *Jubilate.*

V. Abbreviation for *vide, violino, volti,* and VOCE; *Vv., violini.*

Vagabond King, The. OPERETTA by RUDOLF FRIML, 1925, dealing fictionally with the life story of the 15th-century French poet François Villon and his many loves. Villon also helps fight the Burgundians to save Paris. Includes *Only a Rose, Some Day, Love Me Tonight,* and *Song of the Vagabonds.*

vagans (from Lat. *vagari,* wander). A fifth part (*quinta* pars) or voice added to the standard four-part texture of RENAISSANCE sacred vocal music. Its name indicates that there was no set range for such a part.

vaganti (from Lat. *vagari,* wander). Medieval university students who roamed freely from school to school, hence the name, which is derived from the Latin for "wander."

Even though the vaganti lived outside the framework of established society, they were divided into superior and inferior strata, the highest of them belonging to the category of *clericus,* an educated class, and the lowest to the nondescript *goliard* group. The distinctive characteristic of the vaganti was their dedication to poetry and music. Not being constrained by the strictures of the church, they indulged their fancy in songs glorifying the delight of the senses, drink, and secular games. The famous student song, still heard in European universities, *Gaudeamus igitur,* expresses this joy of living. It includes the verse, typical of the spirit of the vaganti, "Meum est propositum in taberna mori" (it is fated that I should die in a tavern). The most remarkable collection of songs by the vaganti is the *Carmina Burana,* discovered in 1803 in the Benediktbeuren (Bura Sancti Benedicti) monastery in Bavaria.

Many of the songs in the Carmina Burana were popularized in a 1937 ORATORIO by CARL ORFF.

Vaisseau fantôme, Le. *See* FLYING DUTCHMAN, THE.

Valkyries, The. *See* WALKÜRE, DIE.

Vallee, Rudy (born Hubert Prior Vallée), popular American singer, saxophonist, bandleader, and actor; b. Island Pond, Vt., July 28, 1901; d. Los Angeles, July 3, 1986. Vallee studied clarinet and saxophone in his youth. He was educated at the University of Maine and at Yale University, receiving a B.A. degree in 1927. He concurrently performed in nightclubs and VAUDEVILLE.

In 1928 Vallee gained fame when his band was engaged at N.Y.'s Heigh-Ho Club. His nasal-crooned rendition of *My Time Is Your Time,* a popular favorite, became his theme song. He struck a responsive chord with such numbers as *THE WHIFFENPOOF SONG* and *I'm Just a Vagabond Lover.* From 1929 to 1939 he was a leading performer on radio. He also starred in his own variety show and appeared in many forgettable films.

Vallee made a remarkable comeback when he starred in the hit Broadway musical *How to Succeed in Business Without Really Trying* in 1961, a title that aptly described his own lucrative career. He also appeared in the film version of the show made in 1967. He tried to persuade municipal authorities to name the street on which he lived after him, but without success.

◄

A 1996 Royal Ballet production of La Valse. *(Robbie Jack/Corbis)*

Valse, La. Choreographic symphony by MAURICE RAVEL, 1919–20, first performed in Paris. The WALTZ rhythm is purposely dimmed as though perceived through an acoustical fog, but gradually the familiar shape becomes more and more dominant until it overwhelms the senses with a powerful explosion of sound.

La Valse is Ravel's savage parody on the world of France's World War I enemies. The work was first performed as a ballet in Paris in 1928. There is also a two-piano version from 1921.

Valse Boston. *See* HESITATION WALTZ; *see also* WALTZ.

Valse triste. INCIDENTAL MUSIC for strings by JEAN SIBELIUS, 1903. The work was composed as part of the play *Kuolema* (Death) by Sibelius's brother-in-law, Arvid Järnefelt, produced in Helsinki.

Next to *FINLANDIA,* this is Sibelius's most popular work. It is lyric and full of natural grace, yet there are interesting harmonic progressions not often found in traditional waltz movements. Sibelius later rescored the work for chamber orchestra and conducted its first performance in Helsinki in 1904.

Valses nobles et sentimentales. Piano SUITE by MAURICE RAVEL, 1911, inspired by FRANZ SCHUBERT's waltzes, first performed in Paris. Ravel orchestrated this suite the following year, when it was performed as a ballet, *Adélaïde, ou Le Langage des fleurs,* in Paris.

value. The time duration of a NOTE or REST relative to (*a*) other notes in the same MOVEMENT, or (*b*) the standard WHOLE NOTE or any other note.

MUSICAL INSTRUMENT

---

valve (Ger. *Ventil*). In brass wind instruments, a device for diverting the air current from the main tube into an additional side tube. This lengthens the AIR COLUMN and therefore lowers the PITCH of the instrument's entire SCALE.

The valve system came into use about 1815. Before that time, trumpets, horns, and other brass could play only NATURAL (HARMONIC) tones above a single FUNDAMENTAL. In the orchestral scores of classical works, the parts of trumpets and horns, commonly set in a variety of pitches, compelled the player either to use several instruments in different KEYS or to manually insert extra tubing (CROOK) to change the length of the air column. Modern instruments eliminate this laborious procedure with the aid of three or more valves. As a result, a full CHROMATIC scale can be played. Valves may be operated with piston or rotary mechanisms.

valve bugle. *See* SAXHORN.

vamp. In popular music and JAZZ, an improvised introduction or accompaniment. It usually consists of a succession of CHORDS played against a repeated figure in the bass, to a set rhythmic pace.

Van Beinum, Eduard. *See* BEINUM, EDUARD VAN.

Varèse, Edgard (Edgar) (Victor Achille Charles), French-born American composer; b. Paris, Dec. 22, 1883; d. N.Y., Nov. 6, 1965. Varèse's paternal grandfather was Italian, and his other grandparents were French. He spent his early childhood in Paris and in Burgundy and began to compose early in life.

PEOPLE IN MUSIC

In 1892 Varèse's parents went to Turin, where he took private lessons in composition with Giovanni Bolzoni, who taught him without charge. Varèse gained some performing experience by playing percussion in the school orchestra. He stayed there until 1903, then went to Paris.

In 1904 Varèse entered the Schola Cantorum, where he studied composition, COUNTERPOINT, and FUGUE

◄

Edgard Varèse. (New York Public Library)

with Albert Roussel, preclassical music with Charles Bordes, and conducting with VINCENT D'INDY. He then entered the composition class of Charles-Marie Widor at the Paris Conservatory in 1905.

In 1907 Varèse received the *bourse artistique* (art's prize) offered by the City of Paris. At that time he founded and conducted the chorus of the University Populaire and organized concerts at the Château du Peuple. He became associated with musicians and artists of the AVANT-GARDE, meeting CLAUDE DEBUSSY, who showed interest in his career. In 1907 he married the actress Suzanne Bing with whom he had a daughter. Together they went to Berlin, at that time the center of NEW MUSIC. The marriage was not successful, and they separated in 1913.

Romain Rolland gave Varèse a letter of recommendation to RICHARD STRAUSS, who in turn showed interest in Varèse's music. Rolland was also instrumental in arranging a performance of Varèse's symphonic poem *Bourgogne,* which was performed in Berlin in 1910. The hostile reception that he encountered from Berlin critics for *Bourgogne* upset Varèse, who expressed his unhappiness in a letter to Debussy. However, Debussy responded with a friendly letter of encouragement, advising Varèse not to pay too much attention to critics. Later in life, Varèse destroyed the manuscript of the work.

The greatest experience for Varèse in Berlin was his meeting and friendship with FERRUCCIO BUSONI, whose theories of music were very influential on the young composer. Also while in Berlin, Varèse composed industriously, mostly for orchestra. The most ambitious of these works was a SYMPHONIC POEM, *Gargantua,* but it was never completed. Several other works, including an unfinished opera, were lost under somewhat mysterious circumstances.

As early as 1913 Varèse began to look for new ways to perform and compose music. Upon his return to Paris, he worked with the Italian musical FUTURIST LUIGI RUSSOLO on this question, although, unlike Russolo, industrial noise as a new type of musical resource did not interest him. He served briefly in the French army at the outbreak of World War I but was discharged because of a chronic lung ailment.

In 1915 Varèse went to N.Y., where he met the American writer Louise Norton. They set up a household together, and in 1921, when she obtained a divorce from her previous husband, they were married.

As in Paris and Berlin, Varèse had chronic financial difficulties in the U.S. The royalties from his few published works were minimal, and in order to supplement his earnings he accepted a job as a piano salesman. He also appeared in a minor role in a John Barrymore silent film in 1918. Some welcome aid came from the wealthy patron Gertrude Vanderbilt, who sent him monthly allowances for a short time.

Varèse also had an opportunity to appear as a conductor. As the U.S. considered entering the war against Germany, there was a demand for French conductors to replace the German music directors who had held a monopoly on American orchestras. In 1917 Varèse conducted the Requiem of HECTOR BERLIOZ in N.Y. In 1918 he conducted a concert of the Cincinnati Symphony Orchestra in a program of French and Russian music. He also included an excerpt from RICHARD WAGNER's *Lohengrin,* thus defying the general wartime ban on German music. However, he apparently lacked that indefinable quality that makes a conductor, and he was forced to cancel further concerts with the Cincinnati Symphony Orchestra.

Eager to promote the cause of modern music, Varèse organized a symphony orchestra in N.Y. with the specific purpose of giving performances of new and unusual music. It presented its first concert in 1919. In 1922 he organized with Carlos Salzedo the International Composers' Guild, which gave its inaugural concert in N.Y. that year. In 1926 he founded, in association with a few progressive musicians, the Pan American Society, dedicated to the promotion of music of the Americas. He also became a naturalized U.S. citizen.

From 1926 to 1936 Varèse intensified his study of the nature of sound, working with the acoustician Harvey Fletcher and with LEON THEREMIN, then resident in the U.S. These studies led him to the formulation of the concept of ORGANIZED SOUND. The sounds used by the composer would themselves determine the organization of a composition.

The resulting product was unique in modern music. Characteristically, Varèse attached to his works titles from the field of mathematics or physics, such as *Intégrales, Hyperprism* (a projection of a prism into the fourth dimension), *Ionisation,* and *Density 21.5* for solo flute. The last work was commissioned by Georges Barrère (1876–1944) and named for the atomic weight of platinum. The score of his large orchestral work *Arcana* derived its inspiration from the writings of the medieval Swiss philosopher Paracelsus.

Later in his career, in the 1950s, an important development was Varèse's application of ELECTRONIC MUSIC. This first appeared in his work *Déserts* and, much more extensively, in his *Poème électronique,* commissioned for the Brussels World Exposition in 1958.

The unfamiliarity of Varèse's style and the tremendous difficulty of his orchestral works led them to be performed only rarely. Among conductors, only LEOPOLD STOKOWSKI was bold enough to put Varèse's formidable scores *Amériques* and *Arcana* on his programs with the Philadelphia Orchestra. They evoked cries of derision and outbursts of righteous indignation from the public and the press.

An extraordinary reversal of attitudes toward Varèse's music took place within Varèse's lifetime, resulting in an increased interest in his works. Also, musicians themselves learned to overcome the rhythmic difficulties presented in Varèse's scores.

Thus Varèse lived to witness this long-delayed recognition of his music as a major stimulus of modern art, and his name joined those of IGOR STRAVINSKY, CHARLES IVES, ARNOLD SCHOENBERG, and ANTON WEBERN among the great masters of 20th-century music. In 1955 Varèse was elected to membership in the National Institute of Arts and Letters and in 1962 in the Royal Swedish Academy. Like Schoenberg, Varèse refused to regard himself as a revolutionary in music. Indeed, he professed great admiration for his remote predecessors, particularly those of the NOTRE DAME SCHOOL, representing the flowering of the ARS ANTIQUA.

On the centennial of his birth in 1983, festivals of Varèse's music were staged in Strasbourg, Paris, Rome, Washington, D.C., N.Y., and Los Angeles. In 1981 FRANK ZAPPA, a sincere admirer of Varèse's music, staged in N.Y. at his own expense a concert of Varèse's works. He presented a similar concert in San Francisco in 1982.

NICOLAS SLONIMSKY, a relative beginner as a conductor, was the first to perform and record *Ionisation*. It is said that scientists working on the atomic bomb at Oak Ridge in 1940 played this recording of *Ionisation* for relaxation and stimulation in their work.

variable meter. Systematic use of changing meters in consecutive MEASURES of a composition.

This metrical system was introduced by Boris Blacher in his piano work *Ornamente,* composed in 1950. The device is deceptively simple: the first measure has two eighth notes, the second measure has three eighth notes, etc., following the ascending arithmetical progression, then reversing the process to follow a descending progression. Other German composers adopted Blacher's variable meters, among them Karl Amadeus Hartmann in his concerto for piano, wind instruments, and percussion, and HANS WERNER HENZE in one of his string quartets.

variation(s) (It. *variazioni*). One of a set or series (or a set or series) of transformations of a THEME by means of harmonic, rhythmic, and melodic changes and embellishments.

Variations for Orchestra. Work by ARNOLD SCHOENBERG, 1928, op.31, written in a consciously ordained method of composition with 12 TONES, first performed in Berlin. In this work Schoenberg utilizes the familiar sequence of tones B–A–C–H (B♭, A, C, B♮), which is woven into the basic 12-tone subject.

Variations on a Nursery Song. Work for piano and orchestra by ERNST VON DOHNÁNYI, 1914, first performed in Berlin, with the composer as soloist. The nursery song of the title is the French air *Ah, vous dirai-je maman,* celebrated as the alphabet song in all languages.

The SCORE is dedicated to "the enjoyment of lovers of humor and to the annoyance of others."

Variations on a Rococo Theme. Work for cello and orchestra by PIOTR ILYICH TCHAIKOVSKY, 1877, first performed in Moscow. Tchaikovsky was not sure of the meaning of the word ROCOCO and asked his friend Fitzenhagen, the cellist to whom the SCORE is dedicated, to explain it. Fitzenhagen said rococo meant carefree enjoyment.

There are seven variations on the carefree (but hardly 18th-century) theme.

Variations on a Theme by Frank Bridge. Work for string orchestra by BENJAMIN BRITTEN, 1937. It was written as an act of homage to his teacher and first performed at the Salzburg Festival.

The theme was taken from Bridge's *3 Idylls* for string quartet of 1907. There are 10 variations in all.

variety show. Theatrical entertainment that includes all kinds of popular presentations, from singing and dancing to magician acts, animal tricks, and comic skits. The variety show is the successor to VAUDEVILLE, in that it became most popular on radio and television after live theatrical vaudeville had all but disappeared.

var-sŏh-vē-ah′nǎh

Varsoviana (It.; Fr. *varsovienne*). A MAZURKA named for the city of Warsaw that became very popular in the middle of the 19th century in France and Germany. At various times in the 19th and 20th centuries, Polish nationalists used the tune to express their feelings of national pride, particularly as they sought to separate themselves from Russian control.

voh-d′vēl′

vaudeville. A word serving as an umbrella for several genres of French origin, all of which share a satirical or comic tone. These include:

1. *Vau de Vire,* named after a city in Normandy, a rural SONG incorporating the elements of daily life, from the 15th century.

2. *Voix de ville* (city voices), a 16th-century urban response to the earlier genre, with more courtly lyrics and simple tunes; much of the music was akin to the dances of the period and influential on the CHANSONS.

3. The term *vaudeville* became prevalent in the 17th century, representing simple strophic airs, continuing the traditional concerns with daily matters. The genre was very popular; the tunes were so well known that they were not included in manuscripts.

4. The *comédie en vaudevilles* made the vaudeville a theatrical genre in the late 17th and early 18th centuries. These light, often parodic comedies alternated dialogue and pantomime with witty and satirical couplets, generally set

to well-known popular AIRS. The style gradually gave way to the OPÉRA-COMIQUE.

5. The *vaudeville final* applied one element of the *comédie en vaudevilles* to comic opera, German and Italian as well as French. In this style, all the characters of a work came onstage at the end and restored order to the proceedings, expressed their feelings, and gave a moral. Composers as early as Jean-Jacques Rosseau and as recent as IGOR STRAVINSKY used the form.

6. In the 19th century, the musical comedy (separate from opéra-comique) evolved increasingly in the direction of a variety show, whether the continental vaudeville, the English MUSIC HALL, or the American vaudeville and VARIETY SHOW.

Vaughan, Sarah (Lois), African-American JAZZ and popular singer and pianist; b. Newark, N.J., March 27, 1924; d. Los Angeles, April 3, 1990. Vaughan began to study music as a child. After winning an amateur singing contest at Harlem's Apollo Theater in N.Y. in 1942, she joined the Earl Hines band in the dual role of singer and pianist. She then played and sang with the bands of Billy Eckstine in 1944–45 and John Kirby in 1945–46.

In 1947 Vaughan married jazz trumpeter George Treadwell. He encouraged her to pursue a solo career as a jazz and pop singer. He successfully arranged for her to sing on radio, television, and on tours throughout the world. In the '50s, Vaughan focused on a jazz repertoire, but by the '60s she was recording more pop material. She returned to jazz in the '70s and '80s, making many appearances at jazz festivals.

In 1980 Vaughan appeared at both CARNEGIE HALL and the Apollo Theater, where her career began; both appearances drew great acclaim. She continued to record and perform until late in the decade, when illness forced her to retire. She died in 1990.

Vaughan Williams, Ralph, English composer; b. Down Ampney, Gloucestershire, Oct. 12, 1872; d. London, Aug. 26, 1958. His father, a clergyman, died when Vaughan Williams was a child, after which the family moved to the

PEOPLE IN MUSIC

PEOPLE IN MUSIC

residence of his maternal grandfather at Leith Hill Place, Surrey. There he began to study piano and violin. In 1887 he entered Charterhouse School in London and played violin and viola in the school orchestra.

From 1890 to 1892 Vaughan Williams studied harmony, composition, and organ at the Royal College of Music in London. He then enrolled at Trinity College, Cambridge, where he took courses in composition and in organ, earning his music degree in 1895. He returned to the Royal College of Music for further study the following year. In 1897 he went to Berlin for further instruction with Max Bruch, and in 1901 he received his doctoral degree in music from Cambridge. Dissatisfied with his academic studies, Vaughan Williams decided, in 1908, to seek advice in Paris from MAURICE RAVEL in order to acquire the technique of modern orchestration that emphasized color.

In the meantime, Vaughan Williams became active as a collector of English FOLK SONGS. In 1904 he joined the Folk Song Society. In 1905 he became the conductor of the Leith Hill Festival in Dorking, a position that he held, off and on, until his old age.

In 1906 Vaughan Williams composed three *Norfolk Rhapsodies,* introducing the essential elements of his national style. He discarded the second and third of the set as not satisfactory in reflecting the subject. In 1903 he began work on a choral symphony inspired by Walt Whitman's poetry entitled *A Sea Symphony* (Symphony No. 1). He completed it in 1909. There followed in 1910 *Fantasia on a Theme of Thomas Tallis,* scored for string quartet and double string orchestra. In it Vaughan Williams evoked the POLYPHONIC style of the 16th-century English composer.

After composing this brief but popular work, he engaged in a much grander SCORE, *A London Symphony* (Symphony No. 2), intended as a musical glorification of the city. Despite the inclusion of immediately recognizable quotations of the street song *Sweet Lavender* and of the Westminster chimes in the score, Vaughan Williams emphatically denied that the score was a representation of London life. He even suggested that it might be more aptly entitled "Symphony by a Londoner," finally declaring that the work must be judged as a piece of ABSOLUTE or abstract music. Yet prosaically minded commentators insisted that *A London Symphony* realistically depicted in its four movements the scenes of London at twilight, the hubbub of Bloomsbury, a Saturday evening reverie, and, in conclusion, the serene flow of the Thames River. Concurrently with *A London Symphony,* Vaughan Williams wrote the ballad opera *Hugh the Drover,* set in England in 1812 and reflecting the solitary struggle of the English against Napoleon.

At the outbreak of World War I in 1914 Vaughan Williams enlisted in the British army and served in Salonika and in France as an officer in the artillery. After the armistice he was a professor of composition at the Royal College of Music in London from 1919 to 1939. He also conducted the London Bach Choir from 1920 to 1928. In 1921 he completed *A Pastoral Symphony.* An interesting innovation in this score is the use of a wordless vocal solo in the last movement. In 1922 he visited the U.S. and conducted this work at the Norfolk (Connecticut) Festival. In 1932 he returned to the U.S. to lecture at Bryn Mawr College.

In 1930 Vaughan Williams wrote a MASQUE, *Job,* based on the British poet/mystic William Blake's *Illustrations of the Book of Job.* It was first performed in a concert version, then presented on the stage in London in 1931. His Fourth Symphony, in F minor (1931–35), first performed by the BBC Symphony Orchestra in London in 1935, presents an extraordinary deviation from his accustomed solid style of composition. Here he experimented with DISSONANT harmonies in conflicting tonalities, bristling with angular rhythms.

Vaughan Williams always professed great admiration for JEAN SIBELIUS. In addition to the harmonious kinship between the two great contemporary nationalist composers, there was the peculiar circumstance that each in his Fourth Symphony ventured into the domain of modernism. Both were taken to task by astounded critics for such musical experimentation.

A peripheral work was Vaughan Williams's *Fantasia on Greensleeves,* arranged for harp, strings, and optional flutes. This was the composer's tribute to his fascination with English folk songs. He had used it in his opera *Sir John in Love,* after Shakespeare's *The Merry Wives of Windsor,* performed in London in 1929.

Sinfonia antartica may well be compared in its realism with the ALPINE SYMPHONY of RICHARD STRAUSS.

Vaughan Williams dedicated his Fifth Symphony in D Major (1938–43) to Sibelius as a token of his admiration. In the Sixth Symphony in E Minor (1944–47) Vaughan Williams returned to the normal serene style, although it has its turbulent moments and an episode of folksy dancing exhilaration.

Vaughan Williams was 80 years old when he completed his challenging *Sinfonia antartica* (Symphony No. 7), scored for soprano, women's chorus, and orchestra. The music was an expansion of his sound track for the motion picture *Scott of the Antarctic* (1947–48) on the doomed 1912 expedition of Robert Scott to the South Pole. Here the music is almost geographic in its literal representation of the regions that Scott explored. In *Sinfonia antartica* Vaughan Williams inserted, in addition to a large orchestra, several keyboard instruments and a wind machine. In the epilogue of the work, he used quotations from Scott's journal. *Sinfonia antartica* was first performed in Manchester in 1953.

In the Eighth Symphony, Vaughan Williams once more returned to the ideal of absolute music. The work is conceived in the form of a NEOCLASSICAL suite. However, faithful to the spirit of the times, he included in the score such modern instruments as VIBRAPHONE and XYLOPHONE, as well as gongs and bells.

In his last symphony, Vaughan Williams at age 85 could still assert himself as a modern composer. For the first time, he used a trio of saxophones, with a pointed caveat that they should not behave "like demented cats" but rather retain their romantic character. Perhaps anticipating the inevitable, he added after the last bar of the score the Italian word *niente*. The Ninth Symphony was first performed in London in April 1958, just months before Vaughan Williams's death.

It is a testimony to his extraordinary vitality that after the death of his first wife Vaughan Williams married at age 80 the poet and writer Ursula Wood. In the following year he once more visited the U.S. on a lecture tour to several American universities.

In Vaughan Williams's works, there seems to have been no intention of adopting any particular method of composition. Rather, he used a great variety of procedures integrated into a distinctively personal and thoroughly English style, nationalistic but not isolationist. Vaughan Williams was particularly adept at exploring the modern ways of modal COUNTERPOINT, with tonality freely shifting between MAJOR and MINOR TRIADS. In this way, he astutely evokes MEDIEVAL and BAROQUE styles while still using modern techniques. Thus Vaughan Williams combines the modalities of the Tudor era with the sparkling POLYTONALITIES of the modern age.

In addition to the works mentioned above, Vaughan Williams composed the opera RIDERS TO THE SEA, after the drama by John Millington Synge (1925–32; London, 1937), and incidental and film music. His vocal music includes *Songs of Travel* for voice and piano, to texts by Robert Louis Stevenson (1904); *Toward the Unknown Region* for chorus and orchestra, after Walt Whitman (1905–07); *On Wenlock Edge,* song cycle for tenor, piano, and string quartet *ad libitum,* to poems from A.E. Housman's *A Shropshire Lad* (1909); *Five Mystical Songs* for baritone, optional chorus, and orchestra (1911); *Flos Campi,* suite for viola, wordless mixed chorus, and small orchestra (1925); *Five Tudor Portraits* for mezzosoprano, baritone, chorus, and orchestra (1936); *Serenade to Music* for 16 solo voices and orchestra (1938); and *10 Blake Songs* for tenor and oboe (1958), as well as other English songs, arrangements of English folk songs, Anglican choral music, HYMN tunes, and CAROLS.

His orchestral works include *In the Fen Country,* symphonic impression (1904); *The Lark Ascending,* romance for violin and orchestra (1914–20); *Fantasia on Sussex Folk-Tunes* for cello and orchestra (1930); Suite for viola and small orchestra (1934); *Five Variants of "Dives and Lazarus"* for string orchestra and harp (1939); Concerto Grosso for string orchestra (1950); and concertos for violin, piano, oboe, and tuba. Among his chamber works are three string quartets (1898; 1909; 1942–44), Piano Quintet in C Minor, with double bass (1905), Phantasy Quintet for two violins, two violas, and cello (1912), Double Trio for string sextet (London), and Violin Sonata in A Minor (1954). He also composed keyboard pieces and made collections of religious songs, including *The Oxford Book of Carols.* He wrote lectures and articles, reprinted in *National Music and Other Essays* published in 1963, and collected folk songs.

PEOPLE IN MUSIC

Velvet Underground. (Members: Guitar/vocal/songwriter: Lou[is Alan] Reed, b. N.Y., March 2, 1942; Viola/bass/keyboards: John Cale, b. Garnant, South Wales, Dec. 3, 1940; Guitar: Sterling Morrison, b. Aug. 29, 1942, East Meadow, Long Island; d. Poughkeepsie, N.Y., Aug. 30, 1995; Drums: Maureen "Mo" Tucker, b. N.J., 1945; Nico [born Christa Päffgen], b. Cologne, Oct. 16, 1939; d. Ibiza, Spain, July 18, 1988.)

The Velvet Underground had a brief and relatively unnoticed existence from 1965 to 1970, but later had a profound influence on emerging ROCK styles (punk, new wave, grunge).

Lou Reed, one-time leader of the Velvet Underground, in 1990. (Neal Preston/Corbis) ▶

After graduating from Syracuse University, Lou Reed worked on the edges of the pop music industry. He worked as a professional songwriter in N.Y., while also performing with groups like the Primitives and the Warlocks (not the same group from which the GRATEFUL DEAD developed). In 1966 he recruited John Cale, and together they formed the Velvet Underground. Cale came from a background of playing avant-garde modern music with LA MONTE YOUNG. So, from the start, the Velvet Underground was a different type of rock group, combining ATONAL and DISSONANT musical accompaniment with lyrical topics not often found in pop songs (drug addiction, sado-masochistic sexual encounters, etc.).

The group was initially produced by Andy Warhol as part of his N.Y. multimedia organization The Factory, and toured under the auspices of his Exploding Plastic Inevitable. However, the aesthetic of the Velvets was closer to the earthy films of Paul Morrissey than to Warhol's deadpan irony, and it did not take long before the group separated from Warhol. The group produced four studio albums before its demise.

Another noteworthy performer with the Velvets was Nico (born Christa Päffgen), a German-Hungarian model and singer. Warhol convinced the group to take her on, and she contributed vocals on their first album and tour. She later recorded several solo albums, some produced by Cale. Other members of the Velvets were Agnus MacLise, a percussionist who joined and left early in the group's history; Maureen "Mo" Tucker, who replaced MacLise and remained with the group until 1969 (she has produced a few solo albums over the years); Sterling Morrison, guitarist, the only member to stay with the group during its entire history, but also the only one to quit music entirely (for an academic career); and the Yule Brothers—Doug, a bassist and guitarist who replaced Cale in 1968, and Billy, who replaced Tucker in 1969.

Two of its members had important careers after leaving the Velvets. After leaving the group, Cale's experimentation continued with his first solo album, *Vintage Violence* (1969). He subsequently collaborated with TERRY RILEY on *The Church of Anthrax* (1971) and *The Alchemy in Peril* (1972) and with Brian Eno in 1974. Other albums include *Paris 1919* (1973), *Fear* (1974), *Helen of Troy* (1975), *Honi Soit* (1981), and *Caribbean Sunset* (1984). As a producer, he worked with several early punk groups.

Reed left the group in 1970 and began exploring different sides of his musical personality. There was the accessible hard rock and balladry of *Transformer* (1972; including his biggest hit *Walk on the Wild Side,* a satire on life at The Factory), *Rock 'n' Roll Animal* (1974), *Coney Island Baby* (1976), *Blue Mask* (1981), *New Sensations* (1984), and *Magic and Loss* (1992). Reed composed two brilliant concept albums, the harrowing *Berlin* in 1973 and the streetwise *New York* in 1989, and an unadulterated, utterly anarchistic display of uninhibited white noise, *Metal Machine Music,* from 1975.

Reed and Cale reunited 20 years after Cale left to compose and perform the suite *Songs for Drella,* in memory of Warhol in 1989. They in turn joined with Morrison and Tucker for a European reunion tour in 1993.

Vendredis, Les. Sixteen pieces in two sets for string quartet, 1899. These were composed by various Russian composers, including ALEXANDER BORODIN, NIKOLAI RIMSKY-KORSAKOV, ALEXANDER GLAZUNOV, and ANATOLI LIADOV, in honor of their weekly meetings on Fridays (Vendredis) held at the house of the publisher Mitrofan Belaiev in St. Petersburg in the 1880s and 1890s.

Venetian school. A style of composition that developed in Venice during the 16th century, with the participation of several important organists from northern Europe.

The center of the Venetian school was the cathedral of St. Mark (San Marcos) with its magnificent architectural plan of symmetric enclaves, making it ideal for the performance of ANTIPHONAL choral works of truly STEREOPHONIC quality. The first acknowledged master presiding over the principal organ at San Marcos was Adrian Willaert, from Bruges, appointed *maestro di capella* (director of the church's music program) in 1527. He instructed the great Italian madrigalist ANDREA GABRIELI in the art of CHROMATIC MODULATION. In turn, Andrea taught his nephew GIOVANNI GABRIELI to adapt choral techniques to the treatment of the orchestra, especially in the contrasting alternation of massive sonorities, popularizing the ECHO.

A long series of great organists at St. Mark's included Claudio Merulo and the theorist GIOSEFFO ZARLINO. Undoubtedly, the Venetian school of composition, orchestration, and choral treatment exercised a profound influence on composers in Germany, among them Hieronymous Praetorius, MICHAEL PRAETORIUS, and Hans Leo Hassler. It was also a powerful influence on BAROQUE instrumental and choral music, at the same time that the Florentine DRAMMA PER MUSIC monopolized the development of OPERA.

Vengerova, Isabelle (Isabella Afanasievna). *See* SLONIMSKY, NICOLAS.

Venuti, Joe (Giuseppe), Italian-born American JAZZ violinist; b. Lecco, April 4, 1898; d. Seattle, Aug. 14, 1978. Venuti was taken to the U.S. as a child and reared in Philadelphia. There he received a thorough classical training on the violin,

PEOPLE IN MUSIC

but after meeting the jazz guitarist Eddie Lang, he turned to popular music.

In the mid-1920s, Lang and Venuti went to N.Y., where they were quickly hired by popular band leader Paul Whiteman. They also recorded in various smaller ensembles with a wide variety of jazz players.

In 1935 Venuti formed his own band and led it until 1943. He then went to the West Coast, where he became a studio musician in Hollywood. His great merit was to make the theretofore-suspect violin a respectable instrument among the swingers of California.

Venuti continued to work through the '50s, '60s, and into the early '70s. At that time, a revival of interest in SWING music, particularly as played on stringed instruments, led him to a second career as a popular performer on the jazz circuit. Venuti recorded prolifically with many accompanists and toured internationally. He continued to play until his death in 1978.

Vêpres Siciliennes, Les. *See SICILIAN VESPERS, THE.*

verbalization. Using verbal instructions to tell musicians how to perform a piece, rather than traditional musical notation.

This practice developed in the 20th century and was probably originated by KARLHEINZ STOCKHAUSEN. One of his pieces represents a parabolic curve with the following inscription: "Sound a note. Continue sounding it as long as you please. It is your prerogative." JOHN CAGE elevated verbalization to the degree of eloquent diction. Earle Brown and Morton Feldman are inventive verbalizationists.

Some classic examples of this type of score include:

LA MONTE YOUNG tells the player: "Push the piano to the wall. Push it through the wall. Keep pushing."

Nam June Paik dictates: "Cut your left arm very slowly with a razor (more than 10 centimeters)."

Philip Corner limits himself to a simple command: "One anti-personnel type CBU [cluster bomb unit] will be thrown into the audience."

verbunkos (Hung.; from Ger. *Werbung,* recruiting). Hungarian recruiting dance, popular in the later 18th and early 19th centuries. It was performed by a group of hussars led by their sergeant to entice young men to join the army (before involuntary conscription was imposed by the Austrians). The verbunkos essentially consists of a slow (LASSÚ) and fast (FRISS) section, which alternate as necessary.

Its musical elements are embodied in FRANZ LISZT's *Hungarian Rhapsodies* and works by composers from LUDWIG VAN BEETHOVEN and FRANZ SCHUBERT to ZOLTÁN KODÁLY and BÉLA BARTÓK.

Verdi, Giuseppe (Fortunino Francesco), Italian opera composer whose genius for dramatic, lyric, and tragic stage music has made him a perennial favorite of opera enthusiasts; b. Le Roncole, near Busseto, Duchy of Parma, Oct. 9, 1813; d. Milan, Jan. 27, 1901. Verdi's father ran a tavern, and it was there that the young musician first heard music. A local organist, Pietro Baistrocchi, noticed his love of musical sound and took him on as a pupil. When Baistrocchi died, Verdi, still a young child, took over some of his duties at the KEYBOARD. His father sent him to Busseto for further training. There he began academic studies and also took music lessons with Ferdinando Provesi, director of the municipal music school.

At the age of 18 Verdi became a resident in the home of Antonio Barezzi, a local merchant and patron of music. Barezzi supplied him with enough funds so that he could go to Milan for serious study. Surprisingly, in view of Verdi's future greatness, he failed to pass an entrance examination to

PEOPLE IN MUSIC

Giuseppe Verdi. (New York Public Library)

the Milan Conservatory. The registrar, Francesco Basili, reported that Verdi's piano technique was inadequate and that in composition he lacked technical knowledge. Verdi then turned to Vincenzo Lavigna, an excellent musician, for private lessons and worked industriously to master COUNTERPOINT, CANON, and FUGUE.

In 1834 Verdi applied for the post of *maestro di musica* in Busseto, and after passing his examination received the desired appointment. In 1836 he married a daughter of his patron, Barezzi. Tragedy intervened when their two infant children died, and his wife succumbed in 1840. Verdi deeply mourned his loss, but he found solace in music.

In 1838 Verdi completed his first opera, *Oberto, conte di San Bonifacio.* A year later, he moved to Milan. He submitted the score of *Oberto* to the directorship of La Scala. It was accepted for performance, which took place that year, with satisfactory success. He was now under contract to write more operas for that renowned theater. His comic opera *Un giorno di regno* was performed at La Scala in 1840, but it was not successful.

Somewhat downhearted at this reverse, Verdi began composition of an opera, *Nabucodonosor* (the title was later abbreviated to *Nabucco*). It was staged at La Scala in 1842, scoring considerable success. Giuseppina Strepponi (b. Lodi, Sept. 8, 1815; d. Sant' Agata, near Busseto, Nov. 14, 1897), a prominent SOPRANO, created the leading female role of Abigaille. Although she was in vocal decline, Strepponi became a great favorite of Verdi's.

Nabucco was followed by another successful opera on a historic subject, *I Lombardi alla prima Crociata,* produced at La Scala in 1843. The next opera was *Ernani,* after Victor Hugo's drama on the life of a revolutionary outlaw. The subject suited the rise of national spirit, and its 1844 production in Venice won great acclaim. Not so popular were Verdi's succeeding operas through 1846.

In 1847 Verdi produced in Florence his first Shakespearean opera, *Macbeth.* In the same year he received a commission to write an opera for London. The result was *I Masnadieri,* based on Friedrich von Schiller's drama *Die Räuber.* It was produced at Her Majesty's Theatre in London in 1847, with JENNY LIND in the leading female role.

Verdi time line

1813	Born
1834	Appointed *maestro di musica* in Busseto
1836	Marries the daughter of his patron, Barezzi
1838	Completes his first opera, *Oberto, conte di San Bonifacio*
1842	The opera *Nabucco* is staged at La Scala, Milan
1844	The opera *Ernani* is produced in Venice
1847	Produces in Florence his first Shakespearean opera, *Macbeth*
1851	The opera RIGOLETTO is performed for the first time at the Teatro La Fenice in Venice
1853	Two important first performances: the opera IL TROVATORE in Rome and the opera LA TRAVIATA in Venice
1855	*Les Vêpres siciliennes,* Verdi's first French opera, is staged in Paris
1857	The opera *Simone Boccanegra* is staged at the Teatro La Fenice in Venice
1859	Marries his leading lady, Giuseppina Strepponi, the same year his *Un ballo in maschera* is first performed in Rome
1862	Attends the first performance of his *La forza del destino* in St. Petersburg

1943

1864	Elected to membership in the Académie des Beaux Arts in Paris
1867	*Don Carlos,* after Schiller's famous drama, is first heard at the Paris Opéra
1869	*Rigoletto* is first heard in Cairo
1870	*Aida,* Verdi's second commission for Cairo, is staged on Christmas Eve
1875	Nominated a senator to the Italian parliament
1887	Verdi's second Shakespearean opera, OTELLO, is premiered at La Scala
1893	*Falstaff,* to a LIBRETTO by Boito, is performed at La Scala
1897	Strepponi dies, and Verdi founds a home for aged musicians in Milan, the Casa di Riposo per Musicati
1898	Verdi's last work, *Four pezzi sacri,* is published
1901	Dies

During Verdi's stay in Paris he renewed his acquaintance with Strepponi. After several years of cohabitation their union was legalized in a private wedding in Savoy in 1859.

A commission from Paris followed, for which Verdi revised his opera *I Lombardi alla prima Crociata* in a French version, renamed *Jerusalem.* It was produced at the Paris Opéra in 1847, followed by the Italian production at La Scala in 1850. This was one of several operas by him and other Italian composers where mistaken identity was the chief dramatic device.

In 1848 Verdi produced his opera *Il Corsaro,* after Lord Byron's poem *The Corsair.* There followed *La battaglia di Legnano,* celebrating the defeat of the armies of Barbarossa by the Lombards in 1176. Its premiere took place in Rome in 1849, but Verdi was forced to change names and places so as not to offend the central European powers that dominated Italy. Two subsequent operas were not successful.

Verdi's great triumph came in 1851 with the production of *Rigoletto,* fashioned after Victor Hugo's drama *Le Roi s'amuse.* It was performed for the first time at the Teatro La Fenice in Venice in 1851 and brought Verdi lasting fame, entering the repertoire of opera houses around the world. The ARIA of the libidinous duke, *La donna e mobile,* became one of the most popular operatic tunes throughout Europe.

This success was followed by even greater acclaim with the productions in 1853 of *Il Trovatore* in Rome and *La Traviata* in Venice. Both captivated world audiences without diminution of their melodramatic effect on succeeding generations in Europe and America—despite the absurdity of the action represented on the stage. *Il Trovatore* resorts to the common device of unrecognized identities of close relatives, while *La Traviata* strains credulity when the lead soprano sings enchantingly and at great length despite her struggle with terminal consumption.

Another commission from Paris resulted in Verdi's first French opera, *Les Vêpres siciliennes,* after a LIBRETTO by Scribe to GAETANO DONIZETTI's unfinished opera *Le Duc d'Albe.* The action deals with the medieval slaughter of the French occupation army in Sicily by local patriots. Despite the offensiveness of the subject to French patriots, the opera was given successfully in Paris in 1855.

Verdi's next opera, *Simone Boccanegra,* was produced at the Teatro La Fenice in 1857. This was followed by *Un ballo in maschera,* staged in Rome in 1859, based on the original

LIBRETTO written by Scribe for Daniel-François-Esprit Auber's opera *Gustave III.* It is based on the story of the assassination of King Gustave III of Sweden in 1792. But the censors would not permit the murder of a king to be shown on the stage, and Verdi was compelled to transfer the scene of action.

Unexpectedly, Verdi became a factor in the political struggle for the independence of Italy. The symbol of the nationalist movement was Vittorio Emanuele, the future king of Italy. Demonstrators painted the name of Verdi in capital letters, separated by punctuation, on fences and walls of Italian towns (V.E.R.D.I., the initials of Vittorio Emanuele, Re D'Italia), and the cry "Viva Verdi!" became code for "Viva Vittorio Emanuele Re D'Italia!"

In 1861 the composer received a commission to write an opera for the Imperial Opera of St. Petersburg. He selected the mystical subject *La forza del destino.* The premiere took place in St. Petersburg in 1862, and Verdi made a special trip to attend. He then wrote an opera to a French text, *Don Carlos,* after Schiller's famous drama. It was first heard at the Paris Opéra in 1867, with numerous cuts, not restored until a century had elapsed after the initial production. (Verdi wrote three versions in all, none of which contain all the music he wrote for the opera.)

In June 1870 Verdi received a contract to write a new work for Cairo, where *Rigoletto* had been performed a year before. The terms were most generous, with a guarantee of 150,000 francs for the Egyptian rights alone. The opera, based on life in ancient Egypt, was *Aida.* The original libretto was in French, and Antonio Ghislanzoni prepared the Italian text. It had its premiere in Cairo on Christmas Eve 1871, with great pomp and circumstance. Verdi stubbornly refused to attend despite persuasion by a number of influential Italian musicians and statesmen. He declared that a composer's job was to supply music, not to attend performances. The success of *Aida* exceeded all expectations. The production was hailed as a world event, and the work itself became one of the most famous in opera history.

After GIOACCHINO ROSSINI's death in 1868, Verdi conceived the idea of honoring his memory by a collective composition of a REQUIEM, to which several Italian composers would contribute a movement each. Verdi reserved the last section, *Libera me,* for himself. He completed the score in 1869, but it was never performed in its original form. The death of the famous Italian poet Alessandro Manzoni in 1873 led him to write his great *Messa da Requiem.* This became known simply as the *Manzoni Requiem,* and he incorporated in it the section originally composed for Rossini. The Requiem received its premiere on the first anniversary of Manzoni's death, in Milan. It was criticized as being too operatic for a religious work, but it remained in musical annals as a masterpiece.

After a lapse of some 13 years of rural retirement, Verdi turned once more to Shakespeare. The result this time was *Otello,* its libretto by Arrigo Boito, a master poet and composer who rendered Shakespeare's lines into Italian with extraordinary feeling. It received its premiere at La Scala in 1887. Verdi was 79 years old when he wrote yet another Shakespearean opera, *Falstaff,* also to a libretto by Boito, who used materials from *The Merry Wives of Windsor* and the two parts of *Henry IV. Falstaff* was performed for the first time at La Scala in 1893. The score reveals Verdi's genius for subtle comedy coupled with melodic invention of the highest order.

Verdi's last composition was a group of sacred choruses—Ave Maria, Laudi alla Vergine Maria, Stabat Mater, and Te Deum—published in 1898 as *Four pezzi sacri.* In the Ave Maria, Verdi made use of the so-called SCALA ENIGMATICA.

Innumerable honors were bestowed upon Verdi. In 1864 he was elected to membership in the Académie des Beaux Arts in Paris, where he filled the vacancy made by the death of GIACOMO MEYERBEER. In 1875 he was nominated a senator to the Italian parliament. Following the premiere of *Falstaff,* the king of Italy wished to make him Marchese di Busseto, but he declined the honor. After the death of Strepponi in 1897, he founded in Milan the Casa di Riposo per Musicisti, a home for aged musicians. For its maintenance, he set aside 2.5 million lire.

In January 1901, Verdi suffered a massive stroke. He died six days later at the age of 87.

Historic evaluation of Verdi's music changed several times after his death. When the opera world was dominated by RICHARD WAGNER and his followers, Verdi was denigrated as a purveyor of "barrel-organ music." However, when Wagner in turn fell out of favor, modern composers, music historians, and academic theoreticians discovered unexpected attractions in the flowing Verdian melodies, easily modulating harmonies, and stimulating symmetric rhythms.

verismo (from It. *vero,* true). Literally "truth" or realism in operatic plots. From the 1890s, a type of operatic naturalism. The two most famous examples are PIETRO MASCAGNI's *Cavalleria Rusticana* and RUGGERO LEONCAVALLO's *Pagliacci.*

    Soon the vogue spread into France with the production of *Louise* by GUSTAVE CHARPENTIER. In Germany verismo assumed satirical and sociological rather than naturalistic forms in the works of KURT WEILL, ERNST KRENEK, and PAUL HINDEMITH. In England, BENJAMIN BRITTEN's *Peter Grimes* is veristic in both subject and execution.

vĕr-ēz′mŏh

Verklärte Nacht (Transfigured Night). String SEXTET by ARNOLD SCHOENBERG, 1899, based on the poem by Richard Dehmel (1863–1920), which Schoenberg wrote long before he initiated his 12-TONE method. It was first performed in Vienna in 1902.

    The poem describes the acceptance by a woman's lover of paternity of a child conceived by another man. The score is almost Wagnerian in its expansive harmonies. It was arranged for string orchestra in 1917 and used as the score for the ballet *The Pillar of Fire* in 1942.

Verlag (Ger.). Publishing house, company, or imprint.

Vers la flamme (Toward the Flame). Characteristic piano piece by ALEXANDER SCRIABIN, 1914. It describes the perpetual ascent toward the regenerating flame that lies at the heart of the composer's unique mystical theories. The music, without KEY SIGNATURE or TONALITY, is extremely delicate and subtly nuanced.

vers mesuré (Fr., measured verse). A movement in 16th-century French poetry in which writers had their lyrics follow the rules of Greek and Latin prosody. The champion of this approach was Jean-Antoine de Baïf (1532–89). The music adaptation was created by doubling the basic note value for long syllables as a substitute for the tonal accents of speech. Orlando di Lasso, Claude Le Jeune (c.1528–1600), and Jacques Mauduit (1557–1627) contributed to the genre, known as MUSIQUE MESURÉE.

verse. 1. In GREGORIAN CHANT, a scriptural portion for solo voice, introduced and concluded by a short choral passage. 2. A STANZA, usually serving as the opening part of a popular song (followed by a REFRAIN CHORUS or transitional BRIDGE).

verse-anthem. One in which VERSES (soli, duets, trios, quartets) predominate over CHORUSES. *Verse-service,* a choral service for solo voices.

verset. 1. A short VERSE, usually forming one sentence with its RESPONSE, for example:

Vers. *O Lord, save Thy people,*
Resp. *And bless Thine inheritance.*

2. A short PRELUDE or INTERLUDE for organ, replacing a VERSE in the MASS. Composers began to compose versets that took advantage of the organ's capabilities and the technical opportunities of POLYPHONIC writing. This greatly extended practice led to increasing domination over proper congregational singing, which alarmed church authorities ever vigilant over the purity and simplicity of PLAINCHANT.

versicle. An exhortation intoned by the CELEBRANT in Roman Catholic or Anglican CANONICAL HOURS, sung in LITANY style with congregational or choral responses. The best known is the Benedicamus Domino, used to close the service.

vertical flute. Generic term for the end-blown flute (e.g., RECORDER, SHAKUHACHI, TIN WHISTLE), as opposed to the TRANSVERSE FLUTE.

The famous papal declaration *Moto proprio* of 1903 specifically warned against the spread of instrumental POLYPHONY in church services.

MUSICAL
INSTRUMENT

Vespers (from Lat. *vespera,* evening; Anglican, Evensong). Originally, the seventh CANONICAL HOUR of the Divine Office of the Roman Catholic daily LITURGY, now the fifth hour, celebrated at dusk, about 6:00 P.M.

Vespers is the most important service in the Office with respect to music, because it includes a variety of CHANTS, HYMNS, and a MAGNIFICAT. Secular forms are commonly admitted in the Vespers, and this dispensation encouraged composers to set Vespers and Magnificats as independent works in a POLYPHONIC style. CLAUDIO MONTEVERDI wrote several Vespers, and WOLFGANG AMADEUS MOZART composed two for large ensemble.

Vespri Siciliani, I. *See* SICILIAN VESPERS, THE.

Vestale, La. Opera by GASPARE SPONTINI, 1807, first produced in Paris.

A Roman captain, Licinio, is busy conquering Gaul. In distress, his betrothed applies for a position as a vestal virgin. However, Licinio refuses to guard her virginity. Upon return to Rome, he invades the vestal premises, extinguishing the holy flame in the process. The poor bride is sentenced to death for her failure to protect the flame, but at the last moment before her execution, a bolt of lightning strikes the scene and relights the sacred fire. This celestial intervention is interpreted to be of divine origin, and the lovers are reunited in matrimony.

The opera was highly successful. HECTOR BERLIOZ considered it a masterpiece in the Gluckian and Cherubinian traditions. It was performed for over a century, but then fell out of the repertory.

Ironically, *La Vestale* has been restaged as part of the BEL CANTO revival begun in the 1950s. This despite the fact that it shares little with the works of VINCENZO BELLINI, GAETANO DONIZETTI, and their contemporaries.

Vexations. A one-page piano piece by ERIK SATIE, c.1893, which he stipulates should be repeated 840 times.

In 1963 in N.Y., a group of dedicated AVANT-GARDE musicians carried out Satie's instructions literally, using a five-pianist tag team. The total duration of this marathon performance was 18 hours and 40 minutes.

MUSICAL INSTRUMENT

vibraphone (vibraharp). A PERCUSSION instrument introduced in the U.S. early in the 20th century. In its popular form it consists of suspended metal bars in KEYBOARD arrangement, which, when struck with mallets, produce tones that are amplified by resonator tubes below the bars. A motor-driven propeller mechanism creates the VIBRATO that gives the instrument its name.

Although occasionally used by classical composers—ALBAN BERG included it in the score to his unfinished opera, *Lulu*—it is primarily known as a popular and jazz instrument. One of the first to popularize the instrument was LIONEL HAMPTON; other well-known players include Milt Jackson and Gary Burton.

MUSICAL INSTRUMENT

vibraslap. A shaker manufactured around 1970 to replace the Latin American QUIJADA DEL BURRO. In the genuine jawbone, the teeth rattled percussively when struck with the palm of the hand, or brushed with a stick. The vibraslap is a wooden shell with small metal pieces inside that rattle when it is struck.

vibration(s) (Ger. *Schwingung*). Periodic oscillations of a flexible sounding body, such as a string or a column of air, which produce definite PITCHes. The unit of vibration is a CYCLE covering the fluctuation of an acoustic body, first to one side, then to the other, returning it to its original position. The frequency of such units per second (cycles per second, or cps; also known as hertz, or Hz), determines the sounding tone.

The human ear is capable of perceiving vibrations from about 16 cps to several thousand cps. The lowest A on the piano keyboard has 27½ vibrations per second, and the high C on the keyboard vibrates at 4,224 cps.

The loudness of a tone depends on its AMPLITUDE, the width of the distance traveled by the sounding body from its original (at rest) position to its most extreme departure from it. Frequency (pitch) and amplitude (DYNAMIC level) are independent of each other.

Vibrations are cumulative in their wave motion. Unrelated objects can be set in motion by contact with *sympathetic vibrations* accrued in this manner. Suspension bridges, with their considerable flexibility, are notoriously vulnerable to accumulated sympathetic vibration.

Other flexible acoustical bodies will respond to a sympathetic tone by trying to resonate with it—objects such as candelabras, glass chimes, chandeliers, wall mirrors, and champagne glasses will break if a singer hits a particularly high and piercing note. ENRICO CARUSO, a member of the Metropolitan Opera touring company that was in San Francisco for its 1906 earthquake, exclaimed, "I knew that high B flat would cause trouble."

More colloquially, a mood or relationship is often described as having good or bad "vibes."

vibrato (It.). 1. In singing, a timbral effect by letting the stream of air out of the lungs about eight times per second through the rigid vocal cords. Ideally, the pitch should remain the same to avoid an irrelevant TRILL. Wind instrument playing may also be affected by vibrato use. 2. On bowed string instruments, a widely used effect involving a slight oscillation of the pitch through a barely perceptible motion of the left hand and finger pressure on a sustained tone.

vē-brăh'tŏh

Vocal and instrumental vibrato assists in the projection of sound. It was the subject of great performance practice debates, as to proper use, prior to the mid-19th century (much as TEMPERAMENT was debated).

Vicentino, Nicola, noted Italian music theorist and composer; b. Vicenza, 1511; d. Rome, 1575 or 1576. Vicentino was a pupil of the Flemish composer Adrian Willaert in Venice. He then became maestro and music master to Cardinal Ippolito d'Este in Ferrara and in Rome. In 1563–64 he was *maestro di cappella* at Vicenza Cathedral, and by 1570 he was in Milan as rector of St. Thomas. He died during a plague.

PEOPLE IN MUSIC

Vicentino had a unique theory about Greek composition. He believed the ancient composers used six different DIATONIC, ENHARMONIC, and CHROMATIC SCALES. He composed a book of madrigals for five voices, published in Venice in 1546, to support this theory. In 1855 he described an instrument called the *arcicembalo,* having six keyboards, with separate strings and keys for distinguishing these scales. Other musicians at the time objected to these ideas, and eventually Vicentino's theories were discredited.

In chromatic composition, Vicentino was followed by Cipriano de Rore and Carlo Gesualdo. His work paved the way for the MONODIC style and the eventual dropping of the church MODES. His surviving works also include MOTETS.

PEOPLE IN MUSIC

Vickers, Jon(athan Stewart), Canadian tenor; b. Prince Albert, Saskatchewan, Oct. 29, 1926. Vickers sang in church choirs as a boy. He engaged in a mercantile career to earn a living and served as a manager in Canadian Woolworth stores. He then was employed as a purchasing agent for the Hudson's Bay Company and moved to Winnipeg. He won a scholarship at the Royal Conservatory of Music of Toronto, where he studied voice with George Lambert.

Vickers made his operatic debut in 1952 at the Toronto Opera Festival as the Duke of Mantua. In 1957 he sang Riccardo at Covent Garden in London, and the next year he appeared as Siegmund in *Die Walküre* at the Bayreuth Festival. In 1959 he sang at the Vienna State Opera, and in 1960 he made his debut at the Metropolitan Opera in N.Y. as Canio. He sang Florestan at Milan's La Scala and Siegmund at the Chicago Lyric Opera in 1961. In 1966, 1967, and 1968 he appeared at HERBERT VON KARAJAN's Easter Festivals. He sang Otello at Expo 67 in Montreal in 1967. In 1975 he appeared as Tristan with the Opéra du Québec. In 1985 Vickers sang GEORGE FRIDERIC HANDEL's Samson at Covent Garden in a production marking the 300th anniversary of the composer's birth. In 1968 he was made a Companion of the Order of Canada.

Throughout the years, Vickers continued to make occasional appearances as a soloist with orchestras and as a recitalist throughout Canada. His remarkable career came to a close with his retirement in 1988.

Vickers was acknowledged as one of the principal HELDENTENORS of his era. In addition to roles already noted, he excelled as HECTOR BERLIOZ's Aeneas, as well as Don Alvaro, Don Carlos, and Parsifal.

Victoria, Tomás Luis de, Spanish organist and composer; b. Avila, 1548; d. Madrid, Aug. 20, 1611. He was a choirboy at Avila Cathedral. In 1565 Victoria went to Rome. To prepare himself for the priesthood, he entered the Jesuit Collegium Germanicum. His teacher may have been GIOVANNI PIERLUIGI DA PALESTRINA, who from 1566 to 1571 was music master at the Roman Seminary, at this time amalgamated with the Collegium Germanicum. The Italian master is known to have befriended his young Spanish colleague, and when Palestrina left the seminary in 1571, it was Victoria who succeeded him as maestro.

In 1569 Victoria had left the Collegium Germanicum to become singer and organist in the Church of Sta. Maria di Montserrato, posts he held until 1564. From this time forward he also officiated frequently at musical ceremonies in the Church of S. Giaccomo degli Spagnuoli. He taught music at the Collegium Germanicum from 1571, becoming its maestro di cappella in 1573. It moved to the Palazzo di S. Apollinaire in 1574 and to the adjoining church in 1576, where he remained as maestro di cappella for a year.

In the summer of 1575, Victoria was ordained a priest. Earlier that year he had received a benefice at Leon from the pope, and in 1579 was granted another benefice at Zamora, neither requiring residence. In 1577 he joined the Congregazione dei Preti dell'Oratorio. He served as chaplain at the Church of S. Girolamo della Carita from 1578 until 1585. This was the church where St. Philip Neri held his famous religious meetings, which led to the founding of the Congregation of the Oratory in 1575.

Although Victoria was not a member of the Oratory, he must have taken some part in its important musical activities, living as he did for five years under the same roof with its founder (St. Philip left S. Girolamo in 1583). He is known to have been a close friend of Juvenal Ancina, a priest of the Oratory who wrote texts for many of the LAUDI SPIRITUALI sung at the meetings of the Congregation.

Victoria served as chaplain to the king's sister, the Dowager Empress Maria, at the Monasterio de las Descalzas in Madrid from at least 1587 until her death in 1603. He also was maestro of its convent choir until 1604, then its organist

PEOPLE IN MUSIC

Victoria was about the same age as Palestrina's two sons, Rodolfo and Angelo, who were students at the seminary.

until his death. His last work, a Requiem Mass for the Empress Maria, his masterpiece, was published in 1605.

A man of deep religious conviction, Victoria expresses in his music all the ardor and exaltation of Spanish mysticism. He is generally regarded as a leading representative of the Roman school. However, it should be remembered that, before Palestrina, this school was already profoundly marked by Hispanic influences through the work of Christóbal de Morales (c.1500–c.1553), Francisco Guerrero (1528–1599), Bartolomé de Escobedo (c.1500–1563), and other Spanish composers residing in Rome. Thus Victoria inherited at least as much from his own countrymen as from Palestrina. In its dramatic intensity, rhythmic variety, tragic grandeur, and spiritual fervor, his music is thoroughly personal and thoroughly Spanish.

Beginning with a volume of MOTETs dedicated to his chief patron, Cardinal Otto Truchsess, Bishop of Augsburg in 1572, most of Victoria's works were printed in Italy, in very fine editions, an indication that he had the backing of wealthy patrons. A volume of MASSES, MAGNIFICATs, motets, and other church music published in Madrid in 1600 is of special interest because it makes provision for organ accompaniment. Victoria published 11 books of considerable variety, including motets, Masses, PSALMS, Magnificats, PROPRIA for the saints, ANTIPHONS, HYMNS, and the Requiem for Empress Maria.

Victrola. Trademark for the phonograph made by the Victor Talking Machine Company. It was later considered a generic term (like GRAMOPHONE) for any 78-rpm record player.

vidalita (Sp., little life). A popular Argentinian carnival SONG in a characteristically combined rhythm of $\frac{3}{4}$ and $\frac{6}{8}$. The name comes from the constant recurrence of the word *vidalista* at the end of every verse.

Vie en Rose, La. Song by Luis Guglielmi (pseudonym Louisguy) and the French chanteuse EDITH PIAF, 1947, who popularized it.

Vie Parisienne, La. OPÉRA-BOUFFE by JACQUES OFFENBACH, 1866, first performed in Paris. Two young swains await the arrival by train of their mutual object of adoration, but she spurns them both. Frustrated, one tries to seduce a Swedish baroness, while the other assumes the role of an admiral in the Swiss navy. Secret trysts are held, and a traveling Brazilian sings an infectious *matchiche* (MAXIXE). There are easily penetrable disguises, but at the end each suitor finds a complementary damsel.

La Vie Parisienne is an affectionate spoof on life under the emperor Napoleon III.

Viennese school. Historical designation of at least two styles of composition centered around the capital of Austria. The term was first proposed by the German writer and musician Christian Friedrich Daniel Schubart (1739–91), who defined the main characteristics of the Vienna school as "an organization without pedantry, graceful form, and an intelligent understanding of the nature of wind instruments." Aesthetically, the *first Viennese school* is distinguished from its contemporary Berlin school by its songful and attractive treatment of melodic material and harmonic formations. The Vienna school embraces the period 1750–1830, with FRANZ JOSEPH HAYDN, WOLFGANG AMADEUS MOZART, and LUDWIG VAN BEETHOVEN dominating. Ironically, none of these CLASSIC masters were born in Vienna, although they lived a good portion of their lives there.

The *second Viennese school* refers to a group of composers of the first half of the 20th century, mainly ARNOLD SCHOENBERG, ALBAN BERG, and ANTON WEBERN and their disciples. These composers wrote in the 12-TONE style, with the aim, in the words of Webern, "to say in new terms something that was said before."

Some musicologists see the first Viennese school's ideas continued in the works of FRANZ SCHUBERT and even the Strauss family in the late 19th century.

Vieuxtemps, Henri, celebrated Belgian violinist and composer; b. Verviers, Feb. 17, 1820; d. Mustapha, Algiers, June 6, 1881. Vieuxtemps's first teacher was his father, an amateur musician. He continued his training with Lecloux-Dejonc. At age six he made his debut in Verviers. After performing in Liège in 1827, he gave several concerts in Brussels in 1828, where he attracted the notice of the great French violinist Charles de Bériot, who accepted him as a pupil. Vieuxtemps studied with Bériot until 1831.

PEOPLE IN MUSIC

In 1833 Vieuxtemps's father took him on a concert tour of Germany. He continued his studies in Vienna, where he received lessons in COUNTERPOINT from Simon Sechter. In 1834 he performed as soloist in the LUDWIG VAN BEETHOVEN Violin Concerto in Vienna, scoring a notable success. In 1834 he made his British debut with the Philharmonic Society of London. After training in composition from Antoine Reicha in Paris in 1835–36, he set out on his first tour of Europe in 1837.

During his constant travels, Vieuxtemps composed violin concertos and other violin works. These quickly became part of the standard repertoire, and he performed them in Europe to great acclaim. He made his first American tour in 1843–44. In 1844 Vieuxtemps married the pianist Josephine Eder (b. Vienna, Dec. 15, 1815; d. Celle-St. Cloud, June 29, 1868). In 1846 he was engaged as a professor at the St. Petersburg Conservatory, remaining in Russia for five seasons.

In 1853 Vieuxtemps recommenced his concert tours in Europe. He paid two more visits to the U.S., in 1857–58 (with Sigismond Thalberg) and in 1870–71 (with Christine Nilsson). He was a professor of violin at the Brussels Conservatory from 1871 to 1873. A stroke, affecting his left side, forced him to end all concert activities, but he continued to teach privately. He went to Algiers for rest and died there, with one of his most prominent pupils, Jenö Hubay, at his side.

With Bériot, Vieuxtemps stood at the head of the French school of violin playing. Contemporary accounts speak of the extraordinary precision of his technique and of his ability to perfectly sustain a flowing melody. The expression *le roi du violon* (the king of the violin) was often applied to him in the press.

As a composer, Vieuxtemps is best known for his seven violin concertos (1836; 1840; 1844; c.1850; 1861, *Grétry;* posthumous, 1883; posthumous, 1883). He wrote much violin music with orchestra or piano, including two cello concertos (Paris, 1877, c.1883). Among his chamber pieces are three string quartets (1871, 1884, 1884) and a Viola Sonata (1863).

Vieuxtemps had two brothers who were musicians: (Jean-Joseph-) Lucien (1828–1901) was a pianist and

> ♫
>
> Vieuxtemps's influence on Russian concert life and violin composition was considerable.

teacher who studied with Edouard Wolff in Paris. He made his debut at a concert given by his elder brother in Brussels in 1845. He devoted himself mainly to teaching there and also wrote a few piano pieces. (Jules-Joseph-) Ernest (1832–96) was a cellist who appeared with his elder brother in London in 1855. He was solo cellist in the Italian Opera Orchestra there before going to Manchester to be principal cellist of the Hallé Orchestra in 1858.

vihuela (Sp.). 1. A generic name for Spanish chordophones, in the 15th century, both bowed and plucked, descendants of the Arab 'UD. 2. A Spanish plucked chordophone of the 16th century, similar to the guitar but with between six and seven COURSES of strings (the guitar had four). There is a reference to a vihuela with five pairs of strings and one *chanterelle,* the short, high string found centuries later on the banjo. In the 17th century, the vihuela declined in favor of the guitar.

Villa-Lobos, Heitor, Brazilian composer of great originality and unique ability to re-create native melodic and rhythmic elements in large instrumental and choral forms; b. Rio de Janeiro, March 5, 1887; d. there, Nov. 17, 1959. Villa-Lobos studied music with his father, a writer and amateur cellist. After his father's death in 1899, Villa-Lobos earned a living by playing cello in cafés and restaurants. He also studied cello with Benno Niederberger.

From 1905 to 1912 Villa-Lobos traveled in Brazil to collect authentic folk songs. In 1907 he entered the National Institute of Music in Rio de Janeiro, where he studied with Frederico Nascimento, Angelo Franca, and Francisco Braga.

In 1912 Villa-Lobos made an expedition into the interior of Brazil, where he gathered a rich collection of Indian songs. In 1915 he presented in Rio de Janeiro a concert of his compositions, creating a sensation by the exuberance of his music and the radical character of his technical idiom. He met the pianist ARTHUR RUBINSTEIN, who became his ardent admirer. For him Villa-Lobos composed the transcendentally difficult piano solo *Rudepoema.*

In 1923 Villa-Lobos went to Paris on a Brazilian government grant. Upon returning to Brazil in 1930, he was active

MUSICAL
INSTRUMENT

PEOPLE IN MUSIC

in São Paulo and then in Rio de Janeiro in music education. He founded a conservatory under the sponsorship of the Ministry of Education in 1942.

Villa-Lobos introduced bold innovations into the national program of music education, with emphasis on native culture. He compiled a *Guia pratico* (practical guide) for teachers, containing choral arrangements of FOLK SONGS of Brazil and other nations, and also introduced his own method of SOLFÈGE for teaching singing.

In 1944 Villa-Lobos made his first tour of the U.S., conducting his works in Los Angeles, Boston, and N.Y. In 1945 he established in Rio de Janeiro the Brazilian Academy of Music, serving as its president from 1947 until his death. He made frequent visits to the U.S. and France during the last 15 years of his life.

Villa-Lobos was one of the most original composers of the 20th century. He lacked formal academic training. However, far from hampering his development, this allowed him to evolve a personal technique of composition. An ardent Brazilian nationalist, he resolved from his earliest attempts to use authentic Brazilian song materials as the source of his inspiration. Yet he avoided using actual quotations from popular songs. Rather, he wrote melodies that are authentic in their melodic and rhythmic content.

In his desire to bring Brazilian folk music into the classical work, Villa-Lobos composed a series of extraordinary works. For example, in his *Bachianas brasileiras,* Brazilian MELORHYTHMS are treated in Bachian COUNTERPOINT. He also composed a number of works under the generic title *Chôros,* a popular Brazilian dance form, marked by incisive rhythm and balladlike melody.

An experimenter by nature, Villa-Lobos devised a graphic method of COMPOSITION, using geometrical contours of drawings and photographs as outlines for melody. In this manner he wrote *The New York Skyline* in 1939, using a photograph for guidance.

Villa-Lobos wrote over 2,000 works. These included four operas, including *Magdalena* (1948) and *Yerma* (1953–56), based on the play by Federico García Lorca, and seven ballets. His Brazilian-style orchestral works include nine *Bachianas Brasileiras* and fourteen *Chôros* for various instrumental combinations.

Villa-Lobos also composed 12 symphonies, two sinfoniettas, five piano concertos, a Guitar Concerto, two cello concertos, a Harp Concerto, and a Harmonica Concerto. Among his chamber works are 17 string quartets and three piano trios. He also composed choral works and piano pieces, including the three *Prole do Bebe* suites (including the popular *Polichinello*).

villancico (Sp.). A term applied to different varieties of Spanish and Latin American vocal music, starting in the 15th century.

  bĕl-yăhn-sē′cŏh

Spanish villancicos have included vernacular love songs with STANZAS and REFRAIN. Imitative POLYPHONIC choral pieces, including the Christmas villancico, increasingly influenced by the MADRIGAL, developed in the 16th century. The BAROQUE religious villancico had an expanded formal structure, and later incorporated the RECITATIVE and ARIA. The genre was prohibited in Spain in the mid-18th century, although performances continued into the next century.

In Latin America the genre is mentioned in the 16th century. Villancicos of the 17th and 18th centuries are solely ecclesiastical and liturgical in purpose, incorporating instrumental music, song, and dance. Italian influences came into play in the 18th century. Many related genres evolved in Latin America, and literally hundreds of villancicos have survived.

villanella (It.; Fr. *villanelle, villanesca*). A lighthearted secular song that originated in Naples in the 16th century. Its musical format was marked by a deliberately rustic style. It was cultivated by educated composers who wished to combat the domination of the more refined MADRIGAL. Often such villanellas were of topical content and regional in application.

  vĕl-lăh-nel′lăh

The term is used by some modern composers to refer to a kind of instrumental rustic dance.

villotta. Song genre, related to the VILLANELLA, popular in Italy during the RENAISSANCE. Its melodic and rhythmic structure combines elements of courtly dances and traditional refrains.

vīnā (S. Ind.; N. Ind., *bīn*). 1. Generic term for Indian CHORDOPHONES. Originally, this was the name for a family of arched HARPS (up through the first millennium A.D.), but later it was more widely applied. 2. A highly developed stick ZITHER. It is now similar in shape to the more modern Indian LUTE (i.e., SITAR), with a body replacing the stick and a gourd resonator at the upper end. The seven strings comprise four melody and three DRONE, played with fingers or a PLECTRUM. The player is seated, with the upper end of the instrument resting on the shoulder.

Vingt-quatre Violons du Roi (24 Violins of the King). A string ensemble known as *la grande bande* that was attached to the courts of Louis XIII, Louis XIV, and Louis XV, comprising 24 violins and other string instruments. *La petite bande* had only 16 players. The ensemble was made famous by JEAN-BAPTISTE LULLY, who conducted it for many years, until his death.

viol. A generic type of bowed string instrument that attained universal popularity in the 17th century. Its antecedents include the medieval FIDDLE.

Viols differ from the violin family in having a fretted FINGERBOARD and a variable number of strings (usually six); the shape of the body also differs. It was made in four sizes, like the violin, by which it was superseded. At first three sizes of viols were in use, classified by their French names: *dessus de viole* (top or TREBLE viol), *taille de viole* (TENOR viol), and *basse de viole* (BASS viol). The bass viol was called VIOLA DA GAMBA and was the precursor of the modern cello. An ensemble of viols was called in England a chest or CONSORT of viols.

The viols were tuned like the LUTE, in fourths above and below the central interval, which was a third. The bass viol was tuned D, G, C, E, A, and D, the tenor viol was tuned A, D, G, B, E, and A, and the treble viol was tuned an OCTAVE above the bass viol. To these was added the *pardessus de viole,* tuned a fourth above the treble viol.

viola (It.; Ger. *Bratsche*). The alto violin. A bowed string instrument with its four strings tuned C_0, G_0, d^1, a^1, a fifth lower than the violin.

Physically, the standard-sized viola is only one-seventh larger than the violin. Its lower range is not properly accommodated in acoustical terms; thus its quality of tone lacks the brilliance of the violin and the deep singing quality of the cello. Its melancholy, philosophical sonority occupies a more subtle, less clichéd place in musical expressivity.

Except for HECTOR BERLIOZ's *Harold in Italy* (which has an important viola part but can't be considered a true CONCERTO), few composers wrote viola concertos until the 20th century, when prominent violists Lionel Tertis, William Primrose, and Karl Doktor commissioned numerous works from leading composers.

viola bastarda (U.K., lyra viol). VIOLA DA GAMBA sized between the bass and tenor VIOLS, with two DRONE strings and five playing strings, tuned alternatively in fifths or fourths in the manner of the LIRA DA BRACCIO. Its strange name may derive from its shape or its tunings. It was popular in the early BAROQUE period.

viola da braccio (It., viola for the arm). An obsolete bowed stringed instrument held at the shoulder, the precursor of the modern violin.

viola da gamba (It., viol for the leg; Ger. *Kniegeige,* knee violin). A family of bowed stringed instruments that evolved from the medieval FIDDLE around the beginning of the second millennium A.D. The gambas, as they are known colloquially, are similar in shape to the violin family, with subtle differences—sloping shoulders, C holes, wider bridge and fingerboard, and bows held with palm up—and not so subtle ones—being held vertically, supported on the lap or between the player's calves, having six instead of four strings, and having frets.

The gambas were commonly used in the late RENAISSANCE and BAROQUE periods. There were six principal instruments: soprano, alto, tenor, and three basses of different sizes. There is much virtuoso solo music for gamba and

vē-ô'lah

MUSICAL INSTRUMENT

MUSICAL INSTRUMENT

brah'chŏh

MUSICAL INSTRUMENT

gahm'băh

MUSICAL INSTRUMENT

many treatises on its playing. The instrument was also featured in BASSO CONTINUO. The viola da gamba has been one of the leading instruments in the early music revival.

dăh-moh′rĕh

MUSICAL
INSTRUMENT

viola d'amore (It., viol of love; Ger. *Liebesgeige*). A bowed CHORDOPHONE in the middle range, for at least part of its history supplied with sympathetic strings. The viola d'amore, first reported in the early BAROQUE period, is the size of the violin but lacking its perfect proportions. The number of strings varies from five to seven, its sympathetic metal strings imparting a silvery resonance to its sound.

The mysterious name of the viola d'amore may have the prosaic explanation that its scroll above the pegbox was often made in the shape of Cupid's face. The viola d'amore was very popular in Baroque music, and JOHANN SEBASTIAN BACH used it in several of his works. In modern times the viola d'amore was mostly used for its evocative value, as in the *Sinfonia domestica* of RICHARD STRAUSS. PAUL HINDEMITH wrote a chamber CONCERTO for it.

MUSICAL
INSTRUMENT

viola pomposa (*violino pomposa;* It.). A viola with an extra string (usually e^2), used during the middle half of the 18th century. Despite later claims, JOHANN SEBASTIAN BACH never invented nor scored for such an instrument, but it is found in scores of GEORG PHILIPP TELEMANN.

MUSICAL
INSTRUMENT

violetta (It.; Fr. *violette*). 1. fiddle or small viola of the 16th century. 2. In the 18th century, the viola (alto violin).

MUSICAL
INSTRUMENT

violin (It. *violino;* Fr. *violon;* Ger. *Violine, Geige*). The best known, most expressive, and most artistic instrument of the string family.

The violin has an oval body modified by two elliptic depressions across its waist. There are two symmetrical SOUND HOLES in the shape of large cursive f's. The body of the violin has the function of a RESONATOR box, with resonance at its strongest at the vibrating center. There are four strings, tuned g^0, d^1, a^1, and e^2, that are held at the lower end (nearest the player) by a TAILPIECE and supported by a BRIDGE above it.

A Paris violin shop. (Owen Franken/Corbis)

The strings are maintained in their tension by four pegs in a pegbox (at the end farthest from the player). A fingerboard is placed under the strings. There are no FRETS on the fingerboard to guide the violinist as the GUITAR or VIOLA DA GAMBA player is guided on his or her instrument. The violinist must therefore develop a secure sense of placement of the finger to play in tune. The strings are activated into sound by a bow strung with horsehairs, or by being plucked with the fingers (PIZZICATO).

The first plausible ancestor of the violin was the Arab RABĀB, which penetrated into Western Europe where it became known as the REBEC. In England, the rebec was called the FIDDLE. The shapes of these instruments varied until the present form was fashioned by the great violin makers of Cremona in the late 17th century. The most celebrated of the Cremona masters was ANTONIO STRADIVARI (or Stradivarius). There are some 540 Stradivarius violins in existence, although the authenticity of some is still in doubt.

The secret of the art of Stradivarius and his workshop has been probed by generations of violin manufacturers. They have sought the solution in the peculiar quality of the wood from the forests of the Cremona region, or the quality of the varnish. The drawings of violins and other string instruments that Stradivarius left behind do not shed light on his mysterious skill. Attempts have been made, using the most modern tools of analytical science, to create perfect copies of the Strads, but in vain.

While their monetary value depends on pedigree, some "Strads," as they are affectionately known, have fetched between half a million and a million dollars.

The violin became a favorite instrument in the hands of early virtuosos of the 17th and 18th centuries. Its technique expanded through many ingenious devices such as HARMONICS, DOUBLE-STOPS, and pizzicato. Violin virtuosity attained new heights with NICCOLÒ PAGANINI, whose wizardry on the instrument was documented in detail by contemporary reports. The great era of violin virtuosity was attained in the 19th century, which numbered, besides Paganini, such illustrious artists as Joseph Joachim, PABLO DE SARASATE, and EUGÈNE YSAŸE.

In the 20th century, virtuoso violinists came increasingly from Eastern Europe, especially Russia. Later in the century, ultra-modernist composers demanded the execution of such unusual techniques as quadruple-stops under the bridge, indeterminate high notes beyond the fingerboard, pizzicato GLISSANDO, and QUARTER TONES.

There are two standard placements for the two violin sections in the orchestra: either the *first violins* are in front, to the conductor's left, and the *second violins* to the right, in front (the traditional layout until the 20th century, still used by some conductors), or the seconds are also on the left, behind the firsts. The first violinist, sitting nearest the audience to the left of the conductor, is called leader in England, konzertmeister in Germany, violon solo in French, and concertmaster in America.

violin family. The familiar four-stringed bowed instruments, constructed in four sizes: violin, viola, violoncello, and double bass.

violin-conductor score. A PARTICELLA used in 19th-century theater orchestras, particularly in Italian opera houses. It usually includes the first violin part, the harmony on the second staff, and the bass line.

vē-ŏh-lē′nŏh pik′kŏh-lŏh

MUSICAL
INSTRUMENT

violino piccolo (It.; Ger. *Quartgeige, Halbgeige*). A small violin, tuned a perfect fourth above the standard violin, used to play in the upper registers. The instrument held sway during the BAROQUE era, but, as Leopold Mozart reported, the improvement of technique made the piccolo instrument unnecessary. It continues to be used as a children's instrument.

violoncello (It., cello; Fr. *violoncelle*). The most songful instrument in the lower range of the string family. The word *violoncello* is a diminutive of *violone;* thus, "little big viola."

vē-ŏh-lŏhn-chel′lŏh

The cello has four strings, tuned as C_0, G_0, d^0, and a^0, an octave below the viola. The instrument is an enlarged version of the violin and viola. It resembles a VIOLA DA GAMBA without frets and is placed between the knees, but it is held in place by a floor spike and rests on the shoulder.

Until the 20th century, few cellists achieved the kind of worldly success had by NICCOLÒ PAGANINI and other wizards of the violin. However, this century has brought forth numerous virtuosi, including PABLO CASALS, MSTISLAV ROSTROPOVICH, Lynn Harrell, Jacqueline Du Pré, and YO-YO MA testifying to the instrument's power of musical communication.

Violoncello piccolo (small cello), is a name attached to the five-string cello used in some works by Baroque composers.

violone (It., large viola). Synonym for the largest of the VIOLA DA GAMBAS, the bass or double bass, with a bottom string tuned to D_0. It was a contemporary of and an influence on the instrument that eventually became the even lower-pitched double bass, but the violone usually had five or six strings, whereas the double bass had three or four.

vē-ŏh-loh′něh

MUSICAL
INSTRUMENT

virelai (Fr., from *virer,* turn, twist). A medieval French fixed form, with the BALLADE and RONDEAU, that dominated French song and poetry in the late Middle Ages and early RENAISSANCE. Although there were many variations, the basic formula was in five parts, ABBAA: the principal A section, containing the REFRAIN; the two B sections, with different but matching texts plus first (*ouvert*) and second (*clos*) endings; A, but with a matching text rather than the refrain; a repetition of the first A.

vēr-eh-lā′

Its name incorporates both dance and poetic (*lai*) origins. Guillaume de Machaut was the greatest exponent of the genre, mostly composing MONOPHONIC examples.

virginal. 1. KEYBOARD instrument of the HARPSICHORD family, extremely popular in the 16th and 17th centuries.

MUSICAL
INSTRUMENT

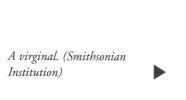

A virginal. (Smithsonian Institution)

The origins of the name is uncertain. A natural surmise, that it refers to the unmarried British queen Elizabeth, is refuted by earlier German publications in which the term was already used. Other conjectures are that virginals possessed a virginal sound and a sweet voice, or that the word is derived from the Latin *virga* (rod), by analogy to the jack, an essential part of the virginal's mechanism.

The virginal is a single-strung, plucked keyboard instrument, with the strings placed within a rectangular shape running right to left. Notable is the location of the relatively small keyboards (less than four octaves) at the left or right side of the virginal's playing area. Instruments were built throughout Europe, with particular skill in Flanders by the Ruckers family. While the virginal retained a role similar to the CLAVICHORD's, that of a home instrument, the louder harpsichord eventually replaced the virginal.

2. A term for all harpsichord family instruments, commonly in use in England at the same time of the particular instrument's height. Thus, a collection of music published in 1611 bore a title that was revealing but at the same misleading: *Parthenia, or The Maydenhead of the first musicke that was ever printed for the Virginalls*. It included dances, mostly PAVANS and GALLIARDS, by British composers of the time. However, they could be played on any plucked keyboard instrument (or arranged for LUTE).

virtuosity (from Lat. *virtus,* ability, value). A display of great proficiency by an instrumentalist or vocalist, called a *virtuoso.*

The concept dates to the BAROQUE period, with the loss of religious restrictions on compositional excess and the rise of new MONODIC TEXTURES. A virtuoso must possess above all else superlative technique. The first virtuosos in this sense were church organists. Of these, GIROLAMO FRESCOBALDI acquired legendary fame. His biographers claim that 30,000 people flocked to hear him play at St. Peter's in Rome. In later centuries, the term *virtuoso* was applied mostly to instrumentalists, particularly pianists and violinists.

During the ROMANTIC era, the idea of "virtuosity" took on new meaning. A virtuoso was someone who tempted fate, who dared to be godlike in his or her powers. FRANZ LISZT and FRÉDÉRIC CHOPIN were revered as giants, men whose virtuosity was testimony to their spirituality.

Today, our heroes have feet of clay. Virtuosos are now recognized as ordinary people who just happen to be able to do extraordinary things musically. We no longer see this as a sign of intense spirituality, even though we may be profoundly moved by such a performance.

The term *virtuoso* is not limited to classical performers. JAZZ saxophonists and ROCK electric guitarists are often compared and analyzed as much as their classical counterparts.

Vishnevskaya, Galina (Pavlovna). *See* ROSTROPOVICH, MSTISLAV (LEOPOLDOVICH).

Vitry, Philippe de (Philippus de Vitriaco), famous French music theorist, composer, poet, and churchman; b. Vitry, Champagne, Oct. 31, 1291; d. Meaux, June 9, 1361. There are six towns in Champagne named Vitry, and it is not known in which of these Vitry was born. He was educated at the Sorbonne in Paris, where he later was *magister artium* (instructor in the arts).

Vitry was ordained a deacon early in life, and from 1323 he held several ecclesiastical offices. He was canon of Soissons and archbishop of Brie. He became a clerk of the royal household in Paris, and about 1346 was made counselor of the court of requests (*maître des requetes*). From 1346 to 1350 he was also in the service of Duke Jean of Normandy (heir to the throne), with whom he took part in the siege of Aiguillon in 1346. When Duke Jean became king in 1350, he sent Vitry to Avignon on a mission to Pope Clement VI, who appointed him bishop of Meaux in 1351.

PEOPLE IN MUSIC

Vitry was known as a poet and a composer, but his enduring fame rests on his ARS NOVA, a treatise expounding a new theory of MENSURAL NOTATION, particularly important for its development of the principle of BINARY RHYTHM. It also gives the most complete account of the various uses to which colored notes were put. Of the four treatises attributed to Vitry, only the last 10 of the 24 chapters of *Ars nova* are now considered authentic.

Although most of Vitry's musical works are lost, a MOTET, with TENOR only, survives.

Vivaldi, Antonio (Lucio), renowned Italian composer; b. Venice, March 4, 1678; d. Vienna, July 28, 1741. Vivaldi

PEOPLE IN MUSIC

Because of his red hair, Vivaldi was called *il prete rosso* (the red priest).

Antonio Vivaldi. (New York Public Library) ▶

was the son of Giovanni Battista Vivaldi (b. Brescia, c.1655; d. Venice, May 14, 1736), a violinist who entered the orchestra at San Marco in Venice in 1685 under the surname of Rossi, remaining there until 1729. He was also director of instrumental music at the Mendicanti from 1689 to 1693. Antonio was trained for the priesthood at S. Geminiano and at S. Giovanni in Oleo and was ordained in 1703.

In 1703 Vivaldi became *maestro di violino* at the Pio Ospedale della Pietà, where he remained until 1709. The Ospedale was an orphanage for young women, who were groomed for courtly careers as musicians. During this period his first published works appeared. In 1711 he resumed his duties at the Pietà, and was named its maestro de' concerti in 1716.

In 1711 Vivaldi's set of 12 concertos known as *L'estro armonico,* op.3, appeared in print in Amsterdam. It proved to be the most important music publication of the first half of the 18th century. His first known opera, *Ottone in Villa,* was given in Vicenza in May 1713, and soon thereafter he became active as a composer and impresario in Venice. From 1718 to 1720 he was active in Mantua, where the Habsburg governor Prince Philipp of Hessen-Darmstadt made him *maestro di cappella da camera,* a title he retained even after leaving that town.

In subsequent years Vivaldi traveled widely in Italy, bringing out his operas in various music centers while retaining his association with the Pietà. About 1725 he became associated with the CONTRALTO Anna Giraud (or Giro), one of his voice students. Her sister, Paolina, also became a constant companion of the composer, leading to speculation by his contemporaries that the two sisters were his mistresses, a contention he denied.

Vivaldi's *La cetra,* op.9 (two books, Amsterdam, 1727), was dedicated to the Austrian emperor Charles VI. From 1735 to 1738 he once more served as maestro di cappella at the Pietà. He also was named *Maestro di Cappella* to Francis Stephen, Duke of Lorraine (later the Emperor Francis I) in 1735.

In 1738 Vivaldi visited Amsterdam, where he took charge of musical performances for the centennial celebration of the Schouwburg theater. Returning to Venice, he found little favor with the theater going public. As a result, he set out for Austria in 1740, arriving in Vienna in June 1741, but dying a month later. Although he had received large sums of money in his day, he died in poverty and was given a pauper's burial at the Spettaler Gottesacher (hospital burial ground).

Vivaldi's greatness lies mainly in his superb instrumental works, most notably some 500 CONCERTOS, in which he displayed an extraordinary mastery of RITORNELLO form and ORCHESTRATION. More than 230 of his concertos are for solo violin and strings, and another 120 or so are for other solo instruments (VIOLA D'AMORE, cello, flute, oboe,

Vivaldi time line

1678 — Born

1703 — Is ordained a priest and becomes *maestro di violino* at the Pio Ospedale della Pietà, where he remains until 1709

1711 — *L'estro armonico,* op.3, a set of 12 concertos, appears in print in Amsterdam

1711–18 — Is once again at the Pietà, where he is named *maestro de' concerti* in 1716

1713 — *Ottone in Villa,* his first known opera, is staged in Vicenza

1718–20 — Active in Mantua, where he is named *maestro di cappella da camera*

1725 — Composes his *Il cimento dell'armonia e dell'inventione,* op.8, in two books, containing his most popular work, *The Four Seasons*

1727 — *La cetra,* op.9 is published in Amsterdam

1735 — Is named *maestro di cappella* to Francis Stephen, Duke of Lorraine

1735–38 — Serves once again as *maestro di cappella* at the Pietà

1738 — Conducts musical performances for the centennial celebration of the Schouwburg theater in Amsterdam

1741 — Travels to Vienna, where he dies a pauper

bassoon) or multiple instruments and strings. In some 60 *concerti ripieni* (string concertos sans solo instrument), he honed a style akin to operatic SINFONIAS. He also wrote about 90 SONATAS.

Only 21 of his operas are extant, some missing one or more acts. A few have been revived in recent years, including *Tito Manlio* (1719), *Farnace* (1727), *Orlando (furioso)* (1727), *La fida ninfa* (1732), *Montezuma* (1733), and *L'Olimpiade* (1734). He also composed eight SERENATAS, 31 solo CANTATAS with BASSO CONTINUO, and nine solo cantatas with instrument(s) and basso continuo.

Vivaldi composed four ORATORIOS, including *Juditha triumphans devicta Holofernes barbarie* (1716). His sacred vocal works include seven MASSES or Mass sections, PSALMS, HYMNS, ANTIPHONS, and MOTETS.

> Of the many collections of Vivaldi's works published during his lifetime, *Il cimento dell'armonia e dell'invenzione*, op.8 (two books, 1725) includes his most popular work, *The Four Seasons*. Each concerto illustrates a season of the year and is accompanied by a sonata.

Vive la Compagnie. Anonymous German military song, c.1838, now known under its French title.

vocal. Pertaining to the voice, or suitable for the singing voice. *Vocal cords,* the two opposed ligaments set in the larynx, whose vibration, caused by expelling air from the lungs, produces vocal tones; *vocal glottis,* the aperture between the vocal cords; *vocal quartet,* chamber piece for four singers; group of four solo singers within a larger group.

vocal score. The ARRANGEMENT of any work for voice(s) and ensemble (up to an orchestra) as a score for voice(s) and piano REDUCTION, for rehearsal purposes and, when resources are limited, actual performance.

vōh-căh-lēz′   **vocalise** (Fr.). A vocal ÉTUDE or composition, sung on open vowels, without text. Vocal music sometimes uses vocalise as a technique for part of its duration, such as the *Bell Song* from LÉO DELIBES's *Lakme* or *Bachianas Brasileiras No. 8* by HEITOR VILLA-LOBOS. Other primarily orchestral pieces may include a passage for solo or choral vocalise, such as CLAUDE DEBUSSY's *Nocturnes* (*Sirènes*), GUSTAV HOLST's *The Planets* (*Neptune*), and CARL NIELSEN's Third Symphony (second movement).

vocalization. Singing exercise comprising a melody sung without words. SCALES and ARPEGGIOS are common vocalizations used to prepare the vocal cords for performance.

Vogelquartett (Bird Quartet). String quartet by FRANZ JOSEPH HAYDN, 1781 (op.33, no. 3), in the key of C major. It was nicknamed because some of the TRILLS and MORDENTS in its melodies sound like an aviary in mild turmoil. The quartet is part of a six-work set known as *Gli Scherzi* for its use of SCHERZO (or scherzolike) movements instead of the older, statelier MINUET.

voice (It. *voce;* Ger. *Stimme;* Fr. *voix*). 1. Human vocal production of musical TONE, divided into six principal ranges: SOPRANO, MEZZOSOPRANO, CONTRALTO (ALTO), TENOR, BARITONE, and BASS. Animal vocal sounds are considered voices, with those of birds called SONGS (although whale songs are not produced through the mouth). But all lack the facility and variety of the human voice. In contemporary scores, voice parts constantly call for untraditional sounds, and sometimes speech replaces musical production altogether. *See* SINGING. 2. A part or line, vocal or instrumental.

voice exchange (Ger. *Stimmtausch*). 1. Medieval compositional technique in which two POLYPHONIC voices take up a portion of each other's music immediately and in the same range, creating the effect of a repetition of the original material. 2. In SCHENKERIAN ANALYSIS, an exchange of NOTES between two polyphonic voices over a span of time, not necessarily in the same range.

voice leading. The art of arranging voices in a POLYPHONIC composition so that each part has a logical continuation without competing with the continuation in others. Depending on the harmonic (TONAL, CHROMATIC, ATONAL) context and the strictness of the contrapuntal "rules" in force at the time, voice leading is usually easier to describe as a series of prohibitions against certain practices, rather than by what is allowed.

voice production. A pedagogical hypothesis that the human voice can be directed or projected physiologically from the head, the chest, or the epiglottis by conscious effort. Of course, the only source of the human voice is the larynx, and the only resonator is the pharynx, but even serious professional singers are convinced that the lower notes travel from the vocal cords to the thoracic cavity and that the head tone (voice) is monitored from the top of the head.

With the invasion of the U.S. by Italian singing teachers late in the 19th century and by Russian singers after World War I, the mythology of voice production assumed the status of a science. One Russian singer who organized an American opera company urged his students to "exercise the muscles of the brain" and was quite unimpressed when he was told that the brain had no muscular network.

There is no harm in using the terms *chest voice* and *head tone* (voice) if both the teacher and the student understand that they are using metaphors. It must be remembered, however, that great natural singers like ENRICO CARUSO and FEODOR CHALIAPIN developed their glorious voices never knowing whether they sang from the chest, head, or epiglottis.

voicing. Instrument TUNING, especially the balancing of multiple strings or pipes in keyboard instruments.

Voivoda, The. *See* VOYEVODE, THE.

Volare. Alternate if better-known name for the Italian popular song *Nel Blu Dipinto Di Blu* by Domenico Modugno, 1958, immensely popular then and over the years.

Volga Boatmen's Song. A famous Russian FOLK SONG. Its Russian title is *Burlaki* (boatman haulers), that is, men who pulled boats upstream on the Volga River while singing a heaving strain.

The AEOLIAN melody is also associated with funerals, which, given its doleful character, is not surprising.

The Volga boatmen are also the subject of a celebrated painting by I.E. Repin (1844–1930).

Volkstümlich (Ger.). Like a FOLK SONG, but newly composed; neotraditional.

fohlks′tim′liyh

Volkstümliches Lied, an ostentatiously simple German art song that emulates the melodic and rhythmic construction of a genuine folk song; *Lorelei* by P.F. Silcher is one example.

A neotraditional composer's goal would be that one of his or her songs is so popular that it, too, is mistaken for a genuine folk song, is often performed and recorded, and is thereby a substantial source of royalties. In the U.S., JEROME KERN's *Ol' Man River* or the songs of neotraditional musicians such as STEPHEN FOSTER and BOB DYLAN are the equivalent of the German genre.

volta (*lavolta;* It., the turn). A dance of Provençal origin, popular in Western European courts between 1550 and 1650.

vŏhl'tăh

The volta is in $\frac{3}{4}$ or $\frac{3}{2}$ time, at a relatively slow lilt. A true couples dance, it features individual jumps by the dancers followed by a well-coordinating lift of the female by the male partner. Each of the three jumps occur simultaneously with a ¾ (280°) turn. It is mentioned in William Shakespeare, and examples are found in LUTE, KEYBOARD, and ensemble arrangements.

voluntary. A partly or wholly improvised organ piece used in Anglican church services. As the name indicates, such a piece is freely "volunteered," stylistically speaking.

Traditionally, it was written in a POLYPHONIC idiom, containing elements of IMITATION and of a cheerful nature. English composers of the 17th and 18th centuries wrote many such voluntaries, not necessarily for organ or for religious settings. Eventually British organists applied the term to any kind of improvisation, particularly one using the loud cornet stop. The best known is Jeremiah Clarke's *Trumpet Voluntary* (composed sometime before 1700), long thought to be by HENRY PURCELL. Its subtitle, *The Prince of Denmark's March,* suggests its mood and milieu.

Von Stade, Frederica, American MEZZOSOPRANO; b. Somerville, N.J., June 1, 1945. Von Stade was educated at the Norton Academy in Connecticut. After an apprenticeship at the Long Wharf Theater in New Haven, she studied at the Mannes College of Music in N.Y.

PEOPLE IN MUSIC

Although von Stade reached only the semi-finals of the Metropolitan Opera Auditions in 1969, she attracted the attention of Rudolf Bing, its general manager. He arranged for her debut with the company in N.Y. as the third Boy in WOLFGANG AMADEUS MOZART's *DIE ZAUBERFLÖTE* in 1970. She gradually took on more important roles there before going to Europe, where she gave an arresting portrayal of Cherubino at the opera house at the palace of Versailles in 1973.

In 1974 von Stade sang Nina in the premiere of Thomas Pasatieri's *The Seagull* at the Houston Grand Opera. In 1975 she made her debut at London's Covent Garden as Rosina, subsequently attaining extraordinary success in lyric mezzosoprano roles with the world's major opera houses. She also pursued an extensive concert career, appearing regularly with the Chamber Music Society of Lincoln Center. In 1988 she sang the role of Tina in the premiere of Dominick Argento's *The Aspern Papers* at the Dallas Lyric Opera, and in 1990 she appeared in recital in N.Y.'s Carnegie Hall. Her Metropolitan Opera engagements throughout the 1990s included Rosina (1992), Cherubino (1993), and Périchole (1996).

Von Stade's memorable roles include Dorabella, Idamante, Adalgisa in *NORMA,* Charlotte in *Werther,* Mélisande, Octavian, and Malcolm in *La Donna del lago.* She has also proved successful as a crossover artist, especially in Broadway musical recordings.

fohr-trah **Vortrag** (Ger.). Rendering, INTERPRETATION, performance, style, delivery, execution. *Vortragsstück* (performance piece), a composition calculated to appeal to the general public; *Vortragzeichen,* EXPRESSION mark.

Votive Mass. Roman Catholic MASS celebrated at the express wish of an individual votary.

vōx **vox** (Lat., voice). 1. In medieval Latin nomenclature, a sound produced by any source. 2. In the theory of ORGANUM, *vox principalis* is the part with the CANTUS FIRMUS; *vox organalis,* the added CONTRAPUNTAL voice.

Vox angelica (angelic voice), a 4′ stop corresponding to the 8′ vox humana; *vox harmonica,* human voice; *vox hu-*

mana (human voice), an 8′ reed stop, with a (fancied) resemblance to the human voice; *vox organica,* wind instruments or organ.

Voyevode, The (The Voivoda). Symphonic ballad by PIOTR ILYICH TCHAIKOVSKY, 1891, first performed in Moscow. This work has no connection with Tchaikovsky's 1869 opera of the same name, but is inspired by Aleksandr Pushkin's translation of a poem by Adam Mickiewicz (1798–1855).

Tchaikovsky himself referred to this SCORE as "a piece of rubbish."

Voyevode, The (The Voivoda). Opera by PIOTR ILYICH TCHAIKOVSKY, 1869, to a libretto based on Aleksandr Ostrovsky's play *A Dream on the Volga,* first performed in Moscow.

The story deals with the attempt by the head of a Volga community to abduct a young woman engaged to another. He has a prophetic dream of his downfall, which comes true when he is dismissed from office by the czar. His intended victim is now free to marry her beloved.

Tchaikovsky destroyed the opera, but orchestral parts were later discovered. Pavel Lamm, the great restorer of fragmentary Russian operas, reconstructed the work.

Výlety pana Broučka. *See* EXCURSIONS OF MISTER BROUČEK, THE.

Waart, Edo (Eduard) **de,** Dutch conductor; b. Amsterdam, June 1, 1941. Waart was a member of a musical family. His father sang in the chorus of the Netherlands Opera. De Waart first studied piano, then at 13 took up the oboe. At 16, he entered the Amsterdam Muzieklyceum, where he studied oboe and later cello, graduating in 1962. During the summer of 1960 he attended the conducting classes in Salzburg given by Dean Dixon.

De Waart played oboe in the Amsterdam Philharmonic in 1962–63, then joined the Concertgebouw Orchestra. He also studied conducting with Franco Ferrara in Hilversum, where he made his debut as a conductor with the Netherlands Radio Philharmonic in 1964. Later that year, De Waart went to the U.S. and was one of the winners in the Mitropoulos Competition in N.Y. In 1965–66 he was assistant conductor with the N.Y. Philharmonic.

Upon his return to Amsterdam in 1966, De Waart was appointed assistant conductor of the Concertgebouw Orchestra, accompanying it on a tour of the U.S. in 1967. He also organized the Netherlands Wind Ensemble, with which he established his reputation through extensive tours.

In 1967 De Waart became a guest conductor of the Rotterdam Philharmonic, serving, from 1973 to 1979, as its chief conductor. He led it on several tours of Europe and the U.S. In 1971, 1972, and 1975 he was a guest conductor of the Santa Fe Opera in New Mexico and also conducted opera in Houston. In 1976 he conducted at Covent Garden in London.

In 1974 De Waart made a successful debut with the San Francisco Symphony, becoming its principal guest conductor in 1975 and its music director in 1977. In 1979 he made his first appearance at the Bayreuth Festival. He resigned as music director in San Francisco in 1986 to serve in that capacity with the Minnesota Orchestra in Minneapolis until 1995. At the same time, he held other positions in Zurich and Sydney, Australia.

On Jan. 24, 1998, Waart made his Metropolitan Opera debut in N.Y., conducting *Die Zauberflöte*. From 1999 he was music director of the Netherlands Opera.

De Waart represents the modern generation of symphony and operatic conductors. He carefully follows each score, to present both classical and modern pieces as faithfully as possible. He avoids any unnecessary showmanship.

Wacht am Rhein, Die. A rousing patriotic German hymn by Carl Wilhelm, 1840, which called on the Germans to keep "watch on the Rhine."

It became famous during the Franco-Prussian War of 1870–71. The Germans not only maintained their watch on the Rhine but actually crossed the river in Alsace and appropriated the city of Strasbourg. It was renamed Strassburg, until its recovery by France after World War I.

Wagner, Cosima, daughter of FRANZ LISZT and the Countess Marie d'Agoult, first wife of HANS (Guido) VON BÜLOW, second wife of (Wilhelm) RICHARD WAGNER; b. Bellagio, on Lake Como, Dec. 24, 1837; d. Bayreuth, April 1, 1930. Cosima received an excellent education in Paris. She married the famous conductor Hans von Bülow in 1857. There were two daughters of this marriage, Blandine and Daniela, while the third daughter, Isolde, was Wagner's child, as was the fourth, Eva, and the son, Siegfried. A divorce from von Bülow followed in 1870, with the marriage to Richard Wagner taking place a few weeks later.

PEOPLE IN MUSIC

A woman of high intelligence, practical sense, and imperious character, Cosima emerged after Wagner's death as a powerful personage in all affairs regarding the continuance of the Bayreuth Festivals, as well as the complex matters pertaining to the rights of performance of Wagner's works all over the world.

Wagner, Siegfried (Helferich Richard), German conductor and composer, son of (Wilhelm) RICHARD and COSIMA WAGNER; b. Triebschen, June 6, 1869; d. Bayreuth, Aug. 4, 1930.

PEOPLE IN MUSIC

RICHARD WAGNER named the *Siegfried Idyll* for his son, Siegfried, and it was performed in Wagner's house in Triebschen on Christmas Day, 1870.

His parents were married in 1870, and Siegfried was thus legitimated.

Siegfried studied with ENGELBERT HUMPERDINCK in Frankfurt am Main, then pursued training as an architect in Berlin and Karlsruhe. During his tenure as an assistant in Bayreuth from 1892 to 1896, he studied with his mother, Hans Richter, and Julius Kniese. From 1896 he was a regular conductor in Bayreuth, where he was general director of the festival productions from 1906.

In 1915 Siegfried married Winifred Williams, an adopted daughter of Karl Klindworth. In 1923–24 he visited the U.S. in order to raise funds for the reopening of the Bayreuth Festspielhaus, which had been closed during World War I. He conducted from memory and left-handed.

In his career as a composer, Siegfried was greatly handicapped by inevitable comparisons with his father. He wrote 12 operas, orchestral works, vocal pieces, and chamber music.

MUSICAL INSTRUMENT

Wagner tuba. A brass instrument introduced by RICHARD WAGNER in *DER RING DES NIBELUNGEN*. It was made in two sizes, tenor and bass. Its funnel-shaped mouthpiece helps to create a tone somewhere between the TUBA and the TROMBONE. ANTON BRUCKNER, IGOR STRAVINSKY, and RICHARD STRAUSS also used the Wagner tuba.

PEOPLE IN MUSIC

Wagner, (Wilhelm) **Richard,** great German composer whose OPERAS, written to his own librettos, radically transformed the concept of stage music; b. Leipzig, May 22, 1813; d. Venice, Feb. 13, 1883. The antecedents of Wagner's family, and his own origin, are open to controversy. His father was a police registrar in Leipzig who died when Wagner was only six months old. His mother, Johanna (Rosine), née Pätz, was the daughter of a baker in Weissenfels. It is possible that she was an illegitimate offspring of Prince Friedrich Ferdinand Constantin of Weimar.

Eight months after her husband's death, Johanna Wagner married the actor Ludwig Geyer in 1814. This hasty marriage generated speculation that Geyer may have been Wagner's real father. Wagner himself entertained this possibility, pointing out the similarity of his and Geyer's prominent noses.

The problem of Wagner's origin arose with renewed force after the triumph of the Nazi party in Germany. Hitler's adoration of Wagner was put in jeopardy by suspicions that Geyer might have been Jewish. If Wagner was indeed Geyer's natural son, then he himself was "tainted" by Semitic blood. To answer this question, Nazi biologists and archivists delved anxiously into Geyer's own ancestry. Much to their relief, it was found that Geyer, like Wagner's nominal father, was the purest of Aryans.

Geyer was a member of the Court Theater in Dresden, and the family moved there in 1814. Seven years later Geyer died, and in 1822 Wagner entered the Dresden Kreuzschule, where he remained a pupil until 1827. CARL MARIA VON WEBER often visited the Geyer home, and these visits nurtured Wagner's interest in music. In 1825 he began to take piano lessons from a local musician, and also studied violin.

Wagner showed strong literary inclinations, and, under the spell of Shakespeare, wrote a tragedy, *Leubald*. In 1827 he moved with his mother back to Leipzig, where his uncle Adolf Wagner gave him guidance in classical reading. In 1828 he was enrolled in the Nikolaischule. While in school he had lessons in harmony with Christian Gottlieb Müller, a violinist in the theater orchestra.

In 1830 Wagner entered the Thomasschule, where he began to compose. He wrote a string quartet and some pi-

◀

Portrait of Richard Wagner by Ferdinand Bac, 1880. (Gianni Dagli Orti/Corbis)

Wagner time line

1813	Born
1822–27	Studies at the Dresden Kreuzschule
1828–30	Studies in Leipzig at the Nikolaischule and the Thomasschule, where he begins to compose
1832	His first published work, a piano sonata, is published by Breitkopf & Härtel, the same year in which he composes an opera, *Die Hochzeit*
1833–34	Composes second opera, *Die Feen*

1834 — Becomes music director with Heinrich Bethmann's theater company in Magdeburg

1836 — Leads the premiere of *Das Liebesverbot* (as *Die Novize von Palermo*) in Magdeburg and also marries the actress Christine Wilhelmine (Minna) Palner

1837–39 — Serves briefly as music director of the Königsberg town theater, then as music director of the theater in Riga

1839 — Arrives in Paris, eking out his existence by making piano arrangements and writing articles for the *Gazette Musicale*

1842 — *Rienzi* is accepted for production in Dresden

1843 — Wagner conducts the first performance of *Der fliegende Holländer* in Dresden, where, a year later, he is named Second Hofkapellmeister

1845 — Conducts the first performance of *Tannhäuser* in Dresden

1849 — Active as a revolutionary, an order is issued for his arrest, causing him to leave Dresden

1850 — Franz Liszt conducts *Lohengrin* in Weimar

1851 — Expounds upon his radical theories of music in his first important text, *Oper und Drama*

1852 — Completes work on the libretto for *Der Ring des Nibelungen*

ano music. That same year, his overture in B-flat major was performed at the Leipzig Theater, under the direction of Heinrich Dorn. Determined to dedicate himself entirely to music, he became a student of Theodor Weinlig, cantor of the Thomaskirche, from whom he received thorough training in COUNTERPOINT and composition.

The year 1832 was a productive one for Wagner. His first published work, a piano sonata in B-flat major, to which he assigned the opus number 1, was brought out by the prestigious publishing house of Breitkopf & Härtel. Later that year, he wrote an overture to *König Enzio*, performed at the Leipzig Theater, followed by another overture in C major, which was presented at a Gewandhaus concert. Wagner's first major orchestral work, a symphony in C major, was performed at a Prague Conservatory concert that year; a year later, it was played by the Gewandhaus Orchestra in Leipzig, when Wagner was just 19 years old. Finally, he also wrote an opera in 1832, *Die Hochzeit*. An introduction, a septet, and a chorus from this work have survived.

Early in 1833, Wagner began work on a second opera, *Die Feen*, to a LIBRETTO after Carlo Gozzi's *La Donna serpente*. Upon its completion in early 1834 he offered the score to the Leipzig Theater, but it was rejected. In the summer of 1834 he began to sketch out a new opera, *Das Liebesverbot*, after Shakespeare's play *Measure for Measure*. That summer he obtained the position of music director with Heinrich Bethmann's theater company, based in Magdeburg. He made his debut in Bad Lauschstadt, conducting WOLFGANG AMADEUS MOZART'S *DON GIOVANNI*.

In 1836 Wagner led the premiere of his opera *Das Liebesverbot*, presented under the title *Die Novize von Palermo*, in Magdeburg. Bethmann's company soon went out of business. Wagner, who was by that time deeply involved with Christine Wilhelmine (Minna) Palner, an actress with the company, followed her to Königsberg, where they were married later that year. In Königsberg he composed the overture *Rule Britannia*, and in 1837 he was appointed music director of the Königsberg town theater. His marital affairs suffered a setback when Minna left him for a rich businessman by the name of Dietrich.

In 1837 Wagner went to Riga as music director of the theater there. Coincidentally, Minna's sister was engaged as a singer at the same theater. Minna soon joined her and reconciled with Wagner. In Riga Wagner worked on his new opera, RIENZI, der letzte der Tribunen, based on a popular novel by Edward Bulwer-Lytton.

In 1839 Wagner lost his position in Riga. He and Minna, burdened by debts, left town to seek their fortune elsewhere. Along the way, their ship encountered a fierce storm and was forced to drop anchor in the Norwegian fjord of Sandwike. They made their way to London, then set out for Boulogne. There Wagner met GIACOMO MEYERBEER, who gave him a letter of recommendation to the director of the Paris Opéra.

Wagner and Minna arrived in Paris in 1839 and remained there until 1842. He was forced to eke out a meager subsistence by making piano arrangements of operas and writing occasional articles for the *Gazette Musicale*. In 1840 he completed his overture to *Faust* (later revised as *Eine Faust-Ouvertüre*).

Soon Wagner found himself in dire financial straits. He owed money that he could not repay, and later that year was confined for three weeks in debtors' prison. In the meantime he had completed the libretto for *DER FLIEGENDE HOLLÄNDER*. He submitted it to the director of the Paris Opéra, but the director had already asked Paul Foucher to prepare a libretto on the same subject. The director was willing, however, to buy Wagner's scenario for 500 francs, which Wagner accepted in 1841. Louis Dietsch brought out his treatment of the subject in his opera *Le Vaisseau fantôme* at the Paris Opéra a year later.

In 1842 Wagner received the welcome news from Dresden that his opera *Rienzi* had been accepted for production. It was staged there in 1842, with considerable success. *Der fliegende Holländer* was also accepted by Dresden, and Wagner conducted its first performance there in 1843. Later that year, he was named Second Hofkapellmeister in Dresden, where he conducted a large repertoire of classic operas, among them *DON GIOVANNI, LE NOZZE DI DIGARO, DIE ZAUBER-FLÖTE, FIDELIO,* and *DER FREISCHÜTZ.* In 1846 he conducted a

1855 Conducts a series of eight concerts with the Philharmonic Society of London

1858 Moves to Venice

1859 Still pursued by the authorities for his revolutionary affiliations, he takes refuge in Switzerland, where he completes the score of *Tristan und Isolde*

1860 Once again in Paris, Wagner conducts three concerts of his music at the Théâtre-Italien

1862–63 Granted amnesty, Wagner settles in Biebrich, and also travels in Vienna, Prague, St. Petersburg, and Moscow

1864 Gains the support of King Ludwig II of Bavaria and settles in Munich

1865 Forced to leave Munich, he travels to Switzerland, where, now estranged from Minna, he takes up with Liszt's married daughter, Cosima von Bülow, with whom he fathers his first child, a daughter, Isolde

1867 Completes *Die Meistersinger,* which is given its first performance one year later in Munich under von Bülow in the presence of King Ludwig

1868 Settles with Cosima in a villa in Triebschen, on Lake Lucerne

1869 A second child is born to Wagner and Cosima, a son, Siegfried

1870 — Cosima obtains a divorce from von Bülow, and she and Wagner are married in Lucerne

1872 — The cornerstone is laid for the grand theater in Bayreuth dedicated to the production of Wagner's works

1873 — Wagner begins to build his own home in Bayreuth, which he calls *Wahnfried* (free from delusion)

1876 — The premiere of *Der Ring des Nibelungen* takes place, under the direction of Hans Richter

1878 — Begins publishing the *Bayreuther Blätter*

1882 — Completes *Parsifal* in Palermo, which is performed at the Bayreuth Festival, Wagner's last appearance as a conductor

1883 — Dies, after a massive heart attack; his body is interred in a vault in the garden of Wahnfried

memorable performance there of LUDWIG VAN BEETHOVEN's Ninth Symphony.

Wagner also led the prestigious choral society *Liedertafel* in Dresden. He wrote several works for this group, including the "biblical scene" *Das Liebesmahl der Apostel.* He was also preoccupied during those years on the score for TANNHÄUSER, completing it in 1845 and conducting its first performance in Dresden that same year. He subsequently revised the score, which was staged to better advantage there in 1847. Concurrently, he began work on LOHENGRIN, which he completed in 1848.

Wagner's efforts to have his works published failed, leaving him again in debt. Without waiting for further performances of his operas already publicly presented, he drew up the first prose outline of *Der Nibelungen-Mythus als Entwurf zu einem Drama,* the prototype of the epic *Ring* cycle. In 1848 he began work on the poem for *Siegfrieds Tod.* At that time he joined the revolutionary Vaterlandsverein and was drawn into active participation in the movement, culminating in an open uprising against the Saxon government in May 1849. An order was issued for his arrest, and he had to leave Dresden.

Wagner made his way to Weimar, where he was cordially received by Franz Liszt. He then proceeded to Vienna, where a Professor Widmann lent him his own passport so that Wagner could cross the border of Saxony on his way to Zurich. There he made his home in July 1849, with Minna joining him a few months later.

Shortly before leaving Dresden Wagner had sketched two dramas, *Jesus von Nazareth* and *Achilleus,* both of which remained unfinished. In Zurich he wrote a number of essays expounding his philosophy of art. One of his theories was that all elements of a musical production—music, story, scenery, orchestration, and so on—should contribute equally to expressing the production's theme.

In 1850 Wagner was again in Paris. There he fell in love with Jessie Laussot, the wife of a wine merchant. However, she eventually left Wagner, and he returned to Minna in Zurich. In 1850 Liszt conducted the successful premiere of *Lohengrin* in Weimar. In 1851 Wagner wrote the verse text of *Der junge Siegfried* and prose sketches for DAS RHEINGOLD and *DIE WALKÜRE.* In 1852 he finished the text of *Die Walküre* and of *Das Rheingold.* He completed the entire libretto of *DER RING DES NIBELUNGEN* in 1852, and it was privately printed in 1853.

In 1853 Wagner began composition of the music for *Das Rheingold,* completing the full score in 1854. In 1854 he commenced work on the music of *Die Walküre,* which he finished in 1856. In 1854 he became friendly with a wealthy Zurich merchant, Otto Wesendonck (1815–96), and his wife, Mathilde (Luckemeyer) Wesendonck (b. Elberfeld, Dec. 23, 1828; d. Traunblick, near Altmünster on the Traunsee, Austria, Aug. 31, 1902). Otto was willing to give Wagner a substantial loan, to be repaid out of his performance rights. The situation became complicated when Wagner developed an affection for Mathilde, which in all probability remained platonic. She wrote the famous *Fünf Gedichte* (*Der Engel, Stehe still, Träume, Schmerzen, Im Treibhaus*), which Wagner set to music as studies for *Tristan und Isolde.* The album was published as the *Wesendonck-Lieder* in 1857.

In 1855 Wagner conducted a series of eight concerts with the Philharmonic Society of London. His performances were greatly praised by English musicians. He had the honor of meeting Queen Victoria, who invited him to her loge at the intermission of his seventh concert.

In 1856 Wagner made substantial revisions in the last dramas of *Der Ring des Nibelungen,* changing their titles to *SIEGFRIED* and *GOTTERDÄMMERUNG.* Throughout these years he was preoccupied with writing a new opera, *Tristan und Isolde,* permeated with the dual feelings of love and death. In 1857 he prepared the first sketch of *Parzival* (later *PARSIFAL*).

In 1858 Wagner moved to Venice, where he completed the full score of the second act of *TRISTAN UND ISOLDE.* The Dresden authorities, acting through their Austrian confederates and still determined to bring Wagner to trial as a revolutionary, pressured Venice to expel him from its territory. Once more Wagner took refuge in Switzerland. He stayed in Lucerne, where he completed the score of *Tristan und Isolde* in 1859.

That autumn Wagner moved to Paris, where Minna joined him. In 1860 he conducted three concerts of his music at the Théâtre-Italien. Napoleon III became interested in his work and in 1860 ordered the director of the Paris Opéra to produce Wagner's opera *Tannhäuser*. After considerable work, revisions, and a translation into French, it was given at the Opéra a year later. It proved a fiasco, however, and Wagner withdrew it after three performances. For some reason the Jockey Club of Paris led a vehement protest against him. The critics also joined in this opposition, mainly because the French audiences were not accustomed to mystically ROMANTIC, heavily Germanic operatic music.

The insults hurled against him by the Paris press make extraordinary reading. The comparison of Wagner's music with the sound produced by a domestic cat walking down the keyboard of the piano was a favorite critical device. The French caricaturists exercised their wit by picturing him in the act of hammering a poor listener's ear.

In an amazing turnabout, the German philosopher Friedrich Nietzsche, a worshipful admirer of Wagner, published a venomous denunciation of his idol in *Der Fall Wagner* in 1888. Wagner made music itself sick, he proclaimed. But at the time Nietzsche himself was already on the borderline of madness.

Politically Wagner's prospects began to improve. In 1860 he was informed of a partial amnesty by the Saxon authorities. That year he visited Baden-Baden, his first visit to Germany in 11 years. Finally, in 1862 he was granted total amnesty, which allowed him access to Saxony. In 1861 Otto Wesendonck had invited Wagner to Venice. Free from political persecution, he could now go there without fear. While in Venice he returned to a scenario he had prepared in Marienbad in 1845 for a comic opera, DIE MEISTERSINGER VON NÜRNBERG. In 1862 he moved to Biebrich, where he began composing its score. Minna, after a brief period of reconciliation with Wagner, left him, settling in Dresden, where she died in 1866.

In order to repair his financial situation, Wagner accepted a number of concert appearances, traveling as an orchestral conductor to Vienna, Prague, St. Petersburg, Moscow, and other cities in 1862–63. In 1862 he gave in Vienna a private reading of *Die Meistersinger*.

In 1864 Wagner's fortunes changed spectacularly when King Ludwig II of Bavaria (1845–86) ascended the throne

Oscar Wilde remarked in *The Picture of Dorian Gray*, "I like Wagner's music better than anybody's. It is so loud that one can talk the whole time without people hearing what one says."

and invited him to Munich with the promise of unlimited help in carrying out his various projects. In return, Wagner composed the *Huldigungsmarsch,* which he dedicated to his royal patron. The published correspondence between Wagner and the king is extraordinary in its display of mutual admiration, gratitude, and affection. Still, difficulties soon developed when the Bavarian Cabinet told Ludwig that his lavish support of Wagner's projects threatened the state's economy. Ludwig was forced to advise him to leave Munich. Wagner took this advice as an order, and late in 1865 he went to Switzerland.

A very serious difficulty arose in Wagner's emotional life, when he became intimately involved with Liszt's daughter Cosima, then the wife of the conductor HANS VON BÜLOW. Von Bülow was an impassioned supporter of Wagner's music. In 1865 Cosima von Bülow gave birth to Wagner's daughter, whom he named Isolde after the heroine of his opera that Bülow was preparing for performance in Munich. Its premiere took place with great acclaim, two months later, with von Bülow conducting.

That summer, Wagner prepared the prose sketch of *Parzival* and began to dictate his autobiography, *Mein Leben,* to Cosima. In 1866 he resumed the composition of *Die Meistersinger.* He settled in a villa in Triebschen, on Lake Lucerne, where Cosima joined him permanently in 1868. He completed the full score of *Die Meistersinger* in 1867. In 1868 von Bülow conducted its premiere in Munich in the presence of King Ludwig, who sat in the royal box with Wagner.

In 1869 *Das Rheingold* was produced in Munich. In 1870 *Die Walküre* was staged there. In 1870 Cosima and von Bülow were divorced, and shortly thereafter Wagner and Cosima were married in Lucerne. Late in 1870 Wagner wrote SIEGFRIED IDYLL, based on the themes from his opera. It was performed in their villa in Bayreuth on Christmas morning, the day after Cosima's birthday, as a surprise for her. In 1871 he wrote the *Kaisermarsch* to mark the victorious conclusion of the Franco-German War. He conducted it in the presence of Kaiser Wilhelm I at a concert in the Royal Opera House in Berlin in 1871.

Later that year in Leipzig Wagner made public his plans for realizing his cherished dream of building his own theater

A son, significantly named Siegfried, was born to Cosima and Wagner in 1869. The mythical Siegfried, of course, was the hero of the *Ring* Cycle.

in Bayreuth for the production of the entire cycle of *Der Ring des Nibelungen*. In late 1871 the Bayreuth town council offered him a site for a proposed Festspielhaus (festival house), and in 1872 the cornerstone was laid. Wagner commemorated the event by conducting a performance of Beethoven's Ninth Symphony (this was his 59th birthday). In 1873 Wagner began to build his own home in Bayreuth, which he called *Wahnfried* (free from delusion). In order to complete the building of the Festspielhaus, he appealed to King Ludwig for additional funds. Ludwig gave him 100,000 talers for this purpose.

Now the dream of Wagner's life was realized. During the summer of 1876 *Der Ring des Nibelungen* went through rehearsals. King Ludwig attended the final dress rehearsals, and the official premiere of the cycle took place in August 1876, under the direction of Hans Richter. In all, three complete productions of the *Ring* cycle were given that month.

King Ludwig was faithful to the end to Wagner, whom he called "my divine friend." In his castle Neuschwanstein he installed architectural representations of scenes from Wagner's operas. Soon Ludwig's mental deterioration became obvious to everyone, and he was committed to an asylum. There, in 1886, he overpowered the psychiatrist escorting him on a walk and dragged him to his death in the Starnberg Lake, drowning himself as well.

The spectacles in Bayreuth attracted music lovers and notables from all over the world. Even those who were not partial to Wagner's ideas or appreciative of his music went to Bayreuth out of curiosity, PIOTR ILYICH TCHAIKOVSKY among them. Despite world success and fame, Wagner still labored under financial difficulties. He even addressed a letter to an American dentist practicing in Dresden (who had treated Wagner) in which he tried to interest him in arranging Wagner's permanent transfer to the U.S. He voiced disillusionment in his future prospects in Germany. Wagner said he would be willing to settle in the U.S. provided a sum of $1 million would be guaranteed by American bankers and a comfortable estate for him and his family could be found in a warm part of the country. Nothing came of this particular proposal. Wagner did establish an American connection when he wrote, for a fee of $5,000, a *Grosser Festmarsch* for the observance of the U.S. centennial in 1876, dedicated to the "beautiful young ladies of America."

In the middle of all this, Wagner became infatuated with Judith Gautier. Their affair lasted for about two years from 1876 to 1878. He completed the full score of *Parsifal* (as it was now called) in 1882, in Palermo. It was performed for the first time at the Bayreuth Festival that year, followed by 15 subsequent performances. At the final performance, in 1882, Wagner stepped to the podium in the last act and conducted the work to its close. This was his last appearance as a conductor. He went to Venice in the fall of 1882 for a period of rest (he suffered from angina). Early in 1883 he suffered a massive heart attack and died in Cosima's presence. His body was interred in a vault in the garden of his Wahnfried villa in Bayreuth.

Wagner's role in music history is immense. Not only did he create works of great beauty and brilliance, but he generated an entirely new concept of the art of music, exercising influence on generations of composers all over the globe. RICHARD STRAUSS extended Wagner's grand vision to symphonic music, fashioning the form of a TONE POEM that uses leading motifs and vivid programmatic description of the scenes portrayed in his music. Even NIKOLAI RIMSKY-KORSAKOV—as far as he stood from Wagner—reflected the spirit of *Parsifal* in his own religious opera, *The Legend of the City of Kitezh*. ARNOLD SCHOENBERG's first significant work, *Verklärte Nacht*, is Wagnerian in its color.

Wagner's reform of opera was incomparably more far-reaching in aim, import, and effect than that of CHRISTOPH WILLIBALD GLUCK. Gluck's main purpose was to counteract the predominance of the singers. This goal Wagner accomplished through insistence upon the dramatic truth of his music. When he rejected traditional opera, he did so in the conviction that such an artificial form could not serve as a basis for true dramatic expression. In its place he gave the world a new form and new techniques. So revolutionary was Wagner's art that conductors and singers had to undergo special training in the new style of interpretation in order to perform his works. Thus he became the founder of interpretative conducting and of a new school of dramatic singing, so that such terms as "Wagnerian tenor" and "Wagnerian soprano" became a part of musical vocabulary.

Wagner condemned the illogical plan of Italian opera and French grand opera. To quote him, "The mistake in the art-form of the opera consists in this, that a means of expression (music) was made the end, and the end to be expressed (the drama) was made a means." Wagner's new artwork creates its own form. Continuous thematic development of basic motifs (melodic themes) becomes a fundamental procedure for the logical cohesion of the drama. These highly individualized generating motifs, appearing singly, in bold relief, or subtly varied and intertwined with other motifs, present the ever-changing soul states of the characters of the drama. They also form the connecting links for the dramatic situations of the total artwork, in a form of musical declamation that Wagner described as *Sprechsingen*.

In the domain of melody, harmony, and orchestration, Wagner's art was as revolutionary as was his total artwork on the stage. He introduced the idea of ENDLESS MELODY, a continuous flow of DIATONIC and CHROMATIC TONES. The TONALITY became fluid and uncertain, producing an impression of unattainability, so that the listener accustomed to CLASSIC MODULATORY schemes could not easily feel the direction toward the TONIC.

The prelude to *Tristan und Isolde* is a classic example of such fluidity of harmonic elements. The use of long unresolved DOMINANT NINTH CHORDS and the dramatic TREMOLOS of DIMINISHED SEVENTH CHORDS contributed to this state of musical uncertainty, which disturbed critics and audiences alike. But Wagnerian harmony also became the foundation of the new method of composition that adopted a free flow of modulatory progressions. Without Wagner the chromatic idioms of the 20th century could not exist.

In orchestration, too, Wagner introduced great innovations. He created new instruments, such as the so-called WAGNER TUBA, and he increased his demands on the virtuosity of individual orchestral players. The demanding flight of the BASSOON to the high E in the overture to *Tannhäuser* could not have been attempted before the advent of Wagner.

Wagner became the target of political contention during World War I when audiences in the Allied countries associated his sonorous works with German imperialism. An even greater obstacle to further performances of Wagner's music arose with the rise of Hitler. Hitler ordered the mass slaughter of the Jews. Hitler was also an enthusiastic admirer of Wagner, who himself entertained anti-Semitic notions (see his essay *Judaism in Music,* 1850). Ergo, Wagner was guilty by association of mass murder. Can art be separated from politics, particularly when politics become murderous? Jewish musicians in Tel Aviv refused to play the prelude to *Tristan und Isolde* when it was put on the program of a symphony concert under ZUBIN MEHTA and booed him for his intention to inflict Wagner on Wagner's philosophical victims.

Several periodicals dealing with Wagner were published in Germany and elsewhere. Wagner himself began issuing *Bayreuther Blätter* in 1878 as an aid to understanding his operas. This journal continued publication until 1938. Remarkably, a French periodical, *Revue Wagnerienne,* began appearing in 1885, at a time when French composers realized the tremendous power of Wagnerian aesthetics. It was published sporadically for a number of years. A Wagner Society in London published, from 1888 to 1895, a quarterly journal entitled, significantly, *The Meister.*

A lesser-known aspect of Wagner's musical output was several arrangements and adaptations he made of various composers' works. He also devoted a large amount of his enormous productive activity to writing. Besides the dramatic works he set to music, he wrote several plays, librettos, scenarios, and novellas. He also expounded his theories on music, politics, philosophy, and religion in numerous essays. Notable among them are *Die Kunst und die Revolution* (1849, Art and Revolution), *Das Kunstwerk der Zukunst* (1849, The Artwork of the Future), and *Oper und Drama* (1851; revised 1868, *Opera and Drama*). His lengthy autobiography appeared in an abridged edition in Munich in 1911 (English translation as *My Life,* London and N.Y.).

wait (wayt, wayte). A town watchman in the Middle Ages whose duty was to keep order in the streets at night and announce the time by playing a brass instrument. Waits often serenaded incoming travelers in their stagecoaches. They were also employed to provide music for ceremonial occasions.

In Germany, waits were called *Stadtpfeifer.* The music that they played was collected under the designation TURM-MUSIK.

Waits, Tom, idiosyncratic American songwriter and performer; b. Pomona, Calif., Dec. 7, 1949. Waits began his career playing in Los Angeles clubs as a singer, pianist, and guitarist, sometimes with his group, Nocturnal Emissions. After being signed by FRANK ZAPPA's manager in 1972, he produced his first record album, *Closing Time* in 1973.

Waits slowly rose from cultdom to stardom through such songs as *Ol' '55, Shiver Me Timbers, Diamonds on My Windshield,* and *The Piano Has Been Drinking.* Noteworthy albums of this period include *Nighthawks at the Diner, Small Change, Foreign Affairs,* and *Heartattack & Vine.* He made a number of recordings for the Asylum label, then switched to Island. With the album *Swordfishtrombones* in 1983, he expanded his accompaniment to include a broad spectrum of exotic instruments.

Waits wrote the score for Francis Ford Coppola's film *One from the Heart* in 1982, and six years later made the concert movie *Big Time.* He also collaborated with his wife, Kathleen Brennan, on the stage show *Frank's Wild Years* in 1987, which includes the pastiches *Temptation* and *Innocent When You Dream.*

Among artists who have performed his music are BETTE MIDLER, Crystal Gayle, BRUCE SPRINGSTEEN, the EAGLES, and the Manhattan Transfer. He also made frequent appearances as a film and stage actor.

Waits is a jazz songwriter who regards the beatniks of the 1950s as his primary inspiration. His imaginative lyrics are full of slang and focus on the sad characters who populate cheap bars and motels. He accompanies his gravelly voice and delivery with rough instrumentation, but always with sensitive musicianship and ironic pathos.

Wake Up Little Susie. Second single and first No. 1 hit for the EVERLY BROTHERS in 1957. Teen lovers oversleep while parked in a car at a drive-in movie, then face trouble for

PEOPLE IN MUSIC

In 1993 Waits created a performance work, *The Black Rider,* in collaboration with Robert Wilson and William S. Burroughs.

breaking the girl's curfew. The song was actually banned from radio play on some stations. A '50s dilemma delivered in perfect two-part harmony. Written by Felice and Boudleaux Bryant.

***Waldstein* Sonata.** Nickname of LUDWIG VAN BEETHOVEN's piano sonata No. 21, op.53, in C major (1803–04), dedicated to Count von Waldstein, a friend and patron of Beethoven. The opening movement is remarkable for its dramatic intensity in the low register.

Waldteufel (born Lévy), (Charles-) **Émile,** French conductor and composer of light music; b. Strasbourg, Dec. 9, 1837; d. Paris, Feb. 12, 1915. His father, Louis (1801–84), and his brother, Léon (1832–84), were violinists and dance composers, and his mother was a pianist. In 1842 the family went to Paris, where he studied piano with his mother and then with Joseph Heyberger. He subsequently audited a class at the Paris Conservatory, enrolling as a student there in 1853, but leaving before completing his courses.

Waldteufel became a piano tester for the manufacturer Scholtus. He also taught piano and played in soirées and, when he had time, composed dance music for salons. In 1865 he became court pianist to the Empress Eugénie and in 1866 conductor of the state balls.

Waldteufel's first WALTZ, *Joies et peines,* published at his own expense in 1859, was an immediate success, and he became known in Paris high society. In 1867 he published another successful waltz with the German title *Vergissmeinnicht.* Then followed a series of waltzes that established his fame as a French counterpart to JOHANN STRAUSS (II), the most famous being *Les Patineurs* (The Skaters; 1882). His dance music symbolized the *gai Paris* of his time as fittingly as the music of Strauss reflected the gaiety of old Vienna.

Waldteufel lived most of his life in Paris, but he also filled conducting engagements abroad, visiting London in 1885 and Berlin in 1889.

Walker, George (Theophilus), African-American pianist, teacher, and composer; b. Washington, D.C., June 27, 1922. Walker studied at the Oberlin College Conservatory

PEOPLE IN MUSIC

PEOPLE IN MUSIC

of Music, earning his master's degree in 1941. He then entered the Curtis Institute of Music in Philadelphia, where he studied piano with Peter Serkin, composition with Rosario Scalero and GIAN CARLO MENOTTI, and chamber music with Gregor Piatigorsky and William Primrose. He was awarded an artist diploma there in 1945.

Walker also took piano lessons with Robert Casadesus in Fontainebleau in France, receiving a diploma in 1947. He obtained his D.M.A. from the Eastman School of Music in Rochester, N.Y., in 1957. That same year, he earned a Fulbright fellowship for travel to Paris, where he took courses in composition with NADIA BOULANGER.

In 1945 Walker made his debut as a pianist, and subsequently appeared throughout the U.S. and abroad. He was also active as a teacher, holding appointments at Dillard University in New Orleans in 1953, the New School for Social Research in N.Y., the Dalcroze School of Music in 1961, Smith College from 1961 to 1968, and the University of Colorado in 1968. In 1969 he was appointed a professor at Rutgers, the State University of New Jersey, where he was chairman of the composition department there in 1974. In 1975 he was also named Distinguished Professor at the University of Delaware and adjunct professor at the Peabody Institute in Baltimore.

In 1969 he received a Guggenheim fellowship, and in 1971 and 1974 two Rockefeller fellowships for study in Italy. In 1982 he was made a member of the American Academy and Institute of Arts and Letters, and in 1988 he received a Koussevitzky Foundation grant. He won the Pulitzer Prize in 1996.

In his music Walker maintains a median modern line with an infusion of black folk idioms. Among his orchestral compositions are Trombone Concerto (1957), *Antiphonys* for chamber orchestra (1968), *Variations* (1971), Piano Concerto (1975), *Dialogues* for cello and orchestra (1975), *In Praise of Folly*, overture (1980), Cello Concerto (1981), *An Eastman Overture* (1983), two sinfonias (1984, 1990), and *Orpheus* for chamber orchestra (1994).

Walker's chamber pieces include two string quartets (1946, 1968), Cello Sonata (1957), two violin sonatas (1957, 1979), *Music for Three* for violin, cello, and piano

(1970), *Music for Brass, Sacred and Profane* for brass quintet (1975), and Viola Sonata (1990). Among his piano compositions are four sonatas (1953, 1957, 1975, 1985). His vocal works include a MASS for vocal soloists, chorus, and orchestra (1977), a Cantata for soprano, tenor, boys' chorus, and orchestra (1982), and *Poem* for soprano and chamber ensemble, after T. S. Eliot's *The Hollow Men* (1986).

walking bass. In JAZZ, a bass figure moving up and down in DIATONIC and CHROMATIC steps in broken OCTAVES in even EIGHTH NOTE rhythms. It was first associated with piano BOOGIE-WOOGIE, but became principally associated with jazz double bass playing in the swing era.

Walküre, Die. The second music drama of RICHARD WAGNER's cycle *DER RING DES NIBELUNGEN,* 1876, premiered at the first Bayreuth Festival.

Die Walküre begins with the meeting of Siegmund and Sieglinde, the long-separated mortal children of Wotan. Unaware of their kinship, they feel a strong attraction toward each other. Sieglinde shows Siegmund the magical sword, Nothung, which Wotan drove deep into a tree and which can be pulled out only by a hero. Siegmund performs the task. Sieglinde becomes enraptured, and she abandons her brutal husband, Hunding, and flees with her brotherly lover.

But Wotan has to come to the aid of Hunding and orders his nine warlike daughters, the Valkyries, to attack the lovers. Wotan's favorite Valkyrie, Brünnhilde, disobeys Wotan's orders by trying to help Siegmund. However, Siegmund is killed by Hunding when Wotan shatters the magic sword in Siegmund's hands. (Wotan rewards Hunding by killing him with a wave of his hand.) As Brünnhilde's punishment, Wotan takes her immortality away, places her on a high rock, puts her to sleep, and surrounds the rock by a ring of fire. Only a hero can break through the fire and rescue her. As the following opera of the *Ring* (*Siegried*) relates, this hero will be Siegfried, son of Sieglinde, who died in childbirth.

The most famous symphonic episode from the opera is *The Ride of the Valkyries,* in which the sturdy Teutonic amazons disport themselves on top of cloud-covered rocks. Wag-

1993

ner's thematic use of the arpeggiated AUGMENTED TRIADS here is notable. *The Magic Fire,* illustrating Brünnhilde's imprisonment by a fiery ring, is another popular tableau in the opera. In it, the most important leading motives of the opera, including Wotan's imperious command, Brünnhilde's lament, the slumber motive, and the sparkling magic fire itself, are all combined in a gorgeous Wagnerian mixture.

PEOPLE IN MUSIC

Wallen, Errollyn, versatile English composer and formidable pianist; b. Belize City, Belize, April 10, 1958. After studies at Goldsmiths' and King's College, London University, where she earned her master's degree, Wallen worked as a performer and composer in POP, JAZZ, and CLASSICAL settings. She also set up her own recording studio and wrote for film, television, and radio.

Wallen wrote and presented *The Music Machine,* a youth program for BBC Radio 3 series (April 1994), and also contributed to *Backtracks,* a series for London's Channel 4 about music composition for film. She formed Ensemble X, comprised of players from pop, jazz, and classical worlds, to perform her music.

Wallen's music has been recorded and broadcast throughout Europe, Africa, and Australia. She has worked with a variety of artists across genres, including Courtney Pine, Juliet Roberts, Peter Gabriel, and Claudia Brucken. Her output ranges from large orchestral works to choral compositions and string quartets, from ballets and operas to pop songs.

Wallen's compositions are remarkably eclectic and include *In Our Lifetime* (1992), a ballet in celebration of Nelson Mandela's release from prison, choreographed by Christopher Bruce for London's Contemporary Dance Theatre; *Waiting,* a ballet (1993); *Concerto for Percussion and Orchestra* (1994, a BBC commission); *LOOK! NO HANDS!,* opera (1996), to a LIBRETTO by Cindy Owens, presented at the Nottingham Concert Series in a program devoted entirely to her work; *Hunger* (1997), a large-scale instrumental work; and *Meet Me at Harold Moore's* (1998), her first, impeccably produced, solo album.

PEOPLE IN MUSIC

Waller, "Fats" (Thomas Wright), noted African-American jazz pianist, organist, singer, bandleader, and composer; b.

N.Y., May 21, 1904; d. Kansas City, Mo., Dec. 15, 1943. As a child, Waller had private piano instruction and studied violin and double bass in school, but his most significant early lessons came from the player piano and nickelodeon pianists whom he studiously imitated. At 14 he was playing organ professionally in a Harlem theater, and at 16 he received piano training from Russell Brooks and JAMES P. JOHNSON. He claimed that he later had some lessons from Leopold Godowsky and studied composition with Karl Böhm at the Juilliard School of Music.

In 1922 Waller began to make recordings and in 1923 made his first appearance on the radio. He subsequently made frequent broadcasts as a singer and pianist. In 1928 he made his debut at N.Y.'s CARNEGIE HALL as a piano soloist. That year, with the lyricist Andy Razaf, he composed most of the music for the all-black Broadway musical *Keep Shufflin'*. They then collaborated on the shows *Load of Coal* and *Hot Chocolates* in 1929. He worked with Ted Lewis (1930), Jack Teagarden (1931), and Billy Banks's Rhythmakers (1932) before organizing his own band, Fats Waller and his Rhythm, in 1934.

In 1935 Waller relocated to the West Coast and appeared in the Hollywood films *Hooray for Love* and *King of Burlesque*. In 1938 and 1939 he toured Europe. In 1943 he appeared in the Hollywood film *Stormy Weather* leading an all-star band.

Waller was a leading exponent of STRIDE piano, playing with a delicacy and lightness of touch that belied his considerable bulk of almost 300 pounds. Much of his popularity was due to his skills as an entertainer. He was especially effective in improvising lyrics to deflate the sentimentality of popular songs.

A musical tribute to Waller, the revue *Ain't Misbehavin'*, was one of the great successes of the N.Y. theater season in 1978.

Waller's hit song, *Ain't Misbehavin'*, was performed by LOUIS ARMSTRONG in the original production of *Hot Chocolates* on Broadway.

Walpurgis Night (Ger. *Walpurgisnacht*). The feast day of St. Walpurgis, an eighth-century English abbess, celebrated on May 1.

Halloweenlike Walpurgis Nights are celebrated at the reputed locale of the witches' sabbath, the peak of Mt.

PEOPLE IN MUSIC

Brocken in the Harz Mountains. Faust attends one in Goethe's play, and FELIX MENDELSSOHN based his secular cantata *Die erste Walpurgisnacht* in 1833 on this scene. HECTOR BERLIOZ presents a witches' sabbath in the final movement of his *Symphonie fantastique*. CHARLES GOUNOD includes a scene during Walpurgis Night in his opera *FAUST*.

Walter, Bruno (born Bruno Walter Schlesinger), German-born American conductor; b. Berlin, Sept. 15, 1876; d. Beverly Hills, Calif., Feb. 17, 1962. Walter entered the Stern Conservatory in Berlin at age eight. A year later, he performed in public as a pianist but at 13 decided to pursue his interest in conducting.

In 1893 Walter became a coach at the Cologne Opera, where he made his conducting debut. In the following year he was engaged as assistant conductor at the Hamburg Stadttheater, under GUSTAV MAHLER. This contact was decisive in his career, and he became in subsequent years an ardent champion of Mahler's music, conducting the premieres of Mahler's posthumous Symphony No. 9 and *Das Lied von der Erde*.

During the 1896–97 season, Walter was engaged as second conductor at the Stadttheater in Breslau. He then became principal conductor in Pressburg, and in 1898 at Riga, where he conducted for two seasons. In 1900 he received the important engagement of conductor at the Berlin Royal Opera under a five-year contract. However, he left this post in 1901 when he received an offer from Mahler to become his assistant at the Vienna Court Opera.

Walter established himself in Vienna as an efficient opera conductor. He also conducted in England, making his first appearance there in 1909, with the Royal Philharmonic Society in London. He remained at the Vienna Court Opera after the death of Mahler. In 1913 he became Royal Bavarian Generalmusikdirektor in Munich. Under his guidance, the Munich Opera gave brilliant performances, particularly of WOLFGANG AMADEUS MOZART's works.

Seeking greater artistic freedom, Walter left Munich in 1922 and gave numerous performances as a guest conductor with European orchestras. He conducted the "Bruno Walter Concerts" with the Berlin Philharmonic from 1921 to 1933, and from 1925 he also conducted summer concerts of the Salzburg Festival. His performances of Mozart's music there set a new standard. He also appeared as pianist in Mozart's chamber works.

In 1923 Walter made his American debut with the N.Y. Symphony Society, appearing with it again in 1924 and 1925. From 1925 to 1929 he was conductor of the Städtische Oper in Berlin-Charlottenburg, and in 1929 he succeeded WILHELM FURTWÄNGLER as conductor of the Gewandhaus Orchestra in Leipzig, but continued to give special concerts in Berlin. In 1932 he was guest conductor of the N.Y. Philharmonic, acting also as soloist in a Mozart piano concerto. He was reengaged during the next three seasons as associate conductor with ARTURO TOSCANINI. Walter was also a guest conductor in Philadelphia, Washington, D.C., and Baltimore.

With the advent of the Nazi regime in Germany in 1933, his engagement with the Gewandhaus Orchestra was canceled. Walter was also prevented from continuing his orchestra concerts in Berlin. He filled several engagements with the Concertgebouw in Amsterdam and also conducted in Salzburg. In 1936 he was engaged as music director of the Vienna State Opera, but this was terminated with the Nazi annexation of Austria in 1938.

Walter, with his family, then went to France, where he was granted French citizenship. After the outbreak of World War II in 1939, he sailed for the U.S., establishing his residence in California and eventually becoming a naturalized American citizen. He was guest conductor with the NBC Symphony Orchestra in 1939 and also conducted many performances of the Metropolitan Opera in N.Y., making his debut leading a performance of *FIDELIO* in 1941.

From 1947 to 1949 Walter was conductor and musical adviser of the N.Y. Philharmonic, returning regularly as guest conductor until 1960. He made recordings with the Columbia Symphony Orchestra, which was created for him, and also conducted in Europe from 1949 to 1960.

Walter achieved the reputation of a perfect classicist among contemporary conductors, his interpretations of the masterpieces of the VIENNA SCHOOL being particularly notable. He is acknowledged to have been a foremost conduc-

Walter gave his farewell performance in Vienna with the Vienna Philharmonic in 1960.

tor of Mahler's symphonies. He also composed his own music, including two symphonies, a string quartet, piano quintet, piano trio, and several albums of songs.

PEOPLE IN MUSIC

Walton, Sir William (Turner), English composer; b. Oldham, Lancashire, March 29, 1902; d. Ischia, Italy, March 8, 1983. Both his parents were professional singers, and Walton himself had a fine singing voice as a youth. Sir Hugh Allen, organist of New College, advised him to develop his interest in composition and sponsored his admission to Christ Church at an early age. Walton entered the Cathedral Choir School there and began to compose choral pieces for performance. However, he never graduated, and instead began to write modern music in the manner that was fashionable in the 1920s.

Walton's talent manifested itself in a string quartet he wrote at the age of 17, which was accepted for performance for the first festival of the International Society for Contemporary Music in 1923. In London he formed a close association with the Sitwell family, a literary clan including the noted writer Edith Sitwell. They provided Walton with residence at their manor in Chelsea, where he lived off and on for some 15 years. Fascinated by Edith's oxymoronic verse, at the age of 19 Walton set it to music bristling with novel jazzy effects in brisk, irregular rhythms and modern harmonies. Under the title *Façade,* it was first performed in London in 1923, with Sitwell herself delivering her poetry. As expected, the show provoked an outburst of indignation in the press and undisguised delight among many in the audience.

However, Walton soon turned to writing music in a NEOCLASSICAL manner, including his CONCERT OVERTURE *Portsmouth Point,* first performed in Zurich in 1926, and the comedy-overture *Scapino* in 1941. His biblical ORATORIO *Belshazzar's Feast* of 1931 reveals a deep emotional stream and nobility of design that place Walton directly in line from GEORGE FRIDERIC HANDEL and EDWARD ELGAR among English masters. Walton's symphonic works show him as an inheritor of the grand ROMANTIC tradition, and his concertos for violin, for viola, and for cello demonstrate an adroitness in beautiful and effective instrumental writing.

Walton was a modernist in his acceptance of new musical styles, but he never deviated from fundamental TONALITY and formal clarity. Above all, his music was profoundly national, unmistakably British in its inspiration and content. Quite appropriately, he was asked to contribute to two royal occasions: he wrote *Crown Imperial March* for the coronation of King George VI in 1937 and *Orb and Sceptre* for that of Queen Elizabeth II in 1953.

Walton received an honorary doctorate from Oxford University in 1942, and in 1951 he was knighted. He spent the last years of his life on the island of Ischia off Naples with his Argentine-born wife, Susana Gil Passo.

waltz (Ger. *Walzer,* from *walzen,* turn around; Fr. *valse;* It. *valzer*). The quintessential ballroom dance in $\frac{3}{4}$ time, which was first performed in Austria toward the end of the 18th century. Choreographically, it consists of a pair of dancers moving around an imaginary axis, resulting in a movement forward.

In the 18th century the waltz was regarded as a vulgar dance fit only for peasant entertainment. In 1760 waltzing was specifically forbidden by government order in Bavaria. The waltz received its social acceptance in the wake of the French Revolution, when it became fashionable even in upper social circles on the continent. England withstood its impact well into the 19th century.

The first representation of a waltzlike dance on the stage occurred during a performance of the opera *Una cosa rara* by Martin y Soler in Vienna in 1786. The waltz attained its social popularity during the Congress of Vienna in 1815. At that time it was known under the name of *Wienerwalzer.* In France the *valse* assumed different forms, in $\frac{3}{8}$, $\frac{3}{4}$, or $\frac{6}{8}$ time, as an ANDANTE (*sauteuse*), ALLEGRETTO, ALLEGRO (*jeté*), or PRESTO. In the 20th century, an American waltz misnamed *Valse Boston* (in reality, a HESITATION WALTZ) spread all over Europe about 1920.

As a musical form the waltz generally consists of two repeated periods of eight bars each. The earliest printing of a waltz in this form was the publication of 12 concert waltzes by the pianist Daniel Steibelt in 1800. These were followed by a collection of waltzes by Johann Nepomuk Hummel

The close physical contact between male and female waltzing partners was considered shocking when it was first seen.

published in 1808. These concert waltzes were extended by the insertion of several TRIOS, multiple REPRISES, and a CODA, lasting nearly half an hour in all.

During the 19th century, the concert waltz became a favorite among composers for piano, beginning with CARL MARIA VON WEBER, and finding its greatest artistic efflorescence in the waltzes of FRÉDÉRIC CHOPIN. LUDWIG VAN BEETHOVEN canonized the waltz in his famous *Diabelli Variations* (op. 120), based on a waltz tune.

The waltz grew into an industry in Vienna. Joseph Lanner and JOHANN STRAUSS (I) composed hundreds of waltz tunes to be played in Viennese restaurants and entertainment places. JOHANN STRAUSS (II) raised the waltz to its summit as an artistic creation, which, at the time, served the needs of popular entertainment. He was justly dubbed "The Waltz King" (*Walzerkönig*). Strauss wrote many other popular works, including *Tales of the Vienna Woods, Voices of Spring, Vienna Blood,* and *Wine, Women, and Song* (*see* WEIN, WEIB, UND GESANG). All these waltzes were really chains of waltz movements.

Gradually the waltz, like the MINUET, assumed a legitimate concert form. HECTOR BERLIOZ has a waltz movement in his *Symphonie fantastique,* PIOTR ILYICH TCHAIKOVSKY includes a waltz in his Fifth Symphony, and GUSTAV MAHLER has one in his Ninth.

MAURICE RAVEL parodied the Viennese waltz gloriously in *La Valse.*

Waltzing Matilda. An Australian song, 1903, the words fitted to an old Scottish tune (published 1818) and published in Sydney. Matilda is not a girl's name but Australian slang for a knapsack, and waltzing refers to bouncing, not dancing. Strangely, the song is in $\frac{4}{4}$ rather than $\frac{3}{4}$ time.

The song became tremendously popular among Australian troops during the two world wars, and has assumed the status of an unofficial national anthem. The song was placed in modern perspective by the Australian singer/songwriter Eric Bogle. His powerful antiwar song *And The Band Played "Waltzing Matilda"* describes the horrific battle of Gallipoli in World War I.

War and Peace. Opera by SERGEI PROKOFIEV, begun in 1941 and given its first complete stage production in

Leningrad, 1948. Prokofiev did not specify the number of acts and emphasized that the production should be announced as being in 13 scenes.

Originally, Prokofiev planned to have the opera presented in two parts on two consecutive evenings, but eventually he compressed it to fit a single evening. The cast of characters numbers 72 singing and acting *dramatis personae*. The score attempts with considerable success to embrace the epic breadth of Leo Tolstoy's great novel from which the LIBRETTO was extracted by Prokofiev and his second wife, Myra Mendelson. The work went through more or less continuous revision until 1952.

The last version of the opera opens with a choral epigraph, summarizing the significance of Napoleon's invasion of Russia in 1812. Interlaced with military events are the destinies of the Rostov family and the dramatic story of Pierre Bezuhov. The concluding words of the victorious Field Marshal Kutuzov, "Russia is saved," were unquestionably intended to echo the recent Russian experience in fighting off another invasion, that of Hitler.

The musical style is profoundly Russian in spirit, but there are no literal quotations from folk songs. The melodic, rhythmic, and harmonic realization is recognizably that of Prokofiev's own.

War of the Buffoons. *See* GUERRE DES BOUFFONS.

War Requiem. ORATORIO by BENJAMIN BRITTEN, 1962, written to commemorate the restoration of the Cathedral of Coventry, destroyed by bombing in World War II. The text includes six movements from the traditional Latin REQUIEM MASS and nine wartime poems by Wilfred Owens, who was killed in action shortly before the 1918 armistice. The work is scored for soprano, tenor, baritone, chorus, boys' choir, organ, small ensemble, and full orchestra.

Warfield, William (Caesar), African-American baritone and teacher; b. West Helena, Ark., Jan. 22, 1920. Warfield studied at the Eastman School of Music in Rochester, N.Y., graduating in 1942. He sang in opera and musical comedy, giving his first N.Y. song recital in 1950, with excellent criti-

PEOPLE IN MUSIC

cal acclaim. He subsequently toured Europe in the role of Porgy in GEORGE GERSHWIN's *Porgy and Bess.* He married the soprano LEONTYNE PRICE in 1952 (they were divorced in 1972).

In 1974 Warfield was appointed a professor of music at the University of Illinois, and in 1984 he was elected president of the National Association of Negro Musicians. With A. Miller, he published *William Warfield: My Music and My Life* (Champaign, Ill., 1991). In 1994 he became a professor of music at Northwestern University.

PEOPLE IN MUSIC

Waring, Fred(eric Malcolm), American conductor of popular music and inventor of sundry kitchen appliances; b. Tyrone, Pa., June 9, 1900; d. Danville, Pa., July 29, 1984. Waring learned music at his mother's knee. His father was a banker who gave speeches at spiritual revivals and temperance meetings.

Waring took up the BANJO at 16, and organized a quartet that he called the Banjazzatra. He studied engineering and architecture at Pennsylvania State University. He retained his love for gadgets throughout his musical career. In 1937 he patented the Waring blender, for whipping food or drinks to a foam. Another invention was a traveling iron.

Waring acquired fame with his own band, the Pennsylvanians, which played on national tours at concert halls, hotels, and college campuses. The group was particularly successful on radio programs sponsored by tobacco companies and the Ford Motor Company. His repertoire consisted of wholesome American songs, many his own. Among his soloists on special programs were BING CROSBY, HOAGY CARMICHAEL, IRVING BERLIN, and FRANK SINATRA.

Waring had a natural streak for publicity. He once bet that he could lead a bull into a Fifth Avenue china shop, and succeeded, without breaking a single piece of crockery. He was a friend of President Dwight Eisenhower. In 1983 President Ronald Reagan awarded him the Congressional Gold Medal. He continued to lead youth choral groups, giving a concert at Pennsylvania State University a day before he suffered a stroke, and two days before his death.

Warlock, Peter. *See* HESELTINE, PHILIP (ARNOLD).

washboard (rubboard; Fr. *frittoir*). Traditional American instrument made from the at one time common household item.

In the days before washing machines, laundering was performed on a corrugated metal or glass washboard. Musicians discovered that by running metal picks over the washboard's surface, they could create a jagged rhythmic accompaniment for dance music. Some musicians also added bells or gongs to the top of the washboard, to give them additional percussive sound effects.

Washington, Dinah (born Ruth Lee Jones), African-American singer of blues and popular music; b. Tuscaloosa, Ala., Aug. 8?, 1924; d. Detroit, Dec. 14, 1963. Washington's family went to Chicago when she was fairly young. She began playing piano and singing in the church choir. She won an amateur singing contest at the age of 15, leading to some local club appearances.

At a Chicago club, Washington was heard by VIBRAPHONE player/bandleader LIONEL HAMPTON, who hired her as his lead vocalist. She remained with the Hampton band from 1943 to 1946, scoring hits with *Evil Gal Blues* and *Salty Peppa Blues.*

After World War II, Washington began touring as a solo act. She switched to the popular R&B style for her late '40s hits, including BLOW TOP BLUES. Then, in the mid-'50s, she began performing a combination of standards, pop songs, and JAZZ and BLUES numbers. She scored her biggest hit in 1959 with *What a Diff'rence a Day Makes.* A year later, she was singing duets with popular singer Brook Benton on the uptempo numbers *Baby (You Got What It Takes)* and *A Rockin' Good Way (to Fall in Love),* both top-10 pop hits. Her last major hit came in 1961 with the slow pop-ballad *September in the Rain.*

Washington was known for her upbeat personality and love of life. She spent money lavishly on furs, cars, and jewelry. She was married seven times, and also had numerous affairs. A heavy drinker, she died from an apparent lethal mixture of pills, perhaps combined with alcohol.

Wasitodiningrat, (Ki) **K.R.T.** (Kanjeng Raden Tumengung, a title of honorary royal status), important Indonesian com-

MUSICAL INSTRUMENT

In Cajun music, the washboard was transformed into a metal vestlike suit. The player could rub his own belly, as it were, and create a syncopated rhythm.

PEOPLE IN MUSIC

poser and performer; b. Yogyakarta, Java, March 17, 1909. His former names are Wasitolodoro, Tjokrowasito, and Wasitodipuro. Wasitodiningrat was born in the Pakualaman Palace, one of three principal courts of central Java, where his father was director of musical activities. Wasitodiningrat studied dance from the age of six, graduating from the SMA National High School in 1922.

Wasitodiningrat became music director of the Yogyakarta radio station MAVRO in 1934 and remained there through the Japanese occupation, when the station was called Jogja Hosokjoku. In 1945 the station became RRI (Radio Republic Indonesia), and he served as director there again in 1951.

Between 1951 and 1970 Wasitodiningrat taught dance at the Konservatori Tari and the Academy Tari, both in Yogyakarta, and music at the Academy Karawitan in Surakarta. He also founded and directed the Wasitodipuro Center for Vocal Studies in Yogyakarta. In 1953 he toured Asia, North America, and Europe.

In 1961 Wasitodiningrat became associated with the new dance/theater form *sendratari,* later becoming music director for P.L.T. Bagong Kussudiardjo's troupe. He succeeded his father as director of the Pakualaman GAMELAN in 1962. In 1971 he joined the faculty of the California Institute of the Arts as master of Javanese gamelan. He also taught workshops at both the Los Angeles and Berkeley campuses of the University of California.

Wasitodiningrat is a leading performer and composer of central Javanese music. The Pakualaman gamelan's recordings are considered among the finest of the style, and one is included in the 40 minutes of music installed in the spacecraft VOYAGER, intended to represent Earth's music to outsiders. His numerous awards include a gold medal from the Indonesian government honoring his devotion to Javanese music. He frequently performs with his daughter, Nanik, and her Balinese husband, Nyoman Wenten.

Water Music. Orchestral divertimento by GEORGE FRIDERIC HANDEL, 1717. It was written for King George I of England, to be played on an open barge during the king's sailing party on the Thames River. Three orchestral SUITES were subsequently drawn from it, consisting of various AIRES, HORN-PIPES, MINUETS, and other dances. The publishers seized on its success and printed numerous arrangements under the title *The Celebrated Water Musick.*

Waters, "Muddy" (born McKinley Morganfield), African-American BLUES singer, leading exponent of the Chicago blues style; b. Rolling Fork, Miss., April 4, 1915; d. Westmont, Ill., April 30, 1983. His parents were separated, and he was reared by his maternal grandmother on a plantation near Clarksdale, Mississippi. She called him "Muddy" because of his childhood habit of playing in the mud. His playmates called him "Waters," and he accepted the name "Muddy Waters" when he began to sing and play guitar.

In 1941 ALAN LOMAX and John Work recorded Waters's singing for the Library of Congress. This encouraged him to try his luck in commercial recording. In 1943 he moved to Chicago, where he had his first successes, and, indeed, he soon earned the nickname "King of Chicago Blues." He used electric amplification on his guitar and soon assembled a band—including piano, harmonica, bass, and drums—that became the model for all electric blues outfits. Thus Waters was the most important of the acoustic rural blues musicians to make the transition to electric urban blues in the 1940s.

Waters played electric blues in England in 1958. This struck holy terror into the ears and hearts of purist British folk-song experts, but he recruited to his cause young enthusiasts, among them Mick Jagger.

Waters was a popular performer in his hometown of Chicago from the '50s through his death in the early '80s. By the '60s, he was touring on the blues circuit throughout the U.S. and around the world. He appeared in the Band's last concert in 1976, which was subsequently made into the film *The Last Waltz.* In his later years, the Texas blues guitarist Johnny Winter worked with Waters professionally as a performer, producer, and all-around champion. Waters died in 1983.

Watts, André, brilliant American pianist; b. Nuremberg, June 20, 1946. He was born in a U.S. Army camp to an

PEOPLE IN MUSIC

Mick Jagger and his friends named their famous band the ROLLING STONES after Waters's early hit song *Rollin' Stone.* The rock journal *Rolling Stone* also owes its name to Muddy's song. BOB DYLAN created his own rock tune *Like a Rolling Stone* as an unconscious tribute.

PEOPLE IN MUSIC

André Watts, c. 1970.
(Corbis/Bettmann)

African-American soldier and a Hungarian woman. His mother gave him his earliest piano lessons. After the family moved to the U.S., he studied at the Philadelphia Musical Academy.

At the age of nine, Watts made his first public appearance playing the FRANZ JOSEPH HAYDN Concerto in D Major at a children's concert of the Philadelphia Orchestra. His parents were divorced in 1962, but his mother continued to guide his studies. At 14 he played CÉSAR FRANCK's *Symphonic Variations* with the Philadelphia Orchestra. In 1963, at age 16, Watts became an instant celebrity when he played FRANZ LISZT's First Piano Concerto at one of the televised Young People's Concerts with the N.Y. Philharmonic, conducted by LEONARD BERNSTEIN.

Watts's youth and the fact that he was partly black contributed to his success, but it was the grand and poetic manner of his virtuosity that conquered the usually skeptical press. Still, he insisted on completing his academic education. In 1969 he joined the class of Leon Fleisher at the Peabody Conservatory of Music in Baltimore, obtaining his artist's diploma in 1972.

In the meantime he developed an international career. Watts made his European debut as soloist with the London Symphony Orchestra in 1966, then played with the Concertgebouw Orchestra in Amsterdam. Later that year he played his first solo recital in N.Y., inviting comparisons in the press with great piano virtuosos of the past. In 1967 he was soloist with the Los Angeles Philharmonic under ZUBIN MEHTA on a tour of Europe and Asia.

On his 21st birthday, Watts played the Second Piano Concerto of JOHANNES BRAHMS with the Berlin Philharmonic. In 1970 he revisited his place of birth and played a solo recital there with sensational success. He also became a favorite performer at important political occasions. Watts played at President Richard Nixon's inaugural concert at Constitution Hall in 1969, at the last coronation of the Shah of Iran, and at a festive celebration of the President of the Congo.

In 1973 Watts toured the Soviet Union. That same year, he received an honorary doctorate from Yale University, and in 1975 he was given another honorary doctorate by Albright College. In 1976 he played a solo recital on live network television. He was also the subject of a film documentary.

In 1988 Watts celebrated the 25th anniversary of his debut with the N.Y. Philharmonic as soloist under Mehta in the Liszt First Concerto, the Beethoven Second Concerto, and the Rachmaninoff Second Concerto in a concert telecast live on PBS. That same year he also received the Avery Fisher Prize. In 1995 he marked the fortieth anniversary of his debut.

wavelength. The length of a SOUND WAVE, marking the crests (or other corresponding points) of two successive waves. Lower sounds have longer wavelengths, and higher sounds have shorter wavelengths. In other words, the wavelength is inversely proportional to the FREQUENCY of VIBRATIONS of a given sound.

wa-wa (wah-wah). 1. A trumpet technique (placing the hand in the bell) or MUTE that produces a wavering amplitude effect used principally in JAZZ. 2. An electronic device producing a similar effect on the ELECTRIC GUITAR and other instruments, usually manipulated by a foot pedal.

Waxman (Wachsmann), **Franz,** German-American composer and conductor; b. Königshütte, Dec. 24, 1906; d. Los Angeles, Feb. 24, 1967. Waxman studied in Dresden and

Rock guitarists such as ERIC CLAPTON and JIMI HENDRIX popularized the wa-wa sound in the 1960s.

PEOPLE IN MUSIC

Berlin, then went to the U.S. in 1934 and settled in Hollywood, where he took lessons with ARNOLD SCHOENBERG. He became a successful composer for films, winning an Academy Award in 1950 for his score for *Sunset Boulevard*. He also was active as a conductor, serving as founder-conductor of the Los Angeles Music Festival from 1947 to 1967.

Waxman's other film scores include *Magnificent Obsession* (1935), *Captains Courageous* (1937), *The Philadelphia Story* (1940), *Stalag 17* (1953), *Sayonara* (1957), and *Sunrise at Campobello* (1960). He also composed orchestral and vocal works.

We Shall Overcome. Song of uncertain authorship that has served as the marching hymn of the black civil rights movement after World War II.

The music has been traced to an 18th-century anthem, *O Sanctissima*. The lyrics are based on the 19th-century hymn *I Shall Overcome*. In that version, the singer was celebrating overcoming the temptations of the earth. In the civil rights adaptation, the singers celebrate overcoming racial injustice and prejudice.

Webber, Andrew Lloyd. *See* LLOYD WEBBER, ANDREW.

Webber, Julian Lloyd. *See* LLOYD WEBBER, JULIAN.

Weber, Carl Maria (Friedrich Ernst) **von,** celebrated German composer, pianist, and conductor; b. Eutin, Oldenburg, Nov. 18, 1786; d. London, June 5, 1826. His father, Franz Anton von Weber (1734?–1812), an army officer, played the violin and served as kapellmeister in Eutin. His fondest wish was that Carl Maria follow in the footsteps of WOLFGANG AMADEUS MOZART as a child prodigy.

Carl Maria's mother was a singer of some ability, but she died when he was 11. Franz Anton led a wandering life as music director of his own theater company, taking his family with him on his tours. Although this mode of life interfered with Carl Maria's regular education, it gave him practical knowledge of the stage and stimulated his imagination as a dramatic composer.

PEOPLE IN MUSIC

Constanze Weber, Mozart's widow, was Franz Anton Weber's niece.

Weber's first teachers were his father and his half-brother Fritz, a pupil of FRANZ JOSEPH HAYDN. At Hildburghausen, while with his father's company in 1796, he also received piano instruction from J. P. Heuschkel. The next year he was in Salzburg, where he attracted the attention of Michael Haydn, who taught him COUNTERPOINT. He composed a set of *Six Fughetten* there (published in 1798). As his travels continued, he was taught singing by Valesi (J. B. Wallishauser) and composition by J. N. Kalcher in Munich from 1798 to 1800. At the age of 12, Weber wrote an opera, although it was never performed and the manuscript has not survived.

Through a meeting with Aloys Senefelder, the inventor of lithography, Weber became interested in engraving. He became Senefelder's apprentice, acquiring considerable skill. He engraved his own *Six Variations on an Original Theme* for piano in Munich in 1800. His father became interested in the business possibilities of lithography and set up a workshop with him in Freiberg. However, the venture failed, and Carl Maria turned again to music.

Weber composed a two-act comic opera, *Das Waldmädchen,* in 1800. It was premiered in Freiberg, six days after his 14th birthday, with performances following in Chemnitz that year and in Vienna four years later. In 1801 the family was once more in Salzburg, where Carl studied further with Michael Haydn. He wrote another opera there, then gave a concert in the fall of 1802 in Hamburg. The family then proceeded to Augsburg, where they remained until the fall of 1803, when they settled in Vienna. Weber continued his studies with Abbé Vogler, at whose recommendation he secured the post of conductor of the Breslau Opera in 1804. He resigned this post in 1806 after his attempts at operatic reform caused difficulty with the company's management.

In 1806 Weber joined the court of Duke Eugen of Württemberg-Ols at Schloss Carlsruhe in Upper Silesia. Much of his time there was devoted to composition. In 1807 he was engaged as private secretary to Duke Ludwig in Stuttgart, and also gave music lessons to his children. This employment was abruptly terminated when Weber became innocently involved in a scheme of securing a ducal appointment for a rich man's son in order to exempt him from military service. He accepted a loan of money in return for this favor, which was a common practice at the Stuttgart court. Nonetheless, Weber was arrested in early 1810 and kept in prison for 16 days. This matter, along with several others, was settled to his advantage, only to find him the target of his many creditors, who had him rearrested. Finally, agreeing to pay off his debts as swiftly as possible, he was released and then banished by King Friedrich.

Weber went to Mannheim, where he made appearances as a pianist. He next went to Darmstadt, where he rejoined his former teacher, Vogler, for whom he wrote the introduction to his teacher's edition of 12 JOHANN SEBASTIAN BACH CHORALES. In 1810 Weber's opera *Silvana* was successfully premiered in Frankfurt. The title role was sung by Caroline Brandt, who later became a member of the Prague Opera and eventually Weber's wife.

Weber left Darmstadt in early 1811 for Munich, where he composed several important orchestral works, including the CLARINET concertino, the two clarinet concertos, and the BASSOON concerto. His clarinet pieces were written for the noted virtuoso Heinrich (Joseph) Bärmann (1784–1847). Weber's one-act SINGSPIEL, *Abu Hassan,* was successfully given in Munich in the late spring of 1811. For the rest of that year Weber and Bärmann gave concerts in Switzerland. After appearing in Prague, they went to Leipzig, Weimar, Dresden, and Berlin (attended by King Friedrich Wilhelm III), all in 1812. In late 1812 Weber was soloist at the premiere of his Second Piano Concerto in Gotha.

Upon Weber's return to Prague in early 1813, he was informed that he was to be the director of the German Opera there. He was given extensive authority and traveled to Vienna to engage singers and secure the services of Franz Clement as concertmaster. During his tenure Weber presented a distinguished repertoire, which included LUDWIG VAN BEETHOVEN's *FIDELIO*. However, when his reforms encountered opposition, he submitted his resignation in 1816.

In late 1816 Weber was appointed Musikdirektor of the German Opera in Dresden by King Friedrich August III. He opened his first season in early 1817. That same year he was named Königlich Kapellmeister and began to make sweeping reforms.

Weber and Brandt were married in Prague that year. About this time he approached Friedrich Kind, a Dresden lawyer and writer, and suggested to him the idea of preparing a LIBRETTO on a ROMANTIC German subject for his next opera. They agreed on *DER FREISCHÜTZ*, a fairy tale from a collection of ghost stories by J. A. Apel and F. Laun. The composition of this work, which would prove Weber's masterpiece, occupied him for three years. The score was completed in the spring of 1820.

Gaspare Spontini, director of the Berlin Opera, was a highly influential figure in operatic circles and at court. Spontini considered himself the guardian of the Italian-French tradition in opposition to the new German Romantic movement in music, represented by Weber.

After some revisions *Der Freischütz* was accepted for performance at the opening of Berlin's Neues Schauspielhaus. Weber conducted its triumphant premiere in 1821. The work's success surpassed all expectations, and the cause of new Romantic art was won. *Der Freischütz* was soon staged by all the major opera houses of Europe.

Weber's next opera was *Euryanthe*, produced in Vienna in 1823, with only moderate success. Meanwhile, his health was affected by tuberculosis and he was compelled to spend part of 1824 in Marienbad. He recovered sufficiently to begin the composition of *Oberon*, a commission from London's Covent Garden. The English libretto was prepared by J.R. Planché, based on a translation of C. M. Wieland's verse-romance of the same name. Once more illness interrupted Weber's progress, and he spent part of the summer of 1825 in Ems to prepare himself for the journey to England.

Weber set out for London in early 1826, a dying man. On his arrival, he was housed with Sir George Smart, the conductor of the Philharmonic Society of London. Weber threw himself into his work, presiding over 16 rehearsals for *Oberon*. In the spring, he conducted its premiere at Covent Garden, obtaining a tremendous success. Despite his greatly weakened condition, he conducted 11 more performances of the score, and also participated in various London concerts, playing for the last time a week before his death.

In June, Weber was found dead in his room and was buried in London. His remains were removed to Dresden in

1844. Later, they were taken to the Catholic cemetery in Dresden to the accompaniment of funeral music arranged from motifs from *Euryanthe* for wind instruments as prepared and conducted by RICHARD WAGNER. The next day, Weber's remains were interred as Wagner delivered an oration and conducted a chorus in his specially composed *An Webers Grabe.*

Weber's role in music history is epoch-making. In his operas, particularly *Der Freischütz,* he opened the era of musical Romanticism, in decisive opposition to the established Italianate style. The highly dramatic and poetic portrayal of a German fairy tale, with its aura of supernatural mystery, appealed to the public, whose imagination had been stirred by the emergent Romantic literature of the period. Weber's melodic genius and mastery of the craft of composition made it possible for him to break with tradition and to start on a new path, at a critical time when individualism and nationalism began to emerge as sources of creative artistry.

His instrumental works, too, possessed a new quality that signaled the transition from CLASSIC to Romantic music. For PIANO he wrote pieces of extraordinary brilliance, introducing some novel elements in chord writing and passage work. He was himself an excellent pianist, his large hands giving him an unusual command of the keyboard.

Weber's influence on the development of German music was very great. The evolutionary link to Wagner's music drama is evident in the coloring of his orchestral parts and in the statement of his leading motifs. Finally, he was one of the first outstanding interpretative conducting podium figures.

In addition to his 10 operas (some incomplete or lost) and works for solo wind instrument and orchestra, Weber wrote incidental and interpolated music for more than 25 dramatic works. His other vocal music included concert ARIAS, five MASSES and two liturgical related offertories, and secular CANTATAS. Among his orchestral works are two symphonies (1807, 1807), concertos and concertolike pieces with flute, clarinet (three), bassoon (two), horn, viola (two), cello, piano (three), and harmonichord (a bowed keyboard instrument), concert overtures and other works, and wind ensemble music. Among his chamber pieces are the Piano

Weber's hands were so large that he could play an INTERVAL of a twelfth—quite an unusual capability among pianists.

Quartet in B-Flat Major (1809), *Six Progressive Sonatas* for violin (or flute) and piano (1810), *Seven Variations on a Theme from "Silvana"* for clarinet and piano (1811), Clarinet Quintet in B-Flat Major (1815), *Grand Duo Concertant* for piano and clarinet (1815–16), and Trio for flute, cello, and piano (1819).

Weber wrote prolifically for his own instrument, the piano, but relatively little of it is played. Popular are four sonatas (1812; 1816; 1816; 1822), *Momento capriccioso* in B flat major (1808), *Rondo brillante: La gaite* in E flat major (1819), *AuVorderung zum Tanze: Rondo brillante* in D flat major (1819; made even more famous by HECTOR BERLIOZ's orchestration, 1861), *Polacca brillante L'hilarite* in E major (1819), and several piano duets.

Weber's critical writings on music are valuable, if at times surprisingly conservative. Like many of his day, he had very mixed feelings about Beethoven's later music. Weber also left an autobiographical sketch, an unfinished novel, poems, and other writings.

Weber's compositions are cataloged according to the J. numbers established by F. Jähns in his *Carl Maria von Weber in seinen Werken: Chronologisch-thematisches Verzeichniss seiner sämmtlichen Compositionen* (Berlin, 1871).

Webern, Anton (Friedrich Wilhelm von), remarkable Austrian serial composer and innovator of KLANGFARBEN-MELODIE; b. Vienna, Dec. 3, 1883; d. Mittersill, Sept. 15, 1945. Webern received his first instruction in music from his mother, an amateur pianist. He then studied piano, cello, and theory with Edwin Komauer in Klagenfurt, where he also played cello in the orchestra. In 1902 he entered the University of Vienna, where he studied HARMONY and COUNTERPOINT. He also attended classes in musicology with Guido Adler, receiving his Ph.D. in 1906.

In 1904 Webern began private studies in composition with ARNOLD SCHOENBERG, whose ardent disciple he became. ALBAN BERG also studied with Schoenberg, and together, Schoenberg, Berg, and Webern laid the foundations of what became known as the second Viennese school of composition. The unifying element was the adoption of Schoenberg's method of composition with 12 TONES RE-

Some critics referred to Schoenberg, Berg, and Webern as a Vienna (Unholy) Trinity, with Schoenberg as God the Father, Berg as God the Son, and Webern as the Holy Spirit.

Anton von Webern, c. 1925. (Corbis-Bettmann)

LATED only to one another.

From 1908 to 1914 Webern was active as a conductor in Vienna and in Germany. In 1915–16 he served in the army, and in 1917–18 he was conductor at the Deutsches Theater in Prague. In 1918 he removed the nobiliary particle "von" from his name when such distinctions were outlawed in Austria. He settled in Mödling, near Vienna, where he taught composition privately. From 1918 to 1922 he supervised the programs of the Verein für Musikalische Privataufführungen (Society for Private Musical Performances). This group was organized in Vienna by Schoenberg with the intention of promoting modern music without being exposed to reactionary opposition (music critics were not admitted to these concerts).

Webern was conductor of the Schubertbund in 1921–22, and of the Mödling Male Chorus from 1921 to 1926. From 1922 to 1934, he also led the Vienna Workers' Symphony concerts and the Vienna Workers' Chorus, both sponsored by the Social Democratic Party. From 1927 to 1938 he was a conductor on the Austrian Radio. Furthermore, he conducted guest engagements in Germany, Switzerland, and Spain. From 1929 Webern made several visits to England, where he was a guest conductor with the BBC Symphony Orchestra. For the most part, however, he devoted himself to composition, private teaching, and lecturing.

After Adolf Hitler came to power in Germany in 1933, Webern's music was banned as an example of "degenerate art." After 1938, his works could no longer be published. He eked out an existence by teaching a few private pupils and making piano arrangements of musical scores by others for Universal Edition. After his son was killed in an air bombardment of a train in early 1945, he and his wife fled from Vienna to Mittersill, near Salzburg, to stay with his married daughters and grandchildren.

Webern's life ended tragically when he was shot and killed by an American soldier after stepping outside his son-in-law's residence one evening. The circumstances were shrouded in secrecy for many years, but a full account was finally given in 1961.

Webern left relatively few works, most of short duration (the fourth of his *Five Pieces for Orchestra,* op.10, takes only 19 seconds to play), but in them he achieves the most subtle of expressive means. He adopted the 12-tone method of composition almost immediately after its definitive formulation by Schoenberg in 1924 and extended the principle of nonrepetition of notes to TONE COLORS. In some of his works (e.g., the Symphony, op.21) solo instruments are rarely allowed to play two successive thematic notes. Dynamic marks are similarly diversified.

Typically, in Webern's works, each 12-tone row is divided into symmetrical sections of two, four, or six members. These enter into intricate but invariably logical canonic imitations. INVERSIONS and AUGMENTATIONS are common features. Melodically and harmonically, the intervals of the MAJOR SEVENTH and MINOR NINTH are stressed. Single MOTIVES are brief and stand out as individual particles or lyric ejaculations.

The impact of Webern's works on the general public and on the critics was disconcerting, and upon occasion led to violent demonstrations. However, his extraordinary skill and novelty of technique made this music endure beyond the fashions of the times. Performances of Webern's works multiplied after his death and began to affect increasingly larger groups of modern musicians.

IGOR STRAVINSKY acknowledged the use of Webern's methods in his later works, and numerous JAZZ composers have professed to follow Webern's ideas of tone color. Ana-

PIERRE BOULEZ announced, "Schoenberg is dead! Long live Webern!" in 1952, referring to the greater influence Webern had than his mentor did.

lytical treatises have been published in several languages. The International Webern Festival celebrated the centennial of his birth in Vienna in 1983.

Webern's output includes 31 works with opus numbers and a few unnumbered works. These include the orchestral *Passacaglia,* op.1 (1908), *Six Pieces for Orchestra,* op.6 (1913), *Five Pieces for Orchestra,* op.10 (1911–13), *Five Pieces for Orchestra,* op. posthumous (1913), Symphony for chamber ensemble, op.21 (N.Y.), and Variations, op.30 (1940).

Webern's chamber works include five movements for string quartet and four pieces for violin and piano, op.7 (both 1910), six bagatelles for string quartet, op.9 (1911–13), *Three Little Pieces* for cello and piano, op.11 (1914), String Trio, op.20 (1926–27), Quartet for violin, clarinet, tenor saxophone, and piano, op.22 (1931), Concerto for nine instruments, op.24 (1935), String Quartet, op.28 (1936–38), and Variations for piano (1937). He also made arrangements of works by Schoenberg, FRANZ SCHUBERT, and JOHANN SEBASTIAN BACH.

Among Webern's choral compositions are two CANTATAS: First Cantata, op.29, with soprano and orchestra (1938–39), and Second Cantata, op.31, with soprano, bass, and orchestra (1941–43). He also wrote numerous solo vocal works, mostly with piano accompaniments. These included settings of poems by the German poets Stefan George, Rainer Maria Rilke, and Georg Trakl, as well as biblical texts and nursery rhymes.

Wedding, The. *See* NOCES, LES.

PEOPLE IN MUSIC

Weill, Kurt (Julian), remarkable German-born American composer; b. Dessau, March 2, 1900; d. N.Y., April 3, 1950. Weill was a private pupil of Albert Bing in Dessau from 1915 to 1918. In 1918–19, he studied COUNTERPOINT, COMPOSITION, and CONDUCTING at the Berlin Hochschule für Musik. He was then engaged as an opera coach in Dessau and theater conductor at Lüdenscheid.

In 1920 Weill moved to Berlin and became a student of FERRUCCIO BUSONI at the Prussian Academy of Arts until 1923, where he also studied with Philipp Jarnach. His first major work, the Symphony No. 1 (*Berliner Sinfonie*), was composed in 1921. However, it was not performed in his lifetime. Indeed, its manuscript was not recovered until 1955, and it was finally premiered by the North German Radio Symphony Orchestra in Hamburg in 1958.

Weill turned to the stage for his next large-scale work, the ballet *Zaubernacht* (with song; 1922). Then, influenced by new trends in the German musical theater, he began to write satirical operas in a sharp modernistic manner: *Der Protagonist* (1924–25) and *Royal Palace* (1925–26).

In 1927 there followed a striking SONGSPIEL, *Mahagonny*, to a LIBRETTO by German playwright and social satirist Bertolt Brecht, savagely satirizing the American primacy of money. It was remodeled and presented as the three-act opera *Aufstieg und Fall der Stadt Mahagonny* (The Rise and Fall of the State of Mahagonny; 1929).

▲

A scene from a 1994 London production of The Threepenny Opera. *(Robbie Jack/Corbis)*

Weill interrupted work on the revision of *Mahagonny* to produce his greatest success in this genre, a modern version of JOHN GAY's THE BEGGAR'S OPERA, to a sharp libretto by Brecht. It opened in 1928 under the title *Die Dreigroschenoper,* and subsequently was staged all over Germany, and was also produced in translation throughout Europe.

Although Weill and Brecht grew apart over ideological differences, they produced two smaller works of great influence on later composers: *Der Jasager* (One Who Says Yes; 1930), a "school opera" with Marxist teachings, and *Die*

Sieben Todsünden, a dance-song CANTATA that encapsulates Berlin of the 1920s and early 1930s (and indeed the world that Weill had to abandon).

After the Nazi ascent to power in Germany, Weill and his wife, the singer LOTTE LENYA, who appeared in many of his musical plays, went to Paris in 1933. They settled in the U.S. in 1935, and Weill became a naturalized American citizen in 1943.

Gradually absorbing the modes and fashions of American popular music, Weill adopted the typical form and content of American musicals. In his European productions he had already absorbed elements of American popular songs and JAZZ rhythms. His musicals combine this Americanized idiom with a hint of early-20th-century advanced compositional techniques (ATONALITY, POLYTONALITY, POLYRHYTHMS) and present the result in a pleasing, yet sophisticated and challenging, manner.

As Brecht, Georg Kaiser, and Caspar Neher had been his principal collaborators in Germany, Weill worked with American literary luminaries including Maxwell Anderson, MOSS HART, IRA GERSHWIN, S. J. Perelman, Ogden Nash, Elmer Rice, Langston Hughes, and ALAN JAY LERNER. Some works were too radical or offbeat for their audiences, while others were too operatic. His greatest successes were *Lady in the Dark* (1940), *One Touch of Venus* (1943), *Street Scene* (a "Broadway opera," 1946), and *Lost in the Stars* (1949).

For all Weill's success in American-produced scores, virtually all of his European works were unproduced in the U.S. at the time of his death. But four years after Weill's death, MARC BLITZSTEIN made an English version of *Die Dreigroschenoper,* versified in a modern American vernacular. It was produced as *THE THREEPENNY OPERA* in 1954 and became a long-running N.Y. hit. The show's *Ballad of Mack the Knife* (in German, *Die Moritat von Mackie Messer*), became tremendously successful. The production relaunched Lenya's career, and she appeared in theatrical and film roles into the 1970s. At her death, a Kurt Weill Foundation was established to help assist performances of his works and encourage scholarship.

Many of Weill's works have received first American productions or revivals, and many new recordings have also

Down in the Valley, a one-act "college opera," remains Weill's most-performed English-language work.

been released. Weill's primary reputation as a theatrical composer has obscured attention to other valuable works, such as his two symphonies (1921, *Berliner Symphonie;* 1933, *Pariser Symphonie* or *Three Night Scenes*), Divertimento (1922), Concerto for violin, WOODWINDS, double bass, and PERCUSSION (Paris, 1925), and *Kleine Dreigroschenmusik* for winds (1929).

Among Weill's excellent vocal works are *Recordare* for choir and children's chorus (1923); *Der neue Orpheus,* cantata for soprano, violin, and orchestra (1925); *Vom Tod im Wald,* ballad for bass and 10 wind instruments (1927), *Das Berliner Requiem,* cantata for tenor, baritone, bass, chorus, and 15 instruments (1929); and *Der Lindberghflug,* cantata after a radio SCORE for TENOR, BARITONE, chorus, and orchestra. The original 1929 version was composed with PAUL HINDEMITH, although later that year Weill rewrote it as wholly his own work. Its subsequent titles were *Der Flug des Lindberghs* and finally *Der Ozeanflug,* as a gesture of protest against Charles Lindbergh's militant neutrality toward Nazi Germany. Weill's chamber pieces include two string quartets (1919, 1923) and a Cello Sonata (1920). He also composed film scores, radio and theater scores, and many songs.

Wein, Weib, und Gesang (Wine, Women, and Song). Waltz by JOHANN STRAUSS (II), 1869, among his most popular. The element of wine is represented by the short upbeat suggesting a mild degree of intoxication, and the element of woman is suggested by the flowing waves of accompaniment. The concluding song unites both under its irresistible melodic sway.

Weinberger, Jaromir. *See* SCHWANDA THE BAGPIPER.

Weir, Judith, Scottish composer; b. Aberdeen, May 11, 1954. After studies with JOHN TAVENER in London, Weir received training in computer music from Barry Vercoe at the Massachusetts Institute of Technology in 1973. From 1973 to 1976 she was a student of Robin Holloway at King's College, Cambridge. She also studied with Gunther Schuller and OLIVIER MESSIAEN at the Berkshire Music Center in Tanglewood, Massachusetts, in the summer of 1975.

PEOPLE IN MUSIC

From 1979 to 1982 Weir taught at the University of Glasgow, then held a creative arts fellowship at Trinity College, Cambridge, from 1983 to 1985. She was composer-in-residence of the Royal Scottish Academy of Music and Drama in Glasgow from 1988 to 1991. From 1995 to 1997 she served as the Fairbairn Composer-in-Association with the City of Birmingham.

In her diverse output, Weir has effectively utilized both traditional and contemporary techniques in creating a highly individual means of expression. She is best known for theatrical works, including the operas *A Night At the Chinese Opera* (1986–87), *The Vanishing Bridegroom* (1990), and *Blond Eckbert* (1994). Among her orchestral works are *Music Untangled*, overture (1991; revised 1992) and *Heroische Bogenstricke* (Heroic Strokes of the Bow, 1992).

Weir's chamber pieces include a String Quartet (1990), *I broke off a golden branch* for violin, viola, cello, double bass, and piano (1991), *El Rey de Francia* for violin, viola, cello, and piano (1993), and *Musicians Wrestle Everywhere* for 10 instruments (1994). She also composed numerous keyboard works, as well as vocal pieces, including *Don't Let That Horse* for soprano and horn (1990), *On Buying a Horse* for medium voice and piano (1991), *The Alps* for soprano, clarinet, and viola (1992), *Broken Branches* for soprano, piano, and double bass (1992), and *Two Human Hymns* for chorus and piano (1995).

PEOPLE IN MUSIC

Weisgall, Hugo (David), distinguished Moravian-born American composer and teacher; b. Eibenschutz, Oct. 13, 1912; d. N.Y., March 11, 1997. Weisgall emigrated with his family to the U.S. and became a naturalized citizen in 1926. He studied at the Peabody Conservatory of Music in Baltimore from 1927 to 1932, then had composition lessons with Roger Sessions at various times between 1932 and 1941. He also was a pupil at the Curtis Institute of Music in Philadelphia and pursued academic studies at Johns Hopkins University (Ph.D., 1940). After military service in World War II, he was active as a conductor, singer, teacher, and composer.

Weisgall was founder-conductor of the Chamber Society of Baltimore in 1948 and the Hilltop Opera Company in

1952. From 1949 to 1951 he was director of the Baltimore Institute of Musical Arts, and from 1951 to 1957 he taught at Johns Hopkins University. In 1952 he was made chairman of the faculty of the Cantors' Institute at the Jewish Theological Center in N.Y. He taught at the Juilliard School of Music from 1957 to 1970 and at Queens College of the City University of N.Y. beginning in 1961.

Weisgall served as president of the American Music Center from 1963 to 1973, and in 1966 he was composer-in-residence at the American Academy in Rome. He held three Guggenheim fellowships and received many prizes and commissions. In 1975 he was elected to membership in the National Institute of Arts and Letters, and in 1990 he became president of the American Academy and Institute of Arts and Letters. In 1994 he was awarded its Gold Medal for Music.

Weisgall was a master of all musical idioms, especially vocal ones. He composed 10 operas, four ballets, orchestral works, vocal works, and songs.

Weiss, Silvius Leopold, lutenist and composer; b. Breslau, Oct. 12, 1686; d. Dresden, Oct. 16, 1750. He most likely was a pupil of his father, Johann Jacob Weiss, a lutenist and composer (b. c.1662; d. Mannheim, Jan. 30, 1754).

Silvius was in the service of Count Carl Philipp of the Palatinate in Breslau by 1706. He then was in Italy with Alexander Sobiesky, Prince of Poland, from 1708 to 1714. In 1715 he entered the service of the Hessen-Kassel court and shortly thereafter went to Düsseldorf. In 1717 he joined the chapel of the Saxon court in Dresden, where his status was formalized in 1718. He also traveled as a virtuoso, appearing in Prague (1717), London (1718), Vienna (1718–19), Munich (1722), Berlin (1728), and Leipzig (1739), where he visited JOHANN SEBASTIAN BACH.

Weiss was a foremost performer on and composer for the LUTE. His surviving works number almost 600. He composed the largest corpus of solo lute works (mostly PARTITAS and SUITES) by any composer. They are worthy of comparison with Bach's small number of works for this instrument.

Weiss's brother Johann Sigismund (b. probably in Breslau, c.1689; d. Mannheim, April 12, 1737) was a lutenist,

PEOPLE IN MUSIC

viola da gambist, violinist, and composer. Sometime around 1708 he became a lutenist at the Palatine chapel in Düsseldorf, following it to Heidelberg in 1718 and to Mannheim two years later. In 1732 he was named director of instrumental music there, and later served as konzertmeister and THEORBO player. He was one of the finest composers of the early MANNHEIM SCHOOL.

Silvius's son Johann Adolf Faustinus (b. Dresden, April 15, 1741; d. there, Jan. 21, 1814) was a lutenist and composer. He served as chamber lutenist at the Dresden court from 1763 until his death, and also traveled widely. He composed lute and guitar music.

PEOPLE IN MUSIC

Welk, Lawrence, popular American bandleader and accordionist; b. Strasburg, N.D., March 11, 1903; d. Santa Monica, Calif., May 17, 1992. Welk began playing ACCORDION in German-speaking areas of his native state as a youth. He then performed with his own combos, gaining success as a self-described purveyor of "champagne music." After touring and making numerous radio appearances, he launched his own television program in Los Angeles in 1951. It subsequently was featured on network television from 1955 to 1971.

Welk owed his popularity to his skillful selection of programs containing a varied mixture of semiclassical pieces, western American BALLADS, and POLKAS and other dance tunes. His use of an accordion section in his arrangements, steadfast rhythmic beat, and sentimentalized tempos gave his renditions a sound quality that made him a favorite with widespread audiences.

well temperament. *See* TEMPERAMENT.

Well-Tempered Clavier, The (*Das wohltemperierte Clavier*). Collection of paired PRELUDES and FUGUES by JOHANN SEBASTIAN BACH, in two books (1722, 1742).

Each book contains 24 preludes and 24 fugues in all MAJOR and MINOR KEYS arranged in CHROMATIC order, alternating in major and minor keys. Consequently all odd-numbered preludes and fugues are in major keys, and all even-numbered ones are in minor. The first prelude and fugue in each of the two books is in C major, while the last prelude and fugue in each of the two books is in B minor.

The complete German title of Book 1 of the 48 is rendered into English as follows: "The Well-Tempered Clavier, or preludes and fugues through all tones and semitones, relating to the major 3rd, that is, Ut Re Mi, as well as those relating to the minor 3rd, that is, Re Mi Fa. Compiled and prepared for the benefit and practice of young musicians desirous of learning, as well as for the entertainment of those already versed in this particular study, by Johann Sebastian Bach, Anno 1722."

The term *well-tempered* has often been interpreted to mean the use of equal temperament, but it is actually a late form of meantone temperament (*see* TEMPERAMENT), in which individual keys' characters are maintained. Bach's achievement was a triumph of tonal freedom within its BAROQUE context.

Bach had a precursor in the person of J.C.F. Fischer, who published, a quarter of a century earlier, a collection of 20 preludes and fugues in 19 different keys, characteristically entitled *Ariadne musica neo-organoedum* (alluding to Ariadne, whose guiding thread helped Theseus to find his way out of the Cretan labyrinth). Bach must have known Fischer's work (in fact, some of Bach's fugal subjects are similar to Fischer's).

The description "Clavier" is vague. In Bach's time, the term was applied to all KEYBOARD instruments and could have been either a HARPSICHORD or a CLAVICHORD.

The English Bachologist Ebenezer Prout amused himself by setting the subjects of each one of Bach's 48 fugues to humorous verses, some of merit and wit. For fugue No. 7 of Book 2, he said: "When I get aboard an ocean steamer / I begin to feel sick" (the last two words on a trill). The fugue No. 22 of Book 1, which is rather intricate, inspired him to write, "Oh, dear! What shall I do? It's utterly impossible for me to play this horrid fugue! I give it up!" And the chromatic countersubject of the same fugue is quite emotional: "It ain't no use! It ain't a bit of good! Not a bit, not a bit!"

Werckmeister, Andreas, German organist, organ examiner, music theorist, and composer; b. Benneckenstein, Thur-

PEOPLE IN MUSIC

ingia, Nov. 30, 1645; d. Halberstadt, Oct. 26, 1706. After his studies in Bennungen, Nordhausen, and Quedlinburg, Werckmeister became organist in Hasselfelde, near Blankenburg, from 1664 to 1674. After serving as organist and notary in Elbingerode in 1674–75, he went to Quedlinburg as organist of the collegiate church of St. Servatius and of the court of the abbess and Countess of Palatine, Anna Sophia I. He also was named organist of the Wipertikirche in 1677, and in 1696 he settled in Halberstadt as organist of the Martinikirche.

Werckmeister was highly influential as a music theorist. His explanation of number symbolism in music and its theological basis remains invaluable. But his work maintains its greatest relevance in the area of meantone temperament (*see* TEMPERAMENT), as early music revivalists tackled KEYBOARD tuning issues.

Werfel, Alma Mahler. *See* MAHLER, GUSTAV.

Werk (Ger.). 1. Work, OPUS, composition. 2. An ORGAN KEYBOARD with its own set of pipes; *Orgelwerk*.

A wave of suicides followed the publication of Goethe's novel, among young males in the throes of unrequited love. In some countries, the novel was banned as a result.

Werther. Opera by JULES MASSENET, 1892, first performed in Vienna. The LIBRETTO is extracted from Goethe's celebrated short novel *Die Leiden des jungen Werthers* (The Sorrows of Young Werther, 1774).

Werther is a young man with an overpowering passion for a young woman. She shares his affection but marries a more practical person. Werther does not cease to express his adoration for her. He borrows a pistol from her husband and shoots himself. She rushes to his side, and he has the ultimate satisfaction of dying in her arms while proclaiming the eternal validity of his deathless passion.

In his melodious score, Massenet extracted the last fluid ounce of tearful emotion afforded by the libretto.

Wesendonck, Mathilde (Luckemeyer). *See* WAGNER, (WILHELM) RICHARD.

West Side Story. Musical by LEONARD BERNSTEIN and STEPHEN SONDHEIM, 1957, first performed in Washington,

D.C. It is an undisputed classic of the American musical theater. The idea was developed by choreographer Jerome Robbins jointly with Bernstein.

Two rival youth gangs, the Jets, composed of Italian and Irish boys, and the Sharks, recruited from the Puerto Rican population, fight each other tooth and nail, knife and switchblade, like latter-day Montagues and Capulets. Tony of the Jets is the counterpart of Shakespeare's Romeo, and Maria, sister of the leader of the Sharks, is Juliet. A dance in a school gymnasium sets the scene of mutual distrust between the two gangs. But Tony and Maria arrange for a secret meeting, and their song *Tonight* is one of the most appealing love ballads in American musical theater. Also remarkable is her vivacious confession, *I Feel Pretty.*

The tension between the two gangs erupts in a savage fight ballet (*Rumble*). In a climactic fight, Tony's friend Riff is knifed to death. In revenge, Tony kills Maria's brother, Bernardo. After a tense cat-and-mouse chase, Tony is inexorably shot by a Shark and dies in Maria's arms.

Among other fine numbers are the ballad *Somewhere,* a group of Puerto Rican women debating the advantages of American life in *(I Want to Live in) America,* and a classic comic song, *Gee, Officer Krupke!,* a cynical commentary by the Jets on juvenile delinquency.

The film version of *West Side Story,* released in 1961, earned 10 Academy Awards. Shortly before his death, Bernstein recorded a complete, almost operatic version of the work. Ironically, a large portion of the neighborhood in which *West Side Story* is set was demolished to make way for the Lincoln Center for the Performing Arts, where Bernstein was for many years employed as conductor of the N.Y. Philharmonic.

Westminster Chimes. Tune, c.1794, attributed to William Crotch (b. Norwich, July 5, 1775; d. Taunton, Dec. 29, 1847). In 1860 the Big Ben tower clock at the Houses of Parliament was equipped with a mechanism for sounding the Westminster chimes.

The opening four notes are identical with a phrase that occurs in *I know That My Redeemer liveth* from GEORGE FRIDERIC HANDEL's *Messiah,* no doubt a coincidence. Countless arrangements have been made of the Westminster chimes. RALPH VAUGHAN WILLIAMS interpolated the Big Ben tune in his *London Symphony.*

What's Goin' On? Turbulent social-protest anthem by MARVIN GAYE released in 1971, as well as the title track of a highly influential album.

When Irish Eyes Are Smiling. Song by Ernest R. Ball, 1913, the best known of his contributions to neo-Irish folklore. His other songs in a pseudo-Irish manner were *Mother Machree* (1910) and *A Little Bit of Heaven* (1914). Ball collaborated with the great Irish tenor John McCormack.

When Johnny Comes Marching Home. A Civil War song by Patrick Gilmore, 1863, written under the pseudonym of Louis Lambert. It became a nostalgic ballad of Union soldiers returning home from the battlefields. Because Gilmore and bandmasters of the 19th century freely took credit for folk songs, or even songs by known contemporary composers, it may well be that *When Johnny Comes Marching Home* was an arrangement of a preexisting popular song. The modal character of the tune suggests Irish or Scottish origin.

When the Red, Red Robin Comes Bob, Bob, Bobbin' Along. Song by Harry Woods, 1926. It remains a springtime favorite.

When the Saints was further popularized by LOUIS ARMSTRONG when it became a part of his repertoire after World War II.

When the Saints Go Marching In. African-American SPIRITUAL, of unknown origin, published in 1908. It combines elements of a funeral hymn and a southern dance step. The tune became a standard for early New Orleans JAZZ bands.

Whiffenpoof Song, The. Song of the Yale University Glee Club, 1909. Whiffenpoof was a character in a famous comic strip (and VICTOR HERBERT's OPERETTA *Little Nemo,* 1908). The song was popularized by RUDY VALLEE, himself a Yale man.

While Strolling Through the Park One Day. Song by Robert Ki, 1884. It became tremendously popular among young lovers in N.Y. Soft-shoe steps (tap dance) were usually interpolated during the refrain.

whip (Fr. *fouet;* Ger. *Peitsche;* It. *frusta*). A wooden PERCUSSION instrument having two sections joined at one end. They are clacked together to make the sound of a cracking whip. MAURICE RAVEL uses it in some of his scores, as does EDGARD VARÈSE in *Ionisation.* PIETRO MASCAGNI makes dramatic use of the whip in *Cavalleria rusticana* to announce the entrance of the vengeful husband.

Whispering. Popular song by John Schonberger, 1920. The opening line, "Whispering while you cuddle near me," gives an idea of the sentiment of the song. The song sold millions of copies in sheet music and became a romantic perennial.

whistle (from Old Eng., *whistle;* Fr. *sifflet;* Ger. *Pfeife;* It. *fischio*). Family of short end-blown FLUTES, in numerous forms, dating to prehistory. In its basic form, there are no FINGERHOLES. The whistle can be used as a decoy or signal.

White Christmas. A ballad by IRVING BERLIN, 1942, which became a HYMN, an ANTHEM, and a prayer for G.I.'s in the South Pacific, where Christmas is always green. By 1965 *White Christmas* had sold nearly six million copies in sheet music and over 50 million recordings.

Native American Indians playing small whistles. (Smithsonian Institution)

BING CROSBY made a career with *White Christmas,* but some 300 other performers also covered it.

white noise (sound). All audible tones within a given sound spectrum, heard at once. A common synonym is static.

Whiteman, Paul, American conductor of POPULAR MUSIC; b. Denver, Colo., March 28, 1890; d. Doylestown, Penn., Dec. 29, 1967. Whiteman played viola in the Denver Symphony Orchestra and later in the San Francisco People's Symphony Orchestra. In 1917–18, he was conductor of a 40-piece band in the U.S. Navy.

Whiteman then formed a hotel orchestra in Santa Barbara, California. He then moved the group to Atlantic City, New Jersey, and eventually to N.Y. In 1920 he signed with Victor Records, and three years later he took the band to London on tour. In 1924 he gave a concert in Aeolian Hall in N.Y., at which he introduced GEORGE GERSHWIN's *Rhapsody in Blue,* written for his orchestra, with the composer as piano soloist. In 1926 he made a tour in Europe.

While not himself a JAZZ musician, Whiteman was popularly known as the "King of Jazz" and frequently featured at his concerts such notables of the jazz world as BIX BEIDERBECKE, Frank Trumbauer, and BENNY GOODMAN. BING CROSBY achieved his early fame as a member of Paul Whiteman's Rhythm Boys, a vocal group that performed with the band. Whiteman established the Whiteman Awards, made annually for symphonic jazz compositions written by Americans.

Whithorne (born Whittern), **Emerson.** *See* LEGINSKA (LIGGINS), ETHEL.

Who, The. (Guitar/vocal/songwriter: Pete[r Dennis Blandford] Townshend, b. Chiswick, May, 19, 1945; Vocals: Roger Daltrey, b. Hammersmith, March 1, 1944; Bass; John Entwistle b. Chiswick, Oct. 9, 1944; Drums: Keith Moon, b. Wembley, Aug. 23, 1947; d. London, Sept. 7, 1978.) Popular and influential ROCK band, viewed by some to have been the leading 1960s British group after the BEATLES and ROLLING STONES.

In the early 1960s, Townshend began playing BANJO in a Dixieland jazz group in which Entwistle was trumpeter. They teamed with Entwistle's friend, vocalist Daltrey, and organized a group to which they first gave the name High Numbers. Drummer Moon joined the group in 1964, at which point the group became The Who.

The Who became famous for their high-energy perform-ances. Their stage show in the early years concluded with their smash-ing their instru-ments, a rousing finale that per-fectly expressed teen frustration. In 1965 the group released the single *My Genera-tion,* their first major hit and soon a battle cry for youth rebel-lion. In 1966 they recorded *A Quick One While He's Away,* a mini-rock opera that forecast the group's later development.

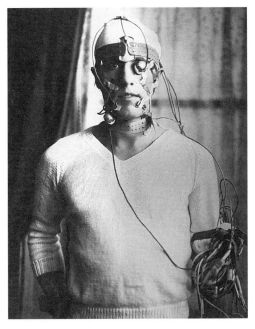

◀

Roger Daltrey in the film version of Tommy. *(Hulton-Deutsch Collection/Corbis)*

Although several well-produced and thoughtful singles had success in the U.K. and the U.S., The Who did not reach worldwide success until the release of the "rock opera" *Tommy* in 1969. Composed mostly by Townshend, it tells the story of a deaf, dumb, and blind boy who becomes a quasi-spiritual leader for his generation. In addition to its massive success as a recording, *Tommy* was long a staple of The Who's live performances. It has been recorded by super-star casts, released as a film, and, in 1993, was realized as a Broadway musical with Michael Cerveris in the title role. The Who recorded a second opera, the more evocative and less plot-driven *Quadrophenia,* in 1973.

In between these milestones the group produced some fine recordings, including *Live at Leeds* (1970), *Who's Next* (1971), and *Who Are You* (1978). After Moon's death, the group continued to work together with new drummer Kenny Jones. A tragic moment in their career occurred at a Cincinnati concert in late 1979 when 11 young people were trampled to death in a rush for the entrance gates. After two more albums, the group disbanded in 1983. The Who has reunited for one subsequent *Tommy* tour and for benefit concerts.

Concurrent with his work in the Who, Townshend produced numerous solo albums, scoring his only major solo hit with 1980's *Let Your Love Open the Door.* Since the band broke up, he has continued to perform and record, including his 1989 opera *Iron Man* and 1993's *PsychoDerelict.*

whole-tone scale. A SCALE consisting entirely of consecutive WHOLE STEPS, whether written as MAJOR SECONDS or DIMINISHED THIRDS. The whole-tone scale gained popularity early in the 20th century when it was used by the IMPRESSIONIST school of composers.

The whole-tone scale is neutral in its polarity. It lacks modality, and the intervallic progression in the whole-tone scale remains the same in melodic ROTATION. The PERFECT FIFTH and FOURTH, cornerstones of tonality, are absent in the whole-tone scale. There is no DOMINANT or SUBDOMINANT, and no LEADING TONE.

FRANZ LISZT was fascinated with the whole-tone scale. He was greatly impressed by the *Fantastic Overture* (1859), which the Russian amateur composer Boris Vietinghoff-Scheel (1829–1901) sent him, in which whole-tone scales were profusely employed. Liszt described its effect as "terrifying to all long and protruding ears." Liszt himself made use of the whole-tone scale in his *Divina Commedia,* illustrating the *Inferno,* and he used it systematically in his posthumously published organ and late piano pieces.

But it was CLAUDE DEBUSSY who elevated the whole-tone scale from a mere exotic device to a poetic and expressive medium. Its great capacity for change and adaptability greatly attracted Debussy and his followers as an alternative to a DIATONIC scale. A very interesting application of the whole-tone scale occurs in Debussy's *La Mer.* The principal theme of the first movement is in the AEOLIAN MODE, while in the third movement it appears as a progression of whole tones. The first and the last sections of Debussy's *Voiles* for piano (*Préludes,* Book 1) consist of whole tones with the middle section providing a contrast in the PENTATONIC scale.

ALBAN BERG used an alternation between the two distinct whole-tone scales (beginning on C and on D♭) in his *Nacht* (*7 Frühe Lieder,* 1907).

With the gradual decline of pictorial and sensorial programmaticism in contemporary music, the whole-tone scale sank into disuse. Eventually it joined the subculture of film music. Cinematic Nazis advance on the screen to the sound of whole-tone scales in the trombones. Mad scientists hatch murderous schemes to blow up the world in mighty progressions of whole tones. When Jean Harlow, in her screen biography, climbs up the ladder in the studio before her final collapse, she is accompanied by delicate whole-tone PIZZICATOS. The whole-tone scale is also used, wittily, in satirical comment on pompous personages in animated cartoons.

Widor, Charles-Marie (-Jean-Albert), French organist, pedagogue, and composer; b. Lyons, Feb. 21, 1844; d. Paris, March 12, 1937. Widor's father, an Alsatian of Hungarian descent, was organist at the church of St.-François in Lyons and active as an organ builder.

PEOPLE IN MUSIC

Widor was a skillful improviser on the ORGAN while still a boy and became organist at the Lyons lycée (school) at 11. After studies in Brussels, he became organist at St.-François in 1860 and gained fame by giving provincial concerts. In 1870–71 he held a provisional appointment as organist at St.-Sulpice in Paris, which became permanent

◄

Charles Marie Widor, c. 1900. (Michael Nicholson/Corbis)

in 1871. He remained in this position until 1934. That year, he played his *Pièce mystique* there, composed at age 90.

Around 1880 he began writing music criticism under the pen name "Aulétès" for the daily *L'Estafette.*

In 1890 Widor became professor of organ and in 1896 professor of composition at the Paris Conservatory. In 1910 he was elected a member of the Académie des Beaux-Arts, of which he became permanent secretary in 1913. He had many distinguished pupils, including ALBERT SCHWEITZER, with whom he collaborated in editing the first five volumes of an eight-volume edition of JOHANN SEBASTIAN BACH's organ works, published in N.Y. from 1912 to 1914.

As a composer Widor wrote copiously in many forms but is best known for his solo ORGAN music, especially the 10 "symphonies" (SUITES, 1876–1900). A master organ virtuoso, he won great renown for his performances of Bach and for his inspired IMPROVISATIONS. Other Widor organ works include the *Suite latine* (1927), *Three nouvelles pièces* (1934), and eight SONATAS. He also composed three OPERAS, two BALLETS, incidental music, five SYMPHONIES—including three with organ—two piano CONCERTOS, one cello concerto, and other orchestral works. He also composed chamber works, piano music, and sacred and secular vocal works, with instrumental and orchestral accompaniment. Widor also wrote books on music history and performance.

Wieck, Clara Josephine. *See* SCHUMANN, CLARA (JOSEPHINE) WIECK.

Wieck, (Johann Gottlob) **Friedrich.** *See* SCHUMANN, CLARA (JOSEPHINE) WIECK.

PEOPLE IN MUSIC

Wieniawski, Henryk (Henri), famous Polish violinist, teacher, and composer; b. Lublin, July 10, 1835; d. Moscow, March 31, 1880. His mother, Regina Wolff-Wieniawska, was a talented pianist. Henryk began training with Jan Hornziel and Stanislaw Serwaczynski in Warsaw.

Upon the advice of his mother's brother, Edouard Wolff, who lived in France, Henryk was taken to Paris, where he entered the Conservatory at the age of eight. In his second year he entered the advanced class of Lambert Massart. At the age of 11 he graduated with first prize in violin, an unprecedented event in the annals of the Paris Conservatory.

After further private studies with Massart from 1846 to 1848, Wieniawski made his Paris debut in 1848, in a concert accompanied by his brother at the piano. He gave his first concert in St. Petersburg shortly thereafter, playing four more concerts there. He then played in Finland and the Baltic provinces. After several successful appearances in Warsaw, he returned in 1849 to Paris, where he studied composition with Hippolyte Collet at the Paris Conservatory, graduating in 1850.

From 1851 to 1853 Wieniawski gave about 200 concerts in Russia with his brother. He also devoted much time to composition. By age 18, he had composed and published his virtuoso First Violin Concerto, which he played with extraordinary success in Leipzig that same year. In 1858 he appeared with ANTON RUBINSTEIN in Paris and in 1859 in the Beethoven Quartet Society concerts in London, where he appeared as both violist and violinist.

In 1860 Wieniawski went to St. Petersburg and was named solo violinist to the czar, and also concertmaster of the orchestra and first violinist of the string quartet of the Russian Musical Society. He likewise served as professor of violin at the newly founded conservatory from 1862 to 1868. He continued to compose and introduced his greatly esteemed Second Violin Concerto in St. Petersburg in 1862, with Rubinstein conducting.

In 1872 Wieniawski toured the U.S. with Rubinstein. One of their featured works was LUDWIG VAN BEETHOVEN'S *KREUTZER* SONATA, which they performed about 70 times. When Rubinstein returned to Europe, Wieniawski continued his American tour. He returned to Europe in 1874, gave several concerts with Rubinstein in Paris, and in the same year succeeded HENRI VIEUXTEMPS as professor of violin at the Brussels Conservatory. He resigned in 1877 owing to an increasingly grave heart condition.

Wieniawski suffered a heart attack during a concert in Berlin on Nov. 11, 1878. However, he still agreed to play several concerts in Russia, making his farewell appearance in Odessa in April 1879. His last months were spent in Moscow, where he was taken to the home of Nadezhda von Meck, PIOTR ILYICH TCHAIKOVSKY'S patron, in 1880.

Wieniawski was married to Isobel Hampton, an Englishwoman. Their youngest daughter, Irene (1879–1932), wrote music under the pen name Poldowski.

Wieniawski was undoubtedly one of the greatest violinists of the 19th century. He possessed a VIRTUOSO technique and an extraordinary range of DYNAMICS. He was equally distinguished as a chamber music player. As a composer, he remains best known today for the two violin concertos and an outstanding set of etudes. He also composed numerous other orchestral works as well as pieces for solo or two violins.

His brother Jósef (b. Lublin, May 23, 1837; d. Brussels, Nov. 11, 1912) was a distinguished pianist, teacher, and composer. His nephew Adam Tadeusz Wieniawski (b. Warsaw, Nov. 27, 1879; d. Bydgoszcz, April 21, 1950) was a composer.

Will You Love Me in December as You Do in May? Song by Ernest R. Ball, 1905, with words by James Walker, destined to become mayor of N.Y. Walker selected it as his theme song for his political campaigns. It was eventually played at his funeral.

William Tell. Opera by GIOACCHINO ROSSINI, 1829, his last stage work, first performed in Paris under the French title *Guillaume Tell.* The opera is rarely performed in its entirety, but its overture is an extremely popular concert piece; its final section was the theme for *The Lone Ranger* radio and television series.

William Tell is a Swiss patriot and a remarkable archer. The brutal governor of the province tests his marksmanship by ordering Tell to split, with an arrow, an apple placed on the head of Tell's young son. William passes the test, then turns the weapon on the tyrant and kills him with a single shot.

Williams, "Cootie" (Charles Melvin), African-American jazz trumpeter and bandleader; b. Mobile, Ala., July 24, 1908; d. N.Y., Sept. 15, 1985. Williams took trumpet lessons with Charles Lipskin. He made his way to N.Y. and joined groups led by Chick Webb and Fletcher Henderson. From 1929 to 1940 he was a member of DUKE ELLINGTON'S

PEOPLE IN MUSIC

band. After working with BENNY GOODMAN in 1940–41, he led his own groups until rejoining Ellington's band in 1962. He left in 1975 but continued to perform until 1983. He was one of the leading JAZZ trumpeters of his era, equally adept at open and muted playing.

Williams, (Hiram) **Hank,** American country music singer, guitarist, and songwriter; b. Georgiana, Ala., Sept. 17, 1923; d. Oak Hill, Va., Jan. 1, 1953. Williams sang church hymns and learned to play organ at a very early age, then took guitar lessons from a black street singer. At 12 he won a prize in an amateur contest in Montgomery, Alabama, singing his own song, *W.P.A. Blues.* At 14 he formed his own band, Hank Williams and His Drifting Cowboys.

PEOPLE IN MUSIC

In 1946 Williams went to Nashville, and in 1949 he joined the famous GRAND OLE OPRY there, where he was an instant success with his rendition of *Lovesick Blues.* Its recording sold over a million copies. Williams's yodeling on this recording was an updated version of Jimmie Rodgers's popular style, and it became his trademark. He was also among the first country musicians to feature a STEEL GUITAR in his band, whose singing sound was also greatly popular among fans.

In 1950 he put out several recordings of his own songs, *Long Gone Lonesome Blues, I Just Don't Like This Kind of Livin', Why Don't You Love Me?,* and *Moanin' the Blues,* which were all successful. His subsequent releases were *Hey, Good Lookin'; Your Cheatin' Heart; Move It on Over; Cold, Cold Heart;* and *Jambalaya (on the Bayou).*

However, hard touring, heavy drinking, and a painful back problem—which led to an addiction to pain-killing drugs—took their toll on Williams's health. He died en route to a performance on New Year's Eve 1952.

Williams's son, (Randall) Hank Williams, Jr. (b. Shreveport, La., May 26, 1949), is also a successful country-western singer, guitarist, and songwriter. His career was also hampered by alcohol and drug problems. In 1975 he sustained severe injuries while mountain climbing, but he eventually resumed his career. Williams is one of the few sons of a popular performer who has established a long career based solely on his own merits as a performer and songwriter.

Williams, John (Christopher), remarkable Australian guitarist; b. Melbourne, April 24, 1941. He first studied with his father, the guitarist Leonard Williams. When he was 14 he performed in London, then took guitar lessons with AN-DRÉS SEGOVIA at the Accademia Chigiana in Siena from 1957 to 1959. In 1958 he made his formal debut at London's Wigmore Hall. From 1960 to 1973 he was a professor of guitar at the Royal College of Music in London. Following successful tours to the Soviet Union in 1962 and the U.S. and Japan in 1963, he performed with outstanding success on regular tours of Europe, North and South America, Australia, and the Far East. In 1980 he was made an Officer of the Order of the British Empire. In 1988 he appeared in the London Promenade Concerts with the National Youth Jazz Orchestra. In 1989, and again in 1994, he toured in the U.S. In 1995 he toured the Far East and also gave recitals in Europe. In 1997 he played concerts in Chicago, N.Y., China, Greece, and Scandinavia.

Williams's repertoire is truly egalitarian in its scope. While he is admired for his performances of the standard works for the guitar, he has done much to expand the repertoire by giving premieres of scores by Leo Brouwer, ANDRÉ PREVIN, Peter Schulthorpe, TŌRU TAKEMITSU, and Nigel Westlake. In addition, he has found success in JAZZ and POP genres.

Williams, John (Towner), enormously successful American composer and conductor; b. N.Y., Feb. 8, 1932. Williams grew up in a musical atmosphere, his father being a film studio musician. He began piano lessons and later learned to play trombone, trumpet, and clarinet.

In 1948 the family moved to Los Angeles, where he studied orchestration with Robert van Epps at Los Angeles City College and composition privately with MARIO CASTEL-NUOVO-TEDESCO. He also took piano lessons with Josef Lhévinne at the Juilliard School of Music in N.Y.

Williams began his career as a composer, arranger, and conductor for films and television. He wrote the film SCORES, rich in sounding brass and tinkling cymbals, for *Close Encounters of the Third Kind, Superman, The Empire Strikes Back, Raiders of the Lost Ark, E.T. The Extraterrestrial,* and *Re-*

turn of the Jedi. He won Academy Awards for *Fiddler on the Roof* (1971), *Jaws* (1975), and *Star Wars* (1977). The record albums for these background scores sold into the millions.

Among his nonfilm works are *Essay* for strings (1966), Symphony (1966), *Sinfonietta* for wind ensemble (1968), Concerto for flute, strings, and PERCUSSION (1969), Violin Concerto (1974–76), Tuba Concerto (1985), *Celebration Fanfare* for orchestra (1985), *The Five Sacred Trees,* CONCERTO for bassoon and strings (1992–94), and Cello Concerto (1994).

In 1980 Williams was chosen conductor of the Boston Pops Orchestra, succeeding the late ARTHUR FIEDLER, who had held that post for almost 50 years. Williams declared openly that no one could hope to equal Fiedler in charisma and showmanship, but he said he would try his best to bridge the gap. He largely succeeded, and diversified his appeal to Boston Pops audiences by playing selections from his own sparkling film scores. He stepped down from his post in 1993.

Williams, Mary Lou (born Mary Elfrieda Scruggs), African-American jazz pianist, composer, and arranger; b. Atlanta, May 8, 1910; d. Durham, N.C., May 28, 1981. Williams began her career as a pianist in Kansas City with the saxophonist Andy Kirk (to whom she was married for a time). In 1931 she became pianist and arranger for Kirk's Twelve Clouds of Joy band and provided him with such songs as *Walkin' and Swingin', Twinklin', Cloudy,* and *Little Joe from Chicago.* She then worked with DUKE ELLINGTON, BENNY GOODMAN, and others.

PEOPLE IN MUSIC

In 1945 Williams composed the BEBOP hit *In the Land of Oo-Bla-Dee* for DIZZY GILLESPIE. After becoming a Roman Catholic in the early '50s, she composed a number of religious works, including *St. Martin de Porres* and three MASSES. Her *Music for Peace* became popularly known as "Mary Lou's Mass." In 1977 she was named artist-in-residence at Duke University in Durham. She died in 1981.

Williams, Ralph Vaughan. *See* VAUGHAN WILLIAMS, RALPH.

Wills, Bob (James Robert), American country music singer, fiddler, bandleader, and songwriter; b. near Kosse, Tex.,

PEOPLE IN MUSIC

March 6, 1905; d. Fort Worth, May 13, 1975. Wills first took up the MANDOLIN, then began to play the FIDDLE. Through his association with local black musicians, he learned BLUES and JAZZ as well. In 1928 he organized his own group, the Wills Fiddle Band.

In 1930 the vocalist Milton Brown joined the group, which also included Wills's brother Durwood as guitarist. Within a year, they were performing on radio under the sponsorship of Burrus Mills as the Light Crust Doughboys. In 1932 they recorded together, but shortly thereafter Brown left to form his own group and was replaced by Tommy Duncan, who would become Wills's longtime lead singer. The group lost their affiliation with Burrus Mills in 1933.

After settling in Tulsa, Oklahoma, in 1934, Wills became a fixture on station KVOO. His group was now known as the Texas Playboys. From 1942 he was active with the group on the West Coast, and also appeared in grade B cowboy films. He gained popularity with his composition *Take Me Back to Tulsa* and *San Antonio Rose*. In 1968 he was elected to the Country Music Hall of Fame.

PEOPLE IN MUSIC

Willson, (Robert Reiniger) **Meredith,** American flutist and composer of musicals; b. Mason City, Iowa, May 18, 1902; d. Santa Monica, Calif., June 15, 1984. Willson learned to play the flute as a child, then went to N.Y. and studied at the Damrosch Institute from 1919 to 1922 and received instruction in flute from Georges Barrère from 1920 to 1929. He was first flutist in JOHN PHILIP SOUSA's band from 1921 to 1923 and a member of the N.Y. Philharmonic from 1924 to 1929. He then became a musical director for various radio shows.

For the 30th anniversary of the San Francisco earthquake, Willson wrote a symphony, which he conducted in its first performance there in 1936. His second Symphony was first played by the Los Angeles Philharmonic in 1940. He wrote other symphonic works, band pieces, and a choral work, *Anthem of the Atomic Age.*

However, Willson devoted himself mainly to the composition of popular music, in which he revealed a triple talent as a performer, writer, and composer. He appeared as a comedian on a radio program, *The Big Show.* He engaged in comic banter with Tallulah Bankhead, closing with an inspirational hymn, *May the Good Lord Bless and Keep You,* which became popular as an anthem. Willson achieved his greatest triumph with his musical THE MUSIC MAN, for which he wrote book, lyrics, and music. It opened in late 1957 and became an immediate success. The show contained the ever-popular chorus *76 TROMBONES* and many other hits.

Willson's subsequent musicals were *The Unsinkable Molly Brown,* produced in late 1960, for which he wrote the musical score, and *Here's Love,* produced in 1963, an adaptation of the film *Miracle on 34th Street. The Music Man* and *The Unsinkable Molly Brown* were made into films.

Willson was also active as an arranger and orchestrator in Hollywood. He helped Charlie Chaplin in arranging the score for his anti-Fascist film, *The Great Dictator,* in 1940.

Wilson, Brian (Douglas). *See* BEACH BOYS, THE.

wind band (Ger. *Harmoniemusik;* Fr. *harmonie*). 1. A company of performers on WIND INSTRUMENTS. 2. The wind instruments in the orchestra; also, the players on, or parts written for, the same.

wind instruments (Ger. *Blaserinstrumente;* Fr. *instruments à vent*). Instruments whose tones are produced by wind (compressed air) blown through a tube. In the Western classical orchestra, these are divided into the WOODWIND and BRASS families.

In a score, onstage, or in the pit, these instruments are grouped together, highest member of each family at the top (with the exception of the HORN and SAXOPHONE, which are placed in the score between the two wind families).

While the modern woodwind family includes instruments made of metal and MOUTHPIECES with no, one, or two reeds, the brass family is more homogeneous: all are made of metal, have coiled tubing, a flared opening called a bell, and a cup or cuplike mouthpiece, and can use MUTES. The only unusual feature is the TROMBONE's having a slide rather than VALVES to change pitch.

The loudest members of the families are the OBOE and TRUMPET, and care must be taken with balancing the winds'

MUSICAL
INSTRUMENT

The organ is not usually considered a wind instrument, although it uses a hybrid wind-keyboard technology.

DYNAMIC levels. Horns and bassoons match well with each other in chordal writing, and in prevalve days the bassoons often stood in for the horns (for example, in LUDWIG VAN BEETHOVEN's Fifth Symphony, first movement). *See also* BRASS INSTRUMENTS; WOODWIND INSTRUMENTS.

wind machine (Ger. *Windmaschine*). An instrument designed to imitate the sound of a strong, whooshing wind gust. It usually is made up of a large barrel covered with cloth. When the barrel is rotated manually with the aid of a crank, the cloth rubs against a fixed piece of wood. This creates the windlike sound. Pitch and dynamic level can be altered by the speed of rotation.

Composers who have used the wind machine include RICHARD STRAUSS (*Alpine Symphony; Don Quixote*), MAURICE RAVEL (*Daphnis et Chloé*), DARIUS MILHAUD (*Les Choéphores*), ARNOLD SCHOENBERG (*Die Jakobsleiter*), and RALPH VAUGHAN WILLIAMS (*Sinfonia antartica*).

Winter Dreams. Title of PIOTR ILYICH TCHAIKOVSKY's First Symphony, 1868, in G minor, first performed in Moscow. The first two movements carry titles, *Dreams During a Winter Journey* and *Somber Land, Misty Land*. There follows a SCHERZO and FINALE.

PEOPLE IN MUSIC

Wittgenstein, Paul, Austrian-born American pianist; b. Vienna, Nov. 5, 1887; d. Manhasset, Long Island, N.Y., March 3, 1961. His brother was the famous philosopher Ludwig Wittgenstein. Paul studied with Malvine Brée, Theodor Leschetizky, and Josef Labor. He made his debut as a pianist in Vienna in 1913.

Serving in World War I, he lost his right arm at the Russian front, was a prisoner of war, and was repatriated in 1916. Wittgenstein developed a superb left-hand technique and soon began commissioning works specifically for single-hand. These included concertos from RICHARD STRAUSS, MAURICE RAVEL, SERGEI PROKOFIEV, ERICH KORNGOLD, BENJAMIN BRITTEN, and others. He gave the world premieres for all except the Prokofiev, which he found unsuitable.

After appearing in the major European musical centers and making an American tour in 1934, Wittgenstein emigrated to the U.S. in 1938, becoming a naturalized citizen eight years later. He taught privately in N.Y. from 1938 to 1960, and at the Ralph Wolfe Conservatory in New Rochelle from 1938 to 1943 and at Manhattanville College of the Sacred Heart from 1940 to 1945.

John Barchilon's novel *The Crown Prince* (1984) is based on Wittgenstein's career.

Wizard of Oz, The. The 1939 musical film with excellent songs by HAROLD ARLEN and E. Y. Harburg, based on the Frank Baum children's novel. There was an earlier stage version from 1903 with a difficult plot and songs, but it in no way equaled the later film and was quickly forgotten.

The film tells the story of Kansas-born Dorothy, who lives on a farm. Injured in a cyclone, she dreams she is transported to a wonderful kingdom called Oz (the film changes from stark black and white to vivid Technicolor at this point). There she encounters a good witch, who tells her that she must visit the Great Wizard in order to find her way back home again. Meanwhile, she encounters three others on the road to Oz, including a Cowardly Lion (who wants to be brave), a Tin Man (in search of a heart), and a Scarecrow (looking for a brain).

◄

Judy Garland is named "The Lollipop Queen" by some happy Munchkins in The Wizard of Oz, *1939. (Corbis-Bettmann)*

The trio happily "follow the yellow brick road" to Oz but encounter several obstacles on their trip. The Wicked Witch of the West (as opposed to her sister, the good witch of the East) seeks to thwart their plans. Eventually, she is killed by the forces of good. The four travelers reach Oz, discover the Wizard (who turns out to be something of a carnival huckster), and earn their prizes.

The score includes many memorable songs, particularly the beautiful OVER THE RAINBOW. It was sung by the incomparable JUDY GARLAND who portrayed Dorothy in the film.

Wohltemperiertes Klavier, Das. *See* WELL-TEMPERED CLAVIER, THE.

Wolf, Hugo (Filipp Jakob), famous Austrian composer, one of the greatest masters of the LIED; b. Windischgraz, Styria, March 13, 1860; d. Vienna, Feb. 22, 1903. His father, Philipp Wolf (1828–87), was a gifted musician from whom Hugo received piano and violin lessons at a very early age. He later played second violin in the family orchestra.

While attending the village primary school from 1865 to 1869, Wolf studied piano and theory with Sebastian Weixler. In 1870 he was sent to the Graz regional secondary school but left after a single semester. In 1871 he entered the St. Paul Benedictine Abbey in Carinthia, where he played violin, organ, and piano. In 1873 he was transferred to the Marburg secondary school and remained devoted to musical pursuits. In 1875 he went to Vienna, where he became a pupil

PEOPLE IN MUSIC

Hugo Wolf, c. 1880. (Michael Nicholson/Corbis) ▶

Hugo Wolf

at the conservatory, studying piano, harmony, and composition.

When RICHARD WAGNER visited Vienna in 1875 Wolf went to see him, bringing along some of his compositions. The fact that Wagner received him at all, and even said a few words of encouragement, gave Wolf great impetus toward further composition. But he was incapable of submitting himself to academic discipline, and soon difficulties arose between him and the conservatory authorities. He openly expressed his dissatisfaction with the teaching, which led to his expulsion in 1877.

Wolf then returned to his native town, but after a few months at home he decided to go to Vienna again, where he managed to support himself by giving music lessons to children in the homes of friends. By that time he was composing diligently, writing songs to texts by his favorite poets: Goethe, Lenau, and Heine.

Wolf had an unhappy encounter with JOHANNES BRAHMS in 1879, who advised Wolf to study COUNTERPOINT before attempting to compose. This embittered the young musician, and he became determined to follow his own musical inclinations without seeking further advice. That same year he met Melanie (née Lang) Köchert, whose husband, Heinrich Köchert, was the Vienna court jeweler. By 1884 she had become Wolf's mistress and a great inspiration in his creative work.

After serving a brief and unhappy tenure as second conductor in Salzburg in 1881, Wolf returned to Vienna in 1882. The following year, he became music critic of the weekly *Wiener Salonblatt.* He took this opportunity to indulge his professional frustration by attacking those not sympathetic to new trends in music. He was particularly critical of Brahms, thus antagonizing the influential Eduard Hanslick and other admirers of Brahms. But he also formed a coterie of staunch friends who had faith in his ability.

However, Wolf was singularly unsuccessful in his repeated attempts to secure performances for his works. He submitted a string quartet to the celebrated Rose Quartet, but it was rejected. Finally, Hans Richter accepted for the Vienna Philharmonic Wolf's SYMPHONIC POEM *Penthesilea,* but the public performance was a fiasco, and Wolf even accused Richter of deliberately sabotaging the work. Later he reorchestrated the score, eliminating certain crudities of the early version.

In 1887 Wolf resigned as music critic of the *Wiener Salonblatt* and devoted himself entirely to composition. He became convinced that he was creating the greatest masterpieces of song since FRANZ SCHUBERT and ROBERT SCHUMANN, and stated his conviction in no uncertain terms in his letters. Wolf's incredible egotism may have masked his own insecurity about his talents and the constant criticism he faced. Yet he was about to experience a turn for the better in the critical reaction to his works.

In 1888 Rosa Papier became the first artist to sing one of Wolf's songs in public. Shortly thereafter, Wolf himself played and sang several of his songs at a meeting of the Vienna Wagner-Verein. In late 1888 he made his public debut as accompanist in his songs to the tenor Ferdinand Jager, which proved the first of many highly successful recitals by both artists. Soon Wolf's name became known in Germany. He presented concerts of his own works in Berlin, Darmstadt, Mannheim, and other musical centers. He completed the first part of his great cycle of 22 songs, *Italienisches Liederbuch,* in 1891, and composed the second part (24 songs) in five weeks, in the spring of 1896.

While Wolf could compose songs with a facility and degree of excellence that were truly astounding, he labored painfully on his orchestral works. An early symphony was never completed, nor was a violin concerto, and the work on *Penthesilea* took him a disproportionately long time.

In 1895 Wolf began to compose his opera, *Der Corregidor.* Working feverishly, he completed the vocal SCORE with piano accompaniment in a few months. The orchestration took him a much longer time. *Der Corregidor* had its premiere in Mannheim in 1896. While initially a success, the opera failed to find wide appeal and was soon dropped from the repertoire. Wolf subsequently revised the score, and its new version was brought out in Strasbourg in 1898. He never completed his second opera, *Manuel Venegas,* although fragments were presented in concert in Mannheim in 1903, a week after his death.

In the meantime Wolf's fame grew. A Hugo Wolf-Verein was organized at Berlin in 1896 and did excellent work in furthering performances of Wolf's songs in Germany. Even more effective was a similar group in Vienna, founded by Michel Haberlandt in 1897 (and disbanded in 1906).

As appreciation of Wolf's remarkable gifts as a master of lied began to find recognition abroad, tragedy struck. By early 1897 he was a very ill man, both mentally and physically. According to Wolf, GUSTAV MAHLER promised to use his position as director of the Vienna Court Opera to mount a production of *Der Corregidor*. When the production failed to materialize, Wolf's mental condition disintegrated. He declared to friends that Mahler had been relieved of his post and that he, Wolf, had been appointed in his stead.

In the fall of 1897 Wolf was placed in a private mental institution. After a favorable remission, he was discharged in early 1898 and traveled in Italy and Austria. After his return to Vienna, symptoms of mental derangement manifested themselves in even greater degree. In the fall of 1898 he attempted suicide by throwing himself into the Traunsee in Traunkirchen but was saved and placed in the Lower Austrian provincial asylum in Vienna. He remained in confinement, gradually lapsing into complete insanity.

Wolf died at the age of 42 and was buried near the graves of Schubert and Beethoven in Vienna's Central Cemetery. A monument was unveiled in the fall of 1904. His mistress plunged to her death from the fourth-floor window of her home in Vienna in 1906.

Wolf's significance in music history rests on his songs, about 300 in number, many of them published posthumously. He certainly earned the nickname "the Wagner of the lied." Wolf accepted the Wagnerian idiom through natural affinity as well as by clear choice. The elaboration of the accompaniment and the incorporation of the vocal line into the contrapuntal scheme of the whole are Wagnerian traits. But with these external similarities, Wolf's dependence on Wagner's models ceases.

In his intimate penetration of the poetic spirit of the text, Wolf appears a legitimate successor to Schubert and Schumann. Wolf's songs are symphonic poems in miniature, artistically designed and admirably arranged for voice and piano, the combination in which he was a master.

Wolf usually grouped his lieder by poet or chronology. Only two cycles have a programmatic concept: *Spanisches Liederbuch,* 44 songs based on translations of Spanish poetry by Geibel and Heyse (1889–90), and *Italienisches Liederbuch,* 46 songs based on translations of anonymous Italian poems by Heyse, in two books: 22 songs (1890–91) and 24 songs (1896). Individual collections are based on the poetry of Mörike (1889), Eichendorff (1889), Goethe (1890), Keller (1891), and others. About 90 lieder unpublished during his lifetime survive.

Besides lieder, Wolf composed some choral works, an opera, and some symphonic works, many incomplete.

wolf tone (Ger. *Wolfton*). Undesirable sound effects, produced in the course of playing an instrument in the usual manner, due to imperfect construction.

A particular PITCH will sound much louder or softer than its neighbors, due to an irregularity of RESONANCE that enhances or dampens the sound. String instruments are most likely to succumb to this effect. Cellists offset the effect by playing slightly out of tune, squeezing the instrument between their knees, or using a *wolf mute* behind the bridge. Other instruments susceptible to the wolf were the old BASSOON, the early VALVE HORN, and the pipe ORGAN of any era.

Wolff, Christian, French-born American composer and teacher; b. Nice, March 8, 1934. Wolff's family came to the U.S. in 1941, and he became a naturalized citizen in 1946. He studied piano with Grete Sultan from 1949 to 1951 and composition with JOHN CAGE in 1950–51. Wolff then pursued training in classical languages at Harvard University, receiving a bachelor of arts degree in 1955. After studying Italian literature and classics at the University of Florence in 1955–56, he returned to Harvard, earning his Ph.D. in comparative literature in 1963.

From 1962 to 1970 Wolff taught classics at Harvard, and in 1971 he joined the faculty of Dartmouth College to teach classics, comparative literature, and music. He was made professor of music and of classics there in 1978. He also was a guest lecturer at various institutions of higher

PEOPLE IN MUSIC

learning and contributed articles on literature and music to many publications.

Wolff evolved a curiously static method of composition, using drastically restricted numbers of PITCHES. He used three different pitches in his *Duo for Violinist and Pianist* (1961), four in the trio for flute, cello, and trumpet (1951), and nine in *For Piano I* (1952). Wolff used arithematic patterns to structure his rhythms, and also expressively used RESTS (or silence) within his compositions.

Beginning in 1957, Wolff introduced into his works various degrees of free choice. Sometimes players are required to react to the musical activities of their partners according to spontaneous and unanticipated cues. INDETERMINATE works with choice of instrumentation include *For 5 or 10 Players* for any instruments (1962); *For 1, 2, or 3 People* for any sound-producing means (1964); *Pairs* for any two, four, six, or eight players (1968); *Prose Collection* for variable numbers of players, found and constructed materials, instruments, and voices (1968–71); *Changing the System* for eight or more instruments, voices, and PERCUSSION (1972–73); and *Isn't This a Time* for any saxophone or multiple REEDS (1982).

Among Wolff's chamber works are *Summer* for string quartet (1961); *Wobbly Music* for chorus, keyboard, guitars, and at least two melody instruments (1975–76); *Rock About, Instrumental, Starving to Death on a Government Claim* for violin and viola (1979–80); *Peace March 1* for flute (1983–84), *2* for flute, clarinet, cello, percussion, and piano (1984), and *3* for flute, cello, and percussion (1984); *Leaning Forward* for SOPRANO, BARITONE, clarinet, and cello (1988); and *Emma* for viola, cello, and piano (1989).

Wolff's piano works (solo unless indicated) include *For Piano* I–II (1952, 1953), *Duo for Pianists* I–II (1957, 1958), *For Piano with Preparations* (1959), *Bread & Roses* (1976), *3 Studies* (1976), *Hay Una Mujer Desaparecida* (1979), Preludes (1981), *Piano Song, "I Am a Dangerous Woman"* (1983), and *Rosas* for piano and percussion (1990).

Wolf-Ferrari (born Wolf), **Ermanno,** Italian opera composer; b. Venice, Jan. 12, 1876; d. there, Jan. 21, 1948.

PEOPLE IN MUSIC

Wolf-Ferrari's father was a well-known painter of German descent, and his mother was Italian. About 1895 he added his mother's maiden name to his surname.

Wolf-Ferrari began piano study as a small child but also showed a talent for art. After studying art at the Accademia di Belle Arti in Rome in 1891–92, he went to Munich to continue his training, then turned to music and studied COUNTERPOINT at the Akademie der Tonkunst until 1895. In 1899 he returned to Venice, where his ORATORIO *La Sulamite* was successfully performed. This was followed a year later by the production of his first major opera, *Cenerentola,* which initially proved a failure. However, its revised version for Bremen, produced in 1902, was well received and established his reputation as a composer for the theater.

From 1903 to 1909 Wolf-Ferrari was director of the Liceo Benedetto Marcello in Venice. He then devoted himself mainly to composition. He obtained his first unqualified success with the production of the comic opera *Le donne curiose* in Munich in 1903. The next opera, *I quattro rusteghi,* was produced there three years later and was also well received. There followed his little masterpiece, *Il segreto di Susanna,* in 1909, a one-act OPERA BUFFA in the style of the Italian VERISMO. Turning toward grand opera, Wolf-Ferrari wrote *I gioielli della Madonna.* It was performed in Berlin in 1911 and soon became a repertoire piece everywhere.

Wolf-Ferrari continued to compose, but his later operas failed to match the appeal of his early creations. The most successful of his later works were *Sly, ovvero La leggenda del dormiente risvegliato* (1927) and *Il campiello* (1936). From 1939 to 1945 Wolf-Ferrari returned to teaching, becoming a professor of composition at the Salzburg Mozarteum.

In addition to his operas, Wolf-Ferrari wrote popular orchestral works, including Serenade for strings (c.1893), Kammersymphonie (1901), *Idillio-concertino* for oboe, two horns, and strings (1933), and *Suite-concertino* for bassoon, two horns, and strings (Rome, 1933). Among his chamber works are three violin SONATAS (1895, 1901, 1943), two piano trios (c.1897, 1900), Piano Quintet (1900), and solo piano pieces. His vocal compositions include *La vita nuova,* CANTATA (1901), as well as other large and small choral works.

Wolpe, Stefan, German-American composer and teacher; b. Berlin, Aug. 25, 1902; d. N.Y., April 4, 1972. Wolpe studied theory at the Berlin Hochschule für Musik from 1919 to 1924. After graduation he became associated with choral and theatrical groups in Berlin, promoting social causes and composing songs on revolutionary themes.

PEOPLE IN MUSIC

With the advent of the anti-Semitic Nazi regime in 1933, Wolpe went to Vienna, where he took lessons with ANTON WEBERN. A year later, he traveled to Palestine, where he taught at the Jerusalem Conservatory. In 1938 he emigrated to the U.S., where he devoted himself mainly to teaching. He was on the faculty of the Settlement Music School in Philadelphia from 1939 to 1942, the Philadelphia Academy of Music from 1949 to 1952, Black Mountain College, North Carolina, from 1952 to 1956, and Long Island University from 1957 to 1968. He also taught privately. Among Wolpe's students were ELMER BERNSTEIN, Ezra Laderman, Ralph Shapey, DAVID TUDOR, and MORTON FELDMAN.

Wolpe was married successively to Ola Okuniewska, a painter (1927); Irma Schoenberg (1902–84), a Romanian pianist (1934); and Hilda Morley, a poet (1948). In 1966 he was elected a member of the National Institute of Arts and Letters. His last years were made increasingly difficult by Parkinson's disease. He contributed numerous articles to German and American music magazines.

In his early, social protest compositions, Wolpe drew on FOLK SONGS and JAZZ rhythms, along with traditional harmonies, to appeal to the "common man." Later, he added to this musical stew elements of modern composition, including ATONALITY and many abrupt shifts in METER and DYNAMICS. He also drew on traditional Jewish cantorial music for inspiration. Remarkably, the very breadth of these influences contributed to his clearly identifiable style.

He wrote theatrical works, the best known being the lyric scene *Anna Blume* for musical clown and piano (based on a painting by the German artist Kurt Schwitters; 1929). He also wrote incidental music for two Bertolt Brecht plays: *The Good Woman of Setzuan* (1953) and *The Exception and the Rule* (1960). His orchestral works include *The Man from Midian*, ballet SUITE (1942), Symphony (1955–56), and Chamber Piece Nos. 1 and 2 for 14 players (1964; 1965–66).

Wolpe was prolific as a composer of chamber music. Most of his pieces are scored for between one and four instruments, with larger works including the *Quintet with Voice* for BARITONE, clarinet, horn, cello, harp, and piano (1956–57), *Piece for 2 Instrumental Units* for flute, oboe, violin, cello, double bass, and PERCUSSION (1962–63), and Piece for trumpet and seven instruments (1971).

Wolpe's early piano works drew on folk melodies and harmonies. His *4 Studies on Basic Rows* from 1935–36 was his breakthrough to contemporary techniques. Subsequent important works include *Toccata in Three Parts* (1941), *Battle Piece* (1943–47), *Enactments* for three pianos (1950–53), *Form* (1959), and *Form IV: Broken Sequences* (1969). Wolpe's unjustly neglected songs have a wide breadth of subjects and texts, setting Hölderlin, Fontaine, Tagore, Kokoschka, Mayakovsky, Becher, Albert Einstein, and biblical excerpts.

PEOPLE IN MUSIC

Wonder, Stevie (born Steveland Judkins Hardaway), phenomenally successful African-American soul singer, keyboardist, and songwriter; b. Saginaw, Mich., May 13, 1950. Other sources state that he was born Steveland Judkins or Steveland Morris.

Blinded in infancy by insufficient oxygen in an incubator, Stevie learned to play drums and piano. He improvised his first song, *Lonely Boy,* at the age of 10, and at 12 composed *Fingertips,* which became a hit. He signed with BERRY GORDY, JR., at Motown Records in 1961. Gordy initially promoted him as a virtuoso harmonica player, emphasizing his exceptionally young age by billing him as "Little Stevie Wonder."

In his first recordings, Wonder was a consistent hitmaker who took the Motown teenage formula to its heights. He recorded BOB DYLAN's *Blowin' in the Wind,* Tony Bennett's hit *For Once in My Life,* the BEATLES' *We Can Work It Out,* and his own *Uptight, I Was Made to Love Her, My Cherie Amour,* and *Signed, Sealed, Delivered I'm Yours.* He also appeared in the films *Muscle Beach Party* and *Bikini Beach.*

At age 21, Wonder evolved a new approach to composition, based on SYNTHESIZERS, complete control over his own work, and an interest in the African-American experience.

Beginning with the album *Music of My Mind* in 1972, Wonder showed a greater maturity and musical sophistication. Among the classic hits were *Superstition, Living for the City, You Are the Sunshine of My Life, You Haven't Done Nothing, Higher Ground, Boogie On Reggae Woman, Isn't She Lovely, I Wish,* and *Sir Duke* (a tribute to DUKE ELLINGTON).

After a nearly fatal automobile accident and the breakup of his marriage in the late 1970s, Wonder returned to form. He created memorable songs in his original, pop-oriented style (*I Just Called To Say I Love You* from the soundtrack *The Woman in Red* and *Part-Time Lover*) and in his new, political-flavored mode (*It's Wrong [Apartheid]* and the rap-influenced *Master Blaster [Jammin']*).

Wonder collaborated with PAUL MCCARTNEY on *Ebony and Ivory* (1982) and later with MICHAEL JACKSON on *Get It* (1987). He wrote the soundtrack to Spike Lee's *Jungle Fever* in the mid-'90s.

Wonder has also devoted much time, energy, and money to social causes. He added his voice to a campaign against drunk driving, donated to AIDS and cancer research, and contributed to U.S. for Africa's charity record, *We Are the World,* in 1985.

Happy Birthday from 1980 was part of Wonder's campaign to make Martin Luther King, Jr.'s birthday a national holiday.

Wonderful Town. Musical by LEONARD BERNSTEIN, 1953. Eileen comes to N.Y. from Ohio with her sister. They go through hilarious encounters with various men, including visiting sailors of the Brazilian navy. The nostalgic ballad *Ohio,* in which the sisters bemoan their decision to leave their home state, became a perennial favorite.

woodblocks. *See* CHINESE BLOCKS.

MUSICAL
INSTRUMENT

woodwind(s) (Ger. *Holzblasinstrumente*). Group of instruments in the orchestra originally made of wood and played by blowing (FLUTE, PICCOLO, OBOE, ENGLISH HORN, CLARINET, BASS CLARINET, BASSOON, CONTRABASSOON). In modern times, flutes and piccolos are made of metal, but they are still included in the woodwind category. The SAXOPHONE, a hybrid metal wind instrument, has a reed and clarinet-style key system. It too is classified in the woodwind category. There are some special and rarely used instruments that belong to this group: the once popular RECORDER, the alto and bass flutes, and the HECKELPHONE (a baritone oboe).

Woodwind quintet, a somewhat inaccurate name for an ensemble consisting of four woodwind instruments (flute, oboe, clarinet, bassoon) and the modern valve (French) horn, a brass instrument.

Woody Woodpecker. Song by George Tibbles and Ramey Idriss, 1947, the theme song of a cartoon character created by Walter Lantz. Woody's rapid fanfare figure, immediately recognizable to cartoon aficionados everywhere, captures his zany character perfectly.

PEOPLE IN MUSIC

Work, Henry Clay, American composer of popular songs; b. Middletown, Conn., Oct. 1, 1832; d. Hartford, June 8, 1884. Work was a printer by trade and entirely self-taught in music. His first success was *We Are Coming, Sister Mary* (1853). His subsequent well-known songs include *Kingdom Coming* (1862), *Come Home, Father* (1864), *Wake, Nicodemus!* (1864), *Marching through Georgia* (1865), and *Grandfather's Clock* (1876).

Worms Crawl In, The. Anonymous morbid vermicular ditty, first published in 1923, known to virtually everyone in the English-speaking world. The tune, in minor mode and jig time, is also called *The Hearse Song.*

Wouldn't It Be Loverly? Song by ALAN JAY LERNER and FREDERICK LOEWE, 1956, from the musical MY FAIR LADY. The flower girl Eliza Doolittle dreams of how "loverly" it would be to have warm clothes and a clean, dry place to live.

Wozzeck. Opera by ALBAN BERG, 1925, first performed in Berlin. The LIBRETTO is extracted from *Woyzeck,* an unfinished play by George Büchner, written in 1836.

Wozzeck is a private in the German army, bedeviled by his cruel superiors. A drum major openly brags of his success in seducing Wozzeck's common-law wife, Marie. Provoked beyond endurance, Wozzeck stabs Marie to death. He then goes insane and, trying to wash the blood from his hands, walks into the pond and drowns. The opera concludes with a poignant scene when their child rocks on his wooden horse, not knowing of the tragedy.

Wozzeck is a milestone in the history of modern musical theater. It is a tour de force of formal organization, the entire score being programmed as a series of BAROQUE dance forms and variations. The musical style is tensely ATONAL.

Although *Wozzeck* is now acknowledged as a modern masterpiece, at its first performances German music critics described it as a cacophonous monstrosity.

Curiously, another composer, Manfred Gurlitt (1890–1972), chose the same subject independently from Berg for an opera. His *Wozzeck* was produced in Bremen, 1926, four months after Berg's masterpiece, but could not withstand the comparison and soon faded from the musical scene.

One critic described Berg as being a member of "the shock troops of atonalists … a musical swindler." Another simply called *Wozzeck* "ear torture."

Wreck of the Old 97, The. Song by various authors, 1924, based on the melody of HENRY CLAY WORK's *The Ship That Never Returned* from 1865. It became a famous railroad ballad, commemorating a tragic train wreck.

Wunderbar. Song by COLE PORTER, 1948, from the musical *Kiss Me Kate.* The song parodies the typical Viennese WALTZ, with plenty of extra schmaltz.

Wunderkind. A very talented young musician, heralded as a VIRTUOSO.

No art, no science is revealed at an age so early as that of musical talent. When an anxious and hopeful mother (less frequently, father) notices that her darling child bangs on the keyboard of an upright piano (rarely a baby grand in such families), she perceives the breath of musical genius. The first symptom of *Wunderkindheit* is the possession of PERFECT PITCH, but possession of this precious gift does not guarantee a successful musical career.

Most Wunderkinder are taught piano or violin. There are few Wunderkinder of the cello, and hardly any of a wind instrument. Wunderkinder are often exhibited by their parents as wonders of nature. They are kept chronologically young by cutting down their ages as they outgrow short pants. WOLFGANG AMADEUS MOZART's father advertised his genius son as being eight years old during several successive years. One of the most durable child prodigies was the violinist JASCHA HEIFETZ. He made a sensational American debut at the age of 16 in Carnegie Hall, N.Y. The American Society for the Prevention of Cruelty to Children intervened against the exploitation of Josef Hofmann, who played a LUDWIG VAN BEETHOVEN piano concerto in N.Y. at the age of 11. He was forced to stop public appearances until the age of 16, but this hiatus did not prevent him from becoming one of the greatest master pianists of all time.

Child conductors are a great rarity, but at least one made a meteoric career early in the century: Willy Ferrero, an American-born Italian boy who toured Europe as a symphony conductor at the age of eight, arousing wonderment among audiences in France, Italy, and Russia. He ended his inglorious career as a provincial opera conductor. Another wunderkind conductor was LORIN MAAZEL, who led symphony concerts at the age of nine, eliciting comparisons with a trained seal. He survived, becoming one of the world's leading conductors.

Child composers are even more of a rarity than performing prodigies, Mozart being the greatest among them. FELIX MENDELSSOHN achieved a fantastic mastery of musical composition at a very early age. FRANZ SCHUBERT wrote inspired songs at the age of 17. But neither Beethoven nor JOHANNES BRAHMS were precocious composers. Nor were RICHARD WAGNER, PIOTR ILYICH TCHAIKOVSKY, and IGOR STRAVINSKY.

Erich Korngold drew comparisons with Mozart when he wrote a piano trio at the age of 12. He was introduced to GUSTAV MAHLER, who exclaimed, "Ein Genie! Ein Genie!" He wrote operas at the age of 18, but his star set precipitously in the musical firmament as he grew older.

The number of talented wunderkinder who never made it big is large. Ineffable sadness surrounds the parade of red-cheeked boys and girls whose pictures used to adorn the pages of European and American music magazines of the fin de siècle. Whatever happened to them? Not even the most dogged efforts of musicological bloodhounds could trace most of them to their final retreats in some unknown home for the retired.

Wunderlich, Fritz (Friedrich Karl Otto), noted German tenor; b. Kusel, Sept. 26 1930; d. Heidelberg, Sept. 17, 1966. Wunderlich received his education at the Freiburg Hochschule für Musik. He then sang opera in Stuttgart from 1955 to 1958, Frankfurt from 1958 to 1960, and Munich from 1960. In 1965 he appeared as Don Ottavio at London's Covent Garden.

While still a young man, Wunderlich gained a reputation as a LYRIC TENOR, his performances of WOLFGANG AMADEUS MOZART roles being especially acclaimed for their expressive power. His untimely death (in a mysterious accident) deprived the opera stage of one of its finest and most promising artists.

PEOPLE IN MUSIC

Wuorinen, Charles, American composer and pianist; b. N.Y., June 9, 1938. Wuorinen's family roots originated in Finland. His father was a professor of history at Columbia University, and the environment at home was highly intellectual.

Wuorinen received a fine academic training. He began to play piano and to compose, so they say, at the incredible age of five. He then took lessons in theory with Jack Beeson and VLADIMIR USSACHEVSKY. He received the Young Composers Award from the N.Y. Philharmonic when he was 16 years old. At 18 he wrote his earliest orchestral work, *Into the Organ Pipes and Steeples.* In 1956 he entered Columbia University as a student of Otto Luening, where he composed, in quick succession, three full-fledged symphonies (1958, 1958, 1959). He received his B.A. in 1961 and his M.A. in 1963.

Wuorinen co-founded the Group for Contemporary Music with Harvey Sollberger in 1962. In 1964 he was appointed an instructor in music at Columbia University and taught there until 1971, when he resigned in a flurry of angry controversy over the refusal of the faculty to grant him tenure. After serving as an adjunct lecturer at the University of South Florida in 1971–72, he was on the faculty of the Manhattan School of Music in N.Y. from 1972 to 1979. From 1973 to 1987 he was artistic director and chairman of the American Composers Orchestra in N.Y. In 1984 he be-

PEOPLE IN MUSIC

came a professor at Rutgers, the State University of New Jersey.

In 1968 and 1972 Wuorinen held Guggenheim fellowships. In 1969 he received a commission from Nonesuch Records for a work using synthesized sound, titled *Time's Encomium*. This work was awarded the Pulitzer Prize in music in 1970, an unprecedented honor for a work written expressly for a recording. Wuorinen later arranged it for a regular orchestra. In 1985 he was made a member of the American Academy and Institute of Arts and Letters.

From 1985 to 1987 Wuorinen served as composer-in-residence of the San Francisco Symphony. From 1989 to 1994 he was a visiting professor at the State University of N.Y. at Buffalo.

From his very first attempts in free composition Wuorinen asserted himself as a true representative of the modernistic second half of the 20th century. His works show the influence of IGOR STRAVINSKY's late period, when stark primitivism gave way to austere LINEAR COUNTERPOINT, as well as to EDGARD VARÈSE. He owes a more direct debt to the 12-TONE method of ARNOLD SCHOENBERG. Wuorinen's "time point system," in which pitch, time, and rhythmic divisions relate to one another, is a direct outgrowth of SERIALISM as developed by Schoenberg, ALBAN BERG, and ANTON WEBERN. Wuorinen's system lends itself to unlimited tonal and temporal arrangements, combinations, and permutations.

Enormously prolific, Wuorinen finds it possible to explore the entire vocabulary of serial composition. Most of his works are instrumental, but he also wrote a BAROQUE burlesque entitled *The W. of Babylon (or The Triumph of Love)*, in 1975. Its dramatis personae include an assortment of lascivious French noblemen and ignoble men and women of the 17th century, spouting lewd declarations and performing lecherous acts. Wuorinen wrote two other stage works: *The Politics of Harmony*, masque (1966–67), and *Delight of the Muses*, ballet (1991).

Wuorinen's many orchestral works, in addition to the three numbered symphonies, include two violin concertos (1958; 1971–72), and three piano concertos (1965–66; 1973–74, for amplified piano and orchestra; 1982–83). Among later orchestral works are *Galliard* for chamber orchestra (1987), *Five,* concerto for amplified cello and orchestra (1987), *Bamboula Beach,* overture (1987), *Machault Mon Chou* (1988), *Delight of the Muses* (1991; also as a ballet, 1992), Saxophone Quartet Concerto (1992), *The Mission of Virgil* (1993), and *Windfall* (1994).

Among Wuorinen's many chamber works are three wind quintets (1956, 1958, 1977); three numbered string quartets (1970–71; 1978–79; 1986–87); three trios for flute, cello, and piano (1961; 1962; 1972–73); chamber concertos for cello and 10 players (1963), for flute and 10 players (1965), and for tuba, 12 winds, and 12 drums (1969–70); *On Alligators* for eight instruments (1972); *Speculum speculi* for six players (1972); *Tashi* for clarinet, violin, cello, and piano (1975); *Archangel* for bass trombone and string quartet (1977); *Divertimento* for string quartet (1982); Concertino for 15 instruments (1982); *A Doleful Dompe on Deborah's Departure as well as Borda's Bawdy Badinage* for English horn, violin, and cello (1986); Saxophone Quartet (1992); Percussion Quartet (1994); Piano Quintet (1994); *Guitar Variations* (1994); and many solo instrumental works.

Wuorinen also composed various keyboard works (for piano, organ, and harpsichord) and many vocal works, including *The Celestial Sphere,* ORATORIO for chorus and orchestra (1980), MASS for soprano, chamber chorus, violin, three trombones, and organ (1982), *A Solis Ortu* for chorus (1988–89), *Genesis* for chorus and orchestra (1989), and *A Winter's Tale* for soprano and piano (1992; also for soprano, clarinet, horn, string trio, and piano, 1995).

Wynette, Tammy (real name, Wynette Pugh), American country music singer; b. Red Bay, Ala., May 5, 1942; d. Nashville, Tenn., April 6, 1998. Born in Alabama, Wynette was raised in rural Mississippi. She taught herself to play piano and guitar and began singing as a teenager. Her parents split up, and Wynette followed her mother to Birmingham, Alabama, where she worked in various jobs, including as a beautician. At age 17, she was married, although the marriage quickly ended. Meanwhile, she began singing locally, winning a spot on a local radio show and then on Porter Wagoner's popular syndicated country program.

As a helpful glossary to his music, Wuorinen published a manual, paradoxically entitled *Simple Composition,* in 1979.

PEOPLE IN MUSIC

Wynette came to Nashville in the mid-'60s looking to expand her career. She was heard by producer Billy Sherrill, who signed her to Epic records. The pair immediately hit it big with 1966's *Apartment Number 9*, followed immediately by *Your Good Girl's Gonna Go Bad*. Wynette specialized in big-voiced, slightly racy, and confrontational songs, culminating in her 1968 classic, *Stand By Your Man*.

That same year, Wynette began an off-again, on-again relationship with hard-living country singer GEORGE JONES. The two married in 1969 but divorced in 1975. Nonetheless, they recorded many successful duets together, even after their relationship crumbled. Their duo hits included 1973's *We're Gonna Hold On*, 1976's *Golden Ring*, and 1980's *Two-Story House*.

Wynette continued to produce solo hits through the '70s. By the '80s, she began suffering from a series of mysterious illnesses and was hospitalized several times through the decade. Meanwhile, she continued to tour and record as best as she could. In 1992 she had a freak hit in Europe when she was paired with the British techno-rock group KLF on the song *Justified and Ancient*. In 1996 she reteamed briefly with George Jones for a well-received album.

Wynette died in 1998.

PEOPLE IN MUSIC

Wyschnegradsky, Ivan (Alexandrovich), Russian composer, master of MICROTONAL music; b. St. Petersburg, May 16, 1893; d. Paris, Sept. 29, 1979. Wyschnegradsky studied composition at the St. Petersburg Conservatory. In 1920 he settled in Paris and devoted virtually his entire musical career to the exploration and creative realization of music in QUARTER TONES and other microtonal INTERVALS. He had a quarter-tone piano constructed for him and also published a guide, *Manuel d'harmonie à quarts de ton* (Manual of harmony in quarter-tones; Paris, 1932). In 1945 he presented in Paris a concert of his music, at which he conducted the first performance of his *Cosmos* for four pianos, with each pair tuned at quarter tones.

Bruce Mather took interest in Wyschnegradsky's music and gave a concert of his works at McGill University in Montreal that included three world premieres in 1977. With the exception of these rare concerts, Wyschnegradsky remains a figure of legend. He regarded his *La Journée de l'existence* (The Journey of Existence) for narrator, *ad libitum* chorus, and orchestra (to his own text; 1916–17) as his germinal work, opening the path to microtonal harmony. He dated this "awakening to ultrachromaticism" as having occurred in 1918. At his death he left sketches for a short opera in five scenes, *L'Éternel Étranger* (The eternal stranger), begun in 1939 but never completed. Also left unfinished was the ambitious *Polyphonie spatiale* (Spatial polyphony).

Wyschnegradsky wrote quarter-tone works for piano(s), string ensembles (including quartet), voice and piano, chorus, ONDES MARTENOT, and orchestra, works for 3rd-, 6th-, 8th-, 12th-, and 31st- (Fokker) tones, as well as works for standard EQUAL TEMPERAMENT. His *Ainsi parlait Zarathoustra* for orchestra (1929–30; arranged for four pianos, 1936) is considered his masterpiece. He also published several articles on ultrachromaticism and related topics.

Xenakis, Iannis, French composer and music theorist of Greek background; b. Brăila, Romania (of Greek parents), May 29, 1922. At the age of 10, Xenakis was taken by his family to Greece, where he began to study engineering. His schooling was interrupted when he became involved in the Greek resistance movement against the Nazi occupation forces. He was severely wounded in a skirmish in 1945 and lost sight in one eye. Shortly thereafter he was captured, but he managed to escape to the U.S.

In 1947 Xenakis went to Paris and later became a naturalized French citizen. He studied architecture with Le Corbusier and became his assistant from 1948 to 1960. During the same period he took lessons in composition with Heinz Honegger and DARIUS MILHAUD at the École Normale de Musique in Paris and with OLIVIER MESSIAEN at the Paris Conservatory from 1950 to 1953.

He aided Le Corbusier in the design of the Philips Pavilion at the 1958 World's Fair in Brussels, where he met EDGARD VARÈSE, who was then working on his *Poème electronique* for the exhibit. He assisted Varèse, and in return received stimulating advice on the creative potential of the electronic medium.

During his entire career, Xenakis strove to connect mathematical concepts with the organization of a musical composition, using the theory of sets, symbolic logic, and calculus. Unlike chance music, Xenakis's compositions have an internal logic, although it may be difficult for the listener to hear. He published a comprehensive volume dealing with these procedures, *Musiques formelles* (Paris, 1963; English translation, 1971, as *Formalized Music;* second edition, revised, 1992).

Xenakis was founder-director of the Centre d'Études Mathématiques et Automatiques Musicales in Paris in 1966, and founder and director of the Center for Mathematical and Automated Music at Indiana University in the U.S., where he served on the faculty from 1967 to 1972. From 1972 to 1974 he was associated with the Centre National de la Recherche Scientifique in Paris. He was a professor at the University of Paris from 1972 to 1989.

In 1974 Xenakis received the Ravel Medal of France, and in 1975 he was elected an honorary member of the American Academy of Arts and Letters. He received the Grand Prix National de la Musique of France in 1976, and in 1983 he was made a member of the Académie des Beaux-arts of France. In 1987 he received the Grand Prix for music of Paris.

Xenakis's influence on the development of advanced composition in Europe and America is considerable, and several composers have adopted his theories. Xenakis uses Greek words for the titles of virtually all of his works to stress the philosophical derivation of modern science and modern arts from classical Greek concepts. In some cases he uses computer symbols. His use of the computer led him to develop the computer drawing board, UPIC, which he used for both compositional and educational purposes.

Among his many works are:

Metastasis for 61 instruments (a harbinger of KRZYSZTOF PENDERECKI's cluster pieces; 1953–54)

Duel, musical game for two "antagonistic" conductors and two orchestras playing different material, mathematically based on game theory, with the audience determining the winning orchestra (1959)

ST/48-1,240162 (1956–62; ST=stochastic; 48=number of players; 1=first work for this contingent; 240162=24 January 1962, date on which the work was finally calculated by the IBM 7090 computer in Paris as programmed by Xenakis)

ST/10-1,080262 (1956–62; a string quartet version is entitled *ST/4*)

Atrées for 10 players (1956–62; written in homage to Blaise Pascal and calculated by the IBM 7090)

Strategie, musical game for two conductors and two orchestras (1959–62; Venice Festival, 1963; Bruno Maderna's orchestra won over that of Konstantin Simonovic)

Polla ta dhina (Many Are the Wonders) for children's choir and small orchestra, to a text from Sophocles's *Antigone* (1962)

Eonta (Ionian neuter plural of the present participle of the verb "to be"; the title is in Cypriot syllabic characters of Creto-Mycenean origin) for piano, two trumpets, and three tenor trombones (1963–64)

Terretektorh for 88 players scattered among the audience (1966)

Hibiki-Hana-Ma, 12-channel electroacoustic music distributed kinematically over 800 loudspeakers, for the Osaka EXPO '70 (1969–70; also a four-channel version)

Persepolis, light-and-sound spectacle with eight- or four-channel electroacoustic music (1971)

Retours—Windungen for 12 cellists (1976)

Chant des soleils for chorus, children's chorus, winds, and percussion (1983)

Tracées for orchestra (1988)

Sea Nymphs for chorus (1994)

Xenakis also composed many works for solo instruments and a variety of tape pieces.

Xerxes *See* SERSE.

Xochipilli. "Imagined Aztec music" by CARLOS CHÁVEZ, 1940, for wind quartet and Mexican PERCUSSION. It was first performed in N.Y. with the composer conducting.

MUSICAL
INSTRUMENT

---

xylophone (from Grk., wood sound; Ger. *Xylophon;* It. *xilofono, silofono*). A KEYBOARD PERCUSSION instrument with hardwood KEYS arranged and tuned like a piano; each key has a RESONATOR tuned to it. The keys are fastened horizon-

Xylophone player. (James P. O'Brien/University of Arizona School of Music)

tally to two stretched boards and played with two or more sticks or mallets.

Predecessors of the modern xylophone are found in many parts of the world, consisting of a few wooden bars of different lengths producing different tones. They were usually laid out on straw, and therefore became known among explorers as STROHFIEDEL (straw fiddle).

The early xylophone reached its greatest development in Southeast Asia in the 14th century. The instrument had spread westward into Africa, then the Americas, arriving in Europe by the 16th century. Gradually assuming its modern form, the European-American xylophone was imported into Latin America and Africa and became a kind of piano with wooden keys.

Many composers of the 20th century included the xylophone in their symphonic scores, including the *Sabre Dance* from *Gayané* by ARAM KHACHATURIAN. CAMILLE SAINT-SAËNS used it to great effect in his *Danse macabre,* to suggest the bone rattling of disembodied ghosts.

xylorimba (xylo-marimba; It. *silorimba*). A hybrid KEY-BOARD instrument, developed in the early 20th century, with a five-octave range encompassing that of the XYLOPHONE and MARIMBA. Xylorimbas were used in POPULAR MUSIC

The difference between a vibraphone and xylophone is the material from which the keys are made: metal (vibes) vs. wood (xylophone).

MUSICAL INSTRUMENT

and VAUDEVILLE in the 1920s and '30s (as the marimba-xylophone).

It has also been used by classical composers, including ALBAN BERG, IGOR STRAVINSKY, LUIGI DALLAPICCOLA, OLIVIER MESSIAEN, Peter Schat, and Roberto Gerhard.

Yankee Doodle. American patriotic song of mysterious origin. A reference to the title is found in a LIBRETTO to an American BALLAD OPERA produced in 1767. The earliest printing of the tune itself was in 1794.

During the American Revolution the song was already popular. For a long time the British believed that the tune was sung to mock the ragged American revolutionists, but Americans themselves played it as an expression of a certain swaggering confidence in their cause. Because the meaning of the word *doodle* in this context cannot be deciphered, the puzzle of the song's origin is fated to remain unsolved.

Yaravi. *See* HARAWI.

Yasser, Joseph, Polish-born Russian-American organist, conductor, and musicologist; b. Lodz, April 16, 1893; d. N.Y., Sept. 6, 1981. Yasser studied at the Moscow Conservatory, graduating in 1917 as an organist. After several years of teaching organ in Moscow and Siberia, he reached Shanghai in 1921 and conducted a choral society there.

Yasser subsequently emigrated to the U.S. in 1923, serving as organist at Temple Rodeph Sholom in N.Y. from 1929 to 1960. He became interested in how scales are formed, writing a famous theory book, *A Theory of Evolving Tonality,* in 1932. He also contributed several articles to *Musical Quarterly* dealing with QUARTAL HARMONY, which were subsequently published in a book in 1938.

Yeoman of the Guard, The, or The Merryman and His Maid. Operetta by WILLIAM GILBERT and ARTHUR SULLIVAN, 1888, first performed in London. The merryman is a jester who expects to marry the beloved of a man sentenced to

PEOPLE IN MUSIC

death. But the prisoner is unexpectedly reprieved, and the jester's plans are thwarted.

Yes, Sir, That's My Baby. Song by Walter Donaldson, 1925, which became a hit when EDDIE CANTOR sang it. The tune is something of a *tour de force,* because the first 16 syllables consist of only two different notes.

The first four notes are identical with the opening of the HALLELUJAH CHORUS from GEORGE FRIDERIC HANDEL'S *MESSIAH.*

Yes, We Have No Bananas. American nonsense song by Frank Silver and Irving Cohn, 1923.

The composers claimed that their inspiration came from a Greek fruit peddler who nodded his head to signify that yes, he did not have any bananas left. But Greeks nod their heads to signify the negative and shake their heads for the affirmative, so the peddler had perfect ethnic logic on his side.

Yeston, Maury. *See NINE.*

Yip, Yip, Yaphank. Revue by IRVING BERLIN, 1918. Berlin himself took part in the show, which depicted the life of American doughboys (soldiers) in World War I. He made a sensation with his loud lament, *Oh, How I Hate to Get Up in the Morning.*

Berlin originally planned to include a first version of *GOD BLESS AMERICA* in the show, but it was cut for reasons unknown and not revived until the 1930s.

yodel (Ger. *Jodel*). A type of rural singing in the European Alps, especially in Switzerland, characterized by the frequent alternation of FALSETTO tones with chest tones. Its effect is that of a kind of expanded warble. The earliest yodel call is found in a collection entitled *Bicinia Gallica, Latina, Germanica,* published in 1545. A similar technique is used by various groups in Africa.

Yodeling is related to the field holler of the American South. It eventually found its way into country music through the singing of JIMMIE RODGERS.

You Ain't Heard Nothin' Yet. Song by AL JOLSON and others, which he added to his extravaganza *Sinbad* in 1918. The title was Jolson's catchphrase when addressing his audiences.

You Made Me Love You, I Didn't Want to Do It. Song by Jimmy Monaco, 1913, introduced by AL JOLSON in *The Honeymoon Express.* This was the VAUDEVILLE show in which Jolson first assumed the character of a blackface comedian. The song became a TIN PAN ALLEY classic and was featured in several movies.

You Must Have Been a Beautiful Baby. Song by Harry Warren and JOHNNY MERCER, 1938, included in the film *Hard to Get.* A great success, it was incorporated in several movie musicals.

Youmans, Vincent (Millie), American composer of POPULAR MUSIC, including the perennial favorite of songs, *Tea for Two;* b. N.Y., Sept. 27, 1898; d. Denver, April 5, 1946. Youmans took piano lessons as a child but was apprenticed by his father to enter the business world. He served as a messenger in a Wall Street bank, then enlisted in the U.S. Navy, where he also played the piano in a Navy band. He wrote a song, *Hallelujah,* which was picked up by JOHN PHILIP SOUSA, who performed it with his own bands. Later it was incorporated by Youmans in his musical *Hit the Deck* in 1927.

After World War I Youmans earned a living as a song plugger for publishers in N.Y. He produced two musical comedies, *Two Little Girls in Blue* in 1921 and *The Wildflower,* two years later. Both were moderately successful, but he achieved fame with his next production, *No, No, Nanette.* It opened in Detroit in the spring of 1924, then was staged in Chicago. After a 49-week run there, it moved to London, where it was produced in early 1925. It finally reached Broadway in the fall of 1925, and proved to be one of the most beguiling and enduring American musicals.

There followed several other successful musicals: *A Night Out* (1925), *Oh, Please!* (1926), *Rainbow* (1928), *Great Day* (1929), and *Through the Years* (1932). In 1933 Youmans went to Hollywood to complete his score for the film *Flying Down to Rio.* Because of an increasingly aggravated tubercular condition, he retired to Denver in the hope of recuperation in its then-unpolluted environment, and remained there until his death.

PEOPLE IN MUSIC

Its hit song, *Tea for Two,* became a perennial favorite all over the world.

Among Youmans's songs the following were also hits: *Bambalina, I Want to Be Happy, Hallelujah, Sometimes I'm Happy, Great Day, Without a Song, Time on My Hands, Through the Years, Carioca, Orchids in the Moonlight, Drums in My Heart, More Than You Know,* and *Rise 'n' Shine.*

PEOPLE IN MUSIC

Young, La Monte (Thornton), influential American composer of the extreme AVANT-GARDE and early proponent of musical MINIMALISM; b. Bern, Idaho, Oct. 14, 1935. Young studied clarinet and saxophone with William Green in Los Angeles from 1951 to 1954. From 1953 to 1956 he attended Los Angeles City College, and also studied COUNTERPOINT and composition privately with Leonard Stein in 1955–56. He was a pupil of Robert Stevenson at the University of California, Los Angeles, where he earned a B.A. degree in 1958. Young then pursued further training with Lalo Shifrin and Andrew Imbrie at the University of California, Berkeley, from 1958 to 1960. He also attended summer courses in new music in Darmstadt, and subsequently studied ELECTRONIC MUSIC with Richard Maxfield at the New School for Social Research in N.Y. in 1960–61.

In 1963 Young married the artist and illustrator Marian Zazeela, with whom he subsequently gave audiovisual performances in a series of "Sound/Light Environments" in Europe and America. That same year, he edited *An Anthology of Chance Operations, Concept Art, Anti-Art, etc.,* which was published in 1963. Along with his own *Compositions 1960,* it had a strong influence on CONCEPT ART and the FLUXUS movement. Many of his early works consisted of simple (if sometimes ironic) instructions to the performers, as in: "Push the piano to the wall; push it through the wall; keep pushing."

Young's mature work has consisted of created total "sound environments." Listeners can arrive and depart at any time; the musical presentation has been ongoing for several years. In 1970 Young traveled to Northern India to study vocal music with Pandit Pran Nath, who would remain Young's teacher and guru until Nath's death in 1996.

Young has contributed extensively to the study of JUST INTONATION and other "pure" tuning systems; one goal was to create acoustic "clouds" of overtones. He received a Guggenheim fellowship and a grant from the National Endowment for the Arts.

Among Young's extensive list of works, many have titles that are as evocative as the piece itself, including:

Poem for Tables, Chairs, and Benches (moving furniture about; University of California, Berkeley, 1960)

The Well-Tuned Piano (1964–81)

The Tortoise Droning Selected Pitches from the Holy Numbers of the Two Black Tigers, the Green Tiger, and the Hermit (1964)

The Tortoise Recalling the Drone of the Holy Numbers as They Were Revealed in the Dreams of the Whirlwind and the Obsidian Gong, Illuminated by the Sawmill, the Green Sawtooth Ocelot, and the High-Tension Line Stepdown Transformer (1964)

Map of 49's Dream of Two Systems of 11 Sets of Galactic Intervals Ornamental Lightyears Tracery for voices, various instruments, and sine wave drones (1968)

The Subsequent Dreams of China (1980)

The Second Dream of the High-Tension Line Stepdown Transformer for trumpet ensemble (1985)

Young has created several pieces of conceptual music and tape recordings of his own MONOPHONOUS vocalizing achieved by both inspiration and expiration so that the vocal line is maintained indefinitely. He has also performed various physical exercises with or without audible sounds.

Young, Lester (Willis), called Pres or Prez, African-American JAZZ TENOR saxophonist; b. Woodville, Miss., Aug. 27, 1909; d. N.Y., March 15, 1959. Young studied trumpet, alto sax, violin, and drums with his father, then played in his family's band. Turning to the tenor saxophone at 19, he began performing with various groups in the Midwest.

Young was a member of COUNT BASIE's band in 1934, 1936–40, and 1943–44. While serving in the U.S. Army, he was court-martialed for using drugs. Upon his release in

PEOPLE IN MUSIC

1945, he resumed his career, which was plagued by his abuse of alcohol. He continued to perform until shortly before his death.

He made recordings with various jazz notables, including BILLIE HOLIDAY, who dubbed him "Pres" (a contraction of "President") for his outstanding abilities. One of the great jazz saxophonists, he influenced numerous successors through his beautiful long melodic lines, fine phrasing, and inventive solos. Among his famous recordings were *Lady Be Good, Shoe Shine Boy, Lester Leaps In, After Theatre Jump, These Foolish Things, All of Me* (with Holiday), *Pres Returns,* and *Easy Does It.*

Young, Neil, Canadian-born FOLK-ROCK singer, instrumentalist, and composer; b. Toronto, Nov. 12, 1945. After surviving childhood illnesses, Young learned to play banjo and guitar in his youth. Moving to Los Angeles in 1966, he joined Stephen Stills to form BUFFALO SPRINGFIELD, which produced Young's hits *Nowadays Clancy Can't Even Sing, Broken Arrow, Mr. Soul,* and *I Am a Child.*

Young left Buffalo Springfield in 1967 to begin a solo career, which he continued while performing and recording with (David) Crosby, Stills, and (Graham) Nash and scoring hits with their albums *Déjà Vu* (1970) and *Four-Way Street* (1971). Among Young's many solo albums are *Everybody Knows This Is Nowhere* (1969), *After the Goldrush* (with the backup group Crazy Horse; 1970), *Harvest* (his best-selling album; 1972), *Tonight's the Night* (1975), *Zuma* (1975), *Comes a Time* (1978), *Rust Never Sleeps* (1979), *Re-ac-tor* (1981), *Old Ways* (1985), and *Freedom* (1989).

In his songs Young created an effective marriage of folk, country music, and hard rock. Among his best songs are *The Loner, Cinnamon Girl, Down By the River, Southern Man, Only Love Can Break Your Heart, Ohio, Like a Hurricane, Heart of Gold, Country Girl, Helpless, Cortez the Killer, Hey Hey My My,* and *Vampire Blues.*

Young Person's Guide to the Orchestra, The. Orchestral VARIATIONS and FUGUE by BENJAMIN BRITTEN, 1945, premiered in Liverpool, 1946. The variation theme is taken from a piece of incidental music of HENRY PURCELL.

PEOPLE IN MUSIC

Young partnered with the group PEARL JAM for the 1995 recording *Mirror Ball.*

In its original form, Britten's piece is part of an educational film entitled *Instruments of the Orchestra*. With an unpretentious narrative as support, Britten cleverly brought out orchestral families and individual instruments one after another, so a young person can really learn how orchestral instruments sound. The Purcell variations and fugue are often recorded and performed independently of the text.

Young, Victor, American pianist and composer; b. Bristol, Tenn., April 9, 1889; d. Ossining, N.Y., Sept. 2, 1968. Young studied piano with Isidor Philipp in Paris, then toured in England and the U.S. as an accompanist to prominent singers. He held various teaching positions and was music director in Thomas A. Edison's Experimental Laboratory in West Orange, New Jersey, conducting tonal tests and making piano recordings under Edison's personal supervision from 1919 to 1927. He wrote the musical SCORE for one of the earliest sound motion pictures, *In Old California*.

Altogether Young composed some 300 film scores, including *Wells Fargo* (1937), *Gulliver's Travels* (1939), *For Whom the Bell Tolls* (1943), *The Night Has a Thousand Eyes* (1946), *Rio Grande* (1950), *The Quiet Man* (1952), *Shane* (1953), and *Around The World in Eighty Days* (1956). He also wrote orchestral works, piano music, and many popular songs.

PEOPLE IN MUSIC

You're a Good Man, Charlie Brown. Musical by Clark Gesner, 1967, based on Charles Schulz's famous comic strip *Peanuts*.

Charlie Brown engages in all kinds of childhood adventures in the company of Snoopy (beagle and World War I flying ace), Linus (blanket-bearing genius), Lucy (perpetual crank and book reviewer), Patty (mystery woman), and Schroeder (Beethoven-worshiping toy pianist). Includes the title song, *Faithful Friends Always Near Me, Queen Lucy, My Blanket and Me*, and *Book Report*.

The show was revived on Broadway in 1999.

You're the Cream in My Coffee. Song by Ray Henderson, 1928, from the musical *Hold Everything*. An all-time hit, it inspired a parody, "You're the fly in my coffee, / you're the nail in my shoe"—among many others.

Youth Symphony. SERGEI PROKOFIEV's Seventh Symphony, 1951–52, his last, written to glorify the spirit of Soviet youth. Ostentatiously melodious and insistently harmonious, it was written in answer to his Soviet government critics, who claimed his works were tainted by "modern" musical styles. The first performance took place in Moscow in 1952.

Yo-Yo Ma. *See* MA, YO-YO.

Ysaÿe, Eugène (-Auguste), Belgian violinist, conductor, and composer; b. Liège, July 16, 1858; d. Brussels, May 12, 1931. At the age of four Ysaÿe began to study violin with his father, a theater conductor. At seven, he was enrolled at the Liège Conservatory as a pupil of Désiré Heynberg, winning second prize in 1867. In 1869 he left the conservatory in a dispute with his mentor, but was readmitted in 1872 as a pupil of Rodolphe Massart, winning first prize in 1873 and the silver medal in 1874. He then continued his training on scholarship at the Brussels Conservatory with Adam Tadeusz Wieniawski, and later completed his studies with HENRI VIEUXTEMPS in Paris from 1876 to 1879.

In 1879 Ysaÿe became concertmaster of Bilse's orchestra in Berlin. He appeared as a soloist at Pauline Lucca's concerts in Cologne and Aachen. In Germany he met ANTON RUBINSTEIN, who took him to Russia, where he spent two winters. He also toured in Norway. In 1883 he settled in Paris, where he met CÉSAR FRANCK, VINCENT D'INDY, and other contemporary composers, and gave successful concerts.

Ysaÿe formed a duo with the pianist Raoul Pugno and started a long series of concerts with him, establishing a new standard of excellence. In 1886 he married Louise Bourdeau. Franck dedicated his violin SONATA to them as a wedding present, and Ysaÿe's interpretation made it famous. From 1886 to 1898 he was a professor at the Brussels Conservatory. In 1886 he also organized the Ysaÿe Quartet (with Crickboom, Léon Van Hout, and Joseph Jacob).

In 1889 Ysaÿe made successful appearances in England. In 1894 he made his U.S. debut, playing LUDWIG VAN BEETHOVEN's Violin Concerto with the N.Y. Philharmonic

PEOPLE IN MUSIC

CLAUDE DEBUSSY dedicated his string quartet to Ysaÿe's group, which gave it its first performance at the Société Nationale in Paris on Dec. 29, 1893.

and creating a sensation by his virtuosity. He revisited the U.S. many times, with undiminished acclaim. He began his conducting career in 1894 and established in Brussels his own orchestra, the Société des Concerts Ysaÿe.

When the Germans invaded Belgium in 1914, Ysaÿe fled to London, where he remained during World War I. In 1918 he made his debut as conductor with the Cincinnati Symphony Orchestra, and also led the Cincinnati May Festival. He was offered a permanent position as conductor of the Cincinnati Symphony Orchestra, which he held from 1918 to 1922. He then returned to Belgium and resumed leadership of the Société des Concerts Ysaÿe. After the death of his first wife, he married an American pupil, Jeannette Dincin, in 1927.

Ysaÿe's style of playing is best described as heroic, but his art was equally convincing in the expression of moods of exquisite delicacy and tenderness. His frequent employment of TEMPO RUBATO produced an effect of elasticity without distorting the melodic line. He was known for an unorthodox bow grip, which excluded the little finger.

Ysaÿe's works include eight violin CONCERTOS, six sonatas for solo violin (1924), and other solo violin pieces, nine symphonic poems and concertolike works for violin and orchestra, *Poème nocturne* for violin, cello, and strings, *Les Harmonies du soir* for string quartet and string orchestra, *Méditation* for cello and string orchestra (c.1900), *Trio de concert* for two violins, viola, and orchestra, *Amitié* for two violins and orchestra, solo cello sonata, duo-violin sonata, and other CHAMBER MUSIC.

At the age of 70 Ysaÿe began the composition of an opera in the Walloon dialect, *Piér li Houïeu* (Peter the Miner), which was produced in Liège in 1931. The composer was suffering at the time from diabetes, which had necessitated the amputation of his left foot. He began the composition of a second Walloon opera, *L'Avierge di Piér* but had no time to complete it. In 1937 Queen Elisabeth of Belgium inaugurated the annual Prix International Eugene Ysaÿe in Brussels (its first winner was David Oistrakh).

Ysaÿe's younger brother, Théophile (b. Verviers, March 22, 1865; d. Nice, March 24, 1918), was a pianist and composer who participated in the Société des Concerts Ysaÿe as a rehearsal conductor.

PEOPLE IN MUSIC

Yun, Isang, important Korean-born German composer; b. Tongyong, Sept. 17, 1917; d. Berlin, Nov. 3, 1995. Yun studied Western music in Korea during 1935–37 and in Japan from 1941 to 1943. During World War II he was active in the anti-Japanese underground. In 1943 he was imprisoned, then spent the rest of the war in hiding until the liberation in 1945.

Yun became a music teacher in Tongyong in 1946, and later taught in Pusan. In 1953 he became a professor of composition at the University of Seoul, then studied at the Paris Conservatory in 1956–57 and at the Berlin Hochschule für Musik in 1958–59. He also attended summer courses in new music in Darmstadt. He settled permanently in Berlin.

Yun's career was dramatically interrupted when, on June 17, 1967, he and his wife were brutally abducted from West Berlin by secret police agents of South Korea. They were forced to board a plane for Seoul, where they were brought to trial for sedition. He was sentenced to life imprisonment, and his wife was given three years in jail. This act prompted an indignant protest by the government of West Germany, which threatened to cut off economic aid to South Korea. Twenty-three celebrated musicians, including IGOR STRAVINSKY, issued a vigorous letter of protest. As a result of this pressure, South Korea released Yun and his wife after two years of detention, at which time they returned to Germany.

In 1969–70 Yun taught at the Hannover Hochschule für Musik. In 1970 he was appointed lecturer in composition at the Berlin Hochschule für Musik, where he was a professor from 1973 to 1985. In 1971 he became a naturalized German citizen.

After a SERIALIST phase, Yun began producing music marked by a fine expressionistic and coloristic quality and written in an idiom of euphonious DISSONANCE. In the years after his release from South Korean prison, he began composing in more clear-cut musical genres. Among his many compositions are the operas *Der Traum des Liu-Tung* (1965), *Die Witwe des Schmetterlings* (The Butterfly Widow; 1967;

completed in his prison cell and premiered in absentia in Bonn), *Geisterliebe* (1969–70), and *Sim Tjong* (1971–72). His orchestral compositions include *Bara* (1960), *Réak* (1966), Cello Concerto (1976), Double Concerto for oboe, harp, and small orchestra (1977), Clarinet Concerto (1981), three violin concertos (1981; 1983–86; 1992), five symphonies (1983; 1984; 1985; 1986; for baritone and orchestra, 1987), *Gong-Hu* for harp and strings (1984), two chamber symphonies (1987, 1989), Oboe Concerto (1990), and *Silia* (1992).

Yun's many chamber pieces include six string quartets, the first two of which were withdrawn (1959, 1988, 1990, 1992); Octet for clarinet, bassoon, horn, and string quintet (1978); Concertino for accordion and string quartet (1983); Quintet for clarinet and string quartet (1984), Quintet for flute and string quartet (1986); Kammerkonzert I (1990) and II (1990); Wind Quintet (1991); Quartet for trumpet, horn, trombone, and piano (1992); Wind Octet (1994), and many works for solo instruments and solo instruments and piano. He composed a variety of keyboard works (for piano, organ, and harpsichord), as well as numerous vocal works, including *O Licht ...* for chorus, violin, and percussion and *Der Herr ist mein Hirte* for chorus and trombone (both 1981).

yurupari. A very long wooden TRUMPET used by the Amazon Indians in Brazil, which they considered taboo to women and strangers. Oscar Wilde mentions them in his novel *The Picture of Dorian Gray,* speaking of exotic and dangerous hobbies of his hero in whose collection there are "mysterious yuruparis of the Rio Negro Indians, that women are not allowed to look at." The reason for this proscription is not explicitly known.

MUSICAL INSTRUMENT

Z mrtveho domu. *See* FROM THE HOUSE OF THE DEAD.

Zabaleta, Nicanor, Spanish harpist; b. San Sebastian, Jan. 7, 1907; d. San Juan, Puerto Rico, March 31, 1993. Zabaleta began his training in his home town. After further studies in Madrid, he went to Paris to study harp with Marcel Tournier and composition with Eugene Cools. He then toured extensively in Europe, South America, and the U.S.

Zabaleta was noted for his efforts to increase the number of works available for the harp, both by bringing to light neglected compositions of early composers and by prompting modern composers to write harp music. Many harp concertos were written for him by Alberto Ginastera, DARIUS MILHAUD, WALTER PISTON, HEITOR VILLA-LOBOS, VIRGIL THOMSON, and JOSEF TAL.

Zaïde. Unfinished opera by WOLFGANG AMADEUS MOZART, 1779, to a LIBRETTO resembling that of *The Abduction from the Seraglio.* A heroic youth rescues his chosen bride from a sultan's harem. It was not performed until 1866, in Frankfurt, in an arrangement done by various sources.

zamacueca (zambacueca; Sp.). The national song dance of Chile, also called *cueca,* a couple dance in rapid alternating $\frac{3}{4}$ and $\frac{6}{8}$. The popular Argentinean dance ZAMBA is derived from it.

zampogna (*zampoña*). Italian traditional BAGPIPE.

zampoñas (Sp.). Chilean PANPIPES.

Zandonai, Riccardo, Italian composer; b. Sacco di Rovereto, Trentino, May 30, 1883; d. Pesaro, June 5, 1944.

Zandonai was a pupil of Gianferrari at Rovereto from 1893 to 1898, then of PIETRO MASCAGNI at the Liceo Rossini in Pesaro. He graduated in 1902, and for his final examination he composed a symphonic poem for solo voices, chorus, and orchestra, *Il ritorno di Odisseo.*

Zandonai then turned to opera, which remained his favored genre throughout his career. His first opera was *La coppa del re* (c.1906), which was never performed. After writing the children's opera *L'uccelino d'oro* in 1907, he won notable success with his third opera, *Il grillo del focolare,* after Charles Dickens's *The Cricket on the Hearth,* in 1908. With his next opera, *Conchita,* after the novel *La Femme et le pantin* by Pierre Louÿs, in 1911, he established himself as an important Italian composer. The title role was created by the soprano Tarquinia Tarquini, whom Zandonai married in 1917. *Conchita* received its American premiere in San Francisco in 1912.

Zandonai's reputation was enhanced by subsequent works, notably his 1914 opera *Francesca da Rimini,* after Gabriele d'Annunzio. During World War I, Zandonai participated in the political agitation for the return of former Italian provinces. He wrote a student hymn calling for the return of Trieste in 1915.

As *La Femme et le pantin* it was given at the Opéra-Comique in Paris in 1929.

Zappa, Frank (Vincent), outspoken American ROCK artist; b. Baltimore, Dec. 21, 1940, of Italian descent (Zappa means "hoe" in Italian); d. Los Angeles, Dec. 4, 1993. The family moved to California when Frank was young. From his school days Zappa played guitar and organized groups with weird names such as The Omens and Captain Glasspack and His Magic Mufflers. In 1960 he composed the sound track for the low-budget film *The World's Greatest Sinner,* and in 1963 he wrote another for *Run Home Slow.*

In 1965 Zappa joined the RHYTHM-AND-BLUES band the Soul Giants. He soon took over its leadership and thought up the name the Mothers of Invention. The band's first few albums combined many of Zappa's interests: MUSIC CONCRÈTE in the style of EDGARD VARÈSE, raucous, satirical lyrics attacking the hippie lifestyle, and rock 'n' roll—powered guitar riffs. Their self-named first album and its followup, *Freak Out!,* became underground hits. Along with *Absolutely Free*

PEOPLE IN MUSIC

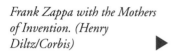

Frank Zappa with the Mothers of Invention. (Henry Diltz/Corbis) ▶

(with *Brown Shoes Don't Make It*), *We're Only in It for the Money,* and *Lumpy Gravy,* these works were the earliest concept albums.

In 1969 Zappa replaced the original Mothers with new musicians, a process he would repeat every few years. Eventually he stopped using the Mothers name altogether. Moving farther afield, Zappa produced a film and SCORE for *200 Motels,* about life on the road as a rock star. He became a cult figure, and as such suffered the penalty of violent adulation. Playing in London in 1971, he was nearly killed when a drunken fan pushed him off the stage into an empty orchestra pit. Similar assaults forced Zappa to hire a bodyguard for protection. In 1982 his planned appearance in Palermo, Sicily, the birthplace of his parents, had to be canceled because a mob rioted in anticipation of the event.

Zappa deliberately confronted the most cherished social and emotional sentiments by putting out such songs as *Broken Hearts Are for Assholes.* His *Jewish Princess* offended the sensibility of American Jews. His production *Joe's Garage* contained Zappa's favorite scatological materials, and he went on analyzing and ridiculing urinary functions in such numbers as *Why Does It Hurt When I Pee?* (ironically and tragically, Zappa died from prostate cancer that went undetected for a decade). Other less sharply directed satires included *Dancin' Fool* and *I Have Been in You.* In 1980 he produced the film *Baby Snakes,* which shocked even the most impervious senses.

Zappa's lyrical disdain and angry attitudes tend to disguise the remarkable development in his music. Having turned rock into a social and versatile medium, he moved into the greater complexities of JAZZ, with an interest in separating performance from recording. His *Hot Rats,* a jazz-rock release, gave the new FUSION music a significant boost. Zappa recorded every performance he ever played, and over the years released them, sometimes in large boxed sets (*Shut Up'n Play Yer Guitar,* 1981; *You Can't Do That on Stage Anymore; Beat the Boots,* two sets).

But Zappa astounded the musical community when he proclaimed his total adoration of the music of Varèse, gave a lecture on him, and supported concerts of his music in N.Y. Somehow, without formal study, he managed to absorb the essence of Varèse's difficult music. This process led Zappa to produce truly astonishing full orchestral scores reveling in artful DISSONANT COUNTERPOINT: *Bob in Dacron and Sad Jane* and *Mo' 'n' Herb's Vacation,* and the cataclysmic *Penis Dimension* for chorus, soloists, and orchestra.

An accounting of Zappa's scatological and sexological proclivities stands in remarkable contrast to his unimpeachable private life and total abstention from alcohol and drugs. An unexpected reflection of Zappa's own popularity was the emergence of his daughter, born Moon Unit, as a rapper on his hit *Valley Girls,* in which she used the vocabulary of growing womanhood of the San Fernando Valley near Los Angeles ("Val-Speak"). His son, Dweezil, is also a musician whose first album, *Havin' a Bad Day,* was modestly successful.

In 1985 Zappa became an outspoken opponent of the activities of the Parents Music Resource Center (PMRC), an organization comprised largely of wives of U.S. senators (and a future vice president) who accused the recording industry of exposing American youth to "sex, violence, and the glorification of drugs and alcohol" through song lyrics. Their demands to the Recording Industry Association of America (RIAA) included the labeling of record albums to indicate lyric content.

Zappa voiced his opinions in no uncertain terms, first in an open letter published in *Cashbox,* then in one to President Ronald Reagan. Finally, in 1985, he appeared at the first of a series of highly publicized hearings involving the

Zappa made art out of his own testimony by taking his own speech and running it through a Synclavier on his album *Zappa Meets The Mothers of Prevention.*

PEOPLE IN MUSIC

Senate Commerce, Technology, and Transportation Committee, the PMRC, and the RIAA, where he eloquently testified for freedom of speech.

Later recordings that make extensive use of the SYN-CLAVIER include *Francesco Zappa* (arrangements of works by the 18th-century Italian composer and cellist who happens to share Zappa's surname) and *Jazz From Hell.* Upon learning of his fatal illness, Zappa went through his entire recorded output, digitalized and remixed it, and sold it outright to the Rykodisc label. The last release before his death was *The Yellow Shark.*

Zarlino, Gioseffo (Gioseffe), Italian music theorist and composer; b. Chioggia, probably Jan. 31, 1517; d. Venice, Feb. 4, 1590. Zarlino received academic training from the Franciscan monks, his teacher in music being Francesco Maria Delfico. In 1537 he took minor orders and in 1539 was made a deacon. He was active as a singer during 1536 and organist in 1539–40 at Chioggia Cathedral. After his ordination he was elected capellano and mansionario of the Scuola di S. Francesco in Chioggia in 1540.

In 1541 Zarlino went to Venice to continue his musical training with Adrian Willaert. In 1565 he succeeded his fellow pupil Cipriano de Rore as maestro di cappella at San Marco, holding this position until his death. He also was chaplain of S. Severo from 1565 and a canon of the Chioggia Cathedral chapter from 1583. His students included G. M. Artusi, Girolamo Diruta, Vincenzo Galilei, and Claudio Merulo.

Zarlino's historical significance rests on his theoretical works, particularly *Le istitutioni harmoniche* in 1558. In this work, he describes the MAJOR and MINOR THIRDS as INVERSIONS within a FIFTH, and consequently, as mutual mirror reflections of component INTERVALS, anticipating the modern theories of Jean-Philippe Rameau, Giuseppe Tartini, Moritz Hauptmann, and Hugo Riemann. He also gives lucid and practical demonstrations of DOUBLE COUNTERPOINT and CANON, illustrated by numerous musical examples. While adhering to the system of 12 MODES, he places the IONIAN rather than the DORIAN mode at the head of the list, thus pointing toward the emergence of the major SCALE as the preponderant mode. He also gives 10 rules for proper syllabification of the text in musical settings.

Zarlino's theories were attacked, with a violence uncommon even for the polemical spirit of the age, by Vincenzo Galilei, his former pupil, in two pamphlets from the 1580s. In reply to the first of Galilei's books, Zarlino published *Sopplimenti musicali* in 1588. In the latter, he suggests EQUAL TEMPERAMENT for the tuning of the LUTE.

As a composer, Zarlino was an accomplished craftsman. He wrote both sacred and secular works.

zarzuela (from Sp. *zarza,* bramble bush). Spanish light OPERA characterized by dance and spoken dialogue. The name is derived from the Royal Palace La Zarzuela, near Madrid, where zarzuelas were performed before the royal court.

thăhr-thw-āl′ăh

The genre appeared in the 17th century. Performances of zarzuelas at the court were interspersed with BALLETS and popular dances fashioned after the spectacles at Versailles. With the massive intrusion of Italian opera into Spain in the 18th century, the zarzuela lost its characteristic ethnic flavor. It was revived by nationally minded composers of the second half of the 19th century, particularly Francisco Asenjo Barbieri, Ruperto Chapí, Tomás Bretón y Hernández, Joaquín Valverde, and Federico Chueca. In the early 20th century composers such as Amadeo Vives, Jésus Guridi, José Maria Usandizaga, Moreno Torroba, and Eduardo Toldrá continued composing in a now dying genre.

Classical composers such as ENRIQUE GRANADOS and MANUEL DE FALLA also wrote zarzuelas.

The modern zarzuela, known as *género chico,* embodied elements of the Viennese OPERETTA, and still later annexed American JAZZ rhythms. Zarzuelas taking up an entire evening were called *zarzuela grande;* a *zarzuelita* is a small zarzuela. *See also* TONADILLA.

Zauberflöte, Die. *See* MAGIC FLUTE, THE.

Zauberharfe, Die (The Magic Harp). Opera by FRANZ SCHUBERT, composed in 1820. This was the only opera by Schubert performed during his lifetime, in Vienna.

Zauberoper (Ger.). A magic opera, in which supernatural forces intervene in human affairs. A typical example is CARL MARIA VON WEBER's *Der Freischütz.*

Zaza. Opera by RUGGERO LEONCAVALLO, 1900, first produced in Milan. A Paris café songstress becomes embroiled in an affair with a married man. Abandoned by him, she finds happiness with her vaudeville partner. Although less successful than the composer's *PAGLIACCI,* the opera enjoys occasional performances.

tzīt   **Zeit** (Ger.). Time. *Zeitmass,* tempo; *Zeitoper* (opera of the times), German operas of the 1920s and early 1930s with distinct sociopolitical themes, driven by a generalized tendency of artists toward the creation of socially relevant art; *Zeitschrift,* newspaper, periodical, magazine, etc.

Zeitmasse. Chamber instrumental work by KARLHEINZ STOCKHAUSEN, 1956, first performed in Munich. This serial piece experiments with constant metric and tempo MODULATIONS.

PEOPLE IN MUSIC

Zelter, Carl Friedrich, German composer and teacher; b. Berlin, Dec. 11, 1758; d. there, May 15, 1832. The son of a mason, Zelter was brought up in the same trade, but his musical inclinations soon asserted themselves. He began training in piano and violin at 17, and from 1779 he was a part-time violinist in the Doebbelin Theater orchestra in Berlin.

From 1784 to 1786 Zelter was a pupil of C.F.C. Fasch. In 1786 he brought out a funeral CANTATA on the death of Frederick the Great. In 1791 he joined the Singverein (later Singakademie) conducted by Fasch, often acting as his deputy, and succeeding him as its conductor in 1800. He was elected associate of the Royal Academy of the Arts in Berlin in 1806, becoming a professor in 1809. In 1807 he organized a Ripienschule for orchestral practice, and in 1809 he founded the Berlin Liedertafel, a pioneer men's choral society that became famous. Similar organizations were subsequently formed throughout Germany, and later in the U.S.

Zelter composed about 100 men's choruses for the Liedertafel. In 1822 he founded the Royal Institute for Church Music in Berlin, of which he was director until his death (the institute was later reorganized as the Akademie für Kirchen- und Schulmusik). His students included FELIX

MENDELSSOHN, GIACOMO MEYERBEER, Carl Loewe, and Otto Nicolai. Goethe greatly admired Zelter's musical settings of his poems, preferring them to FRANZ SCHUBERT's and LUDWIG VAN BEETHOVEN's. This predilection led to their friendship, which was reflected in a voluminous correspondence, *Briefwechsel zwischen Goethe und Zelter* (six volumes, Berlin, 1833–34).

Zelter's songs are historically important, because they form a link between old BALLAD types and the new art of the LIED, which found its flowering in Schubert and ROBERT SCHUMANN. Zelter's settings of Goethe's *König von Thule* and of *Es ist ein Schuss gefallen* became extremely popular. Among his other compositions are a viola CONCERTO (1779), keyboard pieces, and choral works.

Zemlinsky, Alexander (von), Austrian composer and conductor of partly Jewish parentage (he removed the nobiliary particle "von" in 1918 when such distinctions were outlawed in Austria); b. Vienna, Oct. 14, 1871; d. Larchmont, N.Y., March 15, 1942. At the Vienna Conservatory Zemlinsky studied piano and composition from 1887 to 1892. In 1893 he joined the Vienna Tonkünstlerverein, and in 1895 he became connected with the orchestra society Polyhymnia and met ARNOLD SCHOENBERG, whom he advised on technical aspects of CHAMBER MUSIC. Schoenberg always had the highest regard for Zemlinsky as a composer and lamented the lack of appreciation for his music. There was also a personal bond between them, because in 1901 Schoenberg married Zemlinsky's sister Mathilde.

Zemlinsky's first opera, *Sarema*, to a LIBRETTO by his father, was produced in Munich in 1897. Schoenberg made a piano-vocal SCORE of it. Zemlinsky also contacted GUSTAV MAHLER, music director of the Vienna Court Opera, who accepted Zemlinsky's opera *Es war einmal* for performance. Mahler conducted its premiere at the Court Opera in 1900, and it became Zemlinsky's most popular production.

From 1900 to 1906 Zemlinsky served as conductor of the Karlstheater in Vienna. In 1903 he conducted at the Theater an der Wien, and in 1904 he was named chief conductor of the Volksoper. In 1910 he orchestrated and conducted the ballet *Der Schneemann* by the talented 11-year-

PEOPLE IN MUSIC

old WUNDERKIND Erich Korngold. About that time, he and Schoenberg organized in Vienna the Union of Creative Musicians, which performed Zemlinsky's tone poem *Die Seejungfrau* in 1903.

In 1911 Zemlinsky moved to Prague, where he became conductor at the German Opera and also taught conducting and composition at the German Academy of Music beginning in 1920. In 1927 he moved to Berlin, where he was appointed assistant conductor at the Kroll Opera, with Otto Klemperer as chief conductor and music director. When the Nazis came to power in Germany in 1933, Zemlinsky returned to Vienna, and also filled engagements as guest conductor in the Soviet Union and elsewhere. After the Anschluss of 1938 he emigrated to the U.S., which effectively ended his career.

As a composer Zemlinsky followed the post-Romantic trends of Mahler and RICHARD STRAUSS. He was greatly admired, but his works were seldom performed, despite the efforts of Schoenberg and his associates to revive his music. How strongly he influenced his younger contemporaries is illustrated by the fact that ALBAN BERG quoted Zemlinsky's *Lyric Symphony* in his own *Lyric Suite*.

In the latter 20th century a great number of Zemlinsky's works, both operatic and nonoperatic, received revivals. Among Zemlinsky's most popular works are eight completed operas, three symphonies (1892; 1897; c.1903), *Lyrische Symphonie* in seven sections, after Rabindranath Tagore, for SOPRANO, BARITONE, and orchestra (his best-known work; 1922–23), and Sinfonietta (1934). He also wrote chamber works, including four string quartets (1895; 1913–15; 1924; 1936); vocal works, including three psalms for chorus and orchestra: No. 83 (1900), No. 23 (1910), and No. 13 (1935); *Maeterlinck Lieder*, six songs for medium voice and orchestra (1910–13); *Symphonische Gesänge* for voice and orchestra (1929); four volumes of LIEDER to texts by Heyse and Liliencron (1894–97), and songs to words by Dehmel, Jacobsen, Bierbaum, Morgenstern, Ammann, Heine, and Hofmannsthal (1898–1913; 1929–36).

Zero Symphony. Unnumbered symphony by ANTON BRUCKNER, 1863–64, in D minor, first complete performance in Klosterneuberg, 1924. This is the second surviving early symphony of Bruckner. The first, 1863, in F minor, is nicknamed the *School* Symphony. Bruckner actually named the D minor work *Die Nullte* in retrospect (this is also translated as Symphony No. 0). Its music is in a pleasing ROMANTIC vein, but the score lacks the composer's typical philosophical introspection.

zheng (*cheng*). A Chinese half-tube ZITHER, dating from the third century B.C. The zheng was a popular solo instrument of the people, while the QIN was reserved for scholars and

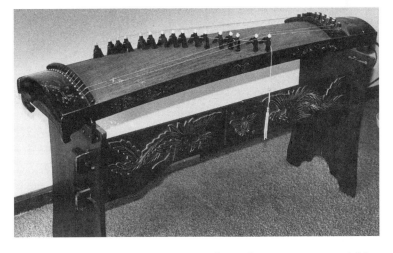

◄

Chinese Zheng. (K. H. Han/Northern Illinois University)

officials in meditation. The number of strings was variable, with 14 as an average. Modern instruments may have 24 or more. In any case, the strings are divided by movable bridges. The zheng is tuned pentatonically. In addition to harmonics, ornaments are performed by applying pressure to the nonplaying side of the bridges (like the Japanese KOTO and Korean *kayago*).

Ziegfeld Follies. Series of spicy REVUES produced by Florenz Ziegfeld (1867–1932), inaugurated in 1907. These revues always featured many beautiful young women (he advertised his shows as "glorifying the American girl"). The shows were produced annually until 1925. Three more shows were produced during Ziegfeld's lifetime, and four more were produced posthumously, the last in 1957. Songs and sketches were by various songwriters and writers.

Showgirls in the Zigfeld Follies. *(Corbis-Bettmann)* ▶

Musically, the most successful editions of the Ziegfeld Follies were those of IRVING BERLIN. Berlin contributed one of his most enduring tunes, *A Pretty Girl Is Like a Melody,* to the 1919 edition. He wrote the entire score and lyrics for the 1927 revue. Other famous participants included Nora Bayes (*Shine On Harvest Moon*), Bert Williams (*Nobody*), FANNY BRICE (*Indian Love Call*), and EDDIE CANTOR. Ziegfeld was also an independent producer, with credits including *Show Boat, Rosalie, Whoopie,* and *Bitter Sweet.*

Zigeunerbaron, Der. *See* GYPSY BARON, THE.

Zimerman, Krystian, Polish pianist; b. Zabrze, Dec. 5, 1956. Zimerman began taking piano lessons at age five with his father. When he was seven he became a pupil of Andrzej Jasinki, with whom he later studied at the Katowice Conservatory.

In 1975 Zimerman won first prize in the Chopin Competition in Warsaw, after which he played with great success in Munich, Paris, London, and Vienna. In 1976 he was a soloist with the Berlin Philharmonic. He made his first U.S. appearance in 1978, and subsequently toured throughout the world to great critical acclaim.

Zimerman's performances of the ROMANTIC repertory are remarkable for their discerning spontaneity. He has also

PEOPLE IN MUSIC

played contemporary works, including the premiere of Witold Lutoslawski's Piano Concerto (1989), which is dedicated to him.

Zimmermann, Bernd (Bernhard) **Alois,** German composer; b. Bliesheim, near Cologne, March 20, 1918; d. Königsdorf, Aug. 10, 1970. Zimmermann studied at the Cologne Hochschule für Musik and at the Universities of Cologne and Bonn until he was drafted for military service during World War II.

After his discharge, Zimmermann became a pupil of Heinrich Lemacher and Philip Jarnach in 1942, and later attended the summer courses in new music of Wolfgang Fortner and René Leibowitz in Darmstadt from 1948 to 1950. He taught theory at the University of Cologne from 1950 to 1952 and at the Cologne Hochschule für Musik from 1957 to 1970.

Plagued by failing eyesight and obsessed with notions of death, Zimmermann reflected these moods in his own music of the final period. His *Requiem für einen jungen Dichter,* a "lingual" for narrator, SOPRANO and BARITONE soloists, three choruses, tape, orchestra, JAZZ combo, and organ (1967–69) sets texts drawn from poems, articles, and news reports concerning poets who committed suicide. He killed himself less than a year after the premiere of this morbid score.

Zimmermann's idiom is mainly EXPRESSIONISTIC, with a melody line of anguished CHROMATICISM. In a sense, he realized the paths opened by ALBAN BERG. The opera *Die Soldaten,* based on a play by J.M.R. Lenz (1958–60; revised 1963–64), took the atmosphere of Berg's WOZZECK several steps further. The explicit presentation of the molestation of innocent civilians by the military brought on a critical and societal storm of protest.

Zimmermann maintained strong religious beliefs. Five days before his death he completed *Ich wandte mich und sah an alles Unrecht das geschah unter der Sonne,* an "ecclesiastical action" after Ecclesiastes and Dostoevsky, for two narrators, bass, and orchestra (1970), a moving final expression of hope. While in his lifetime he was primarily known to limited music circles in Germany, the significance of his music began to be realized after his death.

Zingara, La. Opera by GAETANO DONIZETTI, 1822, first performed in Naples. Zingara, a young Gypsy woman, defies traditional Neapolitan suspicion of Gypsies as thieves and villains by helping to reunite two separated lovers, foiling a joint suicide, and brings them eternal happiness. But, being so wonderful, could she really be a Gypsy? Alas, no—she is revealed as a missing daughter of an unjustly imprisoned nobleman. So much for breaking Gypsy stereotypes!

Zip Coon. Song of unknown origin from a blackface MINSTREL show, 1834, produced in N.Y. As its racist title suggests, the text portrays a Broadway dandy decked out in fine clothes and a silk hat. The melody used is the Anglo-Irish *Turkey in the Straw,* rather than any quasi-African American tune.

tsit′ter

MUSICAL
INSTRUMENT

zither (Ger.). 1. A name given to any simple CHORDOPHONE, with strings that run parallel to its SOUNDBOX. Most are plucked (PSALTERY type), but some are IDIOPHONIC (struck with sticks or beaters; DULCIMER type) or HETEROPHONIC (plucked and struck). 2. A FOLK instrument popular in Bavaria and Austria, capable of considerable harmonic sonority. It is built of a shallow wooden resonating box, with 32 or more strings. It has a fretted FINGERBOARD on the side nearest the player, supporting five melody strings, plucked with the fingers and a metal plectrum worn on the right thumb. The melody strings are stopped with the fingers of the left hand to determine PITCH. *See also* kantele.

zopf (Ger., pigtail). An irreverent description of the type of music composed by wig-wearing BAROQUE musicians. The zopf (stylized pigtail) is familiar from the portraits of JOHANN SEBASTIAN BACH, GEORGE FRIDERIC HANDEL, FRANZ JOSEPH HAYDN, and their contemporaries. WOLFGANG AMADEUS MOZART even wore a zopf as a child.

The Zopf era came to a sudden end at the threshold of the 19th century. LUDWIG VAN BEETHOVEN's portraits show him with tousled hair, but he never wore a wig.

Zorba. Musical by JOHN KANDER and Fred Ebb, 1968, based on Kazantzakis's novel *Zorba the Greek.* The action takes place around a sidewalk café in Athens and follows the fortunes and misfortunes of Zorba. The songs imitate Greek traditional music, especially the sound of the BOUZOUKI, a plucked CHORDOPHONE; among the best songs are Zorba's ballads *The First Time* and *I am Free*.

Zorn, John, innovative American composer and instrumentalist; b. N.Y., Sept. 2, 1953. Zorn plays saxophone, keyboards, duck calls, and other semi-musical instruments in dense, loud aural canvases that have been compared to the works of Jackson Pollock (and also to an elephant trapped in barbed wire).

After a brief college stint in St. Louis and world travels, Zorn became an active contributor to the downtown music scene in N.Y. He performed with a coterie of well-reputed AVANT-GARDE and rock musicians, including guitarists Bill Frisell and Fred Frith, bassist Bill Laswell, pianists Anthony Coleman and Wayne Horvitz, drummers Bobby Previte and David Moss, vocalist Shelly Hirsch, and the Kronos Quartet.

Zorn has created separate groups for different facets of his music: *Naked City* (from late 1980s) and *Masada* (from 1994). His *The Big Gundown* (1987) uses the music of film composer Ennio Morricone (b. 1928) as material to be freely distorted and reworked. His major recordings include *Archery* (1981); *Cobra* (group improvisation, two volumes: 1986, 1994); *A Classic Guide to Strategy* (solo with overdubbing, 1987); *News for Lulu,* with Frisell and George Lewis, trombone (two volumes: 1987, 1989); *Spillane* (1988); *Spy vs. Spy,* playing the music of ORNETTE COLEMAN (1989), *The Book of Heads,* performed by guitarist Marc Ribot (1995); and *Kristallnacht* (1995).

PEOPLE IN MUSIC

Zukerman, Pinchas, Israeli violinist, violist, and conductor; b. Tel Aviv, July 16, 1948. Zukerman began to study music with his father, taking up the violin at age six. He then enrolled at the Conservatory in Tel Aviv, where he studied with Ilona Feher.

With the encouragement of ISAAC STERN and PABLO CASALS, Zukerman became a scholarship student at the Juilliard School of Music in N.Y., where he studied with Ivan Galamian from 1961 to 1967. In 1967 he shared first prize

PEOPLE IN MUSIC

in the Leventritt Competition in N.Y. with Kyung-Wha Chung, then launched a brilliant career as a soloist with major American and European orchestras. He also appeared as both violinist and violist in recitals with Stern and ITZHAK PERLMAN. He subsequently devoted part of his time to conducting, appearing with the N.Y. Philharmonic, Philadelphia Orchestra, Boston Symphony Orchestra, Los Angeles Philharmonic, and many others.

From 1980 to 1987 Zukerman was music director of the St. Paul (Minnesota) Chamber Orchestra. He was principal guest conductor of the Dallas Symphony Orchestra summer music festival from 1990 to 1992, and in 1993 he became a teacher at the Manhattan School of Music in N.Y. During the 1994–95 season, he made a world tour as a conductor with the English Chamber Orchestra.

Zukerman was married to the flutist Eugenia (née Rich) Zukerman (b. Cambridge, Mass., Sept. 25, 1944) from 1968 to 1985. His second wife is the actress Tuesday Weld. His performances as a violinist are distinguished by their innate emotional spirit and modern VIRTUOSO technique.

Zukofsky, Paul, American violinist and conductor; b. N.Y., Oct. 22, 1943. His father, Louis Zukofsky, was a poet who experimented in highly complex verbal forms. Paul began playing the violin at the age of four on a quarter-size instrument, and when he was seven he began lessons with Ivan Galamian. He was soloist with the New Haven (Connecticut) Symphony Orchestra at the age of eight, and made his Carnegie Hall recital debut in N.Y. when he was 13. At 16 he entered the Juilliard School of Music.

From his earliest years Zukofsky was fascinated by ultramodern music. He developed several special techniques, in effect transforming the violin into a multimedia instrument beyond its normal capacities. In 1969 he inaugurated in N.Y. a concert series, Music for the 20th Century Violin, performing works often requiring acrobatic coordination. His repertoire includes all four violin SONATAS by CHARLES IVES, the violin CONCERTOS by William Schuman and ROGER SESSIONS, *Capriccio* by KRZYSZTOF PENDERECKI, and the solo violin works of JOHN CAGE.

PEOPLE IN MUSIC

In 1970 Louis Zukofsky published a novel, *Little,* dealing with the trials and triumphs of the violin wunderkind.

As a violin instructor, Zukofsky held the post of Creative Associate at the Buffalo Center of the Creative and Performing Arts and also taught at the Berkshire Music Center in Tanglewood and at the New England Conservatory of Music. In later years he became active as a conductor. He served as conductor of the Contemporary Chamber Ensemble at the Juilliard School from 1984 to 1989, and also was director of chamber music activities there from 1987 to 1989. From 1989 to 1995 he directed the Schoenberg Institute at the University of Southern California in Los Angeles, where he also taught violin.

Zukunftmusik (Ger.). Music of the future. A term coined by RICHARD WAGNER. His opponents turned this lofty phrase into a derisive description of his music.

zummāra (Arab.). Arab double CLARINET with parallel identical cylindrical pipes and a tremulant sound. It is a descendant of the Egyptian *memet,* dated to 2700 B.C.

zurnā. SHAWM family of wide geographic distribution, with conical bore, flared bell, seven FINGERHOLES, and several ventholes at the lower end. It is found under this and other names in Arab and Slavic regions, Turkey, India, and Indonesia.

Zwei (Ger.). Two. *Zweihändig,* for two hands; *Zweistimmig,* for two voices; in or for two parts.

Zwilich, Ellen Taaffe, American composer; b. Miami, April 30, 1939. Zwilich studied composition with John Boda and violin with Richard Burgin at Florida State University, earning her B.M. degree in 1956, and a M.M. degree six years later.

Zwilich then moved to N.Y., where she continued her violin studies with Ivan Galamian. After playing in the American Symphony Orchestra there from 1965 to 1972, she enrolled at the Juilliard School in N.Y., and studied with ROGER SESSIONS and ELLIOTT CARTER. In 1975 she received a doctor of musical arts in composition from that school, the first woman to receive such a degree.

MUSICAL INSTRUMENT

MUSICAL INSTRUMENT

tsvī

PEOPLE IN MUSIC

In 1983 Zwilich received the Pulitzer Prize in music for her Symphony No. 1 (originally titled *3 Movements for Orchestra*), first performed in N.Y. in 1982. In 1984 she received an award from the American Academy and Institute of Arts and Letters, and in 1992 she was elected to its membership. From 1995 to 1998 she held the first Composer's Chair at CARNEGIE HALL.

Zwilich's music offers a combination of purely technical excellence and a distinct power of communication, while a poetic element pervades the MELODY, HARMONY, and COUNTERPOINT of her creations. This combination of qualities explains the frequency and variety of prizes awarded her from various sources: the Elizabeth Sprague Coolidge Chamber Music Prize, a gold medal at the 26th Annual International Composition Competition in Vercelli, Italy, National Endowment for the Arts grants, a Guggenheim fellowship (1980–81), and the Ernst von Dohnányi Citation. Conductors in the U.S., Europe, and Japan are also eager to program her works. During a 1988 tour of the Soviet Union, ZUBIN MEHTA and the N.Y. Philharmonic presented the world premiere of her *Symbolon* in Leningrad.

Zwilich is best known for her instrumental works, which include three symphonies: No. 1, originally titled *Three Movements for Orchestra* (1982), No. 2, Cello Symphony (1985), and No. 3 (1992); *Concerto grosso* (1985), Flute Concerto (1989), Concerto for bass trombone, strings, timpani, and cymbals (1989), Concerto for horn and strings (1993), and Trumpet Concerto, *American* (1994). Among her chamber works are a String Quartet (1974), Double Quartet for strings (1984), and Quintet for clarinet and string quartet (1990).

Zwilich also composed a BALLET, *Tanzspiel* (1987), *Ceremonies* for band (1988), and several vocal works, including *Immigrant Voices* for chorus, brass, timpani, and strings (1991) and *A Simple Magnificat* for chorus and organ (1994).

Zwischenfalle bei einer Notlandung (Incidents at an Emergency Landing). "Reportage in 2 phases and 14 situations" by BORIS BLACHER, 1966. It is scored for instruments and electronic devices and was first performed in Hamburg.

Index